booksonline

Read this book online today:

With SAP PRESS BooksOnline we offer you online access to knowledge from the leading SAP experts. Whether you use it as a beneficial supplement or as an alternative to the printed book, with SAP PRESS BooksOnline you can:

- Access your book anywhere, at any time. All you need is an Internet connection.
- Perform full text searches on your book and on the entire SAP PRESS library.
- Build your own personalized SAP library.

The SAP PRESS customer advantage:

Register this book today at *www.sap-press.com* and obtain exclusive free trial access to its online version. If you like it (and we think you will), you can choose to purchase permanent, unrestricted access to the online edition at a very special price!

Here's how to get started:

1. Visit *www.sap-press.com*.
2. Click on the link for SAP PRESS BooksOnline and login (or create an account).
3. Enter your free trial license key, shown below in the corner of the page.
4. Try out your online book with full, unrestricted access for a limited time!

Your personal free trial **license key**
for this online book is:

y2xm-aw78-fhnt-qipv

Creating Dashboards with SAP® BusinessObjects™

SAP PRESS is a joint initiative of SAP and Galileo Press. The know-how offered by SAP specialists combined with the expertise of the Galileo Press publishing house offers the reader expert books in the field. SAP PRESS features first-hand information and expert advice, and provides useful skills for professional decision-making.

SAP PRESS offers a variety of books on technical and business related topics for the SAP user. For further information, please visit our website: *www.sap-press.com*.

Loren Heilig et al.
SAP NetWeaver BW and SAP BusinessObjects—The Comprehensive Guide
2012, 795 pp. (hardcover)
ISBN 978-1-59229-384-1

Ingo Hilgefort
Integrating SAP BusinessObjects BI Platform 4.x with SAP NetWeaver
(Second Edition)
2012, 437 pp. (hardcover)
ISBN 978-1-59229-395-7

Ingo Hilgefort
Reporting and Analysis with SAP BusinessObjects (Second Edition)
2012, 501 pp. (hardcover)
ISBN 978-1-59229-387-2

Coy W. Yonce, III
100 Things You Should Know About Reporting with SAP Crystal Reports
2012, 338 pp. (hardcover)
ISBN 978-1-59229-390-2

Ray Li and Evan DeLodder

Creating Dashboards with SAP® BusinessObjects™

The Comprehensive Guide

Galileo Press

Bonn • Boston

Galileo Press is named after the Italian physicist, mathematician and philosopher Galileo Galilei (1564—1642). He is known as one of the founders of modern science and an advocate of our contemporary, heliocentric worldview. His words *Eppur si muove* (And yet it moves) have become legendary. The Galileo Press logo depicts Jupiter orbited by the four Galilean moons, which were discovered by Galileo in 1610.

Editor Laura Korslund
Copyeditor Ruth Saavedra
Cover Design Graham Geary
Photo Credit iStockphoto.com/penfold
Layout Design Vera Brauner
Production Graham Geary
Typesetting SatzPro, Krefeld (Germany)
Printed and bound in the United States of America

ISBN 978-1-59229-410-7
© 2012 by Galileo Press Inc., Boston (MA)
2nd edition 2012

Library of Congress Cataloging-in-Publication Data
Li, Ray.
Creating dashboards with SAP businessobjects / Ray Li,
Evan DeLodder.
p. cm.
ISBN 978-1-59229-410-7 -- ISBN 1-59229-410-3 1. Dashboards
(Management information systems) 2. SAP ERP. I. DeLodder, Evan.
II. Title.
HD30.213.L5185 2012
005.4'37--dc23
2012005023

FSC
www.fsc.org
MIX
Paper from
responsible sources
FSC® C014174

Contents at a Glance

1   Introduction to SAP BusinessObjects Dashboards 19

2   Becoming Familiar with SAP BusinessObjects Dashboards 35

3   Dashboard Tutorial 95

4   UI Component Basics 109

5   Advanced UI Components 221

6   Data Connectivity Basics 335

7   Advanced Data Connectivity 375

8   Special Features 441

9   A Comprehensive Hands-On Example 489

10 Introduction to the SAP BusinessObjects Dashboards SDK 511

11 Get Started with Custom Component Basics 527

12 Implement Advanced Custom Add-On Component Features ... 557

13 Hands-On: Develop Your Custom Add-On Component 581

A   Location Intelligence 611

B   Tips for Using SAP BusinessObjects Dashboards 635

C   The Authors 669

Dear Reader,

Have you ever created a report and been bored by the process? Or created a report and wished you had more control over the design and look? If you've purchased this book, creating interesting, comprehensive, and unforgettable displays with SAP BusinessObjects Dashboards will never again be a problem for you!

Ray and Evan present clear and detailed step-by-step instructions that will make you an expert on creating dashboards in no time. Thanks to their expert writing, tasks such as navigating all of a dashboard's elements, creating an easy-to-use interface, and integrating supplements such as maps will no longer hold any mystery for you. In this updated second edition of their best-selling book, I'm confident that you'll find the extra details that will really help you "wow" your audience. And in addition to all of this, I'm thrilled to be able to offer SAP PRESS's first color online book! (Please refer to *www.sap-press.com* or the inside front cover of this book for more information on how to access this version.)

We at SAP PRESS are always eager to hear your opinion. What do you think about *Creating Dashboards with SAP BusinessObjects—The Comprehensive Guide*? As your comments and suggestions are our most useful tools to help us make our books the best they can be, we encourage you to visit our website at *www.sap-press.com* and share your feedback.

Thank you for purchasing a book from SAP PRESS!

Laura Korslund
Editor, SAP PRESS

Galileo Press
Boston, MA

laura.korslund@galileo-press.com
www.sap-press.com

Contents

Foreword 17

1 Introduction to SAP BusinessObjects Dashboards 19

1.1 What Is SAP BusinessObjects Dashboards? 19
    1.1.1 Who Works with SAP BusinessObjects Dashboards? 19
    1.1.2 Installation 20
    1.1.3 Relationship with Excel 21
1.2 What Can SAP BusinessObjects Dashboards Do? 22
    1.2.1 Data Visualization Capabilities 23
    1.2.2 Data Connectivity Capabilities 27
    1.2.3 Distribution 28
    1.2.4 Changes in SAP BusinessObjects Dashboards 4.0 29
    1.2.5 Extensibility 33
1.3 SAP BusinessObjects Dashboards in the SAP BusinessObjects
    Portfolio 33
1.4 Summary 34

2 Becoming Familiar with SAP BusinessObjects Dashboards 35

2.1 Menu 36
    2.1.1 File 36
    2.1.2 SAP 58
    2.1.3 Edit 62
    2.1.4 View 63
    2.1.5 Format 68
    2.1.6 Data 71
    2.1.7 Help 74
2.2 Toolbar 77
    2.2.1 Standard 78
    2.2.2 Export 78
    2.2.3 Themes 79
    2.2.4 Format 79
    2.2.5 Start Page 80
    2.2.6 Summary 80

2.3	Components Browser	82
	2.3.1 Category	82
	2.3.2 Tree	83
	2.3.3 List	84
2.4	Canvas	84
2.5	Embedded Excel Spreadsheet	85
2.6	Property Panel	85
2.7	Object Browser	88
2.8	Query Browser	89
	2.8.1 Select a Universe	90
	2.8.2 Build Query	90
	2.8.3 Preview Query Result	92
	2.8.4 Usage Options	92
2.9	Summary	93

3 Dashboard Tutorial 95

3.1	Introduction	95
3.2	Choose the Right UI Components	96
3.3	Bind Data	98
	3.3.1 Bind Data for Pie Chart	99
	3.3.2 Enable Drill-Down for the Pie Chart	100
	3.3.3 Bind Data for Label	103
3.4	Connect to External Data	103
3.5	Formatting	104
3.6	Distribute the Output	106
3.7	Summary	108

4 UI Component Basics 109

4.1	Working with Charts	110
	4.1.1 Pie Chart	110
	4.1.2 Column Chart	133
	4.1.3 Line Chart	155
	4.1.4 Bar Chart	163
	4.1.5 XY Chart	164
	4.1.6 Bubble Chart	168
	4.1.7 Area Chart	171

4.2	Selectors	174
	4.2.1 Introduction to SAP BusinessObjects Dashboards Selectors	174
	4.2.2 Select a Single Item	175
	4.2.3 Filter	181
	4.2.4 Checkbox	185
	4.2.5 Ticker	186
	4.2.6 Picture Menus	188
	4.2.7 List Builder	192
4.3	Represent a Single Value	194
	4.3.1 Introduction to Single-Value Components	195
	4.3.2 Slider	195
	4.3.3 Progress Bar	200
	4.3.4 Dial and Gauge	200
4.4	Use Containers to Wrap Several Components	206
	4.4.1 When to Use a Container	207
	4.4.2 How to Use a Container	207
4.5	Build Backgrounds to Assist Layout	210
	4.5.1 When to Use Backgrounds	211
	4.5.2 How to Use Backgrounds	211
4.6	Universe Connectivity	214
	4.6.1 Query Refresh Button	215
	4.6.2 Query Prompt Selector	216
4.7	Summary	219
5	**Advanced UI Components**	**221**
5.1	Advanced Charts	221
	5.1.1 Stacked Column Chart	222
	5.1.2 Stacked Bar and Area Chart	227
	5.1.3 Combination Chart	227
	5.1.4 OHLC Chart	229
	5.1.5 Candlestick Chart	239
	5.1.6 Radar Chart	240
	5.1.7 Filled Radar Chart	243
	5.1.8 Tree Map	245
	5.1.9 Sparkline Chart	247
	5.1.10 Bullet Chart	251

5.2   Advanced Selectors 255
        5.2.1   Accordion Menu 255
        5.2.2   Icon 261
        5.2.3   Play Selector 263
        5.2.4   Calendar 270
5.3   Advanced Single-Value Components 273
        5.3.1   Dual Slider 273
        5.3.2   Spinner 275
        5.3.3   Play Control 276
        5.3.4   Value 278
5.4   Displaying Data in a Table 280
        5.4.1   List View 280
        5.4.2   Spreadsheet Table 285
        5.4.3   Grid 289
5.5   Using Art 292
        5.5.1   Image Component 292
        5.5.2   Shapes 294
        5.5.3   Lines 298
5.6   Use Maps for Geographical Representation 299
5.7   Web Connectivity 304
        5.7.1   Connection Refresh Button 304
        5.7.2   URL Button 307
        5.7.3   Slide Show 312
        5.7.4   SWF Loader 314
5.8   Others 315
        5.8.1   Local Scenario Button 315
        5.8.2   Trend Icon 317
        5.8.3   Trend Analyzer 318
        5.8.4   History 321
        5.8.5   Print Button 324
        5.8.6   Reset Button 324
        5.8.7   Source Data 325
        5.8.8   Panel Set 328
5.9   Summary 333

6   Data Connectivity Basics 335

6.1   Embedded Excel Spreadsheet 336
        6.1.1   Role of Excel 337

6.1.2   How to Use Excel 337
6.2   Import Data from an Excel File 340
6.2.1   When to Import Data from an Excel File 340
6.2.2   How to Import Data from an Excel File 341
6.3   Security Issues Related to Accessing External Data 341
6.3.1   Run Locally 342
6.3.2   Run on a Web Server 343
6.4   XML Data 343
6.4.1   When to Use XML Data 346
6.4.2   How to Use XML Data 347
6.4.3   Practice 357
6.5   Web Service Connection 364
6.5.1   When to Use a Web Service Connection 364
6.5.2   How to Use a Web Service Connection 365
6.6   Excel XML Map 369
6.6.1   When to Use an Excel XML Map 370
6.6.2   How to Use an Excel XML Map 370
6.7   Summary 373

7   Advanced Data Connectivity 375

7.1   Query as a Web Service 376
7.1.1   When to Use Query as a Web Service 376
7.1.2   How to Use Query as a Web Service 377
7.2   SAP NetWeaver BW Connection 385
7.2.1   When to Use SAP NetWeaver BW Connection 386
7.2.2   How to Use SAP NetWeaver BW Connection 387
7.3   Live Office Connection 388
7.3.1   When to Use Live Office Connection 389
7.3.2   How to Insert SAP BusinessObjects Reports in Excel 391
7.3.3   How to Use Live Office Connection 391
7.3.4   Practice 397
7.4   Crystal Reports Data Consumer 399
7.4.1   When to Use the Crystal Reports Data Consumer
Connection 401
7.4.2   How to Use the Crystal Reports Data Consumer
Connection 401
7.4.3   Practice 408

	7.5	Flash Variables	411
		7.5.1 When to Use Flash Variables	412
		7.5.2 How to Use Flash Variables	412
	7.6	FS Command	417
		7.6.1 When to Use FS Command	417
		7.6.2 How to Use FS Command	418
		7.6.3 Practice	421
	7.7	External Interface Connection	424
		7.7.1 When to Use an External Interface Connection	424
		7.7.2 How to Use an External Interface Connection	425
		7.7.3 Practice	427
	7.8	LCDS Connection	431
		7.8.1 When to Use an LCDS Connection	432
		7.8.2 How to Use an LCDS Connection	433
	7.9	Portal Data	435
		7.9.1 When to Use Portal Data	436
		7.9.2 How to Use Portal Data	436
	7.10	Summary	440

8 Special Features 441

	8.1	Drill-Down	441
		8.1.1 When to Use Drill-Down	442
		8.1.2 How to Use Drill-Down	443
		8.1.3 Drill Down from One Chart to Another	444
		8.1.4 Drill-Down on the Same Chart	447
	8.2	Make Smart Use of Dynamic Visibility	452
		8.2.1 When to Use Dynamic Visibility	453
		8.2.2 How to Use Dynamic Visibility	456
		8.2.3 Practice	458
	8.3	Alerts	464
		8.3.1 How to Use Alerts	464
		8.3.2 Practice	465
	8.4	Direct Data Binding	472
		8.4.1 One-Dimensional Binding	473
		8.4.2 Two-Dimensional Binding	474
	8.5	Export	474
		8.5.1 Flash	475
		8.5.2 AIR	475

	8.5.3	HTML	476
	8.5.4	SAP BusinessObjects Platform	476
	8.5.5	PDF	477
	8.5.6	PowerPoint Slide	478
	8.5.7	Outlook	479
	8.5.8	Word	479
8.6	Themes and Colors		479
	8.6.1	How to Apply a Theme	480
	8.6.2	How to Apply a Color Scheme	482
	8.6.3	How to Create a Customized Color Scheme	483
8.7	Summary		488

9 A Comprehensive Hands-On Example 489

9.1	Planning the Dashboard		491
	9.1.1	Plan the Workflow	491
	9.1.2	Plan the UI	492
9.2	Preparing Data		493
	9.2.1	The US Map	494
	9.2.2	The Gauge	495
	9.2.3	The Column Chart	495
	9.2.4	The Line Chart	497
	9.2.5	The Radio Button	500
	9.2.6	The Pie Chart	500
9.3	Organizing Data in Excel		501
9.4	Designing the Dashboard		505
	9.4.1	Position the UI Components	505
	9.4.2	Import the Excel File	506
	9.4.3	Connect to External Data	508
	9.4.4	Adjust the Appearance	509
9.5	Summary		510

10 Introduction to the SAP BusinessObjects Dashboards SDK 511

10.1	About the SAP BusinessObjects Dashboards SDK	511
10.2	About Flex	512
10.3	When to Use the SDK	513
10.4	How to Use the SDK	515
10.5	What Can I Do with the SDK?	518

10.5.1 Flex Applications 520

10.5.2 Data Processors, Connections, and Functions 521

10.6 SDK Best Practices 521

10.6.1 Use Only What You Need 521

10.6.2 Bindings 522

10.6.3 Use Custom Property Sheets 522

10.6.4 Don't Repeat Yourself 522

10.6.5 Develop Test Containers 522

10.6.6 Trace and Alert 523

10.6.7 Development Approaches (MXML versus ActionScript) 523

10.6.8 Styling 523

10.7 SDK Pitfalls 524

10.7.1 Flash Shared Local Objects are Unreliable 524

10.7.2 XLPs and XLXs Should Be Archived 524

10.7.3 Common Component Classes—First in Wins 525

10.8 Summary 525

11 Get Started with Custom Component Basics 527

11.1 Developing Basic Add-On Property Sheets 527

11.1.1 Property Sheet Data Binding 528

11.1.2 Explicitly Setting Property Values 531

11.1.3 Explicitly Getting Property Values 532

11.1.4 Property Sheet Styling 532

11.1.5 Basic Property Sheet Overview 532

11.1.6 Proxy.Bind Explained 542

11.2 Developing Basic Add-On Components 543

11.2.1 Main Component Initialization Event Handler and
Import Statements 544

11.2.2 Private Variables 544

11.2.3 Public Chart Color Variable—xcChartColor 545

11.2.4 Public Chart Series Variable 545

11.2.5 Public Chart Data Variable 546

11.2.6 Chart Building Function 548

11.2.7 Tooltip Function 551

11.2.8 MXML Markup: Grid Lines and Cartesian Chart 552

11.3 Creating Basic Component Packages 552

11.3.1 Basic Component Packaging Steps 553

	11.3.2	Packaging for Special Components	554
	11.3.3	Packaging Best Practices	555
11.4	Summary		555

12 Implement Advanced Custom Add-On Component Features ... 557

12.1	Implementing Advanced Property Sheet Features		557
	12.1.1	Subelement Binding	558
	12.1.2	Persisting Property Sheet Values	560
	12.1.3	Retrieving Persisted Property Sheet Values	561
	12.1.4	Setting Custom Component Property Values	562
	12.1.5	Retrieving Custom Component Property Values	562
	12.1.6	Generating Reusable Property Sheet Patterns	563
	12.1.7	Communicating with External Data Services	565
	12.1.8	Implementing Advanced Component Features	566
	12.1.9	Communicating at the Application Level	577
	12.1.10	Additional Packaging Features	578
12.2	Where to Go from Here: Tips, Tricks, and Resources		579
12.3	Summary		579

13 Hands-On: Develop Your Custom Add-On Component 581

13.1	Creating the Chart		581
13.2	Creating the Flex Component and Property Sheet Project		582
	13.2.1	Creating the Flex Property Sheet	588
	13.2.2	Creating the Flex Component	594
13.3	Creating the Flex Test Container		597
13.4	Creating the Packager and SAP BusinessObjects Dashboards XLX Add-On		597
13.5	Creating the Data Sharing Component		598
	13.5.1	Model Locator	599
	13.5.2	Component Files	600
	13.5.3	SAP BusinessObjects Dashboards Component Files	602
	13.5.4	Property Sheet	603
13.6	Summary		608

Appendices 609

A Location Intelligence 611
   A.1   What Makes Up Location Intelligence? 612
   A.2   Why Location Intelligence Is Important 614
   A.3   How Does Location Intelligence Fit into SAP BusinessObjects
           Dashboards? 615
   A.4   Location Intelligence Options in SAP BusinessObjects
           Dashboards 617
   A.5   Common Location Intelligence Use Cases 621
   A.6   Location Intelligence Best Practices 626
   A.7   Summary 633
B Tips for Using SAP BusinessObjects Dashboards 635
   B.1   Using SAP BusinessObjects Dashboards in an SAP BusinessObjects
           Environment 635
   B.2   Deployment and Migration 643
   B.3   How to Use SAP BusinessObjects Dashboards with
           SAP NetWeaver BW and SAP NetWeaver Portal 644
   B.4   Supported Excel Functions 647
   B.5   SAP BusinessObjects Dashboards Editions 659
   B.6   Tips for Creating a Good Dashboard 662
C The Authors 669

Index 671

Foreword

I recall my excitement when I first picked up the Xcelsius software in 2007, then moved on to build the biggest Xcelsius community on the web. After watching executives salivate over their data once it was transformed into a visual masterpiece, it was clear that this software was more than just a business intelligence tool. It was a game changer in the market, allowing end users to rapidly deploy powerful visual dashboards that could be connected to any data source. Originally built as a tool for Excel users, it quickly became a companion for financial analysts and a toy for senior executives, landing it in the lap of many unsuspecting report developers.

As the founder of *www.EverythingXcelsius.com*, I was truly honored when I was asked to write the Foreword for the second edition of this book. The first edition was a dream come true for our Xcelsius (now renamed SAP BusinessObjects Dashboards) Gurus community. It was the first book ever published to cover the "enterprise" data connectivity layer of Xcelsius, providing best practices for options such as the Query Browser (released in 4.0), Query as a Web Service (QaaWS), SAP BusinessObjects Live Office, and the SAP BICS connector.

It's no secret that connecting SAP BusinessObjects Dashboards to any kind of enterprise data sources has been and continues to be a challenge for many developers. Reading this book is guaranteed not only to give you a jump start, but also a concrete foundation to plan a solid data connectivity strategy for your dashboards. In addition, with the changes to the software after the release of SAP BusinessObjects 4.0, this second edition of *Creating Dashboards with SAP Business-Objects—The Comprehensive Guide* is a must read for all SAP business intelligence customers.

The authors are two of the world's most accomplished visual analytics professionals. Ray Li, a former technical lead at Business Objects prior to its acquisition by SAP, was responsible for integrating the suite of Business Objects tools with the SAP software development in Shanghai, China. As the CTO of location intelligence leader Centigon Solutions, there is no one who has a better command for the SAP BusinessObjects SDK in the market than Evan DeLodder. Evan provides a taste of location intelligence in Appendix A as a treat to you, which will help prepare you for what the industry calls "the next wave of BI."

Whether you're a new or existing SAP customer, there is no other book on the market that will start your journey with SAP BusinessObjects Dashboards more smoothly. I advise you to read through Chapter 1 to develop an understanding of what's new to release 4.0, then use the table of contents to learn at your own pace.

Mico Yuk
http://about.me/micoyuk
Blog: *www.EverythingXcelsius.com*
Company: *www.Benchmarkers.com*

SAP BusinessObjects Dashboards is an outstanding and easy-to-use data visualization tool that allows you to create intuitive, interactive, attractive, and powerful analytics or dashboards with secure connections to your real, live data.

1 Introduction to SAP BusinessObjects Dashboards

This chapter provides a general introduction to SAP BusinessObjects Dashboards (previously known as Xcelsius) 4.0, including what it is, what you can do with it, and how it is positioned in the SAP BusinessObjects Business Intelligence (BI) platform. After reading this chapter you should have a basic understanding of SAP BusinessObjects Dashboards and know whether it's the right tool for your analytic and dashboard requirement.

The content is based on SAP BusinessObjects Dashboards 4.0.

1.1 What Is SAP BusinessObjects Dashboards?

SAP BusinessObjects Dashboards is a flagship desktop product of SAP that allows users to transform plain data into interactive Adobe Flash-style visualizations. Simply speaking, it's a solution to design interactive dashboards that can connect to live data to show key metrics. A user can use it to create a dashboard model that can be deployed in Flash format to web portals, the SAP BusinessObjects BI platform, and desktop applications such as PDF, PowerPoint, or Word.

1.1.1 Who Works with SAP BusinessObjects Dashboards?

Roughly speaking, three kinds of people work with SAP BusinessObjects Dashboards: the *designer* who designs the visualization model, the *end user* who consumes the information of the output dashboard, and the *plug-in developer* who writes Flex codes to create new components.

As a dashboard designer, you may want to use this product to create interactive dashboards to visualize your snapshot or live data and turn data into information for decision support. It's often the SAP consultant, or the IT department who works as a dashboard designer. The value of such a person is that he uses the product to create reliable, visually stunning, and accurate dashboards to access timely and relevant business data.

The end users, often the managing-level business users or decision-makers in a company or government, use the output of the dashboard designer, which is often a Flash file or a PowerPoint slide where the data, often the key metrics, is represented in an intuitive and attractive way to answer business questions more easily and to make wiser decisions for the organization. The benefits are:

1. The dashboard is intuitive—so the user can grasp the information quickly at a glance. Moreover, with data visualized graphically instead of in a plain table, the user can find something behind the data with his experience and instinct.

2. The dashboard is interactive—so the user can work with the dashboard for analysis, such as drill-down and selecting from a map.

3. The dashboard is good-looking—so the user enjoys the process of reading the dashboard and is willing to spend time on business analysis with it.

People with no software experience can also use SAP BusinessObjects Dashboards for noncommercial use or just for fun in their homes. For example, you can create a dashboard showing your family's daily expense division at the end of a month.

Another group of people who are also involved in SAP BusinessObjects Dashboards are developers or programmers who develop plug-ins or new components using the SAP BusinessObjects Dashboards component software development kit (SDK) for their specific use scenarios. They can then either share the new plug-in with others for free or sell it in a marketplace. Such people don't work with SAP BusinessObjects Dashboards directly to design dashboards, but work with some development tool such as Flex Builder or Eclipse to create plug-ins with the Flex programming language.

1.1.2 Installation

SAP BusinessObjects Dashboards can only be installed on Windows systems from Windows XP, Vista, or up to Windows 7, either 32-bit or 64-bit edition.

However, its output, a Flash file (*.swf*) or something else containing the Flash file such as HTML and Adobe PDF (Portable Document Format), is supported by all platforms including Mac OS, Linux, and so on. You can run it as a stand-alone application using Adobe Flash Player or Adobe AIR or through a web browser such as Internet Explorer or Firefox. To run the Flash files, you need to have Adobe Flash Player 9.0.151.0 or above installed. As a result, its output can't run on Apple iPhone or iPad.

The installation requires Adobe Flash Player 9 or higher and Microsoft Office Excel XP or higher installed on your machine. The installer must have administrator privileges to continue.

SAP BusinessObjects Dashboards is a multilingual product, supporting more than 10 languages. It provides a step-by-step guide in your selected language to make your installation process easy.

By default it will be installed to *C:\Program Files\SAP BusinessObjects\Xcelsius*. After installation, you can launch it from your desktop or START menu. It provides an intuitive integrated development environment (IDE) with which you can easily design the dashboard you want by simply dragging and dropping user interface (UI) elements and setting their properties. The user doesn't need to have any programming skill to create a powerful dashboard, thus saving much time for users to get hands-on. Throughout this book you will see exactly what you can do with SAP BusinessObjects Dashboards to present your data and how to do that.

1.1.3 Relationship with Excel

SAP BusinessObjects Dashboards has much to do with Microsoft Excel, as you may have guessed from its previous name, Xcelsius. It was originally designed to turn Excel spreadsheet data into dashboards.

Before the release of SAP BusinessObjects Business Intelligence (BI) 4.0, Microsoft Excel was SAP BusinessObjects' only direct data source—any data could be read from or written into only the embedded Excel spreadsheet. In the new release, Excel is still an important and mostly used data source for dashboards, but a new feature called direct data binding enables the designer to bind live data from Universe queries directly to UI components, without the help of Excel.

Compared to Excel, SAP BusinessObjects Dashboards provides a better look and feel, is more powerful and easier to use, and can be deployed to more environments.

In the meantime, users can still benefit from their experience with Excel to write Excel formulas (for example, HLookup, Match, etc.) for calculation to make a powerful visualization.

1.2   What Can SAP BusinessObjects Dashboards Do?

A skilled designer can create attractive, interactive, and powerful dashboards, with rich intuitive information that the consumer can understand and act upon immediately. This can help executives and business users to better understand their business situations and then make wiser decisions—to understand the past, be clear about the present, and predict the future. It applies to both enterprise and individual uses of data visualization.

Under certain circumstances, the functionalities of SAP BusinessObjects Dashboards may have some limitation in satisfying your needs. To solve such problems, SAP BusinessObjects Dashboards provides a Flex-based software development kit (SDK), which you can use to create SAP Dashboard add-ons for your specific requirements. To do this, you need to be familiar with the Adobe Flex programming language.

You can design your dashboard with rich UI (user interface) elements, connecting to your live data source with one or more kinds of data connectivity, and distribute it to others by either exporting it to a local SWF file and sending it to others or hosting the output in a web application server so that the information consumer can access it with a web browser.

With the help of SAP BusinessObjects Dashboards, you can:

- Create attractive and interactive dashboards, using several kinds of UI controls such as charts and gauges
- Connect dashboards to your real and live data, using one or more kinds of data connectivity provided by SAP BusinessObjects Dashboards such as web service connections and XML data
- Distribute dashboards through several media including Flash, Microsoft Office Word and PowerPoint, and the SAP BusinessObjects BI platform
- Develop an SAP BusinessObjects Dashboards add-on component using the SAP BusinessObjects Dashboards SDK when the existing features have limitations for your specific requirement

In the three following sections, we'll talk more about each of SAP BusinessObjects Dashboards' capabilities of UI components, data connectivity, and distribution.

1.2.1   Data Visualization Capabilities

If you've worked with Excel, you know that when there's too much data, it's difficult to understand and hard to remember what you're seeing in tables. However, by visualizing data with SAP BusinessObjects Dashboards, the consumer can easily and quickly understand the data through the intuitive graphics and even the information behind the data (such as the relative difference between two items) and have an intuitive impression of the visualization and thus can remember the data easily.

An SAP BusinessObjects Dashboards visualization provides insight into complex data and delivers confidence to those who will use it to make decisions. SAP BusinessObjects Dashboards provides several categories of UI elements such as charts, gauges, and maps for data visualization. Each category may contain several kinds of UI components to satisfy different situations. For example, the category *Chart* includes pie charts, stacked column charts, and bubble charts. They can be used to show a part-to-whole contribution or percentage, comparison among counterparts, trends over a period, and so on.

Most charts support drill-down ability, which means you can drill from summary levels to more detailed levels. This is very important and helpful in data analysis. By using drill-down, you can drill from the top level to the more detailed level to find the de facto cause of a problem.

As displayed in Figure 1.1, you can convert data presentation from a static and difficult to understand Excel worksheet to a dynamic, visualized, and easy to understand presentation.

In Chapters 4 and 5 you'll see detailed descriptions of all the UI elements provided by SAP BusinessObjects Dashboards. To help you get acquainted with those UI elements, here we'll show you some simple examples, categorized into percentage, comparison, and interactivity.

Remember, choosing the right UI element as your display medium is one of the most important steps during the design of a good dashboard.

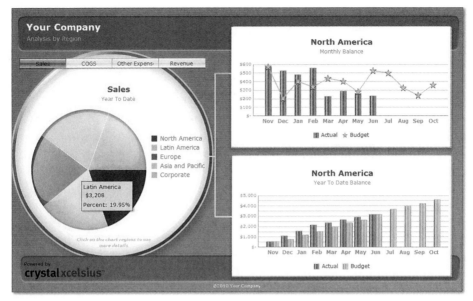

Figure 1.1 A Typical Dynamic Dashboard Created with SAP BusinessObjects Dashboards

Percentage

Sometimes you may want to see the percentage or the part-to-whole contribution of each item to get a rough idea at a glance about who's doing well and who's doing badly. For example, you can use a pie chart to show the contribution of each region to the company's total sales revenue. SAP BusinessObjects Dashboards provides pie charts and radar charts for this situation. Figure 1.2 and Figure 1.3 show examples.

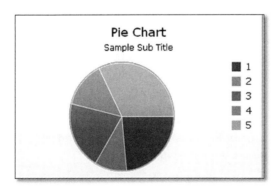

Figure 1.2 A Pie Chart to Visualize Contributions

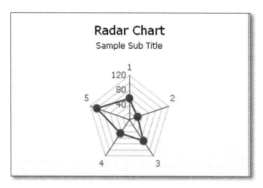

Figure 1.3 A Radar Chart to Visualize Percentages

These figures are just examples. Note that the title, subtitle, color, legend, and so on can all be customized according to your real data. For more information about these charts and how to use them, refer to Chapter 4.

Comparison

You use comparison charts when you want to show the differences among several items instead of the contribution of each item to the total.

SAP BusinessObjects Dashboards provides several charts for comparison such as column charts, bar charts, stacked bar charts, and so on. For example, you can use a column chart to show the sales amounts of all regions or to see the difference between region 1 and region 2. Figure 1.4 shows a column chart together with a stacked column chart.

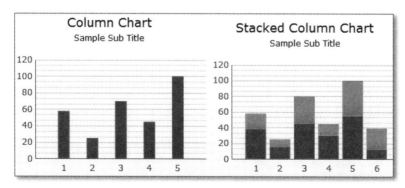

Figure 1.4 A Column and a Stacked Column Chart to Show a Comparison

SAP BusinessObjects Dashboards also provides bubble charts and XY charts for multidimensional comparison and analysis. For example, you can use a bubble chart to compare a group or series of items based on three parameters. It has both X- and Y-axes to represent the item location over the chart area and a Z value to represent the item size. For another example, you can use such charts to represent the market composition information, with the X-axis representing the return on investment (ROI) by industry type, the Y-axis representing the cash flow, and the Z-axis representing the market value. Note that the bigger the bubble is, the higher the Z-value is. Figure 1.5 shows a simple bubble chart.

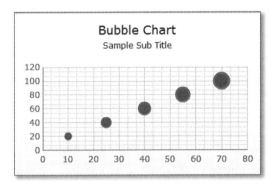

Figure 1.5 A Bubble Chart to Show a Multidimensional Comparison

Interactivity

SAP BusinessObjects Dashboards provides several UI components to make your dashboard interactive including combo boxes, sliders, gauges, maps, fisheye picture menus, and calendars, which work like parameters or filters. The user can see information he's interested in by setting corresponding values from the components. Essentially, such UI components all act as selectors.

For example, you can create a dashboard with a combo box of regions so that the end user can see the information for a specific region instead of all of it by selecting one region from the combo box.

SAP BusinessObjects Dashboards provides maps of many countries as selectors; the user can easily select the region he's interested in. Imagine that you need to select a region or city without a map; you have to select from a large list—either a combo or a radio box.

A map is a very good format to display geographical data. If the default maps can't satisfy your needs, you can use the SDK component to develop a new one, such as a map of your city or one for your organization that has subsidiaries in different countries.

You can also create a gauge-based dashboard in which gauges are available for the user to set values interactively. Such dashboards are usually used for what-if analysis, when you need to change the conditions on the fly to see what will happen in a particular situation. Figure 1.6 shows an example of gauge usage.

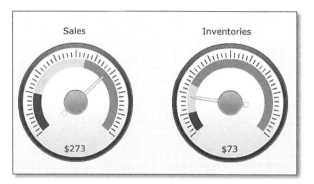

Figure 1.6 A Gauge for Displaying and Setting a Numeric Value

1.2.2 Data Connectivity Capabilities

To make a dashboard really useful and meaningful, you need to bind UI elements to your real and live data. This way, you enable the dashboard to reflect the real status and convey the accurate, up-to-the-minute information, so that it can be really helpful for decision making.

Data connectivity is here to solve such a problem. SAP BusinessObjects Dashboards 4.0 provides several kinds of data connectivity for your specific data sources, so you can provide everyone in your organization with live data and manage multiple data sources by controlling all data connections from one central interface—the Data Manager of SAP BusinessObjects Dashboards.

Generally speaking, there are two ways to reflect real data in your dashboard: Input data in the embedded spreadsheet at design time, or connect to the external data source using one or more kinds of data connectivity.

An Excel spreadsheet is embedded into SAP BusinessObjects Dashboards as the direct data source for UI elements. You can write your data in a separate Excel spreadsheet file and then import it into SAP BusinessObjects Dashboards, input the data directly into the embedded spreadsheet in its workspace, or connect to dynamic data through data connectivity and map the returned data into the embedded spreadsheet or directly to UI components.

You can write the data that is known at the time you create the dashboard, such as the metadata of the dashboard like the titles and creation time, directly in the embedded spreadsheet and bind it to UI elements. This is usually the case when the data will not change and the user is OK seeing the same data each time he views the dashboard.

However, in most cases the data won't be available until runtime. Sometimes the data must be processed by a server before being consumed in your dashboard. Sometimes the data resides in another data source such as an XML file or in another system such as production. To connect to such data, you need to use data connectivity.

A wide range of data connectivity methods are available to satisfy different environments, such as web service connections and XML data and SAP NetWeaver Business Warehouse (BW) connections to connect to a BW query. For example, let's say you're creating a dashboard to show the sales information for each region in each quarter. The data resides in the corporate database, and a web service hosted in a web application server is providing the data you require. In this case, you can create a web service connection to that web service to request data, and feed it to the UI components.

1.2.3 Distribution

Your dashboard is designed to communicate information in the best way and to be consumed by someone else. With SAP BusinessObjects Dashboards, you can export your dashboard into many formats so it can be distributed through several kinds of media. The available distribution methods are explained here:

▶ You can export the dashboard to Macromedia Flash, Adobe AIR, or HTML so it can be viewed stand-alone or from a web browser.

▶ You can export it to desktop applications such as PDF or Microsoft Office documents including Word, Outlook, and PowerPoint so you can send your dashboard via email or present it during a speech. This way you can leverage the large installation of Microsoft Office.

▶ If you are an SAP BusinessObjects user, you can export it to the SAP BusinessObjects BI platform. By doing so, you can use the security settings provided by SAP BusinessObjects so that only people you permit have the right to access your dashboard, and the data they see will depend on their roles.

1.2.4 Changes in SAP BusinessObjects Dashboards 4.0

SAP BusinessObjects 4.0 is a big release with several significant improvements and changes to the product suite. For SAP BusinessObjects Dashboards, most changes are related to SAP BusinessObjects (or the BI platform) or SAP NetWeaver BW. That means that if you're using SAP BusinessObjects Dashboards or working in a non-SAP or non-BusinessObjects environment, most changes in release 4.0 will not affect you. For add-on developers, the change is the support for Flex 4 in its SDK component.

In the rest of this section we'll briefly talk about some changes in SAP BusinessObjects Dashboards 4.0, including those related to SAP BusinessObjects such as direct integration with Universe (Common Semantic Layer), direct data binding, translation and processing servers, and those independent of SAP BusinessObjects such as dynamic coloring.

New Dashboard Design Object

In SAP BusinessObjects Enterprise 3.x, there are two types of objects for dashboards: a dashboard definition file (*.xlf*, referred to as model), which is for the designer and can only be opened by SAP Dashboard (Xcelsius) Design; and the dashboard output, often a Flash file (*.swf*), which is for the end user to view with Flash Player or Internet Explorer.

In SAP BusinessObjects 4.0, a new object type called the dashboard design object was introduced in the Business Intelligence platform, containing both the design model and the output Flash file. When the end user views the dashboard from the SAP BusinessObjects portal, the Flash file is opened. The designer can open it from SAP BusinessObjects Dashboards to change the design, and the Flash file in the object will be automatically updated without the need of re-exporting.

Dashboards created with SAP BusinessObjects Dashboards 4.0 can only be saved to the SAP BusinessObjects 4.0 platform. Older versions are not supported.

Direct Integration with Universe

In Xcelsius, to consume data from a SAP BusinessObjects Universe, you had to either expose data fields of the universe as a Query as a Web Service (QaaWS) and create a QaaWS connectivity, or create a Web Intelligence document on top of the Universe and then use either Live Office or BI Web Service. Either way was a little troublesome.

In SAP BusinessObjects Dashboards 4.0, life can be easier with the embedded Query Browser, where the dashboard designer can connect to a relational universe (Common Semantic Layer, or CSL) and build a query by defining fields, filters, and prompts for the data.

Note that there are also some significant changes to Universe in the 4.0 release, such as multi-data source support with the help of Data Federator, the new information design tool (IDT), and the new postfix *unx* instead of *unv*. The direct integration only works for the new semantic layer—universes created in SAP BusinessObjects 3.x releases can't be used directly here without conversion, nor can you connect to an SAP BusinessObjects 3.x system.

Direct Data Binding

In Xcelsius, the embedded spreadsheet worked as the only direct data source for UI components. The input and output data of any data connectivity needed to be mapped to cells of the embedded Excel file before it could be used with UI components.

In SAP BusinessObjects Dashboards 4.0, you can bind the returned data of a Universe query directly to the UI components without the need to store data in the intermediate Excel spreadsheet. To do this, when setting the data (labels, series values, etc.) of a UI component, you select a Universe query instead of the embedded spreadsheet and select one or more fields from the returned data.

In Xcelsius, the destination of data insertion for some UI components could only be cells in the embedded spreadsheet. Now it can also be a Universe query by binding the destination to a Universe query prompt.

For universes with parameters, a new UI component called Query Prompt Selector has been introduced that can automatically handle prompt value selection behavior based on the metadata of the query prompts defined in the universe. It can handle parameters of single value, single or multiple selection with a list of values (LOV), or single or multiple selection with a cascading list of values. Note that this feature is only available for data returned from Universe queries, but not any other kind of data connectivity.

Text Translation

A dashboard can be multilingual so that it can be used in subsidiaries in different regions of a large multinational corporation.

To do this in Xcelsius, you needed to translate the metadata and data into several languages either inside the embedded Excel spreadsheet or in a database and return localized texts based on the user selection or location.

SAP BusinessObjects Dashboards 4.0 can integrate with the Translation Manager tool by BusinessObjects so that the designer can focus on just the visualization, and the translator can work with just the Translation Manager tool to do the translations. At runtime, the user sees localized text depending on his preferred viewing locale (PVL) defined in the SAP BusinessObjects BI launchpad.

This functionality can only be used when you have exported your dashboard to the SAP BusinessObjects BI platform. The texts in the dashboard that can be translated are most text inputs such as titles, subtitles, series names, and so on and data in the embedded spreadsheet cells that are marked as translatable by the designer via the menu path FILE • TRANSLATION SETTINGS. Note that this is different from translation on the SAP NetWeaver BW side via SAP • TRANSLATION SETTINGS.

Regional Formatting

The display formats of number, currency, date, time, and so on may vary in different regions. For example, you need to decide whether and how to show the thousand separator, whether to insert the correct currency symbol, and more.

To be usable across subsidiaries in different regions of a large corporation, the dashboard needs be able to show data in a format suitable for the corresponding regions. In Xcelsius, this was difficult to achieve.

In SAP BusinessObjects Dashboards 4.0, you can retrieve the user's preferred viewing locale (PVL) specified in the BI launchpad and display the number, currency, date, time, and so on in that format at runtime. Like text translation, to use this feature the dashboard needs be exported to and viewed from the SAP BusinessObjects Business Intelligence platform.

Processing Servers

In SAP BusinessObjects 4.0, a new processing layer is provided to address the performance and scalability requirements of large-scale dashboard deployment. There are two new servers in this release for this purpose. One is the Dashboard Design Processing Server between the dashboard and the data source, which accepts and processes data requests. It can share data among dashboards to reduce database accesses. The other is the Dashboard Design Cache Server for data caching and sharing among different data requests.

These servers are hosted on the SAP BusinessObjects server side, the same as other servers. They are also integrated into the standard SAP BI platform services including auditing and monitoring.

Note that both servers will only take effect when your dashboard is retrieving data from a relational universe (semantic layer), either through a direct Universe query or through Query as a Web Service.

UI Changes

In this edition we'll include the components that were either newly introduced in SAP BusinessObjects Dashboards 4.0 or not covered in the first edition such as bullet charts, sparkline charts, canvas containers, a new connectivity called SAP NetWeaver BW Connection to connect directly to a BW query, and a menu called SAP to save the dashboard object to or open it from the SAP system. They'll be covered in Chapters 2, 4, and 5.

To work with Universe queries, a new view called QUERY BROWSER has been added to list and manage the Universe queries along with two new UI components, the QUERY REFRESH BUTTON and the QUERY PROMPT SELECTOR.

For direct data binding, a new option has been added to the BIND button in the PROPERTIES panel of most UI components.

1.2.5 Extensibility

There are a lot of active forums and communities with plenty of members talking about the design and usage of SAP BusinessObjects Dashboards. During your development, when you meet with some questions, you can check such forums to ask for advice.

SAP BusinessObjects Dashboards brings with it a wide range of UI components and data connectivity methods, but sometimes you may encounter a scenario where you need something new. SAP BusinessObjects Dashboards is extensible in that it provides a software development kit (SDK), which you can use to create your custom UI components and data connectivity. Moreover, some companies are working on developing a new component, and there are many active forums about how to use this product. Also, SAP keeps releasing new features for it, and according to the SAP roadmap, it's the recommended and preferred dashboard tool.

1.3 SAP BusinessObjects Dashboards in the SAP BusinessObjects Portfolio

SAP BusinessObjects Dashboards is the dashboard and visualization component in the SAP BusinessObjects BI portfolio.

In the reporting and analysis category, SAP BusinessObjects provides several outstanding tools: SAP Crystal Reports for detailed and fixed-format reporting, Web Intelligence Rich Client for ad-hoc query and reporting, SAP BusinessObjects Dashboards for dashboarding, SAP Advanced Analysis for self-service multidimensional analysis either within Microsoft Office Excel and PowerPoint or on the web, and SAP BusinessObjects Explorer for self-service analysis.

SAP BusinessObjects Dashboards can work with several other SAP BusinessObjects products in a BI solution such as SAP Crystal Reports, SAP BusinessObjects Web Intelligence, Universe, and SAP BusinessObjects Enterprise, as explained next.

First, it can consume data from SAP Crystal Reports or SAP BusinessObjects Web Intelligence with the help of SAP BusinessObjects Live Office. You can create an SAP Crystal Reports report within a Microsoft Excel document after installing SAP BusinessObjects Live Office. The Excel document can then be used as a data source for SAP BusinessObjects Dashboards. Of course, you can also export your SAP Crystal Reports report directly into an Excel file, but the data won't be updated automatically.

A special kind of data connectivity, Crystal Report Data Consumer, can be used to integrate an SAP dashboard with SAP Crystal Reports with data communication from the SAP Crystal Reports report to the dashboard, as will be explained in Chapter 7.

From Web Intelligence Rich Client, you can expose a block of data as a web service, named Business Intelligence Web Service (often referred to as BI Web Service). SAP BusinessObjects Dashboards can then get data from Web Intelligence documents by creating Query as a Web Service connectivities connecting to the BI Web Services.

Second, it can also consume data from a universe with the help of Query as a Web Service (QaaWS), another SAP BusinessObjects product that exposes data from a Universe query into a standard web service.

Third, with the new Query Browser view, you can create queries on top of relational universes directly within the SAP BusinessObjects Dashboards environment and feed the return data of the Universe query into UI components directly or to the embedded spreadsheet.

Last, SAP dashboards can be exported to an SAP BusinessObjects Business Intelligence platform, thus distributing the dashboards to other users in the organization and using SAP BusinessObjects security mechanisms to control users' access. Other SAP BusinessObjects users can access the dashboard through a browser from the BI portal such as BI launchpad, if they are permitted to.

1.4   Summary

In this chapter we introduced SAP BusinessObjects Dashboards as a powerful yet easy-to-use tool to design dashboards and its targeted designer and end user. As to its functionalities, we talked about its rich set of UI elements and included some figures to give you a rough idea about what it can do. We also talked about its data connectivity to connect to external live data and how to distribute it to other users in several formats. In the next chapter we'll go through the design environment of SAP BusinessObjects Dashboards 4.0 to get you familiar with it.

As a dashboard designer, you need to understand how to use SAP BusinessObjects Dashboards to create efficient, attractive, and powerful dashboards.

2 Becoming Familiar with SAP BusinessObjects Dashboards

SAP BusinessObjects Dashboards 4.0 provides an intuitive integrated development environment (IDE) for creating dashboards. You easily lay out the UI components, create data connectivities, and configure their properties inside the IDE. This chapter will illustrate all of the elements of SAP BusinessObjects Dashboards that you will work with to help you get acquainted with it, including menus, toolbars, the canvas, and the newly introduced components such as the Query Browser.

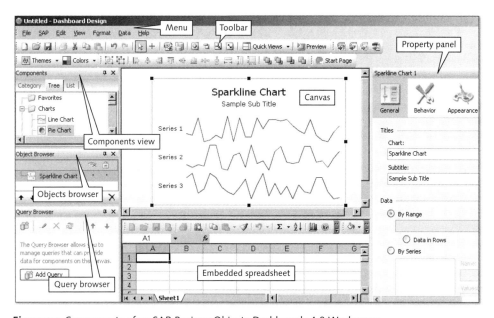

Figure 2.1 Components of an SAP BusinessObjects Dashboards 4.0 Workspace

After reading this chapter you'll understand the purpose of each command in SAP BusinessObjects Dashboards 4.0 and know how to adjust the settings of your dashboard.

Figure 2.1 shows the components of SAP BusinessObjects Dashboards 4.0, including the menus, the COMPONENTS browser, the canvas, the property sheet, and the embedded spreadsheet.

In the rest of this chapter, we'll explain all of these elements separately, including their purposes and how to use them.

2.1   Menu

The menu area lies in the first row of the SAP BusinessObjects Dashboards 4.0 designer workspace. We'll explain each of the items in the following sections.

2.1.1   File

This is the most comprehensive menu in SAP BusinessObjects Dashboards. You can create, open, save, export, set translatable texts, or print your dashboard through this FILE menu, as shown in Figure 2.2. Dashboard preferences such as language, default theme, and preset size are also set here.

If you're in an SAP BusinessObjects environment, you can save the dashboard to the Business Intelligence Platform from here. Note that in Xcelsius 2008 the menu name was SAVE TO ENTERPRISE or OPEN FROM ENTERPRISE, while in SAP BusinessObjects Dashboards, ENTERPRISE is replaced by PLATFORM. Similarly, we now call it the Business Intelligence platform instead of BusinessObjects Enterprise.

New

This is a command group including NEW and NEW WITH SPREADSHEET. You use the NEW command to create a new dashboard from scratch. By selecting NEW WITH SPREADSHEET, you're creating a new dashboard and loading data from an existing Excel file (*.xls* or *.xlsx*) into your dashboard. After selecting this command, you'll see an empty canvas and be prompted to select an Excel file, the data of which will be imported into the embedded Excel spreadsheet.

Figure 2.2 The File Menu

Note that the existing Excel file is only used at import time. When the data has been imported, SAP BusinessObjects Dashboards has nothing to do with it any more. Changes to the Excel file will not affect your dashboard. You can even delete the original file. This also means that changes in SAP BusinessObjects Dashboards will not be reflected in the original Excel file. If you want to get the latest content in the Excel file, you have to import it again from the DATA menu.

Open/Save/Save As

You use the OPEN command to open an existing dashboard design object (*.xlf*) from your file system, either locally or on a network location. Similarly, you use the SAVE or SAVE AS... command to save your design as a dashboard definition file.

When you select the OPEN command, a dialog will prompt you to choose a dashboard design file. Which folder is displayed by default can be customized in the PREFERENCES menu item, either LAST FOLDER OPEN or always to a specified folder.

If the dashboard design file you opened is not of the same version as your SAP BusinessObjects Dashboards software, you'll see a warning message showing the risk.

Open from Platform/Save to Platform

The platform here refers to an SAP BusinessObjects Business Intelligence (BI) platform, which was called an enterprise in Xcelsius 2008. Aside from the file system mentioned in the previous section, you can also open an existing dashboard design object (.xlf) from your SAP BusinessObjects system with the command OPEN FROM PLATFORM or save it there using the command SAVE TO PLATFORM.

Another command is SAVE TO PLATFORM AS, which allows you to save the dashboard design object to the BI platform with another name or into another folder without overwriting the existing object.

In SAP BusinessObjects 4.0, the dashboard design object contains two objects—the definition, which is for the designer, and the Flash output for the end user. After making changes to the dashboard, if you don't want to update the Flash output, select SAVE TO PLATFORM AS • DASHBOARD DESIGN OBJECT. Otherwise, select SAVE TO PLATFORM AS – DASHBOARD DESIGN OBJECT to replace the Flash object.

You may want to use these commands when you're collaborating with your colleagues in designing a dashboard. You can use the SAVE TO PLATFORM command to save your design to the SAP Business Intelligence platform so that you or your colleagues can open it in SAP BusinessObjects Dashboards later to review or continue your development.

When you select any such command, you'll be prompted to log on to an SAP BusinessObjects system as shown in Figure 2.3 if you haven't already established an active session with it. Note that you need to log on to an SAP BusinessObjects 4.0 system, not 3.x.

> **Note**
>
> You need the license of the SAP BusinessObjects Dashboards, Departmental Edition (formerly Xcelsius Enterprise) to use this command. Otherwise, it will be disabled in gray.

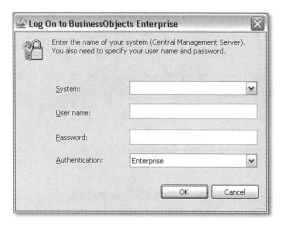

Figure 2.3 The Dialog to Log on to the SAP Business Intelligence Platform

Templates

As you know, the layout including the color, size, and position is very important for an attractive and professional dashboard. SAP BusinessObjects Dashboards provides templates in several categories such as finance, government, HR, and sales.

A template is a fully functional dashboard with predefined layout and data. In some cases, all you need to do before using a template as your working dashboard is to update the data in the embedded spreadsheet.

When you select this command through menu FILE • TEMPLATES, you'll see a dialog showing all available templates, as shown in Figure 2.4.

You can navigate through the dialog to find the template that best fits your requirements. When you've selected a template and clicked the OK button, the template, as a common dashboard design object, is opened in your workspace with all of the UI elements copied to your canvas and the data to your embedded spreadsheet.

Choosing a template means creating a new dashboard from the template. You may treat this operation as NEW FROM A TEMPLATE, not from scratch. If you click this menu item when editing your own dashboard, you'll be asked if you want to save your changes to the old dashboard. That is, if you want to take advantage of a template in the process of designing your dashboard, you have to begin with the template.

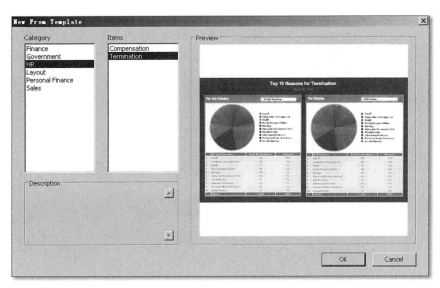

Figure 2.4 Available Templates in SAP BusinessObjects Dashboards 4.0

As mentioned before, SAP BusinessObjects Dashboards templates are common dashboard design source files with the *.xlf* extension. They're copied to your file system during installation. Typically, you can find them in *DASHBOARD_INSTALL_DIR/assets/template*; for example, *C:\Program Files\SAP Business Objects\Xcelsius\assets\template*.

You can add your custom template or category to SAP BusinessObjects Dashboards 4.0 by adding a dashboard definition file (*.xlf*) and its corresponding output, a Flash SWF file to provide a preview, to a folder in the template directory as mentioned above. The next time you launch SAP BusinessObjects Dashboards, you'll see the new template after clicking this menu item. When you select this template, the corresponding definition will be opened in your SAP BusinessObjects Dashboards workspace.

Note that to make this work, the name of the Flash file should be identical to that of the definition file.

Samples

A sample is also a dashboard definition known as an SAP BusinessObjects Dashboards source file with an *.xlf* extension. Its purpose is to illustrate the effect of a feature of SAP BusinessObjects Dashboards 4.0 and how to use it.

SAP BusinessObjects Dashboards 4.0 provides many kinds of samples from which you can learn how to design dashboards. The samples cover the most important features, including alerts, drill-down, dynamic visibility, and trend analyzer.

These samples are also fully functional, with both UI components and data. You can preview the sample to see the effect and check the properties of each component to find out how it's designed. You can then use that feature in your future design.

When you select the SAMPLE command, a dialog will prompt you by showing all of the available samples, as displayed in Figure 2.5. You can click any category in the CATEGORY list to see items belonging to that category displayed in the ITEMS list. To the right of the dialog is a preview of the sample dashboard, and on the bottom left is the description.

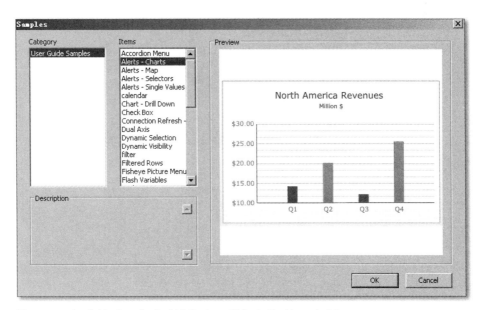

Figure 2.5 Available Samples in SAP BusinessObjects Dashboards 4.0

When you've selected a sample and clicked the OK button, the sample dashboard will open in SAP BusinessObjects Dashboards, as displayed in Figure 2.6. You can then check how it's designed to learn from it or continue your design on top of it.

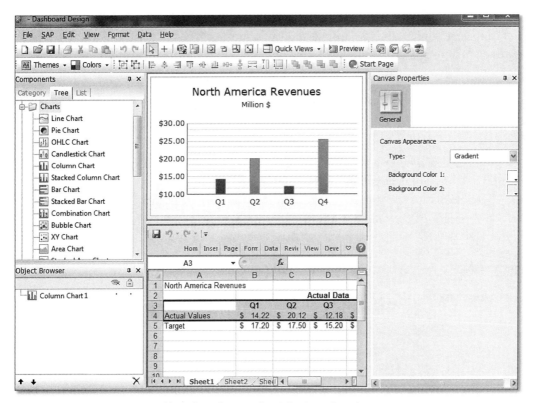

Figure 2.6 Your Dashboard Workspace after Selecting a Sample

You may find that samples are similar to templates and wonder why they're separated. The difference lies in their purpose. The focus of a template is the appearance, showing how to define the dashboard layout to make your dashboard look professional in different scenarios. It focuses on high-level layout and interaction. Samples, on the other hand, focus on some specific functionalities of SAP BusinessObjects Dashboards, showing what you can achieve and how—for example, how to create a dashboard with drill-down and trend analysis capabilities.

Similar to a template, a sample is also a normal dashboard definition file with an *.xlf* extension. These files are copied to your file system during installation. You can find them at *DASHBOARD_INSTALL_DIR/assets/samples*; for example, *C:\ Program Files\SAP BusinessObjects\Xcelsius\assets\samples*. You'll see the definition file (*.xlf*) and its corresponding Flash file (*.swf*) for each sample. For some samples with external data sources, you may also find the data source file, typically an XML or an Excel file.

You can add your custom samples to SAP BusinessObjects Dashboards by adding a dashboard definition file (*.xlf*) and its corresponding output Flash file (*.swf*) to the samples directory as mentioned in the paragraph above. The next time you launch SAP BusinessObjects Dashboards, you'll see the new sample with the name and preview of the Flash file from this menu.

Document Properties

You use this command to set the document properties of the dashboard you're currently working on, such as canvas size and description. Compared to preferences, which we'll talk about later, your changes to document settings only affect the current dashboard and will disappear the next time you launch SAP Business-Objects Dashboards, while preferences control the global settings and will be always effective for future use.

After selecting this command, you'll see a dialog to set document properties as shown in Figure 2.7.

Figure 2.7 Properties in the Document Properties Dialog

Let's discuss each property of this dialog:

▶ CANVAS SIZE IN PIXELS

You set the canvas size of your current dashboard here. The canvas will be stretched or cut to the specified size. SAP BusinessObjects Dashboards 4.0 provides two ways to set the canvas size. One is PRESET SIZE, including 160 * 160, 320 * 320, 640 * 640, 800 * 600, and 1024 * 768, and the other is CUSTOM SIZE, where you can manually set the width and height to fit your requirements. Note that the size is in pixels.

You may only want to set the canvas size here when there's a strict requirement for the size of your dashboard. To adjust the canvas size, you can usually use the four buttons INCREASE CANVAS SIZE, DECREASE CANVAS SIZE, FIT CANVAS TO COMPONENTS, and FIT CANVAS TO WINDOW on the toolbar that we'll explain in Section 2.3.

▶ DESCRIPTION

You can enter text here to describe the current dashboard, such as the purpose and the development status, so that when you or someone else opens your dashboard later, that person can recall what it's about.

> **Note**
>
> The description will only appear here when the user selects DOCUMENT PROPERTIES with your dashboard opened in SAP BusinessObjects Dashboards. It will not appear anywhere in the exported Flash file or the file properties.

▶ FONT

You can set fonts for all texts in your dashboard to make it look better and easier to read. After selecting the option USE GLOBAL FONT, you can set the default font for the texts of all of the UI components, which is Verdana by default. For example, if you select this option and select the font Arial, then the font of all of the text parts, such as title and text, of all of the UI components in this dashboard will be Arial. You can check this in the APPEARANCE – TEXT area in the PROPERTIES panel of any UI component.

After selecting USE GLOBAL FONT, you can choose whether to use device fonts or embedded fonts for your dashboard, as displayed in Figure 2.8.

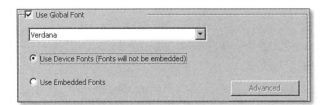

Figure 2.8 Using Device or Embedded Fonts

Use Device Fonts (Fonts Will Not be Embedded) is the default option. This option is recommended for creating dashboards that require the extended character set as defined by Unicode.

As the label Use Device Fonts indicates, the fonts are not embedded into the generated SWF file. At runtime, the Adobe Flash player will render the True-Type font you selected for each UI component, using those installed on the machine where the Flash player is installed. Device fonts also let you display different fonts for different components within one dashboard.

However, depending on the TrueType fonts installed on the end user's machine, the fonts may not display properly. For example, if you choose Courier New for the title of a pie chart and select Use Device Fonts, but the end user's machine has no such font installed, the text may behave badly at runtime.

The Use Embedded Fonts option generates the characters from the TrueType font you select and embeds them into the output SWF file. Because the font is embedded in the SWF file, it displays properly regardless of whether the user's machine has the TrueType font installed. What's more, the texts of your dashboard display exactly the same way on any machine.

You need to be aware that checking this option increases the size of the output file and the time required to load or render the dashboard.

> **Note**
>
> Asian character sets are not supported with embedded fonts due to the large number of characters they require. You must select Use Global Fonts when you are using Asian characters in your dashboard.
>
> In addition, if you select Use Embedded Fonts, you cannot change text fonts through the Properties panel of a UI component. All texts in your dashboard will use the default font you selected.

- ▸ SHOW LOADING STATUS

  If this option is selected, you'll see a message dialog showing the loading status such as CREATING COMPONENTS... and INITIALIZATION COMPLETE when previewing or viewing the dashboard.

  If this option is not selected, when the dashboard is being loaded you will only see the message INITIALIZING....

Preferences

You set global preferences with this command, such as the display language, the default theme, and the default open folder. Let's talk about them one by one.

Document

Figure 2.9 shows the available properties you can set in this tab. Similar to document properties, you can set the canvas size here, which will take effect not only in the current dashboard you are designing but also each time SAP BusinessObjects Dashboards is launched.

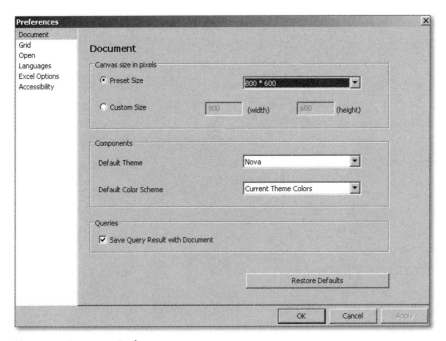

Figure 2.9 Document Preferences

When the canvas size is set both here and in document properties, the one set in document properties takes precedence.

You can also set the default theme and default color schema here. For explanations of the theme and the color schema, please refer to Section 2.2.3 and Chapter 8.

One new configuration item here is SAVE QUERY RESULT WITH DOCUMENT, which, when selected, will save the result data of the Universe queries together with the SAP BusinessObjects Dashboards object. If you've used SAP Crystal Reports, this option is similar to SAVE DATA WITH REPORT.

If you've accidentally made any changes to the settings, you can click the RESTORE DEFAULTS button to revert to the default settings. This button is always available in the PREFERENCES window.

Grid

Here you set whether or not to show gridlines on the canvas and snap components to them. The width and height of the grid are also set here (see Figure 2.10).

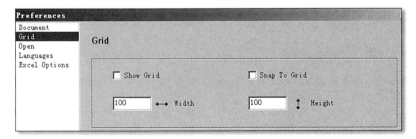

Figure 2.10 Properties to Define for Grid

If you want to show the grid in the canvas to help position and align the UI components, select SHOW GRID. After that, you can set the width and height of the grid. For example, if SHOW GRID is selected with a width of 20 and height of 30 (pixels), the canvas will be filled with rectangles of the size 20 * 30. Figure 2.11 shows the grid on the canvas and the PREFERENCES window.

You can enable SNAP TO GRID to help align components on the canvas. When this option is selected, the components have to be aligned to the gridlines. This can help you align components in a particular direction.

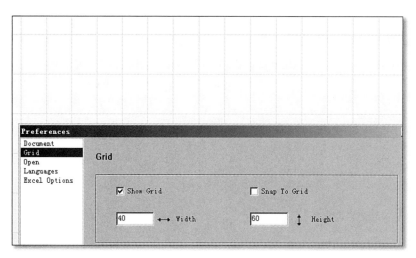

Figure 2.11 The Definition of Grid and the Canvas

Open

With this command you can set the default folder that you'll be prompted to open when you select FILE • OPEN. There are two options:

1. The first option is LAST FOLDER OPEN, which means the folder you opened the last time you used SAP BusinessObjects Dashboards. You may want to use this option if you always want to see related dashboards.

2. The other option is FOLDER, which allows you to specify the path you want. With this option, you'll see the same folder here each time you click the OPEN command. This option is helpful if you're working on several dashboards for one project.

Languages

SAP BusinessObjects Dashboards is internationalized for users in different countries or regions. English is the default language. You can also install one or more language packs on one machine to see menus and commands displayed in your preferred language. More than 10 languages are available including French, German, Chinese, Japanese, and Russian.

You can use this command to select the language for your SAP BusinessObjects Dashboards software, which will affect all user interface texts, including the labels, menus, chart names, and SAP BusinessObjects Dashboards help. Changes to language will take effect after restarting SAP BusinessObjects Dashboards.

One new feature here is that you can also set the default format for currency, as displayed in Figure 2.12. You can define how to display negative values (with a negative sign or in red), how many digits need to be displayed after the decimal point, and whether and how to display the currency symbol as a prefix or postfix. For example, in the United States you may want to display $1000.00, while in China you may choose 1000.

When you've defined your preferences, each field of type CURRENCY will follow that format by default, which you can observe in the PROPERTIES panel. We'll talk about that in Chapters 4 and 5.

> **Note**
>
> The available languages depend on the language packs you selected during installation. Figure 2.12 displays a SAP BusinessObjects Dashboards with only one language pack, simplified Chinese, installed.

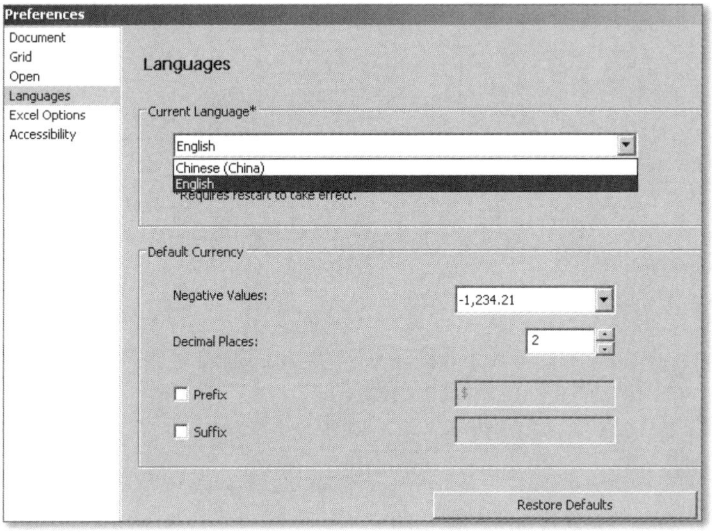

Figure 2.12 Available Languages Depend on Language Packs Installed

Excel Options

Microsoft Excel is the foundation of SAP BusinessObjects Dashboards. Each UI element can only bind to data in the embedded spreadsheet, unless you're using a Universe query, the returned data of which can be mapped to UI components directly without the intermediate Excel file. In other words, usually Excel acts as the only and direct data source that a dashboard element can bind to. You can write data directly in the embedded Excel workbook, put data in another Excel file, and then import it into SAP BusinessObjects Dashboards or connect to an external data source using some form of data connectivity and then map the input and output data to a single cell or cell range in the embedded Excel spreadsheet. From this perspective, Excel acts as the bridge between visualization and the backend data.

No matter what way you choose, you're working closely with the embedded Excel spreadsheet. The PREFERENCES window includes some Excel options as displayed in Figure 2.13.

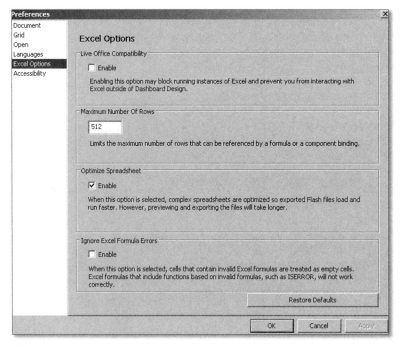

Figure 2.13 Available Excel Options to Customize

▸ MAXIMUM NUMBER OF ROWS
You can set the maximum number of rows that any Excel formula or binding in your dashboard can refer to. For example, you cannot use a list view component to show data across more than the defined rows. For data connectivities, you cannot bind the output values to a cell range of more than the defined rows either.

One more complex example: Suppose you're using several combo box components in your dashboard for the user to make selections. For the convenience of the end user, you want to limit the size of the candidate items of each selector to 10 rows. Suppose the candidates are listed in rows in the embedded spreadsheet. You can set MAXIMUM NUMBER OF ROWS to 10. When the user tries to bind to more rows, SAP BusinessObjects Dashboards will automatically apply the restriction with the warning "Your range has been reduced to the maximum rows allowed."

Note that this number only restricts the maximum rows that can be used in an Excel formula and the bindings of a data connectivity or a UI component. The embedded spreadsheet can still contain as many rows as you want. By default, the number is 512. You can increase or decrease it according to your specific requirements.

► LIVE OFFICE COMPATIBILITY
The LIVE OFFICE COMPATIBILITY option is only useful for SAP BusinessObjects users. You need to enable it before using data in a Live Office-enabled Excel spreadsheet, which means the data in the Excel spreadsheet is a view created from either managed SAP Crystal Reports or managed Web Intelligence documents deployed on an SAP BusinessObjects BI platform.

After you've imported a Live Office-enabled Excel spreadsheet into SAP BusinessObjects Dashboards 4.0, you can make it refreshable against the source data by configuring the Live Office connection in the Data Manager. In this way you can get live data from a Live Office-enabled Excel file from your dashboard, compared to importing data from a common Excel file, where the data is static after it's imported, and you need to re-import the file to get the latest data.

However, there's a drawback when Live Office compatibility is enabled: The performance of other Microsoft Office programs may be affected, and Microsoft Office files might not open or work correctly. If you choose not to enable Live Office compatibility but still want to use data from a Live Office document, the recommended way is to work with Live Office in a stand-alone Excel file outside of SAP BusinessObjects Dashboards and then import that file into it.

► OPTIMIZE SPREADSHEET
You can select this option to optimize the embedded spreadsheet, especially the Excel formulas, so that the exported Flash file can load and run faster. The

drawback is that if you click PREVIEW or EXPORT in dashboard designer, the processing time may be a little longer.

▶ IGNORE EXCEL FORMULA ERRORS

Your formulas written in the embedded spreadsheet may cause errors, such as looking up a value that doesn't exist in the returned data or a divided-by-zero error that you forgot to catch. With this option selected, cells with invalid Excel formulas will be treated as empty.

Note that Excel formulas that include functions based on invalid formulas will not work correctly. As a result, you need think carefully before selecting this option if you have used a function like ISERROR to check validity.

Changes to these items require a restart of SAP BusinessObjects Dashboards to take effect.

Translation Settings

This is a new feature in SAP BusinessObjects Dashboards 4.0 for the designer to select texts in the embedded spreadsheet of the current dashboard to be translated in the Translation Manager, a client tool of SAP BusinessObjects.

For example, you may want your chart title to be localized based on the end user's locale. To do this, click this menu item, add groups in the prompt window, and specify cell ranges that contain texts to be translated, as illustrated in Figure 2.14.

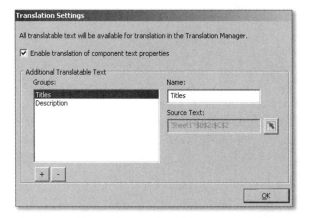

Figure 2.14 Select Cells Containing Texts to be Translated by the Translation Manager

When the dashboard is saved to the SAP Business Intelligence platform, the translator can see these texts in the Translation Manager. He can then translate the texts into several languages. At runtime, depending on the viewer's preferred viewing locale (PVL) defined in the BI launchpad, translated texts for that local are displayed.

The Translation Manager is a separate tool of SAP BusinessObjects for localization of many SAP BusinessObjects products including Universe and Web Intelligence.

Preview

You can switch from design mode to preview mode by clicking this command, where you can see how your dashboard will behave at runtime. This can help you adjust the design of your dashboard. If you have experience in code debugging, you may find these modes to be very similar.

Adobe Flash Player is required to preview your dashboard. To return to design mode, just click this command again.

Export Preview

You can click this command to quickly view how your dashboard behaves in a stand-alone Adobe Flash Player. SAP BusinessObjects Dashboards generates a temp Flash (*.swf*) file and launches Adobe Flash Player in a separate window to play it. The generated Flash (*.swf*) file is located in a temporary folder in your user directory; for example, *C:/Users/ray/AppData/Local/Temp/XC_124/* or *C:/Documents and Settings/ray/Local Settings/Temp/XC_11a4.*

Export

The dashboard is designed to communicate information with others, so you can export your dashboard to a file in several kinds of media and distribute it to the consumer. Depending on the consumer's environment, you need to select one medium to export your dashboard to. No matter what type you choose, the exported dashboard will behave completely the same as what you see when you select PREVIEW or EXPORT PREVIEW.

After clicking this command, you'll see a list of available media types as displayed in Figure 2.15.

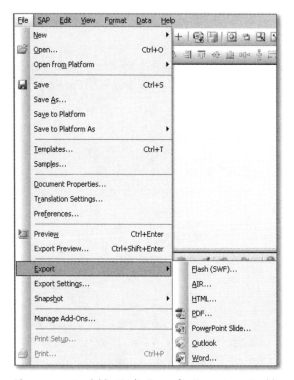

Figure 2.15 Available Media Types for Exporting a Dashboard

You can choose an appropriate type based on your requirement and the environment in which it will be used. We'll provide detailed explanations about when and how to use each type in Chapter 8.

Unlike Xcelsius 2008, here you cannot export your dashboard to the SAP Business Intelligence platform; you can only save.

Export Settings

This command is used to specify what data in what Excel file you want to use for the exported dashboard. You can choose to use current Excel data or another external Excel file.

Use Current Excel Data

This is the default option. The exported dashboard will use the data you see in the embedded Excel spreadsheet, and it will function exactly the same as what you see in preview mode.

Use Another Excel file

Sometimes the data source for the dashboard is initially unavailable to you, the dashboard designer. In this case, you can work against sample data in the embedded spreadsheet, which has exactly the same format as the actual Excel file. When the real data is ready in another Excel file, you can specify it through this command and then export the dashboard. The end user will then see your dashboard reflecting the actual data.

For example, you may need to create a sales distribution dashboard for the month. You know what the data is like and how is it organized in Excel, but the data has not come yet. You can create the dashboard with sample data and export it with another Excel file when you get the data.

Snapshot

You use this command to take a snapshot of your dashboard. In preview mode, you can interact with the dashboard in the same way the end user will. If you find a scenario or combination of settings or data interesting or useful, you can take a snapshot of the dashboard to save the specific status.

SNAPSHOT is similar to export in that both commands export the dashboard to a certain type of file such as Flash or PDF. The difference lies in the initial scenario for the consumer: the default values and what components are visible of an exported dashboard are set in design mode, while you set those for a snapshot in preview mode. Another difference is that the EXPORT command is only available in design mode, while SNAPSHOT is only available in preview mode.

The export methods include:

▶ **Current Excel data**
   SAP BusinessObjects Dashboards 4.0 will generate an Excel spreadsheet file (*.xls*) with the current data values. This file may be different from what you see in the embedded Excel spreadsheet. For example, if you bind a text input to an Excel cell and change its value in preview mode, the generated Excel file will

have the value you entered. This can be a very useful tool for diagnosing or debugging when dashboards are not working as expected.

▶ **PDF**
An Adobe PDF file is generated with the current state of the components. The dashboard is still interactive, with all of the functionalities.

▶ **PowerPoint slide**
A Microsoft PowerPoint file with one slide that contains a Flash (SWF) file with the current state of the components is generated. Similar to what you see via the menu path EXPORT • POWERPOINT SLIDE, one PowerPoint file and one SWF file are generated.

▶ **Outlook**
A Microsoft Outlook email that attaches the Flash (SWF) file with the current state of the components is generated. Similar to what you see via EXPORT • OUT-LOOK, SAP BusinessObjects Dashboards generates a temp SWF file, launches Outlook to create a new email message, and attaches the SWF file.

▶ **Flash**
A Flash (SWF) file with the changes made in preview mode is generated.

▶ **HTML**
Similar to what you see via EXPORT • HTML, one HTML file and one Flash (SWF) file with the current state of the components are generated. You may choose this option to put the HTML file in a web server so that others can access your dashboard with a web browser.

Manage Add-Ons

An add-on is an SAP BusinessObjects Dashboards extension for either UI or data connectivity. It can be developed by SAP BusinessObjects itself, SAP Business-Objects partners, or customers using the SDK, which we'll cover in Chapters 10 to 13. An add-on, either a custom UI component or a data connectivity, is a file with an *.xlx* extension.

If you're using Microsoft Windows 7, you need run SAP BusinessObjects Dash-boards with administrator privileges to launch Add-On Manager. Otherwise, you'll see an error.

After clicking this menu item, you'll see the Add-On Manager, where you can install a new add-on by clicking the INSTALL ADD-ON button and browsing to the *.xlx* file, or remove an already-installed add-on.

Note that there's a link, GET MORE ADD-ONS, on the bottom left of the Add-On Manager. Clicking this link will direct you to the Add-On Marketplace website at *http://ecohub.sdn.sap.com/irj/ecohub/solutions?query=xcelsius* (in Xcelsius 2008, it was *http://www.ondemand.com/information/xcelsius.asp*), where you can download add-ons for your unique business requirements from a list of available ones or sell add-ons that you've developed.

You can also view the details of an existing add-on by simply clicking on it. As shown in Figure 2.16, the name, description, and other information are displayed so that you can easily understand the purpose of the add-on and then decide whether or not to use it.

To uninstall a custom add-on, just click the REMOVE ADD-ON button. You'll be prompted to confirm before actually removing an add-on.

Figure 2.16 Details of an Installed Custom Add-On

2.1.2   SAP

This menu was released after Xcelsius 2008 SP2 (support package). Commands in this menu are used for communicating with SAP NetWeaver BW systems. For example, you can save your dashboard to or open it from a BW system. You can also run the dashboard directly from the BW system if it has SAP Portal installed (SAP NetWeaver Java Engine). The commands are displayed in Figure 2.17.

Figure 2.17 Available Commands in the SAP Menu

There are some prerequisites to use these commands. For example, on the server side, SAP NetWeaver Java and ABAP 7.0 EHP1 (enhancement package) SP5 need be installed; on the client side (the system where SAP BusinessObjects Dashboards is installed), SAP GUI (Graphical User Interface) 7.10 SP12 or higher with the BI add-on needs be installed.

Publish/Publish As

These commands are used to save your dashboard design object to an SAP NetWeaver BW system. The BW system can then act as a central repository so that others can open the dashboard later to continue the design. The other purpose is that you can transport or translate your dashboard design object from one BW system to another, along with other SAP InfoObjects such as cubes and queries.

When your dashboard is published to SAP NetWeaver BW, SAP BusinessObjects Dashboards generates and publishes three files to SAP NetWeaver BW: the dashboard definition file with an *.xlf* extension, the output Flash file (*.swf*), and a text file that contains the texts to be translated in the BW system. The content of the text file depends on what you specified in the TRANSLATION SETTINGS command of the SAP menu.

This is typically used when you use BW queries or query views as your dashboard data source.

Open

You use this command to open a dashboard design model (the definition object with an *.xlf* extension) that you or someone else has published to the BW system, just like the command OPEN FROM PLATFORM to open it from a BusinessObjects system.

If your dashboard doesn't have an active connection to any BW system, you'll be prompted to select a BW system and log on when you click the command OPEN, PUBLISH, or PUBLISH AS, or the SAP NetWeaver BW connection in the connections list in the Data Manager. The screens are similar to what you see when launching the SAP GUI or when connecting to an SAP system from the SAP Crystal Reports designer.

Launch

This command is used to run the dashboard (*.swf*) that has already been published to the BW system. If you haven't published or have failed to publish the dashboard to a BW system, you'll see an error message on clicking this command, asking you to publish the dashboard first.

You may want to use this command to test or debug the dashboard with an SAP NetWeaver BW connection. The reason is that for such dashboards, you can only see the dashboard layout and basic interaction in preview mode, but the data from the BW queries or query views will not be returned.

After you click this command, a web browser will open with the SAP Portal logon screen (if a connection to the SAP Portal already exists and is still active in the same web browser session, this screen is skipped). When you've logged on, the dashboard, along with the data of the BW connection (if the dashboard has such connections), is displayed. The URL to the dashboard visualization is displayed in the web browser, which can be used to create a URL iView, which can in turn be used in other places of the SAP Portal. The URL may be like *http://bwserver. domain:50000/irj/servlet/prt/portal/prtroot/pcd!3aportal_content!2fcom.sap.pct!2f platform_add_ons!2fcom.sap.ip.bi!2fiViews!2fcom.sap.ip.bi.bex?DASHBOARD=ZDF INANA*. Note that the value for the parameter DASHBOARD should be the technical name of your dashboard when it's published to SAP NetWeaver BW.

For example, you can create a daily revenue analysis dashboard that retrieves financial and sales data from BW queries, publishes it to the BW system, launches it, and uses the URL to create a URL iView and assign the iView to a portal page and the user role for sales executives of your company. Then the sales executives can locate and view this dashboard easily every day that log on to SAP Portal.

Disconnect

This command is disabled (in gray) if your dashboard isn't connected to a BW system. If you've established a connection to an SAP NetWeaver BW system (after selecting OPEN or PUBLISH), this command is enabled. If then you want to connect to another SAP system, you must disconnect the current connection first by clicking this command.

Translation Settings

This command is used to select cells in the embedded spreadsheet containing static texts and translate them in an SAP system when the dashboard has been published. This is different from the TRANSLATION SETTINGS command in FILE menu in four ways:

1. The selected texts here are translated in a BW system, instead of by the Translation Manager, which is a BusinessObjects tool.

2. The dashboard needs be published to a BW system to do the translation, instead of to a Business Intelligence platform.

3. The dashboard is viewed from SAP Portal, instead of the BI launchpad of SAP BusinessObjects.

4. Which translated texts are displayed depends on the BW user locale, instead of the SAP BusinessObjects user's preferred viewing locale (PVL) configured in the preferences of the BI launchpad (InfoView).

After clicking this command, you'll see the TRANSLATION SETTINGS window where you add cells with texts to be translated in SAP, as displayed in Figure 2.18.

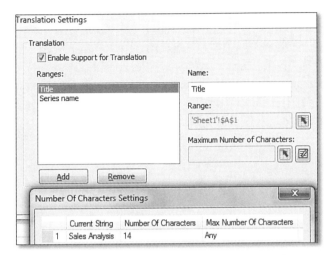

Figure 2.18 Translation Settings for Texts to be Translated in an SAP System

To use this feature, you need select the option ENABLE SUPPORT FOR TRANSLATION first. You can then add ranges of cells containing texts to be translated. However, unlike from the translation in a BusinessObjects system, here you can only select a single cell for each range, as you can see from the figure.

When designing complex dashboards, you may take the length of a text field into consideration. For example, you may have three gauges in a row to display the status of three measures. The length of each title field shouldn't exceed the width of the gauge component. One gauge is titled sales revenue, and you made the gauge just wide enough to hold the title. However, when translated into Spanish, the title becomes *los ingresos porde ventas,* which will disorder your visualization.

To solve such a problem, you need to either take the length of localized texts into consideration at design time and deal with it, or limit the length when it's translated. The MAXIMUM NUMBER OF CHARACTERS field is used in this scenario, as the name indicates. To set the maximum length, you either enter a constant number by clicking the 📝 icon or bind it to a cell in the embedded spreadsheet by clicking the 🔧 icon, as displayed in Figure 2.18.

To remove a cell from being translated, simply click to select it and click the REMOVE button below the list. To disable all translations, deselect the ENABLE SUPPORT FOR TRANSLATION option.

When the dashboard has been published to a BW system, you can proceed with translation of the selected texts, like other BW objects. To do the translation, you may want to create a piece list in the Data Warehouse Workbench (Transaction RSA1) and translate the texts into your target language in Transaction SE36. You can refer to documents about translation on the SAP website, such as *http:// help.sap.com/bp_bw370/documentation/How_To_Translate_BI_Objects.pdf*.

2.1.3 Edit

The EDIT menu is used to undo and redo and perform other copy and paste operations.

Undo/Redo

SAP BusinessObjects Dashboards supports undo and redo of many levels. You may want to use the UNDO command to cancel an operation when you delete a component by accident.

These operations are similar to those in other common applications such as Microsoft Office Word. The hotkeys are also the same: Ctrl+Z for undo and Ctrl+Y for redo.

Copy/Paste/Cut/Delete/Select All

These operations are also very common. You may want to copy or cut a component in the canvas and then paste it to move or duplicate it, or even move it to another dashboard design object opened in another instance of SAP BusinessObjects Dashboards. For example, when multiple INPUT TEXT components in the logon screen of your dashboard need to have the same styles, it's easier to adjust the appearance of one component and copy it for others, instead of dropping new components into the canvas and readjusting them.

SAP BusinessObjects Dashboards also provides a command to select all components in the canvas: SELECT ALL. You can use this command when you want to operate on all of the components; for example, to delete or make alignments.

The hotkeys are also the same as those in other common applications such as Microsoft Office Word; for example, [Ctrl]+[C] for copy, [Ctrl]+[X] for cut, [Ctrl]+[V] for paste, [Del] for delete, and [Ctrl]+[A] for select all.

2.1.4 View

Commands in this menu are used to show or hide certain parts of the workspace, such as the COMPONENTS BROWSER and TOOLBARS, as shown in Figure 2.19. A new menu item introduced in SAP BusinessObjects Dashboard 4.0 is QUERY BROWSER, which did not exist in Xcelsius 2008.

Figure 2.19 View Menu Commands of SAP BusinessObjects Dashboards 4.0

Grid

Use this command to show or hide grids in the canvas. When this command is selected, you'll see grids in the canvas as we showed in Figure 2.12. The grids will disappear when this command is deselected.

Note that the width and height of the grid are set via FILE • PREFERENCES as explained in Section 2.2.1.

Properties/Object Browser/Components/Query Browser

There are three important views in the workspace during your design time, which we'll explain in more detail later in this section. Let's briefly explore the four views:

▶ The PROPERTIES view displays the PROPERTIES panel to show the properties of the canvas (when no component is selected) or one or more selected components, including titles, data, and colors.

▶ The COMPONENTS BROWSER view lists all available UI components by categories or in a list.

▶ The OBJECT BROWSER view lists all in-use components that have been dragged into the canvas of your dashboard.

▶ The QUERY BROWSER view lists all the Universe queries you've created for your dashboard so you can modify or delete them. You can also start to create a new query in this view.

You can show or hide each view by selecting the corresponding command. For example, you may want to hide all of them for a larger canvas to position your components but show the Object Browser when there are many components in the canvas and you want to select some.

Quick Views

At different design stages, you may want to focus on different aspects of your dashboard. For example, you may focus on adjusting the positioning of all components or the properties of a single component or on how the data is retrieved and mapped in the embedded spreadsheet. You can use commands in this menu to display only components you're interested in. The meaning of each quick view is explained in the following list.

▶ CANVAS ONLY
As the name indicates, only the canvas is displayed in the center of the screen, allowing you to focus on positioning the components, as shown in Figure 2.20. This is similar to the effect of hiding the views of PROPERTIES, OBJECT BROWSER, COMPONENTS BROWSER, and QUERY BROWSER, and then dragging the embedded Excel spreadsheet to the lowest workspace.

▶ SPREADSHEET ONLY
When you switch to this quick view, only the embedded Excel spreadsheet is displayed in the screen, as shown in Figure 2.21. You can then focus on:

▶ Data binding
To bind properties of UI components to cells or cell ranges in the spreadsheet or to map input and output of a data connectivity to the spreadsheet

▶ Excel formulas
To calculate new data using Excel functions. For example, you can edit one cell with the formula =Sum(B1:B5).

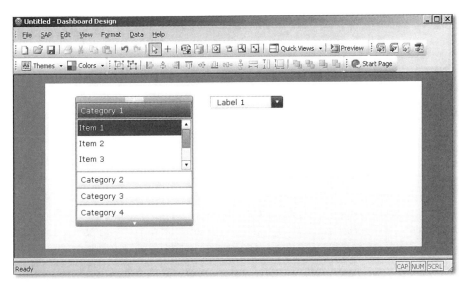

Figure 2.20 Workspace with Canvas Only

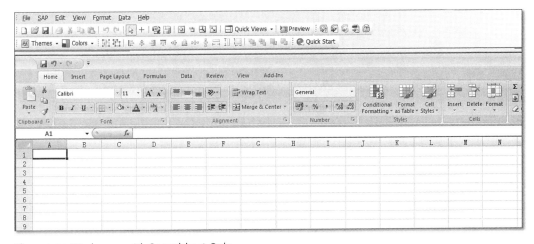

Figure 2.21 Workspace with Spreadsheet Only

► CANVAS AND SPREADSHEET

As indicated by the name, both the canvas and the embedded spreadsheet are displayed with this quick view. You may want to switch to this view when you want to check whether the UI components are displaying the right data as entered in the Excel spreadsheet.

► MY WORKSPACE

You can use this option to return to the default view, with both the canvas and the embedded spreadsheet displayed. Whether other views are shown depends on whether they are displayed before switching to any quick view.

Canvas Sizing

From this menu, you can select INCREASE CANVAS or DECREASE CANVAS to slightly adjust the canvas size (both in width and in height) based on how many components are included in your dashboard and how are they laid out.

For example, click INCREASE CANVAS when you need more space to place additional components on the canvas, and click DECREASE CANVAS when there's too much space left. Note that these two commands alter the size in both the horizontal and vertical directions. That is, both width and height will be changed at the same time.

To adjust either the width or height but not both, you can use some other methods, either changing the canvas size in DOCUMENT PROPERTIES or using a rectangle component to define the layout and then clicking FIT CANVAS TO COMPONENTS.

Another two commands, FIT CANVAS TO COMPONENTS and FIT CANVAS TO WINDOWS, are ways to auto-adjust the canvas size. You can first place your components at will on the canvas and then use FIT CANVAS TO COMPONENTS so that the canvas is just large enough to hold all your components. Sometimes, to make the dashboard look better, you may use INCREASE CANVAS after this to leave some space or gap at the borders.

FIT CANVAS TO WINDOWS, on the other hand, adjusts the canvas to the current window size, that is, the size of the current space left for the canvas surrounded by the toolbar and other parts, as illustrated in Figure 2.22.

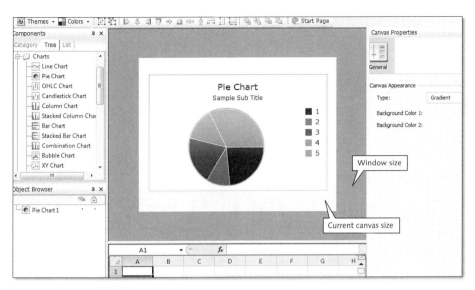

Figure 2.22 Canvas Size and Window Size in Dashboard Design Workspace

In this figure, the current canvas size is in the white background color, and the window size is larger, surrounded by the COMPONENTS BROWSER to the left, the embedded Excel spreadsheet at the bottom, the property sheet to the right, and the toolbar at the top. If you click FIT CANVAS TO WINDOWS now, the canvas will extend to the whole window, as shown in Figure 2.23.

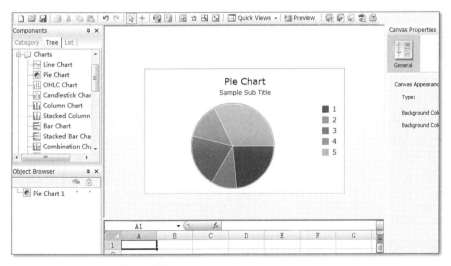

Figure 2.23 Fit Canvas Size to Window

You can compare Figures 2.23 and 2.22 to see the effect of selecting FIT CANVAS TO WINDOW.

Toolbars

You can use this menu to customize what to display in the toolbar. It includes five submenus: STANDARD, THEMES, EXPORT, FORMAT, and START PAGE. See Figure 2.24 for the corresponding parts in the toolbar for each command.

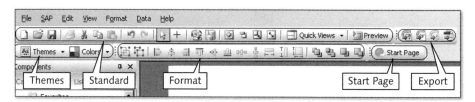

Figure 2.24 Parts of the Toolbar

2.1.5 Format

Commands in this menu are effective in helping you position the UI components in the canvas.

Align

Sometimes you may want to make the components align to each other for a neat look and feel. In SAP BusinessObjects Dashboards 4.0, you can first select two or more components and then set alignment with the ALIGN command, including a direction (to the left, right, center, top, bottom, or middle).

The selection order is very important to the alignment result. The first component you select becomes the base line for alignment. For example, you may have dropped an accordion menu and a pie chart in the canvas. To align them to the top with the accordion menu as the base, you can select the accordion menu first, hold down Ctrl, click the pie chart to select it, and then click ALIGN • TOP.

Space Evenly

Use this menu to adjust spaces between the center points of multiple UI components so that their gaps are equal. There are two commands in this menu: one to adjust spaces horizontally (ACROSS) and the other to adjust spaces vertically (DOWN).

SAP BusinessObjects Dashboards adjusts the spaces by summing the horizontal (or vertical if DOWN is selected) spaces between the center points of every two horizontally (or vertically) adjacent components and calculating the average. Then it rearranges the components horizontally (or vertically) with the average space. As a result, you need to select at least three components to use this command. Otherwise, the commands in this menu are disabled.

If you select components that are vertically aligned and click SPACE EVENLY • ACROSS or select components that are horizontally aligned and click SPACE EVENLY • DOWN, then no change is made, because the spaces in that direction are all zero.

Note
The commands will adjust spaces between the center points of components, not their edges.

Make Same Size

As indicated by the name, you can use commands in this menu to make multiple components be the same size—width, height, or both. For example, let's say you've dragged one pie chart and one column chart into your dashboard, either reflecting the same data or in a drill-down scenario. For a neat look and feel, you want to make the two components the same size. Instead of resizing them using the mouse, you can select them and then click MAKE SAME SIZE IN WIDTH, HEIGHT, or BOTH. You'll find this command very useful during your dashboard development.

Similar to alignment, the first component you select becomes the base. For example, if you click component A and then press Ctrl to select components B and C and then click MAKE SAME SIZE • WIDTH, then the width of components B and C will be adjusted automatically to be equal to that of component A.

Center in Canvas

There are three commands in this menu: VERTICALLY, HORIZONTALLY, and BOTH. As indicated by the name, you can put your components in the center of the canvas using this menu, centered by width, height, or both.

You may want to use this command to leave equal gaps to the borders of your dashboard. To do this, select one or more components and click this menu. You can easily try this out to better understand the feature.

Order

If you place multiple UI components on the canvas they may overlap, and parts of certain components become invisible to the user when there's any component in front of them. In addition to the X (width) and Y (height) coordinates, each component on the canvas has depth in the Z direction. The overlapping among components is determined by the relative depths, the default value of which is defined by the order it's dropped into the canvas. With the ORDER menu, you can change the relative depth of a component, thus changing the overlap relationship.

You use the command BRING TO FRONT to bring the selected component(s) to the foremost, or the top, level. Correspondingly, SEND TO BACK sends the selected component(s) to the backmost, or the bottom, level, so that it acts as the background of other components. For example, let's say you dragged several components including a pie chart and a background (or image component) to the canvas. You may want to set the background component as the dashboard background by selecting it and clicking SEND TO BACK and select the pie chart and click BRING TO FRONT.

To change the depth slightly, you can use BRING FORWARD to move the component one layer closer to the top from its current position. On the other hand, you use SEND BACKWARD to move the component one layer closer to the bottom layer from its current position. You may want to use these commands to switch the relative depth of two adjacent components.

Group/Ungroup

You can include multiple components into one group so that you can move them together without worrying about changing the relative positions by accident. For example, let's say you've perfectly adjusted the relative position of several combo boxes as selectors. Now you want to move them a little down or left. You can select all of them by holding down Ctrl and then moving them together. But it's easy to make the mistake of missing one box, and in the future when you want to move them again, you'll have to select all of them again. A better solution is to organize them into one group and then click on any of the components to move them all.

Another usage of the GROUP command is to set properties for multiple components at once. For example, if you want to show or hide some components at the same time, you can group them and then set their dynamic visibility.

To organize multiple components into one group, just select them all and click GROUP. Then, each time you click one of the components and move it, all components in the group get moved. To ungroup them, just select any component in the group and click UNGROUP.

2.1.6 Data

To make your dashboard reflect real and live data, you need to map your real data to the embedded Excel spreadsheet and bind it to UI components with the help of data connectivity. In the DATA menu, you can import real data from another Excel file or connect to live data. The available commands in the DATA menu are described as follows.

Import

You can use this command to import data from an existing Excel file into the embedded spreadsheet of your design workspace. You may want to use this command when the data is already in an Excel file, typically provided by another department in your company or a third-party provider, and the data will not be updated frequently.

For SAP BusinessObjects users, you can insert the data from SAP Crystal Reports or SAP BusinessObjects Web Intelligence documents into a Live Office-enabled Excel file and use this command to import it into the embedded spreadsheet.

You have to use this command when the data is only available in Excel format but cannot be provided through any of the data connectivities that will be covered in Chapters 6 and 7. For example, the data exists in a legacy system that provides no application programming interface (API) for any external application to retrieve the data.

On clicking this command, you will be prompted to select an Excel file on your local machine or on a network. The Excel file can be either Office 97–2003 (with an *.xls* extension) or Office 2007 or 2010 (with an *.xlsx* extension). After you have selected an Excel file, the data in all sheets of the file will be copied to the embedded spreadsheet. Any change you made to the embedded spreadsheet before will be lost.

Note that after import, SAP BusinessObjects Dashboards has nothing to do with that existing Excel file. This has two consequences. First, you can delete or move that file without affecting your dashboard. Second, changes to that existing Excel file will not be reflected automatically in your dashboard. To solve this, you can import the Excel file again, but any changes made to the built-in Excel spreadsheet, such as new formulas, will be lost or overwritten by the imported Excel file.

Import from Platform

Sometimes the existing Excel file is not sent to you directly or located in a network place. Instead, for security reasons, it may be stored in an SAP Business Intelligence platform so that only certain people with required rights can access it. You can use the IMPORT FROM PLATFORM command to import such an Excel file.

On clicking this command, you'll be prompted to enter credentials to log on to an SAP BusinessObjects Business Intelligence platform 4.0 system. After a successful logon, you'll see the folder hierarchy in that SAP BusinessObjects system, where you can navigate to and select an Excel file. After you've selected an Excel file, the data in all sheets of the file will be copied to the embedded spreadsheet, and any changes you have made to the built-in Excel file will be lost, the same as already discussed.

Export

As mentioned in the two previous sections, you can import the data of an existing Excel file into SAP BusinessObjects Dashboards. On the other hand, you can also export the data in the embedded spreadsheet of your current dashboard to another Excel file with this command.

You may want to use this command when you have adjusted the Excel file format, such as what data is put in what ranges in SAP BusinessObjects Dashboards to satisfy the dashboard needs, and you want the data provider to enter data in that format.

For example, you (the dashboard designer) are working with the HR department (the data provider) to create a dashboard. The HR department delivers the data in an Excel file, but it's very difficult to use in SAP BusinessObjects Dashboards. You then work with SAP BusinessObjects Dashboards to design the UI and specify where to put the data in Excel, such as the employee names, salaries, and last year's average salary. Then you export the data to an Excel file and send it to the HR department as a template for them to enter data.

Connections

The three commands just described are related to data in Excel files. SAP BusinessObjects Dashboards provides many ways to connect to external data sources other than Excel, such as web services and XML data. They can be accessed through this menu.

After clicking this command, you'll see the Data Manager, where connections are defined. You can click the ADD button to create a new connection of the selected type, as shown in Figure 2.25.

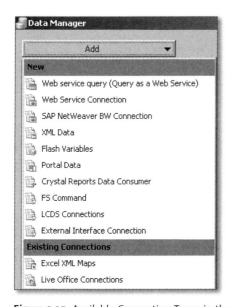

Figure 2.25 Available Connection Types in the Data Manager

You can select a connection type according to your environment and fill in the required parameters in the property pages to define your connection. For example, you need define the service URL, where to bind the input parameters and output results in the embedded spreadsheet, and when to trigger the connection.

You can define several connections of one type, such as web services or XML data. However, for some other types of connection such as a Flash variable, you can only define one connection of that type.

Defined connections are listed in the Data Manager, where you can change their sequences or delete them. To delete a connection, just select it and click the DELETE button at the bottom: X .

If you have several connections that are all set to refresh on load, SAP BusinessObjects Dashboards will load them in the sequence defined in the Data Manager. You can change the sequence by selecting a connection and clicking the MOVE UP or MOVE DOWN button at the bottom: ↑ ↓ . Detailed explanations of the connections will be provided in Chapters 6 and 7.

2.1.7 Help

Like many other SAP products, SAP BusinessObjects Dashboards provides a help document with information about how to use it. You can launch it from this menu.

The help document is a file with a *.chm* (Compiled Help Manual) extension copied to your file system during installation. You can find the help document at *%Xcelsius_DIR%/assets/help/locale/%LANGUAGE%/Xcelsius.chm;* for example, *C:\Program Files\SAP BusinessObjects\Xcelsius\assets\help\locale\en\xcelsius.chm*. Based on the language packs you've installed, you may find the help documents in different languages.

Start Page

The START PAGE is a new view introduced in SAP BusinessObjects 4.0, replacing QUICK START in Xcelsius 2008. After selecting this command, your canvas will be replaced with the view as displayed in Figure 2.26.

The start page displays commands to quickly create a new dashboard or open an existing model, provides a list of recent files, and displays some content from the SAP website. This layout is consistent with many other BusinessObjects products, such as SAP Crystal Reports.

Figure 2.26 Start Page in SAP BusinessObjects Dashboards 4.0

To return to your dashboard development, click either the START PAGE toolbar or follow the menu path HELP • START PAGE again.

License Manager

You use this command to update the license for your SAP BusinessObjects Dashboards installation. After clicking this command, you'll see a window pop up where you can enter your key code for SAP BusinessObjects Dashboards.

The license is written to the registry at *HKEY_LOCAL_MACHINE\SOFTWARE\SAP BusinessObjects\Suite XI 4.0\Xcelsius\Keycodes*. You can also update your license directly in the registry.

About SAP BusinessObjects Dashboards

You can use this command to check the version of SAP BusinessObjects Dashboards you are using. You may want to do this when working with someone else to create a dashboard or when explaining how to reproduce a problem. After clicking this command, you'll see the dialog shown in Figure 2.27.

Figure 2.27 License and Version Information of Your Dashboard Design Installation

The text area in the middle of the window displays the general information of SAP BusinessObjects Dashboards. The line Version 6.0.0.0 means you are using SAP BusinessObjects Dashboards 4.0 without any service pack or fix pack installed. The number structure is [product version].[service pack number].[fix pack number].0.

The second line shows the build number of your installation, from which the software developers can know the source code version your SAP BusinessObjects Dashboards is built upon. The SAP website lists the version and build number for each release of SAP BusinessObjects Dashboards, as listed here:

SAP BusinessObjects Dashboards Release	Version	Build Number
Xcelsius 2008 (RTM)	5.0.0.99	12,1,0,121
Xcelsius 2008 SP1	5.0.0.99	12,1,0,247
Xcelsius 2008 fix pack 1.1	5.1.1.0	12,1,1,344
Xcelsius 2008 SP2	5.2.0.0	12,2,0,608
Xcelsius 2008 fix pack 2.1	5.2.1.0	12,2,1,66
Xcelsius 2008 SP3	5.3.0.0	12,3,0,670
Xcelsius 2008 SP3 fix pack 3.1	5.3.1.0	12,3,1,776
Xcelsius 2008 SP3 fix pack 3.2	5.3.2.0	12,3,2,864
Xcelsius 2008 SP3 fix pack 3.3	5.3.3.0	12,3,3,973
Xcelsius 2008 SP3 fix pack 3.4	5.3.4.0	12,3,4,1038
Xcelsius 2008 SP3 fix pack 3.5	5.3.5.0	12,3,4,1128
Xcelsius 2008 SP4	5.4.0.0	
SAP BusinessObjects Dashboards 4.0	6.0.0.0	14.0.0.760

2.2   Toolbar

The toolbar area is below the menus and above the canvas. It lists some commands that are also accessible from the menus but are more convenient to use, like shortcuts. The commands are categorized into several groups, as displayed in Figure 2.24.

To show or hide toolbar icons, go to the menu VIEW • TOOLBARS and click the corresponding toolbar category name. A checkmark before a toolbar name indicates that the toolbar is currently displayed.

To use a command, just click on it. Depending on your currently selected components, some commands may be disabled. For example, if nothing is selected in the canvas, the COPY and PASTE commands will be disabled.

The purpose of each command in the toolbar and how to use it are briefly explained below, organized by category.

2.2.1 Standard

The standard category includes the following commands:

▸ CREATE, OPEN, and SAVE a dashboard.

▸ PRINT THE SWF FILE prints the current state of the dashboard, which is only available in preview mode. It is disabled if you don't have a printer installed.

Similarly, the items PRINT SETUP, PRINT, and PRINT PREVIEW in the FILE menu are only available when you're in Preview mode and have a printer installed.

▸ CUT, COPY, and PASTE one or more UI components.

▸ Switch the mouse between a select tool and a component tool. When the mouse is a select tool (displayed as an arrow), ▨, you can click on the canvas to select a component. If it's a component tool which is displayed as a plus (+) sign, ⊞, when you click on the canvas, the component selected in the COMPONENTS browser will be created on the canvas.

▸ IMPORT SPREADSHEET and manage data connections.

▸ Change the canvas size.

▸ QUICK VIEWS.

▸ Preview toggles between design mode and preview mode.

2.2.2 Export

This category includes commands to export the dashboard to several file types including PowerPoint, Word, Outlook, and Adobe.

If PowerPoint, Word, Outlook, or PDF is selected, a temp file containing the dashboard content is created, and you can save it to another location you prefer.

Unlike from Xcelsius 2008, with SAP BusinessObjects Dashboards you cannot export your dashboard to the SAP Business Intelligence platform (or BusinessObjects Enterprise); you can only save your dashboard design object to the platform.

Using these commands to export your dashboard may be slightly different from using the menu items. For example, after following the menu path FILE • EXPORT • PDF, you can choose whether to use Acrobat 6.0 (PDF 1.5) or Acrobat 9.0 (PDF 1.8), but if you do this from the toolbar, the exported document will always be in Acrobat 9.0 format.

2.2.3 Themes

The themes category includes commands to change the current theme and the color scheme of your dashboard. Themes and color schemes are used to define the style and colors of UI components. Chapter 8 will provide detailed explanations of them.

▶ **Themes**

Similar to many applications such as the Microsoft Windows operating system, a theme defines the global visualization of styles and properties of all UI components. It provides an easy way to customize the components and maintain a consistent look and feel among all components throughout your dashboard. This concept is called *skins* in some other applications.

To change the theme of your dashboard, click the THEMES dropdown list and select one. Your visualization will be updated immediately, and you can see the change. Note that there can only be one theme per dashboard.

In SAP BusinessObjects Dashboards 4.0, a new theme, Phase, has been added.

▶ **Colors**

Colors define the color schema of your dashboard visualization. The colors of the canvas background; the titles, labels, and values of a text component; and the mouse-over and selected color are defined in the color scheme. For example, a pie chart may have many parts, and the default color of the first, second, and other parts are defined in the color scheme. A color scheme is also included in a theme, but you can further customize your components by changing the color scheme, without changing the theme.

Sometimes you may want to create your own color scheme and reuse it in your dashboards. To do this, you can click CREATE NEW COLOR SCHEME... in the COLORS dropdown list and specify colors for each element in the new window. You can refer to Chapter 8 for more information about this topic.

2.2.4 Format

This category includes commands to:

▶ Group or ungroup more than one component

▶ Align more than one component to the left, right, top, or bottom

▶ Center more than one component horizontally or vertically

- ▶ Space more than two components evenly across or down
- ▶ Make more than one component the same width, height, or both
- ▶ Change the orders of components when there's overlapping on UI components

These commands are also accessible from the FORMAT menu. For a detailed explanation of each command, please refer to Section 2.1.5.

2.2.5 Start Page

This category includes one command, which is used to show or hide the start page. Its effect is similar to selecting HELP • START PAGE. This command was called QUICK START in Xcelsius 2008.

2.2.6 Summary

As a summary of the commands in the toolbar, Table 2.1 shows the toolbar buttons and the corresponding purpose of that command.

Button	Description
	Create a new dashboard
	Open a dashboard definition file (.*xlf*)
	Save the dashboard design to an .*xlf* file
	Print the current dashboard visualization at preview time
	Cut the selected components
	Copy the selected components
	Paste the selected components
	Undo an operation
	Redo an operation
	Change the mouse to the select tool
	Change the mouse to the component tool
	Import data from an external Excel file (.*xls* or .*xlsx*)
	Manage data connections

Table 2.1 Toolbar Buttons and Their Functions

Button	Description
	Increase the canvas
	Decrease the canvas
	Fit the canvas to components
	Fit the canvas to the window
	Export the dashboard to Microsoft Office PowerPoint
	Export the dashboard to Microsoft Office Word
	Export the dashboard to Microsoft Office Outlook
	Attach the dashboard to Outlook
	Group selected components
	Ungroup components in a group
	Align components to the left border of the first selected component
	Center components horizontally
	Align components to the right border of the first selected component
	Align components to the top border of the first selected component
	Center components vertically
	Align components to the bottom border of the first selected component
	Space more than two selected components evenly across the canvas
	Space more than two selected components evenly down the canvas
	Make selected components the same width as the first selected component
	Make selected components the same height as the first selected component
	Make selected components the same width and height as the first selected component
	Bring the selected component to the front
	Send the selected component to the back
	Bring selected component(s) one layer forward
	Send selected component(s) one layer backward

Table 2.1 Toolbar Buttons and Their Functions (Cont.)

2.3   Components Browser

The COMPONENTS browser lists all available UI components of SAP Business-Objects Dashboards 4.0. Some UI components may be excluded if they aren't available to your license. The browser provides three kinds of views (category, tree, and list) to list the components.

2.3.1   Category

The components in this view are listed by category with a thumbnail, including charts, selectors, and maps, as shown in Figure 2.28.

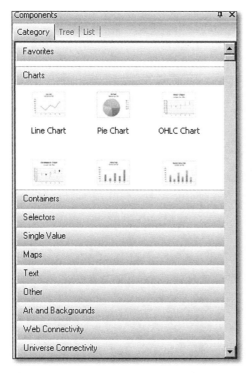

Figure 2.28 UI Components Displayed by Category

You can drag its right border to adjust the width of this view. Depending on its width, there may be one or more components in each row.

This view is helpful to find the right component when you know what type you want to use during design but are not sure what components of that type are available. For example, when you want to use a chart, expand the CHARTS category in this view and see what is inside.

Note that there are two special categories here, FAVORITES and ADD-ONS. FAVORITES lists the components that you frequently use for quicker access. ADD-ONS lists the add-on components that you have installed via the menu path FILE • MANAGE ADD-ONS, as illustrated in Section 2.1.1.

Compared to Xcelsius 2008, a new category called UNIVERSE CONNECTIVITY has been added, with two new UI components.

2.3.2 Tree

This view is very similar to the CATEGORY view except that the thumbnail for each component is smaller, as shown in Figure 2.29.

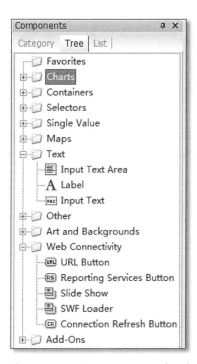

Figure 2.29 UI Components Displayed in a Tree Structure

A component in this view occupies less space than in the CATEGORY view. If you want to see more components in one screen, this view is a better choice.

2.3.3 List

This view lists all components in alphabetical order. In contrast to the CATEGORY and TREE views, components in this view are not grouped and do not have any thumbnail.

You can switch to this view when you want to quickly locate a UI component by its name. For example, if someone told you that a LIST view component can be used to display a wide range of data but you don't know what category it falls into, you can quickly find it in LIST view by its starting letter L.

2.4 Canvas

The canvas is the area where you drag and drop and position UI components to build your dashboard visualization. You can place, position, and resize them on the canvas.

Remember that to change the canvas size, you can use the INCREASE CANVAS, DECREASE CANVAS, FIT CANVAS TO COMPONENTS, and FIT CANVAS TO WINDOWS commands. The default canvas size is set in the menu path FILE • PREFERENCES • DOCUMENT or FILE • DOCUMENT PROPERTIES.

To help arrange your components, you can show grids on the canvas by selecting VIEW • GRID. You can set the grid properties by selecting FILE PREFERENCES.

The canvas background can be a solid color, gradient colors, an image, or no background. To change the canvas background color, or to use an image as your dashboard background, you can click the canvas (not on any component) and set its type and background color or import a background image in its corresponding property sheet, as shown in Figure 2.30.

Figure 2.30 Properties of the Canvas

2.5 Embedded Excel Spreadsheet

As mentioned before, SAP BusinessObjects Dashboards uses Microsoft Excel as its only direct data source (except in the case of Universe queries) and has embedded an Excel spreadsheet along with it since Xcelsius 2008. You can see some sample data in the embedded spreadsheet during dashboard design, which is very intuitive; this may save you a lot of time.

There's no command to directly show or hide the embedded Excel spreadsheet. However, you can click on the borders between it and the adjacent views to resize its space, as displayed in Figure 2.31.

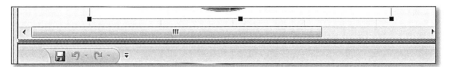

Figure 2.31 Drag the Border to Resize the Embedded Spreadsheet

When you switch to CANVAS ONLY via the menu path VIEW • QUICK VIEWS, the embedded spreadsheet disappears. This is the same result as dragging the border between the canvas and the spreadsheet to the lowest of the workspace.

2.6 Property Panel

Each UI component, including the canvas, has a PROPERTIES panel where you can set its properties including data and appearance. For example, to set the title of a pie chart, you can click to select the chart in the canvas and then enter your text for its title or bind it to a cell in the embedded spreadsheet in the PROPERTIES panel.

Many properties can be bound to a single cell or a range of cells in the embedded spreadsheet or to a Universe query, including but not limited to the following:

▶ Texts
▶ Colors
▶ Data (category labels and values)
▶ Dynamic visibility
▶ Drill down

To bind properties to a single cell or a cell range in the embedded spreadsheet, click the BIND button to the right of the property. You'll be prompted to enter a range. You can enter it directly in the prompt dialog or select a single cell or a cell range in the embedded spreadsheet and then click OK.

To bind properties to the returned data of a Universe query, click the drop-down arrow for that field and choose QUERY DATA. You'll be redirected to a window to select fields of the returned data from a list of Universe queries.

Note that not all fields can be bound directly to a Universe query. For example, you can bind the text of the title or subtitle of a chart only to a cell in the embedded spreadsheet, but not to a Universe query. This is the binding button for such fields (![icon]), which can differ slightly for others (![icon]).

We'll cover how to bind a field directly to a Universe query later. Here we show a simple example of binding to the embedded spreadsheet. To set the title of a pie chart, click on it to open its property sheet and click the BIND button to the right of the chart title text box, as shown in Figure 2.32.

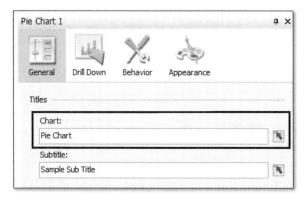

Figure 2.32 Click the Bind Button to Bind the Title of a Pie Chart

Then you'll see a dialog pop up asking you to select a range, as illustrated in Figure 2.33. Though the prompt is SELECT A RANGE, you can still select a single cell. Just click the embedded spreadsheet to select a single cell or a range of cells and click OK in the dialog.

You can also enter the name of the cell or cell range directly in the dialog. For example, enter "Sheet1!$B$4" directly.

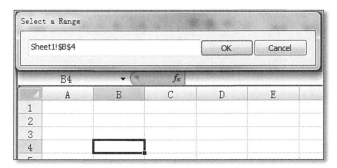

Figure 2.33 Dialog to Select a Single Cell or Cell Range for Binding

When multiple components are selected, the property sheet only displays the properties that are common to all. This way you set the same property for multiple components at once. For example, when two charts are selected, you can set the dynamic visibility property of both in the PROPERTIES panel, but you cannot set the titles, as shown in Figure 2.34.

Figure 2.34 Property Panel for Multiple Components

The properties displayed in the property sheet depends on the selected component(s). A detailed explanation of the PROPERTIES panel will be given in later chapters, where we'll discuss the individual UI components.

To show or hide the PROPERTIES panel, select VIEW • PROPERTIES. You can also click the CLOSE button (✕) in the top right to close it.

2.7 Object Browser

The OBJECT BROWSER lists all components currently used by your dashboard design in a tree hierarchy and in the order of depth. You may want to use this command when you have several components in the canvas and you want to:

▸ Find one component quickly

▸ Lock some components to avoid changing their positions

▸ Hide some components from the canvas to focus on the others

As shown in Figure 2.35 you can hide, lock, delete, send backward, or bring forward a component by clicking the corresponding button in the OBJECT BROWSER.

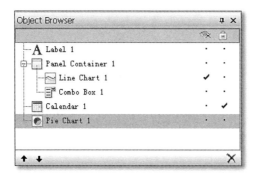

Figure 2.35 Object Browser Showing All UI Components of Your Dashboard

As mentioned before, the components are listed by hierarchy and in order here. As you can see from this figure, the label component is higher than the pie chart, meaning the label is at the back of the pie chart. That is, if they are overlapped, part of the label may be invisible, while the pie chart will always be visible. Also, the line chart and the combo box are displayed as children of the panel container, which means they are inside the panel container.

If it's hard to select one or more UI components from the canvas (for example, when there are too many components), you can easily select them here. What's more, if a component is hidden or locked in a container, you have to select it here and not in the canvas.

2.8 Query Browser

The QUERY BROWSER is a new view introduced in SAP BusinessObjects Dashboards 4.0 so you can create and/or manage Universe queries directly in the dashboard design environment, as displayed in Figure 2.36.

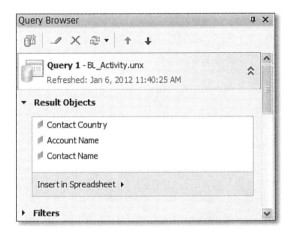

Figure 2.36 Managing Universe Queries Directly in the Query Browser

You can click either the icon on the top left or the ADD QUERY button on the bottom to create a new query. For existing queries, can click the corresponding icons to edit or delete them.

One helpful use of the ADD QUERY button is to reestablish the connection with a SAP BusinessObjects server. Let's say you've created a Universe query and navigated away during direct data binding. When you come back, the session with the SAP BusinessObjects sever may have timed out, and you'll see an error message saying INVALID SESSION when you preview or edit the Universe query. Instead of relaunching SAP BusinessObjects Dashboards, you can simply click this button again to log on to the SAP BusinessObjects server and continue with your work after log on.

After clicking the ADD QUERY button, you'll be prompted to log on to an SAP BusinessObjects 4.0 server if you haven't established an active session yet. After log on, you'll see the Add Query Wizard, which consists of four steps as listed in the following sections.

2.8.1 Select a Universe

The first step is to select a relational Universe that your query is based on, as displayed in Figure 2.37.

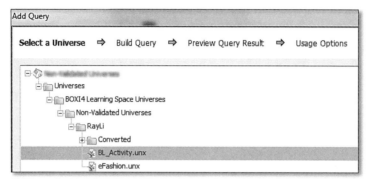

Figure 2.37 Select a Relational Universe

Note that you can only use Universes of new versions created with the Information Design tool. Old Universes in SAP BusinessObjects 3.x environments must be converted before they can be used here. OLAP Universes, such as a Universe based on a BW query, can't be used here.

Depending on your permission in the 4.x environment, the UNIVERSES folder structure and available universes may vary. When you've found your Universe, click NEXT to continue.

2.8.2 Build Query

The Universe may contain a lot of fields with business-meaningful names for different analysis scenarios. Depending on your requirements, you might only use some of the fields, which makes a query.

When you have clicked NEXT in the previous step, SAP BusinessObjects Dashboards will call the Dashboard Design Processing Server on the SAP BusinessObjects server side to read the definition of your selected Universe and display its metadata here, as displayed in Figure 2.38. You may find this very similar to the EDIT QUERY page when you're creating a Web Intelligence report with Web Intelligence Rich Client.

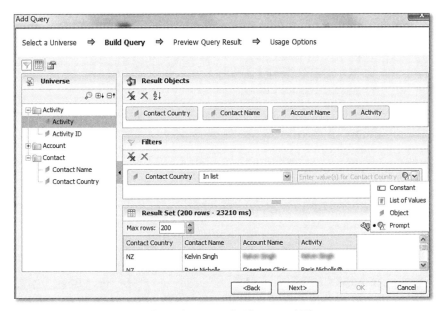

Figure 2.38 Building a Query by Defining Result Objects and Filters

In this page at the left is a list of Universe classes with dimensions, details, or measures; to use them in your dashboard, drag them to the Result Objects area.

The area in the middle right shows the default filters defined in Universe. You can also create your own dashboard filter by dragging the fields you want to filter to the Filters area and then select the operator (Equal To, Between, In List, etc.) and operand (which can be a constant, a list of values, data from another object, or a prompt). The available operands are listed in Figure 2.38. When you select Prompt, you'll see a new window where you can define the prompt, such as its default value and whether it's optional or mandatory.

Another area here is named Data Preview, which shows some rows of the returned data so you can get some idea about what the returned data is like to justify your dashboard design. How many rows of data are returned depends on what's defined in Max Rows. You can increase maximum rows of the preview data if you want to see more data, or decrease it for a faster response in this phase. Also, you can select whether the returned data is to be displayed as a raw value or formatted.

In our sample in Figure 2.38, there are three classes with several dimensions defined in our selected Universe as displayed on the left. For our dashboard we selected the data of four fields, COUNTRY, CONTACT NAME, ACCOUNT NAME, and ACTIVITY for a CRM (customer relationship management) analysis. We want the user to filter the data by countries, so we drag CONTACT COUNTRY to the FILTERS area, choose the operator IN LIST, and choose OPERAND AS PROMPT so the user can select the countries he's interested in at runtime.

2.8.3 Preview Query Result

When you've finished your query, click NEXT to go to the next phase (preview query result) to see whether the returned data is what you want and whether the format is okay. What you see here is exactly what you'll see in the RESULT SET section of the last step, as displayed in Figure 2.38.

2.8.4 Usage Options

This tab is similar to the USAGE tab of other data connectivities and defines how to trigger the Universe query to refresh, as displayed in Figure 2.39.

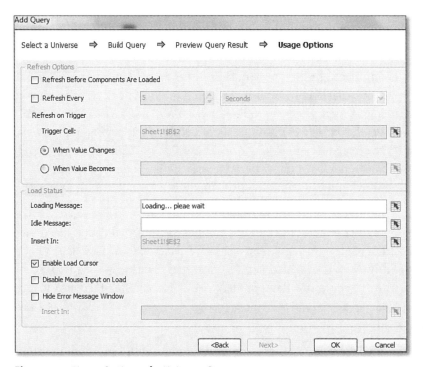

Figure 2.39 Usage Options of a Universe Query

You can select REFRESH BEFORE COMPONENTS ARE LOADED to trigger the Universe query and retrieve its data when the dashboard is loaded. Normally, to improve response speed, we unselect this option and use a trigger cell or the QUERY REFRESH button for the user to explicitly refresh it.

In some scenarios you can select the REFRESH EVERY option and define an interval to trigger the query repeatedly. This is mostly used in real-time BI (for example, to display real-time stock prices or the sales volume of a retail company during a big promotion, such as a Christmas promotion, when the sales may change rapidly and the managers need the data).

Other properties such as TRIGGER CELL and LOAD STATUS are similar to those of common data connectivities and will be covered in Chapter 6.

2.9   Summary

The workspace of SAP BusinessObjects Dashboards 4.0 consists of several parts, such as menus, canvas, the COMPONENTS browser, the PROPERTIES panel, and the new QUERY BROWSER. In this chapter we illustrated the parts and commands you'll use as you work. Being familiar with each part and having a good understanding of what they are used to do will be very helpful and will save you a lot of time. In the next chapter, we'll go through a simple example to warm you up as you design your dashboard.

SAP BusinessObjects Dashboards 4.0 provides plenty of tools and options to create a powerful dashboard. In this chapter, you'll follow a simple tutorial to quickly get started with a dashboard of your own.

3   Dashboard Tutorial

So now you know what SAP BusinessObjects Dashboards is and are familiar with its design environment and commands. Maybe you can't wait to try it out and get a quick hands-on experience with it. Before diving into the rich set of UI components and data connectivities, we'll guide you through a simple example to quickly get started.

In this chapter we'll present a tutorial on how to create a simple dashboard. After reading this chapter you'll be able to describe the steps of creating a dashboard using SAP BusinessObjects Dashboards 4.0, and know where to start to create a dashboard.

3.1   Introduction

In this chapter we'll show you the basic steps of creating a dashboard using SAP BusinessObjects Dashboards 4.0. You can also begin with these steps when creating more complex dashboards. Generally, the required steps to create a dashboard are:

1. Analyze: Understand the requirement, purpose, and audience
2. Design: Define the layout, interaction, data connectivity, and data format
3. Development I: Choose data visualization methods
4. Development II: Choose data connectivity
5. Development III: Visualization format
6. Distribute to the audience

Naturally, similar to other system development, the first thing you need to understand is the business scenario, including but not limited to:

- The purpose of the dashboard
- Who will use it
- Where to get the data
- What the data is like
- How the end user will use it

This applies to complex requirements as well as simple ones. Only when you thoroughly understand them can you choose the right UI components to deliver the right information, find the way to bind and retrieve data, and finally create a professional dashboard that can help the users analyze their business and make a wise decision. The following sections will guide you through a simple dashboard design process.

Suppose that one of your friends asks you to create a dashboard showing the area of each of the continents in the earth. You decide to use a pie chart to show the area for each continent. When the user clicks on one continent, a label below displays text showing the area—very simple, but informative enough. Let's begin with this example.

3.2   Choose the Right UI Components

Once you've made clear the purpose and audience of the dashboard, the first step is to choose suitable UI components to visualize your data. You choose the right components based on the business scenario or the end user's preferences. It's a best practice to think about what UI components to use and how to lay them out outside SAP BusinessObjects Dashboards. For example, you can first draw the dashboard on a piece of paper, thinking about the use scenario and user interactions that will affect the design of the layout.

In our case, we need a pie chart to show and compare each continent's area and a label to show some general information about the selected continent. Detailed explanations of all available UI components will be covered in Chapters 4 and 5.

After dropping one or more UI components onto the canvas, you need to position them to build a logical and easy to use layout. You can use the mouse to move and resize them. If you have too many components, you may want to use the Object Browser to hide, lock, or delete them, as illustrated in Section 2.7.

You can customize each component in its corresponding PROPERTIES panel by changing properties such as the colors, font styles, labels, values, and so on.

For this tutorial, begin by launching SAP BusinessObjects Dashboards 4.0. Open the COMPONENTS view, and in the CATEGORY tab, drag a pie chart from CHARTS and a label from TEXT and drop them onto the canvas. Position them as displayed in Figure 3.1, with the label below the pie chart.

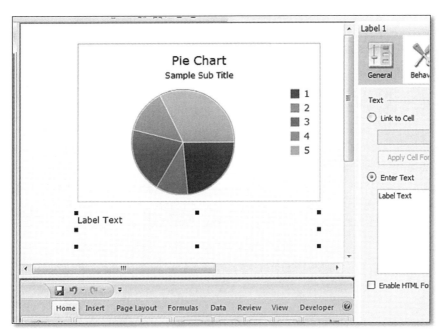

Figure 3.1 The UI Components of Our Sample

For a better layout, align the components to the left and make them the same width by selecting both and then selecting FORMAT • ALIGN • LEFT and FORMAT • MAKE SAME SIZE • WIDTH.

These are all of the components in our simple dashboard. To make it look professional, adjust the canvas size by clicking the FIT CANVAS TO COMPONENTS button on the toolbar to make it just big enough to hold them. Then click INCREASE CANVAS to increase it a little bit, leaving some gap around the borders to make the user feel more comfortable.

3.3 Bind Data

The second step is to bind the UI components to data to reflect real information. You can directly enter static data into the embedded spreadsheet or import it from an existing Excel file (with an *.xls* or *.xlsx* extension). For dynamic data, you need to go one step further by using a type of data connectivity and then bind them to the UI components.

In our tutorial, the continents' areas are static. For simplicity, we directly enter such data into the embedded spreadsheet. For information about how to use the embedded spreadsheet, including the naming convention of each sheet, where to put the data, and how to use color to show different data, please refer to Chapter 6 where we'll discuss the embedded Excel spreadsheet, and Appendix B where we'll discuss some best practices.

Most commonly, you'll be using dynamic data. The actual, live data resides outside of SAP BusinessObjects Dashboards and has to be retrieved with the help of one or more data connectivities, including Universe queries. In such cases, you can write some explanatory sample data in the embedded spreadsheet in this step and wait until the next phase of binding data to map the real data. For example, you can assume that the range Sheet1!$B$2:$C$4 is for the sales information for each region in your company. This way you eliminate the complexity of data connectivity and focus on UI components for now. You can focus on data connectivity later in step 3.

In our tutorial, your data in the embedded spreadsheet should be similar to that in Figure 3.2.

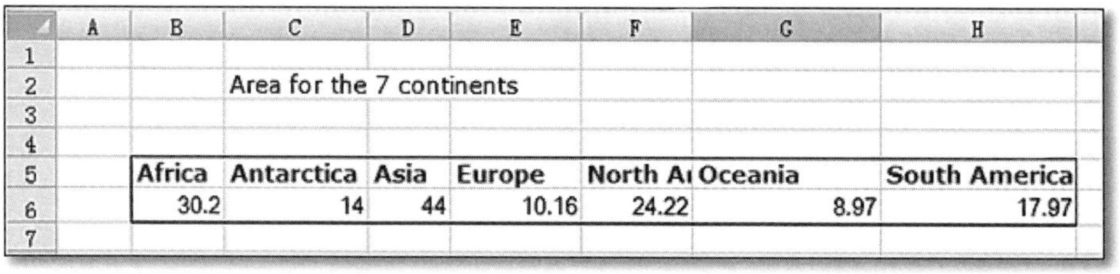

	A	B	C	D	E	F	G	H
1								
2			Area for the 7 continents					
3								
4								
5		Africa	Antarctica	Asia	Europe	North A	Oceania	South America
6		30.2	14	44	10.16	24.22	8.97	17.97
7								

Figure 3.2 Data in the Embedded Spreadsheet

3.3.1   Bind Data for Pie Chart

In this step, let's enrich the pie chart with some meaningful data. To do this, click the pie chart to open the PROPERTIES panel, and in the GENERAL tab, bind properties such as TITLE and DATA SOURCE to cells in the embedded spreadsheet. If the PROPERTIES panel is not displayed, double-click the pie chart or select PROPERTIES in the VIEW menu.

The binding can be divided into three categories, as illustrated in the following subsections.

To a Single Cell

To bind a single-value property to a cell in the embedded spreadsheet, click the BIND button to the right of the property and select a single cell. In our tutorial, we need bind the TITLE property of the pie chart to cell Sheet1!$C$2, where the title is stored, as displayed in Figure 3.3.

Figure 3.3 Title of the Pie Chart Bound to a Cell in the Spreadsheet

You can also enter the title directly in the INPUT field. However, binding it to a cell makes it flexible when you need to update it later.

To a One-Dimensional Cell Range

This is appropriate if you need to bind some property, such as the labels of a combo box, to a one-dimensional list of values; that is, a row or a column in the embedded spreadsheet. To do this, click the BIND button to the right of the property and drag the mouse to select a range of cells in one row or in one column. If you select cell ranges in multiple rows or columns, only the data in the first row or column is used.

In our tutorial, we need bind the VALUES property of the pie chart to cell range Sheet1!$B$6:$H$6, where the sizes of the continents are stored. Similarly, bind the LABELS property to cell range Sheet1!$B$5:$H$5, as shown in Figure 3.4.

Figure 3.4 Data Binding for the Pie Chart

To a Two-Dimensional Cell Range

To bind a two-dimensional list of values to a cell range (multiple rows and columns), click the BIND button to the right of the property and drag the mouse to select a two-dimensional range of cells. SAP BusinessObjects Dashboards will then automatically parse the data using its own mechanism and divide it into categories and series or into several series. For example, you may want to bind the data of a column chart to a two-dimensional cell range in the embedded spreadsheet.

SAP BusinessObjects Dashboards does not support data binding of more than two dimensions.

Now the pie chart displays the data the user is interested in. You can click PREVIEW in the toolbar to have a look at the effect. Let's move on to make it more interactive by adding drill-down ability to the dashboard.

3.3.2 Enable Drill-Down for the Pie Chart

By now the pie chart is displaying the size of each continent. You can get a rough idea of the percentage of each continent at a glance and know the concrete size by moving your mouse over an item. To make the dashboard clearer and more intuitive, we use a label component under the pie chart to show the area of the selected continent in an obvious way.

The purpose behind this is to use another component to show more information about the selected item in a pie chart. It can be as simple as a label or as complex as another chart showing the countries in the continent.

In our example, we enable drill-down on the pie chart so that the name and the area of the selected continent can be inserted somewhere in the spreadsheet. Then we can use that data for the label. To enable drill-down, click on the pie chart to open its PROPERTIES panel, and in the INSERTION tab, select ENABLE DATA INSERTION. You then have the option to select an insertion type and configure its source and destination. Figure 3.5 shows the INSERTION tab of the pie chart.

Figure 3.5 Configure Drill-Down Behavior for the Pie Chart

There are five insertion types for drill-down. You can click the HELP icon () to get an idea of what each type does. The help is like a live video instead of plain text and is very intuitive and easy to understand.

You choose the drill-down type depending on the requirement. We'll provide detailed explanations of each insertion type in Chapter 4 when we talk in more detail about how to use a pie chart.

In INTERACTION OPTIONS, you can configure when the drill-down happens, either on mouse-over or on mouse-click. There's no strict rule about what to choose, and you can just follow your preference. By default, MOUSE CLICK is selected.

SAP BusinessObjects Dashboards also provides a way to specify what item is selected by default. You set the default item by setting its index, starting from 1 as shown in Figure 3.6.

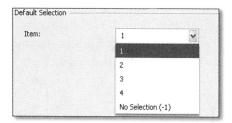

Figure 3.6 Default Selected Item of a Drill-Down

In Xcelsius 2008, service pack 1, you had to select a default item. That is, a drill-down always happened immediately when the pie chart was displayed. However, in certain cases you may want to display nothing until the user manually and explicitly clicks the pie chart to select an item. Since Xcelsius 2008 SP3, you can select nothing as the default by choosing No Selection (-1) as the default selection.

In this tutorial, we insert a column from cell range Sheet1!$B$5:$H$6 into column Sheet1!$C$8:$C$9, as shown in Figure 3.7.

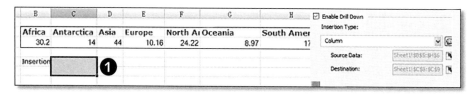

Figure 3.7 Drill-Down Definition of the Pie Chart

Note that the destination is a one-dimensional cell range with two rows and one column, highlighted in yellow ❶. The cell range containing the source data is also highlighted with a thick box, so you can easily distinguish the data from other cells in the embedded spreadsheet.

Color Figures

Go to *www.sap-press.com* to find figures that are mentioned in color, or see the inside front cover to take advantage of a free trial online color version of the book.

3.3.3 Bind Data for Label

As mentioned in the last section, we'll add a label below the pie chart to display more information about the selected continent for the user's better understanding. For example, when Asia is selected, the label displays THE AREA OF ASIA IS 30.2 MILLION KILOMETERS.

You either bind the text of the label to a cell or enter constant text directly. To form a meaningful sentence, we use a string function in the Excel spreadsheet. For example, you select a cell and set its value to:

  =CONCATENATE("The area of ", C8, " is ", C9, " million kilometers.")

> **Note**
>
> Sheet1!$C$8 stores the name of the selected continent, and Sheet1!$C$9 stores its area, which is a number.

You then bind the label to cell Sheet1!$F$8 through the label's PROPERTIES panel, as displayed in Figure 3.8.

Figure 3.8 Binding the Label to a Cell with Excel Formulas

By now the dashboard provides all of the functionalities you wanted: The pie chart displays each continent's area, and the label displays an explanatory text of the selected item when the user clicks on the pie chart.

3.4 Connect to External Data

This step is required if your data isn't finalized at design time and has to be retrieved through a type of data connectivity such as a web service, which can be either your enterprise's service hosted on your web application server or a public service. For example, you can connect to Yahoo! web service to get stock prices given a company's stock code.

In this step, you define the data connectivity in the Data Manager, which is accessible from the menu path DATA • CONNECTIONS, where you map the input and output data to a cell or cell range in the embedded Excel spreadsheet and define when and how to trigger the connections to load the live data.

Because the data in our tutorial is static, we'll skip this step. For information about how to use data connectivity in SAP BusinessObjects Dashboard 4.0, refer to Chapters 6 and 7.

3.5   Formatting

The steps described in Section 3.2 focus on the functionality of the dashboard: choosing the right UI components to visualize data and retrieving the accurate and live data. Now we'll focus on the visual appearance, including the sizing, alignment, positioning, fonts, colors, and so on. If you like, you can also add a background to the dashboard or choose a different theme or color scheme to make it more customized for your specific end user.

You change the canvas size by using the four commands INCREASE CANVAS, DECREASE CANVAS, FIT CANVAS TO COMPONENTS, and FIT CANVAS TO WINDOW in the toolbar or via the menu VIEW CANVAS SIZING. You can also set it via the menu path FILE • DOCUMENT PROPERTIES, but setting it will resize the canvas without taking into account existing UI components.

You change the sizes and alignment of components in the canvas by selecting one or multiple components and using mouse to resize them, or by using commands such as ALIGN TO LEFT and ALIGN TO TOP.

> **Note**
>
> When aligning components and making them the same size, the first component you select becomes the base.

Properties such as fonts, colors, and text alignments are set in the APPEARANCE tab in the properties sheet of the selected component(s), as shown in Figure 3.9.

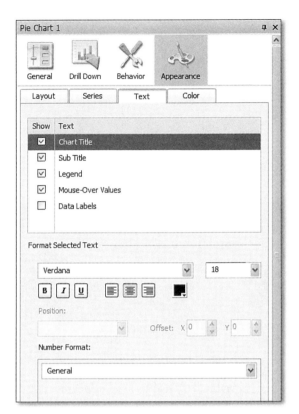

Figure 3.9 The Text Format is Set in the Appearance Tab

We'll explain each property related to the text formats in more details in Chapters 4 and 5. Here we'll just go through an example by setting the font, size, style, and color of the pie chart's title.

To do this, click the pie chart on the canvas to open its properties sheet (if the Properties panel is not displayed, double-click the chart or follow the menu path View • Properties). Select the Appearance tab and then select Text, and you'll see a list of texts that are available for formatting. Here we want to format the title of the pie chart, so click Chart Title, set its font to Verdana, size to 20, style to bold, alignment to center, and color to cyan. Your property sheet should look similar to what's displayed in Figure 3.10.

Pay attention to the checkbox in front of each text. If it isn't selected, the corresponding text will not be displayed in the chart.

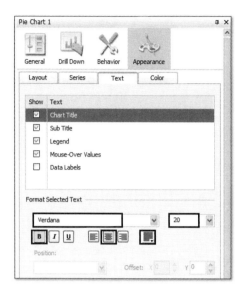

Figure 3.10 Title Formats of the Pie Chart

3.6 Distribute the Output

By now you have created a professional dashboard, not only in appearance, but also in the information it conveys. When you click Preview to have a look at your dashboard, it should look like Figure 3.11. If not, go back to the previous sections to check what you've done.

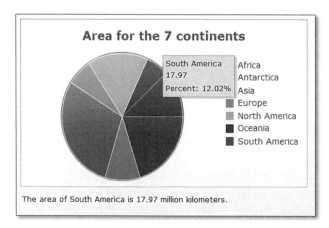

Figure 3.11 Final Effect

As previously mentioned, the purpose of a dashboard is to help communicate information, so we need to distribute the dashboard to others in some manner. Usually, this is the last step of your dashboard development cycle, unless you need some feedback from the end user to modify your dashboard.

Distribution is achieved via the menu path FILE • EXPORT or FILE • SAVE TO PLATFORM or SAP • PUBLISH. SAP BusinessObjects Dashboards 4.0 supports three methods of distribution: to the SAP Business Intelligence platform, to SAP NetWeaver BW, or to a local file. In all three cases, if your dashboard needs to access some external data, you need pay attention to the security issues with Flash Player by either providing a cross-domain policy file or trusting the SWF file (explained in Chapter 6).

If you're an SAP BusinessObjects user, you may want to save the dashboard to the SAP Business Intelligence platform (formerly SAP BusinessObjects Enterprise) so that other SAP BusinessObjects users can access it through the BI portal (BI launchpad for example) if they are permitted to. In Xcelsius 2008, a Flash file was created in your SAP BusinessObjects system. In SAP BusinessObjects Dashboards 4.0, a SAP BusinessObjects Dashboards design object is created, containing both the definition and the output Flash.

In an SAP environment, you can also publish your dashboard to a SAP BW system so it can be stored, transported, or translated like other BW objects. The generated file contains the dashboard definition, the output Flash file, and a text file with the texts to be translated, if any.

In some other cases, you may want to export the dashboard simply to a local file and then either send it directly to others or store it in a web application (for example, your personal website or your company's portal) so others can access it through a web browser. In our tutorial, we simply export it to an SWF file. To do this, save the dashboard and select FILE • EXPORT • FLASH (SWF), as shown in Chapter 2, Figure 2.15.

After setting the file location and file name, you'll find an SWF file generated in your file system. You can then send it to your friend to wait for his "Wow!"

3.7   Summary

In this chapter we explained the typical steps to create a dashboard including how to design, develop, and distribute it. For each step, we illustrated what we need to do and how to do it. In the next chapter, you'll see the detailed illustration of some basic UI components.

SAP BusinessObjects Dashboards provide a rich set of UI components for you to create a nice visual for your audience. In this chapter we'll begin with some commonly used components.

4   UI Component Basics

Is the example in Chapter 3 too simple to meet your requirements? Don't worry; SAP BusinessObjects Dashboards can be more powerful. It provides a large range of UI components to create attractive, powerful, and interactive data visualizations. In this chapter we'll describe some commonly used UI components and what you can do with each of them. After reading this chapter you'll have a clear idea of what UI component you can use in certain scenarios and how to use them.

Some properties are common to most components, such as dynamic visibility, drill-down, text formats, and alerts. Discussing them in a separate section may look clearer but will cause the misunderstanding that they are common to all components and cause confusion about what functionalities are available to what charts. So, instead, we'll discuss them as we meet them.

In this chapter you'll see:

- A list of available UI components including charts and menus
- Descriptions of what you can do with each of them and when and how to use them

After reading this chapter, you'll be able to:

- Describe the UI components provided by SAP BusinessObjects Dashboards 4.0
- Create a more attractive dashboard with more UI components

4.1   Working with Charts

A chart is the most widely-used UI component in data visualization because of its intuitive and attractive appearance. A chart can organize and represent a set of numerical or qualitative data. The data in a chart is represented by symbols in the same or different colors, such as bars in a bar chart, lines in a line chart, and slices in a pie chart.

The main benefit of using a chart is that it eases the understanding of the relationships among multiple parts of the data. You can use them to show, compare, and analyze the values of several items.

In SAP BusinessObjects Dashboards 4.0 you can find many kinds of charts such as pie charts, radar charts, sparkline charts, and bullet charts. All charts share some common purposes, while each has its specific purpose and use scenario. For example, you may use a pie chart to explain the percentages or contribution of different data parts, while a line chart may be a better candidate to show data changes at discrete time points over a period.

To use a chart, just select it from the CHARTS category in the COMPONENTS view, drag and drop it onto the canvas, adjust its position, and set its properties such as colors and data binding.

In this chapter, we'll explain some basic as well as commonly used charts, including what the chart is, its advantages and disadvantages, under what conditions you may want to use it, and how to use it. As a pie chart is the first one we talk about. We'll explain all its features, which means that most features of other charts will simply be ignored in later sections if they have been covered in Section 4.1.1.

In the next chapter we'll discuss some more complex or less frequently used charts such as the radar chart.

4.1.1   Pie Chart

A pie chart is a circular chart that resembles a pie. It uses slices with different colors to represent different data parts. The part-to-whole relationship is built into the pie chart in a quite obvious way. The user can learn the percentage of each part and relative size by simply looking at or moving the mouse over the pie slices and decode the ratio (half, quarter, etc.) in his head.

When to Use a Pie Chart

You may want to use a pie chart to show the relative size, and especially the contribution or distribution of each data part. For example, when you want to explain the sales revenue of each branch and its contribution to the company's total, a pie chart is the best candidate.

You may think that some other kinds of charts, such as a column chart or a bar chart, can also show the size and contribution of each data part. You are partly right. Yes, they can show the size of each part, but they aren't the best way to show the contribution or percentage. For example, in the pie chart showing sales revenue in Figure 4.1, you can easily find out at one glance that Q4 takes up almost exactly one-quarter of the yearly sales revenue and Q2 takes up a little more than one-third.

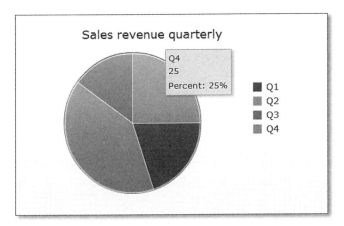

Figure 4.1 A Pie Chart Showing the Contribution of Each Quarter

However, if you use a bar chart (or column chart, which is very similar) in this situation, as displayed in Figure 4.2, it will be difficult to find such information.

As a rule, another factor you need to consider before choosing a pie chart is the whole visualization of your dashboard, including the available space for your chart.

There are different opinions about using pie charts. Some are in favor of them for their good appearance and intuitive part-to-whole relationship, while others think the opposite. One major reason for not choosing a pie chart is that sometimes it's not easy to judge the angles of each part. You may even make a wrong judgment.

Try reading the article from Stephen Few called "Save the Pies for Dessert" to find an in-depth explanation of the pie chart (*www.perceptualedge.com/libary*).

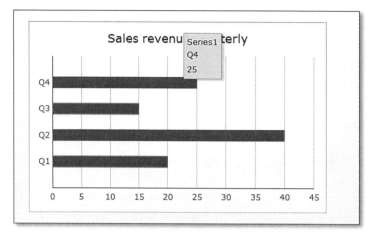

Figure 4.2 The Contribution of a Quarter Isn't Intuitive Enough in a Bar Chart

How to Use a Pie Chart

To use a pie chart in your dashboard design, first select it in the COMPONENTS view and drag and drop it to the canvas.

To set its position and size, use the mouse to move or resize it by clicking it, holding the mouse, and dragging. These two steps are common to all charts in SAP BusinessObjects Dashboards.

A pie chart, like any of the other charts, has a rich set of properties including titles, data, color, and dynamic visibility. You can set these properties in the PROPERTIES panel, which will display when you have selected the pie chart and the PROPERTIES view is enabled (VIEW • PROPERTIES). You can also force display the PROPERTIES panel by double-clicking the chart.

The canvas itself also has a PROPERTIES panel where you define its background color, which can be a solid color, a gradient between two different colors, an image, or nothing. To open the canvas' PROPERTIES panel, click the canvas without touching any UI component.

The properties of a pie chart are categorized into four groups, corresponding to the four tabs in the PROPERTIES view. We'll explain them in the following sections.

General

This category includes the most common and necessary properties to make up a chart—titles and data.

A pie chart can have both a title and a subtitle. Either can be a constant text (entered directly in the fields) or be bound to a single cell in the embedded spreadsheet, which can be either static or dynamically retrieved from a connectivity, with or without Excel formulas.

Generally, the title tells the overall purpose of the chart, and the subtitle gives some additional information. For example, in a quarterly sales revenue report, you can use *Sales Revenue by Quarter* as the title, and show the year as the subtitle so that others can know what year you are talking about. Similarly, if your dashboard contains parameters, you can show the parameter values the user has entered in the subtitle area. This is also a best practice to make your dashboard clear, exact, and easy to understand.

The data of a pie chart contains labels and values, which need to be bound to a row or column in the embedded spreadsheet or a Universe query. As a new feature in SAP BusinessObjects 4.0, you can also bind data directly to a Universe query, which we'll cover in Chapter 8 as a special feature referred to as direct data binding. Here we'll talk about data binding with Excel.

The labels are dimension attributes such as Q1 and Q2, while the values are numeric values such as 25,000 or a percentage of a measure such as sales revenue. The labels will display as legends in the pie chart, and the values will appear when you move the mouse over the slices.

To bind data, click the BIND button to the right of LABELS or VALUES, and then select a cell range in a row or column in the embedded spreadsheet. You can also enter the name of a cell range directly in the input field.

Note that the data parts are arranged clockwise, starting from the fourth quadrant. That is, the first data part appears from the horizontal rightward radius, and the remaining parts follow it clockwise, as illustrated in Figure 4.3.

Understanding this can help you make a better dashboard by adjusting the order of the data parts.

Figure 4.4 illustrates the properties in this category and how they relate to the pie chart and the embedded spreadsheet.

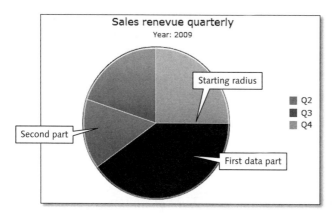

Figure 4.3 Data Parts of a Pie Chart Arranged Clockwise (Starting from the Fourth Quadrant)

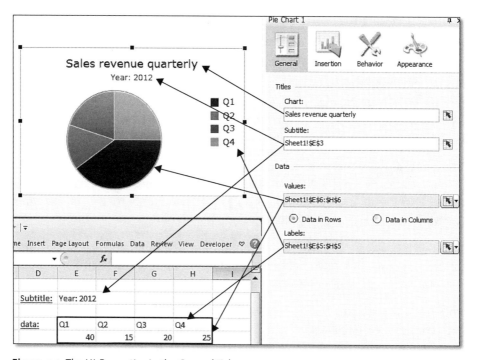

Figure 4.4 The UI Properties in the General Tab

Insertion

Here you define how data is inserted on user interaction. This tab was called DRILL DOWN in previous versions of the software.

To drill down means to move from high-level summary information to a more detailed level or to see more information related to the selected item. The purpose is for the user to understand or find out the reason for something. For example, in a pie chart showing the quarterly sales revenue, you can drill down from a quarter to see more detailed data, such as the monthly data, of that selected quarter. A useful drill down often occurs along a hierarchy; for example, from year to quarter to month or from country to region to state.

Sometimes you may use drill down along no hierarchy. Instead, you just use it as a selector. That is, when the user clicks on a slice on the pie chart, some other information related to your selection is displayed on some other components. The information is updated according to your selection.

Enable Data Insertion

By default the drill-down functionality of a pie chart is not selected. If the values or labels haven't been specified, this option is disabled. To use this functionality, you need select the ENABLE DATA INSERTION checkbox.

In SAP BusinessObjects Dashboards you can insert the position, value, or status list of the selected slice, or a row or column of a two-dimensional cell range, to a cell or cell range in the embedded spreadsheet or to a Universe query prompt. As shown in Figure 4.5, you can click the HELP button (⬤) to the right of the drop-down list to see how to use it.

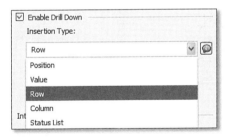

Figure 4.5 Available Insertion Types of Drill-Down in a Pie Chart

Detailed explanations of each insertion type are covered next.

Position
Choose this option if you want to know the index of the selected slice in the pie chart. With this selection, you insert the position of the selected slice into a cell in

the embedded spreadsheet or as the input value for a parameter of a Universe query. The position corresponds to the order of each data part, starting from 1. You can also count the position by looking at the pie chart. Remember, the data parts are arranged from the horizontal rightward radius clockwise.

To bind the position to the embedded spreadsheet, click the BIND button to the right of the DESTINATION field and select a single cell. With each selection, the position of the selected slice is inserted into that cell. For example, if you click the Q2 slice, the content of the target cell becomes 2. If no item is selected (only possible before interaction and if NO SELECTION is the default selection), the target cell is empty, instead of 0.

To bind the position to a Universe query, click the dropdown icon of the BIND button, select QUERY PROMPT, and select one prompt from one of the available Universe queries defined in your dashboard.

If you have done the binding by mistake, click the dropdown icon of the BIND button and select CLEAR BINDING.

Value

Choose this option if you want to know the value of the selected slice. With this selection, you insert the value of the selected slice into a cell in the embedded spreadsheet for future use or a Universe query prompt. The values are specified in the VALUES property in the GENERAL tab.

Similar to position, you need to specify a target cell in the embedded spreadsheet to store the value. With each selection, the value of the selected slice is inserted into that cell. Like the POSITION option, the target cell becomes empty when the pie chart is loaded and NO SELECTION is the default selection.

The way to use the value as the input value for a Universe query parameter or clear the binding relationship is the same as for position.

Status List

The status of a data part refers to whether it's currently selected: 1 for yes and 0 for no. The status list is thus a one-dimensional array with zero or one "1" and others "0".

To bind the status list to the embedded spreadsheet, click the BIND button for DESTINATION and specify a cell range to store the statuses of all data parts. The number of cells should be the same as the number of the data parts. For the selected slice, the corresponding cell contains the value 1, while all other cells are set to 0. If no slice is currently selected, all cells are 0.

If you're going to bind the status list to a Universe query prompt, remember that the value is a one-dimensional array, not a single value.

You may be a little puzzled about the difference between position and status list. You can use both to check what item is selected, and usually you can use position instead of status list. However, sometimes you need to show different components for different parts in the pie chart, and you need to control their dynamic visibilities. In such a case, it's easier to use a status list and control the dynamic visibility of each child component based on the corresponding cell.

Row/Column

With the three options we just discussed, you insert something related to the selected slice into a single cell or a cell range in the embedded spreadsheet or the Universe query prompts. The destination value might be the position or value of the selected data part or a number indicating what data part is currently selected. You can then use the target for further selection, such as in a `VLookup()` or `Match()` function in Excel or for refreshing the data from a Universe query.

However, with ROW or COLUMN the pie chart can behave like a selector. Based on the index of your selected slice, you select a row or a column from a two-dimensional cell range (the source data) and insert it into another row or column or a Universe query prompt (the destination). The source data can be anywhere in the embedded spreadsheet and can have nothing to do with the pie chart. Let's emphasize that again: The pie chart here is just a selector, similar to a combo box or a menu.

With this option, you specify a two-dimensional cell range in the SOURCE DATA field and a row or column in the DESTINATION field, either in the embedded spreadsheet or in a query prompt as a one-dimensional array. With each selection, the corresponding row or column in the source data is inserted into the DESTINATION field. For example, in Figure 4.6 the pie chart shows the total sales for each city in Q1.

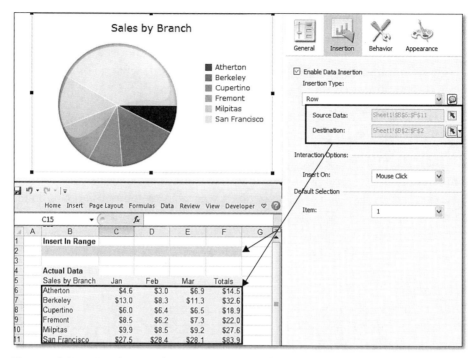

Figure 4.6 Use a Pie Chart to Select a Row or Column from a Cell Range

When the user selects a city, the monthly sales revenue for that city is inserted into another row, which can in turn be used as the data source for another component. In this example, the source data is in cell range Sheet1!$C$6:$G$11, and the destination is in row Sheet1!$C$2:$G$2.

▶ INTERACTION OPTIONS
The interaction options refer to when the drill-down happens—on a mouse click or mouse over a slice, as you can see from Figure 4.7.

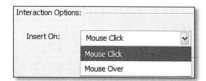

Figure 4.7 Available Interaction Options for Drill-Down of a Pie Chart

You make a selection based on your requirement or preference. The default option is MOUSE CLICK, which is most frequently used. With this option you can move your mouse over the slices to see the value and percentage of each data part and click the one you are interested in to see more detailed data corresponding to your selection.

Otherwise, drill-down is triggered on each mouse-over action. Select this option if you want the user to see the corresponding detailed data immediately on mouse over, without an extra click.

► DEFAULT SELECTION
Default selection refers to what item is selected by default, without user interaction. By default it is 1, which means the position or value of the first item is inserted into the target, or the first row or column in the cell range specified as source data is inserted into the destination. You can assume that SAP Business-Objects Dashboards "clicks" that item automatically, immediately after the pie chart is loaded.

► If you don't want any item be selected at first, choose the last option, NO SELECTION (-1).

Behavior

In this category you set the behaviors of the pie chart, as explained in the following list:

► IGNORE BLANK CELLS
Select this option if you want to ignore the data parts with an empty value (if any) at the end of the range, so that those with a blank value won't be displayed in the pie chart. For example, let's say you're creating a dashboard showing the sales revenue of each sales region. The data is retrieved from another data source, and you're not sure how many sales regions are there at design time. So you have to bind your pie chart to a cell range that is large enough to hold the maximum number of sales regions as far as you can see. The problem is that currently there may not be that many items, and you want to ignore the empty data. To do this, you have to enable IGNORE BLANK CELLS.

In the sample displayed in Figure 4.8, we want to show the sales revenue of each quarter, while at runtime it's only August, so data for Q4 is unavailable and thus empty. Figure 4.8 shows the difference between the pie charts with and without this option selected.

Whether the label for the blank quarter Q4 is displayed depends on whether IGNORE BLANK CELLS is selected.

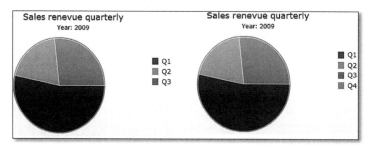

Figure 4.8 The Last Data Parts with 0 Value Aren't Displayed when "Ignore Blank Cells" is Selected

Note

Only the blank cells at the end of the range are ignored.

If the value for Q4 is 0 instead of empty, it won't be ignored, as it's not "blank."

In the sample in Figure 4.8, if the sales revenue for Q2 is empty, it won't be ignored because it's not at the end. However, if the sales revenues of Q3 and Q4 are both empty, both will be ignored.

If you want to ignore all data items with an empty value, not only these at the end, you have a workaround to do this. For example, you can use Excel formulas to rearrange the data for the pie chart, so that the items with an empty value are all placed at the end of the range. Then when this option is selected, all such items will be ignored.

One more note: Whether a cell is considered blank is determined by its value, not its label. That is, if the sales revenue of Q4 isn't empty but you forgot to type Q4 in the Excel spreadsheet, it won't be ignored, though it will have an empty legend.

▶ ENABLE SORTING

As mentioned earlier, the slice for each data part is displayed clockwise in the pie. You can change the order of the data parts by the numeric values or by the labels, in ascending or descending order. To do this, select ENABLE SORTING and select your sorting type as shown in Figure 4.9.

The options are easy to understand. For example, if you choose BY CATEGORY LABELS, the slices are sorted by the category labels in alphabetical order, from A to Z. If at the same time you select REVERSE ORDER, you sort by category labels in alphabetical order from Z to A.

Figure 4.9 Sorting Options for a Pie Chart

▶ Dynamic Visibility

This property is common to all UI components that can be visible. With this property, you have the ability to show one or more components only under a certain condition, when the value of a certain cell is equal to a constant or that of another cell.

To use this property, select a cell in the Status field. Then the Key field is enabled and you can enter a constant or select another cell to compare with. The pie chart will only show when Status matches Key.

If you've set dynamic visibility before and now want to remove it, simply click the Bind button of the Status field and empty the Select a Range field. The constant or cell you specified in the Key field will be automatically removed.

In our example of the sales revenue dashboard, a pie chart is used to represent the data. You may want to enhance it by adding a column chart representing the same information and asking the user to select whether he wants to see the pie chart or the column chart. In such a situation, you use a cell to control the visibility of the two charts. Note that the status cell is bound to a selector, such as a combo box, from which the user selects what chart to see.

In your future development, you'll find dynamic visibility a very useful functionality and will use it a lot. For example, to introduce your dashboard and show others how to use it, you need to provide a help document. You can write the help information in a label and put it in a panel container (let's name it the Help panel). You add a toggle button labeled Help to the dashboard and only show the Help panel when the user clicks the Help button. To achieve this, you insert a certain value to a cell when the user clicks the toggle button and set the dynamic visibility of the Help panel based on that cell.

Dynamic visibility can be set for either a single or multiple UI components. Note that there's no such property for certain UI components that cannot be visible to the end user; for example Canvas Container, History, and Trend Analyzer.

▶ ENABLE DATA ANIMATION

For a better user experience, select ENABLE DATA ANIMATION. As the name indicates, the animation is for the data, or the slices of the pie chart, not the pie chart itself, which is defined by ENTRY EFFECT, as described in the next section.

When this option is selected, the slices of the pie chart appear on the screen with an animation effect. Otherwise, all of the slices of the pie chart appear at the same time. You can try it out with a simple test by dropping a pie chart on the canvas and previewing it with and without this option selected.

▶ ENTRY EFFECT

You use this option to configure how the chart appears on the screen. You can select one effect from the TYPE dropdown list. NONE means no effect, which is the default option. The other three options are FADE-IN, WIPE RIGHT, and WIPE RIGHT-DOWN. You can select one based on your preferences.

With any effect you select, you need to specify the duration in seconds that the entry effect will last. You can enter the duration directly or use the spin button to increase or decrease it at 0.1 second intervals. The suggested duration is 0.2 to 1 second.

Appearance

In this tab you define the visual appearance of a pie chart such as its layout, color, fonts, and so on. This category is divided into several subcategories as illustrated next.

1. LAYOUT

   ▶ CHART AREA

   You can set whether or not to show the chart background on the canvas by selecting SHOW CHART BACKGROUND. The background is a solid area with borders behind the chart, as shown in Figure 4.10.

   The background of the pie chart in Figure 4.10 is the white rectangle area with borders. For a clear look, we changed the canvas background color from white to light gray.

   You then set the margin to control the space between the chart and the edges (borders) of the background by entering a number directly in the MARGIN field or clicking the up or down arrow in the spinner, as displayed in Figure 4.11.

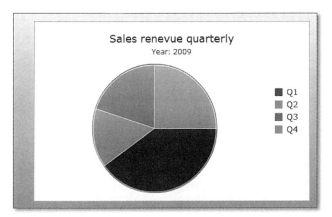

Figure 4.10 The Chart Background of a Pie Chart

Figure 4.11 Set Margins Between Chart and Background Borders

The margins in the four directions can be different. To make them the same, select SAME MARGINS ON ALL SIDES.

You set the color of the background on the COLOR tab. Showing the chart background is a good way to identify the chart area and make it stand out from other components. The chart then appears somewhat above the canvas. If you don't like this effect and want to provide a user experience with the chart integrated into the canvas, you can choose not to show the chart background. The result is displayed in Figure 4.12.

▶ PLOT AREA
The plot area is where the pie itself lies, without the titles or legends. The area is determined by its axes. You can configure whether or not to show the fill, which displays a background to the plot area; and show the border, which displays borders around it.

You can set the color of the fill or the border when it's enabled via the color picker icon to the right of each property.

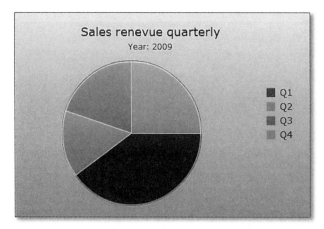

Figure 4.12 Pie Chart Appears Embedded in the Canvas with the Chart Background Hidden

When SHOW BORDER is selected, you have the option to set the border thickness by entering a number directly in this field or clicking the up or down arrow of the spinner. Only an integer is accepted here.

Figure 4.13 shows how these settings affect the chart's look and feel.

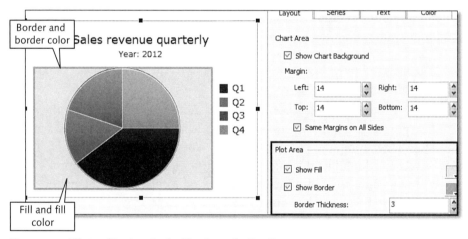

Figure 4.13 Effects of Settings in the Plot Area of a Pie Chart

▶ TITLE AREA
Similar to the plot area, the title area is where the titles (including both the chart title and the subtitle) lie. You can configure whether or not to show the fill (background) or show the border and choose their colors and set the

border thickness when enabled. You make your settings through the corresponding fields.

Figure 4.14 shows how these settings affect the chart's look and feel.

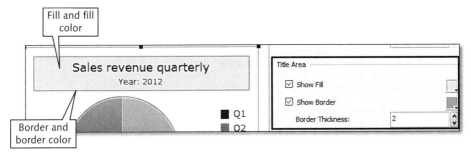

Figure 4.14 Effects of Settings in the Title Area of a Pie Chart

▶ LEGEND

The legend is an explanatory list of the symbols on the chart, typically an inscription or title with an image as an indicator. In the screenshots of our pie chart, the list on the right (e.g., ▪ Q1) displays the legend.

The legend can help the user know the label of each slice from its color; for example, what quarter the slice stands for. Without it, the user has to move the mouse over a slice to know its label.

However, sometimes you may choose not to show the legend to save space for the chart; for example, when the label of some slice is very long and thus requires a lot of space.

When the legend is enabled, you can further set its position in the pie chart to be on the right, left, top, or bottom.

You can set the horizontal offset for the top and bottom, and you can set the vertical offset for the left and right. The offset is 0 by default, which means the legend appears in the vertical or horizontal center. You set the offset by entering an integer in the field or increasing or decreasing it using the spin button with increments of 1.

The purposes of the offset are explained here:

Horizontal offset:

– N > 0: *N* pixels to the right

– N < 0: *N* pixels to the left

Vertical offset:

- N > 0: N pixels to the top

- N < 0: N pixels to the bottom

Similar to the plot area and title area, you can also configure whether or not to show the fill (background) or show the border and set their colors and border thickness when BORDER is enabled.

Generally, you show the fill or border to emphasize the legend, not when you want a tidy and clean appearance.

Figure 4.15 shows the effect of these settings, where the legend is displayed at the top with a horizontal offset of 24 and a border thickness of 3.

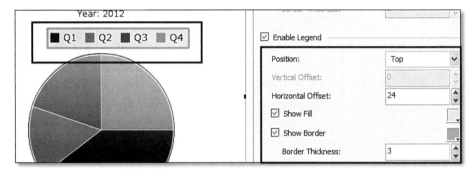

Figure 4.15 Effects of Settings for the Legends of the Pie Chart

2. SERIES

▶ DATA POINT

In this list area, the color of each data point, or slice, of the pie chart is displayed. The default colors of the pie chart are defined by the color scheme your dashboard is currently using. You can customize the color of each data part by clicking the color picker and choosing the color you prefer. This property is useful if you want to use specific colors for certain data parts.

▶ TRANSPARENCY

By default, the pie chart is solid. You set the transparency level with the TRANSPARENCY property. The minimum value is 0, which means solid (no transparency), and the maximum is 100, meaning it's fully transparent, and thus no slice is visible.

You can move the slider bar to adjust the transparency or enter an integer in the field. If you want a transparency level of 50%, enter "50". Note that decimals are not accepted here. If you enter a decimal value such as "32.6", it will be rounded up to 33.

▶ LINES

You use this option to control whether or not to show a line between every two adjacent slices and around the pie. If SHOW LINES is enabled, you have the option to set the lines' color and thickness.

Figure 4.16 shows the effect of these settings where SHOW LINES is enabled with a thickness of 2 in red (it looks ugly, but it's just for explanation here). Pay attention to the lines between every two slices and around the pie.

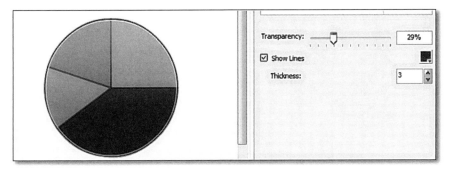

Figure 4.16 Lines Between Every Adjacent Slice of the Pie Chart

▶ TEXT

Here you set the format for all texts that will appear in the pie chart, including the chart title and subtitle, the legend, mouse-over values, and data labels. For each item you can set the format including font, font size, style, alignment, and color. For legends and data labels you can further set their position and offset so they will appear wherever you want them. Note that you cannot customize the positions of the chart title or subtitle or mouse-over values, as they are fixed.

For the color of each text, you can select a color from the color picker window, enter the RGB/HSL value for a custom color, or bind it to a cell in the embedded spreadsheet to make it dynamic. This will be illustrated in the next section discussing color.

One new feature introduced in SAP BusinessObjects Dashboards 4.0 is the functionality to define the content of data labels that appear in the chart for each data part or slice. You can define what information to include in the data label (category label, value, and percentage about part-to-whole), label separator (new line, space, comma, etc.), and where to place it (center, inside end, best fit, etc.). Such labels are always displayed for each part, unlike mouse-over values, which only appear when the user moves the mouse over a data part. Figure 4.17 shows an example where data labels are defined.

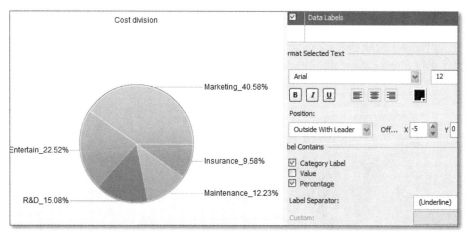

Figure 4.17 Data Labels Displayed for Each Slice

The data label displayed in Figure 4.17 is defined as CATEGORYLABEL_PERCENTAGE. Value is ignored in this label, as we want to highlight the percentage instead of the actual value. For LABEL SEPARATOR we chose UNDERLINE, which can be NEW LINE, COMMA, SPACE, and so on. If you don't find the separator you like here, you can choose CUSTOM and enter you own separator, which can be one or more characters.

You select the position to display the data labels from the POSITION dropdown list. The available positions are CENTER, INSIDE END, and OUTSIDE END. You can also choose BEST FIT to let SAP BusinessObjects Dashboards determine the position. Here we chose OUTSIDE WITH LEADER LINE, which displays a straight line from the label pointing to its corresponding slice.

You can click on another text part to configure its appearance. Figure 4.18 shows the text properties for the legend of a pie chart.

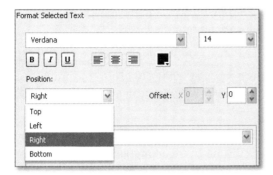

Figure 4.18 Available Properties to Format the Legend of a Pie Chart

The number format defines how the value is displayed. Let's look at the available options:

- GENERAL
Choose this option if you want to display the value as a string.

- NUMERIC
Choose this option for a numeric value such as 3.14.

  You can configure how a negative value is displayed, the number of digits after the decimal point, and whether or not to show a thousand separator, as displayed in Figure 4.19.

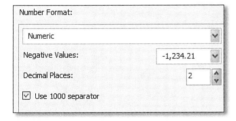

Figure 4.19 Customize the Display Format of a Numeric Value

One new feature is the option to use region-specific formatting that matches your preferred viewing locale (PVL) defined in BI Launchpad. Users can see the numeric values displayed in their specific region, either English, German, Chinese, and so on. To do this, select the DEFAULT NUMBER FORMAT checkbox under the list box.

- CURRENCY
Select this to display the value as a currency. Similar to the NUMERIC

option, you can also configure how a negative amount is displayed and the number of digits after the decimal point.

Using the thousand separator is a must here.

To display the value in a meaningful way, you can also set a prefix and postfix. For example, you can display the currency symbol (e.g., $, USD) as the prefix or postfix.

One new feature added in SAP BusinessObjects Dashboards 4.0 is the ability to set a default currency format by selecting FILE • PREFERENCE, as we discussed in Chapter 2. Corresponding to this feature, there's a new option, DEFAULT CURRENCY FORMAT, just below the number format list box. When this option is selected, the settings you set in the FILE • PREFERENCE menu will be reflected here and used in the pie chart. At runtime, the display format for the CURRENCY fields will match the user's PVL defined in BI Launchpad.

Figure 4.20 shows the effect of setting MOUSE-OVER VALUES to CURRENCY and displaying the currency symbol $ as a prefix. Note that the mouse-over value in Q4 is now displayed as $25.00.

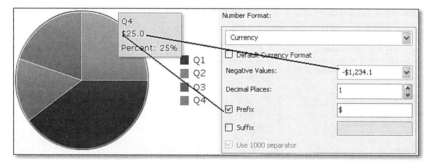

Figure 4.20 Customize the Display Format of a Currency Value

– PERCENT
  Choose this format if you want to display your value as a percentage; for example, if you're showing the year-to-year growth of sales revenue. The value is calculated inside the embedded spreadsheet as (this year's sales revenue – last year's sales revenue) / (last year's sales revenue), such as 0.13. Instead of displaying 0.13 on mouse over, you want the user to see 13%, so you need set NUMBER FORMAT as MOUSE-OVER VALUES AS PERCENTAGE.

  You can set how many digits are displayed after the decimal point.

– DATE/TIME

You can customize how to display a date or time with this property; for example, whether to show the month as March, 3, or 03. You can select one format from the TYPE dropdown list, as shown in Figure 4.21.

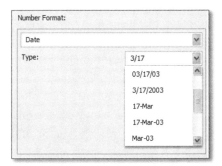

Figure 4.21 Choose a Display Format for the Date Type

3. COLOR

In this tab you set the colors of all elements of a pie chart including the background, the slices, the lines between slices, the title area, the plot area, the legend area, and so on.

If you've enabled CHART BACKGROUND in the LAYOUT tab, you can set the background color here by clicking the color picker to the right of the label BACKGROUND COLOR. In the COLORS window you have several ways to select a color, as displayed in Figure 4.22.

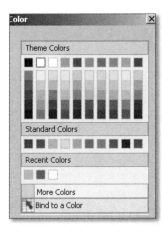

Figure 4.22 Color Window for You to Pick or Define a Color

Click to select one color from the THEME COLORS or STANDARD COLORS area. Click MORE COLORS to open a more complex color window, where you can either select one from the many available colors or manually enter the RGB or HSL value of the color you want. For example, you can enter 0 for red and green and 128 for blue to get the color navy.

A new feature is that you can also bind the color to a cell in the embedded spreadsheet that contains the RBG value of a color in hexadecimal (e.g., for red it's #FF0000, and for pink it's #FFC0CB). The symbol # is optional. This way you can make the color dynamic, by making the text in that cell dynamic. For example, you can write an Excel formula in that cell to specify different colors depending on the season or on the preference passed in from an external application. Follow the same steps to define colors for the title area, plot area, and legend area, including fill and border colors.

Similar to what you do in the SERIES tab, you can also customize the slice colors here by clicking the color picker to the right of each data part. You can also set the line color between every two adjacent slices in this tab, through the color picker for LINE COLOR.

Figure 4.23 shows the configuration items in this tab. Note that TITLE AREA is configurable, while PLOT AREA is disabled due to the different settings in the LAYOUT tab.

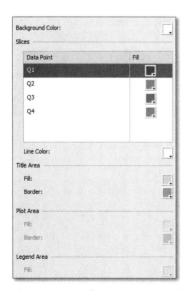

Figure 4.23 Configuration Items in the Color Tab

4.1.2 Column Chart

A column chart uses a column (vertical, tall, and relatively thin) to represent the data for each data part, compared to a slice in a pie chart. The labels are displayed in the horizontal X-axis and the values in the vertical Y-axis. In Section 4.1.4 you'll see bar charts, which use horizontal bars to visualize the data.

A column chart can also have a secondary Y-axis, which we'll illustrate in the following sections.

When to Use a Column Chart

A column chart is mainly used to show and compare the values for different counterparts in a range; for example, to show and compare the sales revenue in each quarter or in each branch. Remember, we use a pie chart to show the percentage or contribution to the total sales revenue of each quarter. This is the difference between a pie and a column chart.

How to Use a Column Chart

The PROPERTIES panel of a column chart is arranged in five categories, as explained next.

General

▶ TITLES

Similar to a pie chart, you can set the chart title, the subtitle, and the title of each axis here. You can either enter text into the corresponding input field or click the BIND button to bind it to a cell in the embedded spreadsheet.

A column chart contains an X-axis to display the category, a Y-axis to display the value, and possibly a secondary axis (vertical) to display the value of another series. You can set titles for each axis. Figure 4.24 shows the effects of these properties.

Note that the field SECONDARY VALUE (Y) AXIS is disabled until you have specified a data series plotting on the secondary axis, which will be explained in the next section.

▶ DATA

You need to specify the labels on the X-axis and one or more series of values on the Y-axis (or the secondary Y-axis) for a column chart. There are two ways to specify the data sources, as illustrated in Figure 4.24.

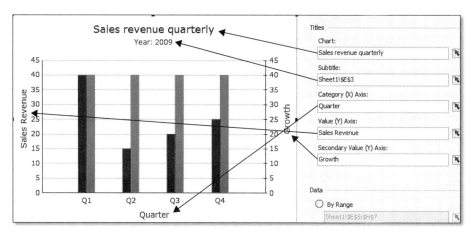

Figure 4.24 Effects of Setting the Titles of a Column Chart

▶ BY RANGE

Click the BIND button to select a cell range as the data source, and depending on the way your data is arranged, select either DATA IN ROWS or DATA IN COLUMNS. SAP BusinessObjects Dashboards will try to determine this automatically, depending on whether there's text instead of numeric values in the first row or column.

As Figure 4.25 shows, the labels (quarter names) are in the fifth row, and the values (sales revenue and growth) are in the sixth and seventh rows, so we select the range 'Sheet1'!$A$3:$E$5 as the data source and select DATA IN ROWS.

	A	B	C	D	E
1	Subtitle	2011 YTD			
2					
3	Quarter	Q1	Q2	Q3	Q4
4	Revenue	27.3	19.8	25.6	37.1
5	Growth	10%	6%	-8%	21%
6					
7					
8					
9					

Data

◉ By Range
'Sheet1'!$A$3:$E$5

◉ Data in Rows   ○ Data in Colu...
○ By Series

Revenue   Name:
Growth

Figure 4.25 Specify a Cell Range as the Data Source of a Column Chart

SAP BusinessObjects Dashboards will automatically treat the first row (or column, if DATA IN COLUMNS is selected) as the label (category) and others as values that will appear in the Y-axis. The data will be reflected in the column chart immediately so you can quickly check whether it's what you want.

SAP BusinessObjects Dashboards can also automatically calculate the series names and values from your specified range. For the example in Figure 4.25, SAP BusinessObjects Dashboards knows that cells A4 and A5 are series names, not values.

► BY SERIES

This option provides more flexibility but more complexity than BY RANGE. Here you need to manually specify a row or column for labels, add one series for each kind of value (or measure), and bind it to another row or column in the embedded spreadsheet or from the Universe queries. You can specify the series name that will appear in the legend area and when the user moves the mouse over the columns.

The typical steps of using this option are:

► Specify a cell range for the category labels that will appear on the X-axis by clicking the BIND button at the bottom. In our case, click the BIND button and select the cell range Sheet1!$F$5:$I$5, where the names of Q1 to Q4 are stored.

With direct data binding, a new feature that we'll illustrate in Chapter 8, you can bind the category labels here directly to the returned data of a Universe query by choosing QUERY DATA after clicking the BIND button, as displayed in Figure 4.26.

Figure 4.26 Binding Category Labels Directly to the Returned Data of a Universe Query

► To clear your direct data binding, simply choose CLEAR BINDING.

► Click the ADD SERIES button ([+]) to add one series for values that will appear in the Y-axis. Then you have the option to set the series name by either entering a text or binding it to a single cell, and to specify the values of this series by binding VALUES to a cell range in the embedded Excel file or to a Universe query. You can also configure whether to show the values on the primary or secondary axis.

▷ In our case, enter "Sales Revenue" in the NAME field, select the range Sheet1!$F$6:$I$6 as the data source for VALUES(Y), and plot it on the primary axis. You can also bind the name to a cell such as Sheet1!$D$5.

▷ Repeat the second step if you want to show other value series. We'll add a second series named GROWTH to show the year-to-year sales revenue growth and plot it on the secondary Y-axis.

▷ To delete a series, click the DELETE button ([-]).

▷ When there are multiple series, there will be multiple columns for each data part. You can use the UP ([^]) or DOWN ([v]) button to change the series order, which defines what column is displayed to the left. Note that the columns of the first series display to the left of those of the second and later series.

Figure 4.27 shows the effect of these settings. The sales revenue for each quarter is displayed on the primary Y-axis in cyan ❶, and growth on the secondary Y-axis in orange ❷. Note that the columns for sales revenue are displayed to the left of those for growth, based on the series order you defined in the list.

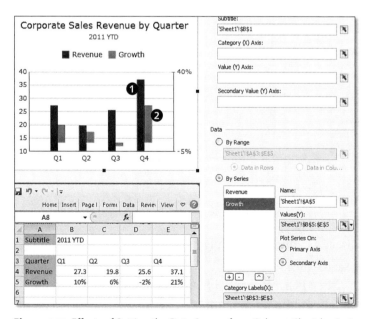

Figure 4.27 Effects of Setting the Data Source for a Column Chart by Series

Insertion

Similar to what we discussed for a pie chart, you can insert the position or value of the current selected data part into a cell, the status list, or a row or column from a cell range to another row or column.

As part of direct data binding, you can also bind the drilled-down data, either a single value or a row or column of data, to the query prompt of a Universe query as the input of the query. In other words, direct data binding is bidirectional: You can bind the output data of a Universe query to a UI component or bind the data of a UI component to the input of a Universe query.

In addition, you can insert the series name of your current selection into a cell. You define the series names in the GENERAL tab. When you click a column in the column chart, its series name is inserted into the target cell. This way you can get to know what column the user is clicking when there are more series in the column chart.

The drill-down behavior is per series. That is, when there are multiple series, the drill-down can be triggered on each series. You may want to use this option to insert a row or column from different ranges into the target. This is different from pie charts, which have only one series.

However, there can only be one insertion type in a column chart, no matter how many series there are. As shown in Figure 4.28, you can select one insertion type and then specify the destination and the source data (if available) for each series.

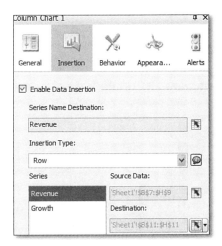

Figure 4.28 Drill-Down Behavior for Each Series with One Insertion Type

The interaction options and default selection are the same as those for pie charts. For more information about what they are and how to use them, refer to the corresponding subsection in Section 4.1.2. The difference is that you can set the default item for each series here.

Behavior

By default, this category is divided into three tabs: COMMON, SCALE, and ANIMATIONS AND EFFECTS. If there's any series plotting on the secondary Y-axis, the SCALE tab is subdivided into a PRIMARY SCALE tab and a SECONDARY SCALE tab.

In the COMMON subtab you can configure following properties:

▶ IGNORE BLANK CELLS

You can choose to ignore cells at the end of the range that are blank by selecting IN SERIES, IN VALUES, or both. Note that for a pie chart you can only ignore blank cells in values.

To ignore cells that are blank in values means that in each series, the last few items with blank values (0 is not blank) are not displayed.

To ignore cells that are blank in series means that the last few blank series (all values are empty) are not displayed. If IN SERIES isn't selected here, even though all values of the last one or more series are empty, spaces will still be reserved for them. If LEGEND is selected, the series name will still be displayed.

If cells blank in values are not ignored, the spaces for them will still be left in the chart, resulting in an unfriendly user experience. For example, if we select two more empty columns in the quarterly sales revenue column chart, Figure 4.29 shows the difference when IGNORE BLANK CELLS – IN VALUES is selected or not.

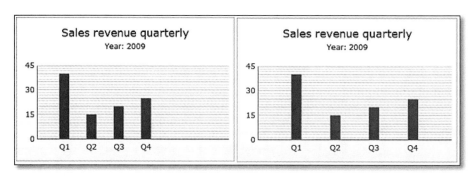

Figure 4.29 Effects of Ignoring End Blank Cells in a Column Chart

As you can see from this figure, the space for the two empty items is still reserved in the left column chart, resulting in a confusing appearance.

We recommend that you always select the two options here to ignore cells at the end of the range that are empty either in series or in values. This is especially useful when you aren't sure about the actual size of the data. For example, the sales revenue of each branch is returned from a data connectivity such as a web service that is mapped to a cell range in the embedded spreadsheet. The number of rows, or the branches, changes every year or month. As a result, you have to talk to the user to agree on the maximum number of branches in the next one or two years and bind the data to a cell range with that number of rows. However, currently there may be fewer branches, and the last few rows are empty. In such a case, you need to ignore the blank end cells.

As mentioned previously, a data item that is empty in value or in series but is not at the end of the range will not be ignored. As a result, you'll see a blank column, or a column without a label, displayed in the column chart. To solve this problem, move the blank cells to the end of the cell range either using Excel formulas or in the backend so that such cells are placed at the end.

▶ ENABLE RUN-TIME TOOLS
When this option is selected, SAP BusinessObjects Dashboards offers a set of functions to enable data scale configuration at runtime. As chart data changes at runtime, you can adjust the scaling options with these tools.

When you select the ENABLE RUN-TIME TOOLS checkbox and three subordinate checkboxes, an icon will be displayed at the top-left corner of the column chart at runtime. When you move your mouse over that icon, a menu list will pop up. What menu items are available is based on your selection of the subordinate checkboxes here.

The options that are available when you select ENABLE RUN-TIME TOOLS are explained in the following:

  ▷ SHOW FOCUS BUTTON
  With this option selected, a FOCUS button will be displayed in the pop-up menu. By clicking the FOCUS button, you rescale the chart axes based on current data.

  ▷ SHOW RESET SCALE BUTTON
  A RESET SCALE button will be displayed in the pop-up menu if you select this

option. You can click the Reset Scale button to rescale the chart axes to those that were initially loaded.

▶ Show Scale Behavior Options

Three status buttons will be displayed in the pop-up menu if you select this option:

- Grow: Auto (Y) axis with Allow Zoom Only selected
- Off: Manual (Y) axis
- Auto: Auto (Y) axis with Allow Zoom Only unselected

You can switch to one of the three options at runtime to change the scaling options. The option you set in the Scale tab at design time will be the default option at runtime. For example, if you select Manual(Y) Axis in the Scale tab, the default option at runtime will be Off.

▶ Enable Range Slider

When this option is selected, a miniature version of the chart is displayed below the chart, with a slider below (for bar and stacked bar charts, the range slider is displayed to the left instead of at the bottom of the chart). The user can move the slider to select a proportion of the data to show on the main chart. This is mainly used when there are many (say, more than 10) items on the chart, making it very crowded. For example, a chart showing daily sales revenue for each day in a month may have 30 columns. With a range slider, you can focus on only a few days among the 30.

By default, all the columns are displayed for the entire data. To display only partial data, you can define the data range by specifying the beginning and end range value as displayed in Figure 4.30.

Figure 4.30 Defining the Beginning and End Position of the Range

You can specify the range by position (e.g., 1–10) or by category label (e.g., JAN–APRIL) of the X-axis. As defined in Figure 4.30, the beginning position is

1 and the end is 5, so only the first five columns are initially displayed in the column chart whose position is from 1 to 5. If the beginning and end positions are equal, only one column will be displayed. If the beginning position is larger than the end, all the data items will be selected and the entire chart will be displayed. Note that the position of the first column is 1, not 0. If 0 is specified for either the beginning or the end position, the entire range is displayed.

In Figure 4.30 we manually entered integers for the positions. You can also bind the beginning or end position to a cell in the embedded spreadsheet to make the selection dynamic, either based on user preference defined on the server side or bound to another selector such as a combo box.

The range can also be defined by the category labels. For example, if the column chart displays the sales revenue of 12 months in a year, you can display only the summer months (April, May, June) at first. To do this, specify April as the category label for the beginning range value and June for the end. Note that the category labels on the X-axis don't need to be displayed in ascending or descending order. The only requirement is that the first occurrence of the label specified as the end should be displayed after that for the beginning. Otherwise, the entire range is displayed.

Defining the beginning and end range value defines which columns are displayed at first. You can define range labels, which are used to divide the miniature chart into several parts with the same number of columns and name them. For example, when displaying the inventory of each material, you can divide them into categories or material groups and define the label for each group. The number of groups depends on how many labels you define here, by either binding to a cell range in the embedded spreadsheet or entering them manually via the two buttons to the right of RANGE LABELS. For example, in a column chart showing the sales revenue of each month, if you define two range labels called FIRST HALF and SECOND HALF, the columns in the miniature chart will be divided into two groups, and if you define four called Q1, Q2, Q3, and Q4, there will be four groups.

As a comprehensive example, Figure 4.31 displays a column chart showing the revenue of each day in June 2012, with the sixth to the tenth days displayed by default. The miniature columns are divided into the groups called 1–10, 11–20, and 21–30.

Pay attention to the labels at the bottom. At preview or runtime you can move the two sliders to select the data you want to see.

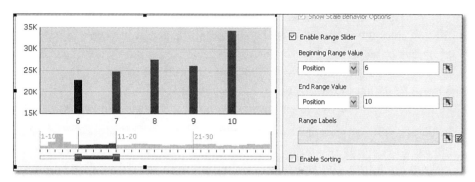

Figure 4.31 Effect of Defining the Range Slider by Position

▶ SCALE

Here you define how the Y-axis behaves, including the minimum and maximum limits, number of major and minor divisions, and so on. Note that this tab may be divided into PRIMARY SCALE and SECONDARY SCALE if you have series plotted on the secondary Y-axis.

▶ AUTO (Y) AXIS

If this option is selected, SAP BusinessObjects Dashboards will automatically calculate the minimum and maximum limits and number of divisions based on the values of data items in all series at runtime. The scale will grow or shrink automatically as data changes.

You can select this option if you aren't sure about the values scale at design time—whether it's several hundred or millions.

Select ALLOW ZOOM OUT ONLY if you want the Y-axis to grow without shrinking when data changes, thus minimizing chart scaling; for example, if you're using a column chart to display the quarterly sales revenue every year, with a combo box for the user to select one year. In the year 2000, the sales revenues are very low, say less than 100, and in 2009, revenues are more than 100 and less than 500. The maximum limit of the Y-axis can grow from 100 to 500 on your selection. If you do not select this option, you'll see an obvious shrinkage of the Y-axis, and the change or shrinkage may happen on every change. In contrast, if the change happens gently without any shrinkage, the user may not even notice it. You may want to select this option when your chart is used in an animation.

Note that the shrinkage will only happen when the scale is growing higher and will not happen when it's decreasing. That is, the scale will change from 100 to

500 when you change the year from 2000 to 2009. But when you change it back to 2000, the scale will remain 500.

With this option selected, you can tune the zoom sensitivity via the slider beneath it. The value determines how much the Y-axis scale will grow on data changes. Moving the slider to the left results in the axis scale increasing by a small factor when the scale of the Y-axis changes. On the other hand, the axis scale increases by a larger factor on data change when you move the slider to the right.

▶ MANUAL (Y) AXIS

Select this option if you aren't satisfied with the result of selecting AUTO (Y) AXIS and want more flexibility. You can manually set the minimum and maximum limits and number of major and minor divisions by entering an integer in the corresponding fields or clicking the BIND button to bind the limit to a cell in the embedded spreadsheet.

The advantage of this option is that it provides more flexibility. For example, when all of the values are very large (e.g., larger than 1,000,000), you can choose to start from 1,000,000 or 500,000. You can also configure how to display the divisions, which we'll explain in the next section.

However, the minimum and maximum limits of the chart are fixed with this option. So don't use this option if you are not sure about the values; in other words, if the values might vary a lot in different situations.

If you still want to control the scale limits on your own in the situation above, you can achieve a perfect chart by binding the limits to cells whose values are dynamic—or calculated from the values to be displayed. For example, you can calculate the limits using Excel functions like MIN or MAX in two cells and bind them to the scale limits.

▶ (Y) AXIS SCALE

Here you define how to position the major and minor divisions on the vertical axis by selecting LINEAR or LOGARITHMIC from the dropdown list.

Linear means dividing the axis into divisions on a linear scale. The divisions are plotted at evenly-spaced intervals.

Logarithmic means plotting the divisions on a logarithmic scale instead of linearly. The divisions are plotted at intervals of the logarithm of the value, instead of the value itself. The spaces between every two adjacent divisions are not even: Smaller values have larger space intervals, while larger values have smaller intervals.

Figure 4.32 shows the difference between these two methods by displaying the same data in two column charts.

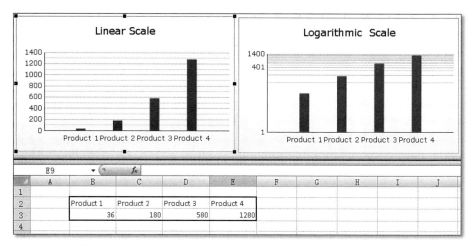

Figure 4.32 Difference Between the Linear and Logarithmic Y-Axis Scale

The LINEAR option is most commonly used in daily work. You may only want to choose LOGARITHMIC when the values are vastly different, covering a large range of data; for example, if the values include 10; 200; and 40,000. If you select LINEAR, the value 10 will be a tiny column. Choosing LOGARITHMIC can reduce the scale to a more manageable range that's more suitable to display on the Y-axis.

▶ FIXED LABEL SIZE
In a column chart, the data label for some value points on the Y-axis may be longer than others (e.g., 40,000 is much longer than 100). For a better look and feel, you can select this option so that the width of the Y-axis labels will not differ too much.

Sometimes the value is very big (e.g., larger than 1,000,000). With FIXED LABEL SIZE selected, you can display abbreviations of the values as labels. For example, instead of displaying 45,000, you can display it as 45K. Click the LABEL ABBREVIATIONS button to customize the abbreviations; that is, what symbol is used to represent thousand, million, billion, and trillion, as shown in Figure 4.33.

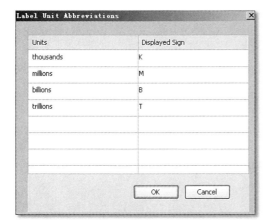

Figure 4.33 Manage Label Abbreviations for Quantitative Values

Use the DISPLAYED SIGN fields to change the abbreviation. However, you cannot create new abbreviations; for example, for hundreds.

Figure 4.34 shows the comprehensive effect, with LOGARITHMIC Y AXIS SCALE and FIXED LABEL SIZE selected. Note that the letter K is used as an abbreviation for thousands.

Figure 4.34 Effects of Setting Scale Properties of a Column Chart

▶ DIVISIONS

In a column chart, the values are represented by columns. The higher the column is, the bigger the value is. Aside from the minimum and maximum limits, you need to display some major and minor divisions so the user can easily see the rough value through its height.

You can define how the divisions are displayed by specifying either the number or the size of divisions. Note that this option is only available if you have selected MANUAL (Y) AXIS. SAP BusinessObjects Dashboards will then automatically calculate where to position the divisions.

You can also define how many minor divisions will appear between every two adjacent major divisions. Depending on your requirements, you need to consider thoroughly before choosing how to define the major and minor divisions. In the PROPERTIES panel, you can see that you can configure them by either entering an integer in the field or by clicking the BIND button.

Figure 4.35 shows a column chart with three major divisions and one minor division in between. Pay attention to the three horizontal lines of values 20, 40, and 60 and the one horizontal line in between.

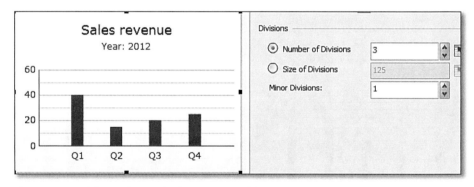

Figure 4.35 A Column Chart with Three Major and One Minor Division

The properties in the ANIMATIONS AND EFFECTS tab are the same as those of a pie chart, and we'll ignore them both here and in any later UI components. For more information about them, please refer to the corresponding part in Section 4.1.1, where we discuss how to use a pie chart.

Appearance

In this tab we define the visual appearance of each part of the column chart, including its color, the position of each text field, and so on.

▶ LAYOUT

Settings here are the same as those for a pie chart, including:

- ▶ Whether to show the chart background and the margin between the chart and, if so, the background border.

- ▶ Whether to show the fill in the plot area or title area and, if so, the color. The fill is a solid background.

- ▶ Whether to show the border in the plot area or title area and, if so, the color and thickness.

You can also configure whether and how to display the legend. For a pie chart, the legends are labels with images, while for a column chart, they are series names with images. When you select ENABLE LEGEND, you can set the position, where it will appear, the vertical and horizontal offset, whether to show the fill and border, and how to do so.

One more thing you can do here is allow the user to hide or show columns of a series at runtime. This is not applicable to a pie chart, which contains only one series. You may want to do this when you want to display several measures (thus series) in the chart and in the meantime allow the user to focus on only a few series by hiding all the other series.

To do this, select the option ENABLE HIDE/SHOW CHART SERIES AT RUNTIME. Then select an interaction type, which can be either CHECKBOX, so a checkbox will be displayed to the left of each legend for the user to select or unselect; or MOUSE CLICK, so there will be no checkbox added and the user just clicks the legend to hide or display the series.

Figure 4.36 shows the effects of these settings, where the fill is shown in the plot and title areas, the border is shown in the title area with a thickness of 2, and the legend is positioned on the right with both fill and border. Also, a checkbox is displayed to the left of each series to allow the user to hide or display each series at runtime with a single click on the checkbox.

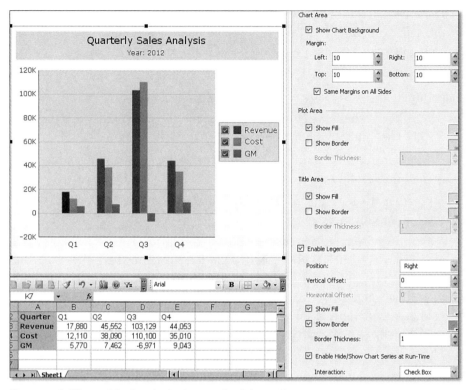

Figure 4.36 Effects of Settings in the Layout of a Column Chart

Now that you understand the effects of each property, you can customize these settings for your dashboard based on your requirements.

▶ SERIES

Here you can set the color of each series through the corresponding color picker and slider. For a pie chart, each data part represents a series, while for a column chart, each measure (sales revenue or growth) is a series, and all data parts in the measure are columns (markers) in the same series.

Here you can also set the width and transparency of the columns for all series with the MARKER SIZE field and the TRANSPARENCY slider. This option is helpful when you have too many or too few items, in which case the columns may become very sparse or very crowded. For a better user experience, you can reduce the marker size when there are too many items (e.g., over 20 products) or increase it when there are too few (e.g., 4 quarters) for a better look and feel.

Note that fill color is per series, but marker size and transparency are for all series.

▶ AXES

You can configure whether and how to show the horizontal and the primary or secondary vertical axis here. When there's a series plotting on the secondary vertical axis, this tab is divided into two tabs: PRIMARY AXES and SECONDARY AXES.

When the primary vertical, the secondary vertical, or the horizontal axis is enabled, you can set its color by selecting one from the corresponding color picker and its thickness via the corresponding spinner.

You can display a tick mark for each major or minor division on the vertical axes. Whether to show the major or minor ticks is also configured here.

You can also define whether or how to show the major and minor gridlines by selecting the corresponding checkboxes. When these checkboxes are selected, the color and thickness of the gridline can also be set via the corresponding color picker and spinner. Figure 4.37 shows the effect of the settings of these properties.

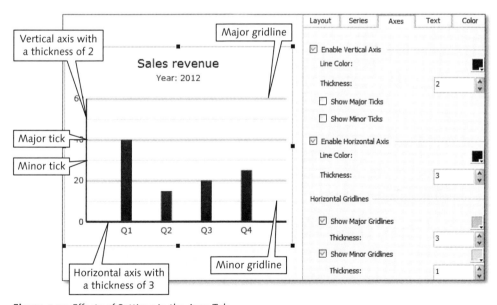

Figure 4.37 Effects of Settings in the Axes Tab

The primary vertical axis is enabled in cyan with a thickness of 2, and the horizontal axis is enabled with a thickness of 3. Both major and minor gridlines are enabled in the same color but different thicknesses, and both major and minor ticks are displayed.

▶ TEXT

Here you can set the formats of all the texts that will appear in the column chart, including the title and subtitle, titles and labels of the horizontal (X, for categories) axis and the primary and secondary vertical (Y, for values) axes, mouse-over values, and so on. You may need to pay more attention to the text formats for legends and range labels.

You can also set the text formats for data labels of each series. The data label will display in the chart for each column for that series. The content of the data label can contain none or all of series name, category label, and value, separated by your specified label separator, which you can select from NEWLINE, UNDERLINE, COMMA, SEMI COLON, PERIOD, SPACE, or any character you have customized. This is similar to a pie chart, as illustrated in Section 4.1.1.

The format includes font, size, style, alignment, and color. For some texts you can also configure where to display them by setting the positions and offsets. Your changes will be reflected in the chart on the canvas at design-time immediately.

Like the settings for a pie chart, you can customize the format to display the value if it's a numeric, currency, percentage, date, or time value. For more details about these formats, please refer to the corresponding section about pie charts in Section 4.1.1.

▶ COLOR

You can set colors for all parts of a column chart here. If SHOW CHART BACKGROUND is enabled (in the LAYOUT tab), you can set the background color from the COLOR PICKER button.

Similar to the SERIES tab, you can also set colors for each series here. The default colors are based on the current color scheme, which by default is determined by the current theme.

As you would do for a pie chart, here you can also set the colors for the fill and border of the title area, plot area, and legend area if you have enabled them in the LAYOUT tab. In addition, you can set the colors for the axes and gridlines, as explained here:

▸ First, the color of the horizontal X axis.

▸ Second, colors of the vertical Y-axis and its corresponding horizontal major gridlines and horizontal minor gridlines.

▸ Third, if one series or more is plotted on the secondary vertical axis, you can also specify colors related to it, including the vertical (secondary) axis and its corresponding horizontal (secondary) major gridlines and horizontal (secondary) minor gridlines.

Alerts

You can show different colors for different data parts of the same series in a column chart with the help of alerts. An alert is used to highlight values under certain conditions by displaying the markers in colors that stand out. This is a very useful feature. For example, you may want to highlight the branches with sales revenues higher than the yearly average or products with sales revenue growth less than 10% so that at a glance the user can determine the items that need be looked into. Typically, you display the poor items in red and the good ones in green.

▸ Enable Alerts

Select this option before using alerts. Note that alerts cannot be enabled when there is more than one series in the column chart. This makes sense, as markers in another series are in different colors, which makes it confusing to have colors representing alerts.

The condition to define alerts is based on the value, either the quantity itself or its percentage of a target. You can choose either based on the business requirements of your dashboard.

There are three options to specify the target if you've selected As Percentage of Target:

▸ **A single cell**
You select a single cell after clicking the Bind button. The value in that specified cell will be used as the target for all values. That is, the percentage of each category item, which will be used in the condition to determine its color, is calculated by dividing the value by that in the target cell.

▸ **A cell range**
Click the Bind button to select a cell range, which can be either a row or a column and should be the same size as the values. For example, there are

four category items in our quarterly sales revenue sample, so the number of cells in this range should also be four. The percentage of each category item will be based on the value in the corresponding cell in the range, by its index.

> **Note**
>
> If you select more cells than there are category items, redundant cells will be ignored. On the other hand, if fewer cells are selected, the remaining targets will be the same as the last one in the specified cell range. Moreover, if there are empty or nonnumeric cells in between, the percentage for the corresponding category item will be 100%.

▶ **Directly entering values**

Instead of binding to a cell or a cell range, you can directly enter values as the target by clicking the ⊞ button next to the BIND button. In the prompt window, you can enter the target value for each category item. If you don't specify a target value for some data items, their corresponding columns will be displayed in the color you specified for no data.

In the prompt window you can add, modify, or delete a target value. You can also change the target orders with the Up and Down buttons, as shown in Figure 4.38.

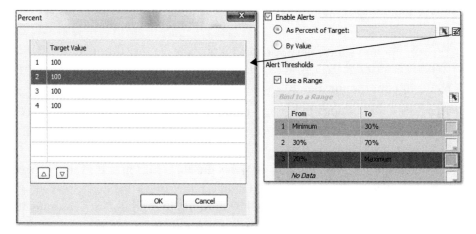

Figure 4.38 Manually Specify Target for Each Data Item

▶ ALERT THRESHOLDS

You set the level for each threshold and the color for each level under ALERT THRESHOLDS. A level is defined in a condition that's based on the absolute value or the calculated percentage of a target of each item.

By default there are three levels, based on a 30/70 division by percentage. Values larger than the FROM value and smaller than or equal to the TO value fall into the corresponding level and are displayed in corresponding colors.

Note that there's a special level called NO DATA at the end, which is used to handle exceptions or data items without a valid TARGET value. If any cell contains an unexpected value (for example, a string when a number is expected), the corresponding data item will fall into the no data level and consequently will be displayed in the color defined for that level. This color is often gray.

You can double-click any field to change its value. Its adjacent levels will be updated automatically according to the new value. The starting and ending limits, MINIMUM and MAXIMUM, cannot be edited. For example, as displayed in the left part of Figure 4.39, 30% appears in both level 1 and level 2. If you change either of them to 40%, the other will be changed automatically to 40%.

Figure 4.39 Alerts Definition is Updated When a Threshold is Manually Updated

To add a level, click the input field on top of the level list and enter a value. Based on its value and the existing levels, a new level will be inserted. If you enter "50" in the screen shown in Figure 4.32 in the input field and click the ADD button or press ⎡Enter⎤, the existing level 30% to 70% will be divided into two: 30% to 50% and 50% to 70%. This happens because 50% falls into the level 30% to 70%. The result is illustrated in Figure 4.40.

Note that for a percentage-based threshold you need to enter the value without the percent sign. That is, to add a threshold of 50%, enter "50" instead of "50%" or "0.5." If you enter "0.5" in the field, SAP BusinessObjects Dashboards will think you are asking for 0.5%.

For value-based thresholds, also enter the value directly.

Figure 4.40 Enter a Threshold to Define New Levels

To delete a level, click the DELETE icon of the corresponding level. Its adjacent levels will be merged automatically so that the existing levels cover all data points. For example, if you delete level 30% to 50%, the To value of the first level will be changed to 50% immediately.

You can click the color picker on the right to set the color for each level. This option is disabled if ENABLE AUTO COLORS is selected, and the colors for each level are defined by SAP BusinessObjects Dashboards according to the current theme.

You may have noticed that these methods use static constant numeric values to define the thresholds or levels. Sometimes dynamic thresholds are required. For example, you might want the user to define the threshold. To achieve this, bind the thresholds to cells in the embedded spreadsheet. Select USE A RANGE and select a cell range from the embedded spreadsheet. SAP BusinessObjects Dashboards will create levels based on the threshold values defined in the cells. For example, say you have 18 in cell F8, 30 in cell G8, and 35 in cell H8. The levels will be less than or equal to 18, larger than 18 but less than or equal to 30, larger than 30 but less than or equal to 35, and larger than 35.

With USE A RANGE selected, you can specify the colors if ENABLED AUTO COLORS is not selected, but you cannot change the values by double-clicking them.

The values in the cells of the range should be in incremental order. That is, the value of the right-hand cell should be bigger than that of the left-hand cell. Note that in the example above, the values are in incremental order (18, 30, 35). If the cell range is in a column, the value of the lower cell should be bigger than that of the upper cell. Otherwise, though the levels definition appears correct, the markers will not fall into any level for a value-based threshold.

▶ COLOR ORDER

This option is useful to generate colors for levels automatically. You can choose whether low values, middle values, or high values are good, which will be displayed in a more agreeable color (e.g., green). Note that the option MIDDLE VALUES ARE GOOD is only available for percentage alerts; that is, for a percentage-based thresholds definition. Choose this option when the value shouldn't be too small or too big; for example, if your inventory shouldn't be below the minimum stock to ensure in-time delivery, nor should it be very high to save money.

By default, LOW VALUES ARE GOOD is selected. If you change it to HIGH VALUES ARE GOOD, the colors of each level will be switched, in a reverse order. That is, given T levels, the color of the Nth level will be switched with that of the $(T-N)$th level, where T is the number of levels and N is an integer between 1 and T.

4.1.3   Line Chart

A line chart uses a series of data points to represent values. Every two adjacent points are connected by one straight line. Similar to the column chart, the category items, or labels, are displayed in the horizontal X-axis. The Y-axis displays the value scale. You can get the value of a label from the Y-coordinate of its corresponding data point. Figure 4.41 shows a typical line chart.

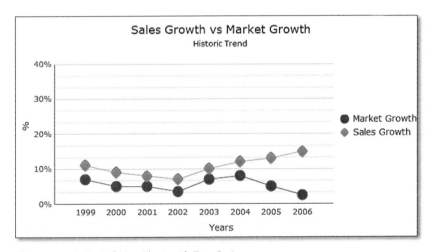

Figure 4.41 A Typical Line Chart with Two Series

Essentially, a line chart is very similar to a column chart in configuration and use. The only difference between them, aside from their different purposes, is that a line chart uses points to represent values, while a column chart uses columns or bars to do so.

In the "How to Use" section, we'll explain only the properties specific to a line chart. We'll ignore or briefly explain the properties that are the same as those in a column or pie chart. For more details, please refer to the corresponding parts in the "How to Use" sections in Section 4.1.1 about pie charts or Section 4.1.2 about column charts.

When to Use a Line Chart

A line chart is often used to illustrate the trend or change in data of certain measures over a period of time. Its focus is the trend of data change. So the labels are often time intervals such as days, months, or years. That's why the line segments are often drawn chronologically.

For example, when you want to see the change, or trend, in sales revenue over months this year, you can choose the line chart. In Figure 4.41, you can easily get an idea about the growth trend in the two measures (sales growth and market growth) over the years from 1999 to 2006.

How to Use a Line Chart

You can drag a line chart from the COMPONENTS view to the canvas and resize it using the mouse, which is the same for all charts. You can set its properties in the PROPERTIES panel, which is divided into five categories, which we discuss next.

General

Similar to the column chart, you can set the data source of all parts in the line chart, including the chart title and subtitle, titles of the category (X) axis and value (Y) axis, labels of the category (X) axis, and values of the Y-axis.

You can add as many series as you want, plotted on either the primary Y-axis or the secondary Y-axis. If a series is plotted on the secondary axis, you can set its title.

The way to set the data items is the same as for a column chart and is explained in the "How To Use" — "General" subsection in Section 4.1.2. A new feature is that you can bind the data of the category labels or series values to either the embedded spreadsheet or directly to a Universe query.

Insertion

The functionality and configuration of insertion are exactly the same as for a column chart, as explained in Section 4.1.2. The only difference the end user will encounter at runtime is that he clicks or puts the mouse over a point, instead of a column or marker.

Behavior

The properties in this category and their uses are exactly the same as those of a column chart, as explained in the "How to Use"—"Behavior" subsections of Section 4.1.2, including whether to ignore empty cells at the end of a range in series or value, whether to enable the runtime tools or range slider, and how and whether to sort by value or by category label in ascending or descending order, dynamic visibility, set the axis scale manually or automatically, show the major or minor gridlines, and enable data animation.

Appearance

As indicated by the name, you can set how the line chart appears through this category, including the font of all texts, the color and thickness of all axes and gridlines, and whether and how to show the fill and border in the chart, title, plot, and legend areas. You can also define whether and how to display the mouse-over values when the user moves the mouse over a point or the data labels for each series that will always be displayed for each point of that series.

All settings and uses are the same as those of a column chart, except for the SERIES tab, where you can select a shape for the data points as markers per series, selecting from a circle, diamond, star, triangle, and cross. For each series, FILL defines the color of the markers, and LINE defines that of the line segments connecting the markers.

You can define the thickness of the line per series, for a clear appearance or to highlight some series among many. This setting is per series.

You can also define whether and how to show the markers. For example, sometimes you just need a line to show the trend and you don't need markers (e.g., round points) to indicate each value. In such a case, you can unselect ENABLE

SERIES MARKERS. This setting applies to all series. Figure 4.42 shows an example of these settings.

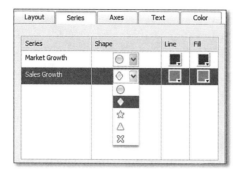

Figure 4.42 Customize Shape and Color of Each Series in a Line Chart

Alerts

Like in column charts, you can enable alerts to highlight outstanding (very good or very bad) items by displaying them in special colors, based on their quantities or their calculated percentages against targets.

Note that with alerts enabled, the color of a marker is defined by the level it falls into, but the color of the line segments, which is defined in APPEARANCE • SERIES, will not be changed.

Practice

Now let's go through a simple hands-on example to get a deeper impression of line charts. Suppose the director of the sales department in your company asks for a dashboard showing the change in sales revenue over each quarter in 2009 and the growth rate on a year-to-year basis.

A line chart is best suited to satisfy his requirement to show the change trend over the period. Start by dragging a line chart from the COMPONENTS panel and dropping it onto the canvas and resizing it a little bigger. Now let's move on, step by step.

Step 1: Prepare the Data

The director has sent you the data in an Excel file. You can either pick up the data you want and enter or paste it into the embedded Excel spreadsheet or import it directly by selecting DATA • IMPORT.

You can use Excel formulas to calculate some data that is required by the chart but not provided in the original data source. For example, the growth over a quarter is not provided by default but is calculated with a formula. The content of cell F8 is =(F6-F7)/F7. You can format the cell in the embedded spreadsheet to be a percentage.

Your data is similar to that displayed in Figure 4.43.

	A	B	C	D	F	G	H	I
2								
3				subtitle:	Year: 2009			
4								
5				Sales revenu	Q1	Q2	Q3	Q4
6				This year	40,000	52,000	35,000	44,000
7				Last year	32,000	46,000	32,000	48,000
8				Growth	25.00%	13.04%	9.38%	-8.33%
9								

Figure 4.43 Data in the Embedded Spreadsheet

Pay attention to the cell index, which we'll refer to shortly in the data binding phase.

Step 2: Specify Data in the General Tab

To make the chart easy to understand, we need to display some useful information in the titles. The title conveys the main purpose of the line chart. Here, we enter the name "Sales revenue quarterly trend."

The subtitle provides supplementary information about the chart. Here, we'd like to show what year we're talking about. The year may be dynamic; for example, selected by the user from a combo box. So we bind it to a cell by clicking the BIND button next to the input field, and click the OK button in the prompt window after selecting the cell Sheet1!$F$3 in the embedded spreadsheet.

The titles of the X- and Y-axes are also displayed, providing additional hints about what each axis shows. These titles are also entered into the input fields.

On the X-axis, we want to display the four quarters. Click the BIND button for CAT-EGORY LABEL(X), and hold the mouse to select the range Sheet1!$F$5:$I$5, where the four quarters are stored.

To show the sales revenue for each quarter of this year, click the ADD button to add a series. Enter the name "Sales revenue," click the BIND button next to VAL-UES(Y), and select the range Sheet1!$F$6:$I$6, where the values are stored. We want them to display on the primary Y-axis, so we leave the default selection PRI-MARY AXIS to plot the series on.

The sales director also wants to see the growth in percentages. We have calculated the growth in Excel using formulas, and now we need to add one series. To do this, click the ADD SERIES button to add another series, bind its name to the cell Sheet1!$D$8 and its values(Y) to the cell range Sheet1!$F$8:$I$8, where the growth values are stored. Here we select SECONDARY AXIS to plot this series on, because the growth is less than 1 or 100%, but the sales revenue, which is plotted on the primary Y-axis, is over 10,000. You can imagine that if the data in these two series is plotted on the same Y-axis, the growth will be almost invisible.

By now your chart and the GENERAL tab should look like Figure 4.44.

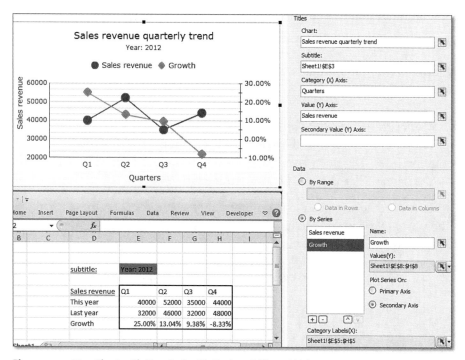

Figure 4.44 Line Chart with Two Series Plotted on Different Y-Axes

Step 3: Set Behavior
We don't need the drill-down functionality for this chart, so we'll ignore the properties in the INSERTION tab. However, if you want the cursor to change to a hand on mousing over a marker, you can still enable INSERTION.

In the BEHAVIOR category, as a best practice always select IN SERIES and IN VALUES for IGNORE BLANK CELLS if blank cells are not specially required.

As shown in Figure 4.44, the sales revenues are in the tens of thousands, which should be abbreviated. So in PRIMARY SCALE, select FIXED LABEL SIZE. Then 60,000 will be displayed as 60K, which is more agreeable to the eye. This is very useful when the number is very large.

We don't want to see too many gridlines in the chart, so decrease MINOR DIVISIONS from the default 2 to 1.

In Figure 4.44, the divisions on the secondary Y-axis are too dense. So in the SECONDARY SCALE tab, select MANUAL (Y) AXIS to manually set the minimum and maximum limits, and set them to –0.2 and 0.3, respectively.

By default, the major divisions are defined with a size of 10, which is not suitable for percentages. We can change SIZE OF DIVISIONS to 0.1 or 0.05 or something like that or just specify how many major gridlines we want. Here we select NUMBER OF DIVISIONS and set it to 4.

Figure 4.45 shows the dashboard effect at this point and the properties in the SECONDARY SCALE tab.

Figure 4.45 The Line Chart after Customizing the Primary and Secondary Scale Tabs

Step 4: Set Appearance

By default, the legend area appears to the right of the line chart. The dashboard seems to be too wide and not very tall, so we want to decrease the width and increase the height. One way to do this is to show the legend area on the top instead of to the right. To do this, select POSITION TO TOP under ENABLE LEGEND in the LAYOUT tab.

In the SERIES tab, we can set the series shape, line color, and fill color. We want a smaller marker size here, so decrease MARKER SIZE from 17 to 12.

We don't want to show the minor gridlines, so unselect SHOW MINOR GRIDLINES in both the PRIMARY AXES and SECONDARY AXES tabs.

For illustration purposes, to highlight the current year, we can display the subtitle with an underline. To do this, select SUB TITLE in the TEXT tab and then click the UNDERLINE button (|u|).

Finally, in preview mode, your dashboard should look like Figure 4.46.

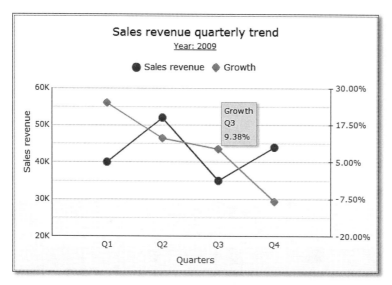

Figure 4.46 The Final Appearance of the Line Chart

You can then export the dashboard to a Flash or PowerPoint slide and send it to the director of sales. From this dashboard he can easily find out that the sales revenue in 2009 keeps bouncing, which is not a good sign. Though the sales revenue in Q4 has increased a lot compared to Q3, the growth keeps going down.

You can find the source file (*sample-Line.xlf*) for this example on this book's web page at *www.sap-press.com*.

4.1.4   Bar Chart

A bar chart uses horizontal bars to represent the data values of one or more series, compared to the vertical columns in a column chart. As a result, the horizontal axis (primary or secondary) shows the values (measure), while the vertical axis shows the category labels (dimension). Except for this difference, a bar chart is very similar to a column chart, not only in the use and configuration, but also in focus. You'll find that their PROPERTIES panels are very alike.

You can imagine the bar chart as a transposition of the column chart, as illustrated in Figure 4.47.

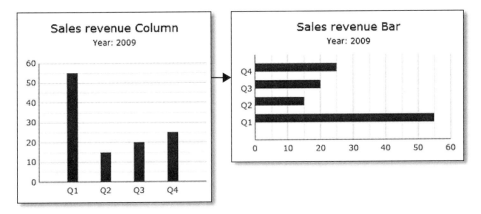

Figure 4.47 A Bar Chart Looks Like the Transposition of a Column Chart

If a series is defined to plot on the secondary axis, there will be a horizontal X-axis on the top, compared to the vertical Y-axis on the right side of a column chart. The new axis is used to display the values of the secondary axis.

When to Use a Bar Chart

A bar chart is often used to compare the values of different category items, which is the same as a column chart. For example, you can use a bar chart to compare the budget plan of each cost center in the current fiscal year.

It's hard to choose between a bar and a column chart for functionality. Some people can see the difference among several values displayed by horizontal bars in a bar chart more easily, while others can't.

As shown previously in Figure 4.40, when the numeric values of the measures vary a lot, a bar chart requires a wider space, while a column chart requires a higher space. Similarly, when there are many category items, a bar chart takes up a taller space, while a column chart takes up a wider space. You need to take this into consideration when there are many UI components on the canvas and there's limited free space.

Another difference is that if the category labels contain many characters (e.g., The United States of America), in a column chart they may be displayed horizontally if it's wide enough and vertically otherwise, but in a bar chart they'll always be displayed horizontally. You can use both charts to display the population of several countries labeled Russia, The United States of America, India, and People's Republic of China to see the difference.

How to Use a Bar Chart

Using a bar chart is exactly the same as for a column chart, as described in Section 4.1.2.

4.1.5 XY Chart

From the name, you know that there are two axes in an XY chart, X and Y, and there will never be a secondary Y-axis. In contrast to other charts such as the column chart, there's no category data. Instead, both axes show values of measures. In addition, an XY chart uses points to represent data, instead of a pie or columns.

The X-axis of a column chart represents the category labels and is discrete. However, in an XY chart, both the X- and Y-axes are continuous to show numeric values.

The XY chart shows a data point at each intersection of the X- and Y-values from the data source. The data points might not appear in the order in which the values appear in the cell range. Instead, the points are shown along the X-axis in ascending order. All points are the same size and color. Similar to other charts, you can enable alerts to set different colors for the points for the data items that you want to highlight. Unlike the line chart, there's no line segment between every two adjacent points.

Figure 4.48 shows a typical XY chart, where sales revenues are displayed on the X-axis and the cost is on the Y-axis.

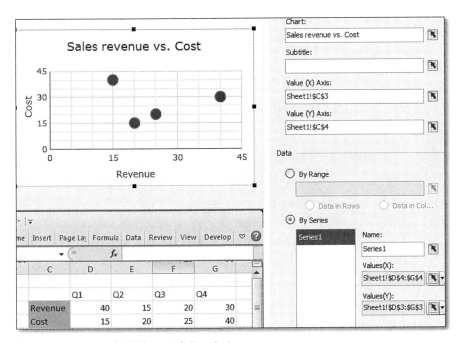

Figure 4.48 A Typical XY Chart with Two Series

As displayed in this figure, there are four points in the chart, one for each quarter, plotted at the intersection of two values of the X- and Y-axes. At each data intersection, that is, for each quarter, a point is shown with an X-coordinate of the sales revenue and a Y-coordinate of the cost. From the figure you can tell that in Q1 the cost is the lowest, but its sales revenue is the best—which is amazing.

When to Use an XY Chart

An XY chart is mainly used to compare the values of different measures for each category item. For example, you can use an XY chart to show the sales revenue against the number of sales people involved every month. You can display the number of sales people on the X-axis and the sales revenue on the Y-axis, and there will be a round point for each month at the conjunction of the X- and Y-coordinate of that month. This way, you can determine roughly whether it's worth adding more sales people to achieve a higher sales revenue.

How to Use an XY Chart

Most functionalities and properties of an XY chart, including titles, drill-down (insertion), fonts, colors, and alerts, are the same as those of a line chart. You'll find the PROPERTIES panels to be very similar. For explanations of each property and how to use it, please refer to the corresponding section for the line chart. Here we will only go through some properties that are specific to an XY chart.

General

You set the data source for all data parts of an XY chart here, including the chart title and subtitle, the title of the X- or Y-axis, and data.

However, you cannot set category labels for the chart. That is, when you select BY RANGE to specify data, don't include any category labels. If you select BY SERIES, you can manually set the series names and values on the X- and Y-axes. Note: Both the X- and Y-axes display numeric values but no categories.

There's no secondary Y-axis here. That is, though you can specify multiple series in this XY chart, they are plotted on the same Y-axis. So pay attention to the minimum and maximum limits of the series when there are multiple series.

Figure 4.49 shows an example of the effects of these settings where the sales revenues are plotted on the X-axis, and the costs in the current as well as the last month are plotted on the Y-axis. A point is displayed for each month.

If BY SERIES is selected, you can bind the values of both the X- and Y- axis to either the embedded spreadsheet or query data, while if BY RANGE is selected, you can only bind data to the embedded spreadsheet.

Note that the VALUES (X) field can be bound to different cell ranges for different series.

Behavior

All settings in this tab are the same as for a line chart, except that in the SCALE tab, you can set the minimum and maximum limits and the scale algorithms for both the Y- and X-axes, as displayed in Figure 4.50.

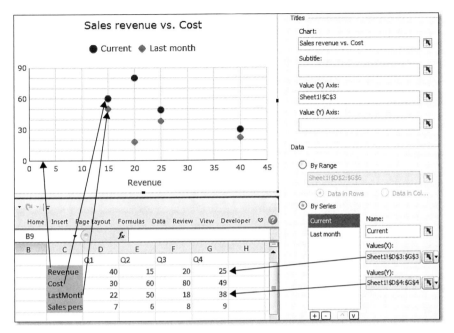

Figure 4.49 Effects of Settings in the General Tab of an XY Chart

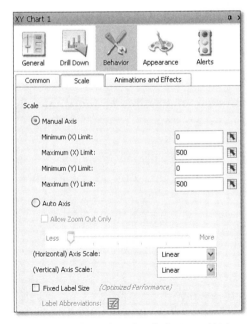

Figure 4.50 The Scales of Both the X- and Y-Axes can be Configured, Unlike in a Line Chart

You can have a look the source file of this example, which can be downloaded at *www.sap-press.com*.

Similarly, the limits can be automatically or manually set and can be either constant numeric values or bound to a cell in the embedded Excel spreadsheet. This is easy to understand, because both axes show numeric values. The scale algorithms can be either linear when the values vary little, or logarithmic otherwise.

Appearance

Here you set how each part of an XY chart appears, including whether and how to show fills and borders, margins, gridlines and ticks, and the font and color of each text. Also, you can allow the user to hide or display a series at runtime by clicking on the legend itself or a checkbox near it. As these settings have been covered in previous sections, we won't repeat them here.

4.1.6 Bubble Chart

A bubble chart looks very similar to an XY chart in that both charts:

▸ Show measure values in both the X- and Y-axes without category labels

▸ Have no secondary X- or Y-axis

▸ Use a circle point to represent the value at each intersection of X and Y values

▸ Have no line segments connecting the points

▸ Are continuous in both the X- and Y-axes

However, a bubble chart is very different from an XY chart, and is more powerful in that it can be used for three-dimensional analysis. The points or markers of a bubble chart are always round, with variable sizes or colors. Each point in a bubble chart is defined in terms of numeric values on three distinct measures, making it possible to be used in three-dimensional analysis. Because both the X- and Y-axes of the bubble chart are numeric scales, the position of each point is nothing but an indicator of the two values. The size, or area, of the point (marker) depends on the magnitude of the third numeric measure. That is, you can tell whether one item is bigger than another by the markers' sizes.

A bubble chart uses the circle size to represent its quantity value, which should always be above zero. If the value is negative, a tiny dot is displayed, and its size never changes, no matter if it's –10 or –100. As a result, the size makes little difference in such a situation. A workaround for such a situation is to duplicate the numeric values into another row, with the negative values changed into positive ones and to display them as a series in the chart. For example, if the values of a measure are (1, 2, –3, 4), you can duplicate them into another row with values (1, 2, 3, 4) and add both series to the chart. The bubble for value –3 will be displayed twice, once a tiny dot in the original series and then as a bubble with a size proportional to its value in the new series. The bubbles for values 1, 2, and 4 are also displayed twice, in the same place and of the same size. Figure 4.51 shows the effect of such a situation at runtime.

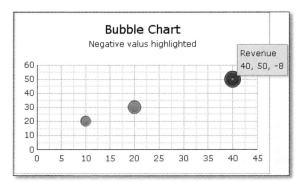

Figure 4.51 Use Two Series to Highlight the Negative Values with an Appropriate Bubble Size

When to Use a Bubble Chart

A bubble chart is often used to compare a group of items based on three different measures on one dimension (category), providing a three-dimensional analysis. For example, you can use a bubble chart to analyze the market share of each vendor by showing the sales revenue on the X-axis and the number of products on the Y-axis. Here the category items are the company names, with three measures: number of products, sales revenue, and competitive ability measured by market share.

When using a bubble chart, you need think carefully about what measures will be associated with the X-axis, the Y-axis, and the Z-axis for the bubble size.

Figure 4.52 shows an example of the chart just described. You can easily find out that, though the sales revenue of the third bubble counting from left to right is not the largest, it has the biggest market share. Similarly, the fourth bubble has the largest sales revenue, and its market size is the second.

169

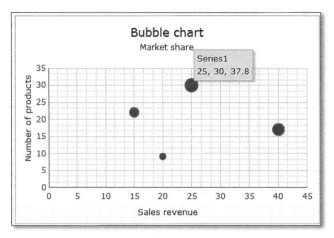

Figure 4.52 A Typical Bubble Chart to Analyze the Relationship Among Market Share, Sales Revenue, and Number of Product Lines

How to Use a Bubble Chart

You set the data source for all data parts in the GENERAL tab. Note that for each series you specify three data sources for values of the X-axis, Y-axis, and size. If BY RANGE is selected, you need to select three rows or columns that will be the values of the X-axis, Y-axis, and size, sequentially, with the data in the first row or column being the value for the X-axis, the second for Y, and the third for size.

The data insertion (drill-down) functionality is the same as that of other charts. You can set the drill-down operation per series, similar to that of a column chart.

In the APPEARANCE tab you can set the marker size for each series. The size of each bubble is not fixed, and the setting here is just a reference. You can try to understand the effect of setting the marker size here by displaying a bubble with a size of 1.

One more word about the size of the marker, or the bubble: The bubble is a circle, the area of which is sequential to the square of its radius. As a result, if the size of one data item is four times larger than that of another, the radius of the bigger one will just be twice that of the smaller one.

The LEGEND area displays the name of the Z-axis in each series such as *Market Share*, not the name of each category item such as *Company A*. So when you mouse over a bubble, you don't know what company the value combination represents. As a workaround, you could use a spreadsheet component below to list the data in a table, as a supplementary explanation. Figure 4.53 shows an example.

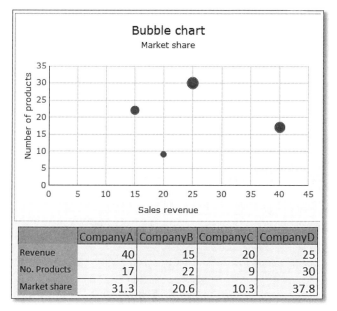

	CompanyA	CompanyB	CompanyC	CompanyD
Revenue	40	15	20	25
No. Products	17	22	9	30
Market share	31.3	20.6	10.3	37.8

Figure 4.53 A Bubble Chart with a Spreadsheet Showing the Actual Data

Refer to *sample-Bubble.xlf* on *www.sap-press.com* for an example.

4.1.7 Area Chart

Similar to a line chart, an area chart uses points plotted on the vertical axis to represent quantitative values on one or more measures of a category. The category items are plotted on the horizontal X-axis. The points are connected by line segments. An area chart is different in that:

▶ The first point of an area chart is displayed on the Y-axis, the X-coordinate of which is 0.

▶ The last point is displayed on the right edge.

▶ The area surrounded by the X- and Y-axes and the lines is filled.

▶ The point size is the same as the line size.

▶ No drill-down or data insertion functionality is supported.

Figure 4.54 shows a typical area chart. Note that the category label of the first data item, Q1, is displayed in the same position as the minimum limit of the Y-axis, which is different from any other kind of chart, where the first item is always displayed some distance away from the starting point of the X- or Y-axis.

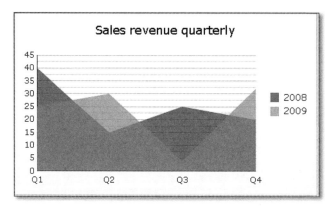

Figure 4.54 A Typical Area Chart

An area chart uses points to represent individual values and areas surrounded by lines and axes to represent totals. One difference here is that the size of each data point is always the same as that of the lines connecting them. In addition, an area chart focuses on the total value, rather than the individual value.

The filled area between the X- and Y-axes and the line segments of one series indicates a quantitative approach to the total value of the measure and over the category items of that series. In Figure 4.54, the chart shows the total sales revenue over four quarters in 2009 and in 2008, and you can get a rough idea of which year has the higher sales revenue through the area's size. Of course, the area size is not equal to the total in the figure, which is the entire year's sales revenue. However, when the sales revenues of multiple years or products are displayed together, you can compare the total of each series from their areas. For example, in Figure 4.54, you can compare the total revenue of 2009 and 2008 by comparing the size of the two areas.

When to Use an Area Chart

Choose an area chart when you want to show and compare the value of each category item, especially to compare the cumulated total value or percentage over a period. The filled area often indicates a cumulative total over time; for example, to display the sales revenue of each quarter, with the area size indicating the total sales revenue each year. You can then compare the sales revenue of each year by the area sizes in different colors for different series.

When there are several series in one area chart, which is usually the case, it's recommended that you display the slower-changing series on the bottom. The reason is that a vastly changing series may introduce the illusion that all series are constantly changing.

How to Use an Area Chart

The PROPERTIES panel of an area chart is divided into three categories: GENERAL, BEHAVIOR, and APPEARANCE. This is quite different from the previously discussed charts, because it does not include data insertion functionalities or alerts. The reason is that the focus of an area chart is the total, not the individual, and there's no marker for you to click.

Most properties and their functionalities are the same as those of other charts, so we'll ignore them here. For details about how to configure them, please refer to the corresponding "How to Use" sections of other charts. In this section we'll only explain some properties that are specific to area charts.

General

This tab is the same as that of many other charts, including the column and line charts. You set the data sources for all data parts of an area chart, including the chart title and subtitle and the titles of the X-, Y-, and secondary Y-axes if a series is plotted on the secondary axis.

This is also where you bind the category labels and the values of each series to a cell range in the embedded spreadsheet or directly to a Universe query. You can choose whether to plot each series on the primary or secondary Y-axis.

If you specify data by range, you can only select a data range from the embedded spreadsheet; the first row or column should be the category items, and each of the subsequent rows or columns will be treated as series values.

Appearance

Similar to what you do for other charts, here you set the appearance including fonts, colors, styles, and alignments of all parts that will appear in the area chart. However, you can only set the fill color for each series; you cannot set the shape or color of the markers, because there aren't any.

4.2   Selectors

Selectors are UI components that the user can work with to make a selection from several items. Typical selectors include the radio button and the combo box. To build an interactive dashboard, you need to provide selectors for the user to either see only the data that he is interested in or choose the visual style he likes.

4.2.1   Introduction to SAP BusinessObjects Dashboards Selectors

The basic functionality of a selector is to provide the user with a way to select something from a list of candidates. From the implementation perspective, a selector inserts the selected values into the destination, which in turn act as the base to update the dashboard, either for dynamic visibility or data refresh.

Some properties are common to all selectors, such as data insertion and dynamic visibility. Very simply put, you use dynamic visibility to show the component only if required, when the content of a specified cell is equal to a constant value or that of another cell in the embedded spreadsheet.

Data insertion, similar to that in the INSERTION tab of a chart, plays a critical role in interactive dashboard models. At design time, data insertion is about specifying three elements: data insertion type, source data (if applicable), and destination, which can either be the embedded spreadsheet or a Universe prompt. There are various types of data insertion, including position, label, value, row, column, filtered rows, and status list, as explained in the "How To Use" section for pie charts.

Note that not all insertion types are applicable for all selector components. The available types are listed in the corresponding dropdown list in the PROPERTIES panel.

4.2.2   Select a Single Item

This section covers some selector components used to select a single item from a list, including combo boxes, radio buttons, list boxes, and label-based menus, as shown in Figure 4.55.

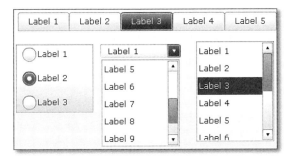

Figure 4.55 Selector Components to Select a Single Item

A combo box is a common UI component in which a vertical dropdown list of candidates displays when it's clicked. The user can then select one from the list.

A list box is very similar to a combo box except that there's no dropdown list, and all candidates are displayed vertically. When not all the candidates can be displayed at the same time, a vertical scroll bar is displayed.

A radio button, on the other hand, lists all candidates vertically or horizontally, with a radio button next to each item. The user can select one of them to make a selection. There will never be a scroll bar, no matter how many candidates there are.

A label-based menu displays the candidates in a vertical or horizontal group of buttons and can be used as a menu for the user to choose from.

When to Use a Single-Item Selector

Choose one of the single-item selectors when you want the user to select a single item from a list of candidates so that other parts of the dashboard will be updated to show only the data relevant to the selection. Based on your dashboard layout or your preferences, choose the one that best fits your design and requirements.

How to Use a Single-Item Selector

To use a selector, drag it from the Components view and drop it onto the canvas. Moving it is similar to moving other components, but you may not be able to resize some selectors horizontally or vertically. For example, you cannot drag a combo box to make it taller. Instead, you can only adjust its height by changing the font size of the label.

The various single-item selectors are used and configured almost in the same way. Basically, you need to specify its data source (called labels) and then define the data insertion behavior—that is, what data will be inserted to what place on user selection.

The Properties panel is divided into the categories General, Behavior, Appearance, and Alerts. Note that a radio button doesn't have an Alerts category.

General

In this tab you set the title, labels, and data insertion behavior for the selector currently selected in the canvas, either a combo box, a radio button, or a label-based menu. For radio buttons and label-based menus, you'll see one more option to set its orientation to horizontal or vertical. Figure 4.56 shows the effects of these settings for a radio button. Note that the labels are displayed horizontally.

The insertions types Position, Row, Column, and Status List are the same as those of a chart, as explained in Section 4.1.1 when we discussed pie charts. Three more types need mentioning here:

▶ Value
The insertion type value is different from that of a pie chart. Instead of inserting one of the values specified for a chart, here you need to specify an array of cells as the source data, and the content of the cell with the same position as the selected label will be inserted into the Destination field, either a single cell in the embedded spreadsheet or a Universe prompt that allows single value.

Click the Hint button () to the right of the Insertion Type field to see an illustration of how this option works.

▶ Label
The insertion type label is similar to the insertion type value of a pie chart in that it inserts one of the labels you have specified. For example, in Figure 4.56, if the user clicks year 2009, the label 2009 is inserted into the destination as a text. Unlike values, you cannot specify source data with this option.

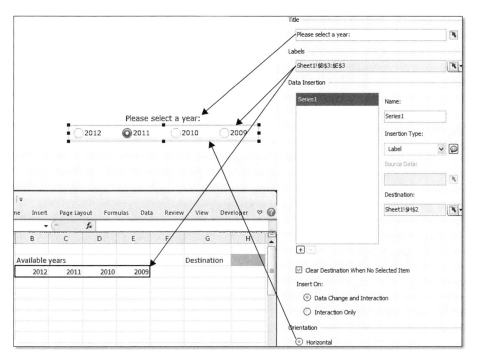

Figure 4.56 Effects of Setting the General Properties of a Radio Button

▶ FILTERED ROWS

This is a special insertion type used to insert one or more rows from a cell range specified as the source data to the destination. The main point here is that this type can be used to select multiple rows from the source data, and the destination can also be multidimensional, while in data insertion for a chart, you only have the ability to select one row or column from source to destination.

SAP BusinessObjects Dashboards filters a cell range based on the value in the first column and compares it with the currently selected label of the selector component. The prerequisite is that the selector is bound to the first column of this cell range. Figure 4.57 shows an example.

Note that we used two list view components in this sample, one to show the source data in the embedded spreadsheet and the other to show the filtered rows. The labels of the label-based menu are bound to the first column of the source data, which contains six cells. You only see three distinct values in the menu because of the insertion type you have chosen.

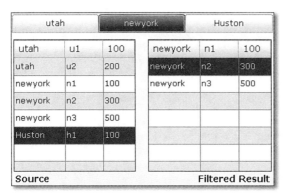

Figure 4.57 Effect of Using the Filtered Rows Insertion Type

You can find the source file of this example (*sample-Selector-FilteredRow.xlf*) on *www.sap-press.com*.

Behavior

In this tab you define the default selected item, dynamic visibility, and animation effect.

The default selected item can be customized by position or label. You can change it to the *N*-th item by selecting LABEL N or N in the dropdown list, or you can select NO SELECTION (NONE) or NO SELECTION (–1) if you want nothing to be selected at first, which means that it needs user interaction to make a selection.

You can also bind it to a cell to make the default selection dynamic. At runtime, the content of that cell will be compared sequentially to all items of the selector, and the first match will be selected. The first item will be selected if no match exists. In Figure 4.49, we can pass the current year from a Flash Var (a data connectivity that will be introduced in Chapter 7) to a cell and bind the selected item of the radio button to that cell. Then, no matter when the user views this dashboard, the current year is always selected by default.

One new selection type, *dynamic*, is added in SAP BusinessObjects Dashboards 4.0, which acts like a combination of the types label and position. You can bind the item to a cell in the embedded spreadsheet, the content of which will be compared with the label first, and if no exact match is found, it will be compared with the position. If there's still no match, the first item will be selected. In this case, the positions of the labels start from 0, which is different from type position, where the position starts from 1. This feature is useful when you want a dynamic default selection and you are not sure what's contained in the item cell. The data is from another component and can be either a label or an index. For example, for a combo box with the labels FOOTBALL, BASKETBALL, and BASEBALL, you choose the selection type DYNAMIC and bind the item to a cell. If the content of the cell is either BASKETBALL or 1, the item BASKETBALL will be selected. If its content is 2, BASEBALL will be selected.

After a user selection, you can insert the selected position or label into a cell in the embedded spreadsheet by clicking the BIND button (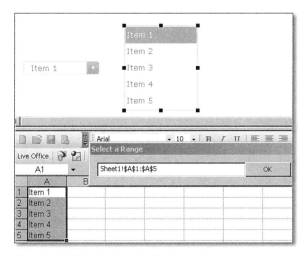) for INSERT SELECTED ITEM. Whether the position or label is inserted depends on what you selected for TYPE, either POSITION or LABEL. Note that this is disabled for the selection type DYNAMIC.

Binding the selected item to a cell is also useful for interaction among multiple components. Say you have a combo box and a list box sharing the same labels, and you want to synchronize their selected items. That is, when the user selects one item on the combo box, the selected item of the list box will change accordingly, and vice versa. You can follow these steps to practice this example:

1. Drop a combo box and a list box onto the canvas.

2. Bind their labels to the same cell range, as shown in Figure 4.58.

Figure 4.58 Data Binding for the Two Selectors

3. Set the insertion type of both components to LABEL and set the destination to cell Sheet1!$B$1.

4. For both components, on the BEHAVIOR tab, in the SELECTED ITEM section, select LABEL (or DYNAMIC) in the TYPE field and bind ITEM to cell Sheet1!$B$1, as displayed in Figure 4.59.

Figure 4.59 Bind the Selected Item of Both Components to the Same Cell

5. To test the selected items, click PREVIEW to run the dashboard, and you'll find that the selected items of two selector components are synchronized. That is, when you select any item in either selector, the selected item of the other one will be immediately updated to the same accordingly.

Refer to *www.sap-press.com* for the dashboard model file called *sample-Selector-SameSelection.xlf*.

You can configure interaction options to define whether the data insertion happens on mouse over or mouse click for some selectors like the list box and label-based menu. Either option has advantages and disadvantages. Choose based on your requirements.

In the ANIMATIONS AND EFFECTS tab, in addition to from the properties ENTRY TYPE and DURATION, which we explained in Section 4.1.1, you can also select ENABLE SOUND to play a sound each time the user makes a selection. The sound file is provided by SAP BusinessObjects Dashboards and cannot be customized.

Appearance
Here you set the formats such as font, color, and position of all texts including the title and the labels, similar to the TEXT and COLOR tabs in a chart. You can also set the transparency level of the component here.

For the candidate items you can set default color, selected color, and mouse-over color, if applicable. This is an easy way to indicate what item is currently selected and provides an enjoyable user experience on mouse over and selection.

Note that if you've configured data insertion to be triggered on mouse over for a combo box or label-based menu (by choosing MOUSE OVER for INTERACTION

Option), when you move your mouse over the item, its color is first changed to the mouse-over color and then to the selected color.

For some components, you can also set the colors of the label background and the horizontal or vertical scroll bar, if any. However, the title of a label-based menu will not be displayed, though you can set its text and format.

The Layout tab is a little different for different selector components. A common property is transparency, which controls the transparency level of the entire component.

Some properties are specific to each component in the Layout tab. For example, you can configure the number of labels displayed for a combo box when the user clicks to display the items list, the button separation space between every two adjacent buttons of a label-based menu, and the marker size of the circle next to each label of a radio button. To see how it affects your dashboard, just modify it and see the immediate change in the component on the canvas.

4.2.3   Filter

SAP BusinessObjects Dashboards provides a special component called Filter to conditionally select one row from a cell range in the embedded spreadsheet. It's also a kind of selector, but it checks the data in a range of cells with multiple fields and categorizes the dimension columns by unique data entries. The dimension columns then form a group of combo boxes, one for each dimension (column), with all of the unique values listed. The number of dimension columns included in the filter is configurable. When the user makes a selection in the filter, the row of data with all dimension values meeting the filter is inserted into the target row.

Note that Filter can only be used to select one record from many. If more than one row meets the filter condition, only the first row is inserted. You may find it somewhat similar to the filtered rows insertion type of the selectors described above.

Let's go through a simple example to better understand how to use this component. Suppose you have a data table of sales measures for different regions and products, as displayed in Figure 4.60.

Region	Product	Sales Revenue	Sales Quantity
East	Phone	350,000	2,350
East	PC	580,000	1,830
West	Phone	425,000	2,815
West	PC	660,000	2,268

Figure 4.60 A Data Table Showing Sales Information for Regions and Products

Now you need to select a combination of one region and one product to show the specific sales figures. For example, you want to see the measures for product PC in region East. Normally you may solve this problem with two combo boxes and get the data with some complex Excel functions, especially when different products are sold in different regions, in which case the candidates of the second combo box have to be dynamic.

The filter component is designed for this kind of scenario: filtering data from multiple columns of conditions. Note that the visual presentation of a filter is a set of combo boxes, each of which displays unique members from one column of conditions. For this example, when you specify the number of filters as two, the filter component includes two combo boxes for the user to select a region and a product, as shown in Figure 4.61. Note that the candidates of each combo box are unique.

Figure 4.61 The Filter Appears as Two Combo Boxes as You Configured

If the user selects WEST and PHONE, the corresponding row [425000, 2815], as displayed in Figure 4.60, will be inserted into the destination. You can then use a chart or some other component to show the measures of the specific PC product in the specific East region.

When to Use a Filter

You might choose a filter component when you have plenty of data, with several dimensions and measures, and you want the user to be able to select a single row by making his choice from a group of combo boxes.

You can achieve the same goal by manually creating several combo boxes and using complex Excel functions such as HLookUp, VLookUp, and so on, which is more complex and does not perform as well. A filter is designed to do this and thus makes it much easier and faster.

How to Use a Filter

The PROPERTIES panel of a filter is divided into three tabs GENERAL, BEHAVIOR, and APPEARANCE, as explained next. We'll ignore BEHAVIOR because it contains nothing special other than selectors.

General

The TITLES field defines the title of each combo box in the filter component. You can click the BIND button to bind the title to a row or column, whose number of cells should be the same as the number of filters. Otherwise, the titles of the last few combo boxes will be empty. You can also manually edit the title for each combo box after clicking the BIND (🗐) button. You may have already found that for other UI components you can only bind TITLE to a single cell, not a cell range here.

Data insertion is also different from other components. For SOURCE DATA, you specify a range of data including both the dimension columns and the values. For DESTINATION, you specify a row to store only the values, without the dimension columns. This means that the numbers of the rows of source and target data are different, while in other components they are the same.

You set NUMBER OF FILTERS to define how many combo boxes that the user can choose from will appear in the filter. If you set the NUMBER OF FILTERS value to N, SAP BusinessObjects Dashboards will generate one combo box for each of the first N columns and list the distinct items in it. So if we denote the number of columns of source data as Ns and that of the destination as Nd, then we should have an equation such as:

$$Ns = Nd + N.$$

You then know how many columns there should be in the cell range you specified in the DESTINATION field. Figure 4.62 shows a sample effect of these settings.

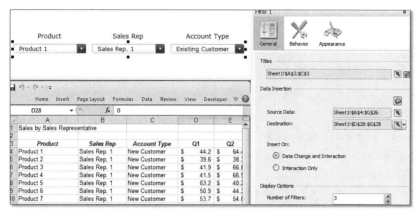

Figure 4.62 Effects of Using a Filter Component to Filter a Large Range of Data

As you can see, the entire cell range, including the products, sales representatives, account type, and sales revenue in each quarter, is specified as source data, but the destination is only a row with four columns to store the sales revenues for four quarters. The first three columns are used as filters, so we set NUMBER OF FILTERS to 3.

As a result, the user chooses one product, one sales rep, and one account type from the filter, and SAP BusinessObjects Dashboards inserts the rows corresponding to these selections, the data of which can then be illustrated in another UI component.

Note that the candidates of each combo box are unique. Unlike other selector components, you don't need to specify labels for a filter. Instead, the labels are determined by the data table specified as the source data. In other words, labels for the selector and data for insertion are combined as the source data.

Appearance

A filter appears as a group of combo boxes. Most properties here, including transparency, text formats and positions, and colors are similar to those of other components.

In the LAYOUT tab you define how many labels will be displayed in the dropdown list when the user clicks the dropdown arrow in each combo box, through NUMBER OF LABELS DISPLAYED. FILTER GAP defines the horizontal gap between every two adjacent combo boxes. LIST TRANSPARENCY defines the transparency level of the dropdown list of the combo boxes.

In the Color tab you can configure the colors of the combo boxes in a filter, including the dropdown button color and its arrow color when it's selected or not selected.

4.2.4   Checkbox

A checkbox in SAP BusinessObjects Dashboards 4.0 is a square box that contains white space (for false, not selected) or a tick mark (for true, selected) with a caption describing its meaning. To toggle the state of a checkbox, simply click the square but not the caption.

When to Use a Checkbox

A checkbox is often used to show a state (selected or not, yes or no, true or false, 1 or 0, etc.) or some preference. For example, you can use a checkbox to control the dynamic visibility of another component. The user can select the checkbox to show that component and unselect to hide it.

How to Use a Checkbox

In the General tab of the Properties panel, you set Title of a Check Box by entering a constant string or binding it to a cell.

In Data Insertion, you bind the source data to a row or column with two and only two cells and bind Destination to a single cell in the embedded spreadsheet.

Note that the first cell contains the content for unselected, and the second for selected. That is, if the default is Selected Item is Unchecked, which can be set in the Behavior tab, the content of the first cell is inserted into Destination by default, and when the user selects the checkbox to change its state, the second value is inserted. In contrast, if Checked is selected as the default Selected Item, the second cell is inserted into Destination by default.

In the Appearance tab, you can set the font size, style, color, and position of the caption. You can also set the colors of the square when it's selected and not selected.

A typical checkbox displays the caption Show Chart on the top and is selected by default.

A toggle button is very similar to a combo box in that both have only two options. It's often used for the user to toggle between two states: on and off. The differences are:

▸ The caption of a combo box can be either a constant string or bound to a cell, while the caption of a toggle button must be bound to two adjacent cells in a row or column, which defines the label of the toggle button when it's selected or unselected. For some special purposes you can make the two cells identical.

▸ The caption of a combo box can be on the top, left, right, or bottom of the square, while the caption can only be in the center of a toggle button. That is, you cannot set the position for the caption.

In addition, in the BEHAVIOR tab of the toggle button's PROPERTIES panel, you can select ENABLE SOUND to play a sound when the user clicks the toggle button. In the APPEARANCE tab you cannot set the font family for the labels, but you can set the on and off colors of both the button and the labels. You can change the colors and check the effects in preview mode.

4.2.5 Ticker

A ticker component displays a group of texts horizontally. One outstanding feature of the ticker is that its candidates continue scrolling horizontally until the user hovers the mouse over the labels.

When to Use a Ticker

When the ticker is not wide enough to display all of the candidates in one screen, the texts scroll but no scroll bar is displayed. This makes the ticker the best-fit component when you want to visualize the labels of many candidate items within a limited space, for user selection or just display. For example, you might use a ticker in your dashboard to list the current prices of several stocks you are interested in.

Figure 4.63 shows a typical ticker.

Figure 4.63 A Typical Ticker

How to Use a Ticker

In the canvas, you can use the mouse to resize the width of a ticker component, but you cannot adjust the height. To slightly change the height, change the font size of LABELS in the TEXT tab under APPEARANCE.

General

Here you specify the title, labels, and value labels of the ticker component. The labels can be bound to a row or column in the embedded spreadsheet, or directly to a Universe query or manually input. But the value labels can only be bound to a row or column in the embedded spreadsheet.

Each label corresponds to one value label in a one-to-one relationship. Both labels and value labels will be displayed together in the ticker, horizontally and one by one as pairs.

Similar to other selectors, in this tab you can also define how the data insertion works per series. You first select a series on the left and then set its insertion type, destination, and source data if possible. Note that the source data can only be a one- or two-dimensional cell range in the embedded spreadsheet, while the destination can be either a single cell or a row or column in the embedded spreadsheet or be bound to a query prompt as a parameter value.

Behavior

The properties here, including INTERACTION OPTIONS, SELECTED ITEM, and DYNAMIC VISIBILITY, are similar to those of other charts. One special group of properties here is TICKER OPTIONS, where you set the item separator, scroll direction, and scroll speed, as displayed in Figure 4.64.

Figure 4.64 Options Specific to a Ticker

The item separator is a symbol with one or more characters that's used to separate different pairs of labels and value labels. Typical separators are "-" and "|". You can use any letters as item separators.

The other two options control the scrolling behavior of the labels. You can choose whether the scrolling occurs to the left or to the right. To adjust scroll speed, move the SCROLL SPEED slider from SLOWER (leftmost) to FASTER (rightmost).

Alerts

Unlike most other selector components, you can enable alerts for a ticker to show labels in different colors based on their corresponding values.

When ALERTS is enabled, there will be a leading icon for each data item, the color of which is defined in ALERT THRESHOLDS according to its corresponding value. Figure 4.65 shows a ticker with both the label and value displayed, a minus sign "–" as the item separator, and alerts enabled.

Figure 4.65 Ticker with Alerts Enabled

Alerts are usually used to display KPIs (key performance indicators) for large numbers of items or to indicate whether stock prices are going up or down. Note that alerts only affect the colors of the round icons, not the labels.

For example, when using a ticker to display stock prices, you can show the stock codes in labels, the current stock prices in value labels, and use alerts to show whether each stock price is going up or down compared to its closing value on the last day or period.

4.2.6 Picture Menus

Picture menus are similar to label-based menus or tickers. In terms of functionality they are essentially the same, in that all are used to select one from a list of candidates and insert the position or value or row to the destination. The difference is that instead of showing literal labels, images are displayed in picture menus.

SAP BusinessObjects Dashboards 4.0 provides two kinds of picture menus: sliding picture menu and fisheye picture menu. Both use images to display options, with slight differences in appearance and user experience.

When to Use a Picture Menu

You can choose a picture menu when you want to construct a more visual and stunning UI for selection. For example, you can use a sliding picture menu to show the financial status of various countries, so that the user can choose a country from a list of vivid pictures instead of from a combo box listing the country names.

How to Use a Picture Menu

We'll go over how to work with the different tabs and areas in the following subsections.

General

In this tab you define the title, labels, and images to display in the sliding or fisheye picture menu. When an image is selected, its corresponding label as defined in LABELS will be displayed.

The images to display in the menu can be either in your local file system or on the Internet. For images in your local file system, you select EMBEDDED, click the IMPORT button, and browse to the file in the prompt window. In this window, click the CLICK TO ADD IMAGES button to add more images and browse to them one by one, as shown in Figure 4.66.

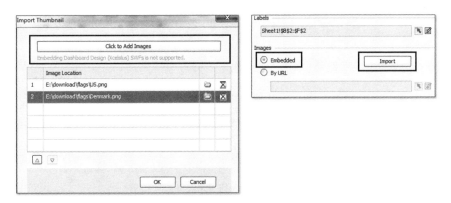

Figure 4.66 *Manage Image Locations in Import Thumbnail Window*

Instead of embedding the images as part of the dashboard, which increases the size of the output SWF file, you can request the images through URLs at runtime. You may want to do this for the following reasons:

▶ Sometimes the images are not available locally. Instead, they are on your company intranet or the Internet.

▶ The images are dynamic images that may change from time to time, and you cannot fix them at design time.

To do this, select BY URL and bind to a cell range containing the image URLs. With this option, you put the URLs of the images in a sequence of cells in the embedded spreadsheet and click the BIND button to bind to them. Or you can click the ![icon] button next to the BIND button to manually enter the URLs, without writing them in Excel and then binding to them.

Both the EMBEDDED and BY URL options have advantages and disadvantages. If the images are embedded, the output visualization file can be used and distributed without those image files, but the file size may be a little bigger. On the other hand, with BY URL, the visualization will not work when those URLs are not accessible and the loading time may be longer, as it needs to visit the URLs to get the image, but the file size can be smaller.

Figure 4.67 shows the effects of these properties of a sliding picture menu. Pay attention to where the title and label are displayed and how the image URLs are stored, bound to, and displayed.

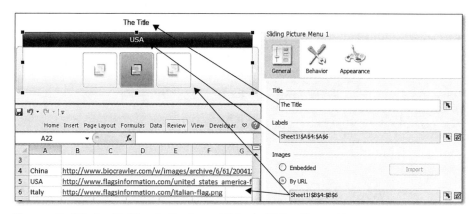

Figure 4.67 Effects of Settings in the General Tab of a Sliding Picture Menu

In this example, the three countries are represented by their national flags in a very intuitive way. The images are referred to by URLs over the Internet or an intranet instead of being embedded.

The supported image types include JPEG, PNG, and GIF. According to the size and resolution requirements of the menu, you can choose image files with a small size so the dashboard can be quickly loaded for a better user experience.

Behavior

Most properties in this category are the same as those of other UI components. One that needs mentioning is interaction options.

▶ INSERT ON

This option defines whether the insertion, as defined in the DATA INSERTION field in the GENERAL tab, occurs on mouse over or mouse click.

▶ SLIDER METHOD

This option is only applicable to a sliding picture menu. It controls how to display the images that are invisible at first due to the menu width. When BUTTONS is selected, you see two arrows to the left and right, which you can click to see more images. If the menu is wide enough to display all images, the two arrows are still displayed but cannot be clicked.

Otherwise, if MOUSE is selected, the two arrows are not displayed and the invisible images appear when you move the mouse over the right or left corner of the menu.

▶ SCROLL SPEED and ZOOM SPEED

You adjust the slider to set how fast the invisible images appear for a sliding picture menu or how fast the images are zoomed for a fisheye menu.

▶ ZOOM SIZE

This option is only applicable to a fisheye picture menu. It controls how an image is magnified on mouse over. The minimum size is 1, meaning no magnification. You can adjust the slider to change this setting.

Differences Between Fisheye and Sliding Picture Menus

These two menu types are the same in functionality and similar in appearance, with some differences illustrated in the following list.

▶ **Magnifying effect**

In a fisheye picture menu, as the user moves the mouse over each item (image) in the menu, that item is magnified. Moreover, the closer the image is to the currently active item, the more it's magnified. This creates an effect similar to that of a fisheye lens.

However, when the user moves the mouse over an item in the sliding picture menu, only the color of that item changes (from the default color to the mouse-over color as defined in the APPEARANCE tab). There's no magnifying effect.

▶ **Resizing option**
At design time, neither the fisheye nor the sliding picture menu can be resized vertically. This is because each image in them has a fixed height defined by SAP BusinessObjects Dashboards, no matter how big the original image is.

The sliding picture menu is a little more flexible here because you can resize it horizontally, thus changing its width at design time. But you cannot resize a fisheye menu horizontally or vertically. SAP BusinessObjects Dashboards controls the width of a fisheye menu depending on the number of images it contains. That is, a fisheye menu is just wide enough to display all of the images at the same time.

At runtime, all images are visible at one glance at a fisheye menu. On the other hand, if the sliding menu is not wide enough to show all images, you can use the arrows to the left or right to scroll through the images. You can also configure the sliding menu to scroll through the images automatically as the user moves the mouse by changing SLIDER METHOD from BUTTONS to MOUSE in the BEHAVIOR category in the PROPERTIES panel.

Figure 4.68 shows the difference between these two menus.

Figure 4.68 Difference Between the Appearance of a Fisheye and a Sliding Picture Menu

Pay attention to the arrows in the sliding menu and the different sizes of the three flags in the fisheye picture menu on the right side of this figure.

4.2.7 List Builder

A list builder is a component that allows the user to choose one or more items from a list of candidates. This is different from all of the other selectors we have discussed so far, with which the user can select only one item at a time.

There are two areas in a list builder component: One lists the candidates that have not been selected, and the other lists the selected items. Figure 4.69 displays a typical list builder.

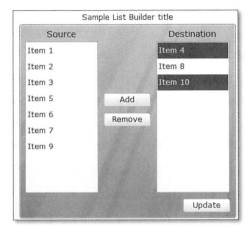

Figure 4.69 A Typical List Builder with Areas for Selected and Unselected Items

When to Use a List Builder

You can use a list builder when you want the user to be able to select multiple items at the same time. For example, you have a chart showing the sales information of various products, and the user can choose one or more products to see their information.

How to Use a List Builder

At runtime, the user can select one or multiple items in the SOURCE area and click the ADD button to move them to the DESTINATION area or select one or more items in the DESTINATION area and click the REMOVE button to delete them. When the user has finished the selection, he clicks the UPDATE button to commit the changes and data insertion will be triggered.

At design time you can move or resize a list builder component on the canvas. A horizontal or vertical scroll bar may appear during your resizing.

The PROPERTIES panel is divided into four areas: GENERAL, BEHAVIOR, APPEARANCE, and ALERTS. There are no special properties here, and their names are self-explanatory. In the next few paragraphs, we'll briefly discuss what you can do in each tab.

In the GENERAL tab you'll see many more configurable properties than many other components have. Here you specify data sources for all data parts that will appear in a list builder component, including the titles of the list builder itself, the SOURCE area, and the DESTINATION area. The LABELS field defines what will be displayed in the SOURCE area and can be bound to either a row or column in the embedded spreadsheet or to a Universe query. You can also specify the texts for the ADD, REMOVE, and UPDATE buttons, for localization or customization.

Fewer data insertion types are supported here, with only label, value, row, and column. You can specify the insertion type as well as the source and destination per series.

In the BEHAVIOR tab you can define what items are selected by default when the dashboard is loaded. You do this by binding the ITEM(S) field to a row or column containing the labels (e.g., Item 1, Item 3) or positions (e.g., 1, 3) of the items to be selected by default.

Another property here is INSERT ITEMS AT RUN-TIME, which when selected will trigger the data insertion defined in the GENERAL tab. This way the DESTINATION field defined in DATA INSERTION in the GENERAL tab will be populated when the dashboard is loaded at runtime.

You set the text formats and colors at different states for all texts for different purposes in the APPEARANCE tab. SAP BusinessObjects Dashboards provides the ability to set the default, mouse-over, and selected colors of the labels and backgrounds of the SOURCE and DESTINATION areas. In addition, you can set the colors of the three buttons in different states (selected or not) and the scroll bars in the SOURCE and DESTINATION areas.

4.3   Represent a Single Value

You may often want to display a single numeric value to display some information or for the user to change. SAP BusinessObjects Dashboards 4.0 provides a special category for such UI components called *single value*, which includes dials, sliders, progress bars, spinners, and more.

4.3.1 Introduction to Single-Value Components

A single-value component is always bound to a single cell in the embedded spreadsheet. When you run the dashboard, you can see or modify the value in that cell. The content in that cell can only be a numeric value.

All single-value components are output controls. That is, any of them can be used to represent a value.

However, not all of them can be used as input to allow user interaction. This depends on the content in the cell the component links to. If the cell contains a formula of any type, the component is interpreted as an output only and allows no user interaction, which means the user cannot change the value. For example, if you have a spinner linked to a cell that doesn't contain a formula, you can modify the value by clicking the Up or Down arrow of the button, thereby modifying the cell value. However, if the cell the spinner links to does contain a formula, such as =SUM(B4:C4), it becomes output-only, and you cannot modify the value.

As a common property, most single-value components have minimum and maximum limits. For some components, you can also enable alerts to show a different color based on the value they stand for. This is a very useful feature. For example, you can use a gauge to show the current debt of your company or family and show it in red when it reaches a limit.

Moreover, unlike most other components, a single-value component has no mouse-over values. That is, the current value will not be displayed when you move your mouse over it.

4.3.2 Slider

The user can move a slider, either horizontal or vertical, to change its value within the range defined by the minimum limit and maximum limit.

When to Use a Slider

You can use a slider component to represent some unit or base value so the user can adjust it to see its effects. For example, you can use a horizontal slider in a dashboard for budget and planning for the user to adjust the price, which affects the potential sales revenue in another chart.

How to Use a Slider

SAP BusinessObjects Dashboards 4.0 provides two kinds of sliders: horizontal and vertical. Some themes may list more, such as Horizontal Slider2, and Vertical Slider2. After dropping any one of these onto the canvas, you can move or resize it as you want.

The Properties panel of a slider is divided into four categories, which we'll discuss next.

General

Here you set the data source of the title and the data for the slider component. For data, enter a single numeric value or bind it to a single cell in the embedded spreadsheet. Its value can be either an integer or a decimal. If an invalid value such as a string is specified as the data, the string will still be displayed as data, but the slider will be in its leftmost position, treating the invalid value as zero.

Two more options are available for the scale: the minimum and maximum limits. With manual selection, you need to specify the minimum and maximum limits by entering constant numeric values or via data binding. With auto selection, there are four options to determine how SAP BusinessObjects Dashboards automatically calculates the scale range:

▶ Value Based
SAP BusinessObjects Dashboards automatically calculates the scale as a range around the numeric value specified in the Data field.

▶ Zero Based
The slider shows a range with 0 as the lower limit and a value larger than the value entered in the Data field as the upper limit.

▶ Zero Centered
The slider shows a range that includes the value and its negative, with zero at the center point. The maximum value of the range is a little bigger than the absolute value in the Data field.

▶ Alert Based
The slider shows a range based on the selected alert method.

You can choose one of these methods based on your requirements or just use the default method—Value Based.

Behavior

You use this tab to control user interaction options. There are many more properties available here than there are in this category of other components.

▶ SLIDER MOVEMENT

This property specifies the increment by which the value increases or decreases when users move the needle, progress bar, slider, or spinner. There are three options:

  ▶ INCREMENT

  You manually input an increment value or bind it to a cell.

  ▶ MAJOR TICKS

  With this option, the value progress moves incrementally only on the major ticks but cannot be finer. That is, the end user can never set a value other than that indicated by any major tick.

  ▶ MAJOR AND MINOR TICKS

  With this option, the value progress moves incrementally only on the major and minor ticks.

▶ LIMITS

This controls how the maximum limit and minimal limit specified in the GENERAL tab work. There are two options for each limit.

  ▶ FIXED

  The end user is not allowed to change the limit set on the GENERAL tab. The value can only be within the fixed limit.

  ▶ ADJUSTABLE:

  The limit set on the GENERAL tab will be the default limit and will be displayed visually. Users can adjust the limit at runtime, through a VALUE component displayed beneath the corresponding limit.

Figure 4.70 shows an example of a horizontal slider where the minimum limit is fixed, while the maximum limit is adjustable.

Figure 4.70 A Horizontal Slider with Fixed Minimum and Adjustable Maximum

Pay attention to the value component below the maximum limit. The user can hold the mouse and drag it higher or lower to increase or decrease the maximum limit.

▶ ENABLE INTERACTION

Unselect this option to not allow the user to move the slider to change the value. The user can still adjust the limits if they're adjustable.

You may want to unselect this option to display a value that is calculated from other fields but that it doesn't make sense to manually change. For example, in a DuPont analysis dashboard, the asset turnover rate is calculated and can't be adjusted.

▶ ENABLE PLAY BUTTON

Play means the value increases automatically once the PLAY button is clicked and stops once the PAUSE button is clicked, which makes up a play sequence. If the ENABLE PLAY BUTTON checkbox is selected, a PLAY button will show on the component, and more options are available as well.

▶ PLAY TIME

This option determines the duration of the play sequence in seconds. The duration should be within the range of 1 to 100 seconds.

▶ AUTO REWIND

This property determines whether the value should rewind to the minimum after reaching the maximum limit.

▶ AUTO REPLAY

This option determines whether the play sequence replays automatically.

When the ENABLE PLAY BUTTON is selected, you'll see a PLAY button (▶) displayed near the component. When the user clicks it, the value will be updated automatically with the increment defined earlier. The duration for each step is defined by the play time divided by the total number of steps in the scale.

Appearance

You use this category to control the layout of a slider component. Similar to the APPEARANCE tab in many other components, here you can set the text formats and colors of all data parts in the component.

You may feel a little strange about the LAYOUT tab, as it's unique to the slider component. Here you can control whether or not to show the ticks. If the ENABLE

TICKS checkbox is selected, ticks will be displayed on the component. The ticks can be automatically scaled with the AUTO SCALE option. Or you can determine how they scale with the MANUAL option.

Similar to the gridlines in a column chart, there are two kinds of ticks, major and minor, as displayed in Figure 4.71.

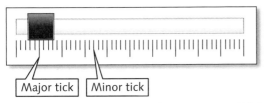

Figure 4.71 Major and Minor Ticks in a Horizontal Slider Component

There are two methods to manually control tick scaling: by number of ticks or by size of divisions. For each option you can configure the settings for both the major and minor ticks:

▶ NUMBER OF TICKS
The MAJOR spinner defines the total number of major ticks on the component, while the MINOR spinner determines the number of minor ticks between every two adjacent major ticks. The number can be either a constant value or bound to a cell in the embedded spreadsheet.

▶ SIZE OF DIVISIONS
The major and minor ticks are defined by the value between them.

In the TEXT tab, you can set whether and how to display the title, current value, and limits of the slider. By default, the current value is displayed to the right. You can set the position and offset to display text elements elsewhere.

Alerts

A slider is used to represent a value that can be good or bad, so it also has an ALERTS tab. You select ENABLE ALERTS and configure the alert ranges and colors the same way you do for other components.

A new property here is ALERT LOCATION, with which you define where to show the alerts. You can highlight any or all of the background, marker, or the value itself. Figure 4.72 shows a horizontal slider with alerts displayed on the background, marker, and value.

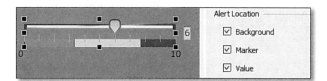

Figure 4.72 Alerts Enabled and Displayed in a Horizontal Slider

4.3.3 Progress Bar

A progress bar is very similar to a slider in representing a single numeric value. One difference is that there's no vertical slider displayed in the progress bar, and the user needs to hold and drag the mouse to decrease or increase the value. Another difference is that the space from the minimum limit to the current value is filled, as shown in Figure 4.73.

Figure 4.73 A Progress Bar Compared to a Slider

A progress bar is often used to convey the progress of a task, such as how much of the sales target has been met. If you are familiar with finance, you may notice that the progress bar is widely used in the DuPont System to represent values such as turnover rate of capital.

Two progress bars are available in SAP BusinessObjects Dashboards 4.0, one horizontal and the other vertical.

The configuration of a progress bar component at design time is exactly the same as that of a slider. Please refer to Section 4.3.2 for details. The only difference at runtime is that here no slider is displayed in the component, and the user needs to hold and drag the mouse to change its value when interaction is enabled.

4.3.4 Dial and Gauge

Dials and gauges are very similar in representing a single value. Both have minimum and maximum limits with a cursor or pointer indicating the current value,

which can be displayed in the bottom center. You can also enable alerts to indicate the status of the current value. At runtime the user drags the cursor up or
down to adjust its value, and the alert is updated.

One difference between a dial and a gauge is that a dial always uses an inside
point to indicate the value, while a gauge can use a needle or an inside or outside
point to do that.

How to Use Dials and Gauges

To use a dial or gauge component, find it by name in the category SINGLE VALUE,
which is further divided into subcategories such as DIAL and GAUGE in the tree of
the COMPONENTS tab view.

The use, both at design time and at runtime, is very similar across all single-value
components. Here we will only explain the properties that are specific to a dial or
gauge component.

General

For a dial, the GENERAL tab is the same as that for a slider.

For a gauge, the data can be more complex, in that a gauge may have multiple
indicators showing multiple values, while a dial can show only one value. You can
select BY RANGE and select a row or column in the embedded spreadsheet that
contains the values to be displayed, or select BY INDICATORS and define the name,
value, and type for each indicator—similar to how you define values by series for
a chart.

The indicator type can be a needle or an inside or outside marker.

Behavior

In this tab the properties DYNAMIC VISIBILITY and ENABLE PLAY BUTTON are similar
to those of other components. Some special properties are illustrated here:

▶ NEEDLE MOVEMENT
You can change the value of a dial or gauge by clicking anywhere in the component and moving your mouse up, down, left, or right to increase or decrease
the value. Here you define how much the value will be updated when the user
drags the needle or marker. Figure 4.74 shows these properties.

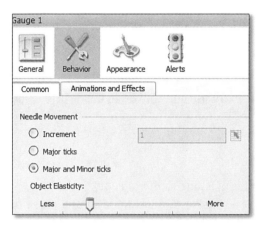

Figure 4.74 Specific Properties of Interaction Options of a Dial or Gauge

  ▸ If you select INCREMENT, you can specify the increment or step value by either entering a constant number or binding it to a cell in the embedded spreadsheet that contains a numeric value. Depending on the scale range of your dial or gauge, you can set this value small (e.g., for percentage, 0.1) or big (e.g., for revenue, 10,000).

  ▸ If you select MAJOR TICKS, the step value will be equal to that of each major tick.

  ▸ If you select MAJOR AND MINOR TICKS, the step value will be that of each minor tick when the user holds and moves the mouse slowly and that of each major tick when he moves the mouse quickly.

You can give each type a try and test the user experience in preview mode before finalizing one.

▸ OBJECT ELASTICITY
Controls the elasticity of the movement of the needle. When it is low, the needle will snap to the new value. Otherwise, the needle will bounce around the new value and finally settle in place. This option is only available for gauges.

▸ LIMITS
Here you specify options for the minimum and maximum limits of the dial or gauge. You have three options: FIXED, ADJUSTABLE, and OPEN.

  ▸ FIXED means the minimum or maximum limit is fixed to the value you specified in the GENERAL tab for SCALE. The user can't change it at runtime.

▸ ADJUSTABLE means the default limit is the value defined in the GENERAL tab, and the user can adjust it through a value component at runtime by dragging the value up or down.

For these two options, when the value has reached the minimum or maximum limit, the user can't drag to make it smaller or bigger. The value can't exceed the limits.

▸ OPEN means there's no minimum or maximum limit to the component. You can keep dragging the needle or marker up or down to make it extremely big or small. With this option selected, you can't set a default value for the limit in the GENERAL tab.

▶ ENABLE INTERACTION

If you just use the dial or gauge to display some information or don't want the user to change the value, you can unselect this option. Figure 4.75 shows the properties here. With ENABLED INTERACTION selected, you can drag the slider to adjust mouse sensitivity, which controls how sensitively the value change reacts to the user's pointer movement. For example, when you move the slider to the right, slighter pointer movements can change the value with large increments. This option is available for value, gauge, and dial components.

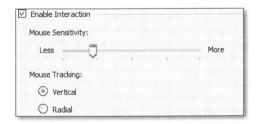

Figure 4.75 Define Mouse Sensitivity Level and Mouse Tracking Direction

▶ MOUSE TRACKING

This defines how the user adjusts the value of the component. Select either VERTICAL or RADIAL. With VERTICAL, users increase the value by dragging the mouse up and decrease it by dragging it down. With RADIAL, users increase the value by dragging the mouse clockwise and decrease it by dragging it counterclockwise. You can select either and have a try in preview mode to better understand the difference before releasing your dashboard to the user. This option is available for gauges and dials.

Appearance

In the LAYOUT subtab you define whether and how to display the major and minor ticks, by specifying either the numbers or the size of the ticks. This is similar to how you define the divisions for a chart.

Another property is RADIAL DEFINITION, which defines the minimum and maximum angles of the minimum and maximum limits. By default the range is –130° to 130°. You can change it to any integer you want.

Practice

A gauge is a very useful component in a professional and good-looking dashboard. In this section we'll create a simple dashboard to demonstrate the use of gauges and sliders through a simple hands-on example.

Consider a simple business scenario: We have revenue and cost data, and we want to calculate and display the margin. You can follow the steps below to create such a visualization.

1. Drag a gauge component and two horizontal slider components onto the canvas and assign titles for them, as displayed in Figure 4.76.

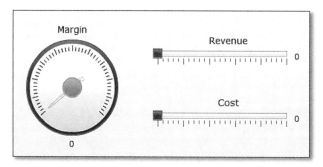

Figure 4.76 UI Layout

2. In the embedded spreadsheet, enter the values for revenue in cell Sheet1!$B$1 and the cost in cell B2, and calculate the margin in cell B3 with Excel formulas =(B1-B2)/B2. Your data in the embedded spreadsheet should look like Figure 4.77.

	A	B
1	Revenue	5000
2	Cost	4000
3	Margin	0.2

Figure 4.77 Data in the Embedded Spreadsheet

3. Bind the data of the revenue slider to cell B1, the cost slider data to B2, and the gauge to B3.

4. Set the data range for each component in the GENERAL tab. Set the range of the revenue slider to [0, 10000], the cost slider to [1000, 8000], and the gauge to [0, 0.5].

5. Enable alerts for the gauge component. On the ALERTS tab, select the ENABLE ALERTS checkbox and then the BY VALUE option. Because a higher margin is better, select the HIGH VALUES ARE GOOD option for COLOR ORDER. In the ALERT THRESHOLDS section, define level [minimum, 0.1] to be red, [0.1, 0.3] to be yellow, and [0.3, maximum] to be green. Figure 4.78 shows what the alerts definition looks like.

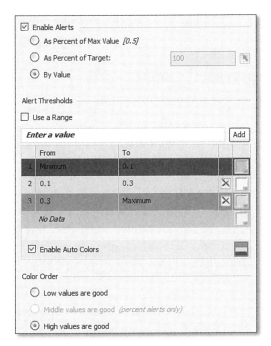

Figure 4.78 Alerts Definition of the Gauge Component

6. Set the display format of the gauge to percentage. To do this, on the APPEAR- ANCE • TEXT tab of the gauge component, select VALUE on the list, and set NUM- BER FORMAT to PERCENT with 2 DECIMAL PLACES.

7. Click PREVIEW to run the dashboard. You can adjust the values of revenue and cost by moving the sliders, and the gauge will display the margin based on the current values of revenue and cost. The color on the gauge will give the user a clear sign of whether the current combination is good or bad, as shown in Figure 4.79.

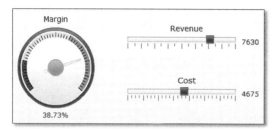

Figure 4.79 Example at Runtime

You can find the source file (*Sample-Gauge.xlf*) of this example at *www.sap-press.com*.

4.4 Use Containers to Wrap Several Components

A container is a special component that can contain other components. Once a component is placed in a container it becomes a subcomponent, or child, of the container. When the container is moved, all of its subcomponents will be moved as well. Subcomponents will not be resized when their container is resized, how- ever.

SAP BusinessObjects Dashboards provides three types of containers: panel, tab set, and canvas. A panel container is just a panel with a title; a tab set is like a tabbed combination of many panels, each with a title; a canvas container is mainly used for ease of development—it's visible at design time but invisible at runtime.

In this section, you'll see how to put groups of UI components into containers so they can be moved or placed together, just like a single component. In addition, you can set dynamic visibility for a group of components by setting that of the container alone.

4.4.1 When to Use a Container

You may want to use a container component to contain other UI components when you have a group of components that will logically work together and, especially, will display or hide together. For example, let's say you want to implement a dialog box that pops up on some situations. You can use a container as the dialog box to hold other components. This way, all components of the dialog will show when the dialog pops up and disappear when the dialog is closed. You only need to set the dynamic visibility once, for the container component only.

A typical use of a panel container is the logon screen, where the user enters his credentials. You create the logon screen using a panel container to host the input fields of username, password, and so on. The entire screen will be hidden when the logon succeeds.

A *tab set* is a good candidate to show rich information for different groups or the same information in different layouts. For example, in one tab you display the change of actual sales revenue in a line chart, and in another you display the budget versus actual cost per cost center. In this case the tab set acts as a selector, and the user can switch among the different tabs to view different information for the same topic.

A *canvas container* is mainly used to control the behavior of multiple components at design time. It's much easier to adjust the position of a container instead of each individual component. Unlike other containers, you needn't set the dynamic visibility of a canvas container to hide it from the end user; it's always invisible to the user. As a result, you needn't care about the layout or appearance of the canvas container.

4.4.2 How to Use a Container

To use a container to wrap components, you just drag and drop the components into the container. When there are many components on the canvas and you find it difficult to move some to the container to form a parent-child relationship, you can use the OBJECT BROWSER view, where you can easily find the component you want.

In the OBJECT BROWSER, you'll observe that containers and their subcomponents are organized in a tree view, as shown in Figure 4.80.

Figure 4.80 Components of a Container Are Displayed Below It in the Object Browser

Panel Container

The available panel container components are listed in the COMPONENTS view under the CONTAINERS category. Depending on the theme you selected, you may see one or more panel containers there. For example, there's only one such component in theme Halo but five in theme Phase.

To use a panel container, find it in the COMPONENTS view and drag it to the canvas. Then, on the canvas or via the Object Browser, you drag other components and drop them into the container to make them subcomponents.

When you're dragging a component into the panel container, there will be a visual effect of a semitransparent rectangle to indicate that the component will be placed "into" the container, as illustrated in Figure 4.81.

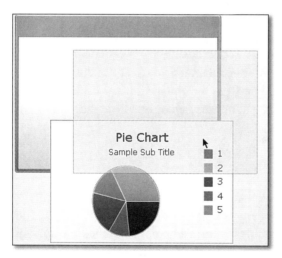

Figure 4.81 Before Dropping the Container onto the Canvas

The PROPERTIES panel of a panel container is very simple. On the GENERAL tab there's only one property, called TITLE, which can be either a constant text or be bound to a single cell in the embedded spreadsheet.

On the SMALL CAPS: BEHAVIOR – COMMON tab you can define whether and how to show the scroll bars of the panel container. There are three options for both the horizontal scroll bar and the vertical scroll bar:

▶ AUTO: With this option selected, the scroll bar appears automatically only when it's needed; for example, when the container is not wide or tall enough to hold all of the components inside.

▶ ON: Select this option to always show a scroll bar.

▶ OFF: No scroll bar is shown, even when the container is not wide or tall enough to display all child components.

Tab Set

It's common to use tabs as the navigation tool in UI design. A tab set is a container component you can use to build a tab-based UI with great ease. You can put different UI components in different tabs and click the title to switch among tabs. Only one tab is displayed on the canvas at a time.

A tab set can be considered as multiple panel containers put together, and you can switch from one tab to another by clicking on the title. In this case the tab set acts like a selector.

By default, there's only one tab in the tab set component. You can add new tabs by clicking the add sign (+) of the tab set and assign the tab set. Assign a name for the newly added tab in the prompt window.

To delete a tab, first click its name to select it and then simply click the minus sign (-) on the top left of the tab set. Note that all components belonging to that tab will be removed at the same time.

You can activate or display one tab by clicking the tab label. You can then add components to this active tab by dragging one or more UI components from either the canvas or the Object Browser and drop them into it. To remove components from one tab, drag them out of the tab with your mouse or change its depth after clicking to select them, using commands such as BRING TO FRONT, SEND TO BACK, BRING FORWARD, or SEND BACK.

The PROPERTIES panel of a tab set component is also simple. There's only one option on the GENERAL tab: TAB ALIGNMENT, which defines whether to place the tab labels on the left, center, or right.

On the BEHAVIOR tab you can define which tab to display by default when the visualization is loaded.

Click the area of each tab below the tab name or click the name of each tab through the Object Browser to select a certain tab instead of the container. You can then set some properties specific to that tab, such as the label of the tab, the scroll bar options, and their colors.

Canvas Container

A canvas container is similar to a panel container in that both are used to wrap components and have no tabs. What's special about a canvas container is that it will not be displayed at runtime, though you can show scroll bars. As a result, you needn't spend time on its appearance such as title or background color, making it a good candidate for grouping several components at design time.

To use a canvas container, just drag it to the canvas and drag other components into it. At design time it's displayed in gray with dashed lines as borders. As a grouping of several UI components, you can still define its properties like dynamic visibility, scroll bars, and entry effect. Though the container will not display at runtime, its scroll bars can, if needed.

4.5 Build Backgrounds to Assist Layout

A background is prebuilt artwork such as an image used to assist the dashboard layout and improve your design. As the name indicates, it acts as the background scenery of the UI components you place on top of it. It can act as the background of the entire dashboard and can also be used to divide the canvas into several parts, each designating a group of related components. You can resize the background to fit its included components.

SAP BusinessObjects Dashboards 4.0 provides several background components in the arts and backgrounds category. Note that the background is related to the theme and color scheme. This means two things:

1. A background can appear in a different color under different themes or color schemes.

2. Some backgrounds may be unavailable for certain themes.

For example, there are six background components in the Nova theme, but only two in iTheme.

4.5.1   When to Use Backgrounds

You can add one or more backgrounds to the canvas to make your dashboard look better or more professional or to make some UI components appear as parts of a whole. By putting some components on top of one background, you provide the appearance that together they form an integrated component. Moreover, you can use backgrounds to divide the canvas into several meaningful parts; for example, one background on the top including the company information such as its name and logo, and another on the bottom including a list builder to select measures and a chart showing the values.

4.5.2   How to Use Backgrounds

A good way to use backgrounds is to design and position them before adding other UI components. That is, design your dashboard against a plain canvas and then position UI components on it.

To add a background to a group of UI components, simply choose one from the COMPONENTS view, drag it to the canvas, and then drag the components on top of it.

If you add backgrounds to UI components already on the canvas and the positions of those components have been adjusted, you can also drop the background onto the correct place. The background will overlap and block those components, however. To solve this, select the background in the Objects Browser and click SEND TO BACK or SEND BACKWARD to move it behind the components.

The PROPERTIES panel of a background is divided into two categories: GENERAL and BEHAVIOR. Because the BEHAVIOR tab is similar to those in other UI components, we'll ignore it here.

General

In this tab you set properties such as the transparency, border scale, and whether or not to block mouse events, as displayed in Figure 4.82.

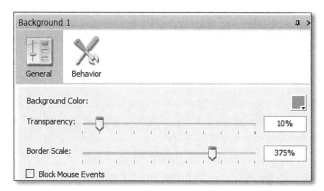

Figure 4.82 Available Properties in the General Tab of a Background

Let's go over the meaning of each property and how to use it:

▶ BACKGROUND COLOR
The default background color of a background component is determined by the color scheme. You can change it with the color picker to make it either static or dynamic.

▶ TRANSPARENCY
This property defines the transparency level of the background. By default it's 0; that is, it's opaque and all UI components behind it are invisible. You may want to change this value for a more interesting user experience.

To change the transparency, move the slider or enter an integer in the input field. If you enter a decimal, SAP BusinessObjects Dashboards will automatically round it up to an integer. Entering nonnumeric text will not change the current value.

▶ BORDER SCALE
The border scale defines the width of the background component's border. You can move the slider to adjust this value or enter an integer in the input field. The smaller the value is, the thinner the borders are.

For most background components, changing this property only affects the border width and nothing else. However, for certain backgrounds, its shape is also changed. Figure 4.83 shows an example of a background component called Background6 in the COMPONENTS view of theme Nova, with a border scale of 100% (left) and 300% (right). Pay attention to the boundaries of the background component and the round corners on the right side of this figure.

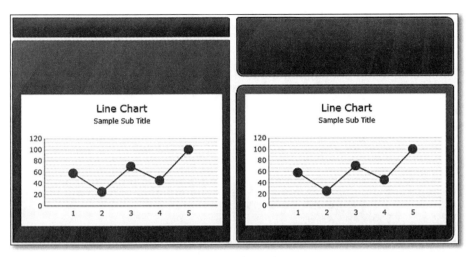

Figure 4.83 Effect of Changing a Background Border Scale

▶ BLOCK MOUSE EVENTS

This option defines whether a mouse-over or mouse-click action on the background component will be passed along to the UI components behind it. Select this if you want to use the background as a mask to prevent the user from clicking some other components. That is, the user can see the components but cannot interact with them.

Two aspects need be considered before using this functionality. First, to prevent the user from clicking the components the background component should be layered on top of other components. Second, to make the components visible, set the transparency of the background to less than 100%.

Figure 4.84 shows an example. The user can see the combo box and the line chart but cannot interact with them.

You can adjust the transparency according to your use scenario for a better look and feel. For example, if you just want the chart to display some information and keep the user unaware of the background, set TRANSPARENCY to 100%. As a result, the background component is completely invisible to the user, and the components behind it accept no user interaction.

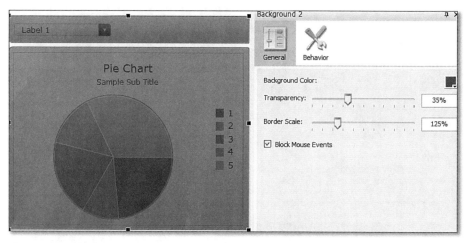

Figure 4.84 A Background Used as a Mask with "Block Mouse Events" Selected

4.6 Universe Connectivity

In the SAP BusinessObjects 4.0 environment, one significant improvement is the wider, easier, and better use of Universes, which is the common semantic layer (CSL) for most SAP BusinessObjects products. A Universe can be directly used not only by SAP BusinessObjects Web Intelligence and SAP Crystal Reports, but also SAP Business Explorer, Advanced Analysis, and SAP BusinessObjects Dashboards. As mentioned before, you can connect to a Universe in SAP BusinessObjects Dashboards and build a query directly within the design environment—with no need to create a query as a web service (QaaWS) or a BI web service from Web Intelligence Rich Client.

What's more, based on the Universe query (or Universe connectivity) you created in SAP BusinessObjects Dashboards, you can bind data of a UI component directly to a Universe query, which means you don't always have to bind your data to the embedded spreadsheet. However, SAP BusinessObjects Dashboards 4.0 can only connect to a relational Universe, which is based on a relational database such as Oracle. If your Universe is based on an SAP BW query, this functionality can't be used.

To create a Universe query inside SAP BusinessObjects Dashboards, a new view called Query Browser is provided, which is covered in Chapter 2, Section 2.8.

A new UI component category, Universe connectivity, is provided including two new UI components to work with Universe: the query refresh button and the query prompt selector. We'll discuss these in the following subsections.

4.6.1 Query Refresh Button

A query refresh button is used to trigger one or more Universe connectivities to refresh, either manually or automatically. It's similar to a connection refresh button, which is used for traditional connection types.

When to Use a Query Refresh Button

Use a query refresh button when you have any Universe connectivity defined in your dashboard, and the data needs to be retrieved at runtime and more than once.

How to Use a Query Refresh Button

To use a query refresh button, just find it in the COMPONENTS BROWSER, drag and drop it to the canvas, resize it, and configure it in its PROPERTIES panel. It's configured the same as a connection refresh button as illustrated in Section 5.7.1 in Chapter 5. Here some principles are outlined.

First, a query refresh button can be used to refresh one or more Universe connectivities, and you can use one or more such buttons in one dashboard. It's a many-to-many relationship between the button and the connectivity.

Second, the query refresh button can be either visible or invisible in the canvas, depending on how you want the end user to use it. If you want to the user to control when to refresh the connectivity, you have to make it visible so that the user can click it. And if you want the connectivity to be refreshed automatically (for example, when the user has made a selection in a fiscal period or cost center or any other parameter), make it invisible and set its trigger behavior. With dynamic visibility, you can also control when to show or hide it.

4.6.2 Query Prompt Selector

A query prompt selector is provided to facilitate the processing of connectivity parameters. It can detect the parameters or variables defined in the Universe connectivities and automatically generate selectors with a list of values.

When to Use a Query Prompt Selector

You may want to drag a query prompt selector component into the canvas so the user can specify parameter values for the Universe connectivity, if any. Depending on how many parameters there are for each Universe connectivity, one or multiple selectors may be generated.

You can also manually add selector components to the canvas and define their properties for each parameter if you need more control on prompts than what's provided by query prompt selectors.

You don't need to consider this component when there's no Universe query defined in your dashboard or the Universe queries don't have parameters.

How to Use a Query Prompt Selector

To use a query prompt selector, just find it in the COMPONENTS view and drop it onto the canvas. You can use as many such components as you want in one dashboard. Normally, you need one query prompt selector for each Universe query that contains interactive prompts.

The query prompt selector's PROPERTIES panel is divided into three tabs.

General

In this tab you define what will be displayed in the selector and when the user makes a selection or input, whether and what Universe queries will be refreshed.

▶ SOURCE PROMPT
This field defines what will be displayed in the selector, including prompt text and list of values. The default is NONE SELECTED, which when selected causes the query prompt selector to remain in its original appearance, and the user needs to enter a parameter value directly into the input field.

When you click the dropdown icon, all prompts defined in all Universe queries in your dashboard will be displayed, from which you can choose one and only one. The appearance of the query prompt selector will be updated immediately.

To go back to NONE SELECTED, just click the CLEAR SELECTION button on the bottom.

Note that here you can't define the prompt text or selection type. They are either hardcoded to ENTER VALUE: and EQUAL when no query prompt is selected, or you must use those defined in the selected prompt. The text for the APPLY button is also fixed.

Figure 4.85 shows two query prompt selectors, one with no source prompt and the other with a source prompt.

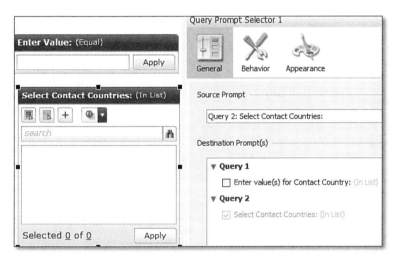

Figure 4.85 Two Prompt Selectors With and Without a Source Prompt

For each selector, the prompt text is displayed on the top as a title with the operator—EQUAL, IN LIST, and so on.

At runtime, for the query prompt selector on the top left, enter a valid value for the parameter and click APPLY. For the one on the bottom left, you click on the SEARCH area to do a search, select one from the list of values with a scroll bar if any, or click the plus sign to manually add one.

If you want to use an existing prompt definition such as the prompt text and list of values, choose a source prompt. On the other hand, if you want to make the selector small and clean, choose NONE SELECTED.

▶ DESTINATION PROMPT(S)
This field lists all the query prompts in your dashboard, and you can select one or more that will be affected when the user changes the prompt values and clicks APPLY. If you selected a query prompt as the source prompt, it will be selected in this area automatically and can't be deselected.

You can select multiple queries here, and all of them will be affected after the user clicks APPLY. By *affected* we mean the parameters defined in the query prompts will be filled with the selected values, not that the queries will be triggered.

▶ SELECTION
When the user has made a selection or manually input some values in the selector, you can insert the selected values, or the user's response to the parameter, into a single cell or a cell range in the embedded spreadsheet for further processing.

▶ REFRESH QUERIES
This area lists the Universe queries in your dashboard instead of prompts, and you can select one or more that will be triggered when the user clicks APPLY. For example, you may have one source prompt for the user to select one or more countries, and upon selection, two Universe queries will be triggered, one to return the sales data in the current year and the other to return the key accounts in the selected countries.

Behavior

A new property here is the ENABLE SEARCH IN LIST OF VALUES checkbox, which is selected by default. When it's deselected, the user won't see the search text and button above the list of values. This property is disabled if no prompt is selected as the source prompt of the selector.

Another property is how to treat the empty values. NO VALUE means nothing or a null, while EMPTY STRING means a text with length 0 (""). If you're familiar with a programming language or the syntax of SAP Crystal Reports, you can easily understand them.

Appearance

In the LAYOUT subtab you define how the list of values and related buttons are displayed. The default is EXPANDED, the effect of which is displayed previously in Figure 4.85. If you want to save space by only displaying the list of values, the search area, and the select all and deselect all buttons when the user clicks a button, choose COLLAPSED.

In the TEXT and COLOR subtabs you define the text formats and colors of every part of a query prompt selector, including how to display the prompt text, the selection type, and so on.

4.7   Summary

In this chapter, we discussed in detail some basic and commonly used UI components provided by SAP BusinessObjects Dashboards 4.0. The topics included what the components are, when and how to use them, and some best practices for using them. For some components, we also included a simple hands-on example for you to quickly get acquainted with the component. In the next chapter we'll go on with the rest of the UI components.

The rich set of UI components in SAP BusinessObjects Dashboards 4.0 contains more than what we discussed in Chapter 4. We'll now cover some of the more complex and advanced components for some special and complex scenarios.

5 Advanced UI Components

In Chapter 4, we looked at some commonly used UI components such as charts, selectors, single-value containers, and backgrounds. With these components, you're already able to build complicated and interesting interactive dashboards. Yet in some cases, we just want more. In this chapter, we introduce some more advanced components including more charts, art and background, maps, and some that provide special functionality such as trend analysis, history preservation, and the new components introduced for direct Universe connectivity.

In this chapter you'll see:

▸ More advanced UI components including more charts, art, maps, and special components

▸ What you can do with each of them and when and how to use them

After reading this chapter you'll be able to:

▸ Describe these advanced UI components

▸ Create a more complicated interactive dashboard than in Chapter 4 using advanced UI components

5.1 Advanced Charts

SAP BusinessObjects Dashboards 4.0 provides a wide range of charts. Chapter 4 covered some basic charts such as pie and column charts. Here we'll show you the rest, some of which are more complex such as the stacked and combination charts. The others may be not that complex but are less frequently used such as the OHLC chart and tree map.

5.1.1   Stacked Column Chart

In Chapter 4 we discussed the column chart, which uses a vertical column to display the value of a data item. The category labels are plotted on the X-axis, and the values on the primary or secondary Y-axis. If you need to display values of multiple measures (or series, e.g., budget and actual cost) in one chart, there will be one column for each measure of each category item.

A stacked column chart is very similar to a column chart. The differences are that a stacked column chart:

▸ Has no secondary vertical axis

▸ Displays only one column per category item, regardless of how many measures are to be displayed

▸ Divides each column vertically into segments in different colors, one for each measure

Figure 5.1 compares a column chart to a stacked chart, both showing the expenses for each category every month.

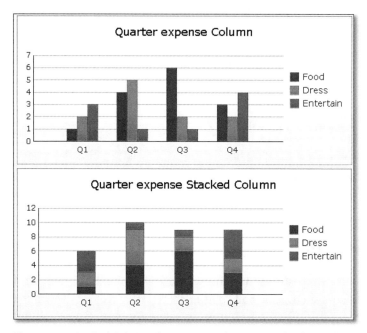

Figure 5.1 A Stacked Column Chart Compared to a Normal Column Chart

The chart on the top is a column chart, while the one below is a stacked column chart. Pay attention to the way the expenses in each category are displayed.

When to Use a Stacked Column Chart

A stacked column chart is used to show the values of different series in one column and at the same time to compare the totals among category items.

It's often used to compare totals over a period of time (Q1, Q2, etc.). However, you can also use it to compare data on other dimensions; for example, over different branches or people. As displayed in Figure 5.1, you can change the category labels from quarters to people, thus comparing the consumption information of each person.

The values of different measures need to be able to accumulated. They can be the revenue or cost of each cost element or the age of each member in a family, but it doesn't make sense to stack the number of employees and the revenue of each segment.

In a column chart, you can compare the values of different measures and of different category items over a period of time, but you cannot compare the total. In a stacked chart, however, each measure of one item is displayed in a different color in one column. Each column represents the total of all values per item, making it easy to see and compare the individual as well as the total values of all category items.

Use a column chart if you want to compare the individuals and a stacked column chart to compare both the individuals and the totals.

How to Use a Stacked Column Chart

The way to add, move, and resize a stacked column chart and set its properties is similar to a column chart. This section will only cover the different aspects.

General

In this tab you set the data sources for all parts of the chart, including the titles, the category labels, and the data values.

To set the titles, enter a text into the field or bind it to a single cell in the embedded spreadsheet after clicking the corresponding BIND button. Such information can only be bound to one cell in the embedded spreadsheet but not to a Universe query.

To set the data, either select a cell range by selecting BY RANGE or manually set the labels to display on the X-axis and series on the Y-axis by selecting BY SERIES.

▶ BY RANGE

With BY RANGE selected, the cell range that you choose as the source should be similar to that displayed in Figure 5.2. After binding, the chart will be updated immediately in the canvas.

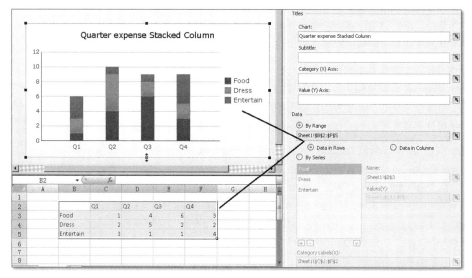

Figure 5.2 The Data Binding of a Stacked Column Chart

SAP BusinessObjects Dashboards can detect the content in your specified range and tries to determine the category labels, the series names, and whether the data is organized by row or by column. Generally, the first row is treated as the category if it contains nonnumeric values, with the first column being the series names. If the detection fails, the category labels will be 1, 2, 3, and so on, and the series names will be Series1, Series2, Series3, and so on.

In Figure 5.2, you can check the difference by selecting range Sheet1!$B$3:$F$5 (without category labels), Sheet1!$C$2:$F$5 (without series names), or Sheet1!$C$3:$F$5 (with neither category labels nor series names) as the data source.

By default, DATA IN ROWS is selected, indicating that the data is read row by row. Depending on your data, you can change it to DATA IN COLUMNS, thus transposing the rows and columns. For the data in Figure 5.2, if you switch to DATA IN COLUMNS, the category labels will become FOOD, DRESS, and ENTERTAIN, while Q1–Q4 will become series names.

▶ BY SERIES

This part will be updated automatically after you select a cell range for BY RANGE. You can select this option after specifying a cell range in BY RANGE to adjust the auto-detected result.

You can also select BY SERIES to manually set the category labels and series from scratch. You then have the option to specify a row or column in the embedded spreadsheet, or the output of a Universe query, as the category labels or the values per series. You can also explicitly set the name of each series, either by entering a text or binding to a single cell in the embedded spreadsheet.

Pay attention to the series orders here. The series defined on the top in the data series area will be displayed on the bottom of the column in the chart. As you can see from Figure 5.2, the series FOOD is defined on the top, while its values are displayed on the bottom of the columns.

Appearance

In this tab you define how each part of the stacked column chart will be visualized, including the margins in four directions to the border of the chart background, whether and how to display the legend and grid lines, and so on.

In SERIES there are two special property items. MARKER GAP controls the horizontal gap between the columns for every two adjacent items.

MARKER OVERLAP controls the horizontal offset between every two adjacent measures in the column for the same item. The default is 100, which means the value of each measure is added straight up the column. The minimum overlap is 0, which means the horizontal offset between every two adjacent measures of each category item is exactly the width of the column.

Figure 5.3 illustrates the effect of setting MARKER GAP to 4 and MARKER OVERLAP to 0. Pay attention to the horizontal offset between DRESS and FOOD for Q1 and that between ENTERTAIN for Q1 and FOOD for Q2.

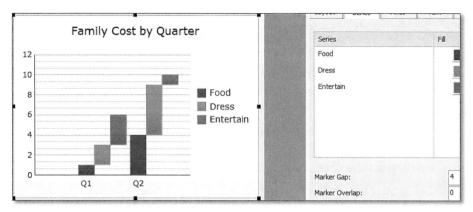

Figure 5.3 Stacked Column Chart with Marker Gap 4 and Marker Overlap 0

In the Text subtab you have the option to define whether to show texts in each part of the chart, and how. For example, with the checkbox Mouse-Over Values selected, you can define the number format of the value that will be displayed on mouse over every column section.

One new property here is Data Labels, with which you can define whether to show labels in each column section, and how. Figure 5.4 shows a sample effect.

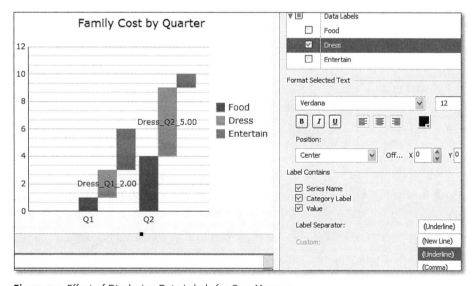

Figure 5.4 Effect of Displaying Data Labels for One Measure

By default, when the user is working with the dashboard, he only sees the columns of different heights and colors. No text is displayed on the columns. If you want to highlight something or give the user a hint about which column shows which information, you can display data labels. As displayed in Figure 5.4, below DATA LABELS is a list of all measures defined in your chart. To display information for one measure, just select its corresponding checkbox and set its style such as font, position, and color. The text of the information can contain the name of the series (or measure), the category label, and the value, which are concatenated as specified for LABEL SEPARATOR (NEW LINE, UNDERLINE, or COMMA). As you can see in Figure 5.4, SeriesName_CategoryLabel_Value (e.g., Dress_Q1_2.00) is displayed for DRESS, and there's no text for the other two series.

Alert

Similar to a column chart, the ENABLE ALERTS checkbox is disabled if more than one series is defined in the GENERAL tab.

5.1.2   Stacked Bar and Area Chart

A stacked bar chart is to a stacked column chart what a bar chart is to a column chart. There's only one horizontal bar for each category label, and values of different measures are stacked horizontally in a bar, one by one and in different colors. The vertical offset between every two adjacent bars for different measures of the same category label can be defined by MARKER OVERLAP in the APPEARANCE – SERIES tab, and that between every two adjacent category labels is defined by MARKER GAP.

Similarly, a stacked area chart is to an area chart what a stacked column chart is to a column chart. The areas are stacked vertically, with each area adding up to the total.

5.1.3   Combination Chart

A combination chart can show series in either columns or points. You can regard it as a combination of a column and a line chart.

When to Use a Combination Chart

A column chart is often used to show and compare values for different counterparts in a range, and a line chart is best suited to show the trend of data change over a period of time. Sometimes you may want to take advantage of both. That's when a combination chart comes into play. A combination chart displays a range of values with a trend line for all of them.

For example, you can use a combination chart to display the actual trade volumes of a stock every day in columns, with a trend line to show the price change over the month.

How to Use a Combination Chart

Using a combination chart is very similar to using a column or a line chart. Its PROPERTIES panel is also divided into the five tabs GENERAL, INSERTION, BEHAVIOR, APPEARANCE, and ALERTS.

General

In this tab we set the chart's data source. The series can be plotted on either the primary or secondary Y-axis. On a typical combination chart, there are often two series in different scales (e.g., one for volume, which is often very large, and the other for growth, which is very small), plotted on different Y-axes. You can add as many series as you want and display each series as either a column or a line chart.

In our example to illustrate a combination chart, we use the volumes and stock prices of SAP AG in the last 10 trading days in 2009, taken from Yahoo! Finance. After setting the chart title and specifying its labels and values, the chart and the GENERAL tab appear as displayed in Figure 5.5.

The configuration items in the INSERTION and BEHAVIOR tabs are the same as those of a pie or column chart, which were illustrated in Sections 4.1.1 and 4.1.2 of Chapter 4 and so are skipped here.

Appearance

In the APPEARANCE tab, you set the fonts, colors, and so on of all text parts and configure whether and how to show the fills, borders, and gridlines.

In the SERIES tab, you can define how to display each series, either as a column or as a line, but there is not a third option.

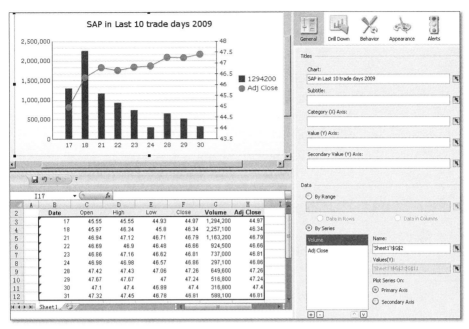

Figure 5.5 Data Binding of a Combination Chart

If you choose to display the values of some series in a line, you can set other properties such as the marker shape, as displayed in Figure 5.6.

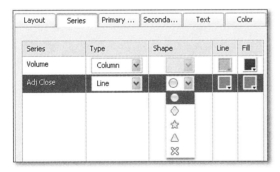

Figure 5.6 Choose How to Display a Series, Column, or Line

5.1.4 OHLC Chart

OHLC stands for open, high, low, and close. An OHLC chart is a special kind of bar chart that is used to illustrate the changes in the price of a stock over time.

Each vertical bar shows the price range (the highest and lowest prices) over one unit of time, for example, one day or one hour, with two horizontal hash marks indicating where the open and close prices were for the stock in that time period.

Figure 5.7 shows a typical OHLC chart that shows the weekly prices of the stock of the New York Stock Exchange-listed company SAP AG. People familiar with the stock market could easily read this chart. For those who are not, the vertical bar illustrates the highest and lowest traded price. The hash mark to the left of the bar illustrates the opening trades, and the hash mark to the right illustrates the closing trades. The blue bars represent higher closing prices, while the red bars represent lower closing prices.

The colors in Figure 5.7 are the default colors defined by the theme being used (blue ❶ and red ❷). You can easily customize the colors in the APPEARANCE tab, similar to what you do to other charts.

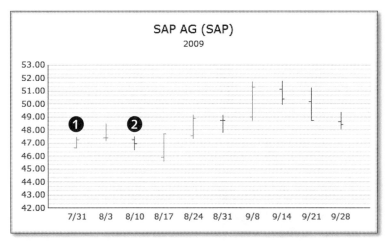

Figure 5.7 Weekly Prices of SAP AG from July 31 to September 28, 2009 in an OHLC Chart

When to Use an OHLC Chart

You use an OHLC chart to show the prices and trends of a stock. There are other types of charts that are commonly used to show stock prices. Some users prefer the simplest line chart, which connects the closing price of the each period to the closing price of the previous time period and the closing price of the following time period. A candlestick chart is another type of chart that is very similar to the OHLC chart.

A line chart is simple, but it conveys less information. The user can only see one series of data, the closing trade of the security. A candlestick chart brings the same amount of information to the user. The only difference between the OHLC chart and the candlestick chart is the appearance of each bar.

How to Use an OHLC Chart

As mentioned before, the OHLC chart is a special kind of column chart or bar chart, so they share a lot of properties in common, but an OHLC chart cannot have a secondary Y-axis. It cannot have alerts. And most importantly, there must be four series of data to be displayed, and each bar must consist of four values, so this means the OHLC chart has some special behaviors that are unlike an ordinary column chart or bar chart.

General

▶ TITLES

You set the chart title, the subtitle, the category (X) axis title, and the value (Y) axis title here, as displayed in Figure 5.8. An OHLC chart doesn't support the secondary Y-axis.

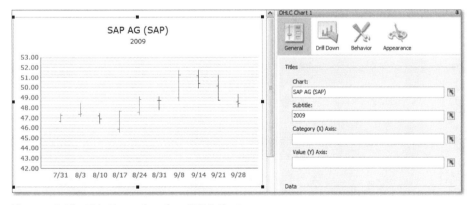

Figure 5.8 The Title Properties of an OHLC Chart

▶ DATA

A typical OHLC chart needs four series of data besides the category labels, which are the opening, highest, lowest, and closing values over a period.

Similar to what you do in the column chart, you also have two ways to bind data: by range or by series.

Generally, you bind the data by range when the data is in a range of continuous cells—in a table form that SAP BusinessObjects Dashboards 4.0 can recognize. If your data is arranged this way, by range is the easier way to bind data, but if your data is not in a range of continuous cells, for example, different series of data are not arranged together or they are even in different Excel sheets, you have to bind the data by series and manually bind each series and the category label.

Now let's see how to bind data for the OHLC chart.

▶ BY RANGE

Again, your data should be in a continuous range of cells, so the four series of data and the category label should be in adjacent cells.

In Figure 5.9, you can see how the data is arranged in the embedded spreadsheet. Column A is the category label; in this case, the date. Column B to column E are opening, highest, lowest, and closing prices, respectively. The sequence of these four series should exactly match the acronym OHLC. And in cell $B$1, we put the series name that appears when the user hovers the mouse over the data point on the chart. Usually this is set to the symbol of some stock.

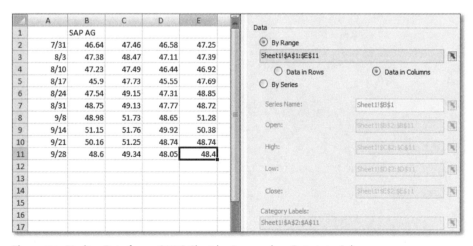

Figure 5.9 Binding Data for an OHLC Chart by Range when Data is in Columns

Figure 5.9 shows an example when the data is in columns. You select the BY RANGE radio button and bind to cell range $A$1:$E$11, and select DATA IN COLUMNS if SAP BusinessObjects Dashboards has not detected that by itself.

- By Series

  Sometimes your data is not arranged in continuous cells, so you have to bind individual series and other properties yourself. You select the By Series radio button and bind the Series Name property, the four series of data, and the category label. The process is similar to when you bind data by series for a column chart.

  In some cases, your data doesn't have a column for the category label, it's separated from the OHLC series, or you don't have the proper series name in the corresponding cell. As long as the OHLC series are in continuous cells, you can use the By Range option and the By Series option together for easier data binding.

  Let's assume that in Figure 5.9 we've inserted another column, Volume, between column A and column B, which makes it impossible to bind the whole range together. The sample data is presented in Figure 5.10. Knowing that the category label is not mandatory for binding by range, you can first select the By Range radio button and bind the range $C$1 to $F$11, which is highlighted in blue ❶ in Figure 5.10.

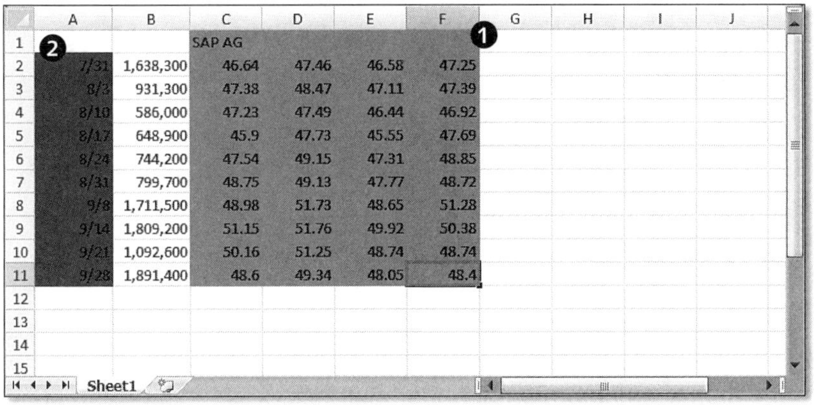

	A	B	C	D	E	F
1			SAP AG			
2	7/31	1,638,300	46.64	47.46	46.58	47.25
3	8/3	931,300	47.38	48.47	47.11	47.39
4	8/10	586,000	47.23	47.49	46.44	46.92
5	8/17	648,900	45.9	47.73	45.55	47.69
6	8/24	744,200	47.54	49.15	47.31	48.85
7	8/31	799,700	48.75	49.13	47.77	48.72
8	9/8	1,711,500	48.98	51.73	48.65	51.28
9	9/14	1,809,200	51.15	51.76	49.92	50.38
10	9/21	1,092,600	50.16	51.25	48.74	48.74
11	9/28	1,891,400	48.6	49.34	48.05	48.4

Figure 5.10 Binding Data when the Category Labels Column and OHLC Data Are Not Continuous

With By Range selected you are not able to bind the category label because this property is under the By Series option and is currently disabled. To do this, you switch to the By Series option. Notice that SAP BusinessObjects Dashboards doesn't discard what is already bound, and the category label is now enabled. As a final step, you bind the category label $A$2 to $A$11, which is highlighted in red ❷ in Figure 5.10.

Now, let's consider another change to the data in the embedded spreadsheet shown in Figure 5.9. This time, the category label and the four series of data are still continuous, but there isn't any cell for series names. The sample data is presented in Figure 5.11.

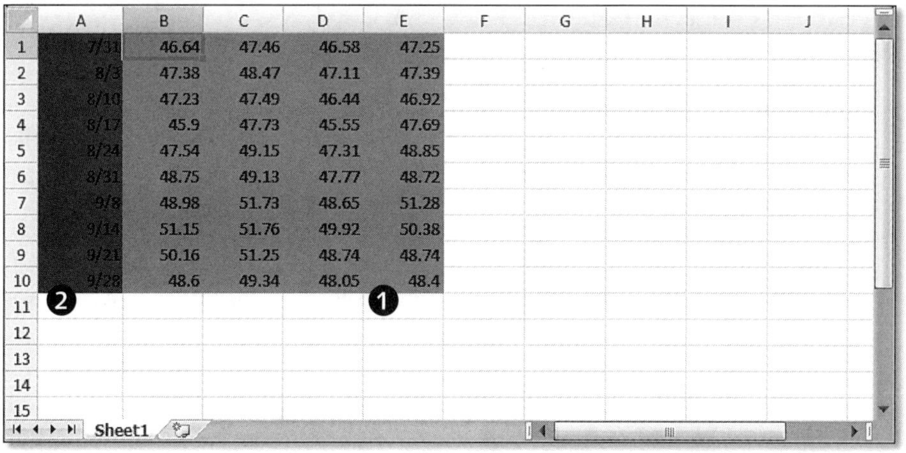

Figure 5.11 Binding Data when the Range Doesn't Contain a Series Name Cell

To easily bind data, you first select BY RANGE and bind to $B$1:$E$10, as highlighted in blue ➊ in Figure 5.11. Don't include the category label column; otherwise, your chart won't display the correct data.

Now that the labels and series values are properly bound, you switch to the BY SERIES option and bind the category label to the range $A$1:$A$10, which is highlighted in red ➋ in Figure 5.11. As for the series name, you can manually enter the name you want or bind it to another cell in the embedded spreadsheet.

Insertion

The OHLC chart also supports drill-down functionality. Clicking on any part of the vertical bar triggers the same insertion.

In the INSERTION TYPE dropdown list, you can select either POSITION, VALUE, ROW, COLUMN, or STATUS LIST, which are almost the same as for a column chart.

When you select the VALUE insert type there's an extra options list, VALUE SET, for which you can select OPEN, HIGH, LOW, or CLOSE, so that the corresponding value is inserted. Figure 5.12 shows the options for VALUE SET.

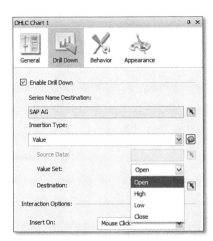

Figure 5.12 The Value Set Option for the Value Insertion Type

Appearance

▶ LAYOUT

Here you can define whether and how to display each part of the chart. There are always two markers for the legend: UP and DOWN. Figure 5.13 shows the effect of showing the legends to the right of an OHLC chart. You can adjust the vertical or horizontal offset to change the position of the legends.

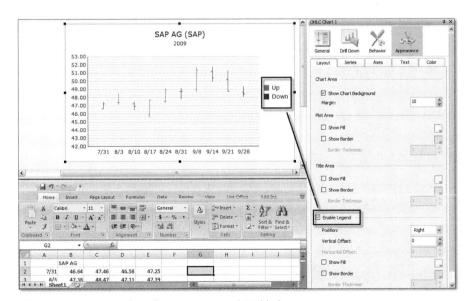

Figure 5.13 An OHLC Chart that Has its Legend Enabled

▶ SERIES

Here you set the positive and negative colors and transparency level of the vertical bars and the legend markers, as displayed in Figure 5.14.

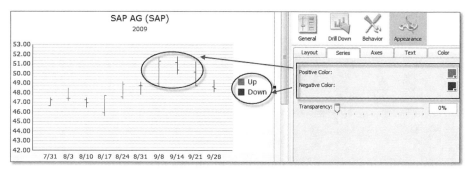

Figure 5.14 Changing Series Color Options for an OHLC Chart

Practice

Now let's go through a simple hands-on example to get more familiar with this component. Suppose you need an OHLC chart to display your company's stock prices for the past three months. For practice, we'll choose Google as our example and plot the daily price from June 2009 to August 2009.

1. **Get the stock prices.**

   You can get the historical prices of Google stock from Yahoo! Finance at *http://finance.yahoo.com*. On the homepage of Yahoo! Finance, enter "GOOG" into the search box and click GET QUOTES. You now go to the Google page. Select HISTORICAL PRICES on the left, enter the START DATE and END DATE, and click the GET PRICES button. The data table shown in Figure 5.15 will be updated according to the dates specified.

2. **Prepare the data source.**

   You can copy the whole price table from the web page into an Excel worksheet. Because Yahoo! Finance lists historical prices retrospectively, you need to sort the data from oldest to newest so they can be correctly plotted on the OHLC chart.

   To do this, select any cell in the data column. Right-click to pop up the context menu. In the SORT submenu, select SORT OLDEST TO NEWEST. Now that the data is correctly sorted, you can add some descriptive text in the Excel worksheet.

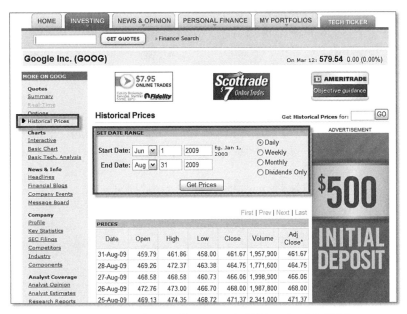

Figure 5.15 Getting Prices of GOOG from June 1, 2009 to Aug 31, 2009

Figure 5.16 shows how the data is organized in an Excel spreadsheet. We added some text so it can be used as the titles of the chart for the user's easy understanding of the dashboard.

	A	B	C	D	E	F	G	H	I	J	K	L
1			Symbol	GOOG								
2			Date Range	From 6/1 to 8/31								
3												
4			Date	Open	High	Low	Close	Volume	Adj Close*			
5			6/1/2009	418.73	429.6	418.53	426.56	3,322,400	426.56			
6			6/2/2009	426.25	429.96	423.4	428.4	2,623,600	428.4			
7			6/3/2009	426	432.46	424	431.65	3,532,800	431.65			
8			6/4/2009	435.3	441.24	434.5	440.28	3,638,100	440.28			
9			6/5/2009	445.07	447.34	439.46	444.32	3,680,800	444.32			
10			6/8/2009	439.5	440.92	434.12	438.77	3,098,700	438.77			
11			6/9/2009	438.58	440.5	431.76	435.62	3,254,900	435.62			
12			6/10/2009	436.23	437.89	426.67	432.6	3,358,900	432.6			
13			6/11/2009	431.77	433.73	428.37	429	2,865,200	429			
14			6/12/2009	426.86	427.7	421.21	424.84	2,918,400	424.84			
15			6/15/2009	421.5	421.5	414	416.77	3,736,900	416.77			
16			6/16/2009	419.31	421.09	415.42	416	3,049,700	416			
17			6/17/2009	416.19	419.72	411.56	415.16	3,490,100	415.16			
18			6/18/2009	415.68	418.69	413	414.06	3,085,200	414.06			
19			6/19/2009	418.21	420.46	414.58	420.09	4,259,100	420.09			
20			6/22/2009	416.95	417.49	401.89	407.35	4,124,400	407.35			
21			6/23/2009	406.65	408.99	402.55	405.68	2,899,600	405.68			
22			6/24/2009	408.74	412.23	406.56	409.29	2,457,800	409.29			
23			6/25/2009	407	415.9	406.51	415.77	3,044,500	415.77			
24			6/26/2009	413.68	428.23	413.11	425.32	3,256,700	425.32			

Sheet1 / Sheet2 / Sheet3

Figure 5.16 GOOG Stock Prices Organized in an Excel Worksheet

3. **Add an OHLC chart and bind the data.**

   Now you launch SAP BusinessObjects Dashboards and create a new dashboard. You first import the Excel file created in the last step into the embedded spreadsheet via the menu path DATA • IMPORT.

   Then you add an OHLC chart to the canvas.

   There isn't a proper series name cell for you to bind everything in one shot, so first, in the GENERAL tab of the PROPERTIES panel, select the BY RANGE radio button and bind the data to range $D$5:$G$69. Then select BY SERIES. The data you specified in BY RANGE will be carried over to the series. You then bind the series name to $D$1 and bind the category label to $C$5:$C$69.

   Now the data is properly set up, as displayed in Figure 5.17.

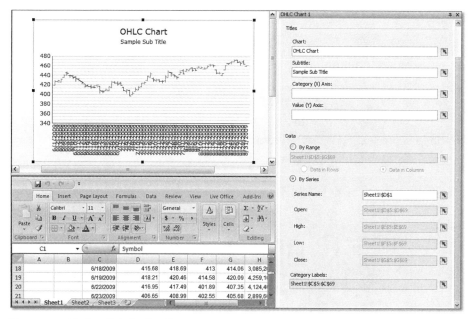

Figure 5.17 Binding Data for the Chart

4. **Add titles and change the appearance.**

   You can see that the OHLC chart on the canvas is already showing stock prices as you want, but there are still some problems in the chart.

   First, the chart titles contain default text and are not very informative. Second, the category labels take up too much space and will not be very useful. Lastly, the series colors are not the ones you are used to.

Now let's solve these problems. In the GENERAL tab of the PROPERTIES panel, bind TITLE to CELL and SUBTITLE to $D$2 so that now you can easily understand what the chart is showing. Switch to the APPEARANCE tab to change the appearance of the chart. In the SERIES tab, change the positive color to green ❶ for higher closing prices. In the TEXT tab, unselect HORIZONTAL (CATEGORY) AXIS LABEL so the dates won't appear.

Figure 5.18 displays the final result of this example.

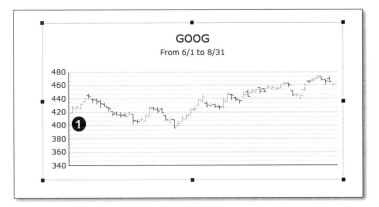

Figure 5.18 The Result of the Example

5.1.5 Candlestick Chart

The candlestick chart is another kind of chart used to illustrate the price changes of stock over time. A candlestick chart is composed of the body and an upper and a lower shadow, which illustrate the highest and lowest traded price of a security during the time interval represented. The body illustrates the opening and closing trades.

Figure 5.19 shows an example of a candlestick chart that displays the same stock price information as the OHLC chart shown in Figure 5.18.

When to Use a Candlestick Chart

Whether to choose a candlestick or an OHLC chart is usually determined by the user's preference. In terms of functionality, they are almost identical. The only difference between these two is the way each data point is represented. In most cases, they can be used interchangeably for the best look and feel.

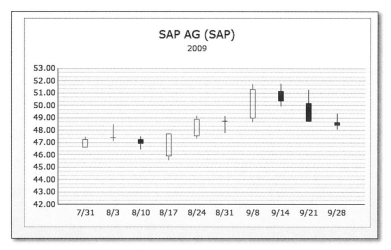

Figure 5.19 Weekly Price of SAP AG in a Candlestick Chart

How to Use a Candlestick Chart

Using a candlestick chart, including moving, resizing, and setting its properties, is exactly the same as using an OHLC chart, as illustrated in Section 5.1.4.

5.1.6 Radar Chart

A radar chart displays data in a radial layout, which makes it a very interesting type of chart. Almost all of the charts we've discussed so far have a category (X) axis and a value (Y) axis. The radar chart doesn't have a category axis but has multiple value axes. In a radar chart, these axes are called vertical axes, and they have the following properties.

▸ All of the vertical axes start from the same center point and end at the perimeter.

▸ All of the vertical axes are the same length.

▸ The separation angles between adjacent axes are all equal.

This makes the radar chart a polygon shape. The number of sides of the polygon or the number of axes is determined by the number of data points each data series has. Each data point is plotted on one vertical axis. The value of the data point is represented as the distance from the center of the chart, where the center represents the minimum value, and the chart edge is the maximum value. All of the data points in a series are connected by straight lines, which makes a series a closed circuit in a radar chart.

Figure 5.20 shows a typical radar chart that is used to illustrate a company's performance in six KPIs for different areas. We can see that for financial and growth metrics, this company gets quite low scores—but quite high scores for the internal process and community metrics.

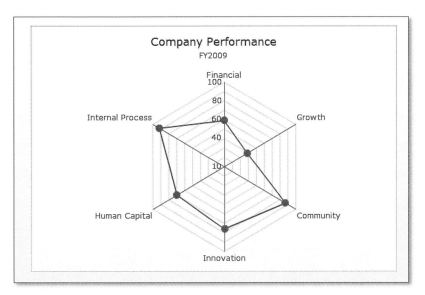

Figure 5.20 Performance Metrics Plotted on a Radar Chart

The radar chart also supports data in multiple series and alerts. However, you cannot enable alerts when you have multiple series of data displayed in a radar chart, just like the other charts that have alerts capabilities.

When to Use a Radar Chart

A radar chart is essentially a line chart wrapped into a circle, where the value (Y) axis starts at the center and ends at the perimeter, and the category (X) axis becomes the perimeter. Technically, this makes using a radar chart quite similar to using a line chart, but actually, the radar chart usually doesn't fit situations in which the line chart works very well.

We've already learned that the line chart is very good at visualizing trends in the data. In Chapter 4, Section 4.1.3, we saw an example of a line chart displaying the historical trends of the market growth and sales growth of a company. Let's see how well the radar chart shows the same data, as displayed in Figure 5.21.

Figure 5.21 Market Growth and Sales Growth Trends from 1999 to 2006 Plotted on a Radar Chart

In this figure, we see a radar chart displaying exactly the same data as that in Chapter 4, Figure 4.34. The problem is that it's impossible to describe the trends of market growth and sales growth from one glance at the radar chart.

The radar chart can also be used to display several aspects of something under investigation. Usually each axis represents a different measure. You can compare values in a single series of data to determine which factor is dominant, or you can compare multiple series of data to find the differences among these items. For example, you can use a radar chart to compare the individual as well as overall ability of NBA players, with each radius representing ability in rebounds, steals, assists, and so on, as displayed in Figure 5.22.

A more typical application of the radar chart is to display the performance metric of an organization for performance management. Usually the radar chart displays KPIs in several important categories and makes visible concentrations of the overall strengths and weakness. Typically, you first need to create several categories or measures to describe the performance. Next, you come to a more important step, standardizing the performance definition. Each category must have a consistent scoring range, for example, 0 to 100. After evaluating and rating each category, you can construct the chart by plotting the ratings on a radar chart. Finally, the most important step is to analyze and interpret the results.

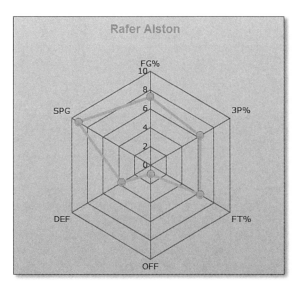

Figure 5.22 NBA Player Abilities in a Radar Chart

How to Use a Radar Chart

The radar chart is essentially another kind of line chart. The methods used to bind the display data, change the appearance, enable alerts, and so on are exactly the same as those illustrated in Chapter 4, Section 4.1.3.

5.1.7 Filled Radar Chart

The filled radar chart is essentially a radar chart whose area is covered by data series filled with a color. The filled radar chart doesn't provide series markers, so it is impossible to enable alerts on a filled radar chart, even if it displays only one series of data.

Figure 5.23 is an example of a filled radar chart that compares the performance of two departments. The point at each axis indicates the value of that measure, while the size of the filled area for each category item indicates the overall performance, which can be the sum of weighted measure values.

As you can see from this figure, it's quite obvious that the performance of department A exceeds that of department B in all aspects.

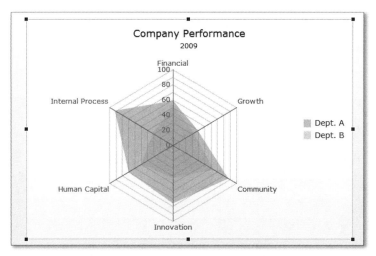

Figure 5.23 Performance Metrics Plotted on a Filled Radar Chart

When to Use a Filled Radar Chart

The filled radar chart is similar to the radar chart. Unless you want to highlight some abnormal values in a single data series, you can always use the two interchangeably. Sometimes a filled radar chart may be preferable because you can compare the areas of two series more easily on a filled radar chart.

A drawback of a radar or filled radar chart is that it requires much more space to visualize the same information than other methods such as a column chart.

How to Use a Filled Radar Chart

Using the filled radar chart is very similar to using the radar chart. For the filled radar chart, you can also set the filled colors of series.

Appearance

▶ SERIES

You can change the filled colors of series in the SERIES tab in the APPEARANCE tab in the filled radar chart's property sheet, which is quite straightforward. The TRANSPARENCY option is very important here. As in Figure 5.24, the transparency is set to 70% by default. Usually, you need a higher transparency value. Otherwise, the department A series will be barely visible because it's covered by the department B series.

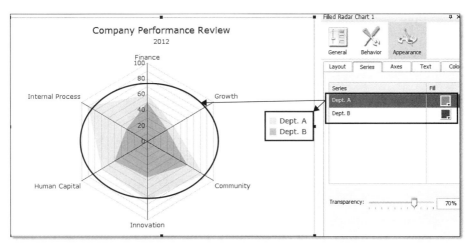

Figure 5.24 Changing Series Color Options for a Filled Radar Chart

5.1.8 Tree Map

The tree map displays a rectangle, which is tiled with smaller rectangles. The size of each rectangle is proportional to a measure of the data and is filled with a color, the intensity of which is related to another measure. The tree map manifests the correlation of two measures, which is very similar to what the XY chart does. Moreover, a tree map appears to be more intuitive to some extent. After all, the differences in color and size are easier to distinguish visually.

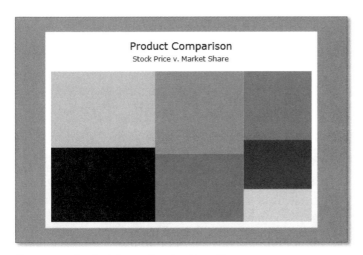

Figure 5.25 Product Comparison in a Tree Map

Figure 5.25 shows a typical tree map that compares seven products in two measures: stock price and market share. The size represents the stock price, and the color intensity represents the market share. From this chart, we can easily discover the following facts:

▸ The company that has a product with a high market share could have a very high stock price (the rectangle in the bottom-left corner).

▸ The company that has a product with a high market share could have a very low stock price (the rectangle in the upper-left corner).

▸ The company that has a product with a low market share could have a very high stock price (the rectangle in the bottom-right corner).

▸ The company that has a product with a low market share could have a very low stock price (the rectangle in the middle right).

Such facts are quite extreme. Maybe the company with a high market share product and low stock price is doing worse than before, so people don't want to keep their stock. You get the idea that the tree map reveals the correlation of two measures.

When to Use a Tree Map

When you want to analyze a situation using two measures, you can choose either an XY chart or a tree map. The tree map may seem more intuitive and more interesting, but it doesn't support alerts, so if you want to highlight data points conditionally, you should choose an XY chart.

How to Use a Tree Map

The ways to bind data and set most of the properties for a tree map are identical to those for an XY chart. You can refer to Chapter 4, Section 4.1.5 for details.

General

In this tab you define the title, subtitle, and data for the tree map. When BY SERIES is selected in the DATA part, you click the plus button to add a series. DISPLAY LABELS refers to the category labels that are members of a dimension (e.g., product, cost center, etc.). VALUES (SIZE) refers to the values of a measure, which are represented by the size of the small rectangle for each category item. VALUES (COLOR INTENSITY) is the values of another measure, which are represented by the color intensity of the rectangles. For example, you can represent the price of each product with rectangle size, and market share percentage with rectangle color intensity.

Appearance

▶ SERIES

You need to specify two colors for each series in the tree map. One is the high color, which is usually dark, and the other is the low color, which is usually a little lighter. Based on these two colors, SAP BusinessObjects Dashboards automatically calculates all the other colors for each rectangle by interpolation so that the intensity of all of the colors is within the range of the high and low colors.

As displayed in Figure 5.26, you can see how the colors of the series are specified. We've changed the high color to purple ❶ and low color to yellow ❷. We've also added red lines ❸ around the perimeter of the whole rectangle and increased their thickness to make it clearer.

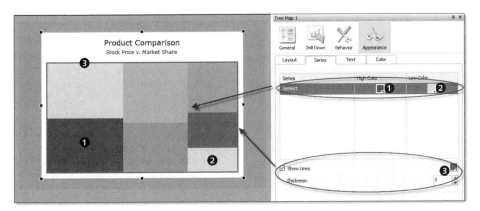

Figure 5.26 Effects of Setting Series Colors in the Appearance Tab

5.1.9 Sparkline Chart

A sparkline chart has one or more lines to show the change trends of certain measures. You can think of it as a combination of one or more line charts, but without any X- or Y-axis.

A sparkline chart is characterized by its small size and dense display. Figure 5.27 shows the stock price change in December 2011 of SAP, Oracle, and Microsoft.

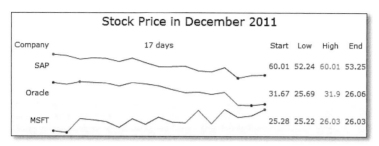

Stock Price in December 2011

Company	17 days	Start	Low	High	End
SAP		60.01	52.24	60.01	53.25
Oracle		31.67	25.69	31.9	26.06
MSFT		25.28	25.22	26.03	26.03

Figure 5.27 A Typical Sparkline Chart Showing Stock Prices Over a Month

It's also possible to highlight or display the start, high, low, and end values of each series. This functionality is similar to the OHLC chart, as mentioned in Section 5.1.4, which shows the four OHLC values per day, not over a period.

When to Use a Sparkline Chart

Based on the theory and characteristics of a sparkline chart, you may use it to display several values in small space. By *several values* we mean there should be several data items, for example, stock price or temperature over a month, sales revenue in the last 10 years or 12 months, or some clinical test data in every 2 seconds in a given minute.

The sparkline chart doesn't look nice when used to display only few (e.g., fewer than five) data points. In such a case you may want to try an OHLC or line chart.

Sparkline charts are mostly used for analysis of the change of stock price, temperature, network traffic, or finance measures over a long period.

How to Use a Sparkline Chart

You can use as many sparkline charts as you want in a dashboard. Its PROPERTIES panel is divided into three tabs as illustrated in the following subsections.

General

Here you specify the data for the chart, either BY RANGE, where you select a cell range in the embedded spreadsheet and let SAP BusinessObjects Dashboards guess its series, or BY SERIES, where you specify the name and values per series. In Figure 5.28, BY SERIES is selected with three measures, the names and values of which are bound to the embedded spreadsheet.

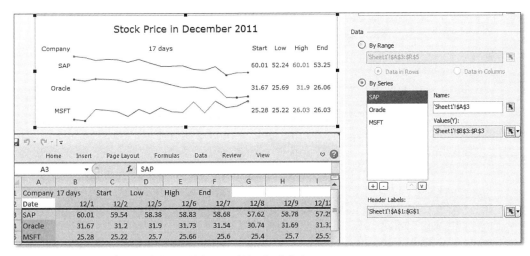

Figure 5.28 Data Binding with Series Values and Header Labels

The HEADER LABELS field at the bottom doesn't mean the category labels of the data points, which is the case for other charts such as a column chart. Think about the components of a sparkline chart: series names, values, and start/high/low/end values. It's not difficult to understand that here the header labels are for the designer to specify the texts to show what the series names and values are about and the four values. In our example in Figure 5.28, the series names refer to companies, so we have "Company" in cell A1; the values refer to stock prices in December 2011, of which 25 days have elapsed, so we have "17 days" in cell B1. The texts in cells C1 to F1 are the labels for the four values and can be your localized text.

Behavior

In this tab you define the chart's behavior. A new property is NORMAL RANGE AREA, which defines a range for "normal" values. The normal range area will be displayed in a different color, which can be defined in APPEARANCE tab, so that data points that fall out of this range can be distinguished.

You can either manually set the low and high values of the normal range, or select AUTO to let SAP BusinessObjects Dashboards make the guess. You can only define one normal range for all series in the chart, so pay attention to the range of the actual values of all series, in case the normal range of one series doesn't make sense with that of another, as their values vary a lot.

Refer to Figure 5.29 for a sparkline chart with NORMAL RANGE enabled and displayed in light blue ❶.

Appearance

In this tab you define the appearance of the chart, mainly the color and position of each part.

In the LAYOUT subtab you define whether and how to display the chart background, plot area, and title area. The horizontal gap is the gap between parts for each series; for example, the gap between the series name and the graphical line. The vertical gap is the gap between every two adjacent series; for example, the vertical gap between two series names (SAP and Oracle). At design time you can adjust the values and see the change in the chart.

In the TEXT tab you define color and format of each text part of the chart, such as the title and subtitle. Other texts, including header labels, series labels, and start/low/high/end values are specific to sparkline charts. You can select the checkbox of each to display it, and then customize its font, color, size, position, offset, and number format—whether it's a date, currency, percentage, or simply text.

Figure 5.29 shows the effect of these settings, where the series labels are displayed to the right of the graphic, all four values are displayed in different colors, and the number format of the start value is specified as currency with the $ symbol.

Figure 5.29 Effects of Settings in the Text Tab

In the COLOR tab most properties are related to the color of each display part. For the normal range area, which we discussed in relation to the BEHAVIOR tab, here you can set its color and transparency. Also, you can define the color of each series. For example, you can display the stock prices of Oracle in a contrasting color (red) to compare others with it. What's more, below MARKERS, you can define whether to show any of the four values start/low/high/end values, and in what shape and what color.

Figure 5.30 shows the effects of these settings, where the normal range color is light blue ❶, lines for the series ORCL are displayed in red, the thickness of all lines is increased to 2 to make them easy to read, the low marker is displayed in red ❷, and the high marker is in green ❸.

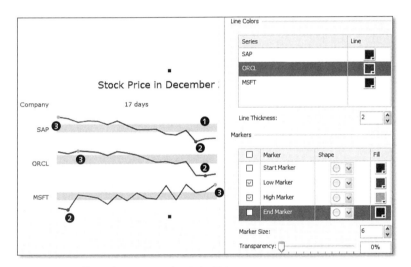

Figure 5.30 Effect of Settings in the Color Tab

You can download this sample sparkline chart from *www.sap-press.com*.

5.1.10 Bullet Chart

A bullet chart is a kind of bar graph that uses a vertical column or horizontal bar to represent the value as well as some comparable values such as a target to indicate the current situation. It looks like a traditional thermometer or a progress bar, with data markers on the X- or Y- axis. One bullet chart can display several bars or columns, one for each series. SAP BusinessObjects Dashboards 4.0 provides two bullet charts, one horizontal and the other vertical.

When to Use a Bullet Chart

A bullet chart can display as much information as a dial, gauge, or progress bar but takes less space and is easier to read. Choose bullet charts when you want to display the values of a measure (e.g., revenue, number of orders) and at the same time compare it with some standards to indicate its status as okay or risky. You can use it for performance measurement, status monitoring, and so on.

As mentioned in Chapter 4, a dial or gauge can attractively display the actual value as well as its status, and a progress bar can show the actual value and current progress. In some situations you may find that these components don't represent rich enough information and takes too much space. If you meet with such a problem during you dashboard development, consider using bullet charts.

How to Use a Bullet Chart

The PROPERTIES panel of the two kinds of bullet charts are the same. We'll discuss the horizontal type here.

General

Here you define the titles, X-axis label, and data for each part per series.

For a horizontal bullet chart, the X-axis displays the data markers for measures. The property HORIZONTAL (X) AXIS defines the label for the X-axis, often the unit or the period of the data. However, in most cases, to make the chart clean, this field is left empty.

Unlike other charts, for a bullet chart you need a comparative value (e.g., a target or average) and scale values (for a normal range) in addition to the primary measure values (e.g., revenue).

If you want to bind data by range, the data for each series should be in the same row or column, with the first cell being the label for that series, the second cell being the sublabel, which is displayed below the label, the third cell being the actual value, the fourth being the comparative value, and the fifth and sixth being the scale values to highlight a normal range.

If you want to be more flexible or when the required data is not in the required sequence one by one, you can choose BY RANGE and specify data for each part of each series. This takes more time but is more flexible.

Here you need to understand the meaning of each field. LABEL is often the name of the series (or measure) such as revenue, customer loyalty, or market share, and SUB-LABEL is the additional information about that series such as unit or department. The PERFORMANCE value is the actual numeric value the series is to display. The COMPARATIVE value is for the actual value to be compared with—often the target by plan or average in the industry. SCALE VALUES is similar to the normal range area of a sparkline chart, which defines a normal value range for each series. Performance values that fall outside this range will be highlighted.

Figure 5.31 shows an example of data binding for a horizontal bullet chart. Note that the actual revenue is displayed in a bar, and the target as a vertical line. For each series the normal area, defined by scale values, is displayed in light gray, and other areas in different colors.

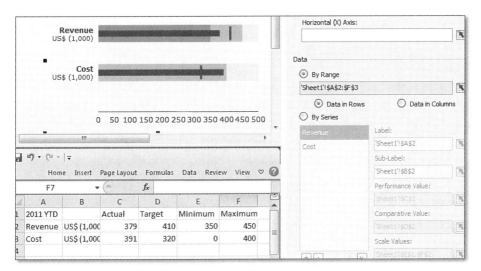

Figure 5.31 Data Binding for a Horizontal Bullet Chart

As you can see from the chart, revenue is a little behind the target but still in the normal range, while cost exceeds the plan by a lot.

Behavior

In the SCALE subtab you define the value scale on the X-axis, the minimum and maximum limits of which can either be manually input or bound or be determined by SAP BusinessObjects Dashboards with AUTO (X) AXIS selected. You can set the SCALE algorithm to LINEAR when the values don't vary too much, or

LOGARITHMIC otherwise. If the values are all too big (e.g., over 10,000), you can select FIXED LABEL SIZE to make the data markers on the X-axis smaller.

One special and very useful feature here is the ability to configure the X-axis scale by series. By default the scale definition is for all series. After selecting CONFIGURE SCALE BY SERIES you have the flexibility to define scale and divisions per series, including the minimum and maximum limits, number or size of divisions and whether to use FIXED LABEL SIZE for each series.

This feature is very useful to make it possible to display the measure of different types in one chart. For example, you can display revenue, cost, profit percentage, number of customers, and growth percentage in multiple bars of one bullet chart. Without this feature it doesn't make sense to include profit percentage, which is between 0 and 100, with revenue, which is often bigger than 100,000. As you can see from Figure 5.32 in the next section, the scale for the series REVENUE and COST is 0–500, while that for PROFIT is 0–40.

Appearance

The APPEARANCE tab for a bullet chart is quite similar to that of other charts like a pie or sparkline chart. In the LAYOUT subtab you define whether and how to show the background, plot, or title area. Most of the time we choose not to display the background or borders, but it's a good habit to show the fill for the plot area to make the chart distinguishable from other charts in the dashboard.

In the SERIES subtab you define colors for each of the four values. PERFORMANCE COLOR is for the bar showing actual value, which is often neutral. COMPARATIVE MARKER COLOR is for the vertical bar to compare the actual value with, which should stand out. SCALE HIGH COLORS and SCALE LOW COLORS are for the colors for areas smaller than the minimum or bigger than the maximum scale values of each series. However, SAP BusinessObjects Dashboards calculates the color for the normal range area as intermediate between scale low and scale high colors.

Bar size determines the height of the bar for each series. Depending on the width of your bullet chart and the number of series, you can increase or decrease it for a better look and feel.

The PERFORMANCE MARKER SIZE field defines the height of the maker, or horizontal bar, for performance (or the actual value). Its value is represented as a percentage of the width of the bullet chart, so if you give it a value of 100%, the width of the performance marker will be the same as the chart. Its value is between 1% and 100% and can be adjusted through either the slider or the input box.

Comparative marker size is the same as performance marker size, except it defines the height of the vertical comparative value bar. Note that the width of this vertical bar cannot be configured.

In the TEXT subtab you can define whether and how to display horizontal axis labels for each series, which are actually the data markers of the values.

Figure 5.32 shows a comprehensive example of a horizontal bullet chart, where its background is not shown, but plot area is displayed in light blue ❶, the comparative marker is highlighted in red with a width of 80% of that of the chart ❷, and X-axis labels for revenue are not displayed, as they are the same as cost.

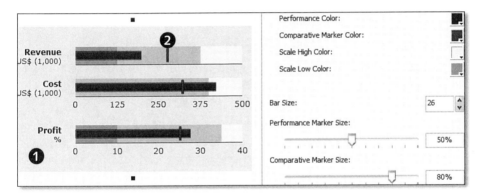

Figure 5.32 A Comprehensive Example of a Horizontal Bullet Chart

5.2 Advanced Selectors

SAP BusinessObjects Dashboards 4.0 provides a wide range of selectors in the Selectors category, some of which are covered in Chapter 4. We'll talk about the rest in this section, such as the accordion menu and play selector.

5.2.1 Accordion Menu

An accordion menu is a two-level menu in which items are categorized into groups. The user can first select a category and then select one of the items within it. The categories are stacked vertically and can be expanded or collapsed. As an example, the CATEGORY tab of the COMPONENTS view is an accordion menu.

When to Use an Accordion Menu

Choose this component when there are too many items to choose from, and they can be categorized into groups. For example, say you're creating a dashboard showing values such as the sales revenue of each branch in your company, which requires the user to select a branch first. The branches in your company are too numerous to display. To help with user selection, you can list them in an accordion menu where the user first selects a sales district and then a branch.

You can select only one item each time. The category cannot be selected; clicking on it will just expand it to list its labels.

How to Use an Accordion Menu

The PROPERTIES panel of an accordion menu is divided into three categories as explained next.

General

▶ TITLE

The title tells the user about the menu and what he needs do. You can customize its location in the APPEARANCE tab by choosing a location from the POSITION dropdown list.

▶ CATEGORIES

The accordion menu is a two-level selector with candidates divided into categories. The typical steps to set up the labels of an accordion menu are:

▷ **Add a category**

Click the ADD button (with a plus [+] sign) below the CATEGORIES list. You can then enter the name of the category in the NAME field or bind it to a cell in the embedded spreadsheet with the BIND button.

▷ **Add labels of the category**

The labels will appear within the category when it's selected. Add the labels by clicking the BIND button to bind them to a row or column in the embedded spreadsheet.

Figure 5.33 shows an accordion menu with one category.

Figure 5.33 An Accordion Menu with One Category

To add more categories, follow the steps on the prior page. To delete a category, select it and click the DELETE button (with a minus [–] sign).

At runtime, the categories are displayed in the order defined here from top to bottom. You can click the buttons to the bottom right of the CATEGORIES list with an up or down symbol to move a category up or down.

▶ DATA INSERTION
Similar to other components, you can select one item from the INSERTION TYPE dropdown list. The options are ROW, VALUE, COLUMN, FILTERED ROWS, and STATUS LIST. Depending on what insertion type you've chosen, you can bind the destination to a cell or a cell range in the embedded spreadsheet. Each time the user makes a selection in the menu, the corresponding value or row is inserted into that cell or cell range.

An accordion menu is more powerful than a normal selector such as a combo box. Only one insertion type and destination can be defined in an accordion menu, but you can define source data for each category. The source data can be a row, a column, or even a cell range with multiple rows and columns. For example, you can display the monthly sales revenue of each branch in a cell range, one row per branch. With this range being the source data, and selecting ROW as the insertion type, you insert the monthly sales revenue of the selected branch to a target row, which can also be used in a column chart.

In CATEGORY LABEL DESTINATION, you can insert the category name of the current selected item to a cell in the embedded spreadsheet.

Clicking the category name will not trigger any data insertion. The user needs to click the items inside each category.

Behavior

▶ SLIDE SPEED
When the user clicks a category that is not currently expanded, it rolls up to

expand its labels. The slide speed controls how fast a category expands when clicked. You can adjust it with the slider, from SLOWER on the left to FASTER on the right.

▶ SELECTED ITEM
Similar to the default selection of a chart or a combo box, you define what category and what label within that category are selected by default. You do this by selecting one from the corresponding CATEGORY or ITEM dropdown list. That category will then be expanded by default.

▶ IGNORE BLANK CELLS
If you don't want to display a category or an item if it's empty, select IN CATEGORIES or IN VALUES. *Empty* means the category or value of an item is blank.

Practice

Now let's go through a simple example to reinforce how to use an accordion menu. Suppose you want to create a dashboard to show and compare the sales revenue and quantity sold of each branch over a period of quarters. Instead of asking the user to select one branch from many in a combo box, we'll use an accordion menu and a column chart to its right to show the values.

1. **Prepare the data.**
Display the values of two measures, sales revenue and quantity sold, of each branch in a range, with one row per branch. Display the sales revenue in each quarter in front of the quantity sold. Display the branches in a column, categorized into sales districts.

Your data should be similar to that displayed in Figure 5.34.

2. **Set up the accordion menu.**
Having planned the data, now let's focus on the UI components. We'll use an accordion menu for the user to select a branch in a quarter, and use a column chart to display the sales information under that condition.

In this step, drag an accordion menu from the SELECTORS category in the COMPONENTS view and drop it onto the canvas. Move and resize it as you want. In step 4 we'll focus on setting up the column chart.

We'll give the accordion menu the title "Please select a branch" to prompt the user, and set it to display on the top left. To do this, click the APPEARANCE tab in the PROPERTIES panel, select the TEXT tab, and then select TITLE and select TOP LEFT in the POSITION dropdown list.

	A	B	C	D	E	F	G	H	I	J
1										
2										
3					Sales revenue				Quantity sold	
4		**South**	Q1	Q2	Q3	Q4	Q1	Q2	Q3	Q4
5		Branch 1	282	309	436	283	15	18	22	10
6		Branch 2	363	447	171	403	17	20	20	18
7		Branch 3	322	112	260	273	22	28	35	26
8		Branch 4	318	330	325	158	25	32	38.7	34
9		Branch 5	114	217	274	146	22	37	45	42
10		Branch 6	167	496	213	420	32	42	25	50
11										
12		**North**								
13		Branch 7	435	443	130	147	18	10	33	38
14		Branch 8	474	260	362	160	11	17	22	39
15		Branch 9	454	387	339	128	15	20	30	14
16		Branch 10	377	625	439	268	22	24	19	28

Figure 5.34 Data in the Embedded Spreadsheet

Now let's set the categories and labels. Click the ADD button below the CATE-GORIES list to create a new category and bind its name to cell Sheet1!$B$4 for sales district South, and bind LABELS to range Sheet1!$B$5:$B$10 for the branches in the South sales district.

Follow the steps to add categories and labels for the sales districts North, East, and West.

By now you can click each category to see its contained items.

3. **Implement data insertion.**

Before this step, nothing happens when the user makes selections in this menu. The menu is used for the user to select a branch to see its sales information. So we'll set INSERTION TYPE to ROW and bind the source data of each category to the cell range containing the sales information of that category.

To do this, select the category SOUTH and click the BIND button next to SOURCE DATA to bind to range Sheet1!$B$5:$J$10, where the branch names and their sales information are stored. Repeat this step for other categories.

The inserted data is inserted into a row, and here we bind DESTINATION to cell range Sheet1!$B$2.

It's better to display the sales district next to the branch name in the column chart, so we'll also insert the category name by binding CATEGORY LABEL DESTI-NATION to cell Sheet1!$A$3.

4. **Arrange the column chart.**

Now it's time to set up the column chart. After positioning it to the right of the accordion menu and making them the same height and aligning them to the top, let's set properties for the column chart.

In the GENERAL tab of the chart's PROPERTIES panel, select BY SERIES to manually set its category labels and values. Bind its category labels to range Sheet1!$C$4:$F$4, where the quarters' names are stored. Add one series called "Sales revenue," bind its values to range Sheet1!$C$2:$F$2, which is the destination of the accordion menu, and plot it on the primary Y-axis. Add another series called "Quantity sold," bind its values to range Sheet1!$G$2: $J$2, and plot it on the secondary Y-axis.

We'd like to show the current branch to avoid confusion about what the data is for. Insert the name of the current sales district, which is the category name of the accordion menu, into cell Sheet1!$A$3 as defined in step 3. Also, the branch name is the first cell of the destination of the menu, Sheet1!$B$2. So we'll use a formula to format a meaningful subtitle for the column chart:

=CONCATENATE("Sales district: ",A3, " Branch: ",B2)

Save it in a cell and bind the subtitle of the column chart to it.

Now we're all done. You can refer to *www.sap-press.com* for the sample model definition file (*.xlf*). Figure 5.35 shows the PROPERTIES panels of both the menu and the chart.

Figure 5.35 Properties Panels of the Two UI Components

The final result of this example is as displayed in Figure 5.36.

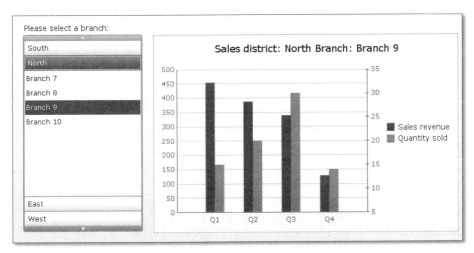

Figure 5.36 Final Result of the Accordion Menu

At runtime, each time the user clicks a category (sales district); its branches are listed below it. When the user selects one branch, its corresponding values are inserted into Destination, shown in the column chart.

5.2.2 Icon

The visual appearance of an icon component is a colorful circle. It's a very useful and unique UI component.

When to Use an Icon

With alerts enabled, an icon is a good way to show whether the value it's bound to is good or bad. You can use it in combination with other components such as a label or a gauge, where the label or gauge component displays the actual value, while the icon indicates its status. An icon is the ideal component to represent the traffic light in green, yellow, or red.

An icon component can have two states, on and off, similar to a checkbox, making it a selector component. In this case, the user can click it to switch its state and see different data or components.

Based on these two functionalities of icons, you may want to use this component either to indicate the status of a data field or to switch between two states, showing different values when it's selected or not.

261

How to Use an Icon

You can move or resize an icon component on the canvas. For example, you can resize it from a circle to an ellipse. Its PROPERTIES panel is divided into four categories, as explained next.

General

If you want the icon component to display a certain value, you can set its label to indicate what value it represents. You can either enter a text in the LABEL field or bind it to a cell in the embedded spreadsheet. The label will only be displayed as a hint on mouse over.

The *display value* is a constant value entered by the designer here or bound to a cell storing the data. It's used in the alerts threshold to determine the color of the icon.

Figure 5.37 shows how the label and display value of an icon component are displayed at runtime.

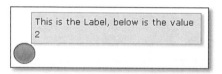

Figure 5.37 Label and Display Value of an Icon at Runtime

If you just want to use an icon as an on/off selector, you can leave the label and the display value empty.

As a selector component, the icon also provides data insertion functionality to choose one from two candidates. At this point it's the same as a checkbox. The source data is a row or column with two cells, and the destination is a single cell to store the selected value. The first cell in the row or column specified in the source data indicates the unselected status, while the second row or column indicates the selected status. Therefore, if the default selected item is unselected, the content in the first cell will be inserted into the destination when the user launches the dashboard. You can configure the default selected item in BEHAVIOR • COMMON.

Appearance

Here you set the transparency level of the component. In the TEXT tab, you set the formats of the label and display value, which will display on mouse over if enabled. However, note that you cannot specify their positions.

One property specific to icons is SHOW ON/OFF. An icon component has two states, on (for selected) and off (for unselected). By default, SHOW ON/OFF is selected, and the icon appears in different colors for the different states. If SHOW ON/OFF is not selected, the data insertion can still work perfectly on user interaction, but the color of the icon will not change between the on and off states. Note that SAP BusinessObjects Dashboards automatically calculates the on color based on its off color, and you cannot specify it. You can unselect SHOW ON/OFF if you have enabled alerts and you don't want the on color to make the colors defined in alerts confusing.

You can set the default color (for unselected) in the COLOR tab only when alerts are not enabled.

> **Note**
>
> The color you specify here is for unselected, no matter what is selected as the default selected item.

Alerts

You can select ENABLE ALERTS if you want to use the icon component as an indicator of the value it represents. For example, you can display the actual value in a label with an icon component alongside to show its status.

5.2.3 Play Selector

A play selector looks like the controller you use when listening to music or playing movies. Typically, it has buttons to play or pause an item, move to the previous or next item, and move to the first or the last item.

SAP BusinessObjects Dashboards provides such a UI component with the five buttons mentioned above to continuously insert a row or column from a cell range such as the source data to another row or column such as the destination. With the play selector component on your dashboard, the user can see data from a large number of items without clicking on each selection. The play selector can automatically insert items one at a time from a large list to a destination, with a movie effect. The user can go backward or forward or pause the play at any time with a simple click.

Figure 5.38 shows a typical play selector.

Figure 5.38 A Simple Play Selector Component

When to Use a Play Selector

Choose a play selector component when you want to display a large list of data one at a time, without requiring user interaction to select the items or when you just want to simulate the effect of a media player.

How to Use a Play Selector

The PROPERTIES panel of a play selector component is divided into three tabs as mentioned in the following subsections.

General

In this tab, define how the data insertion occurs by choosing an insertion type from the dropdown list. Depending on what insertion type you have chosen, you bind the source data to a cell range and the destination to a row or column in the embedded spreadsheet or to a Universe query prompt.

You can add more than one series here without changing the appearance of the play selector. At runtime on user interaction, the insertion happens for all the series so that it's possible to make several data insertions at the same time.

If you don't want data insertion to happen automatically due to a backend data change, choose INTERACTION ONLY. Normally we choose DATA CHANGE AND INTERACTION so the play selector can work together with some other components.

Behavior

In this tab, you can configure common properties like the default selected item, whether to ignore blank cells, dynamic visibility, and animation effects. One interesting property is INTERACTION OPTIONS, which is displayed in Figure 5.39.

Figure 5.39 The Interaction Options of a Play Selector

The following properties are available:

▶ PLAY TIME
This is the amount of time needed for the entire sequence to play from the first item to the last item, if the play selector is configured to play automatically. If you use another UI component such as a column chart to show data in the destination, the display time of each item will be the play time divided by the number of items. You can click PAUSE at runtime to stay on the current item and click one of the other four buttons to quickly leave it.

▶ AUTO PLAY
As indicated by the name, if this option is enabled, the component will play automatically when the dashboard is launched.

▶ AUTO REWIND
If you want the play to rewind automatically, select AUTO REWIND.

▶ AUTO REPLAY
If you want the play to automatically repeat from the first item after reaching the end, select AUTO REPLAY. With AUTO REPLAY enabled, the sequence will keep repeating when you have launched the play and will never stop until you click the PAUSE button.

Appearance

In this tab, you can configure whether or not to show the background, the progress indicator, the REWIND and FORWARD buttons, and the PREVIOUS and NEXT buttons. These parts are displayed in Figure 5.38. You can unselect all of them, leaving only the PLAY button on the screen.

However, you cannot customize the shape of the progress indicator, nor can you configure whether or how to show its major and minor ticks. The reason is that they are fixed by SAP BusinessObjects Dashboards, with 11 major and 4 minor ticks, which are the default settings of a horizontal slider when MANUAL is selected in the play selector's PROPERTIES panel.

Practice

Now let's go through a simple example to see a play selector in use. Suppose you, as the sales director, are to present the sales data and some basic information about each of your company's 10 major branches at the year-end company meeting. It's straightforward to illustrate the sales data in a fancy chart and show the basic information such as location and number of employees in a big label. The best way to talk about the 10 branches one by one would be to use a play selector component, which selects the information from each branch automatically at intervals, and you can go on with your presentation without stopping to select another branch.

Prepare Data

All of the data is placed in a range (either input into the embedded spreadsheet or mapped from the output of some type of data connectivity, which we'll cover in the next two chapters), with one row for each branch. The sales data includes sales revenue for each quarter and the basic information such as the location and number of employees of each branch. Each column represents a data field.

We'll use a column chart to show and compare the sales revenue, and two label components to show the basic information, of the selected branch. No matter what selector component is used, we need to insert the data of a branch from the range to a new row.

The two label components will show the location and the number of employees of the branch. We'll use Excel formulas to make a meaningful name. Set cell G2 to:

=CONCATENATE(G5,": ",G3)

and cell H2 to:

=CONCATENATE(H5,": ",H3)

As a result, the data in the embedded Excel spreadsheet should be similar to what's displayed in Figure 5.40.

	A	B	C	D	E	F	G	H
1								
2		Sales revenues by Branch						
3	**Insertion**							
4								
5			Q1	Q2	Q3	Q4	Location	No. of Employees
6		Branch 1	27.00	34.60	48.70	54.80	Houston	32
7		Branch 2	43.30	52.50	33.50	30.70	Washingtoi	36
8		Branch 3	46.80	23.10	41.80	50.90	London	44
9		Branch 4	36.90	51.90	50.50	54.50	Memphis	48
10		Branch 5	23.60	34.00	32.80	50.70	San Jose	23
11		Branch 6	45.10	35.90	27.70	37.30	City 1	27
12		Branch 7	39.00	28.30	25.30	49.00	City 2	33
13		Branch 8	33.40	47.70	43.80	40.70	City 3	19
14		Branch 9	23.40	24.30	23.30	47.30	City 4	11
15		Branch 10	28.90	49.90	40.90	52.10	City 5	20
16								

Figure 5.40 Data in the Embedded Spreadsheet for the Play Selector

Add Selector

Now that we've planned the data, let's work with the play selector. From the Components view, drag a play selector component from the Selector category and drop it onto the canvas. Move it to the bottom of the canvas for a comfortable look and feel.

We'll use the play selector for the user to select a row from the cell range and insert it into a destination row. For this, in the General tab of the play selector's Properties panel, we'll set Insertion Type to Row and bind the source data to cell range Sheet1!$B$6:$H$15 and the destination to row Sheet1!$B$3:$H$3, as displayed in Figure 5.41.

Figure 5.41 Bindings for Data Insertion of the Play Selector

We don't want the presentation to play automatically, but it's good if we can go backward and forward. For this, unselect Auto Play and Auto Replay in the Behavior tab and leave Auto Rewind selected.

It takes about 20 seconds to talk about each branch. There are 10 branches here, so we'll set Play Time to 20 * 10 = 200 seconds in the Behavior tab. Pay attention to the way we calculate the play time here.

In the Appearance tab, make sure Show Rew/Fwd and Show Prev/Next are selected. You can configure whether or not to show the background or progress indicator as you want.

Add Components for the Selected Branch

By now the play selector is displaying properly and has been configured to insert the data of the selected branch into a row. In this step, we'll add the necessary components to display the data. Let's use a column chart and a label. You can choose other components to represent the same data based on your preferences.

This phase can be divided into three steps as illustrated next.

1. **Lay out the required UI components.**
   Drag a column chart and two label components onto the canvas. Put them on the top of the canvas, above the play selector, with the column chart to the right of the labels. Position the labels vertically. Resize them for an agreeable look and feel.

2. **Set the properties for the column chart.**
   Bind the title to cell Sheet1!$B$2, and the subtitle to cell Sheet1!$B$29, which stores the name of the selected branch. Select By Series for Data, bind the category labels to Sheet1!$C$5:$F$5, which stores the names of the four quarters, add a series named "Sales revenue," and bind its values to Sheet1!$C$3:$F$3, where the sales revenues of the selected branch are stored.

   The General tab of the Properties panel of the column chart should be similar to what's displayed in Figure 5.42.

3. **Set properties for the labels.**
   Bind the two label components to cells Sheet1!$G$2 and Sheet1!$H$2 to show the basic information of the branch. If you want to display more information about the branch, add more labels.

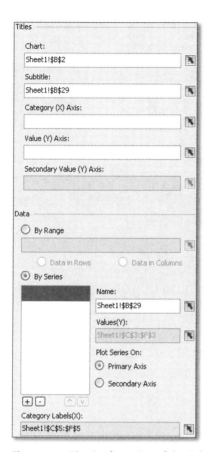

Figure 5.42 The Configuration of the Column Chart

Now we're done. At runtime, click the PLAY button to begin the presentation. The data of each branch will be displayed on the chart along with the labels, in sequence, starting from the first branch. Each lasts for 20 seconds. If you want to spend more time on one of the branches, click the PAUSE button. To quickly go to the next or previous branch, click the corresponding buttons.

Figure 5.43 shows the dashboard at runtime. The left side shows a screenshot from the beginning of the presentation, while the right side shows that the selector has stepped to the fifth branch.

Figure 5.43 The Final Result of the Play Selector

5.2.4 Calendar

A calendar is often used to display dates in years, months, and weeks. A calendar component in SAP BusinessObjects Dashboards is designed for the user to select a single date from a visually intuitive dashboard.

This component is located in the OTHER category in the COMPONENTS view. It can be regarded as a selector for the user to choose one date from many.

There are an almost unlimited number of dates to choose from, making it impossible for a combo box to display the dates for the user to choose from. A calendar component solves this problem by displaying the days of a month in a fixed area, with inside buttons to go to another month or year, as displayed in Figure 5.44.

◄◄	◄	April		2010	►	►►
Mon	Tue	Wed	Thu	Fri	Sat	Sun
			1	2	3	4
5	6	7	8	9	10	11
12	13	14	15	16	17	18
19	20	21	22	23	24	25
26	27	28	29	30		

Figure 5.44 A Typical Calendar Component in SAP BusinessObjects Dashboards

You can click the ◄ or ► button to go to the previous or the next month, and the ◄◄ or ►► button to go the previous or next year.

When to Use a Calendar

You can use a calendar control in your dashboard so the user can select a date from a large range in a user-friendly way.

Without a calendar, you can achieve this with three or four cascading combo boxes for years, months, weeks, and days or with several input fields for the user to enter a date in a quite complex way. Moreover, it takes a lot of effort to calculate the actual date. A calendar control is the most elegant tool for this purpose. Not only is it agreeable to the user, but it also saves a lot of design time.

How to Use a Calendar

You can give the calendar component a title to provide the user a hint about it; for example, "Please select the start date." For a clean look and feel, we often leave this property empty.

General

As a selector component, a calendar supports data insertion, enabling you to insert either the day or date into a single cell as the destination.

▶ DAY
   The day of the month of the selected date is an integer. For example, if the currently selected date is 12/31/2009, the day is 31.

▶ DATE
   The value of the selected date is a variable of the type date. To make the insertion work, you need to set the format of the destination cell in the embedded spreadsheet by right-clicking it, selecting SET CELL FORMAT, and setting its type to DATE. You can then configure how to display the date, such as 03/14/01, 14-Mar-01, and so on.

You make your choice based on the requirements. If you want to display the selected date in a label with a customized format, select DATE and set the destination cell's format. If you just want the numeric value of the day in the month, select DAY.

You can also insert the month or year of the selected date into a single cell in the embedded spreadsheet, also as an integer. However, you cannot insert the week of the selected date into the destination.

Behavior

▶ DEFAULT DATE

You configure what date is displayed by default when the dashboard is launched through DEFAULT DATE. If you want it to display the current date each time the dashboard is launched, select USE CURRENT DATE and leave it to SAP BusinessObjects Dashboards to calculate the selected date.

If USE CUSTOM DATE is selected you can either enter the year, month, and day in the input fields, thus hard-coding the default date, or bind each to a single cell, the value of which can be either calculated or passed from Flash Vars or something like it. If you want more flexibility in controlling the default date, select USE CUSTOM DATE.

▶ CALENDAR LIMITS

No matter what date is displayed and selected by default, the user can select an arbitrary date from the calendar at runtime. If you want to restrict what date can be selected, thus only passing a valid date to the backend, select ENABLE CALENDAR LIMITS and specify the date range that the user can choose from. For example, say you want to compare the sales revenue of each branch on a year-to-year basis, thus requiring the user to select a month first. The month shouldn't be earlier than when your company was founded or later than today.

With ENABLE CALENDAR LIMITS selected, you have the option to set the start and end year and month, as displayed in Figure 5.45.

Figure 5.45 Setting the Minimum and Maximum Year and Month

As you can see from this figure, for each of the four properties, you can either enter a valid integer or bind it to a single cell in the embedded spreadsheet to make it dynamic.

Appearance

In the TEXT tab, you set the formats of each part of the calendar component. The formats include font family, size, style, alignment, and color. Position is only available for the title.

In the COLOR tab, you set the colors or background colors of the many parts of the calendar component, such as the mouse-over color for a date and the button and symbol color of the four buttons (previous and next year and month).

You can get the meanings of most properties simply from their names.

> **Note**
>
> The disabled symbol color and disabled button color are used to show the buttons when the currently displayed month or year is the first or last available one.

For example, if we have defined the calendar limits as January 2010 to March 2010, and the calendar currently displays March 2010, the buttons for the previous year, next month, and next year will be disabled, with a green background and gray color, as displayed in Figure 5.46.

Figure 5.46 Buttons Are Displayed when out of Range

5.3 Advanced Single-Value Components

In Chapter 4 we discussed some basic UI components used to represent a single numeric value such as a gauge that are provided in the single value category. We'll cover the rest of those components in this section.

5.3.1 Dual Slider

As mentioned in Chapter 4, SAP BusinessObjects Dashboards provides horizontal and vertical sliders that can be used both as output components to represent a single value and as input for the user to adjust a value.

A dual slider, as the name indicates, can represent two values. The user can adjust the two values in the same component by moving the sliders.

In the CATEGORY view, there's only one dual slider in the SINGLE VALUE category for some themes, while for some other themes there are two, which are almost identical, differing in the marker shape only, as displayed in Figure 5.47.

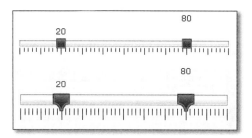

Figure 5.47 Dual Sliders with Different Markers

You can see from this figure that the high value is displayed higher than the low value. This is done to avoid overlapping when the low and high values are equal or very near. Otherwise, the user may have difficulty reading the values when they are equal.

When to Use a Dual Slider

A dual slider component is often used to represent the minimum and maximum values of a field. It makes little sense to represent two unrelated fields.

You can choose this component if you want the user to adjust both the minimum and the maximum values as a range. For example, say you're assigned to create a dashboard where the user can search products with a quantity sold within a certain range. You can use a dual slider for the user to specify the lowest and highest values of quantity sold.

How to Use a Dual Slider

The PROPERTIES panel of a dual slider component is very similar to that of a slider, including the scale, slider movement, and whether and how to show ticks and alerts.

One difference is that you need to specify both the low value and the high value for a dual slider. If you bind either to a cell, the corresponding new value will be inserted into that cell when the user moves the corresponding low or high marker.

The low value can be equal to, but never greater than, the high value. At runtime, you cannot move the low marker in front of the high marker. The case is similar for the high value.

The minimum limit and maximum limit define the scale of the entire slider, similar to a single slider.

The values should conform to the rule that the low value shouldn't be greater than the high value, and both should be within the scale defined by the minimum and maximum limits. Though the default values can break this rule, at runtime, the user will never have a chance to break it after moving the markers.

Another difference is that you cannot select ENABLE PLAY BUTTON for a dual slider, while you can for a common slider.

5.3.2   Spinner

A spinner is an input component with which the user adjusts a value by clicking the up or down arrow or by entering a numeric value. Compared to a slider, it takes less space to display.

A spinner is often used together with other components to help analyze the impact of one value on some other measures.

When to Use a Spinner

Choose a spinner component if you want the user to adjust a value more accurately. With a slider, the user moves the mouse to change the value but it's difficult to make slight adjustments. For example, with a scale of 1 to 100, it's difficult to decrease or increase the value by 1 with a slider, while it's very easy with a spinner.

How to Use a Spinner

To use a spinner, find it in the SELECTOR category or by its name in the COMPONENTS view and drag and drop it onto the canvas. You can use the mouse to resize its width but not to change its height. If you want to change the height, go to the APPEARANCE tab and set the font size for VALUE.

The PROPERTIES panel of a spinner is very similar to that of a slider. Some properties specific to spinners are explained next.

General

In the GENERAL tab, you can set a title for the spinner to show the user what value the spinner represents.

You can enter a numeric value in the DATA field, either an integer or a decimal, as the spinner's default value. You can also bind it to a single cell in the embedded spreadsheet, the value of which is used as the default. At runtime, the new value changed by the user will be inserted into this cell.

You need define the scale for a valid value by setting the minimum limit and the maximum limit.

Behavior

Pay attention to INCREMENT property here, which defines how much the value changes when the user clicks the up or down arrow. At runtime, the user can only change the value to a multiple of the increment you define here. That is, if the default value is 0.2 and the increment is 1, clicking the up arrow will take you to 1, not 1.2. Similarly, if the default value is 3 and the increment is 10, clicking the up arrow will take you to 10, not 13.

As a best practice, make the increment smaller if you want to provide a slighter and thus more accurate adjustment of the value.

The minimum or maximum limit of the spinner's scale can be either fixed to the one you defined in GENERAL tab or be infinite if you choose OPEN instead of FIXED in the corresponding combo box.

If you just want to use the spinner as an output component for value display but not as an input, unselect ENABLE INTERACTION. The value of the spinner can then only be updated when the cell it binds to is updated, while the user can't click to change the value.

Appearance and Alerts

The properties in these two tabs are very similar to those of other components. Pay attention to alerts, which are very useful to display the status of the current value.

5.3.3   Play Control

A play control is an input component for the user to set a numeric value. It looks like a media player with five buttons: PREVIOUS, REWIND, PLAY/PAUSE, FORWARD, and NEXT, similar to the play selector described in Section 5.2.3.

Figure 5.48 shows a sample play control component with the current value on the top, a horizontal slider as the progress indicator in the middle, and the buttons on the bottom.

Figure 5.48 A Play Control Component

You change the value by clicking the PREVIOUS, REWIND, FORWARD, or NEXT button. There is no way to enter a value directly. When you click the PLAY button, the component will automatically increment the value. You can click the PAUSE button to remain on the current value for a longer time or the other four buttons to quickly jump to another value.

A play control differs from a spinner in appearance but is similar in representing and manipulating a single numeric value. On the other hand, its appearance is very similar to that of a play selector, with the difference being that it inserts the current numeric value to a single cell, while a play selector inserts a row or column from a cell range in the embedded spreadsheet to another row or column.

When to Use a Play Control

Choose a play control component either for its unique appearance or because it increments the value at equal intervals automatically without user interaction.

The value you adjust with a play control component is often used in another component. For example, you can use a play control to adjust the product price and analyze the corresponding sales revenue and quantity sold in another chart. Within a reasonable range, the play control automatically increases the price by your specified increment, and the charts help you analyze the impact on sales revenue and quantity sold on each price.

How to Use a Play Control

Let's go over the different settings.

General

Here you set the data and scale of the component, the same way you do for a spinner or a slider. When you bind data to a single cell in the embedded spreadsheet, the value of that cell becomes the default value of the play control when the dashboard is loaded. If the content of that cell is not a numeric value but some characters, it will be treated as 0. When the user updates the value by clicking the PLAY button, the new value is also inserted into that cell.

Behavior

Here you set the user interaction behavior. The increment is the smallest amount that the value can be changed. For example, if the default value is 0 and the increment is 3, then you cannot set the value to 2.

When you click the PREVIOUS or NEXT button, the value is decreased or increased by the amount of the increment. If you click REWIND or FORWARD, the value is changed an amount that is four times the increment amount.

To set the increment, you can either enter a numeric value, integer, or decimal, in the input field or bind it to a cell in the embedded spreadsheet.

The play options, including PLAY TIME, AUTO PLAY, AUTO REWIND, and AUTO REPLAY, are exactly the same as for a play selector. For more information about their meanings and how to use them, refer to the corresponding part in Section 5.2.3.

Appearance

In this tab you can configure whether or not to show each part of a play control component, including the title, the current value, the slider, the REWIND and FORWARD buttons, and the PREVIOUS and NEXT buttons.

As with a play selector, you cannot configure whether or not to show the ticks. There will always be 11 major ticks and 4 minor ticks.

If you want to show both the title and the value, choose a different position for each of them to avoid overlap.

5.3.4 Value

A value component displays a numeric value in a rectangle. It's very similar to a spinner in appearance and properties, described in Section 5.3.2. However, the user adjusts its value by dragging the mouse up or down or double-clicking it and then editing its value inside the component.

You can regard a value component as a grid in the grid component, which we'll describe in Section 5.4.3.

When to Use a Value

Choose a value component when you want to display a single numeric value in your dashboard and at the same time allow the user to adjust the value by dragging the mouse higher or lower.

A value component is the same as a spinner in functionality. The difference is that with a spinner, the user can adjust the value incrementally by clicking the up or down arrow, while with a value he can just drag the mouse to change the numeric value. Usually you choose between them based on your preferences.

How to Use a Value

The PROPERTIES panel of a value is almost the same as that of a spinner, with some differences in BEHAVIOR tab as displayed in Figure 5.49.

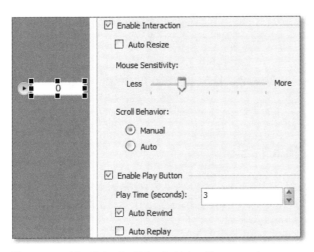

Figure 5.49 The Behavior Tab of a Value Component

You can deselect ENABLE INTERACTION to not allow the user to change the value manually. With interaction enabled, you can set other options like MOUSE SENSITIVITY and scroll direction.

▶ AUTO RESIZE
You can select AUTO RESIZE if you want the component to resize automatically based on the length of the value it's displaying. Pay attention to the length.

▶ MOUSE SENSITIVITY
MOUSE SENSITIVITY defines how sensitive the mouse is during dragging up or down to change the value. You can adjust it by moving the slider from less sensitive on the left to more on the right. Basically, if you want the values to be changed slowly, make the mouse less sensitive. When designing your dashboard, you can try out the least sensitivity by moving the slider all the way to the left, and the most sensitivity to find out the best-fit sensitivity for you.

▶ SCROLL BEHAVIOR
This property controls how the value is changed when you drag the mouse — either AUTO or MANUAL. MANUAL is the default, which means the value is increased or decreased each time you drag the mouse up or down, and it stops when you stop dragging, regardless of whether your mouse button is released or still being held down.

If you select AUTO, the value will keep increasing or decreasing when you hold down the mouse and will stop when you release it. You can choose based on the users' preferences.

Unlike a spinner, you can select ENABLE PLAY BUTTON here, allowing the value to be changed automatically.

5.4   Displaying Data in a Table

SAP BusinessObjects Dashboards 4.0 provides three UI components to display a range of data in a table style: list view and spreadsheet table in the SELECTORS category and grid in the OTHER category.

5.4.1   List View

A list view component displays a range of data in a list view, similar to a common table. You can use it both as a display component and as a selector.

As a display component, a list view displays data in a cell range in the embedded Excel spreadsheet, treating the first row as the header. At runtime, the user can adjust the width of each column but cannot adjust the width of each row. The user can also sort the rows by each data field, in either ascending or descending order, by clicking on the column header.

Using a list view as a selector component, the user can click on a row to choose it, thus triggering the data insertion action. Only one row can be selected at a time.

When to Use a List View

Choose this component when you want to display data in a table-like style, as a supplement to the charts. For example, say you've used a line chart to show the trend of changes in the price of some stock over a period of time. Now you add a list view below the chart to list the prices (or compare them to that of another stock), giving the user more detailed information.

How to Use a List View

The PROPERTIES panel of a list view component is divided into three categories: GENERAL, BEHAVIOR, and APPEARANCE. Most properties are similar to those in other components. In the following section, we'll explain some properties in the GENERAL and APPEARANCE tabs.

General

▶ DISPLAY DATA

You bind display data to a cell range with N rows and M columns in the embedded spreadsheet or some fields of a Universe query that contains the data you want to display. SAP BusinessObjects Dashboards will automatically treat the first row as the column headers and list the rows below in sequence.

SAP BusinessObjects Dashboards automatically defines the width of each row and each column. It determines the width that is exactly enough to display the data. If the width of the list view component is more than enough to display all data fields, the last column will be stretched wider. You can click the CONFIGURE COLUMNS BELOW DISPLAY DATA button to customize the width of each column, as displayed in Figure 5.50.

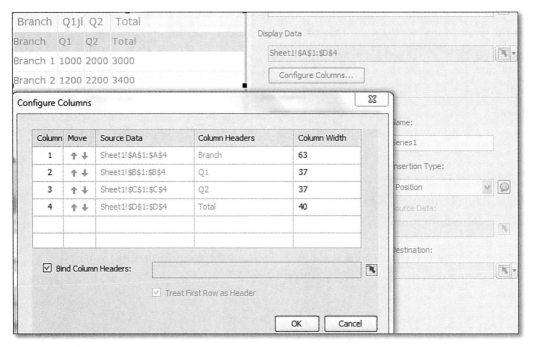

Figure 5.50 Customize Column Headers and Column Width

The column headers default to the texts in the first row. With Bind Column Headers selected, you can bind the headers to another row or column in the embedded spreadsheet. You may want to do this when your display data is all about business data, while the headers are defined elsewhere.

Another way to change the column headers is to unselect Bind Column Headers and then double-click any Column Headers field to enter your new label.

SAP BusinessObjects Dashboards automatically calculates the column widths. To change them, double-click any field and enter a numeric value. If you set zero (0) for the width or leave it empty, SAP BusinessObjects Dashboards will display the column with the minimum width. But this isn't the case for the last column, which will occupy all the space left. Note that the settings here only affect the default width of each column. At runtime, the user can adjust their width by moving the gridlines between adjacent columns.

If the height of the list view is bigger than what's needed, empty rows will be added below the last row, as shown in Figure 5.51.

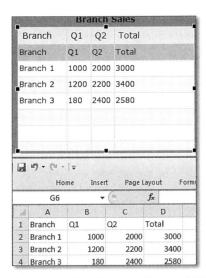

Figure 5.51 Blank Rows are Displayed if There's Extra Space in a List View

In this figure, the embedded spreadsheet is displayed on the bottom, and the list view component in the canvas is displayed on the top. Pay attention to the redundant rows and extra space in the last column.

If the list view component is too small to display the data, a scrollbar will appear horizontally or vertically or both. When you resize the list view on the canvas at design time, the columns widths will not change.

Data Insertion

As a selector, a list view supports data insertion, although only three insertion types are available, as listed next.

▶ POSITION

You insert the position of the selected row into a cell that is bound to DESTINA-TION. The position of the first row is 1.

> **Note**
>
> The position here is the position of the row in the cell range specified for display data, not that of the selected row in list view at runtime. That is, at runtime, you can change the order of rows by sorting on a column. For example, in Figure 5.51, you can sort by total in a descending order, and thus branch 3 will be displayed in the first row. If you click to select the row of branch 3, the position is still 3, not 1.

▶ Value

Similar to the method for other components, you select a row or column as the source data and insert its value into a single cell as the destination.

▶ Row

As for other components, you select a cell range as the source data and insert a row into the destination. The number of rows in the source data should be equal to that of display data.

Appearance

In the Layout tab you can configure whether to show the vertical or horizontal gridlines in the view by selecting the corresponding checkbox. If gridlines are enabled, you can also set their color. However, your changes here will not affect the gridlines in the column; they will always display with default colors.

In the Text tab you can format the title (Branch Sales in Figure 5.51), the headers (Branch, Q1, Q2, and Total in Figure 5.51), and the labels. You can also configure whether and where to show the title.

For a better look and feel, you can set colors for many items in the Color tab. Typically you may want to set the header background color to make it stand out. The rows are displayed in alternating colors with a frequency of 1. That is, the even-number rows are one color, and the odd-numbered rows are another. You can configure the colors of the odd and even rows by specifying Row 1 Color and Row 2 Color, respectively. When you click on a column header, you will see a sort symbol displayed on it, the color of which can be customized in this tab through Symbol Color.

Practice

Figure 5.52 shows a sample list view component at runtime, with the title displayed on the top center, headers centered, and the colors of the header label, header background, row 1 color, and row 2 color customized.

In this screenshot the rows are sorted by total, in ascending order, as indicated by the up arrow in the Total column header. Currently the third row is selected, which is the first row in the embedded spreadsheet. That's why the label below says the currently selected row position is 1, not 3.

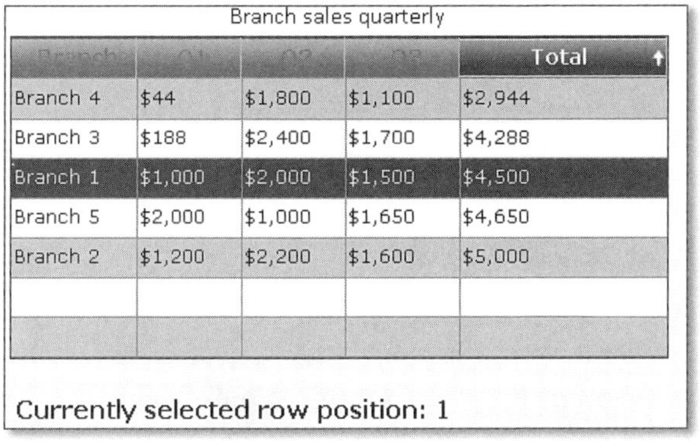

Branch sales quarterly				
Branch	Q1	Q2	Q3	**Total**
Branch 4	$44	$1,800	$1,100	$2,944
Branch 3	$188	$2,400	$1,700	$4,288
Branch 1	$1,000	$2,000	$1,500	$4,500
Branch 5	$2,000	$1,000	$1,650	$4,650
Branch 2	$1,200	$2,200	$1,600	$5,000

Currently selected row position: 1

Figure 5.52 A Practical List View at Runtime

5.4.2 Spreadsheet Table

A spreadsheet table component is similar to a list view in that both display data stored in a cell range in a table style. It can also be used as a selector.

What you see in the embedded spreadsheet is almost exactly what you get in the spreadsheet table. Most formats of the cells in the embedded spreadsheet, including the color and size, are reflected in this component. This is what a list view component cannot do. It only displays the data of the cell range, with all formats ignored.

One limitation of a spreadsheet table is that it currently only supports the font Verdana, which results in some minor differences between the spreadsheet table component and the embedded Excel spreadsheet.

However, a spreadsheet table is not as configurable as a list view. A spreadsheet table:

▶ Doesn't have a title

▶ Doesn't have any column headers

▶ Spaces the columns evenly and doesn't allow the dashboard designer to customize their widths

▶ Provides no alternative color

In contrast to a list view, there are no redundant rows in a spreadsheet table component, nor will there be any extra space for the last column. At runtime, the user cannot adjust the width of a column or sort by any field.

When to Use a Spreadsheet Table

Look at a spreadsheet table component as a duplication of a cell range in the embedded spreadsheet. Like a list view, choose this component if you want to display data in a table style.

The list view and the spreadsheet table components both have advantages and disadvantages. With their different functionalities in mind, you can choose one based on your requirements. For example, if you want the user to be able to sort the records by a data field or display the records in alternating colors, you would choose a list view. On the other hand, if there are specific requirements for the cell formats, especially when you want to display different cells of one row in different formats such as color and data format, you have to use a spreadsheet table, format each cell in the embedded spreadsheet and then bind the display data of the spreadsheet table to that cell range.

Using any other UI component in SAP BusinessObjects Dashboards 4.0, you cannot display a row of data in different formats. As you can see from Figure 5.53, the second cell in the second row is black text with a yellow gray and aligned to the middle, while the third cell in the third row is in a different color and aligned to the right.

If there's too much data to display (for example, over 100 rows and 10 columns), using a spreadsheet table may introduce a severe performance problem because it will copy the format of the many cells into the spreadsheet table component. In this case, if it's not necessary to retain the formats of the cells, you should use a list view instead.

Figure 5.53 shows a case when a spreadsheet table has to be used.

Branch	SalesRevenue				Quantity sold		
	Q1	Q2	Q3	Total	Q1	Q2	Q3
Branch 1	1000	2000	1500	4500	34	22	28
Branch 2	1200	2200	1600	5000	49	88	30
Branch 3	188	2400	1700	4288	12	19	15
Branch 4	44	1800	1100	2944	66	39	71
Branch 5	2000	1000	1650	4650	42	33	29

Figure 5.53 A Spreadsheet Table View at Runtime

Pay attention to the different colors of the cells, and note that the column headers are in two rows. No other component can achieve this effect.

To better understand the differences, you can compare Figure 5.53 to Figure 5.52 in the previous section, where we discussed list views.

How to Use a Spreadsheet Table

To use a spreadsheet table component, drag it from the SELECTORS category and drop it onto the canvas. You can move or resize a spreadsheet table component in the canvas.

If scroll bars are not enabled in the PROPERTIES panel, the resizing happens both horizontally and vertically simultaneously; you cannot resize it on one direction only. Unlike in a list view, when resized, the width and the height of each column and row are increased or decreased in proportion. For example, there will be no more redundant rows when the spreadsheet is stretched very tall.

The PROPERTIES panel is divided into three categories: GENERAL, BEHAVIOR, and APPEARANCE.

General

▶ DISPLAY DATA

Here you bind display data to a cell range in the embedded spreadsheet. Note that there will be no column header in the table. If you want to show the column headers, often in the first row of the component, set the background color in the embedded Excel spreadsheet.

For example, to display a spreadsheet table as displayed in Figure 5.53, the source data in the embedded Excel spreadsheet should be as displayed in Figure 5.54.

	B	C	D	E	F	G	H	I	J
1									
2		Branch		SalesRevenue				Quantity sold	
3			Q1	Q2	Q3	Total	Q1	Q2	Q3
4		Branch 1	1000	2000	1500	**4500**	34	22	28
5		Branch 2	1200	2200	1600	**5000**	49	88	30
6		Branch 3	188	2400	1700	**4288**	12	19	**15**
7		Branch 4	44	1800	1100	***2944***	66	39	71
8		Branch 5	2000	1000	1650	**4650**	42	33	29

Figure 5.54 Data in the Embedded Spreadsheet Should Already be Formatted

Keep in mind that you can select any range you want in the embedded spreadsheet, and the spreadsheet table will display it almost exactly the same. Note that the colors of each cell are retained, but bold and italic are not. However, underlining is retained, though it works a little strangely. You may notice that underlining is not displayed at first, and you need resize the spreadsheet table component a little to see it.

▶ DATA INSERTION

As a selector, the spreadsheet table supports data insertion operations. Only two types are available: position and row. Their meanings and how to use them are the same as in a list view, as explained in Section 5.4.1.

Behavior

▶ ROW SELECTABILITY

One property specific to the spreadsheet table is row selectability, which indicates what rows can be selected. Only a selectable row can be selected to trigger data insertion and changes into another color when selected. Typically, you may want to unselect the header rows to make them unselectable so that it makes no difference when the user clicks on them.

▶ ENABLE SCROLL BARS

By default, scroll bars are disabled when the component takes up just enough space to hold its contents. If you resize the spreadsheet table component to make it smaller, the entire component, including the width, height, and font sizes, are reduced in proportion to adjust to the new size.

When you select this option, resizing the component to make it smaller or larger will not affect its size. Instead, the component remains the same size, and a scroll bar is displayed when necessary. What you're resizing is a transparent "container" to display the table, not the component itself. You can test this by resizing the spreadsheet table with ENABLE SCROLL BARS selected.

You can set the horizontal and vertical scroll bar to ON, OFF, or AUTO. The scroll bar will always show if ON is selected and never show if OFF is selected. If AUTO is selected, the scroll bar will only show when the space is insufficient to display the entire component. For a clean look and feel, it's suggested that you select AUTO.

The property TABLE SCALE defines how much space is used to display the spreadsheet table component. Increasing it will increase the size of the component, while decreasing it will decrease its size. The size of the component is related to the increase or decrease and has nothing to do with its actual value. However, changing this value will never affect the size of the space, or container, that holds the component.

Appearance

SAP BusinessObjects Dashboards will automatically insert a gridline for each row and each column when SHOW GRIDLINES is selected. Otherwise, there will be no gridlines in the component. However, if you've defined gridlines for cells in the embedded spreadsheet, these gridlines will always appear, whether SHOW GRIDLINES is selected or not.

You can customize the colors in many parts of the spreadsheet table component in the COLOR tab, including the gridline color and the row selected color.

5.4.3   Grid

In terms of visual appearance, a grid component displays a range of data in a table style. Each cell is the same size, in contrast to a list view or a spreadsheet table. Moreover, there's no column header in a grid component.

As to the functionalities, a grid component differs from a list view and a spreadsheet table in that besides having the data represented in a table format, the user can modify the values. As a result, a grid can act as both an input and an output component.

Figure 5.55 shows a typical grid, where the sales revenues of each branch in the last five years are listed together in a grid. You could create a chart on top of the grid and change the values for any variable in the grid to analyze its impact.

	FY05	FY06	FY07	FY08	FY09
Atherton	$19.7	$17.1	$18.3	$14.8	$19.8
Berkeley	$14.4	$17.0	$16.4	$16.7	$19.3
Carmel	$18.8	$13.5	$18.7	$13.9	$15.7
Cupertino	$12.0	$16.2	$17.5	$17.8	$13.8
Fremont	$19.2	$15.6	$19.6	$15.9	$14.4
Irvine	$18.9	$14.6	$16.7	$12.1	$13.9
Milpitas	$18.7	$17.8	$14.0	$18.5	$13.7
Orange County	$17.0	$19.4	$17.1	$17.3	$17.3
San Francisco	$14.4	$14.0	$13.9	$15.4	$18.3

Figure 5.55 A Typical Grid Showing Multiple Values

When to Use a Grid

Choose a grid if you want to display multiple values together and/or give the user the ability to change values at runtime. For example, when making your budget plan, you can display the relative expenses and incomes in a grid, which the user can modify to analyze the budget on the fly. In addition to numeric values, you can also use a grid to show texts, such as the names of branches in your company.

How to Use a Grid

You can use a grid as an output component to represent data in a table, similar to a list view or a spreadsheet, but you cannot use it as a selector.

You can also use it as an input component, allowing the user to manipulate each value. To change the value, the end user can either drag his mouse up or down to make the value bigger or smaller in the cell or double-click the value and then modify it directly. From this perspective, a grid is similar to a gauge or a dial, which can also be either input or output components. However, a gauge can only display one value, while a grid can display more.

The grid's PROPERTIES panel is divided into four categories, as explained in the following subsections.

General

Click the BIND button below DATA and bind it to the cell range in the embedded spreadsheet containing the values you want to display. At runtime, when the user makes changes to the values of certain cells, the new values are written back to the cell range defined here. This property is for the grid as an output.

Scale, on the other hand, is for the grid as an input. You can edit the value of a cell in the grid by either dragging your mouse up or down or double-clicking the value and entering a new value. Scale here defines the range of a valid value. That is, you cannot enter a value, or drag the value to, less than the minimum limit or greater than the maximum limit. If you enter a value beyond the scale, the new value will not be accepted.

The original data may not fall into the scale you define here. For example, if a value is 120.3, and the scale you define is 0 to 100, when launched, the grid will show 120.3. However, if you change the value to be within that range, you will have no chance to revert to the original value, which is beyond the scale.

To define the limit, enter an integer or bind it to a cell in the embedded spread-sheet.

Behavior

▶ INCREMENT

As we mentioned, you can change a value in the grid by dragging the mouse up or down. Increment defines how much the value is increased or decreased on each move. You can either enter a constant integer in the input field or bind it to a cell in the embedded spreadsheet, which contains the step value. For example, you can let the user customize this value through an input control, pass it to the embedded spreadsheet through Flash Var or something else, and bind the increment to that value.

▶ LIMITS

As mentioned in the "General" section, you can set the limits of a valid value that the user can change the old value to. If you don't want to set maximum or minimum limits for the values, you can set it to OPEN instead of FIXED in the corresponding dropdown list.

When OPEN is selected, the corresponding limit property in the GENERAL tab is disabled.

▶ ENABLE INTERACTION

If you want the user to be able to change the values, thus making a grid an input component, select ENABLE INTERACTION. Then you have the option to control mouse sensitivity and scroll behavior, which controls the way the user uses the mouse to change the value.

These two properties are exactly the same as those of a value component, as described in Section 5.3.4. Briefly, mouse sensitivity defines how sensitive the mouse is when you drag up or down to change the value, and scroll behavior controls how the value is changed when you drag the mouse; you can select either AUTO or MANUAL. For more information, please refer to Section 5.3.4.

Appearance

Two properties specific to a grid component are the vertical margin and horizontal margin, which control the space between every two vertically or horizontally adjacent grids. By default, they are both 0, leaving a minimal space between every two adjacent grids. You can adjust them to create an agreeable look and feel.

In the TEXT tab you can set the number format of the values. Note that there's one special format called FROM SPREADSHEET, which uses the format you specify for each cell. Only the number format you set in the embedded spreadsheet is kept—not the color, font style, or alignment.

Alerts

You can enable alerts in this tab to show different colors for different values based on the alert thresholds you define here.

Using alerts is the same as for other components such as a column chart. You can refer to the corresponding sections for more information.

5.5   Using Art

SAP BusinessObjects Dashboards 4.0 provides some special UI components in the art and backgrounds category to enhance your design. In Chapter 4, we introduced some backgrounds, and here let's talk about art.

5.5.1   Image Component

You can use the image components to add graphics, logos, custom JPEG backgrounds, and SWF movies to your dashboard. Adding artwork can help make your dashboard more appealing and professional.

The image component supports the following file formats.

► JPG
► PNG
► GIF
► BMP
► SWF

> **Note**
>
> The SWF file can also be generated from SAP BusinessObjects Dashboards itself, but these SWF files can only be linked out of the main presentation rather than embedded in it. This will be further explained in the next section.

When to Use an Image Component

You use image components to include a logo or use a graphical background for your dashboard. There is really no restriction on using images, but keep it in mind that too many images may distract the users from the really useful information they need, so we recommend using images only when necessary.

How to Use an Image Component

To use an image component, first drop it onto the canvas. Then click the IMPORT button to select the external image or Flash file you want to import into the dashboard model.

General

Prior to selecting the file, if you select the RESIZE IMAGE TO COMPONENT option, the image will automatically fit itself to the current size of the image component. Otherwise, the image component will be resized to show the image at its actual size.

When importing external files into the image components, you must choose whether or not to embed the file. If you choose to embed a loaded image, it becomes a part of the completed model so that you can publish and distribute your model as a stand-alone file. If you choose not to embed the file, the file will be loaded into the exported dashboard when needed at runtime. SAP Business-Objects Dashboards will generate a subfolder with the same name as the SWF file during export and put the images in that folder.

The main advantages of embedding files are as follows:

▶ Embedded files enable you to distribute your entire dashboard in a single file.

▶ Dynamic visibility is faster because reloading is not necessary.

▶ Embedded files maintain their state when hidden with dynamic visibility.

The main advantages of not embedding files are as follows:

▶ Runtime performance might increase because the external files are unloaded when they are hidden with dynamic visibility.

▶ Load times will be shorter for the application because external files are loaded only when necessary.

▶ The dashboard does not need to be re-exported if the external file changes.

Based on the advantages and disadvantages you can choose whether to select the EMBED FILE option.

If you are importing an SWF file generated by Xcelsius or SAP BusinessObjects Dashboards itself, you'll see a warning message informing you that this kind of file can't be embedded into the model you're editing and can only be linked to it. This doesn't mean you can't embed a dashboard generated by SAP Business-Objects Dashboards itself. It means the SWF will not be embedded but will be linked, and when your dashboard is exported, a subfolder will be generated that contains the SWF file you want to embed.

You can change the transparency level of the image and block the mouse event on it. To hide the background color of the SWF file so that the components behind it are visible, you can select the HIDE SWF BACKGROUND COLOR checkbox.

5.5.2   Shapes

In addition to images and flash movies, sometimes you might want some simple drawings on your canvas. SAP BusinessObjects Dashboards 4.0 provides shape and line components. We'll discuss lines in the following section. Here we'll show you two shape components: rectangle and ellipse. As their names suggest, you can draw rectangles and ellipses on your canvas. You can also fill them with colors.

When to Use Shapes

Shapes are often used to assist in layout the same way background components do, but background components all have their own visual styles. They could have rounded corners, shadow effects, special drawings on them, and fixed gradient patterns. So, what if you want pure shapes or you want the gradient pattern you like to group relevant components together?

Figure 5.56 shows an example of using shapes to assist in layout.

As you can see from this figure, we used three rectangle components to divide the canvas into three sections, and we set gradient fills inside them. The idea is basically the same as using background components, but with shapes everything is nice and clean. There are no fancy effects at all, just rectangles with fills. It's the information that users care about most, not the artwork, so it could be a good idea if there is no flashy artwork to distract them from the most important information on the dashboard.

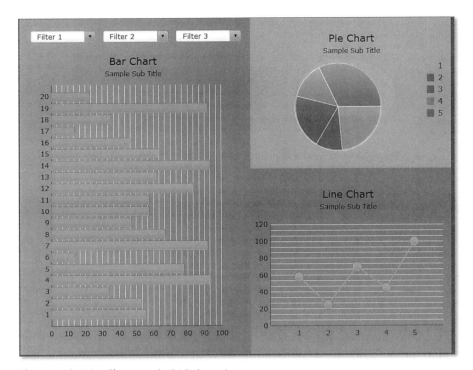

Figure 5.56 Using Shapes to Assist in Layout

How to Use Shapes

You add the rectangle component and the ellipse component the same way you add other components, but there is a trick to how to resize them. If you want to maintain the ratio of the two sides of a rectangle or the two axes of an ellipse, you can hold down $\boxed{\texttt{Shift}}$ while you resize the component on the canvas. The ratio is now locked. This is particularly useful when you want to create a square or a perfect circle. First, add the component to the canvas. By default, the rectangle component creates a square and the ellipse component creates a perfect circle, so you just hold down $\boxed{\texttt{Shift}}$ to resize the component to the size you want and it's done.

Now let's take a look at the properties specific to shapes components.

General

► ENABLE BORDER

By default, rectangles and ellipses have a black border of thickness 1. You can change the color, thickness, and transparency of the borders. As you can see in

Figure 5.57, we've created an ellipse with an orange border ❶ and adjusted the border's thickness to 6 and transparency to 80%.

Figure 5.57 The Border Properties for the Rectangle and the Ellipse Components

▶ FILL

You can fill the rectangle or the ellipse with colors. There are four fill types:

▶ This first type is NONE, which simply means the shape is no filled with anything. With nothing filled, the inside of the shape is transparent. Another component that overlaps with the shape component is visible even if it lies beneath the shape.

▶ The second type is SOLID. It just fills the shape with a single color. You can choose the color you want. And if you still want to see the overlapped components that lie beneath the shape, you can give the fill a higher transparency setting. Figure 5.58 shows a rectangle with a solid fill and transparency 50% so that the bubble chart behind it is still visible.

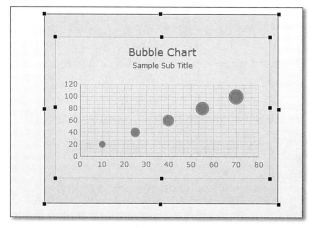

Figure 5.58 A Rectangle Filled with 50% Transparent Solid Light Gray that Covers a Bubble Chart

296

▶ The third type is LINEAR(GRADIENT). When you select this type, the properties GRADIENT PREVIEW and ROTATION are enabled. To define the gradient, use the markers under the color stripe in the GRADIENT PREVIEW property. Click on each marker to set the color to the transparency of the corresponding position on the color stripe. You can also add more markers by clicking on the position you want on the color stripe. To remove redundant markers, simply drag these markers away, and they'll disappear instantly. You can also rotate the gradient to create a tilted gradient. Refer to Figure 5.59 to see this type of fill.

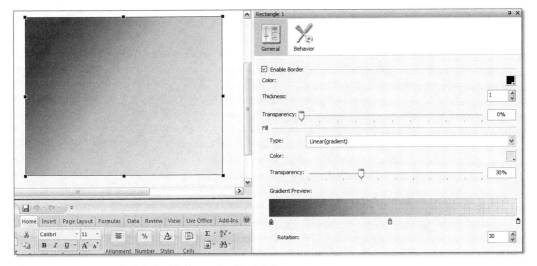

Figure 5.59 A Rectangle Filled with Linear Gradient Colors

▶ The last type is RADIAL(GRADIENT). It works similarly to linear gradient but in a different gradient direction. You should work with the color stripe to set up the gradient colors. The leftmost marker represents the color in the center, and the rightmost marker represents the color on the outer ring. See Figure 5.60 for an example of this type of fill.

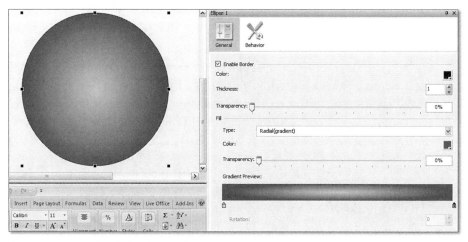

Figure 5.60 A Circle Filled with Radial Gradient Colors

5.5.3 Lines

You can use lines as separators of components on the canvas. They can also indicate logical relationships among components.

When to Use Lines

Choose to use one or more lines in your dashboard to connect UI components together. Figure 5.61 shows an example of using lines to indicate logical relationships among components.

In this figure, we use a vertical line and several horizontal lines to connect three sliders to the left and the label to the right. It's very clear from the presentation that the net profit is calculated from the cost per item, quantity sold, and sales price.

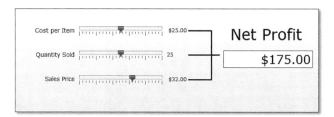

Figure 5.61 Using Lines to Indicate Logical Relationships Among Components

How to Use Lines

To use a line component, drag a vertical or horizontal line from the COMPONENTS view and drop it onto the canvas, where you can change its length.

Lines are very simple to use. There are not many properties you need to set for them. You may want to change the line color and thickness in the PROPERTIES panel, which is very straightforward, so we'll ignore it here.

5.6   Use Maps for Geographical Representation

A map component is a graphical representation of a region, either a continent, a country, or a state, from which the user can choose one place. They're widely used due to their intuitive and visual representation of each candidate item. Imagine the experience of choosing a state from a plain combo box compared to a vivid US map.

SAP BusinessObjects Dashboards 4.0 contains several prebuilt map components for many countries, areas, and continents. You can use map components for geographical representation.

A map acts like a combination of charts and selectors. They display data for each region when you point the mouse over the region, and when you select one of the regions, data insertion occurs so you can get additional information about the region selected.

You can also create alerts on a map component, thus displaying different colors for different regions based on their values of some measure, as displayed in Figure 5.62.

When to Use Maps

When you have data concerning different regions, how are you going to present it? Maybe you'd use ordinary charts such as a pie chart or column chart, or you'd simply put the data in a spreadsheet table, but in some cases, displaying this data on a map is more appealing and intuitive.

Instead of plain text in a table, slices in a pie chart, or columns in a column chart, the user gets a real map to look at. It's easier for him to locate a specific region to get related information.

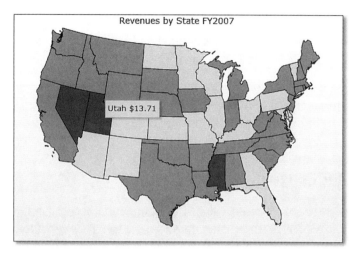

Figure 5.62 A Map Showing Revenues by State in FY2007 with Alerts Enabled

For example, if we need to know the sales revenue YTD for California, we simply point to the bottom-left region of the map for the US to get the answer, because we know California is in that part of the country. On the other hand, if a spreadsheet table or a chart is used, we may need to search for the label California to get the same information.

You can consider map components for better geographical representation of information and selection. The predelivered maps are limited. If you want special maps for your city or your organization, you can find a way to develop a new map component such as using an AnyMap component.

How to Use Maps

You can customize your maps by working with the following tabs and areas.

General

▶ Title

Each map can have a title. By default, the title is the name of the component itself. For example, in Figure 5.63, the map component USA has the default title USA. According to your needs you can change it to anything you want, for example, USA Population Distribution.

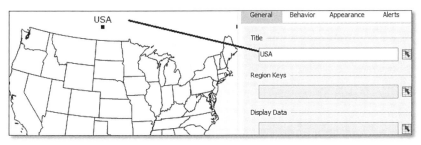

Figure 5.63 Title Property of a Map Component

▶ REGION KEYS

This property is unique to map components. To understand what this property means, we first need to explain how map components work internally.

We already know how a pie chart arranges its data parts (to recap, data items are arranged clockwise, starting from the fourth quadrant), but how do map components associate data with each region? Each region in the map has its own identifier, which is called the region key in SAP BusinessObjects Dashboards. To populate the map with information, your data must include a row or a column associated with the rest of the data to match the region keys defined in the map.

Figure 5.64 shows an example of how the regions keys are related to the map.

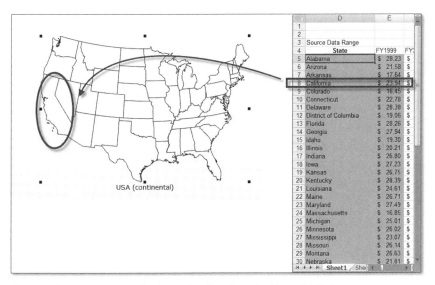

Figure 5.64 A Region Key That's Used to Populate the Map with Data

In this figure, you can see an example of how data is organized in the embedded spreadsheet and how the map is populated with data. We'll discuss the display data soon. At the moment, you need to understand that the region key enables the map to know which value is set to which region.

Each region in the map has a default region key, but it's likely that the regions in your data don't match the default region keys defined by the map component. For example, you have postal abbreviations for the US states in your data, but by default SAP BusinessObjects Dashboards uses the full names of the states as region keys. You don't need to manually change the regions in your data because SAP BusinessObjects Dashboards allows you to enter your own region keys or, in other words, to change the default keys. That's also what the region keys property does. You can do this by clicking the CHANGE icon (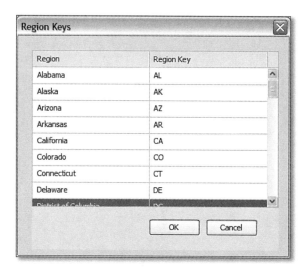) to the right of the REGION KEYS field and editing the names in the REGION KEY column for each item in the window that pops up as illustrated in Figure 5.65.

You can also bind the region keys to specific cells. This saves a lot of typing, but it's only possible when your data is sorted in the same order as the regions listed in the REGION KEYS dialog box. Otherwise, you may still have to edit the region keys manually.

Figure 5.65 Customized Region Keys with US Postal Abbreviations

You can find all of the default region keys in the Excel file *MapRegions.xls* in the folder *C:\Program Files\SAP BusinessObjects\Xcelsius\assets\samples\User Guide Samples*, assuming you've installed SAP BusinessObjects Dashboards in the default location. This Excel spreadsheet is organized in several worksheets. Each map component has a corresponding sheet listing all of the regions in the map. The first sheet is a map index that makes it very easy to navigate to a specific map.

► DISPLAY DATA
You should already know that your data must include an extra region key column or row, so your data will always contain two columns or rows, the first one of which is the region key column or row. It's worth noting that your data doesn't need to be sorted in any order, nor does it need to cover all of the regions defined in the map.

► DATA INSERTION
The map components support two insertion types: row and column. This is similar to other kinds of selectors, but the key to correctly setting up data insertion is that the source range has to include the region row or column so that when you click a region on the map, SAP BusinessObjects Dashboards knows which corresponding row or column in the source region to insert.

Appearance

► LAYOUT
You can define the transparency level by moving the slider or entering an integer in the input field. You may want to add some transparency effect to the map for a nice look and feel.

► TEXT
Unlike other charts that only show mouse-over values when you point to a data point, map components also show mouse-over labels when you point to a region on the map, so in the TEXT tab, you can set the text appearance of both.

► COLOR
You can define five kinds of colors for the map, as illustrated in Figure 5.66.

When the map is used for output only—that is, when data insertion is not enabled for the map—all of the regions are filled with the default color. In this case, you cannot interact with the map, so the color won't change when you point your mouse over a region or click on a region. Regions are always filled with the default color.

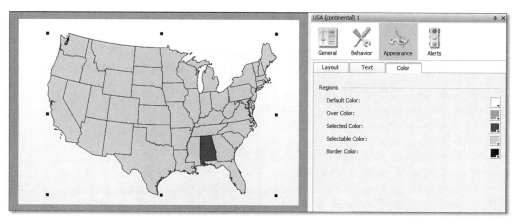

Figure 5.66 Changing Colors of the Map

If you've enabled data insertion, regions are filled with the default color when no values are associated with them and are filled with the selectable color when values are associated with them. Regions with associated values change to the mouse-over color when you point your mouse over them and to the selected color when you selected them by clicking on them.

The lines that separate individual regions are drawn in the border color.

Alerts

You use alerts similarly to the way you use them with other charts, but note that if you select the AS PERCENT OF TARGET option, the cells you bind for this option must also include the region key column or row.

5.7   Web Connectivity

SAP BusinessObjects Dashboards web connectivity functionality allows you to further extend the reach and use of your dashboards. In this section, we'll explain the features of the UI components in the web connectivity category.

5.7.1   Connection Refresh Button

A connection refresh button is a normal rectangular button with a label on top of it. Unlike a toggle button, it has only one state. Each click on it has the same effect.

When to Use a Connection Refresh Button

The connection refresh button is used in conjunction with the data connectivity of your dashboard, which will be covered in Chapters 6 and 7. You may skip this section for now and return here after reading the chapters about data connectivity.

A connection refresh button is used to provide a way for the user to manually trigger one or more connections on the dashboard whenever he wants. This provides more flexibility for the user. Without such a button, the connectivity is triggered on loading the dashboard or at intervals, or when the value of a certain cell in the embedded spreadsheet has changed or has become equal to something. If there's a logon panel in your dashboard, you can add such a button in the logon panel for the user to submit his logon info.

A connection refresh button can't be used to refresh Universe queries. To provide a way for the user to manually and explicitly refresh one or more Universe queries, use a query refresh button, covered in Chapter 4.

With a connection refresh button you can also set the trigger behavior of multiple connections together, or in batches, instead of setting it for the connections one by one. That is, if some connections are triggered the same way, you can set the trigger behavior for all of them here instead of repeating the same steps for each.

Now that you understand what a connection refresh button can do, when to use it will be obvious.

How to Use a Connection Refresh Button

Its Properties panel is divided into three categories, as illustrated next.

General

In this tab you define the label and related data connectivities of this button, as displayed in Figure 5.67.

▶ LABEL
  Here you set the label of the button, which will display on top of it. You can set it by either entering a text in the LABEL field or clicking the BIND button to bind the text to a single cell in the embedded spreadsheet. By default, the label is REFRESH, indicating its purpose. You can customize it to make it more meaningful or easier to understand, such as "Click to Refresh" and so on. Usually, you can bind it to a cell with a localized name for it.

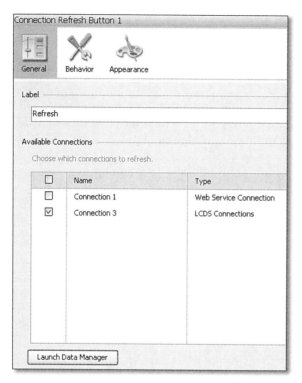

Figure 5.67 Properties in the General Tab for a Connection Refresh Button

▶ AVAILABLE CONNECTIONS

All data connectivities of any type that you have defined in this dashboard through the Data Manager will be listed in the table here with their names and types. You can select the checkbox in front of each connectivity to select it, or unselect the checkbox to unselect the connectivity. This button will then be linked with all of the selected connections. As a result, clicking this button at runtime will trigger all related connectivities at the same time.

The Data Manager, where you define the data connectivities, can be accessed by either selecting DATA • CONNECTIONS, clicking the MANAGE CONNECTIONS button in the toolbar, or pressing Ctrl+M. Another way is provided here: the LAUNCH DATA MANAGER button below the Connections table, which when clicked, will launch the Data Manager.

Additions or deletions of data connectivities in the Data Manager will be reflected here when you return to this PROPERTIES panel.

Behavior

One property specific to the connection refresh button is trigger behavior, which defines how to trigger all of the connectivities selected in the GENERAL tab.

On this tab you can set the trigger behaviors for multiple connectivities in one place, without repeating the action for each connectivity. For example, if multiple connections are triggered by the same cell, you can use a connection refresh button to set this trigger behavior for them all here. To avoid users triggering them manually, you can hide the button at runtime.

If you want all selected connectivities to be triggered on loading the dashboard, select REFRESH ON LOAD.

If you want to trigger the selected connectivities based on the value change event of a certain cell, click the BIND button of TRIGGER CELL to bind it to a single cell in the embedded spreadsheet. You then have the option to set the connections to be triggered either on value change or when the value of that cell has become equal to something—either a constant text or the value of another cell.

Appearance

If you don't want to display the rectangle of the button, unselect SHOW BUTTON BACKGROUND.

The transparency defines how transparent the button's background is. You can adjust it by moving the slider from 0 on the far left to 100% on the far right. If you set TRANSPARENCY to 100%, the effect is the same as unselecting SHOW BUTTON BACKGROUND.

5.7.2   URL Button

The URL button component allows you to add a link to your dashboard. It looks like a normal button, similar to the connection refresh button described above. However, it can open the URL specified when clicked. Clicking on it makes no change but redirects the user to another URL, either in the same window or in a new window.

The URL can be either manually entered or dynamically determined if it's bound to a cell in the Excel worksheet. More interesting, it's also possible to trigger the link without the user actually clicking the button with the help of a trigger cell.

With a trigger cell, you can configure the link to be triggered when the content in that cell changes or becomes equal to something.

When to Use a URL Button

Usually, your dashboard provides high-level, aggregated information. SAP BusinessObjects Dashboards, as an information visualization tool, is not very good at processing data or displaying a large quantity of data. Hence, it isn't a good idea to display a large volume of data or performance-extensive data processing with it.

When the user wants to drill down to more detailed information, the URL button component enables the user to navigate to the right information from the dashboard. For example, you can create a dashboard showing high-level data and provides a URL button that can redirect the user to a report with more detailed information, which might be created using SAP Crystal Reports, SAP Business-Objects Web Intelligence, and so on.

So choose a URL button when you want the user to see the content of one URL at runtime.

How to Use a URL Button

Let's go over the different options and settings that are available.

General

▶ LABEL

This is the label on the button. You can manually enter the value or bind it to a cell in the Excel worksheet.

▶ URL

Similar to the label property, you can also manually enter the value or bind it to a cell in the Excel worksheet for the URL property. If your URL contains special characters such as space, comma, or Chinese characters—which is often the case for URLs with parameter values—select ENCODE URL so that those special characters can be URL Encoded.

▶ WINDOW OPTIONS

The window options controls where the URL will be opened. Normally, the NEW WINDOW option is selected so that when the URL button is clicked, a new browser window will be launched and navigate to the URL.

Another option here is THIS WINDOW. With this selection, when the URL button is clicked, the target URL will be opened in the same window as the dashboard. There is no way you can return to the previous state of the dashboard. You can use the BACK button of the web browser to load the dashboard's SWF again, but you'll lose the interactions you've done. All the components on the canvas will return to their initial state.

Behavior

▶ TRIGGER BEHAVIOR

Normally, you click on the URL button to open the target URL, but the trigger behavior allows you to open the URL without clicking the button. You can trigger the URL button when a cell in the Excel worksheet changes or becomes a specific value.

Appearance

▶ LAYOUT

Sometimes you don't want the URL button to look like a button. You might want to make it look more like a traditional link, for example. If that is the case, you can unselect the SHOW BUTTON BACKGROUND checkbox to make the button disappear. Only the label is left.

▶ COLOR

You can change the default color and pressed colors for both the button and the label. That makes four color options. The button and label are in default colors when the button isn't pressed, and they're in pressed colors when the mouse is clicked on the button.

Practice

Now let's go through a simple example to get more familiar with the URL button. Suppose you need to create a column chart to compare the sales revenue in the fourth quarter in 2009. The user would like a link to the homepage of the company's website on the upper-right corner of the column chart. The user also wants to be able to click on the columns in the column chart to open the detailed sales reports of the corresponding quarter. The detailed sales reports are hosted on your web application server, and you have access to them with a parameterized URL.

Adding a link to the homepage is pretty straightforward, but it seems impossible to open a URL when you click on the column chart. Nevertheless, we can click on columns in a chart when the column chart enables drill-down. And when the column chart has enabled drill-down, it can insert data corresponding to the column clicked to some target range of cells. This would result in changes to some cells, and these cells could in turn be used as trigger cells of the URL button, which in turn opens the URL. Understanding this, we can start building this dashboard.

1. **Create the column chart.**

   You should already be very familiar with the column chart component. Figure 5.68 shows the column chart for this example. Note that you need to enable drill-down so that the columns respond to mouse clicks. We'll insert the row that contains both the label and the value into cell range C1:D1.

Figure 5.68 A Column Chart with Drill-Down Enabled

2. **Add the link to the homepage.**

   Drag a URL button component to the canvas and move it to the upper-right corner of the column chart. Keep the URL button component selected and edit its label and URL in PROPERTIES panel. For example, we set the label to HOMEPAGE and the URL to something like *"http://www.mycompany.com."*

Here we want a hyperlink-like button as shown in Figure 5.69, so we continue to edit the appearance of the URL button. In the APPEARANCE property sheet of the URL button, we unselect the SHOW BUTTON BACKGROUND checkbox in the LAYOUT tab, underline the label text and make it blue in the TEXT tab, and change the pressed color for the label to the same blue as the default color. Now we've properly set up a link to the company's homepage.

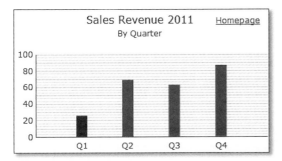

Figure 5.69 A URL Button Linked to the Homepage

3. **Add the link to the sales reports.**

   The last step is to add another URL button, which will open the detailed sales reports for the currently selected quarter. To do this, drag another URL button component and drop it onto the canvas. In the embedded spreadsheet, we need to enter the URL information. In this example, we'll put the base URL in the $F$8 cell, which in our case is *"http://localhost:8080/report.jsp?quarter=."*

   Then in the $F$9 cell, we add the formula =$F$8&$C$9 to concatenate the base URL with the inserted quarter name. Now we can continue to set up the new URL component. Bind the URL to the $F$9 cell, specify $F$9 as the trigger cell, and select the option to trigger the URL button when the value changes.

Now you can preview the dashboard and try clicking on the columns in the column chart. It will work, but there's another problem. We don't need the second URL button on the canvas. There are two ways to hide it. The first way is to put the URL button beneath the column chart. The other way is to prevent the button from showing its background and its label. Choose whichever way you like to hide the URL button.

5.7.3 Slide Show

As its name implies, you can display an image or an SWF in your dashboard with a slide-show effect with this component. The slide show is used to display images and SWF movies, but unlike the normal image component, the slide show component doesn't require you to import the source file. Instead, the slide show component will load the image or SWF movie from the URL that you specify at runtime. By binding this URL to a cell in the Excel worksheet, it's pretty easy to create dynamic slide show effects.

When to Use a Slide Show

Choose a slide show component to display a slide show of a number of pictures. If you only need to display a single static image, you can use the normal image component covered in Section 5.5.1.

One typical use of a slide show is to bind a URL property to a single cell in the embedded spreadsheet and change its content from time to time at runtime. Each time the URL in the cell changes, the slide show component loads the image or SWF file from the new location and transmits from the previous (current) image to the new one in your specified transition and easing types.

How to Use a Slide Show

To add a slide show button to your dashboard, simply drag one from the Components view and drop it on the canvas. You can move or resize it as needed.

Its Properties panel is divided into three categories, as explained next.

General

Here you specify the URL of the image or SWF file to be loaded at runtime. You can either manually enter the URL in the text box below URL (JPEG or SWF File) or bind it to a cell in the embedded spreadsheet. As the title indicates, if you're going to display an image, its type can only be JPEG. BMP or TIF images can't be displayed in a slide show component.

The URL should be accessible at runtime. Progressive JPEGs and JPEGs with CMYK coloring are not supported here.

If you input the URL here, the image or SWF file in that location will be accessed and displayed in the dashboard in your specified transition type only once. On the other hand, if you bind the URL to a cell in the embedded spreadsheet, you can change the cell content at runtime and see the easing effect of the previous image and the transition effect of the new one.

If the image or SWF file specified by the URL is in another domain, you need to consider the Adobe security restrictions such as providing a cross-domain policy file to allow access.

The other property in this tab is APPLICATION DOMAIN, a complex technical concept that defines which domain the SWF will be loaded into. The available options are NEW, CURRENT, and COMPATIBLE. They are all related with LCDS (Adobe LifeCycle Data Services) connections, which we'll cover in Chapter 7, Section 7.8. For more information about them, you can refer to the Adobe website at *http://www.adobe.com/products/livecycle/dataservices/*.

Behavior

You can set the transition behavior here.

▶ TRANSITION TYPE

You can choose among different ways to transition between slides. This is similar to the transition animation in PowerPoint. All of the transition types the slide show component supports have their counterparts in PowerPoint.

▶ EASING TYPE

There are three easing types that you can choose from.

▷ SLOW IN

The transition begins slowly and accelerates as it progresses.

▷ SLOW OUT

The transition begins quickly and slows down as it progresses.

▷ SLOW IN AND OUT

The transition begins slowly and increases in speed until the middle of the transition. The transition then decelerates until it is finished.

▶ TRANSITION TIME

This is the amount of the time it takes for the transition between two slides. A smaller number is better for smooth transitions, while a larger number may be better for performance.

Appearance

▶ SIZING METHOD

Usually the original size of your image will not be the same as the size of the slide show component, so the SIZING METHOD option lets you choose how the images are sized within the bounds of the slide show component. There are three options: ORIGINAL SIZE, STRETCH, and SCALE.

> ▶ Select the ORIGINAL SIZE option if you want your image to maintain its size. If the slide show component is not as large as the image, the areas of the image that extend outside of the slide show component are not shown. This is often used when you want to highlight only part of the image and you don't want to lose the resolution of the image. Combining the HORIZONTAL ALIGNMENT and VERTICAL ALIGNMENT options, you can choose which part of the image will be visible.

> ▶ If you select the STRETCH option, the image will be stretched to fit the bounds of the slide show component. You can ensure that the whole image is displayed, but you will make the image blurry. Moreover, the image could also be distorted if its aspect ratio is changed.

> ▶ However, the SCALE option will ensure that the aspect ratio of the image is maintained. Hence, to fit the image into the bounds of the slide show component, the slide show component may not be fully filled. There could be blank space at the top and bottom or at the left and right of the slide show component.

▶ HORIZONTAL ALIGNMENT

This option defines how images are horizontally aligned to the bounds of the slide show component. You can choose from center, left, and right.

▶ VERTICAL ALIGNMENT

This option defines how images are vertically aligned to the bounds of the slide show component. You can choose from middle, top, and bottom.

5.7.4 SWF Loader

An SWF loader is quite similar to a slide show in that both load an image or SWF file at runtime without embedding it.

You can use either to include another dashboard created by Xcelsius or SAP BusinessObjects Dashboards in your current dashboard to form a parent/child relationship. If the child dashboard is in your local file system, use a URL such as *D:\\links\sales-region.swf*. If it's hosted in your SAP BusinessObjects server, use the OpenDocument syntax to load it.

The only difference between an SWF loader and a slide show is that an SWF loader doesn't provide an easing or transition effect when the URL of the image or SWF file changes.

Using an SWF loader, including its source URL, dynamic visibility, transparency, and sizing method, and so on, is the same as for a slide show component, so we won't cover it here.

5.8   Others

In this section, we discuss some UI components in the OTHER category in the COMPONENTS view of SAP BusinessObjects Dashboards 4.0. There are two exceptions here: Calendars are covered in Section 5.2.4 about advanced selectors, and grids are in Section 5.4.3 as a component to display data in a table.

5.8.1   Local Scenario Button

A local scenario button is used to save the status under certain conditions to or load it from your local computer, making it perfect for saving the states of a what-if analysis. No new dashboard is created on your file system—only the status or state that is saved with the dashboard file.

When you click the local scenario button at runtime, it appears as a button with three menus: LOAD, SAVE, and DELETE, as displayed in Figure 5.70.

Figure 5.70 Buttons in a Local Scenario Button

Note that the LOAD and DELETE buttons are disabled if you haven't saved a scenario to your local machine. You can save many scenarios, each with a unique and meaningful name. Later you can load a scenario to restore it to its original state, even after closing the dashboard.

These scenarios are saved to the user's local machine, so they are unavailable to load if the dashboard is opened on a different machine.

When to Use a Local Scenario Button

Use this component when the user will be performing some interactive analysis with your visualization. For example, in a what-if analysis you may want to save some analysis results or snapshots for later use.

With the local scenario button component, you can save current dashboard states on your local computer and then load them later.

How to Use Local Scenario Button

The PROPERTIES panel of a local scenario button is very simple at design time, though it is divided into three categories.

In the GENERAL tab, you set the label that will appear as the button title by either entering a text or binding it to a single cell. You may have noticed that you can customize only the label, which is SCENARIO by default. You cannot customize the other three labels—SAVE, LOAD, and DELETE. This is a limitation of SAP Business-Objects Dashboards 4.0.

There is little to do with the local scenario button at design time. At runtime, the user can make full use of it for a complete analysis.

The functionalities of the SAVE, LOAD, and DELETE buttons are explained next.

Save

When the user selects the SAVE menu item, a dialog will prompt him to enter the scenario name. Current states of the dashboard can be saved for future use. The saved scenario is stored on the local computer and associated with the dashboard file (*.swf*). If that file is renamed or moved on the same computer, the scenario is still available. However, if the visualization file is emailed or copied to other computers, saved scenarios will not be available on the destination computer.

Load

When the user selects the LOAD menu item, a dialog will prompt him to pick one saved scenario from a list. The dashboard will be restored to the previously saved state.

Delete

Selecting the DELETE item results in a dialog prompt. Users can select a scenario to delete. This operation is unrecoverable, so be cautious here.

5.8.2 Trend Icon

A trend icon is an output component that represents a single numeric value. It looks like a colored circle or ellipse with an icon inside indicating whether the value is positive, not changed, or negative. Unlike the icon component discussed in Section 5.2.2, which can be used as both an input and an output, a trend icon component can only act as an output.

A trend icon is often used to show the trend of a value change. For example, to show whether the sales revenue is going up or down compared to the previous month or year. This is different from an icon component, which is used to show the status of a current value, indicating whether it's acceptable or in danger.

When to Use a Trend Icon

Use one or more trend icon components in your dashboard when you want to show the trend of a value change. A typical usage is in the DuPont Financial analysis system, to indicate whether each measure such as asset-liability ratio or rate of return is getting better or worse.

A trend icon is often used in conjunction with a single-value component such as a horizontal slider or a horizontal progress bar to show the trend together with the actual value of the current (or previous) period. Moreover, you can also add an icon component to further show the status of the value, indicating whether it's good or bad.

How to Use a Trend Icon

You can move or resize a trend icon on the canvas. In its PROPERTIES panel, you bind its data to a single cell in the embedded spreadsheet that contains the value of a certain measure, and set colors of the icon for when the value is positive, zero, and negative.

Figure 5.71 shows the design, the data in the embedded spreadsheet, and the PROPERTIES panel of the trend icon of one measure in a DuPont system: retained profit. In this dashboard, the horizontal progress bar shows the current value, and the trend icon on the top right indicates whether it's higher or lower than that of the previous period.

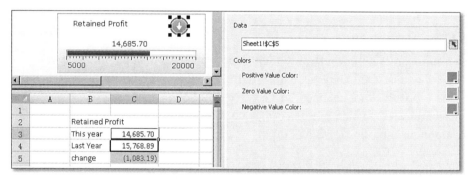

Figure 5.71 Use of a Trend Icon in a DuPont System

Note that the trend icon is bound to cell Sheet1!$C$5, which stores the difference between this year and last year.

5.8.3 Trend Analyzer

A trend analyzer is a background component that will not appear in the dashboard, similar to the history component, which we'll describe in Section 5.8.4.

This component is more complex and powerful than a trend icon. At runtime, it reads input numeric data and generates output with a predefined trend analysis algorithm such as linear, logarithmic, and power. If the data pattern is unknown, the trend analyzer has the option to determine the best fit data trend line for the input data. It then inserts the output to a row or column in the embedded spreadsheet, which can be used in your dashboard as a trend line.

The calculation only occurs at runtime. Each time the source data changes, SAP BusinessObjects Dashboards will recalculate the trend.

When to Use a Trend Analyzer

You can use a trend analyzer when you want to analyze the trend of a series of numeric values using a mathematical method and display it in your dashboard next to the actual values.

How to Use a Trend Analyzer

There's only one tab in the Properties panel of a trend analyzer component: General.

Data refers to the source numeric values the trend that will be analyzed. You set Data by clicking the Bind button to bind it to a row or column containing the values.

You then select a trend/regression type as the algorithm to use for the analysis. If you aren't sure about what you should choose, select Best Fit to leave it to SAP BusinessObjects Dashboards to choose one for you. Otherwise, select one from the six types listed here:

▶ Linear
A linear function is used to calculate the values distribution. The output values of a linear regression are distributed in a straight line in the dashboard. If the goal of your dashboard is prediction or forecasting, you can use linear regression to fit a predictive model to an observed data set.

▶ Logarithmic
Select this if your focus is probability analysis. Unlike linear regression, the output values of this and the other four methods are distributed in a curved line to fit the values.

▶ Polynomial
Choose this type to help analyze gains and losses over a large data set. If you select this type, you have another option to specify the order, between 2 and 6. An order 2 polynomial trend line generally has only one hill or valley. Order 3 generally has one or two hills or valleys.

▶ Power
Choose this type if you want to compare values that increase at a specific rate. Note that you cannot use Power if your data contains zero or negative values

▶ Exponential
Choose this type when your data values rise or fall at increasingly higher rates. Like Power, don't use this type if your data contains zero or negative values.

Some knowledge of mathematics is required to understand each trend and regression type. Alternatively, you can get a rough idea about how each type processes data by looking at the sample shapes of the lines in Figure 5.72.

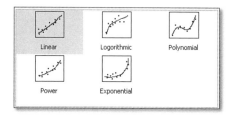

Figure 5.72 Available Algorithms to Calculate Trends

If you trust the ability of SAP BusinessObjects Dashboards, select BEST FIT, and it will choose one algorithm based on your data.

Figure 5.73 shows a sample with two trend analyzer components to analyze the trend of a stock price, one with BEST FIT and the other with LOGARITHMIC selected. A combination chart is used to show the two trends and the actual values. The trend calculated with best fit is displayed with circles, while that calculated with the logarithmic algorithm is displayed with x's.

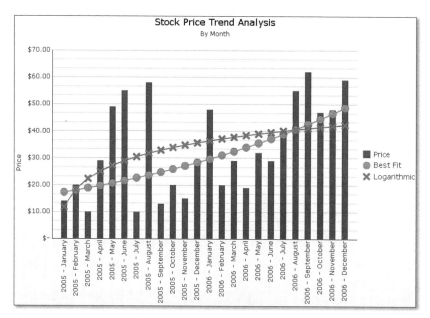

Figure 5.73 Trend Lines of the Same Data with Two Different Algorithms

5.8.4 History

You use a history component to track and display the history of changes of a selected cell. At runtime, the value of a certain cell may change over time.

History is a background component without a visual presentation at runtime. It just tracks value changes of one specified cell and stores the history in an array.

When to Use History

With a history component, you can capture and store the history of value changes. Sometimes you use a single input control to receive multiple values. In such a case, history can be used to store all values entered via the same input control for further processing.

How to Use History

To use history in your dashboard, find the HISTORY component (History) under the OTHER category in the COMPONENTS view and then drag and drop it onto the canvas.

Unlike other UI components, it can be placed anywhere on the canvas, and it will not show up at runtime. Moreover, it cannot be resized because it's meaningless to do so.

Its PROPERTIES panel is rather simple, with only a GENERAL tab. DATA refers to the cell you want to monitor. You bind it to a single cell in the embedded spreadsheet. If multiple cells are selected, only the first one will be used.

Bind DATA DESTINATION to a row or column of cells to store the history of the value change, as displayed in Figure 5.74.

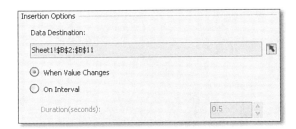

Figure 5.74 The Number of Cells in the Destination Determines How Many History Values Will Be Kept

The size of the cell range you specify as the data destination determines the maximum number of values that will be stored for history tracking. Once the data change history entries exceed the length of the data destination array, the earliest value will be eliminated. This is a kind of first-in, first-out behavior.

As displayed in Figure 5.74, you need to select one of the two options below DATA DESTINATION. If you select the WHEN VALUE CHANGES option, a new entry of data change history will be created only when the monitored value changes. Otherwise, if you select ON INTERVAL, a new entry will be created on the specified interval basis, even if no changes are made to the monitored value. Generally, you can choose based on the actual business requirement.

Practice

Now let's go through a simple example to see how to use a history component. To show the data-change-tracking function, we need a value that changes over time. This can either be accomplished by manual input at runtime or by setting up the automatic value change.

In this example we'll choose a play control component, covered in Section 5.3.3, to enable automatic value change.

Set Up Play Control

First, place a play control component on the canvas and insert its value into a single cell by binding its data property to Sheet1!$B$3. Leave other properties of the play control unchanged. Figure 5.75 shows the properties of this play control component.

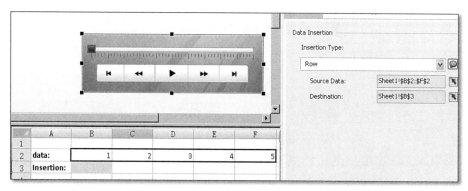

Figure 5.75 The Bindings of the Play Control

Set Up History Component

With the monitored value set up, we can proceed to track data changes with the history component. To do this, add a history component to the canvas and simply bind the DATA field to the monitored cell Sheet1!$B$3. We'll bind the data destination to a row with three cells, thus tracking the last three values of that cell. If you want to track more changes, simply bind to a row or column with more cells.

Because the data changes automatically, we'll select the option to insert a new entry when the value changes. Figure 5.76 shows the PROPERTIES panel of the history component.

Figure 5.76 Properties of the History Component

We're almost done. To display the history tracking at runtime, we'll add a spreadsheet table component to the canvas and bind its display date to the data destination of the history component, which is Sheet1!$B$4:$D$4.

Now you can click PREVIEW to test the dashboard, and click the PLAY button of the play control component. As the value of the monitored cell changes, a new entry of data is inserted into the destination array and pushes the others out. The three most recently changed values are stored in the data destination array because the length of destination array is three.

Figure 5.77 shows a screenshot of this dashboard at runtime when the play selector steps to 2. Note that the spreadsheet displays three numbers—0, 1, and 2—which means the current, or the latest, value is 2, and the previous value is 1.

As you can see from this figure, as the play control plays, the content of the destination cells, as shown in the spreadsheet table component above, changes from empty empty empty to empty empty 0 to empty 0 1, and so on.

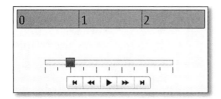

Figure 5.77 Final Result

5.8.5 Print Button

The PRINT button is used to print your dashboard. It will appear in your dashboard but will not be in the printed result (either a PDF or a paper copy). Moreover, all components that do not appear in the visualization at the time you print it at runtime, such as the history and the trend analyzer, will not be printed.

Add a print button to your dashboard if you want to provide the end user such an ability. The user can click the button to print the dashboard to paper and send it to others for further processing.

A print button looks like a regular a button, so its PROPERTIES panel is very simple. One property specific to this component is print scale, in BEHAVIOR • COMMON.

By default, SCALE TO FIT PAGE is selected so that the dashboard will always be printed to one page. If the dashboard crosses over a page, either in width or in height, SAP BusinessObjects Dashboards will automatically zoom it out to fit on one page. Otherwise, the dashboard will just be printed as it is.

If you want to always zoom the dashboard in or out with a constant percentage, select SCALE TO and specify a percent as the zoom value. The software will always zoom in or out to that scale, regardless of the dashboard's actual size. For example, you can set SCALE to 100% to always print it as is, without fitting it to the page. As a result, if the visualization is wider than the page you are using, it will be split into two pages.

5.8.6 Reset Button

You use a reset button to return the dashboard to its original state. When using this component, keep in mind that *original state* means the original scenario when you ran it, including the values in the embedded spreadsheet and what components are displayed. This sounds very simple but may cause confusion.

Add a reset button to your dashboard if you want the user to be able to revert to the original state. For example, in a what-if analysis, the user may adjust the values of several variables to analyze their impacts. Sometime later, he gets in a mess and wants to see the default values. Instead of rerunning the dashboard, he can simply click the RESET button.

Another example is when your dashboard requires the user to select a value for a parameter before retrieving live data for it. The user may need to set another value for the parameter. In such a case, instead of using dynamic visibility, a reset button would be better.

Suppose you want to show the sales revenue and some other values of each branch, among many branches of your company. Instead of retrieving all of the data at once, you provide a parameter prompt panel with a combo box for the user to select a branch first. When the user runs the dashboard, what he sees immediately is a combo box listing all branches. When he's made his selection and clicked the SUBMIT button (often a connection refresh button), another request is sent to the server requesting live data about that branch. On data return, the parameter prompt panel disappears, and the charts showing the values display. If he wants to see data on another branch, clicking the RESET button will direct the user to the parameter prompt screen.

The PROPERTIES panel is very simple, similar to that of a print button. A few of the variables you set are label, background color, button color, text format, transparency level, and dynamic visibility.

5.8.7   Source Data

You use a source data component to push data into other cells by changing the component's selected index. You can push the value of a single cell in the source row or column to another cell such as the destination, or a row or column from the source range to another row or column.

At runtime, this component will not be displayed in the dashboard, like a history or a trend analyzer.

When to Use Source Data

Choose this component if you want to display the content of an arbitrary cell or row based on the user's selection or some other criteria.

An example is a simple dashboard of a quiz. You have a cell range containing many questions from several categories, such as "How long will the grass stay alive without water?" in the category NATURE. Each category corresponds to a row or column. At runtime, questions from a random category are displayed.

To do this, you generate the index by either using the Excel function Rand() or the user's age, preference, and so on. You then use a source data component to insert the row or column with the questions from that category to another row or column, which will be displayed by components in the dashboard. The source data component makes the insertion based on the value of a cell that stores the user's selection.

You may think you can achieve the same thing with complex Excel functions such as HLookup(). However, it's more difficult, and thus error-prone, and results in poor performance at runtime because HLookup() is very expensive to run.

How to Use Source Data

The PROPERTIES panel of a source data component is very simple. In the GENERAL tab, you define the data insertion behavior by selecting an insertion type from VALUE, ROW, and COLUMN, and do the binding for the source data and destination correspondingly. If you're going to insert a single value, select the insertion type VALUE, and bind SOURCE DATA to a row or column and DESTINATION to a single cell. Otherwise, bind SOURCE DATA to a cell range and DESTINATION to another row or column.

In the BEHAVIOR tab, set the selected item index by either entering an integer or binding it to a single cell that stores the index. The item index begins with 1. In the example given in "When to Use Source Data," we bound SELECTED ITEM INDEX to the cell that contains the formula to calculate a random integer; for example, =ROUND(RAND() * 10, 0).

Practice

If you aren't clear about when or how to use a source data component, this example may help you. Suppose you want to add a saying to an existing dashboard so that each time the user runs the dashboard (or every day), he will see a proverb. This also brings more individuality to your dashboard.

1. **Prepare the data.**

   As displayed in Figure 5.78, many proverbs are placed in row 'Sheet1'!$B$2:$B$12 (you can add more interesting proverbs if you like). Only one of them will be selected each time. We plan to insert it into cell 'Sheet1'!$B$1. Also, we need to generate a random integer each time the user runs the dashboard, so we'll calculate it in cell 'Sheet1'!$D$1, which is a formula, =ROUND(RAND() * 12, 0).

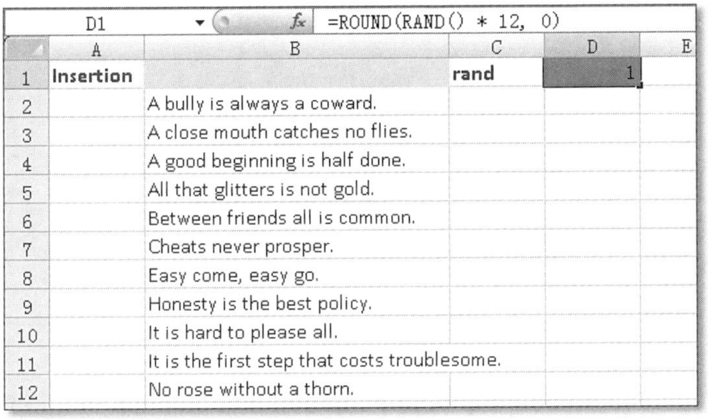

	D1	▼	⟳	f_x	=ROUND(RAND() * 12, 0)		
	A		B		C	D	E
1	Insertion				rand	1
2		A bully is always a coward.				
3		A close mouth catches no flies.				
4		A good beginning is half done.				
5		All that glitters is not gold.				
6		Between friends all is common.				
7		Cheats never prosper.				
8		Easy come, easy go.				
9		Honesty is the best policy.				
10		It is hard to please all.				
11		It is the first step that costs troublesome.				
12		No rose without a thorn.				

Figure 5.78 Data Structure in the Embedded Spreadsheet

2. **Set up the source data component.**

   We'll use the source data component to insert one proverb from a column, so we'll select VALUE as the insertion type and bind SOURCE DATA to column 'Sheet1'!$B$2:$B$12 and DESTINATION to cell 'Sheet1'!$B$1, as we planned in the first step.

   The insertion is based on the random integer stored in cell 'Sheet1'!$D$1, so in the BEHAVIOR TAB, we'll bind SELECTED ITEM INDEX to this cell.

   Figure 5.79 shows the PROPERTIES panel of the source data.

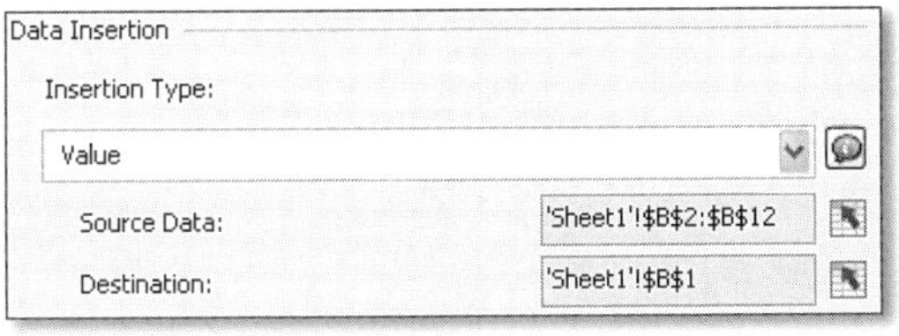

Figure 5.79 Data Bindings of the Source Data Component

As the last step, add a label to show the randomly selected proverb.

Figure 5.80 shows the final screenshot. Note that the proverb displayed is selected randomly.

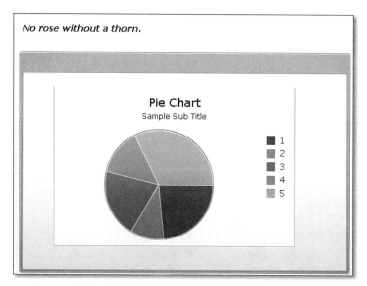

Figure 5.80 Final Result

5.8.8 Panel Set

You can use a panel set to display several dashboards or images within one scene, making it possible for users to navigate among multiple visualizations without leaving the presentation. You can either embed the files into the dashboard or simply link to them to reduce the dashboard size.

SAP BusinessObjects Dashboards provides several kinds of layouts for you to position the SWF or image files, each of which can be maximized for the user to focus on a certain aspect at runtime.

When to Use a Panel Set

Choose a panel set when you want to display several dashboards or images in your presentation.

For example, say you have created several dashboards for different sales districts or different product categories. Traditionally, you would open them one after another during your presentation. With a panel set, you can display them all together in one screen, making it possible to explain all without leaving your presentation.

How to Use a Panel Set

Let's go over the different options and settings that are available.

General

▶ LAYOUT

First, you need define what the panel set looks like by choosing one layout from the 27 in the list. Each divides the panel set component into several child panels, each of which can then contain an SWF or a JPEG image.

▶ PANEL TITLES

To name the child panels, you bind PANEL TITLES to a single cell or a row or column, depending on the layout you have chosen. Briefly, the number of cells you bind PANEL TITLES to should be equal to the number of child panels the chosen layout divides the panel set into. For example, if you select LAYOUT4, which divides the component into three child panels, you need to bind PANEL TITLES to a row or column with three cells. If the row or column contains only two cells, the name of the last child panel will be empty.

▶ CONTENT

Depending on the selected layout, one or more panels may be displayed in the PANELS list. You can click on one of them to set its content and the DROPDOWN MENU LABELS.

There are three kinds of content types, as explained next.

▶ NONE

If you want to leave the panel empty, select NONE.

▶ EMBEDDED JPEG OR SWF

Select this type if you want to embed the SWF or JPEG file into the current dashboard. Then you can click the IMPORT button to launch a window where you select one or more JPEG or SWF files to display in this panel, as shown in Figure 5.81.

In the window shown in this figure, click the CLICK TO ADD IMAGES button to create a new entry for a JPEG or SWF file.

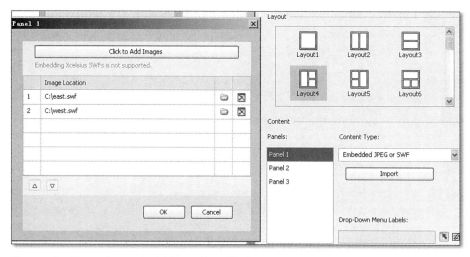

Figure 5.81 Choose Images to Add from Your File System

As noted in this window, embedding SWFs created by Xcelsius or SAP BusinessObjects Dashboards is not supported. If you click the FOLDER icon to browse to an SWF file, the software will check if it's exported from Xcelsius or SAP BusinessObjects Dashboards and reject it with an error message as displayed in Figure 5.82.

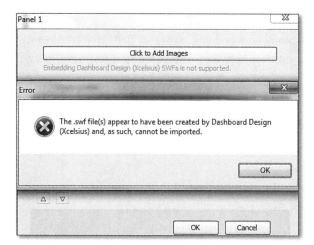

Figure 5.82 An Error Message Is Displayed if You Choose an SWF Created by SAP BusinessObjects Dashboards

This is very frustrating, because usually the SWFs we want to embed or link here are also created by Xcelsius or SAP BusinessObjects Dashboards. However, there's a workaround. The steps are:

1. Click the CLICK TO ADD IMAGES button.

2. Browse to an SWF file not created by Xcelsius or SAP BusinessObjects Dashboards.

3. Click OK to close the browse window.

4. Double-click the IMAGE LOCATION field and replace it with the path of the SWF you want, which is created by Xcelsius or SAP BusinessObjects Dashboards 4.0.

   In preview mode, you'll find that the SWF, though created by Xcelsius or SAP BusinessObjects Dashboards 4.0, is successfully loaded in the panel set with full functionalities.

   Some available operations in this window are that you can double-click the location or click the FOLDER button to edit it, click the DELETE button to delete an image or SWF, or click the up or down arrow on the bottom to change the order of the imported items.

   ▶ BY URL

   If you want to create a link to the SWF or JPEG files instead of embedding them into the current dashboard, select this type. You can then click the BIND button to bind the URLs to a row or column in the embedded spreadsheet containing the absolute or relative file paths. If you don't want to store the URLs in the spreadsheet, click the 📝 button to enter the URLs in the pop-up window.

   When you select either BY URL or EMBEDDED JPEG OR SWF, you can further set the names of the SWFs or JPEGs through dropdown menu labels. You do this by either clicking the BIND button (📑) to bind the names to a row or column in the embedded spreadsheet or clicking the 📝 button to manually enter them.

   These names will appear in the dropdown menu of each child panel, so you can choose one SWF or image from the menu. Obviously, the number of names should be the same as the number of SWFs or JPEGs you defined for this child panel.

   You can repeat the steps listed above for each of the other child panels.

Behavior

▶ PANEL BEHAVIOR

With the ENABLE MAXIMIZE BUTTON selected, a maximize button () will be displayed on the top right of each child panel. The user can click it to expand that child panel to display it on the entire panel set component. When the child panel is maximized, the user can click the button again to revert it to the normal size. A window animation is played on each click. This feature is useful when you want to emphasize different sets of data at different times during a presentation.

The zoom speed defines how long it takes the window animation to go from normal to maximized. You can adjust this setting by moving the slider below, from slower on the left to faster on the right.

▶ SELECTED ITEM

The selected item defines what SWF or JPEG is displayed by default for each child panel. You do this by selecting a panel first and then selecting the default item for it.

▶ IGNORE BLANK CELLS

With this option selected, the SWF or JPEG will not be listed in the dropdown menu if its corresponding label is blank. Its label is regarded as blank only when it's bound to a cell in the embedded spreadsheet and that cell is blank. If you haven't bound the dropdown menu labels to any cell or cell range, or the length of the target is less than that of the SWFs or JPEGs, the labels are not blank but will be generated automatically by SAP BusinessObjects Dashboards. As a result, items will not be ignored in this situation.

Note: If the number of cells of the row or column the dropdown menu labels are bound to is higher than that of the included SWFs or JPEGs, the extra labels will be ignored.

Appearance

By default, a header on the top of a child panel shows its name and the name of the currently selected SWF or JPEG (if any). If you don't want to display this, to save space or based on your preferences, unselect SHOW PANEL HEADERS.

The property NUMBER OF LABELS DISPLAYED defines how many labels are listed in the dropdown menu of each child panel. If the number you specify here is smaller than the actual number of labels, a vertical scroll bar will appear.

Figure 5.83 shows a sample panel set component at runtime. This panel set uses a layout with three parts. The left side shows the sales information for each region, where the user selects a region from the dropdown menu. The top-right part shows a gauge the user can use to adjust the unit, and a photo is displayed on the bottom right. You can operate on each SWF as normal.

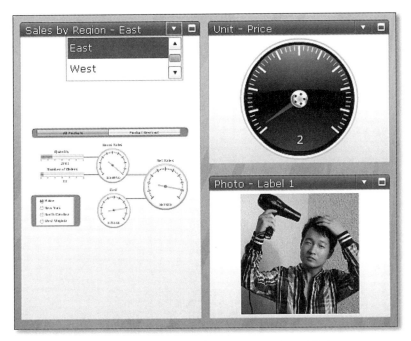

Figure 5.83 A Panel Set Used to Divide the Canvas into Several Parts

5.9 Summary

In this chapter, we discussed some complex and less frequently used UI components in SAP BusinessObjects Dashboards 4.0. Some components share most common properties with others such as data binding and alerts, so we did not explain them here. Others have many specific properties such as rectangles, play control, and OHLC charts, which we illustrated extensively. We hope you have a big picture of what amazing dashboards you can create with SAP BusinessObjects Dashboards and that you choose the best-fit UI components for your own dashboard. In the next chapter we'll talk about data connectivities.

No matter how good your dashboard looks, without reflecting the live, actual business data, it's just a nice looking, static image and won't be useful. SAP BusinessObjects Dashboards provides several kinds of data connectivity to retrieve live data and make your dashboard not only attractive, but functional and powerful.

6 Data Connectivity Basics

In Chapters 4 and 5, we discussed all of the powerful UI components in SAP BusinessObjects Dashboards 4.0. However, a dashboard is not only a graphical UI. To make real business sense, you need to add meaningful data to it. SAP BusinessObjects Dashboards provides a wide range of methods to access your data, called *data connectivity*, which are accessible from the Data Manager within the software.

The available data connectivities can be divided into several categories. Some are specific to the SAP BusinessObjects environment, such as Query as a Web Service and Live Office. Some are specific to the SAP NetWeaver BW environment such as SAP NetWeaver BW Connection. Some are used for communication between the SWF and its container (either Adobe Flash Player or a web browser) such as Flash Variables and External Interface connections. Some are for the dashboard to retrieve live data from a web application server (Tomcat, WebLogic, etc.), such as Web Service Connection and XML data. If your license permits, you can use several kinds of data connectivity in a single dashboard.

You can also retrieve live data with Universe queries, which are accessible from the Query Browser but not from Data Manager, so they're not covered here. For more information about how to connect to a relational Universe and create a query on top of it, refer to Chapter 2, Section 2.8.

In this chapter, we'll illustrate some types of data connectivity that you can use to connect the dashboard to your own data, including local Excel files, remote web services, and XML data.

After reading this chapter you'll be able to:

▶ Describe some basic data connectivity methods

▶ Know how to connect to an external data source using one or more types of data connectivity

6.1 Embedded Excel Spreadsheet

SAP BusinessObjects Dashboards embeds an Excel spreadsheet in its workspace below the canvas. Supported versions include Microsoft Office Excel 2003, XP, 2007, and 2010. This is a fully functional instance of Excel, where you can add, delete, or modify data directly without having to import or reimport an Excel spreadsheet file, just like in a normal stand-alone version of Excel.

The appearance of the embedded Excel spreadsheet is the same as when you launch Excel directly as a stand-alone application. Your customization of Excel will be reflected here, including the language and layout. All of the menus and toolbars are also available here, and you can create as many sheets as you like.

Excel is only required at design time for data manipulation and binding. The data in Excel is incorporated into the dashboard output, and it's not required at runtime. That is, the designer cannot function without Excel, but the user can. This helps the wide distribution of the output, not only in Windows, but also in other operating systems such as Linux or Unix.

An idle or "rogue" Microsoft Excel process hanging in the computer will block SAP BusinessObjects Dashboards from starting up, with the error message displayed in Figure 6.1, when you try to launch the software.

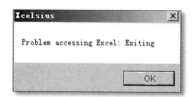

Figure 6.1 SAP BusinessObjects Dashboards Cannot Start Up if an Idle Excel Instance Is Running

This problem may occur when you have launched Excel or SAP BusinessObjects Dashboards before, and it crashed and stopped improperly. As a result, a rogue

Excel process is still there, though you cannot see it. To solve this, press `Ctrl`+`Alt`+`Del` to launch the Task Manager, locate the idle Excel process, and end it. You can then launch SAP BusinessObjects Dashboards successfully.

If you're working with both SAP BusinessObjects Dashboards and a stand-alone Excel, always launch SAP BusinessObjects Dashboards first and then Excel.

6.1.1   Role of Excel

Usually the embedded Excel spreadsheet works as the direct data source for all UI components and the only interface for all external data sources, unless you're using Universe queries for direct data binding, which is illustrated in Chapter 8, Section 8.4. That is, you bind a property of a UI component to a cell or cell range in the embedded Excel spreadsheet, and all external data sources should be mapped here. The embedded Excel spreadsheet is the bridge between UI components and data connectivity. From this perspective, Excel acts as a *data model* for SAP BusinessObjects Dashboards.

In the meantime, Excel can also act as a *calculation engine* for the software to calculate new fields based on the existing data. Most Excel formulas are supported here, providing the dashboard designer more flexibility in calculating new data from existing fields. This is helpful when some data is unavailable or shouldn't be provided by the data source but should be calculated on top of it; for example, to calculate percentages.

As you'll see shortly, some types of data connectivity can be triggered when the value of a cell changes or becomes equal to something. From this perspective, Excel acts as an *eventing model* for SAP BusinessObjects Dashboards.

6.1.2   How to Use Excel

You can bind the properties of UI components and map the input and output of external data sources to a cell or cell range in the embedded Excel spreadsheet.

Plan First

Before designing your dashboard, you should plan how many sheets you need, what cell will be used for what purpose, and so on. During this planning time, you need to think not only about the cells for the UI components' properties and for data input and output, but also about your calculation and rearrangement of them.

It's a best practice to give descriptive names to the sheets and explanatory labels for a cell or a cell range and to use colors and borders to highlight and distinguish them. For example, you use a data connectivity to access external data, the output of which is a cell range with 4 columns and 10 rows. Before binding the output in the Data Manager, plan what area will be used to store the output and highlight the columns and rows with colors or borders. Then you can easily see where to bind the output in the Data Manger. Here, we'll just provide an overview of how to use Excel, and we'll cover it in more detail in the appendix.

Figure 6.2 shows an example of a well-planned design in Excel.

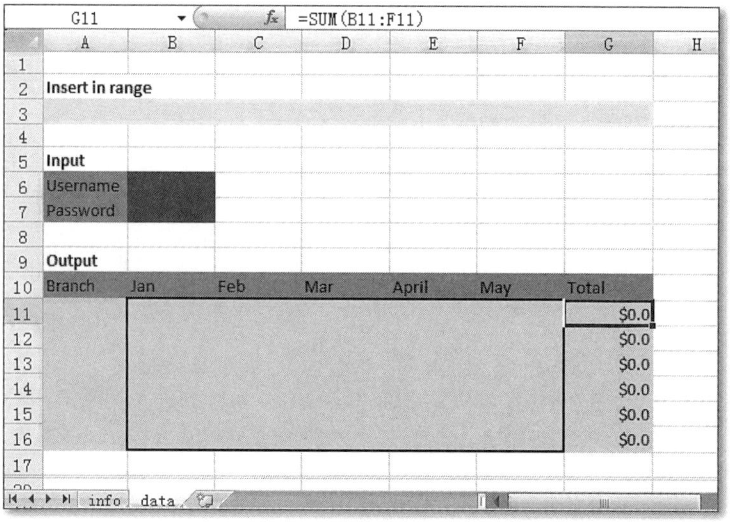

Figure 6.2 Example of a Well-Planned Design in Excel

Some metadata, such as the author and the purpose of this dashboard, is placed in a sheet called INFO. The actual data, including input, output, and calculated data is placed in the DATA sheet and highlighted with colors and cell borders. Note that the destination cells of data insertion or drill-down of UI components are also highlighted for easy understanding of the design.

Sometimes it's difficult to design on an empty Excel spreadsheet and imagine the business meaning and format of a cell. To make the design simpler, you can write some sample values next to the mapped cells in another row or column or range.

The data of the embedded Excel spreadsheet can also be exported with all sheets included. To do this, first switch to preview mode and then follow the menu path FILE • SNAPSHOT • CURRENT EXCEL DATA.

If you use data connectivity and map the output of the external data source to the embedded Excel spreadsheet, the output is not really written to Excel. Remember, the data is only mapped, not written. That means the content of the embedded Excel spreadsheet will not be changed after a preview, and you won't be able to see the output data in the spreadsheet.

Resize

You can resize the area to display the embedded Excel spreadsheet, both in width and in height. The behavior is a little different for Excel 2007 and 2003. If you're using Excel 2007, the ribbon area, the toolbars, and the menus are all visible by default when the space is high enough. However, they'll disappear when the height is decreased to some limit to save space for the cells. If you decrease the width, the menus and the ribbon area will shrink. This is simpler for Excel 2003: The toolbars just show or hide depending on the space size, and a horizontal scrollbar will appear if the width isn't adequate.

Working with the embedded Excel spreadsheet here is no different from what you would normally do. You can fill in texts or numbers in a cell, set its formats including fonts and colors, set border styles, create calculated cells, and so on. You can also create multiple sheets to store different data and give them descriptive names. For example, you can have an Info sheet to store metadata such as the author, the purpose, and the target audience of the dashboard and another sheet called DATA to store the input and output values of a data connectivity.

Copy and Paste

You can copy and paste texts or formulas from or to the embedded Excel spreadsheet. The copy and paste operation can happen between two dashboards or between SAP BusinessObjects Dashboards and a stand-alone Excel instance. Note that both the data and its format are copied. It's helpful when your data resides in multiple Excel files and you want to copy it into the embedded Excel spreadsheet to design your dashboard.

However, formulas cannot be copied between the embedded Excel spreadsheet and a stand-alone one. Only the result data is copied. For example, in SAP BusinessObjects Dashboards, you have the letter A in cell Sheet1!B2, letter B in Sheet1!B3, and the formula =CONCATENATE(Sheet1!B2, Sheet1!B3) in cell Sheet1!C2. When you copy cell Sheet1!C2 and paste it into a cell, say Sheet1!D1, in a stand-alone Excel file, the copied content is "AB" instead a formula.

Copying and pasting between two dashboards instances is also supported. That is, you can design two dashboards simultaneously by running two SAP BusinessObjects Dashboards design instances at the same time and copy and paste data between them. You'll find this functionality useful when you're learning from a dashboard designed by an expert, and you try to create an excellent dashboard from scratch. However, if the two dashboards are not opened at the same time, copy and paste between them is not supported. So when you have copied something from one dashboard design instance and then you open or create another dashboard design model file (*.xlf*) via the menu path FILE • OPEN or FILE • NEW or restart the software, the copied data gets lost and thus cannot be pasted.

6.2   Import Data from an Excel File

You can import data from an existing Excel file into the embedded spreadsheet of your dashboard. The Excel file can be either Office 97-2003 (with an *.xls* extension) or Office 2007 or 2010 (with an *.xlsx* extension), located either on your local machine, on a network, or in an SAP BusinessObjects Business Intelligence platform (a BOE system). Once imported, the embedded spreadsheet will be identical to the source file, with all changes you have made to it lost.

6.2.1   When to Import Data from an Excel File

You may want to use this option when the data source of your dashboard is an Excel file provided by someone else. At design time, you can agree with the data provider on what data is stored in what cells in the Excel file. Then you can begin your design and import data from the Excel file when it's ready.

You must use this option if the data is only available in Excel format but cannot be provided through any of the data connectivity methods in the Data Manager. For example, the data might exist in a legacy system that provides no application programming interface (API) for external calls. Imagine the case when your data is in an SAP R/3 system.

6.2.2 How to Import Data from an Excel File

Importing data from an Excel file is very straightforward. You can do this by selecting DATA • IMPORT to locate a file on your local file system or a network. You can also import data from an Excel file on an SAP BusinessObjects BI platform, via the menu path DATA • IMPORT FROM PLATFORM.

After being imported, the data in all sheets of the Excel file will be copied to the embedded spreadsheet inside SAP BusinessObjects Dashboards. You need do this with caution, as all data that existed in the embedded Excel spreadsheet will be overwritten, and any change you have made to the spreadsheet will be lost. Moreover, this operation is unrecoverable.

If you already have some UI components bound to cells in the embedded Excel spreadsheet, SAP BusinessObjects Dashboards will try to maintain the binding relationship. The binding will work perfectly after importing data if the names of the cells or cell ranges are still available. For example, let's say you've bound the title property of a pie chart to cell Sheet1!$B$2. It will still be bound to Sheet1$B$2 after import if there's such a cell. However, if there's no sheet named Sheet1 in the source Excel file, the binding will be removed because the software cannot find such a cell.

Note that after you've imported data from an existing Excel file, SAP Business-Objects Dashboards has nothing to do with that file any more. First, this means that you can delete or move that file without affecting your dashboard. Second, changes to the existing Excel file will not be automatically reflected in your dashboard. To solve this, you can import that Excel file again, but any changes made to the built-in Excel spreadsheet, such as formulas, will be overwritten by the imported Excel file.

6.3 Security Issues Related to Accessing External Data

In the following sections we'll discuss some basic data connectivity types that you use in the Data Manager to connect your dashboard to external data. The external data source can be an XML file on your local file system or a web service via HTTP.

Your dashboard can either be run locally as a Flash file or inside a Microsoft PowerPoint/Word document, or be hosted on a web application server. At run-time or in preview mode, Adobe Flash Player is used to play the output. This is where the security issue arises.

Adobe Flash Player version 9 or later includes security restrictions that restrict the output (Flash, PDF, PowerPoint, etc.) to access local files or HTTP services. If you don't grant the output permission to access the resources, you'll get an error message on launching the dashboard or in preview mode, as displayed in Figure 6.3 (Adobe Flash Player 10 is used here).

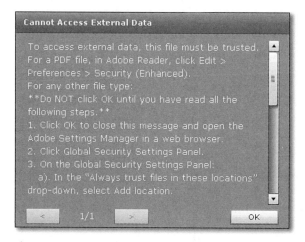

Figure 6.3 Error Window When Flash Player Isn't Granted Access

The security issue includes two situations, when your dashboard is run locally or on a web server, as explained next.

6.3.1 Run Locally

If your dashboard is exported to a file on your local file system such as a Flash or PowerPoint file, you need to add that file to the trusted locations in the Adobe Flash Player Settings Manager so it can access external resources.

The Adobe Flash Player Settings Manager is not a tool or setting on your local machine. Instead, you have to set it over the web. To open the manager, go to *http://www.macromedia.com/support/documentation/en/flashplayer/help/settings_manager04.html.*

In this web page you'll find an area called GLOBAL SECURITY SETTINGS PANEL. Note that you need have the Flash Player add-on installed for your web browser to see the Settings Manager panel. In the panel, select ALWAYS ALLOW, click ADD LOCATION, and browse to the folder or the dashboard file (SWF, PowerPoint, HTML, etc.).

Now you've marked your dashboard as trustworthy, and it can access external resources. You can reopen the dashboard to have a try.

6.3.2 Run on a Web Server

Sometimes you may export the dashboard to a Flash or an HTML file and host it on a web application server. Or you can follow the menu path FILE • SAVE TO PLATFORM so the user can view it through the SAP BusinessObjects BI launchpad. The user can then access it through a URL such as *http://webserver:port/xxx/dashboard.html*. If it connects to an HTTP service hosted on another server, you must provide a cross-domain policy file (typically, a cross-domain XML file) in the web server root. Otherwise you'll get an error message because Adobe Flash Player doesn't allow an SWF file to access data that resides in a domain different from the web domain from which the SWF originated.

The cross-domain policy file grants the Adobe Flash Player permission to access data in a given domain. It controls which SWF files, running on which domains, can access resources on your web server. It's a simple XML file placed on a folder in your web server. The folder differs for each kind of web server. For example, the folder is *TOMCAT/webapps/root* if you're using Tomcat to host your dashboard.

For more details about the cross-domain file, search for it over the Internet or refer to *http://kb.adobe.com/selfservice/viewContent.do?externalId=tn_14213&sliceId=2*.

6.4 XML Data

XML is a set of rules for encoding documents electronically. It can be used to represent almost arbitrary data structures—not only XML files, but also web resources—with great simplicity, generality, and usability. That's why it's now widely used in many situations. For example, you can get the stock price of one or more companies from Yahoo! Finance with one URL, which provides the data in an XML format.

In SAP BusinessObjects Dashboards, XML data is any data source encoded in an XML format, either from a file or over the web available in the HTTP protocol. With this data connectivity you can connect your dashboard to a wide range of external data sources.

The XML data connectivity is identified as a URL, pointing to either a file or a service starting with *http://*. The URL can accept input parameters, which enables you to use one URL for different user inputs. Don't undervalue this property. This enables you to write back to your data source. For example, you can bind user input to one or more cells in the embedded spreadsheet, concatenate them to the URL in key-value format, and trigger the connectivity. The server will then get the user input and write it to the data source after processing. If you're familiar with web programming, you may know this is achieved by the HTTP GET method.

The standard XML schema can be very flexible and complex, as you'll see in the next section about web service connections. In SAP BusinessObjects Dashboards 4.0, the data from an XML data connectivity needs be mapped to a cell range in the embedded spreadsheet with a row-column structure. SAP BusinessObjects Dashboards provides limited support for XML data, with some requirement for the XML data format. Generally, to be able to be consumed by SAP BusinessObjects Dashboards, the returned XML data should be in the following format.

```
<?xml version="1.0" encoding="UTF-8"?>
<data>
<variable name="any string here">
  <row>
    <column> column value 1 </column>
    <column> column value 2 </column>
    . . .
  </row>
  . . .
</variable>
. . .
</data>
```

The following are principals for using XML data in SAP BusinessObjects Dashboards:

▶ The XML data may or may not contain the header `<?xml version="" />`. However, if there are some Asian characters in the XML data, you need the header to specify the encoding type to read them correctly.

▶ The XML body should be within a node named `data`.

▶ The first row below the node `data` should be `<variable name="any string here">`. In `name` you can put anything to explain the meaning of this data. You can have several variable nodes in the XML data.

▶ Inside the tag variable is a list of row nodes. A row indicates a row of data, mapped to a row in Excel. A row can contain one or more columns, mapped to a column in Excel. You can have as many rows as you want, but the number of columns should not exceed 256.

▶ Inside each row is a list of columns. The content of each column node represents the content of the mapped cell.

If the data source resides in an XML file, the file content should be the same as shown above. If it's exposed as an HTTP service, the service should also return exactly the same content in its output stream. This is intuitive: Excel is two-dimensional, and SAP BusinessObjects Dashboards can only bind data to a cell range, with *N* rows and *M* columns.

For example, let's say you're going to show the sales revenue and quantity sold of two companies. To be consumed by SAP BusinessObjects Dashboards, the content in XML format should look like this:

```
<data>
<variable name="any string here">
  <row>
    <column>Company A</column>
    <column>300,000</column>
    <column>1200</column>
  </row>
  <row>
    <column>Company B</column>
    <column>420,000</column>
    <column>1560</column>
  </row>
</variable>
</data>
```

The data will be mapped to a cell range B3:D4 with two rows and three columns in the embedded Excel spreadsheet, as shown in Figure 6.4.

	A	B	C	D	E
1					
2					
3		Company A	300,000	1200	
4		Company B	420,000	1560	
5					

Figure 6.4 Output of XML Data Connectivity Mapped to a Cell Range in an Embedded Spreadsheet

When you use XML data in your dashboard, you can configure how and when the data will be refreshed against the source. We'll provide a detailed explanation about how to use it in Section 6.4.3.

6.4.1   When to Use XML Data

You can use this data connectivity type when the data source is provided in XML format, either as a file or as a service with an HTTP protocol. You can also use it to send data to external applications in an XML format; for example, to export data in the spreadsheet to an XML file.

XML File

This is the case when someone collects the data and puts it in an XML file or when the data is generated automatically by some program and saved into an XML file. The file can be located either in a file system or on a network.

XML Service over HTTP

Sometimes it isn't practical to save data in a physical file. For example, the data is dynamic and varies a lot depending on different conditions. In such situations, you can expose the data as an HTTP service.

If you're familiar with Java, you can simply write a Java Servlet to expose the data. The Java Servlet can be hosted in any Java web application server such as Tomcat. In addition to returning data as an XML string, it can also accept input parameters.

This is very powerful. It enables SAP BusinessObjects Dashboards to connect to almost any data source, only if it can be accessed and processed by the Java programming language and exposed as an XML string. This is also a practical combination of experts in dashboard designing and experts in Java programming, which work together to create a fancy and powerful dashboard.

For example, say your sales data is stored in the database (either transactional or data warehouse) and you want to create a dashboard showing measures about sales, where the user can choose what years, branches, or products to see. To achieve this, the Java experts write code to access the database, calculate the required values, and return the data in a Java Servlet. The dashboard designer then creates a dashboard connecting to the servlet.

The user's default web browser may cache the URL defined in the XML data connectivity. That is, if you request data with the same URL (its parameter included) twice within a short period (before the web browser considers the cached URL as expired), the web browser won't send the request to the web application server. Instead, it returns the cached page content. To avoid this, you can simply disable your web browser from caching. A better way is to append a redundant parameter with `Rand()` as its value. For example, you can update the URL for the XML data connectivity by concatenating `&redundant_param=RAND()` to the real URL in the cell in the embedded spreadsheet.

6.4.2   How to Use XML Data

To connect to XML data, first you need to add one such connectivity by launching the Data Manager, clicking ADD, and selecting XML DATA from the dropdown list.

The Data Manager can be launched either from the menu DATA • CONNECTIONS, from the toolbar, or via the keyboard shortcut [Ctrl]+[M].

You can create as many XML data connectivities in one dashboard as you want and set their properties. Set the properties of an XML data connectivity in the PROPERTIES panel to its right. In the following sections, we'll illustrate the purposes of the properties.

Definition

In this tab you define the location and format of the XML data connectivity, as displayed in Figure 6.5.

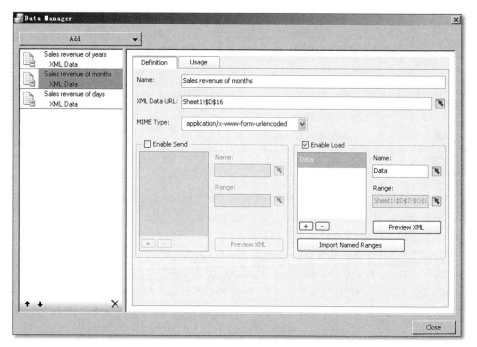

Figure 6.5 Defining XML Data Connectivity

The properties for the XML data are explained here:

▶ NAME

Here you specify the name of this connectivity. The name can be any string but should be meaningful enough to explain what it's about. It will appear in the connectivity list, where the name will help you easily locate the one you want.

▶ XML DATA URL

Here you specify where the XML data source resides. You can enter the URL in the input field or bind it to a cell in the embedded Excel spreadsheet. When the URL has to be concatenated by the values in several cells or be passed in from a Flash variable, you need save it in a cell and bind the URL to it.

If the source is an XML file on the file system, the URL should be something like *file:// D://salesXMLdata.xml, D://salesXMLdata.xml*, or *\\my-file-server\data\ salesXMLdata.xml*. The prefix, *file://*, isn't required. You can also use a relative path here, such as *.../data/salesXMLdata.xml*, which locates the file in the *Data* folder in the same directory as the output at runtime. For example, if you specify the URL as *.../data/salesXMLdata.xml* and export the dashboard as an SWF file to the folder *E:/samples,* then to make it work, the file *salesXMLdata.xml* should be available in the folder *E:/samples/data.*

If there's space in the file name, you can either leave it alone or encode it as %20. For example, you can use either *D:/sales XML data.xml* or *D:/sales%20 XML%20data.xml.*

The content of the XML file is not burned, or embedded, into the output, which means the XML file should be available at the dashboard's runtime. If you use a relative or network path to locate the XML file, ensure that it's accessible when the user launches the dashboard.

To be able to access the XML file, the output (SWF, PDF, PowerPoint, etc.) must be declared as trusted. Refer to Section 6.3 for how to do this.

If the source is an HTTP service such as a Java Servlet, you need to specify the full URL such as *http://myserver:poart/context/salesXMLdata.do.* Unlike for an XML file, the *http://* prefix is required.

You can also use a relative path such as *.../salesXMLdata.do.* The path is relative to where the dashboard originates.

If the HTTP service resides on a domain other than the dashboard, you need a cross-domain policy file to grant access to the dashboard. Refer to Section 6.3 for more information.

▶ MIME TYPE
You select a MIME type from the dropdown list for the data source. There are two options here, TEXT/XML for human-readable text that is defined in RFC 3023 (available at *http://tools.ietf.org/html/rfc3023*) and APPLICATION/X-WWW-FORM-URLENCODED for nonstandard files documented in HTML 4.01 Specification, Section 17.13.4.1 (available at *http://www.w3.org/TR/html401/interact/ forms.html#h-17.13.4.1*). You can refer to these websites for an in-depth understanding of the two types.

If the data source is an XML file, there's no difference between these two options. On the other hand, if it's an HTTP service such as a Java Servlet, you make your selection based on the content type specified in the source. Usually, either is all right, and you can just leave it unchanged to use the default type.

▶ ENABLE LOAD
Select this option if you want the XML data specified in the URL to be loaded into the dashboard when the connection is triggered. It may seem strange that you have to select this option to get data from the URL: Why would you add an

XML data connectivity if you don't want to load XML data into your dashboard? Well, most of the time you don't have to, but imagine a scenario in which you want to submit some information to the server through this URL and don't need to get the result. In this case, you just need to select ENABLE LOAD, which we'll explain shortly.

The XML data is loaded into the embedded spreadsheet. Each variable node, as explained in Section 6.4.1, corresponds to one range.

To add a range, click the ADD button with a plus (+) sign below the range list.

The range name should be the same as that specified in the variable node. For example, if you have a node `<variable name="Sales info">` in the XML data, you need to specify "Sales info" as the range name here. Similar to many other properties, you can enter the name in the input field or bind it to a cell.

In addition to the name, you need to specify a cell range in the embedded Excel spreadsheet to store the data within that variable node. The numbers of rows and columns in the cell range should match those inside the variable node.

If there's more than one variable node in the XML data, you can repeat the previous steps to add more ranges.

To delete a range, click to select it from the list and then click the button with a minus (–) sign. The PREVIEW XML button is used to show you what your data should be like, not to preview the data specified in the URL. Clicking it will generate a temporary XML file in your system's *TEMP* directory (for example, *C:\Users\Ray\AppData\Local\Temp*) according to the settings here and open it in your default Internet browser. For example, let's say you've defined two ranges here, one called Range_0 bound to cell range Sheet1!$E$3:$G$4, which has two rows and three columns, and the other called Range_1 bound to range Sheet1!$E$5:$E$6 with two rows and one column. Clicking the PREVIEW XML button will direct you to a web page that shows a temporary XML file. Figure 6.6 displays the content of the XML file and the settings.

This functionality is helpful for troubleshooting when you think the format of your XML data is correct but it cannot be displayed properly in your dashboard. You can then check the format of your data to see what your dashboard is asking for.

You use the IMPORT NAMED RANGES button to import all named ranges you have created in the embedded Excel spreadsheet. A named range is a cell range with a name, which you can create with the following four steps.

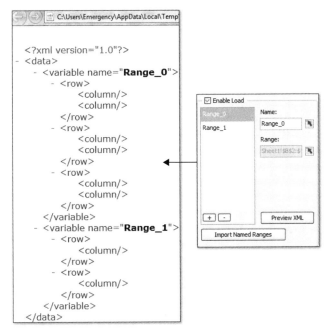

Figure 6.6 Accepted Structure of the XML Content Displayed in a Browser Window after Clicking "Preview XML"

1. Select the cell range to be named.

2. Click the NAME BOX to the left of the formula bar.

3. Type a one-word name for the list, for example, "FruitList." No spaces are allowed.

4. Press ⌈Enter⌉.

Figure 6.7 shows some named ranges.

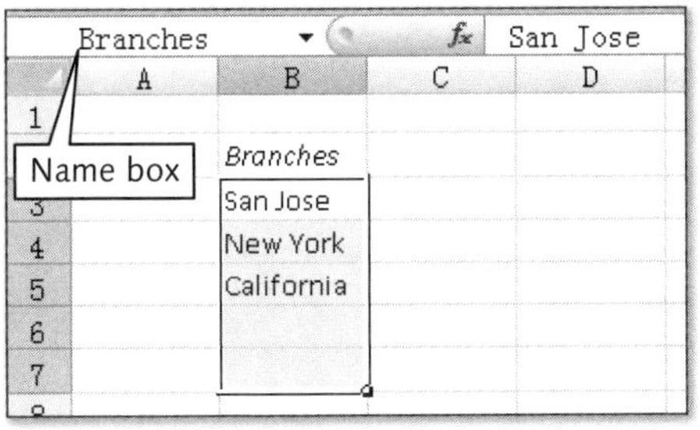

Figure 6.7 Name a Cell Range for Future Reference

After creating a named range, you can select a name in the Name Box dropdown list to select its corresponding cell range. The name can also be used in formulas, such as a SUM calculation.

As we mentioned before, it's a best practice to plan ahead what cells are used for what purpose. For example, you can first define a cell range, Sheet2!$B$3:$B$7, to store all branches and another range for all products. The cells may later be used as the source of a combo box for the user to choose what branch he wants to see. Then in the Data Manager, instead of selecting the ranges one by one, click the Import Named Ranges button to automatically import all of them. Note that clicking this button makes no change if there's no named range in the Excel spreadsheet.

Select Enable Send if you want to send data to the URL. For example, you can send the username and password you entered in the logon panel to the URL, or you can export data from the embedded Excel spreadsheet to an external service. You define what data to send by adding one or more ranges, just like what you do in the enable load step.

You can click Preview XML to see the format of the data that will be sent to the URL. However, you cannot import named ranges here.

All of the data will be included and wrapped into an XML string, the format of which is the same as that discussed in the section above. Name the ranges with care. They will be part of the generated XML string, so the URL should be able to parse them.

This option is very useful if you want to export data to an external service at runtime. A typical use is to export the data to an Excel file. To do this, define the cell ranges containing the data you want to export, and write an HTTP service (e.g., a Java Servlet if you are familiar with Java Enterprise Edition [JEE]) to process the sent XML string and export it to an Excel spreadsheet.

Usage

In this tab, shown in Figure 6.8, you configure when to trigger the data connectivity and how to inform the user about the status.

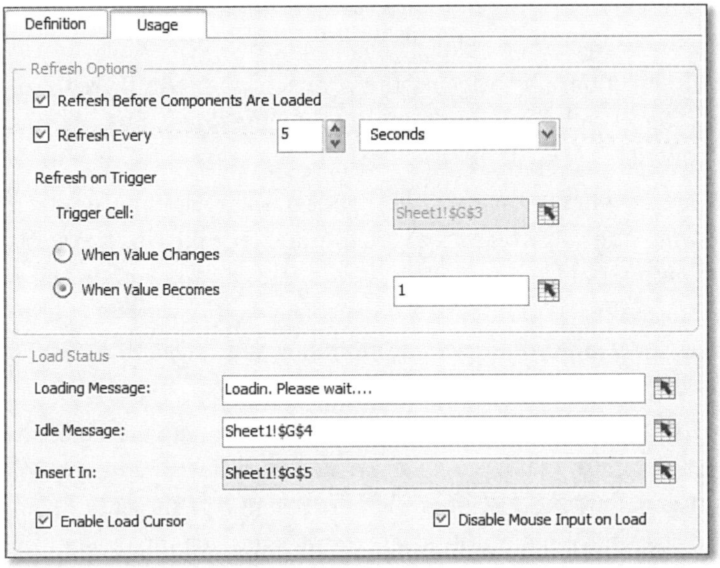

Figure 6.8 Usage Tab of an XML Data Connectivity

The available properties in this tab are illustrated here:

▶ REFRESH BEFORE COMPONENTS ARE LOADED
Select this option if you want to trigger this data connectivity (load the data) automatically each time before any component is loaded. SAP BusinessObjects Dashboards will load data from the specified URL first, before building the UI components. When the UI components appear on the screen, they'll be filled with data.

Select this option when the user isn't required to interact with specific values. Instead, you load data under default conditions to the dashboard.

▶ REFRESH EVERY
Select this option if you want to trigger the data connectivity at intervals. A typical usage is listing stock prices, which requires up-to-date data. When this option is selected, you can specify the interval as N seconds, minutes, or hours. SAP BusinessObjects Dashboards will then load data at each interval from the time when the dashboard is loaded.

▶ REFRESH ON TRIGGER
The previous two options require a user interaction to trigger the connection (the user can't control when to load data). REFRESH ON TRIGGER provides the

user with the ability to control when to load the data. Basically, SAP Business-Objects Dashboards listens to the value-change event of a cell, which is triggered by a user interaction, and triggers the connection as configured. You need to provide a trigger cell that is used as the source, the value of which is listened to by the software.

Then you can choose when to trigger the connection: each time its value changes or only when the value reaches a certain point. For the latter, you can either enter a value or bind it to another cell. Each time the source cell is updated, SAP BusinessObjects Dashboards will check whether the value of the source cell is equal to the one you specified and, if it is, will trigger the connection.

You can use the first type of trigger in many situations; for example, to create a drill-down chart. Suppose you're going to create a dashboard with one column chart on the top showing the monthly sales revenue of the entire company and one pie chart for the monthly sales revenue and quantity sold of the month selected in the column chart. To provide such data, follow these steps:

▶ Create an XML data connectivity to retrieve yearly sales revenues for all the branches, and select REFRESH BEFORE COMPONENTS ARE LOADED.

▶ Bind the data for the pie chart. Enable drill-down for it, and insert the identifier of the selected branch into a cell (say, cell Sheet1!$D$2).

▶ Create another XML data connectivity to retrieve monthly sales revenue and quantity sold for a given branch. The URL of this connectivity should contain the value of the cell in step 2, which stores the identifier of the selected branch (for example, *http://server:port/services/getBranchData?branchId=xx*). Set this connectivity to trigger on cell Sheet1!$D$2 when the value changes.

▶ Bind data for the column chart.

Figure 6.9 shows an example where the user clicks on a month in the column chart on the top, and then the pie chart on the bottom left is updated to show the information of each branch in that month; when the user clicks on a branch in this pie chart, the pie chart on the bottom right is updated to show the quantity sold every week at that branch in that month. Each time the user clicks on a different month in the column chart, the second data connectivity is triggered, and the pie chart on the bottom left is updated. For the second pie chart, the steps are similar.

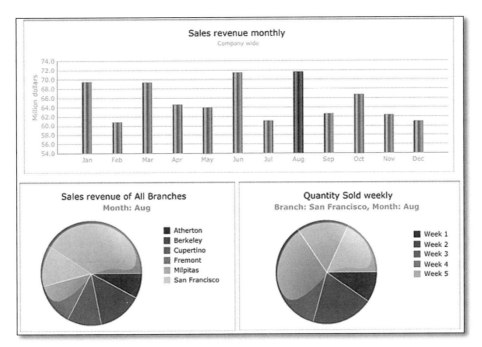

Figure 6.9 XML Data Connection Triggered Whenever the Content of a Cell Changes

You can also achieve this by returning the monthly data for each branch along with the yearly data, but this may cause performance problems if it takes a lot of time to query and parse the monthly data for each branch in the backend. What's more, what if the user wants to drill down from the column chart to see the daily sales revenue of a selected branch in a selected month?

Here's one more example, of the WHEN VALUE BECOMES option. Suppose there's an XML data connectivity requesting some confidential data in your dashboard. Not all people who can see the dashboard have the right to access data from this specific connectivity. You achieve this requirement with a shared secret. You and the user who has the right to access the data agree on a shared password. In your dashboard you provide an input field for the user to input the password. You bind the input field to a cell in the embedded spreadsheet. In the USAGE tab of that XML data connection, you bind TRIGGER CELL to the cell for the input field and then select WHEN VALUE BECOMES. This way, only users who enter the correct shared password can trigger the connection.

Load Status

An XML data connectivity is either loading or idle. When it's been triggered and the result XML has not returned, it's in loading status. Otherwise, it's idle. In this section of the screen (see Figure 6.8), you can set the loading message and the idle message by either entering text in the input field or binding it to a cell.

You use the INSERT IN field to select a cell in the embedded Excel spreadsheet where either the loading or the idle message will be inserted, depending on the load status of the connectivity. You can then bind a label component to this cell, thus displaying the status of the connectivity on the screen.

Select ENABLE LOAD CURSOR if you want to display a busy cursor when the connectivity is loading. The cursor will become a busy cursor (⧖) when the connectivity is loading and go back to its usual shape when the connectivity is idle. This allows the user to know by the shape of the cursor that the connectivity is being loaded.

Select DISABLE MOUSE INPUT ON LOAD if you don't want the user to take any action while this connection is loading. You can select this to prevent the user from sending another request unintentionally while the previous request is still being loaded. For example, let's say you have a pie chart showing the sales revenue of each branch, and each time the user selects a branch, another connectivity is triggered to request some other information about that branch. When the information from one branch is being loaded, you may want to disable the user's ability to click on the pie chart to select another branch. Otherwise, if the information of the latter branch returns before that of the former one, the user will see incorrect data.

Load status can be very useful to create an interactive dashboard. For example, the user may get confused when the connection takes a lot of time to return the XML data and he can see nothing indicating the load status: Is it still loading, or has it already finished, with nothing returned? Displaying a LOADING... label and/ or showing the cursor as busy is a simple way to reassure the user that the system is still processing the data. With the help of dynamic visibility and some other functionalities, you can make the interface better: showing the loading status in an image in front of all other UI components and preventing user interaction during loading.

6.4.3 Practice

It's easy to understand how to set up an XML data connectivity, but that doesn't mean it's a simple function. It can be very powerful and flexible. With XML data connectivity, you can connect your dashboard to almost any kind of data source.

Let's go through a simple hands-on example to see how to fetch live data using XML data, with a three-level drill-down. After this example, you might be able to drill-down four or more levels.

Suppose your boss wants to see the sales revenue of each year since the company was founded. Upon clicking a year, he wants to see the value of each month in that year; upon clicking a month, he wants to see the sales revenue and/or the quantity sold each day.

Plan the Data

The scenario is almost unachievable by placing all of the required data in the embedded spreadsheet at design time or by retrieving data of all measures for all years, all months, and all days with one request, mapping it to cell ranges in the embedded spreadsheet, and binding each chart to them. Instead, we'll request data for each chart separately, passing the selected year or month to the server.

There will be three ranges in the embedded spreadsheet, one for each chart. Drill-down is enabled for each chart (not necessary for the last one). Your embedded spreadsheet should look like Figure 6.10.

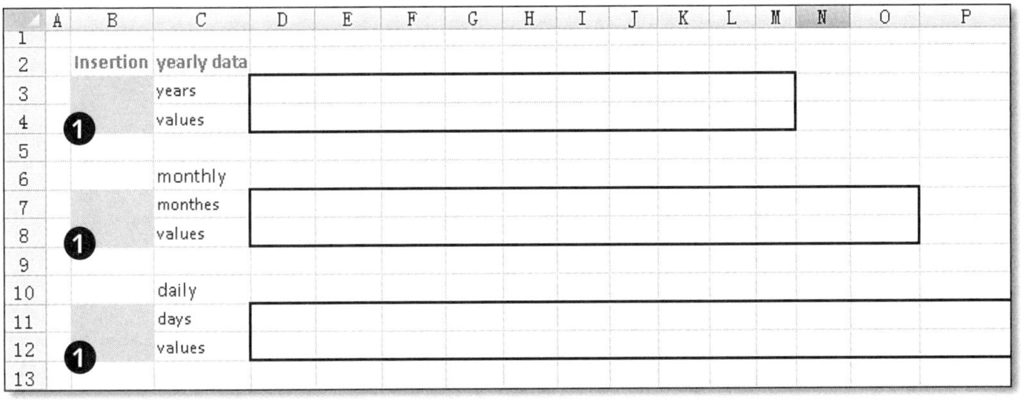

Figure 6.10 Data Structure in the Embedded Spreadsheet

In this example, only the values of one measure are returned, so each range has only two rows—the first for labels and the other for values. Assume our company is less than 10 years old, so we simply leave 10 columns for the yearly data.

Similarly, there are 12 and 31 columns for monthly and daily data, respectively. Note that for some months, there are fewer than 31 days. We chose the maximum number here to avoid missing any data.

For each chart, the selected year, month, or day will be passed to the backend server for further processing to retrieve data for the next level. So we insert the selected item into a column, as highlighted in yellow ❶.

Write Java Servlets in the Server Side

After planning the data, we need something to provide data that's accessible over HTTP. Here we choose Java Servlets to process input parameters and return data in an XML format, assuming you are familiar with Java Enterprise Edition (JEE).

The logic is the following:

▶ If no parameter is passed in, return the data of all available years.

▶ Otherwise, if only a year is passed in as an input parameter, return the data of all months of that year.

▶ Otherwise, if both a year and month are passed in, return the data of all days in that month.

The following shows the sample code to process this logic, using Apache Struts 1 Framework. For more information, please refer to *http://struts.apache.org/*.

```
import org.apache.struts.action.Action;
public class GetSalesRevenueAction extends Action {
    public ActionForward perform(ActionMapping actionMapping,
     ActionForm form, HttpServletRequest request,
     HttpServletResponse response) {
    int year = request.getParameter("year") == null ? 0 :
      Integer.parseInt(request.getParameter("year"));
    int month = request.getParameter("month") == null ? 0 :
      Integer.parseInt(request.getParameter("month"));
    List<SalesRevenue> resultData = new Array List<SalesRevenue>();
    if(year == 0) resultData = getDataOfYears();
    else if(month == 0) resultData = getDataOfMonths(year);
```

```
    else resultData = getDataOfDays(year, month);
    String ret = wrapToXML(resultData);
    response.setContentType("text/xml");
    response.getWriter().println(ret);
    response.getWriter().flush();
    response.getWriter().close();
}


    protected String wrapToXML(List<SalesRevenue> resultData) {
    StringBuffer ret = new StringBuffer();
    ret.append("<?xml version=\"1.0\" encoding=\"UTF-8\" ?>");
    ret.append("<data>");
    ret..append("<variable name=\"Data\">");
    ret.append("<row>");
    for(SalesRevenue item : resultData) {
        ret.append("<column>").append(item.label).append("</column>");
        ret.append("<column>").append(item.value).append("</column>");
    }
    ret.append("</row>");
    ret.append("</variable>");
    ret.append("</data>");
    }
}

class SalesRevenue {
    public String label;
    public String value;
    …..
}
```

The three methods of getDataOfYears(), getDataOfMonths(String year), and getDataOfDays(String year, String month) all return a list of SalesRevenue. Their content is omitted. Briefly, what they do is something like querying the data source and wrapping the result into structures of SalesRevenue. You can enrich the class SalesRevenue to include more data fields on your own.

Pay attention to the function wrapToXML(), which wraps a list of SalesRevenue to an XML string that conforms to the format required by SAP BusinessObjects Dashboards. After programming, you need deploy it as a web application hosted on a web application server such as a Tomcat. Let's assume the URL to call this servlet is *http://localhost:8080/sales/getSalesRevenue.do.*

Set Up XML Data Connectivity

Now that the server is ready, let's define the XML data connectivities that will retrieve live data for us. There will be three such connectivities in our dashboard, one per chart.

Before adding the three connectivities in the Data Manager, we need to build the URLs for them. We store the servlet in a cell for reference; for example, Sheet1!$D$14.

The URL to get the data of all years is the same as the base URL. The URL to get the data of all months is the base URL with &year=[selected year] appended, so the formula in the cell for the second connectivity is:

=CONCATENATE(D14,"&year=",Sheet1!$B$3)

Sheet1!$B$3 stores the numeric value of the selected year.

The URL to get the data of all days in a month is similar. Figure 6.11 shows the URL definitions in the embedded spreadsheet.

	D17	▾		*fx*	=CONCATENATE (D14, "&year=", B3, "&month=", B7)							
	A	B	C	D	E	F	G	H	I	J	K	L	M
13													
14			base URL	http://localhost:8080/sales/getSalesRevenue.do									
15			year URL	http://localhost:8080/sales/getSalesRevenue.do									
16			month URL	http://localhost:8080/sales/getSalesRevenue.do&year=									
17			day URL	http://localhost:8080/sales/getSalesRevenue.do&year=&month=									
18													

Figure 6.11 Concatenate URLs for XML Data Connectivities

Pay attention to the formula for cell D17 about the URL to get daily values.

Now we launch the Data Manager and select ADD • WEB SERVICE CONNECTION to create the connection to get yearly values. In the connection's PROPERTIES panel, name it "Sales revenue of years" to distinguish it from the other two, bind XML DATA URL to the cell containing its value (Sheet1!$D$15), select ENABLE LOAD and name the range "Data," and bind it to range Sheet1!$D$3:$M$4, as defined in the planning phase. The range is named Data as defined in the XML data returned from the Java Servlet, <variable name=\"Data\">.

We want to show the sales revenue of all years when the user launches the dashboard. In the USAGE tab, select REFRESH ON LOAD.

Repeat the steps above to add and configure the other two connectivities, but set the REFRESH OPTIONS of the second connectivity to WHEN VALUE CHANGES for trigger cell Sheet1!$B$3, which contains the selected year, and that of the third connectivity to WHEN VALUE CHANGES for Trigger Cell Sheet1!$B$7, which contains the selected month.

Figure 6.12 shows the PROPERTIES panel of the XML data connectivity to retrieve monthly data of a particular year.

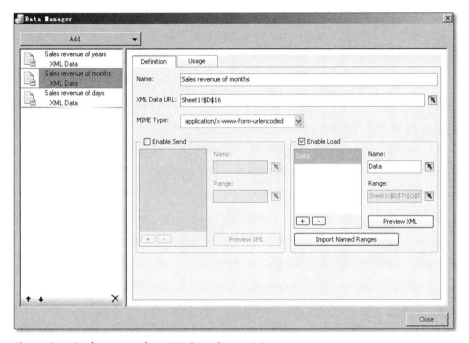

Figure 6.12 Configuration of an XML Data Connectivity

Set Up Charts

In this phase, we focus on adjusting the visual appearance and configuring the charts, including data binding and drill-down behavior.

Drag three column charts to the canvas, two on the top with equal size to show the data of years and months and one on the bottom to show daily data. Select the top two charts and follow the menu path FORMAT • MAKE SAME SIZE • BOTH and FORMAT • ALIGN • BOTTOM. Select the chart on the top left and the one for days and select FORMAT • ALIGN • LEFT.

You may want to use a line or combination chart to show the data for all days in one month to better visualize the trend. For simplicity, we'll just use a column chart here, the same as the other two.

The chart on the top left is for years, so enter the name "Sales revenue yearly" in its PROPERTIES panel, select BY SERIES, and bind its category labels to row Sheet1!$D$3:$M$3, where the years are mapped. Click the button with a + sign to add a series, and bind its values to Sheet1!$D$4:$M$4, where the sales revenues of all years are mapped. Figure 6.13 displays the PROPERTIES panel of the column chart for monthly sales revenue.

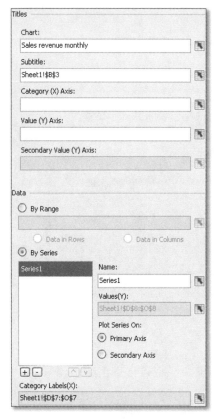

Figure 6.13 Configuration of the Column Chart Showing Monthly Value

The number of years may be less than 10, so the last few cells may be empty in range Sheet1!$D$3:$M$4. To avoid empty markers on the column chart, select IGNORE BLANK CELLS • IN SERIES AND IN VALUES in the BEHAVIOR tab.

It makes little sense to display series names on the chart. Moreover, showing them is a waste of space. So in Appearance • Layout, unselect Enable Legend to hide them.

The most important thing is drill-down. Select Enable Drill Down in the Drill Down tab. We want to insert both the name and sales revenue of the selected year, so we'll select Column as the insertion type, click Series1, and set the source data to range Sheet1!$D$3:$M$4 and the destination to column Sheet1!$B$3:$B$4, as defined in the planning phase.

Repeat the steps above to set data and binding for the other two charts. To show the user the context of the other two charts, bind the subtitle of the second chart to Sheet1!$B$3, which contains the selected year, and that of the third chart to Sheet1!$B$7, which contains the selected month.

Now we're done! At runtime, the sales revenues for each year, for each month of the first year, and for each day of the first month of the first year are displayed in the three charts by default. When the user selects another year from the first chart, the values in the other two charts are changed accordingly. Figure 6.14 shows a screenshot at runtime.

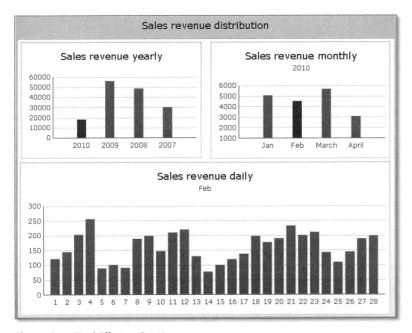

Figure 6.14 Final Effect at Runtime

Pay attention to the subtitles of the second and third charts, which are the selected year (2010) of the first chart and the selected month (February) of the second chart.

6.5 Web Service Connection

A web service is a service hosted by a web server over the HTTP protocol. Its messages are in XML (or JSON, often used in the RESTful web service) format, following the SOAP (Simple Object Access Protocol) standard. It can be developed in many kinds of programming languages and hosted in many web application servers. There's often a machine-readable description of its operations and message structures written in WSDL (Web Service Description Language).

In SAP BusinessObjects Dashboards 4.0, the web service connection is somewhat similar to the XML data connectivity in that both use XML to format the return data. However, a web service connection can be more complex. The return data of an XML data connectivity just follows XML format, and it doesn't need to follow the SOAP standard or provide a WSDL description. What's more, there are significant limitations to its format: Its root node must be named data, followed by a node hierarchy of variable, row, and column. Nothing else is permitted.

A web service connectivity is more powerful than an XML data connectivity. It's required to follow only the XML standard, with no restriction to the node names or hierarchy. Compared to XML data, a web service connection provides a more sophisticated structure and more control over the output.

Similar to an XML data connectivity, a web service connection can also be used for data source write-back. As you'll see, this connectivity accepts input parameters that can be bound to cells in the embedded spreadsheet. That is, you can save user input in the embedded spreadsheet and send it to the server. The server can then write the data back to the data source after processing. If you are familiar with web programming, you may know that this is the HTTP POST method, compared to GET in an XML data connectivity.

6.5.1 When to Use a Web Service Connection

You should anticipate using a web service connectivity when the data source is exposed as a standard web service. One exception here is Query as a Web Service, which is a product of SAP BusinessObjects that also exposes data as a web service. For such data, you choose connectivity of the type Query as a Web Service instead of a web service.

6.5.2 How to Use a Web Service Connection

To add a web service connectivity, launch the Data Manager and select WEB SERVICE in the ADD dropdown list. A web service connection will then be added to the connection list. You can create as many web service connectivities as you want in one dashboard and set their properties by clicking a web service connectivity to open its PROPERTIES panel.

Definition

In this tab you define the URL of the web service, set values for input parameters, if any, and bind the output values to cell ranges in the embedded spreadsheet, as displayed in Figure 6.15.

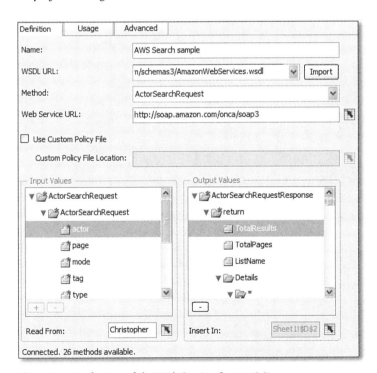

Figure 6.15 Definition of the Web Service Connectivity

The configuration items in this tab are explained here:

► NAME
Similar to what you did for an XML data connectivity, enter a descriptive name for the web service as its purpose. This can help you quickly identify a connectivity in the list to the left if there are many connections on your dashboard.

► WSDL URL
To use a web service, you need know its WSDL URL and enter it here. The WSDL describes the available methods and structure of both input and output.

You click the IMPORT button after entering the WSDL URL. SAP Business-Objects Dashboards will then connect to that URL and parse its definition. If it's unavailable or doesn't have a valid format, the software will pop up an error message saying UNABLE TO LOAD URL. If everything is all right, all the methods will be displayed in the METHOD dropdown list below, with all input and output values in the corresponding lists.

Note that each time you modify the WSDL URL, even just adding or deleting a character in the field, all methods and input and output values of the previous WSDL will be removed. If you have bound the input or output values to a cell or cell range in the embedded spreadsheet, the binding will also be removed; you have to rebind them. So if you don't want to change the WSDL, be careful to avoid modifying the URL.

For simplicity, you can use existing public web services. Amazon.com provides a collection of web services for developers to query or to manage their shops, called Amazon Web Service (AWS). For more details, please visit *http://aws.amazon.com/*.

In the rest of this chapter, we'll use an AWS to illustrate how to use a web service connectivity. In the WSDL URL field enter the WSDL URL *http://xml.amazon.com/schemas3/AmazonWebServices.wsdl*, which we can use for searching.

► METHOD
After importing the WSDL URL, SAP BusinessObjects Dashboards will parse it and list all available methods (or operations) in the METHOD dropdown list. You can select only one method here. If you want to use multiple methods from this web service, add one web service connectivity for each method.

► WEB SERVICE URL
The available web service URLs are also defined in the WSDL, so you'll see this field filled after clicking IMPORT. If there are many, you need to select the one

you want to use for this connection from the dropdown list. However, the WSDL just defines the methods and structures. At runtime, the request is sent to the web service URL, not the WSDL URL.

You can also bind the web service URL to a cell, giving you the ability to change it at runtime. For example, you can copy the default web service URL to a cell and then replace the host with another cell (e.g., use an Excel formula to change the URL to =CONCATENATE("http://", Sheet1!$A$2," /onca/soap3"). At runtime, you can then ask the user to select the host from a combo box and insert it into Sheet1$A$2 (you can use this method when migrating from a development environment to testing). Or you can pass the web service URL through Flash Variables, which we'll explain in Chapter 7, Section 7.5. You may want to bind the web service URL to a cell to make it dynamic when you need migrate your dashboard from a development environment to a production environment.

▶ USE CUSTOM POLICY FILE

As mentioned in Section 6.3, security issues need to be considered if your dashboard accesses resources from another domain. This is a policy caused by Flash Player.

By default, Flash Player only searches for the policy files in the root location of a web server, which makes it a little inconvenient for a site administrator to place those files in the root directory. In such cases, you can use your own custom policy file, which can be placed anywhere.

To do this, select the USE CUSTOM POLICY FILE checkbox and then either enter the custom policy file location in the text box or bind it to a cell in the embedded spreadsheet.

▶ INPUT VALUES

The mandatory and optional input variables or parameters of the web service are listed here. For each variable, you can either enter the value in the READ FROM field or bind it to a cell in the embedded spreadsheet by clicking the BIND button. For example, you may want to add an input label to the dashboard for the user to enter an author name and send it to the web service so that only books by that author are returned.

All values are treated as text, whether it's an integer, date, currency, and so on. For the web service to work perfectly, you need to make be clear about the accepted format of each value. For example, if the web service requires a month for the search to begin with, you need know whether you should enter 200910 or 2009.10 or something else.

All values you specify here will be passed to the web service URL as key-value pairs.

▶ OUTPUT VALUES
A web service may return several data fields, categorized into classes, which are all listed here. A folder icon next to a field indicates a class, and a file icon indicates a field. You can choose the data you are interested in and insert it into the embedded spreadsheet.

Some fields have only one value, such as the TOTALRESULTS field, as shown previously in Figure 6.15. As a result, this field should be bound to a single cell. On the other hand, other fields, such as DETAILS in Figure 6.15, may have several values and should be bound to a column.

If you want to insert all fields of a class into the embedded spreadsheet, click on the class and bind it to a cell range. The number of columns of the range should be the same as the number of fields within the class, and the number of rows should be the same as the number of returned records. If you aren't sure how many records are returned, use the maximum number that will return or that you want. Pay attention to the maximum number of rows that you can bind to, which by default is 512. If you want to increase the number of rows allowed, go to FILE • PREFERENCE and modify the setting in EXCEL OPTIONS, as explained in Chapter 2, Section 2.1.

Microsoft Excel is two-dimensional, so you cannot insert a class with subclasses into a cell range. That is, you can either bind a field to a cell or a column, or bind a class with no subclass to a cell range in the embedded spreadsheet.

Usage

In this tab you define when to trigger the connection and how to deal with load status, the same as for an XML data connectivity.

Advanced

This tab is specific to this connectivity. You may want to use this tab when the web service requires some information to be passed in the SOAP header. That information should be as defined by the web service you are requesting.

You can either enter the information in HTML format in the SOAP header field or click the BIND button to bind it to a cell in the embedded Excel spreadsheet containing the required information. For example, the web service may require user credentials to be passed in the SOAP header, and you can enter something like the following to the field.

```
<soap:Header>
<userName>Ray</userName> <password>abcd</password>
</soap:Header>
```

If the data is bound to a cell, SAP BusinessObjects Dashboards will automatically insert the SOAP header tag into it. That is, in the cell you don't need to include the `<soap:Header>` tag, but only:

```
<userName>Ray</userName> <password>abcd</password>.
```

6.6 Excel XML Map

One powerful feature of Microsoft Office Excel (2003, 2007, and 2010) is that it supports user-defined XML schemas. You can map data from one or more XML files into cell ranges in an Excel file, with or without the XML Schema (*.xsd* files). Excel automates most of the processes for you, including XML parsing and filtering.

XML is widely used in representing and storing data. For example, sales revenue may be exported into an XML file from your SAP ERP system. By mapping XML elements into an Excel file, you can further process the data without leaving Excel, which might be your everyday tool, and refresh it to retrieve the latest data.

SAP BusinessObjects Dashboards provides an Excel XML map connectivity so you can create dashboards based on data in an XML file by mapping data from XML files into an Excel file and then importing the Excel file into SAP BusinessObjects Dashboards. The link to the original XML files will be retained. Similar to other connectivities, you can define when to trigger such connections to get the latest data. To get the data, the XML file must be available when the connection is triggered.

6.6.1 When to Use an Excel XML Map

You may want create connectivities of this kind when the data source is always in XML files, which may or may not need further processing in Excel. A typical usage is when the sales department asks you to create a dashboard showing the monthly sales status, but they have no way to expose the relative data through a web service or Java Servlet. Instead, their application can only export the data into an XML file. The sales department has agreed with you on the location of the exported XML files.

You can then connect to the XML files in your dashboard through Excel XML Map. At runtime, the XML file is updated monthly, when the user exports data to it. The latest data will be updated in the dashboard immediately after the user clicks a refresh button or does anything else that will trigger the connections, without the need to reimport the Excel file.

You are really creating dashboards based on data in XML files. At design time, the Excel spreadsheet acts as a visualization tool in the workspace, so you can better understand the XML schema and easily bind UI components to cells. At runtime, Excel acts as a bridge between your dashboard and the data source—XML files in a specified location.

6.6.2 How to Use an Excel XML Map

The steps to use an Excel XML map connectivity in your dashboard are as follows.

1. **Import Data from XML File(s) into Excel.**
   How to import XML files into an Excel file is not the focus of this book. Very simply put, you first open the XML file in Excel, from the menu path FILE • OPEN. If you're using Excel 2007 or 2010, you'll see more options available in the XML group in the DEVELOPER tab, which is unavailable by default. To enable it, you need to launch Excel outside SAP BusinessObjects Dashboards and select FILE • OPTIONS. In the new window, EXCEL OPTIONS, go to CUSTOMIZE RIBBON and make sure the node DEVELOPER is selected. For more detailed information, please refer to the Microsoft website at:

   ▸ *http://office.microsoft.com/en-us/excel/HP102063971033.aspx* for Microsoft Office Excel 2007

   ▸ *http://office.microsoft.com/en-us/excel/HA011019641033.aspx* for Excel 2003

You can also import XML files directly into the embedded spreadsheet inside SAP BusinessObjects Dashboards. In this case, for Excel 2007 and 2010, access the XML file via the DEVELOPER tab in the ribbon area and click the IMPORT button. For Excel 2003, the process is a little different in that you need click the XML SOURCE button. To show this button, right-click your Excel toolbar and click CUSTOMIZE. Navigate to the COMMANDS tab, select DATA, and scroll down to the XML DATA source option. Click and drag the XML SOURCE button onto your toolbar.

2. **Import the Excel file into your dashboard.**
   This step is required if you launch Excel outside SAP BusinessObjects Dashboards and import data from one or more XML files into an Excel file.

   To import the Excel file, simply click the IMPORT SPREADSHEET button in the toolbar, or select DATA • IMPORT/IMPORT from SAP BusinessObjects Enterprise. We discussed this subject in more detail in Chapter 2, where we covered menus.

3. **Add Excel XML map connections.**
   After importing the Excel file, or the XML file directly, you'll see the data in the embedded spreadsheet. You can then create dashboards based on the data. However, this is just a static snapshot of the source XML file and cannot be refreshed to retrieve live data, because by now, SAP BusinessObjects Dashboards doesn't know that the data is from an external XML file.

   To solve this problem, add Excel XML map connections by clicking EXCEL XML MAPS in the ADD dropdown list in the Data Manager. However, if you do this when the embedded spreadsheet contains no mapping to an XML file, nothing will happen.

   Clicking EXCEL XML MAPS triggers SAP BusinessObjects Dashboards to detect any existing mapping to XML files in the embedded spreadsheet and automatically generate one connectivity for each mapping. Later when we talk about Live Office Connection, you'll find it very similar.

Properties Panel

In our example, we assume that the finance department exports the data about monthly reimbursement amounts into an XML file called *Expense.xml* in the folder *D:/finance*. Figure 6.16 shows the PROPERTIES panel of the detected Excel XML map connection.

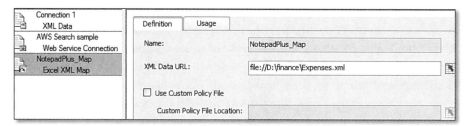

Figure 6.16 Definition of an Excel XML Map Connection

In the DEFINITION tab, the NAME field displays the name of the XML mapping, which cannot be changed here, but only in Excel. Taking Excel 2007 as an example, you can change the name by clicking SOURCE in the XML group of the DEVELOPER tab in the ribbon area.

The XML data URL defines where to locate the XML file. You can specify it by either entering a constant file path in the input field or clicking the BIND button to bind it to a cell in the embedded spreadsheet.

The URL can be of any protocol as long as it's valid. As displayed in the figure, the default URL is the one selected on mapping the XML file which is: *file://finance\Expenses.xml.*

You can also point to a network place, such as: \\192.168.0.4\finance\Expenses.xml.

This is helpful if you're working in a corporate environment, where different departments can share folders over a file server.

By binding the URL to a cell, you make it possible for it to be dynamically based on some condition. For example, you can point to different XML files based on the user selection via some selectors such as a combo box, using if...then...else logic in Excel. If the information about the user who is viewing the dashboard can be passed in, you can also point to different files based on the current user, thus controlling the data security inside your dashboard.

The USAGE tab is exactly the same as that of any other connectivity, where you control how to trigger this connection. For more information about this tab, please refer to the corresponding paragraphs in Section 6.4, where we discussed the XML data connectivity.

6.7 Summary

In this chapter we discussed the embedded Excel spreadsheet, which acts as the bridge between UI components and source data. We also talked about some commonly used, basic data connectivities you can use to retrieve live data from external data sources, the output of which you can bind to cell ranges in the embedded spreadsheet. With the help of such data connectivities, you enable your dashboard to reflect real and live data.

In addition to being user friendly and visually engaging, SAP Business-Objects Dashboards is also very powerful in connecting to external live data. Such advanced connectivity allows you to connect to data in an SAP environment system or consume data from an HTML page or Flash Player.

7   Advanced Data Connectivity

In Chapter 6 we discussed the embedded Excel spreadsheet in the SAP Business-Objects Dashboards workspace, which acts as the direct data source each UI component or data connectivity can bind to. To connect to external and live data sources, we discussed importing data from an external Excel file and using XML data and web service connectivity, which returns data in a simple or standard XML format over HTTP.

This is not the whole story. SAP BusinessObjects Dashboards provides several more types of data connectivity for you to pass data to or from your dashboard, such as Query as a Web Service, which is specific to an SAP BusinessObjects environment; SAP NetWeaver Business Warehouse (BW) Connection, specific to an SAP NetWeaver BW system; and Flash Variables, which is common to all environments.

In this chapter we'll illustrate all of the data connectivity methods not covered in Chapter 6, including Query as a Web Service, Flash Variables, FS Command, External Interface Connection, and SAP NetWeaver BW Connection.

After reading this chapter you'll be able to:

▶ Describe all data connectivity methods available in SAP BusinessObjects Dashboards

▶ Understand the use scenario of each type of data connectivity

▶ Know when to use what type of data connectivity and how

7.1   Query as a Web Service

This connectivity is specific to the SAP BusinessObjects environment. You can use such connectivities in your dashboard to retrieve data from Query as a Web Services and then a Universe. It can be created either from the Query as a Web Service Designer or by publishing a block of data as a web service in Web Intelligence Rich Client.

You may get a little confused about why we need this data connectivity when we already have XML data and web services, which can connect to almost any kind of data source. The disadvantage of these two connectivities is that you need programming effort to retrieve data from your data source and wrap it into an XML string in the format required by SAP BusinessObjects Dashboards, while Query as a Web Service is a product, and all you need is some configuration to make it work, without any programming effort.

Query as a Web Service is hosted in an SAP BusinessObjects environment by a web application server such as Tomcat. It cannot function without an SAP BusinessObjects environment, which is responsible for processing its requests and responses.

7.1.1   When to Use Query as a Web Service

Choose Query as a Web Service (QaaWS) to expose your data when:

▶ It's better and easier for the client to consume web service data.

▶ You can connect to the data source by a Universe.

▶ You're inside an SAP BusinessObjects environment.

In SAP BusinessObjects Dashboards, you can use this connectivity to connect to one or more Universes and, consequently, one or more data sources. You can create as many such connectivities as you want in one dashboard.

Figure 7.1 shows the workflow from SAP BusinessObjects Dashboards to the data source with this kind of connectivity.

A typical use of Query as a Web Service is to create a trusted and attractive BI dashboard against SAP NetWeaver BW systems using SAP BusinessObjects Dashboards by building Universes on top of SAP NetWeaver BW queries (one Universe per BW query) and then building one or more query as a web service for each Universe. Then inside SAP BusinessObjects Dashboards, one or more QaaWS connectivities can be created to retrieve the actual business data stored in SAP NetWeaver BW.

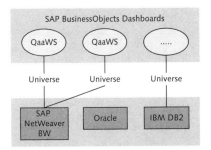

Figure 7.1 Workflow Using QaaWS in SAP BusinessObjects Dashboards

7.1.2 How to Use Query as a Web Service

To connect to a Query as a Web Service, launch the Data Manager, click ADD, and select WEB SERVICE QUERY (QUERY AS A WEB SERVICE) from the dropdown list. You can create as many connectivities as you want in one dashboard.

The PROPERTIES panel for this connectivity is divided into two tabs, as described in the following sections. In this section we talk about the meaning of each method, web service URL, how to transport your dashboard with QaaWS connections from the development environment to test or production, binding of input and output values, and trigger options.

Definition

This tab is very similar to that of a web service connectivity.

▶ NAME
You give the connection a descriptive name instead of Connection 1 or Connection 2 to make it meaningful and distinguishable when there are several connections in the list to the left.

▶ WSDL URL
In the WSDL URL field, enter the WSDL URL of the query as a web service. The WSDL URL should be provided by the person who has created the QaaWS. You can find the URL in Query as a Web Service Designer, as displayed in Figure 7.2. Click the TO CLIPBOARD button to copy the WSDL for the selected QaaWS.

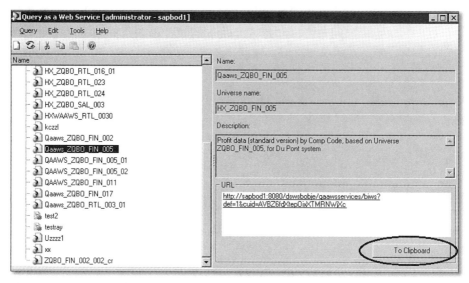

Figure 7.2 WSDL URL of a QaaWS Found Using this Client Tool

If you're using a QaaWS created in Web Intelligence Rich Client by publishing a block, you can get the WSDL URL either from the Web Intelligence Rich Client or QaaWS Designer.

Then in the PROPERTIES panel, you can paste it in the WSDL URL field. Note that in your copied URL might be a property def=1, and you need change it to WSDL=1; otherwise you'll see an error message saying UNABLE TO LOAD URL. You may also encounter such an error if the host name (e.g., sapbod1) can't be parsed in your computer, in which case you may consider using the fully qualified domain name, or use IP instead of the name.

Clicking IMPORT will trigger SAP BusinessObjects Dashboards to connect to the specified WSDL URL and parse it. Here, Query as a Web Service behaves just like a normal web service, and all of its available methods, web service URLs, input parameters, and output values will be displayed in the corresponding fields, as displayed in Figure 7.3.

Note that the WSDL URL can only be input into the text area and can't be bound to the embedded spreadsheet.

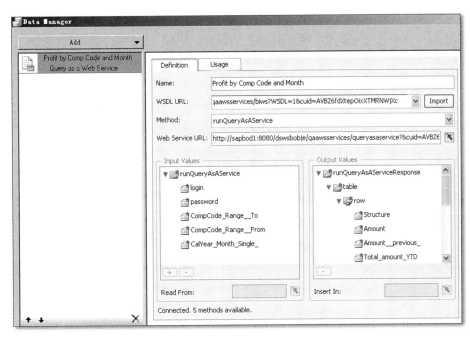

Figure 7.3 Metadata of a QaaWS after You Import Its WSDL URL

▶ WEB SERVICE URL

The web service URL is the actual URL that SAP BusinessObjects Dashboards will connect to to retrieve data at runtime. It's different from the WSDL URL, which is just accessed and used at design time to retrieve its defined method and input/output values.

When you've imported a WSDL URL, any change to the WSDL URL field, even just adding or removing a single character, will clear all the results of clicking the IMPORT button. That is, all of the bindings you have made to the input and output fields of the QaaWS will be lost. However, changes to the WEB SERVICE URL field will not affect other bindings. That's why in most cases when you're going to transport your dashboard from a development environment to test or production, you should leave the WSDL URL field unchanged and only change the Web Service URL field when you have to. For example, you can bind WEB SERVICE URL to a cell in the embedded spreadsheet so it can be passed from another connectivity such as Flash Variables or FS Command. During development you use the web service URL from the SAP BusinessObjects development environment and pass it from Flash Variable into the dashboard. When you are to transport your dashboard to a test or production environment, just change the passed-in value. This way you needn't modify the dashboard definition to transport it.

▶ CUSTOM POLICY FILE

At runtime your dashboard is essentially an SWF file. Due to the security restrictions of Adobe Flash, if the SWF is run locally, you need to add the file or PowerPoint/Word applications trusted. And if the SWF is hosted on a web server, any web server that your dashboard connects to for live data must have a cross-domain policy file to allow access to it.

In SAP BusinessObjects Dashboards 4.0 a new feature is the ability to specify your custom policy file for each QaaWS connectivity by selecting USE CUSTOM POLICY FILE and setting the file's path by either entering it in the input field or binding it to a cell in the spreadsheet. The path can be either absolute or relative. For more information about what a cross-domain policy file is and how to use it, please refer to Chapter 6, Section 6.3 or the Adobe website.

▶ METHOD

This field lists all available methods of the QaaWS. Each method may have different input parameters and output values. You can only elect one per connectivity. If you want to use more methods of one Query as a Web Service, create more connectivities.

Click the dropdown arrow to see the available methods in this Query as a Web Service, as displayed in Figure 7.4.

Figure 7.4 Available Methods of a Query as a Web Service

The available methods for a QaaWS created from the QaaWS Designer and from Web Intelligence Rich Client are different. Figure 7.4 shows the methods for the first case. Generally, the methods are divided into two categories, one to query data and the other to list candidate values (list of values [LOV]) of each input parameter, if any.

▶ **To Query Data**

This category, with the two methods `runQueryAsAService` and `runQueryAs-AServiceEx`, is common to all Query as a Web Service resources.

The method `runQueryAsAService` is selected by default, and you can use it to get the data most of the time. It retrieves the data defined in the query as a web service application, with prompt values bound by the user for parameters.

The other method in this category, `runQueryAsAServiceEx`, is generated for index-aware prompts. It does the same work but provides another functionality: Instead of explicitly specifying the value for a parameter, you can just enter its index. You can find the change in the INPUT VALUES area when switching from method `runQueryAsAService` to method `runQueryAsAServiceEx`.

For more information about these two methods, you can refer to the User Guide for Query as a Web Service, which can be found at *www.help.sap.com*.

▶ **To Get LOV**

You use the methods in this category to retrieve the candidate items, or list of values, of the input parameters. The method name is structured like `valueOf_xxx`, where `xxx` is the parameter name. For example, in Figure 7.4, there's one method called `valuesOf_CalYear_Month_Single_`, which is for parameter `CalYear_Month_Single` defined in the backend.

There will be one method for each parameter, no matter if it's optional or mandatory.

This category contains no method if no parameter is defined in this Query as a Web Service.

Use this method to help the user specify values of input parameters, to avoid wrong inputs or confusion caused by the user not knowing the valid format of each parameter value. For example, you can use this method to create a query as a web service connectivity called "LOV of parameter XX" to retrieve the list of values of a parameter. You insert the result into a cell range and display it in the dashboard using a combo box. Then you create another query as a web service connectivity to query the data with the method `runQueryAsAService`. You can bind the input parameter XX listed in the INPUT VALUES area to the cell that contains the selected value of the combo box. This way, the value selected from the combo box is always valid and thus can be accepted by `runQueryAsAService`.

► INPUT VALUES

This area lists all input parameters defined for the selected method of the Query as a Web Service. You can click on each parameter and set its value by either entering a constant text directly in the input field at the bottom of this area or click the BIND button to bind it to a single cell in the embedded spreadsheet.

As you can see from Figure 7.3, there are two parameters you need to specify values for in INPUT VALUES: login and password. They're used to log on to the SAP BusinessObjects system, which then communicates with the backend data source if necessary. However, you can't specify the authentication type here. Depending on the selected authentication type when defining the QaaWS, which can be Enterprise, SAP, or Windows AD, you may need to enter a different username and password. If your dashboard is to run in an InfoView or BI Launchpad, you needn't enter the username or password here, as your dashboard can reuse the session.

> **Note**
>
> If the parameter is to accept a range of values (requiring a `From` and a `To` value), Query as a Web Service will automatically break into two single-value parameters, one for `From` and the other for `To`, each of which can be bound to a single cell.

Sometimes there are some additional parameters other than user credentials. For example, to retrieve the number of products sold, you need to provide the calendar month to specify the date range. The parameter `valuesOf_CalYear_Month_Single_` in Figure 7.4 is an example of this. When specifying a value for this parameter, either entering it or binding it to a cell, you need to specify the value format: If you want to see the number of products sold in a month, say, August 2009, should you enter 200908, 2009/08, or something else? If the parameter is an SAP variable, it may be something like [0CALMONTH]. [200908]. To determine the exact format, you need to contact the person who created or developed the data source on which the Universe is based. For example, in an SAP NetWeaver BW environment, you need to contact the person who created the BW queries.

If the parameter is optional, you can simply leave it empty if you don't want to specify any value for it. Clicking any folder node, such as the method name here, has no effect.

▶ OUTPUT VALUES

This area lists all of the structures and data fields returned by the previously selected method, including some metadata about the result of the query, such as a message indicating whether the query succeeded or failed. You can select a data field or a structure to bind it to a cell or cell range in the embedded spreadsheet so they can be further used by other UI components to display the data the user has requested.

The data returned from the query is always a list of rows. A row is composed of several data fields, called columns. You can either click a single data field to bind all its values to a single cell, row, or column or click the row to insert all rows returned to a cell range. The number of cells of the target range should be equal to the number of data fields inside that row (structure), and the number of rows should be equal to the number of records returned, that is, how many records satisfy the query condition, defined by the values you specified for the input parameters in the INPUT VALUES area. If you don't know how many records will be returned, use the maximum number that will return, but don't exceed the limit specified in SAP BusinessObjects Dashboards in the menu path FILE • PREFERENCE • EXCEL OPTIONS • MAXIMUM NUMBER OF ROWS.

For the Query as a Web Service used in Figure 7.3, we bound rows to cell range Sheet1!\$C\$2:\$F\$8, with seven rows and four columns. We select seven rows because seven is the maximum number of rows of data we want to accept in the dashboard, no matter how many there are in the backend. Similarly, four is the number of fields in each row: STRUCTURE, AMOUNT, AMOUNT_PREVIOUS, and TOTAL_ACCOUNT_YTD.

The methods and input/output values are those of the QaaWS created from the Query as a Web Service Designer. Figure 7.5 shows the available methods for QaaWS created in Web Intelligence Rich Client by publishing a block of data:

You can see that's there's no method for retrieving an LOV for any parameter, but there's one new method called `Drill_Area_Activity` and one called `GetReportBlock_Area_Activity`, where `AreaActivity` is the name of the QaaWS defined within Web Intelligence Rich Client.

The purpose of method `GetReportBlock` is the same as `runQueryAsAService` mentioned above, to get the block data of SAP BusinessObjects Web Intelligence. You specify values for each parameter and get the returned data by binding table –> row in OUTPUT VALUES to a cell range in the embedded spreadsheet.

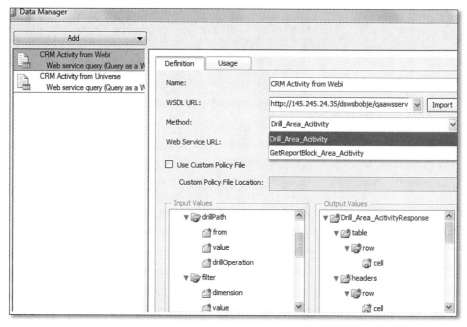

Figure 7.5 Available Methods of a QaaWS Created in Web Intelligence Rich Client

The other method, Drill, is especially useful when you want to drill in the dashboard, similar to what you do in the SAP BusinessObjects Web Intelligence report along some hierarchy. Its OUTPUT VALUES area is the same as that of the method GetReportBlock, while in INPUT VALUES you can set DRILLPATH and FILTER. For DRILLPATH, the property FROM refers to the name of the hierarchy level you want to drill from, for example, country or region in an organization hierarchy. You then specify the value of a node in the hierarchy level in the VALUE field, for example, China for country or South China for region. If you're working with SAP NetWeaver BW, you need provide the technical name instead of a description of the hierarchy node. The property DRILLOPERATION defines the drill direction—whether to drill down or roll up. It can only be either of two values: UP or DOWN, which are case-insensitive. For FILTER, you can define a dimension (e.g., country, calendar year), value (e.g., China, 2011-12), and operator (=,<>, >, etc). When the connection is triggered, only data satisfying the filter and drill conditions will be returned.

Some additional and useful input parameters are available for such QaaWS. For example, if you want to get data from the instance of the SAP BusinessObjects

Web Intelligence report instead of refreshing it, click GETFROMLATESTDOCU-MENTINSTANCE or GETFROMUSERINSTANCE and set its READ FROM value to 1. This way you can schedule your SAP BusinessObjects Web Intelligence report to run in the backend to speed up the response of the dashboard at runtime.

Similar information is also available in OUTPUT VALUES. When you scroll down in this area, you can find some output fields such as USER, DOCUMENTNAME, LAS-TREFRESHDATE, CREATIONDATE, SCHEDULESTARTTIME, and SCHEDULENDTIME. For example, you can retrieve data from the latest instance by setting GETFROMLAT-ESTDOCUMENTINSTANCE to 1 in INPUT VALUES and binding SCHEDULESTARTTIME and SCHEDULEENDTIME to cells in the embedded spreadsheet and then to LABELS in the dashboard to tell the user when the data is retrieved.

Usage

In this tab you configure how and when to load the data by setting the connection to be triggered when you load the dashboard, on intervals counted from the time when the dashboard is loaded, or by listing a certain cell in the embedded spreadsheet.

Also, you can set the load message and idle message here, which will inform the user about the connectivity's status. This functionality may be especially useful for this connectivity, because it often takes a long time to load data from the data source (such as SAP NetWeaver BW), in which case the data needs to be processed by Query as a Web Service, Universe, and the database one by one.

A new property here is whether to convert date/time values to Greenwich Mean Time (GMT). You may want to select this option when your dashboard is used across regions in different time zones and you want to make the value and format of date/time fields consistent.

7.2   SAP NetWeaver BW Connection

A dashboard is used to display highly aggregated data for high-level executives to easily understand the situation and find something behind the data. However, retrieving plenty of detailed transaction data into a dashboard and calculating the aggregation on the fly is almost impossible. That's why in most cases the data for a dashboard is from a data warehouse where the data is loaded from several business systems and aggregated. Such a data warehouse is often referred to as an enterprise data warehouse (EDW) or integrated data warehouse (IDW), which can be SAP NetWeaver BW, SQL Server Analysis, or Oracle and so on.

With the help of some high-performance appliance such as SAP HANA it's possible to read transaction data directly from the business system into memory and calculate the aggregation on the fly, without the need to load data periodically and save the aggregation in additional tables.

With SAP NetWeaver BW Connection you can connect to a BW query directly from your dashboard, without extra steps such as creating a Universe on top of the query, exposing the data of fields from the Universe as a query as a web service or of a block from Web Intelligence Rich Client as BI Web Service, and consume it in dashboard.

7.2.1 When to Use SAP NetWeaver BW Connection

You can use SAP NetWeaver BW Connection when you want to read data from a BW query. Multiple such connections are allowed in one dashboard.

The benefit is that you can connect to data in SAP NetWeaver BW systems directly. However, if your requirement is complex and the BW query itself can't provide the required data or format, you may have to use the traditional method of using SAP BusinessObjects Web Intelligence or SAP BusinessObjects Live Office to format data from the BW query in the way you want.

Before choosing this approach you also need to make sure your environment meets the prerequisites. At design time you need have SAP GUI with patch 901 or above installed on the same machine as SAP BusinessObjects Dashboards. The SAP NetWeaver BW system you are connecting to needs to have SAP NetWeaver 7.0 enhancement package 1 SP5 patched. Both the ABAP and Java engine of your SAP NetWeaver BW system need be installed, with single sign-on between them configured.

Also, you need be aware that data loading in SAP NetWeaver BW is usually done once a day, so if your dashboard is expected to show live data, this connection is not the right choice.

7.2.2 How to Use SAP NetWeaver BW Connection

To add this connectivity, click the ADD drop-down list in the Data Manager and choose SAP NETWEAVER BW CONNECTION. Give it a meaningful name to understand its purpose and source.

Next, click the BROWSE button to the right of the QUERY field to select a query from the SAP NetWeaver BW system. If you haven't connected to any SAP NetWeaver BW system in your design session yet, a list of available SAP NetWeaver BW systems will prompt you, the same as what you see in the SAP GUI logon pad.

After selecting a query, you'll see its metadata including input variables and output data in a cross-tab. For each input variable, you can either enter its value or bind it to a cell in the embedded spreadsheet. Keep in mind that you need to provide the technical name of the dimension the variable is based on. To check the technical name format, run Transaction MDXTEST in SAP GUI and expand each variable after selecting the cube or the query.

Many kinds of returned metadata besides the cross-tab data itself are listed in the OUTPUT VALUES area. The output data is two-dimensional, containing several rows of data in several fields that can be bound to a cell range, as displayed in Figure 7.6.

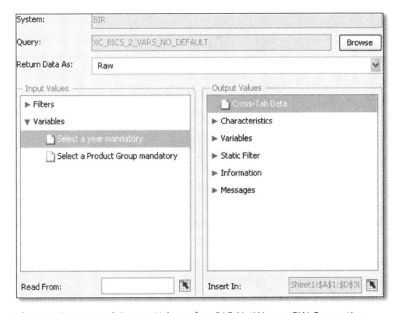

Figure 7.6 Input and Output Values of an SAP NetWeaver BW Connection

There's a new DATA PREVIEW tab for the BW connection so that you can get a quick idea about what the returned data is like. The USAGE tab is the same as that of any other connectivity except for one new property, USE DEFAULT QUERY DATA. You can select this option to use the SAP BEx query default values.

7.3   Live Office Connection

Live Office Connection is used to connect to SAP BusinessObjects Live Office documents to retrieve data from SAP Crystal Reports or SAP BusinessObjects Web Intelligence documents. The purpose is to create a dashboard based on data from one or more SAP Crystal Reports or SAP BusinessObjects Web Intelligence documents, instead of directly from the data source, and to take advantage of these SAP BusinessObjects products.

SAP BusinessObjects Live Office (which we'll just refer to as Live Office) is a product in the SAP BusinessObjects suite that is an integration with Microsoft. It's an add-in of the Microsoft Office products family. With Live Office, you can insert SAP Crystal Reports and SAP BusinessObjects Web Intelligence documents into a Microsoft Office document, including Word, Excel, Outlook, and PowerPoint. The inserted reports can be refreshed within your Microsoft Office document, which is why it's called SAP BusinessObjects Live Office. With Live Office, you access up-to-date information from your familiar Microsoft Office products that you use every day to do your job and make important business decisions. It gives you real-time data that is verifiable and easily refreshed. Live Office allows information workers to work in their most familiar environment: to consume live data within a Microsoft Office document.

When an SAP Crystal Reports or SAP BusinessObjects Web Intelligence document is inserted into Microsoft Office Excel, the Excel document can be used as the data source for SAP BusinessObjects Dashboards. Based on the Excel document, a Live Office connection can be set up within SAP BusinessObjects Dashboards so that the dashboard can fetch live data by refreshing the report. This way, the Excel document with Live Office acts as the bridge between your visualization and an SAP BusinessObjects report, making the visualization data live.

In an enterprise deployment, the dashboards should be refreshable to reflect the latest data. There are many data connection types you can use to make the dashboard refreshable. However, Live Office works in the most "enterprise" way, meaning it connects to the SAP BusinessObjects Business Intelligence platform and consumes data from SAP Crystal Reports and SAP BusinessObjects Web Intelligence documents. These infrastructures are all existing enterprise-level BI assets proven to be secure, performance scalable, and enterprise-class reporting tools that ensure you get the expected data format.

7.3.1 When to Use Live Office Connection

Choose Live Office Connection when you want to create a dashboard on top of data in SAP Crystal Reports or SAP BusinessObjects Web Intelligence documents. If somebody has already created these documents, you only need to go through this section to learn how to use them. However, if you need to create the SAP Crystal Reports or SAP BusinessObjects Web Intelligence documents as middleware, some knowledge these two products is required.

There are two scenarios when you would choose this data connectivity type, as described in the following sections.

Security Restriction

One scenario in which you would use this connectivity is when the dashboard designer doesn't have the right to access the database directly but, for security reasons, can only access other SAP BusinessObjects reports. In such cases, the dashboard designer cannot retrieve data from the data source through any other connectivity. He can only see and access the data exposed from an SAP Crystal Reports or SAP BusinessObjects Web Intelligence document, which has limited the data.

Special Data

Another scenario is when data required in your dashboard cannot be provided directly in the data source, nor can it be calculated with Excel formulas in the embedded spreadsheet, but it can be generated with the help of SAP Crystal Reports or SAP BusinessObjects Web Intelligence such as section suppress and formulas. This is a way to combine the strengths of all three of the SAP BusinessObjects reporting tools: SAP Crystal Reports, SAP BusinessObjects Web Intelligence, and SAP BusinessObjects Dashboards. To use this, you need know the strengths of each to make the best use of them.

For the first scenario (security restriction), it's often natural and obvious to use Live Office Connection because the data is only available through Live Office documents. However, for the scenario of special data, whether to choose Live Office Connection is not that obvious at first. Usually, you'll try to connect to the data source directly through Query as a Web Service or XML data and later find it difficult or even impossible to fulfill all of the requirements, either in data or in format. After some tries, you may find Live Office Connection as the last resort to calculate the required data or expose data in the required format in SAP Crystal Reports or SAP BusinessObjects Web Intelligence before consuming them in your dashboard.

For example, let's say you're going to create a dashboard showing sales revenue by goods in different price ranges, That is, the profits of all goods sold at prices less than $10, between $10 and $20, more than $30, and so on. Suppose the backend data source is SAP NetWeaver BW, where such data is stored in an Info-Cube. The sales revenue of each price range is not stored in the data source, because the range definition may change from time to time. Sometimes the user may want to further divide the range, for example, into less than $5, between $5 and $10, between $10 and $15, and so on. It's difficult to calculate such data in a Universe and then in Query as a Web Service, nor can you do it inside the embedded Excel spreadsheet. So how do you do this?

If you are familiar with SAP Crystal Reports, you may think to get the data using grouping with a specified order. The steps to get such data in SAP Crystal Reports are:

1. Connect to the data source with the corresponding driver (SAP NetWeaver BW MDX, for example).
2. Group on product price through GROUP EXPERT, and select IN SPECIFIED ORDER in GROUP OPTIONS. Then create a group called "Less than $10" with the condition "Product Price Is Less Than $10." Similarly, create named groups for the other price ranges.
3. Create a summary field in the group header as a sum of sales revenue.
4. Hide the DETAIL section.

Now the report has one row per price range. You can then insert this SAP Crystal Reports report into an Excel document through the Live Office menu and connect to it from your dashboard through a Live Office Connection. This way you get the data you want in your dashboard by taking advantage of SAP Crystal Reports.

In these circumstances, you have to generate the required fields in an SAP Crystal Reports or Web Intelligence document and then connect to it from SAP Business-Objects Dashboards through a Live Office Connection.

As mentioned in the previous section, you can also use a query as a web service connection to connect to an SAP BusinessObjects platform. The difference is that QaaWS can only consume data from a query on top of a Universe but cannot create new fields based on the existing fields.

In short, you need to use Live Office Connection when it's the only data source you can access or when you have to take advantage of SAP Crystal Reports or SAP BusinessObjects Web Intelligence to get the data you need in your dashboard, and you cannot provide it otherwise.

7.3.2   How to Insert SAP BusinessObjects Reports in Excel

After installing SAP BusinessObjects Live Office, you'll see one more menu called LIVE OFFICE in Excel. You can click a submenu (for Excel 2003) or an icon in the ribbon area (for Excel 2007 or 2010) to insert an SAP Crystal Reports or SAP BusinessObjects Web Intelligence document or a Universe query into your Excel spreadsheet. A running Central Management Server (CMS) must be available now for you to choose a report or a Universe from. The SAP BusinessObjects web service is used to verify the user to log him on to the CMS, so it must be also available.

You can insert multiple reports into a single Excel file through the Live Office menu in one or more sheets.

7.3.3   How to Use Live Office Connection

Unlike the data connectivities discussed in previous sections, with the default embedded spreadsheet, selecting LIVE OFFICE CONNECTION from the ADD drop-down list in the Data Manager will not add the connection to the list. Instead, this menu is used to detect all reports inserted into the Excel file after it has been imported.

Steps to Use Live Office Connection

The basic steps to use Live Office Connection from SAP BusinessObjects Dashboards are as follows:

1. **Enable Live Office compatibility.**

   For the Live Office document to work, you need to have enabled Live Office compatibility via the menu path FILE • PREFERENCE as described in Chapter 2.

   If you have installed Live Office on your machine, SAP BusinessObjects Dashboards can detect it and ask you if you want to enable it.

   Note that enabling Live Office compatibility may affect the performance of other Microsoft Office programs. If you choose not to enable the Live Office Compatibility mode, you can still work with Live Office, but you need to create a Live Office document with SAP Crystal Reports or SAP BusinessObjects Web Intelligence outside of SAP BusinessObjects Dashboards and then import it into the spreadsheet.

2. **Import the Excel file with SAP BusinessObjects Live Office enabled.**

   When you've created your Excel spreadsheet containing the required reports, click the IMPORT or IMPORT FROM ENTERPRISE button in the DATA menu to import it into your dashboard. As mentioned in Chapter 2 when we discussed the DATA menu, all data in the Excel file will be copied to the embedded spreadsheet, overwriting all changes you've made to it.

3. **Add Live Office Connection.**

   After importing the Excel file, you'll see the data in the embedded spreadsheet, with all data and sheets copied. You can create dashboards based on this data. However, it's static and cannot be refreshed to retrieve live data because by now, SAP BusinessObjects Dashboards doesn't know the data is from an SAP Crystal Reports, SAP BusinessObjects Web Intelligence document, or a Universe query.

   To solve this, select LIVE OFFICE CONNECTION from the ADD dropdown list in the Data Manager. This won't add a new connection like you do for other connectivity types, but will force SAP BusinessObjects Dashboards to detect all reports inserted into the Excel file and create a connection for each report object. You can then configure when to trigger these connections to get live data. The parameters of the reports will also prompt when the corresponding connection is triggered.

If you've inserted two parts of a single report into the Excel file, the number of Live Office connections detected will be equal to the number of report parts, not the number of reports. That is, there will be two connections, not one, though the data is from one report.

Properties Panel

Selecting LIVE OFFICE CONNECTION in the ADD dropdown list of the Data Manager will force SAP BusinessObjects Dashboards to detect all SAP BusinessObjects reports contained in the imported Excel file and create a connection for each report part. That's why you may get a little confused that nothing happened after selecting LIVE OFFICE CONNECTION when no report is inserted into the Excel file.

Figure 7.7 shows the PROPERTIES panel after the SAP BusinessObjects reports in the Excel file are detected. We've inserted two SAP Crystal Reports documents into the Excel file, which is why you see two Live Office connections in the list.

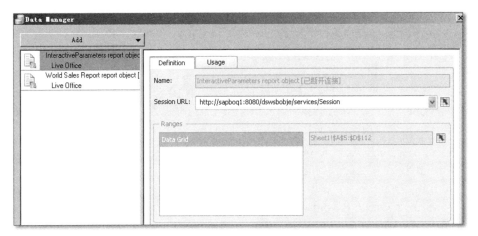

Figure 7.7 Properties of an SAP BusinessObjects Live Office Connection in Data Manager

If your Excel spreadsheet contains more than one view, you can choose one, some, or all of the views listed in the VIEWS area of the DEFINITION tab. Only the data from the views you choose will be refreshed when their corresponding Live Office connections are refreshed.

The properties in this tab are explained in the following list.

▶ NAME
The NAME field is disabled because the name is carried over automatically from the definition of the Live Office report object, so you cannot change it.

▶ SESSION URL
The SESSION URL field points to the SAP BusinessObjects web service, which is used to connect to Live Office data at runtime. You'll find the item *http://<webserver>:8080/dswsbobje/services/session* in the dropdown list as a hint about the URL. In our example, we're using *http://sapboq1:8080/dswsbobje/services/Session*. In some situations you may need to use a fully qualified domain name by adding the domain name after the server name, which is sapboq1 here.

▶ RANGES
In the RANGES area, you can bind data ranges of the Live Office–enabled Excel file to the embedded spreadsheet. By default, the bindings will be detected and configured automatically. There are two situations when you might want to bind the data to another range.

First, the auto-configured cell range may not be able to cover all possible values. For example, with default parameter values, the data from 10 sales regions is returned, which is bound to a cell range with 10 rows. However, with some parameter values, there may be more than 10 rows. So we need to rebind the data to a cell range with the maximum number of rows we want to accept.

Second, we may want to bind the data to the same location as it is bound to in the old Excel file. For example, in the Excel file, the data is inserted into a range starting from the first row. But in the embedded spreadsheet, some of the first rows are reserved for our other use, and we want to move them down.

The USAGE tab is similar to that of other connectivities. Here, you can configure how to use the connectivity, such as how to trigger the connection.

At preview time, when the connection is triggered, you'll be prompted to enter credentials to log on to the SAP BusinessObjects system to retrieve the report data. However, if the dashboard has been saved to an SAP BusinessObjects BI platform and the user accesses it through BI Launchpad, the credentials of the logged-on user will be used to retrieve the data, without the need to log on again.

Pass Parameters from a Dashboard to SAP BusinessObjects Live Office

Sometimes the report object you inserted into the Live Office-enabled Excel file may contain parameters. For the dashboard to work perfectly, you need to provide some way for the user to input values for those parameters and retrieve the corresponding data.

To make it work, first you need to bind the parameters of the SAP Crystal Reports or SAP BusinessObjects Web Intelligence to cells in the Excel file, before importing it into dashboard. To do this, go to the Live Office object and click MODIFY OBJECT/PROMPT SETTING. You'll see the prompt options shown in Figure 7.8.

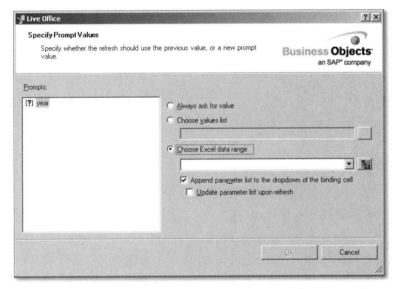

Figure 7.8 Prompt Settings for a Parameter in SAP BusinessObjects Live Office

For each parameter, the following three options are available:

▶ ALWAYS ASK FOR VALUE
Each time the document is refreshed, a prompt dialog will ask users for parameter values.

▶ CHOOSE VALUES LIST
Parameter values are prespecified here.

▶ CHOOSE EXCEL DATA RANGE
Bind parameter values to Excel range cells.

The third option is the most flexible one. Note that when imported into SAP BusinessObjects Dashboards, the report also retrieves values from these cells as its parameter values. This is the most important step to make the process work. In SAP BusinessObjects Dashboards, we can then bind input UI components to the cell(s) that are bound to parameter values. The user can then change values through the UI components, triggering the Live Office connections and consequently refreshing the report objects.

Sometimes you'll note that the PROMPT SETTING menu item is grayed out. The prerequisites of an active prompt setting include:

▶ The reports inserted as Live Office objects must include parameters.

▶ The Live Office object has been refreshed on demand, and prompts have been brought out at least once.

The first prerequisite is ensured at report creation time. For the second item, let's take a look at SAP BusinessObjects Live Office refresh options. Go to the Live Office object and select REFRESH OPTIONS. A dialog will prompt you as displayed in Figure 7.9.

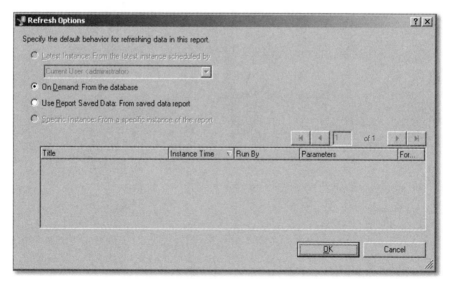

Figure 7.9 Refresh Options for a Parameter in SAP BusinessObjects Live Office

There are four refresh options you can choose from.

▶ LATEST INSTANCE
This option is applicable when the report has instances. Each time the object is refreshed, data will be retrieved from the last scheduled instance. In this case, no prompts are needed. If the SAP Crystal Report or SAP BusinessObjects Web Intelligence document hasn't been scheduled successfully before, this option is disabled.

▶ ON DEMAND
The object will be refreshed against the database, and prompts will show up if there are any.

▶ USE REPORT SAVED DATA
The object will be refreshed against data saved along with the report. No prompts are needed.

▶ SPECIFIC INSTANCE
The object will be refreshed against the data from one specified instance. No prompts are needed.

To activate the PROMPT SETTING menu item, select ON DEMAND. Then refresh the object to bring up the prompt dialog and notify the program that this object has parameters.

7.3.4 Practice

In this sample, the report is an SAP BusinessObjects Web Intelligence document with one parameter. The user can select one year and see the quantity sold across states for that selected year.

You can follow these steps to complete the example:

1. Create an SAP BusinessObjects Web Intelligence document based on the eFashion sample Universe from your SAP BusinessObjects system. It's a simple vertical table with two objects: STATE and QUANTITY SOLD. Add the YEAR object as a prompt query filter. Save this SAP BusinessObjects Web Intelligence document and export it to your SAP BusinessObjects system.

2. Create a Live Office-enabled Excel file and insert the SAP BusinessObjects Web Intelligence report created in the previous step through the LIVE OFFICE menu.

3. Ensure that the REFRESH option selected is ON DEMAND, and refresh the Live Office object to bring up the prompt dialog.

4. Configure the PROMPT SETTING to bind the prompt value to cell $K$1, as shown in Figure 7.10.

	A	B	C	D	J	K	L
1	State	Quantity sold				2006	
2	California	17769					
3	Colorado	5116					
4	DC	6491					
5	Florida	4830					
6	Illinois	6519					
7	Massachusetts	5269					
8	New York	19109					
9	Texas	25193					

Figure 7.10 Data of the SAP BusinessObjects Live Office Document in the Embedded Spreadsheet

5. Save the Excel file to your local disk, and import it into a newly created dashboard in SAP BusinessObjects Dashboards.

6. Add Live Office connections in the Data Manager. In the auto-detected connectivity, specify a valid session URL. Leave the data binding as the default because this is a simple sample and we don't need to reserve extra space for potential data growing.

7. On the USAGE tab of the Live Office Connection PROPERTIES panel, configure the connection to refresh on trigger, and set TRIGGER CELL to Sheet1!$K$1, which is the cell to hold parameter values as defined in step 4. Specify it to refresh on value changes.

8. Add a column chart to the canvas. Add one series to bind to the QUANTITY SOLD column, and bind the category labels to the STATE column. This column chart displays the quantity sold across states.

9. Add a combo box to the canvas. Enter "2004", "2005", and "2006" to cells Sheet1!$D$1, $D$2, and $D$3, respectively, and bind labels to these three cells. This is just a sample, so we'll just hardcode them. In your real business, these candidate items should be read from a Live Office object too, which could be refreshed when the visualization is loaded.

10. For the DATA INSERTION options of the combo box, select the insert type LABEL, and set DESTINATION to cell Sheet1!$K$1, which is bound as the prompt value of the Live Office object and is set as the trigger cell of Live Office Connection. At runtime, when the value of this critical cell changes, the Live Office connection will be refreshed, and the value of this cell will be passed to the underlying report to retrieve the data.

Click PREVIEW to test the dashboard you've just created. Select among different year values, and you'll see that the data in the column chart changes accordingly; it's processed by SAP BusinessObjects Live Office and then SAP BusinessObjects Web Intelligence behind it. The effect is illustrated in Figure 7.11.

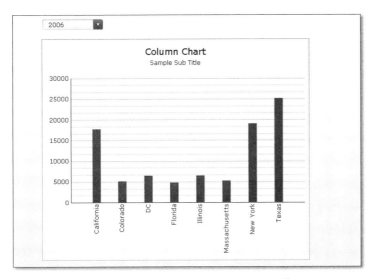

Figure 7.11 Final Effect Using SAP BusinessObjects Live Office Connections

7.4 Crystal Reports Data Consumer

SAP Crystal Reports is the SAP BusinessObjects flagship product for detailed reporting. It allows report designers to create highly formatted reports from any data source and deliver them via email, Microsoft Office, Adobe PDF, or embedded in enterprise applications. SAP Crystal Reports has greatly improved its interactivity feature, which empowers business users to easily manipulate data for deeper business insight.

The Crystal Reports Data Consumer connectivity allows you to insert dashboards created with SAP BusinessObjects Dashboards into SAP Crystal Reports and feed live data from SAP Crystal Reports into your dashboard. This way you leverage and improve existing SAP Crystal Reports documents and add the power of SAP BusinessObjects Dashboards to new SAP Crystal Reports documents. The integration of SAP BusinessObjects Dashboards and SAP Crystal Reports is one of the interactivity enhancements in SAP Crystal Reports 2008. This integration enables report designers to embed beautiful and interactive visualizations into SAP Crystal Reports and link report data to the visualizations, with the help of this connectivity defined in SAP BusinessObjects Dashboards.

Figure 7.12 shows a simple report in the SAP Crystal Reports 2008 designer environment with an SAP dashboard embedded.

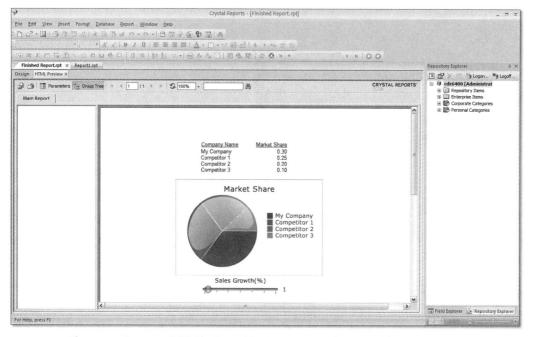

Figure 7.12 Insert an SWF File Created by SAP BusinessObjects Dashboards into SAP Crystal Reports

You need to be familiar with SAP Crystal Reports to understand this section. You should already be able to create basic reports in SAP Crystal Reports.

7.4.1   When to Use the Crystal Reports Data Consumer Connection

SAP BusinessObjects Dashboards is primarily a data visualization tool, while SAP Crystal Reports is better at data processing, complex formatting, and accurate printing. Because of their different features, they are used in different scenarios to meet different requirements.

Choose this type of connectivity if you want to combine the advantages of both SAP Crystal Reports and SAP BusinessObjects Dashboards, providing intuitive analysis and formatted enterprise-level reporting into one SAP Crystal Reports document.

With the development of the business intelligence infrastructure, end-users' demands also grow. The consumers of the formatted reports may ask for more intuitive charts, easier data access, or even what-if scenario models inside the reports. Their primary concern is still the detailed information, but adding an interactive and nice-looking dashboard can improve efficiency. This is the situation in which you should consider using the Crystal Reports Data Consumer connection to provide data to your dashboard models embedded into SAP Crystal Reports.

If the user's focus is primarily on data visualization itself, you don't need to bother embedding the dashboard into SAP Crystal Reports. You should use another kind of data connectivity to pull live data from the data sources into your dashboard.

7.4.2   How to Use the Crystal Reports Data Consumer Connection

To embed a dashboard into SAP Crystal Reports, you need to work with both SAP BusinessObjects Dashboards and SAP Crystal Reports designer. Usually, you create an SAP Crystal Reports report first to prepare data for the dashboard. Then you design the dashboard and configure the Crystal Reports Data Consumer connection, which is required for linking with SAP Crystal Reports data later. Once you have both the SAP Crystal Reports and dashboard models ready, you insert the exported SWF document into the SAP Crystal Reports document, and finally, you set your dashboard to receive real-time SAP Crystal Reports data. Again, we assume you already have adequate skills to build dashboards and SAP Crystal Reports documents, so here we focus on configuring the Crystal Reports Data Consumer connection and linking SAP Crystal Reports data.

Connection

Add the Crystal Reports Data Consumer connection in the Data Manager by selecting this type in the ADD dropdown list. You can add only one connection of this type in a single dashboard, which is the same as Flash Variables and Portal Data. Figure 7.13 shows the PROPERTIES panel of the Crystal Reports Data Consumer connection.

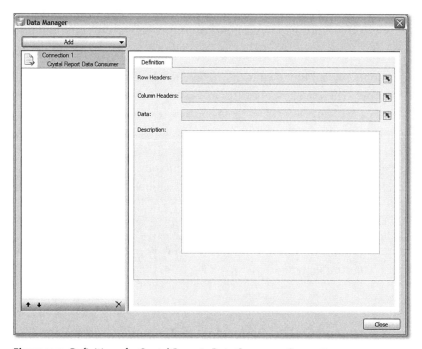

Figure 7.13 Definition of a Crystal Reports Data Consumer Connection

As shown in this figure, the Crystal Reports Data Consumer connection pulls three types of data from SAP Crystal Reports and populates the embedded Excel spreadsheet with that data. These three types of data, row headers, column headers, and data range, essentially form a cross-tabulation, or cross-tab. A cross-tab is a very efficient way to display measures with two dimensions. It can provide greater insight than a simple vertical table or a horizontal table within a smaller space. If your work involves analyzing data in Excel, you're probably familiar with the PivotTable functionality, which in essence, creates a cross-tab.

Figure 7.14 shows an example comparing a vertical table with a cross-tab created by PivotTable functionality in Excel.

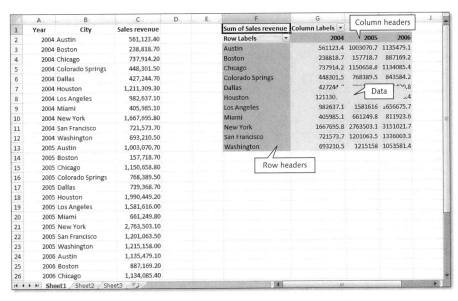

Figure 7.14 Data Bindings for a Crystal Reports Data Consumer Connection

As you can see from this figure, both tables provide the same information; that is, sales revenue by year and city. If the data was presented in a vertical table, it would not fit in one screen, and moreover, it would be hard to determine the relationships among each of the values. However, the cross-tab consists of only 10 rows of data, and you can easily compare sales revenue in different years for the same city or vice versa. We've marked what each of the three types of data correspond to in Figure 7.14. You can see that SAP BusinessObjects Dashboards refers to column labels in a pivot table as column headers, and row labels as row headers.

Cross-tabs are very useful and important in SAP BusinessObjects Dashboards. For example, when you bind data by range for a chart that supports multiple series of data (a column chart for instance), you can bind all of the information needed — the series name, values, category labels — all at once if you organize your data into a cross-tab. How are you going to create a similar column chart if your data is in a vertical table, as shown in Figure 7.14? It would be very hard or even impossible to achieve this.

Now let's consider the difference between Query as a Web Service connections and Live Office connections that we discussed in previous sections in this chapter. QaaWS connections usually bring back data as vertical tables, while Live Office connections can leverage other SAP BusinessObjects reporting capabilities to receive data as cross-tabs. This can determine which type of connection to use, depending on whether a chart with multiple series of data is needed. For the Crystal Reports Data Consumer connection, a cross-tab is the best way to organize your data. That's why we recommend that you always organize your data in cross-tabs if possible.

You may wonder what to do if your data has only one series. If that is the case, you can omit the binding for row headers or column headers to link to a vertical table or a horizontal data table. However, be aware that you don't need to bind all three of these types of data. You can even bind only the row header, only the column header, or only data, although that would hardly be useful.

In the DESCRIPTION text box, enter some information to describe how to bind the data later in SAP Crystal Reports. This could become necessary if the dashboard designer and the SAP Crystal Reports designer are not the same person or are in different development groups, so that the SAP Crystal Reports designer may be confused about the format of the data the dashboard requires. It's a best practice to document how to bind data in this text box.

Integration with SAP Crystal Reports

After you've built the dashboard, with a Crystal Reports Data Consumer connection properly set up, you export it to an SWF file via the menu path FILE • EXPORT • SWF. Next you open a report in SAP Crystal Reports 2008 Designer and insert the SWF file into the report by selecting INSERT FLASH in the INSERT menu. A dialog box will pop up as displayed in Figure 7.15, in which you can choose an SWF file and specify whether to embed it into the SAP Crystal Reports document or create a link to the original SWF file only. To save you trouble when you migrate the SAP Crystal Reports document to another environment, select the EMBED option, though it may slightly increase the size of the SAP Crystal Reports document.

Figure 7.15 Insert an SWF Object into SAP Crystal Reports 2008

Now that you've added the SWF file exported by SAP BusinessObjects Dashboards into SAP Crystal Reports, you need to link it to the SAP Crystal Reports data. To do this, launch Flash Data Expert in the context menu of the Flash object. The Flash Data Expert interface is divided into two parts. On the left, available fields in the report are listed, and you can drag them into the boxes below to bind a field to row headers, column headers, or data. Each of these three boxes is only available if the corresponding part in the Crystal Reports Data Consumer is bound to cells in the Excel file.

For example, the dashboard designer needs a horizontal table of data, so he binds only the row headers and data in the Crystal Reports Data Consumer connection. Then there will be only the INSERT ROW LABEL box and the INSERT DATA VALUES box in the Flash Data Expert for you to bind SAP Crystal Reports data to. On the right, the PREVIEW window shows what the dashboard looks like under the current binding configuration. The description entered in the Crystal Reports Data Consumer connection is displayed in the PREVIEW window, which is useful for others to understand your idea.

As displayed in Figure 7.16, we inserted the YEAR field into the column headers, STORE NAME into the row headers, and SALES REVENUE into the data values. The figure shows the preview of the data and the dashboard model.

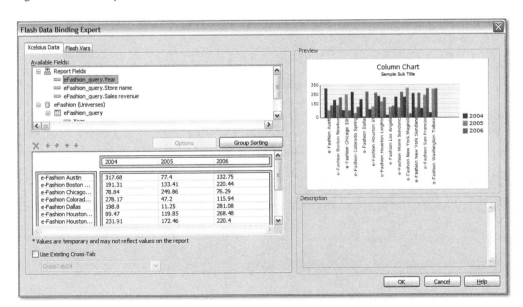

Figure 7.16 Data Mapping in the Data Binding Expert Inside SAP Crystal Reports

The Flash Data Expert has a close relationship with the cross-tab feature in SAP Crystal Reports. When you specify data in the Flash Data Expert, SAP Crystal Reports generates the cross-tab data and passes it to the embedded dashboard. SAP Crystal Reports has to summarize any data that can't be directly available in the database to calculate the aggregated values.

Now let's see how an SAP Crystal Reports–native cross-tab is created. Figure 7.17 shows the Cross-Tab Expert in SAP Crystal Reports. To define the cross-tab data, you insert zero or more fields into rows, columns, and summarized fields.

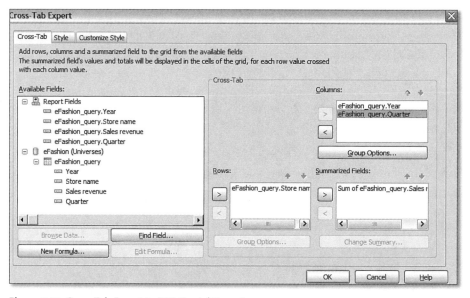

Figure 7.17 Cross-Tab Expert in SAP Crystal Reports

When you already have a native SAP Crystal Reports cross-tab in the report, you can feed it directly to the dashboard in the Flash Data Expert as illustrated in Figure 7.18. As explained above, when you specify rows, columns, and data in the Flash Data Expert, you're essentially creating a native SAP Crystal Reports cross-tab, so if you only need the data for SAP BusinessObjects Dashboards instead of actually displaying the cross-tab in the report, you don't need to create a cross-tab in SAP Crystal Reports and use this option.

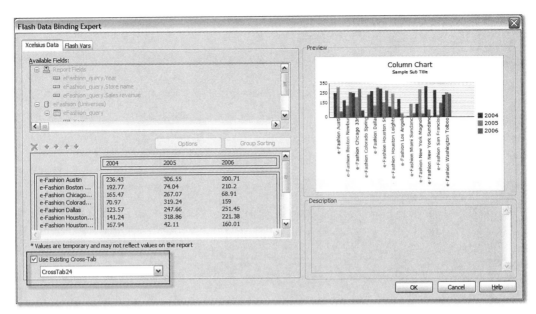

Figure 7.18 Flash Data Expert in SAP Crystal Reports

Flash Variables

You can also pass data from SAP Crystal Reports to the embedded dashboard using Flash Variables if the dashboard has a Flash Variable connection, which we'll cover in the next section. In Figure 7.19, you can see that the Flash Data Expert for this Flash object has no DATA tab, but only a FLASH VARS tab, where you can bind a field or a formula to a Flash Variable.

Using Flash Variables to connect to SAP Crystal Reports data has nothing to do with the Crystal Reports Data Consumer connection. As long as there is a Flash Variable connection defined in the dashboard, you can pass data into it through the Flash Data Expert using Flash Variables. This was primarily used with Xcelsius 4.5, in which the Crystal Reports Data Consumer connection was not yet provided.

To work with SAP BusinessObjects Dashboards, you can use these two methods interchangeably, but the Crystal Reports Data Consumer connection is easier to use. For the Flash Variables connection, you usually have to create Excel formulas to transform the data to the format the Flash Variable connection requires: either CSV or XML.

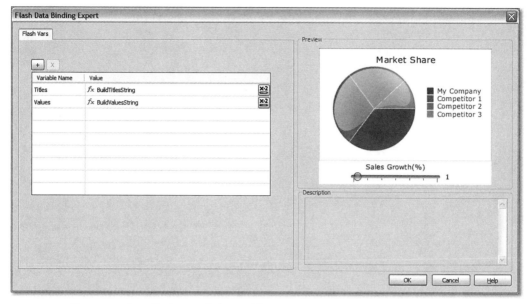

Figure 7.19 Data Binding as Flash Variables

Therefore, we recommend using the Crystal Reports Data Consumer connection instead of the Flash Variables connection for SAP BusinessObjects Dashboards models. But if you're still using Xcelsius 4.5, you have to use the Flash Variables connection.

7.4.3 Practice

In this practice, we'll create an SAP Crystal Reports document connecting to the eFashion sample Universe from your SAP BusinessObjects system. You can use any data source you'd like if you don't have access to an SAP BusinessObjects system. You'll also build a column chart that will display multiple series of data.

1. **Create the SAP Crystal Reports document.**
   Launch SAP Crystal Reports Designer 2008 or 2011, follow the report creation wizard, and select the eFashion Universe as the data source. Then build a query to include the four objects Year, Quarter, Store Name, and Sales Revenue. Insert all four fields from the query into the DETAILS section in the report. Your report should look like Figure 7.20.

3/28/2010			
Year	Quarter	Store name	Sales revenue
2004	Q1	e-Fashion Austin	197,890.70
2004	Q1	e-Fashion Boston Newbury	92,595.50
2004	Q1	e-Fashion Chicago 33rd	256,453.80
2004	Q1	e-Fashion Colorado Springs	131,796.90
2004	Q1	e-Fashion Dallas	150,687.00
2004	Q1	e-Fashion Houston 5th	166,035.00
2004	Q1	e-Fashion Houston Leighton	244,183.00
2004	Q1	e-Fashion Los Angeles	308,928.00
2004	Q1	e-Fashion Miami Sundance	137,529.70
2004	Q1	e-Fashion New York Magnolia	333,357.80
2004	Q1	e-Fashion New York Sundance	222,625.30
2004	Q1	e-Fashion San Francisco	210,292.40
2004	Q1	e-Fashion Washington Tolboc	208,324.40
2004	Q2	e-Fashion Austin	154,038.50
2004	Q2	e-Fashion Boston Newbury	70,902.70

Figure 7.20 Data in the SAP Crystal Reports Document

2. **Create the dashboard using SAP BusinessObjects Dashboards.**

   Drag a column chart component onto the canvas, resize it to the size you want, and change the title of the chart to something descriptive; for example, "Sales Revenue by Store." Click the FIT CANVAS TO COMPONENTS button in the toolbar to shrink the canvas to avoid unnecessary blanks. You can increase the canvas a little by clicking the INCREASE CANVAS button in the toolbar for a better look and feel.

   The chart will display sales revenues from all of the e-Fashion stores over several years. Each year will have its own series of data, and data will be in columns, so you'll put years on column headers and store names on row headers.

   Before you actually bind cells, you may want to go back to SAP Crystal Reports to see how many years and how many stores there are so you'll know how big a data range to bind. In the report, you can find that there are 3 years of data for 13 stores. It's a good habit to bind a range bigger than you need because the volume of data might increase in the future, and you can leverage the IGNORE END BLANK CELLS feature of SAP BusinessObjects Dashboards charts to avoid unnecessary blanks.

   So the range $B$1 to $F$5 will be column headers and will be filled with years; the range $A$2 to $A$16 will be row headers and will be filled with store names; the range $B$2 to $F$16 will be data values and will be filled with sales revenue data. Binding these ranges for the column chart is a little bit tedious. Because there is no data in the range, SAP BusinessObjects Dashboards can't make a perfect guess if you bind by range, so you need to bind each series manually. You need to add five series. Each series name is bound to a cell in the column headers' range. Each series' values are bound to a column in the data values' range. The category labels will be bound to the row headers' range. Don't forget to enable both the IGNORE VALUES and IGNORE SERIES options in the behavior property sheet.

Now that the data is properly planned and bound to the column chart, you need to add a Crystal Reports Data Consumer connection and bind the column headers range, the row headers range, and the data range. This should be very easy. And you should put some instruction in the description field to tell the SAP Crystal Reports developer, yourself in this case, that the column headers should be years and the row headers should be store names.

When you've finished, the workspace of your dashboard should look like Figure 7.21. When everything is set, export the dashboard to an SWF document.

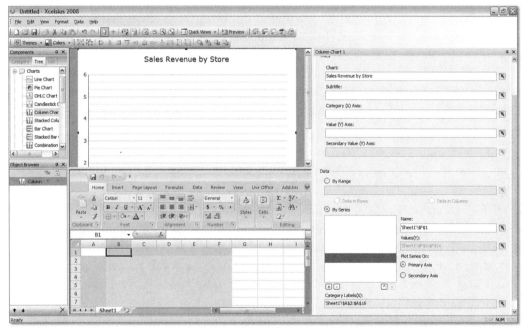

Figure 7.21 Data Binding for the Column Chart in SAP BusinessObjects Dashboards

3. Embed the dashboard into SAP Crystal Reports.

Switch back to the SAP Crystal Reports Designer. Now you'll insert the SWF file into the report. Select INSERT • FLASH to insert the SWF file into the REPORT HEADER section. Right-click the Flash object you just added and launch the Flash Data Expert in the context menu. Then drag YEAR to the column header,

STORE NAME to the row header, and SALES REVENUE to the data to finish the data binding.

You've finished this example. You can now preview the report to see the final result. It should look like Figure 7.22.

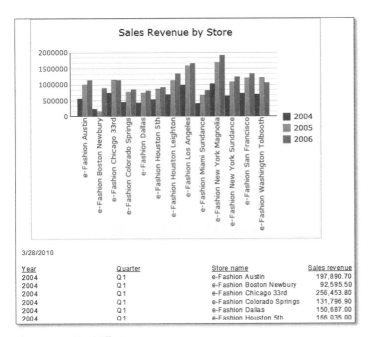

Figure 7.22 Final Effect

7.5 Flash Variables

Flash movies are usually hosted by a container, either the Adobe Flash Player or an HTML file. Thus, they are integrated with other parts of the container. If there's no way for Flash movies to communicate with the outer container that hosts them, the Flash technology will not be flexible. Adobe provides technologies for Flash movies to interact with their containers. Flash Variables is one of those technologies, and it's an efficient method of importing variables into Flash movies.

Later in this chapter, you'll learn about more complicated technologies that enable interactivities such as method invocation.

In SAP BusinessObjects Dashboards 4.0, the Flash Variables connectivity allows you to pass data to your dashboard directly from the container. Flash Variables itself is only a string of characters, but SAP BusinessObjects Dashboards automatically encodes the variables for you so that the value of each variable can be mapped to a cell range in the embedded spreadsheet. Moreover, named ranges, which we mentioned in Chapter 6 when we discussed the XML data connectivity, are also supported to leverage your effort in Excel and reduce the time required to set up each variable.

7.5.1   When to Use Flash Variables

The Flash Variables technology is often used when a Flash movie needs some information that's only available when the movie is first initialized. Usually, such information is provided by the container of the Flash movie. This holds true for the Flash Variables connections in SAP BusinessObjects Dashboards.

For example, let's say you're integrating your dashboard into a legacy web application. The dashboard will compare data pulled from the database with data the user enters on the page via HTML controls. You can use the Flash Variables connection to import data into the dashboard from the HTML container.

You may think you can use another connectivity such as XML Data to retrieve such data on loading the dashboard. You can, but imagine another scenario where the data required by SAP BusinessObjects Dashboards cannot be retrieved by any other data connectivity. For example, your dashboard is wrapped in an HTML file of a web application hosted on a web application server. The user needs to log on to the web application by entering his username and password before accessing the HTML file. Inside your dashboard, you need to retrieve the credentials such as username and password of the user who is currently accessing it. You have no other way to get his provided credentials but Flash Variables.

In such a case, you can use a Flash Variables connectivity to pass in the global session variables, so the Flash movie can get the serialized session or token and reuse them inside the Flash movie itself.

7.5.2   How to Use Flash Variables

To use a Flash Variables connection, launch the Data Manager and select FLASH VARIABLES in the ADD dropdown list. In contrast to other connectivity types, to which many connections can be added in one dashboard, you can only add one Flash Variables connection. If one is already added, you'll find the FLASH VARI-ABLES option grayed out in the ADD dropdown list.

This is easy to understand. Because a single Flash Variables connection can manage as many Flash variables as you want, there is essentially no need to create multiple Flash Variables connections for one dashboard.

The PROPERTIES panel of a Flash Variables connectivity has only one tab, as displayed in Figure 7.23.

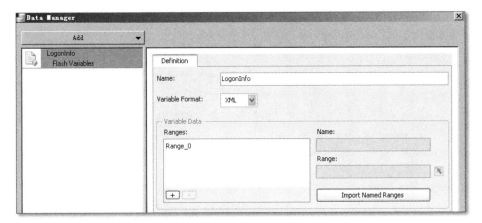

Figure 7.23 Definition of a Flash Variables Connection

The meanings of each property and how to use them are explained next.

Definition

▶ NAME
   You can enter a descriptive name for the connection. Although there will be only one Flash Variables connection, a descriptive name will be helpful.

▶ VARIABLE FORMAT
   We've mentioned that Flash variables are simple strings. When a single Flash variable is bound to a range of cells in the Excel worksheet, the software applies some kind of encoding method to format the data. The variable format option is where you can specify this encoding method. You can select the CSV format or the XML format.

For example, let's say you have a range of three cells that the value of a Flash variable will fill in. Now let's show what the value of the Flash variable should be for both formats. In the CSV format, the value of the variable would be:

```
January,Febrary,March
```

In XML format, the value of the variable would be:

```
<data><row><column>FRANCE</column></row><row><column>SPAIN</column>
</row><row><column>COLOMBIA</column></row></data>
```

You can see that this format is identical to the one the XML data connection requires.

▶ VARIABLE DATA

You can add one or more ranges here. You specify a name and bind a range in the Excel worksheet for each range. A corresponding Flash variable will be created for each range, and the value of variable will fill the range in the Excel worksheet.

Named ranges can be leveraged here for easy creation of variables. Simply click IMPORT NAMED RANGES to quickly import all of the named ranges, like we did for an XML data connectivity. The names and ranges of all named ranges that you have defined will be automatically specified in the corresponding NAME and RANGE fields.

Passing Variables

After setting up the Flash Variables connection, you won't be able to see any effect without putting the generated SWF movie into a container. The easiest way is to use the export to HTML functionality in SAP BusinessObjects Dashboards to generate a default HMTL container of the flash movie. The user can then see your dashboard by accessing the HTML file through a web browser such as Internet Explorer, Google Chrome, Firefox, Safari, and so on.

Normally, if you specify the file name of the exported HTML file as *visualization.html*, the generated HTML file will look like:

```
<HTML>
<HEAD>
<TITLE>visualization.swf</TITLE>
</HEAD>
<BODY>
```

```
<OBJECT classid="clsid:D27CDB6E-AE6D-11cf-96B8-444553540000"
codebase="http://fpdownload.adobe.com/pub/shockwave/cabs/flash/
swflash.cab#version=9,0,0,0"
WIDTH="690" HEIGHT="490" id="myMovieName">
<PARAM NAME="movie" VALUE="visualization.swf">
<PARAM NAME="quality" VALUE="high">
<PARAM NAME="bgcolor" VALUE="#FFFFFF">
<PARAM NAME="play" VALUE="true">
<PARAM NAME="loop" VALUE="true">
<PARAM NAME=bgcolor VALUE="#FFFFFF">
<EMBED src="visualization.swf" quality=high bgcolor=#FFFFFF
WIDTH="690" HEIGHT="490"
NAME="myMovieName" ALIGN="" TYPE="application/x-shockwave-flash"
play="true" loop="true"
PLUGINSPAGE="http://www.adobe.com/shockwave/download/
index.cgi?P1_Prod_Version=ShockwaveFlash">
</EMBED>
</OBJECT>
</BODY>
</HTML>
```

If the *visualization.xlf* file has a Flash Variables connection defined inside it, the generated HTML will become:

```
<HTML>
<HEAD>
<TITLE>visualization.swf</TITLE>
</HEAD>
<BODY>
<OBJECT classid="clsid:D27CDB6E-AE6D-11cf-96B8-444553540000"
codebase="http://fpdownload.adobe.com/pub/shockwave/cabs/flash/
swflash.cab#version=9,0,0,0"
WIDTH="690" HEIGHT="490" id="myMovieName">
<PARAM NAME=FlashVars VALUE="COUNTRIES=%3Cdata%3E%3Crow%3E%3Ccolumn%3E
FRANCE%3C%2Fcolumn%3E%3C%2Frow%3E%3Crow%3E%3Ccolumn%3ESPAIN%3C%2F
column%3E%3C%2Frow%3E%3Crow%3E%3Ccolumn%3ECOLOMBIA%3C%2Fcolumn%3E%3C
%2Frow%3E%3C%2Fdata%3E">
<PARAM NAME="movie" VALUE="visualization.swf">
<PARAM NAME="quality" VALUE="high">
<PARAM NAME="bgcolor" VALUE="#FFFFFF">
<PARAM NAME="play" VALUE="true">
<PARAM NAME="loop" VALUE="true">
```

```
<PARAM NAME=bgcolor VALUE="#FFFFFF">
<EMBED src="visualization.swf" quality=high bgcolor=#FFFFFF
WIDTH="690" HEIGHT="490"
NAME="myMovieName" ALIGN="" TYPE="application/x-shockwave-flash"
play="true" loop="true"
FlashVars="COUNTRIES=%3Cdata%3E%3Crow%3E%3Ccolumn%3EFRANCE%3C%2Fcolumn
%3E%3C%2Frow%3E%3Crow%3E%3Ccolumn%3ESPAIN%3C%2Fcolumn%3E%3C%2Frow%3E
%3Crow%3E%3Ccolumn%3ECOLOMBIA%3C%2Fcolumn%3E%3C%2Frow%3E%3C%2Fdata%3E"
PLUGINSPAGE="http://www.adobe.com/shockwave/download/
index.cgi?P1_Prod_Version=ShockwaveFlash">
</EMBED>
</OBJECT>
</BODY>
</HTML>
```

We've highlighted the additional information in the second HTML file in bold. You need an extra PARAM tag whose NAME attribute is always FlashVars, and the VALUE attribute is the variable key value pairs. The format is variable_name= variable_value. If there are multiple variables, they'll be concatenated by "&" signs, such as:

```
variable_name1=variable_value1&variable_name2=variable_value2.
```

In our example, there's only one parameter, named COUNTRIES, and its value is an encoded XML string, because we have chosen XML as the variable format.

The other thing to add is the FlashVars attribute in the EMBED tag. Its value should be the same as that of the VALUE attribute mentioned above. You must make these two changes simultaneously to make the Flash variable work on all browsers.

You may also notice that the texts have been URL encoded, which is an encoding scheme to avoid non-ASCII characters in URLs. For strings inside Flash Variables, URL encoding is required, so special characters such as <, >, &, =, and spaces will be changed to something like %3C and %20.

Now when you open this HTML document in your web browser, the SWF movie is loaded, and the values are assigned to the COUNTRIES Flash variable, the range corresponding to which will be updated. You can modify the values of the Flash variable in the HTML document to change what you want to see on the dashboard and, more practically, you can automatically generate the HTML document via a web application.

7.6   FS Command

FS Command is an Adobe Flash technology that enables Flash to communicate with the Flash Player or the program hosting the Flash Player such as a web browser, through JavaScript. For example, Flash can use FS Command to execute a piece of JavaScript statement in a web browser.

With FS Command connectivity, your dashboard can invoke JavaScript code written in its container, either the Flash Player or a web browser.

If you are familiar with the ActionScript language, you may know the function `fscommand` with the two parameters `command` and `parameters`. This data connectivity is similar to the ActionScript function `fscommand`. You can refer to the following website for more information about its use: *http://www.adobe.com/support/ flash/action_scripts/actionscript_dictionary/actionscript_dictionary372.html*

7.6.1   When to Use FS Command

Choose an FS Command connectivity when you want to control the behavior of the dashboard's container (either the Flash Player or the host such as a web server) from inside the dashboard. For example, you can maximize the browser window or display an alert message using JavaScript when the user has done something from within the dashboard.

Another scenario in which you might choose an FS Command connectivity is when you want to pass data from your dashboard to its container. For example, you can pass data about your dashboard, such as the currently selected value from a combo box, to a piece of JavaScript code run on the web server for further processing. This is faster than passing the data to a web service or XMLL data connectivity running on a web application server. One disadvantage is that the JavaScript code may be interpreted differently by different web browsers such as Internet Explorer and Google Chrome.

7.6.2 How to Use FS Command

To use FS Command in your dashboard to call JavaScript codes, launch the Data Manager, click ADD, and select FS COMMAND from the dropdown list. You can create multiple connectivities of this type in one dashboard.

The PROPERTIES panel of an FS Command connectivity is described next.

Definition

In this tab there are only three properties: NAME, COMMAND, and PARAMETERS, as displayed in Figure 7.24.

▶ NAME
Like the other data connectivity methods described in the sections above, you name the connection here with a description text instead of Connection 1 or Connection 2, to make it distinguishable when there are several connections in the list to the left. A typical name should indicate the purpose or functionality of that connectivity.

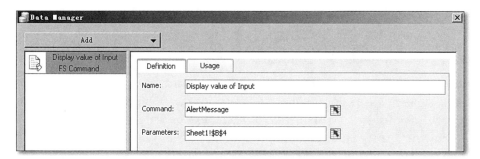

Figure 7.24 Definition of an FS Command Connection

▶ COMMAND and PARAMETERS
In these two fields you specify what command to invoke and the parameters. If your dashboard runs in Adobe Flash Player, the command can only be one of the predefined commands. However, if it's wrapped inside an HTML file and run in a web browser, you can use the name of any JavaScript function here, thus making it possible for your dashboard to call any JavaScript function.

For the latter case, at runtime, your dashboard doesn't call the command directly. Instead, in the HTML file with your dashboard embedded, you write a `myMovie_DoFSCommand` function using JavaScript with the parameters `command` and `properties`, as shown below.

```
function myMovieName_DoFSCommand(command, args)
```

In this function, `myMovieName` is the ID of your dashboard as an embedded SWF object in the HTML file; that is, the `NAME` attribute of the `EMBED` tag or the `ID` property of the `OBJECT` tag in the HTML file. When the connectivity is triggered, the command and parameters configured here will be passed to this function as `command` and `args`, respectively.

Now let's return to how to specify the values for these two fields. In the COMMAND field, specify the name of the JavaScript function that you want to call or invoke by either entering a text in the input field or clicking the BIND button to bind it to a single cell in the embedded spreadsheet. The PROPERTIES field works the same way. The accepted values of these two fields are different when the dashboard is run in an Adobe Flash Player or in a web browser, as explained below.

If the container of your dashboard is the Flash Player, you must enter the name of one of the predefined commands here and, correspondingly, the name of one of the supported parameters of that command, if any. The supported commands and their required parameters are listed below.

▶ `Quit`

  ▹ `Parameter`: no parameter accepted

  ▹ `Purpose`: Use this command if you want to close the Adobe Flash Player to terminate the presentation. You can provide a toggle button labeled CLOSE in your dashboard for the user to close the Flash Player. Clicking the button will trigger the connectivity and thus close the Flash Player.

▶ `Fullscreen`

  ▹ `Parameter`: true or false

  ▹ `Purpose`: Use this command if you want to enable the user to set the Flash Player to full-screen mode or return it to normal menu view. Specify true for full-screen mode and false for normal view.

▶ `Allowscale`

  ▹ `Parameter`: true or false

- ▶ Purpose: Specifying false sets the Flash Player so that your dashboard is always drawn at its original size and is never scaled. Specifying true forces it to scale to 100% of the player.

- ▶ **Showmenu**

  - ▶ Parameter: true or false

  - ▶ Purpose: Specifying true enables the full set of context menu items in the Flash Player. If you want to restrict the user's access to them, specify false to hide all of the context menu items except ABOUT FLASH PLAYER.

- ▶ **Exec**

  - ▶ Parameter: path to the application

  - ▶ Purpose: Use this command if you want to execute an application from within the Flash Player. This command runs only in the subdirectory *fscommand*. In other words, if you use this command to call an application, the application must reside in a subdirectory called *fscommand*.

- ▶ **Trapallkeys**

  - ▶ Parameter: true or false

  - ▶ Purpose: Specifying true sends all key events, including accelerator keys, to the onClipEvent(keyDown/keyUp) handler in the Flash Player.

However, if your dashboard is wrapped by an HTML file and run in a web browser, you can send any message in the two parameters command and parameters. The messages are sent to the JavaScript function with the special name myMovieName_DoFSCommand in the HTML file, as mentioned before. This function can either display or process the messages or call other JavaScript functions based on what command is passed in. This makes it possible for your dashboard to call any JavaScript function from within it, with myMovieName_DoFSCommand as the proxy.

Usage

An FS Command connectivity can only be triggered by a cell when its value has changed or has become equal to something. Unlike other connectivities such as web services, it cannot be triggered on loading the dashboard or at intervals.

You trigger the FS Command connectivity the same way you would trigger any other connectivity described above. You can refer to the corresponding sections for more information.

Figure 7.25 shows a sample USAGE tab of an FS Command connectivity, where it's triggered when the value of cell Sheet1!$B$2 changes.

Figure 7.25 Trigger Option of an FS Command Connection

7.6.3   Practice

Let's go through a simple example to see how to use an FS Command connection. Suppose we're going to create a dashboard with an input text and a toggle button. When the user clicks the button, the text of that input text will be displayed with a JavaScript alert. You can follow these steps to complete this example.

1. **Set up the UI components.**
   From the COMPONENTS view, drag an input text and a toggle button onto the canvas. Bind the destination of the toggle button to cell Sheet1!$B$2. Bind the content and destination of the input text to cell Sheet1!$B$4 so that its value is written to that cell.

2. **Set up the FS Command connectivity.**
   Launch the Data Manager to add an FS Command connection. On the DEFINITION tab, enter "AlertMessage" for COMMAND, and bind PARAMETERS to cell Sheet1!$B$4, where the content of the input text is stored, as shown in Figure 7.26.

   On the USAGE tab, bind the trigger cell to Sheet1!$B$2 and set it to trigger WHEN VALUE CHANGES, as shown in Figure 7.25.

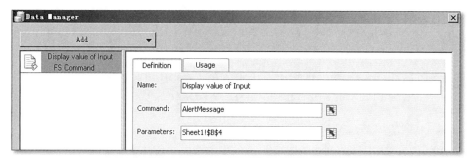

Figure 7.26 Definition of the FS Command Connection

Now each time the user clicks the toggle button, the value in cell Sheet1!$B$2 is changed, and this FS Command connection is triggered.

3. **Edit the JavaScript codes.**

We want to run the dashboard in a web browser, so we need to write an HTML file containing it. To do this, follow the menu path File • Export • HTML and specify its file name and location. An HTML file and an SWF file will be generated.

The proxy JavaScript function called myMovieName_DoFSCommand will not be generated automatically. To add it, we need to find the name of the dashboard by opening the HTML file in a text editor and identify the NAME attribute of the EMBED tag or the ID property of the OBJECT tag, as displayed below.

```
<OBJECT classid="clsid:D27CDB6E-AE6D-11cf-96B8-444553540000"
codebase="http://fpdownload.adobe.com/pub/shockwave/cabs/flash/
swflash.cab#version=9,0,0,0"
WIDTH="800" HEIGHT="600" id="myMovieName">
<PARAM NAME="movie" VALUE="fscommand_handson.swf">
…
</OBJECT>
```

Or:

```
<EMBED src="fscommand_handson.swf" quality=high bgcolor=#FFFFFF
WIDTH="800" HEIGHT="600" NAME="myMovieName" ALIGN=""
TYPE="application/x-shockwave-flash" play="true" loop="true"
PLUGINSPAGE="http://www.adobe.com/shockwave/download/
index.cgi?P1_Prod_Version=ShockwaveFlash">
</EMBED>
```

Depending on your web browser, either the OBJECT or the EMBED tag will be used.

The ID of the dashboard is myMovieName in either case, so we add a JavaScript function called myMovieName_DoFSCommand in the HTML file, below the <BODY> tag. The content of the proxy function, and some related functions, are listed below.

```
<SCRIPT LANGUAGE="JavaScript">
function myMovieName_DoFSCommand(command, args) {
    alert ("The content in the Input Text is: " + args);
    if(command == "purpose1")
        func1();
    else if(command = "purpose2")
        func2(args);
}
function func1() {
    ...
}
function func2(args) {
    ...
}
</SCRIPT>
```

Note that the function myMovieName_DoFSCommand() can not only directly display or process the input parameters inside it, but can also call other JavaScript functions based on the input command to further process the parameters.

You can either open the HTML file directly, or put it on a web server so that others can access it through a web browser. Each time the user clicks the toggle button, the content of the input text will be displayed. Depending on the real requirement, you can further process the passed-in value.

If you open the HTML file directly with a web browser, you will need to set the SWF file as trusted so it can access the HTML file, as we discussed in Chapter 6 when we covered the security issues involved with accessing external data.

Figure 7.27 is a screenshot of the HTML file at runtime.

You can get the source file of this dashboard at *www.sap-press.com*.

Figure 7.27 Final Effect

7.7 External Interface Connection

Similar to FS Command, External Interface is an Adobe Flex technology that enables communication between Flash and its container such as an HTML page. It's a fantastic way to communicate with JavaScript directly from Flash. A dashboard is compiled into Flash, so this technology can be leveraged to enable communication between the dashboard and its container.

External Interface is very similar to FS Command but is more flexible in that you can pass as many arguments as you want to any JavaScript function on the HTML page and receive a return value. It can work in the opposite direction as well, from JavaScript to Flash.

With this connectivity, data from the SWF file can now be passed into or out of a specific cell range, using push/pull technology. Note that the communication is initialized by the container. In other words, it's the JavaScript that invokes the External Interface exposed by your dashboard.

7.7.1 When to Use an External Interface Connection

In some cases you might want to control the dashboard from the outside. For example, you might retrieve a stock price from a provider over the web (e.g., from Yahoo! Stock), do some calculation using JavaScript, and then feed the result into your dashboard. In such a case, you can wrap the dashboard SWF file and JavaScript code in one HTML file. The output of the JavaScript is then sent to the SWF file via an External Interface connection.

One more powerful use of this connectivity is when you want to enable communication between two dashboards, both created by SAP BusinessObjects Dashboards or Xcelsius. For example, say you've created two complex dashboards, one to display sales revenue for each branch and the other to display information about a branch such as its map and images. You may want to use this connectivity to pass the selected branch between them.

Choose this type of connectivity when you want to either pass external data into a cell or cell range of the dashboard or send data inside a cell or cell range of the dashboard to an external application.

7.7.2 How to Use an External Interface Connection

To add an External Interface connection, launch the Data Manager, click ADD, and select EXTERNAL INTERFACE CONNECTION from the dropdown list. A connectivity of this type will be added to the CONNECTIONS list with default properties. You can create as many connections of this type as you want in one dashboard.

You pass external data into your dashboard or pass data from inside your dashboard to external applications. To do this, specify a cell range in the embedded spreadsheet as the source of the data sent out or the destination of the data passed in, and specify whether it can be read, written, or both. Once you understand this mechanism, you'll know what to do with the PROPERTIES panel of an External Interface connection.

In the PROPERTIES panel, click the button with a plus (+) sign to add a range, which will be used as the source, the destination, or both. The properties are per range, as explained next.

▶ NAME
  Specify a name for the range by either entering a text in the RANGE NAME field or clicking the BIND button to bind it to a single cell in the embedded spreadsheet. This name is not used only to make the range descriptive and easy to understand. It will be used in an external JavaScript function later.

▶ RANGE TYPE
  You then set the RANGE TYPE by selecting one from the dropdown list. If you want to pass a single value, select CELL and later bind RANGE to a single cell in the spreadsheet. Similarly, select ROW/COLUMN if you want to pass data in a one-dimensional array, and select TABLE if the data is two-dimensional, with multiple rows and columns.

▶ RANGE

Depending on what range type you have selected, you specify the range by clicking the BIND button to bind to a cell, a row or column, or a table in the embedded spreadsheet. For inbound communication, external data will be inserted here. For outbound communication, data in the specified cell range will be sent to external applications.

▶ ACCESS

Here you specify the access type of the cell range by selecting READ, WRITE, or READ/WRITE. If the data of the cell range will be sent to external applications, select READ. If the cell range is used as the destination of data passed in from external applications, select WRITE. If both might be used, select READ/WRITE.

You can add as many ranges as you want in one External Interface connection by clicking the button with a + sign. To delete a range that you defined before, simply click to select it and click the button with a minus (–) sign.

Note that unlike the other connectivity types described above, you cannot change the name of the connectivity. You have to use the default names Connection 1, Connection 2, and so on.

Figure 7.28 shows a screenshot of the PROPERTIES panel of an External Interface connection. Note that there's no USAGE tab here, where you might want to define when to trigger the connection. The reason for this is that this connectivity is triggered not by itself, but by JavaScript functions in its container HTML file.

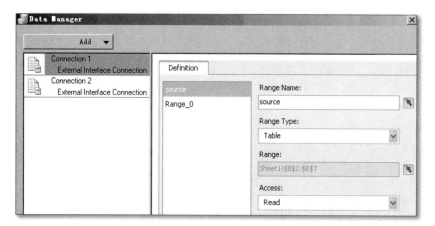

Figure 7.28 Definition of an External Interface Connection

7.7.3   Practice

This example will cover how to write data from JavaScript to your dashboard (inbound) and how to read data from your dashboard to JavaScript (outbound). The user accesses the dashboard by visiting the HTML file containing the SWF file from a web browser.

1. **Plan the data.**

   We plan to use a cell range as both the source of and destination for data communication between our dashboard and its container, which is an HTML file in this example. For simplicity, we'll use a cell range with two rows and two columns, as displayed in Figure 7.29.

   Default values are filled in that cell range.

	A	B	C	D	E	
1						
2		cell range as both source and destination				
3		11	23			
4		35	48			
5						

Figure 7.29 Data Structure in the Embedded Spreadsheet

2. **Design your dashboard.**

   To simulate both read and write, the user needs be able to see and manipulate the data in the cell range. To make it simple, we'll drag a grid component from the COMPONENTS view, drop it onto the canvas, and bind its data to cell range Sheet1!$B$3:$C$4. The data in this cell range is displayed in the grid component, and the user can change the data in the cell range within the grid.

   The PROPERTIES panel and data of the grid should look like Figure 7.30.

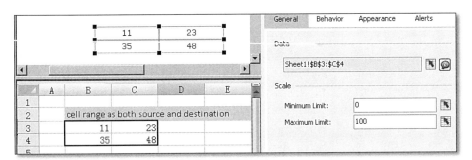

Figure 7.30 Bindings of the Grid

427

3. **Set up an External Interface connection.**

In this step, we'll launch the Data Manager and add one External Interface connection. Its PROPERTIES panel is very simple. We bind its range to Sheet1!$B$3:$C$4, which stores the values of the grid component, set its range type to TABLE because it's a two-dimensional range, and set its access type to READ/WRITE to support both directions.

Figure 7.31 shows the PROPERTIES panel of this connectivity.

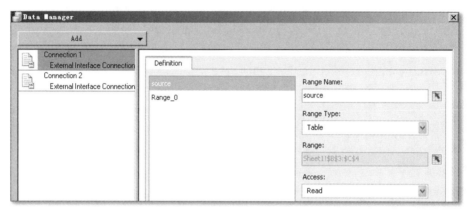

Figure 7.31 Definition of the External Interface Connection

4. **Write the JavaScript code.**

Now the work on the dashboard side is finished. Before going on to the Java-Script code, we need to export the dashboard to an HTML file. To do this, follow the menu path FILE • EXPORT • HTML and set the file location and name. An SWF file will be generated along with its HTML container.

The HTML file is designed to simulate the two communication directions between the SWF file and its HTML container. We'll use four input texts to display the value from the SWF file. The user can also manipulate the value in each input text, which will be written back to the SWF file.

To get data from the SWF file, use `myMovieName.getDataSource(rangeName)`, where `myMovieName` is the ID of the SWF object in the HTML container, and `rangeName` is the name you specified as RANGE NAME in the connectivity's PROPERTIES panel. Like FS Command, the ID of the SWF object is either the `NAME` attribute of the `EMBED` tag or the `ID` property of the `OBJECT` tag, depending on what web browser the end user is using.

To write data back to the SWF file from the HTML file using JavaScript, use `myMo-vieName.setDataSource(rangeName, data)`.

The pieces of JavaScript code in the HTML file are illustrated below.

```
<SCRIPT LANGUAGE="JavaScript">
    function writeToSWF() {
    ma = new Array(2);
    ma[0] = new Array(2);
    ma[0][0] = document.getElementById("a1").value;
    ma[0][1] = document.getElementById("b1").value;
    ma[1] = new Array(2);
    ma[1][0] = document.getElementById("a2").value;
    ma[1][1] = document.getElementById("b2").value;
      myMovieName.setDataSource("Data",ma);
    }
    function readFromSWF() {
    document.getElementById("a1").value =
      myMovieName.getDataSource("Data")[0][0];
    document.getElementById("b1").value =
      myMovieName.getDataSource("Data")[0][1];
    document.getElementById("a2").value =
      myMovieName.getDataSource("Data")[1][0];
    document.getElementById("b2").value =
      myMovieName.getDataSource("Data")[1][1];
    }
</SCRIPT>

<form id="f1">
    <input type="text" size="15" id="a1"/>
    <input type="text" size="15" id="b1"/> <p/>
    <input type="text" size="15" id="a2"/>
    <input type="text" size="15" id="b2"/> <p/>
    <input id="btn_write" type="button" value="Write"
      onclick="writeToSWF()"/>
    <input id="btn_read"  type="button" value="Read"
      onclick="readFromSWF()"/>
</form>
```

Four input texts are added to the HTML file to simulate the grid component for both input and output.

429

The JavaScript function `writeToSWF()`, used to write the values of the four texts manipulated by the user through the web browser back to the SWF file, is triggered by clicking the WRITE button. Pay attention to the line `myMovieName.setDataSource("Data",ma)` in this method.

However, the JavaScript function `readFromSWF()` is used to read data from the SWF file into the four texts in the HTML file and is triggered by clicking the READ button. Pay attention to the line `myMovieName.getDataSource("Data")[0][0]` in this method.

As a result, data between these four HTML texts and the dashboard is exchanged via an External Interface connection. Figure 7.32 shows the original state of the dashboard and the four HTML text fields on launching the HTML file compared to the state when the READ button is clicked.

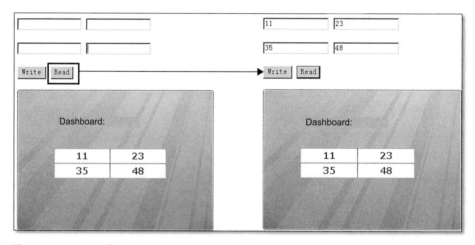

Figure 7.32 Data in the Dashboard is Read into the HTML Page

The user can modify the values in either the SWF file or the four HTML text fields. Clicking the READ button will fill the four HTML text fields with the values in the SWF file, and clicking the WRITE button will overwrite the SWF file with the values in the HTML text fields. Figure 7.33 shows the states before and after the WRITE button is clicked.

To make this work in your environment, you need to set the SWF file as trusted so it can access the HTML file. Do this in the Adobe Flash Player Settings Manager as described in Chapter 6, Section 6.3.

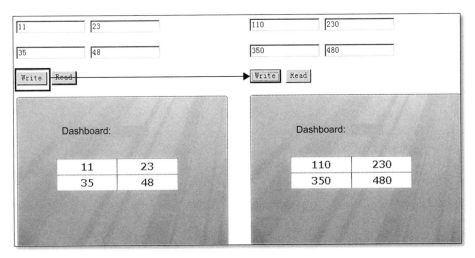

Figure 7.33 Data in the HTML Page is Written to the Dashboard

7.8 LCDS Connection

An LCDS connection is used to connect to Adobe LifeCycle Data Service (LCDS) to retrieve real-time data there. This is one aspect of the integration between SAP BusinessObjects and Adobe, similar to exporting your dashboard to Adobe AIR, as mentioned previously in Chapter 1, Section 1.2.4 and later in Chapter 8, Section 8.5.2.

Adobe LiveCycle Data Services is a component of Adobe LifeCycle Enterprise Suite (ES), which provides an up-to-the-second view of your business data. In terms of programming, it is a scalable and optimized framework that abstracts the complexity of creating easy-to-use, personalized, and interactive applications of RIAs (rich Internet applications). It runs on a web application server such as Tomcat or JBoss to provide real-time transactional services, enabling RIAs to pull and aggregate information from core enterprise applications, and feeds outside the firewall. The supported protocols for data communication between LCDS and SAP BusinessObjects Dashboards include HTTP, RMTP (Real-Time Messaging Protocol), and AMF (Action Message Format). For more information about LCDS, please refer to the Adobe website at *http://www.adobe.com/products/livecycle/dataservices/*.

LCDS needs some configuration before it can be accessed from SAP Business-Objects Dashboards. You need to add the XLCDSServlet to the LCDS server and configure it in the SAP BusinessObjects Dashboards -config files. Figure 7.34 shows the configurations you need for SAP BusinessObjects Dashboards to connect to LCDS, cited from the Adobe website.

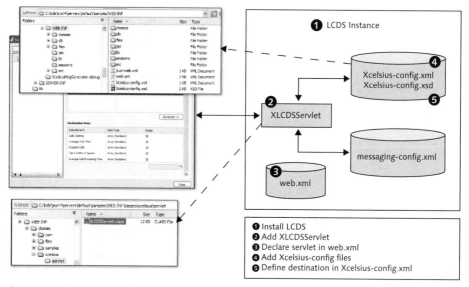

Figure 7.34 Required Configurations for the LCDS Server

With this connection you can stream real-time data from Adobe LifeCycle Data Service into your SAP BusinessObjects Dashboards dashboard at runtime, thus creating low-latency, highly scalable, and data-consistent dashboards or widgets.

Most SAP BusinessObjects Dashboards 4.0 connectivities we mentioned, such as XML data and web services, are used to retrieve live data from the server. An LCDS connection is used to retrieve real-time data, in that it must be able to quickly detect and respond to information, and the latency should be very low, sometimes within milliseconds. This is required by dashboards in real-time applications for stock trading or call center monitoring systems.

7.8.1 When to Use an LCDS Connection

Choose an LCDS connection when the data is provided from the Adobe LifeCycle Data Service or when you want to create a real-time dashboard.

7.8.2 How to Use an LCDS Connection

To add this type of connection, launch the Data Manager and select LCDS CON-NECTION in the ADD dropdown list. You can create as many connections of this type as you want in a single dashboard.

To use an LCDS connection, you need to be able to access the server hosting Life-Cycle Data Service. You can configure this connectivity from its PROPERTIES panel.

Definition

This is the only tab in the PROPERTIES panel, as displayed in Figure 7.35. Similar to the External Interface connection, you cannot set the connection name.

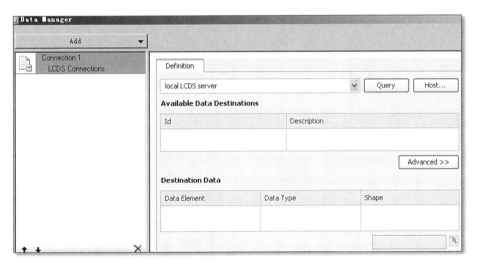

Figure 7.35 Definition of an LCDS Connection

The properties are explained as follows.

▶ HOST
First, you need to select a host from the dropdown list to be associated with this LCDS connection. If no host exists, click the HOST button to manage hosts, including adding, editing, or deleting a host.

Figure 7.36 shows the hosts manager and the window to add a host after clicking ADD.

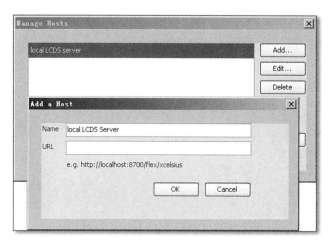

Figure 7.36 Add a Host through the Hosts Manager

As displayed in the figure, you specify a name for the host for easy identification and the URL for the LCDS server to connect to. The basic structure of the URL is:

http://<server name>:<port>/<LCDS context path>/xcelsius

In our example, we use *http://localhost:8700/flex/xcelsius.*

After selecting a valid and available LCDS host, click the QUERY button to trigger SAP BusinessObjects Dashboards to retrieve information on what feed destinations are available from this host. All available data destinations and data elements of the LCDS host will be displayed in the corresponding area in this tab.

▶ AVAILABLE DATA DESTINATIONS
This area lists all of the available data destinations of the LCDS server you selected from the dropdown list, including the ID and description of each. You can select one as the feed destination to bind to your dashboard.

Click the ADVANCED button to make additional settings for the selected data destination. In CHANNEL TYPE, you specify the type of channel, or communication protocol, that's currently being used. Similarly, the CHANNEL URL field indicates the URL associated with the selected data destination.

Click the ADVANCED button again to collapse these additional fields.

▶ DESTINATION DATA
This area lists all of the available data elements from the selected LCDS host. For each data element, you can click the BIND button on the bottom right to

bind it to a single cell, a row or column, or a cell range with multiple rows and columns in the embedded spreadsheet, which will be used to store the data.

The type of each data element is either NUMBER (for numeric values), TXT (for string), or TRUE/FALSE (for Boolean values). It can also be an array of any type, for example, NUMBERS. Moreover, the type can be three-dimensional as an array of arrays; for example, ARRAY (NUMBERS).

The SHAPE field defines the shape, or structure, of the data returned for this element. The shape can be any of the three listed here:

▶ SINGLETON
This shape is for single values. You need to bind it to a single cell in the embedded spreadsheet.

▶ 1D
This shape is for one-dimensional data, that is, data in a row or column. The corresponding data type should be an array of some type, for example, ARRAY (NUMBERS). Its output data should be bound to a row or column in the embedded spreadsheet.

▶ 2D
This is when the data is two-dimensional, that is, in a table of one or multiple rows and columns. The corresponding data type should be an array of an array of some type, for example, ARRAY (ARRAY [TXT]). Consequently, its returned data should be bound to a table in the embedded spreadsheet.

7.9   Portal Data

With SAP BusinessObjects Dashboards you can create dashboards within the portal environment. Supported portals include IBM WebSphere and Microsoft SharePoint.

The portal data connectivity is for communication between dashboards (SWF) hosted in portals. One dashboard can provide data to another as a provider, and the one using the data acts as the consumer. You can define parameters in your dashboard so that the user can customize the values of those parameters within the portal.

With a portal data connection, you can connect your dashboard to SharePoint lists. Also, dashboards can communicate with one another, making it possible for users to adjust values in one dashboard and see the results in another. This is especially useful for a what-if analysis or when you need drill-down from one chart to another.

7.9.1 When to Use Portal Data

You may want to use this type of connectivity when your dashboard is to be hosted in a portal and you want to enable data communication between the dashboard and the portal or between the provider dashboard and the consumer. With the help of the portal, you can define parameters inside your dashboard, the values of which the user can set through the portal. This way, the user can customize the behavior and even the appearance of the dashboard. For example, you can define parameters that control colors in the dashboard, so the user can customize the color schema according to his preferences.

To use this type of connectivity, you need to be able to access the portal hosting the dashboards.

7.9.2 How to Use Portal Data

To add a portal data connection, launch the Data Manager and select Portal Data from the Add dropdown list. Like Flash Variables, you can create only one portal data connection per dashboard. The connection will become disabled when there's already one such connection defined in your dashboard.

In the Properties panel of a portal data connection, what properties are available depends on the connection type. You can select a connection type from the dropdown list, which we'll explain in the following sections.

None

Choose this type if your dashboard doesn't need to communicate with another dashboard. Instead, define some parameters in your dashboard, and specify that you want the users to customize their values from within the portal. By specifying the values they want, different users can see different effects and/or different data of the same dashboard in the portal.

Figure 7.37 shows the Properties panel for a portal data connectivity.

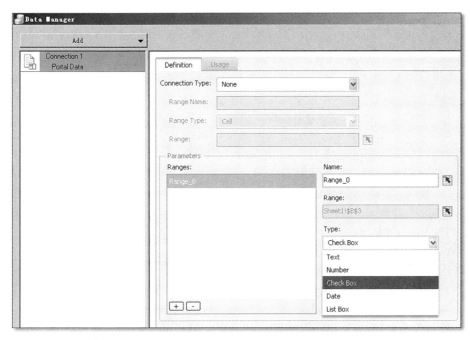

Figure 7.37 Definition of a Portal Data Connection with Type "None"

The RANGE area lists the definitions of all parameters of your dashboard. For each parameter, you need to configure three properties as listed here:

▶ NAME
Define the name of the parameter by entering a text directly in the input field or clicking the BIND button to bind to a single cell in the embedded spreadsheet.

In SharePoint, the name will be displayed in the PROPERTIES dialog box for this dashboard. This parameter will not be listed as a parameter in SharePoint if its NAME field is blank. NAME is a mandatory property for such a connection.

▶ RANGE
Here you click the BIND button to select a cell range in the embedded spreadsheet, which will be used to store the values the user will specify for this parameter in the portal. Based on the parameter type, you can bind to a single cell or a cell range.

▶ TYPE

Here you set the type of the parameter. Depending on your scenario, you can choose from TEXT, NUMBER, CHECK BOX, DATE, and LIST BOX.

Select TEXT to set any text-based data within your dashboard, for example, chart titles, greeting messages, and so on.

You use NUMBER to set any numeric data. A typical use of this type is to customize the alert thresholds used in the ALERTS tab of a UI component such as a column chart or an icon. You can also select this type for the user to customize the number of major or minor divisions in a column chart.

CHECK BOX is useful for toggling the value of a cell between 0 and 1. Choose this type so the user can control whether to show certain components using dynamic visibility.

You use DATE to define a calendar date in your dashboard. It sets the format to DATE and uses a true date value within the dashboard. For example, you can choose this type so the user can specify the date period he is interested in before requesting the data.

For the types listed above, the user can specify any value. The potential problem is that the user may not be clear about the accepted value format and thus may enter an invalid value, resulting in confusion or causing the application crash. To restrict user input, you can select LIST BOX, which enables the designer to build user selection options (a list of values) into the parameters. This way, the user can select only from values provided at design time, which are always valid.

When LIST BOX is selected, two more options become available. ENTRIES sets what entries are available for the user to select. You can bind it to a row or column in the embedded spreadsheet, where the candidate items are stored. You use DEFAULT SELECTION for selecting which entry's value will be used by default if the user does not make a selection.

Consumer

Choose this type of connection if you want your dashboard to accept data from another web part within the portal, acting as a consumer. This will add a portal consumer connection to your dashboard. Figure 7.38 shows the PROPERTIES panel when CONSUMER is selected.

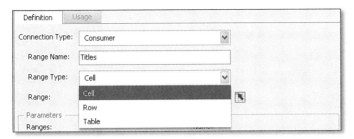

Figure 7.38 Definition of a Portal Data Connection with Type "Consumer"

As you can see from this figure, in addition to the properties in PARAMETERS mentioned above, there are three important selections to configure in the PROPERTIES panel of the consumer connection: RANGE NAME, RANGE TYPE, and RANGE, which we'll explain here.

▶ RANGE NAME

You set RANGE NAME by entering a text. It will be displayed when connecting web parts together in portals. Like the NAME property in PARAMETERS mentioned above, RANGE NAME is mandatory; without it the web parts cannot be connected.

▶ RANGE TYPE

RANGE TYPE defines the amount of data that will be passed.

  ▶ CELL consumes a single value from another web part.

  ▶ Row is a single row with multiple columns, which is similar to the shape type 1D described for LCDS connections. With this type, your dashboard consumes an array of data that will be passed in.

  ▶ TABLE represents data in multiple rows and columns, similar to the shape type 2D described for LCDS connections.

Usually, you will choose CELL or Row, to consume data from another dashboard. You may only want to choose TABLE to consume data from a portal list.

▶ RANGE

RANGE is the area in the embedded spreadsheet of your dashboard that the incoming data will be written to. Depending on what you select in RANGE TYPE, you may bind it to a single cell, a row or column, or a table with multiple rows and columns.

Provider

Choose this type of connection if you want the dashboard to provide data to another web part. In this case, only web parts from SAP BusinessObjects Dashboards can be used to consume information from a dashboard that's using the PROVIDER connection.

The properties in the DEFINITION tab are exactly the same as when you select CONSUMER. You can refer to the section above for information about how to use them.

One more tab, USAGE, is activated only when you select PROVIDER. Similar to many other types of connectivity, in the USAGE tab you define whether you want your dashboard to send data based on the value of a single cell in the embedded spreadsheet, either when it changes or when it becomes equal to something.

7.10　Summary

In this chapter we discussed some advanced types of data connectivity provided by SAP BusinessObjects Dashboards 4.0, such as Query as a Web Service and Crystal Reports Data Consumer in an SAP BusinessObjects environment, SAP NetWeaver BW Connection in a BW system, LCDS connection in the Adobe LifeCycle Data Service, and Flash Variables and FS Command to pass data from the container into the dashboard. In Chapters 6 and 7, we have described all the connections in SAP BusinessObjects Dashboards, and you should now have a big picture of them to help you choose the best ones to retrieve the live data you need to create a powerful, efficient, and attractive dashboard.

In the previous chapters we discussed all of the UI components and data connectivity options available in SAP BusinessObjects Dashboards 4.0. Some of the functionalities, such as drill-down and dynamic visibility, are common to most UI components are very useful.

8 Special Features

In Chapters 4 through 7 we discussed all of the UI components and types of data connectivity provided by SAP BusinessObjccts Dashboards 4.0. Some features, such as drill-down and alerts, are common to most UI components and are useful enough to be widely used in creating dashboards. When introducing each UI component, we talked a little bit about how to use these features in that particular UI component. This may not be comprehensive enough for you to understand them at a higher level, as features on top of UI components.

In this chapter, we'll describe some special features that are not only useful but also widely used, from a general rather than a specific UI component's perspective.

After reading this chapter you'll be able to:

▶ Describe those special features common to most UI components

▶ Be clear about what feature to use to achieve a requirement before choosing the UI components

8.1 Drill-Down

Drill-down is a commonly used technique in reporting and analysis. For example, in a pie chart showing quarterly sales revenue, you can drill down from a quarter to see more detailed data (such as the monthly data) about that selected quarter. This is to some extent similar to navigating through the file system in your computer, from the high-level folders (e.g., *My Computer*) to the drivers (*C:*) to folders (*My Documents*) and files.

You may know that the drill-down functionality is also supported in SAP Crystal Reports (a product of SAP BusinessObjects), where the drill-down is defined by groups you've created through the Group Expert. The drill-down happens from a group to its subgroup. Each time you click (when you view the report through a web browser) or double-click (through the designer) on a group, its child data is displayed in a separate window or tab.

You can also drill down along the hierarchy defined in a Universe in SAP BusinessObjects Web Intelligence. Unlike SAP Crystal Reports, you drill in the same block without opening a new tab. This is more straightforward.

Sometimes you might use drill down along no hierarchy. That is, you just use the function as a selector. For example, when you click on a slice on a pie chart, some additional information related to that selection is displayed on other components. The information changes according to your selection.

In SAP BusinessObjects Dashboards, there's a Drill Down tab in the Properties panels of many UI components, and you need to enable drill-down to use it. In this section, we'll take a closer look at how drill-down is used in dashboard design.

8.1.1 When to Use Drill-Down

Usually a dashboard is used to present high-level aggregated data with intuitive charts to maximum the efficiency of information consumption for the end user. In a more sophisticated dashboard design, users can view detailed data from high-level data, along with a certain hierarchy. For example, users are first presented with a column chart displaying sales for each country. By selecting one country, users can view sales for each region of that country and even go a step further to each city in one region. This example is a classic drill-down path along the region hierarchy.

Sometimes you can also drill down along paths not within a hierarchy. For example, the user is first presented with a chart displaying the sales revenue of each country. On clicking one country, the user sees the graphic location or population or some other information about that country. In such scenarios, the drill-down feature is used as a selector.

In general, when you want to allow users to view data from a high level to details, this drill-down technique is your best-fit choice.

8.1.2   How to Use Drill-Down

Three elements are required to make a drill-down:

1. High-level aggregated data

2. Detailed data

3. The linkage between them

In a dashboard, the high-level data and detailed data are represented with charts or table components, and the linkage between them is implemented with data insertion. When the user selects any part of the high-level data, data corresponding to the selection is inserted into a destination that will affect the detailed data.

Almost all chart components have an INSERTION tab on the PROPERTIES panel. This chart component is where the high-level data is presented and data insertion is configured. Figure 8.1 shows two typical INSERTION tabs.

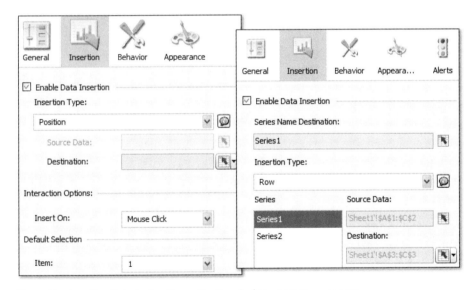

Figure 8.1 Insertion Tabs in the Properties Panel of Most UI Components

Some typical properties in this tab are briefly explained as follows.

▶ ENABLE DATA INSERTION
Select the ENABLE DATA INSERTION checkbox to enable drill-down. Note that this checkbox will be active only after the data source has been configured in the GENERAL tab.

▶ Series Name Destination
For a multiseries chart, the name of the series selected will be inserted into the destination cell specified here.

▶ Insertion Type
Candidate types include position, value, row, column, and status list. Refer to Chapter 4, Section 4.1 for detailed descriptions of these data insertion types.

▶ Source Data and Destination
With a specified insertion type, bind the source data (if applicable) and destination here. If the component has multiple series, the source data and destination can be configured for each series.

Source Data can only be bound to a cell range in the embedded spreadsheet, while Destination can be bound either to a single cell or cell range in the embedded spreadsheet or to a Universe query prompt.

▶ Interaction Options
Specify what action triggers a drill-down: mouse click or mouse over.

▶ Default Selection
Determine the default selection when the visualization is initially loaded. Choose No Selection (–1) if you don't want to keep any default selected item.

8.1.3 Drill Down from One Chart to Another

Usually, drill-down is performed from one chart to another. The first chart shows the highest-level aggregated data, while the other chart(s) shows more detailed data. The UI component used to show more detailed data can be anything. It does have to be a chart.

To start, enable drill-down for the first chart. If there are more charts, enable drill-down for all charts that are not on the last level. Depending on how your data is arranged, either static or dynamic and retrieved from a server, you select the appropriate data insertion type and source and destination data.

In the following example, we'll create two charts to display quarterly sales and a breakdown by product line. Follow these steps:

1. **Plan the data.**
   In this simple example, both the high-level and detailed data are stored in a cell range in the embedded spreadsheet. You can regard it as real data returned from some data connectivity such as a web service connectivity.

Figure 8.2 shows how we store the data in the spreadsheet. The TOTAL column is calculated within the embedded spreadsheet using Excel formulas to sum up values of the products.

	A	B	C	D	E	F	G
1							
2			Total	Phone	Desktop	Laptop	Service
3		Q1	800	150	230	300	120
4		Q2	830	190	220	280	140
5		Q3	860	240	180	290	150
6		Q4	910	260	200	280	170
7		Insertion					
8							

Figure 8.2 Data Arranged in a Two-Dimensional Cell Range

If the data is dynamically retrieved from a connectivity at runtime, you can map it to a range from the second to the sixth row; for example, range Sheet1!$D$2:$I$6, with cells in the first row ($D$2:$I$2) storing the product names, and other cells ($D$3:$I$6) storing the values of all products in all quarters. The number of columns depends on how many products you have.

2. **Set up the chart showing high-level data.**
   We'll use a column chart to show and compare the total sales revenue of all products in each quarter. To do this, drag a column chart from the COMPONENTS view. Drop it on the canvas, and bind its category label to column Sheet1!$B$3:$B$6 with quarter names and its values to column Sheet1!$C$3:$C$6 with sales revenues of all four quarters.

   What's more important in this step is to set up the drill-down behavior. When the user has clicked a quarter, the sales revenue for each product of that quarter should be picked out. To do this, set INSERTION TYPE to ROW, and insert a row from the cell range Sheet1!$B$3:$I$6 containing all products and their sales revenues in each quarter to the row Sheet1!$B$8:$I$8 as the destination.

   Figure 8.3 shows the INSERTION tab of this column chart.

3. **Set up the chart showing detailed data.**
   Select a chart to present the data. We'll use a pie chart to show the contribution of each product to the quarter's total sales revenue.

   To do this, drop a pie chart onto the canvas and align it with the bottom of the column chart. We'll bind its labels to row Sheet1!$D$2:$I$2, where the names of the available products are stored, and its values to row Sheet1!$D$8:$I$8, where the sales revenues of all products in that selected quarter are inserted. To indicate what quarter the pie chart is about, bind its subtitle to cell Sheet1!$B$8.

Figure 8.3 Drill-Down Definition of the Column Chart

Sometimes the last columns in Sheet1!$D$2:$I$2 and Sheet1!$D$8:$I$8 may be empty when there are fewer than six products. To avoid empty series, select IGNORE BLANK CELLS • IN VALUES in the BEHAVIOR tab.

Figure 8.4 shows a screenshot of the dashboard at runtime. Q1 is selected by default, and the sales revenue of each product in Q1 is displayed in the pie chart. Whenever the user clicks another quarter, the data corresponding to that quarter is inserted into another row, causing the pie chart to change.

You can easily extend or improve this dashboard to satisfy your real needs. For example, add one more chart to show more detailed data from a certain part of the second chart, making the dashboard a three-level drill-down.

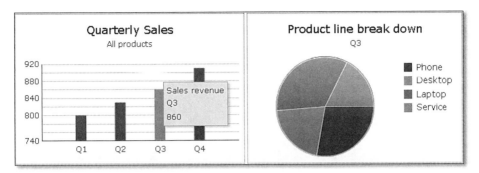

Figure 8.4 Effect of Drill-Down from One Chart to Another

8.1.4 Drill-Down on the Same Chart

Sometimes you might want to perform drill-down on the same chart. For example, a chart displays the yearly sales revenue, and users can drill down by clicking one column to view the monthly sales for that year on the same chart. Drill-down on the same pie chart is very attractive and intuitive to the user. This provides a more direct drill-down experience compared to that on multiple charts, which is more like data linking than drill-down.

Before you get very experienced with charts, you may take it for granted that drilling down on the same chart is very simple. Just use the single chart to represent data from a high-level to a detailed level. However, you'll soon find out that something unexpected will occur. For example, let's say we want to create a dashboard where the user is first presented with the sales revenue of each quarter, and on clicking a quarter, the user will see the sales revenue by product lines in that quarter. On launching the dashboard, you may find that instead of displaying the high-level data, the chart just displays the sales revenue by product in the first quarter.

This occurs because the chart automatically drills down to the lowest level, though there's been no user interaction. In our example, the chart does display the high-level data, which is the sales revenue of each quarter, at first. However, because drill-down is enabled and the first quarter is selected by default (if you haven't changed the DEFAULT SELECTION item in the DRILL DOWN tab), the chart automatically drills down to display data in the lower level of the selected quarter. That's why you see the sales revenue by product in the first quarter instead of the high-level data of each quarter.

This problem can be solved by setting the DEFAULT SELECTION item to NO SELECTION (–1), as displayed in Figure 8.5.

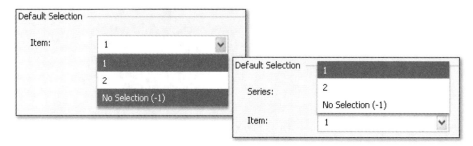

Figure 8.5 Set No Default Selection to Avoid Auto Drill-Down

However, this only solves the problem when the drill-down occurs on only the first level. That is, the drill-down only happens when the user clicks a data element in the first chart, but doesn't happen when the user clicks a data element in the second chart. If you want to provide a dashboard with four or more levels of drill-down, this problem will still occur.

One possible requirement is that the user should first be presented with a chart showing the sales revenue of each quarter. On clicking a data element, the user should see the sales revenue of each product in that quarter. One step further, when the user clicks a product, the chart should display the weekly sales revenue of that product in that quarter. Figure 8.6 illustrates this requirement.

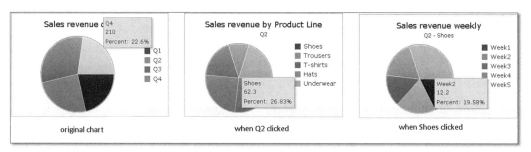

Figure 8.6 Three-Level Cascading Drill-Down on Three Charts

Setting the DEFAULT SELECTION item of the pie chart to NO SELECTION results in the chart displaying the highest-level data to start, which is what we want. However, if you click any quarter, the chart displays the weekly sales revenue of some product, instead of the sales revenue of each product in that quarter. The reason is that when you click a quarter, the selected item of the pie chart changes from No Selection (–1) to the index of the selected quarter (for example, if Q2 is selected, the selected item is now 2). As a result, after displaying the sales revenue of each product, the chart immediately changes to display the weekly sales revenue of the second product, which is *Trousers* in our case.

Figure 8.7 illustrates what you'll actually see. We'll ignore how to get the data for now—we'll explain it shortly.

Figure 8.7 Actual Behavior of the Three-Level Drill-Down on the Same Chart

So far, we've explained whether it's possible to achieve drill-down with one level or more on the same chart and how to achieve one-level drill-down. Enabling drill-down with more than one level on the same chart is more difficult, but is achievable with some workarounds.

First, the data at each drill-down level needs be mapped to the same row or column in the embedded spreadsheet, because we only have one chart to display it. Second, you cannot retrieve all of the data at the start, map it to a cell range, and insert a row or column in data insertion. Instead, all of the data must be retrieved at runtime, with the identifier of the currently selected item passed to the server as a parameter. Figure 8.8 shows what the data should be like in the embedded spreadsheet.

	A	B	C	D	E	F	G	H	I	J	K
1											
2		insertion	live data	suppose there're at most 8 items, so D3:K5							
3			label								
4			value								
5			identifier if requried								
6											
7			base URL	http://server:port/services/.../getdata							
8			URL to fetch data	http://server:port/services/.../getdata?parentId=							
9											

Figure 8.8 Data in Embedded Spreadsheet for Multilevel Drill-Down

As you can see from this figure, the data is always mapped to a single cell range of Sheet1!d3:k5, whether the user is currently on the first, second, or third drill-down level. (The number of columns in this range should be the maximum number of fields you want to accept, in all three levels. If your data contains more than eight fields, feel free to enlarge the range.) Consequently, we need do something to get the data to correspond to the user's behavior through some kind of data connectivity and map it to that cell range. We use an XML data connectivity that connects to a Java Servlet. As you can see from Figure 8.8, the URL for the connectivity is dynamically concatenated in cell Sheet1!$D$8 by adding the key of the currently selected item to the base URL. Let's go over the steps to request the data:

1. At first, nothing is selected. The XML data connectivity is triggered on loading the dashboard with the URL *http://server:port/services/.../getdata?parentId=.*

2. On the server side, the servlet processing this request will find that the parentId is empty, so it will return the highest-level data; that is, the sales revenue of each quarter.

3. The user sees the sales revenues of all quarters and clicks on the one he is interested in; for example, Q2. The XML data connectivity in our example is configured to be triggered when value of cell Sheet1!$D$8 changes. So when the user clicks Q2, the value of that cell changes to *http://server:port/services/.../getdata?parentId=Q2*, and the XML data connectivity is triggered with the new URL.

4. On the server side, the servlet processing this request will find that the parentId is Q2, so it returns the data of Q2; that is, the sales revenue of each product in Q2.

5. The user sees the sales revenue of all products in Q2. However, the user's selecting Q2 in step 3 makes the current selected item of the pie chart become item 2. As a result, the second product is selected automatically and immediately. Consequently, the value of cell Sheet1!$D$8 changes to *http://server:port/services/.../getdata?parentId=Product2*, and the XML data connectivity is triggered again with the new URL.

6. On the server side, the servlet processing this request will find that the parentId is now Product2, so it returns the data of Product2; that is, the sales revenue of each week in Q2 for Product2.

7. The user sees the sales revenue of Product2 for all weeks in Q2.

Auto drill-down happens again when the user clicks on the chart, though not for the first screen, which displays the highest-level data.

If you really want to enable drill-down for more than one level on the same chart, you can try the workaround explained next.

> **Note**
>
> The principle is to return one more items for the previously selected item, with a special identifier that the server will use and a value of 0 to make it invisible in the pie chart. On the server side, when receiving this special identifier, return nothing so that the content of the cell range remains unchanged, and thus the pie chart remains unchanged.

To illustrate this workaround, we'll go back through the steps of communication between the server and client, beginning from step 4, because the first three steps are the same.

1. On the server side, the servlet processing this request will find that the parentId is Q2 and the index of the selected item is 2, so it queries the data source for the data of Q2, that is, the sales revenue of each product in Q2.

   Instead of returning the data directly to SAP BusinessObjects Dashboards, we add one more item here. As mentioned above, the item has a value of 0 and a special identifier, say, –1. This item is placed in the second position, because the index of the selected item (quarter) is 2.

   To help you understand it, the returned data is:

Shoes	–1	Trousers	T-shirts	Hats	Underwear
62.3	0	56.9	43.5	22.8	46.7

2. The user sees the sales revenue of all products in Q2. Because the value of the second item is 0, the user will not see it and thus cannot click it.

Like the case explained previously, the user's selecting Q2 in step 3 makes the current selected item of the pie chart become item 2. As a result, the second product is selected automatically and immediately. However, the identifier of the second product is now –1, not Product2. Consequently, the value of cell Sheet1!$D$8 changes to *http://server:port/services/.../getdata?parentId=-1*, and the XML data connectivity is triggered again with the new URL.

3. On the server side, the servlet processing this request will find that the parentId is now –1. It then understands that this is triggered automatically by SAP BusinessObjects Dashboards, not by the user's intention because it's invisible. So it returns nothing. As a result, the content in cell range Sheet1!$C3$D5 remains unchanged. Consequently, the content of the chart is also unchanged. The user still sees the sales revenue of each product in Q2. The auto drill-down is bypassed in this way.

4. The user clicks the product he is interested in, such as Product3. Consequently, the value of cell Sheet1!$D$8 changes to *http://server:port/services/.../getdata?parentId=Product3*, and the XML data connectivity is triggered again with the new URL.

5. On the server side, the servlet processing this request will find that the parentId is now Product3. It returns the data of Product3; that is, the sales revenue of each week in Q2 for Product3.

8.2   Make Smart Use of Dynamic Visibility

As the name indicates, dynamic visibility is a feature that allows both the designer and the end user to show or hide a UI component dynamically, based on some condition at runtime. In other words, you define what components are displayed on the dashboard at what time. In SAP BusinessObjects Dashboards, this feature is common to most UI components.

You can define the dynamic visibility of either a single or a group of UI components at design time by checking the value of a single cell in the embedded spreadsheet. The UI component(s) is only visible when the value is equal to a constant text value or that of another single cell. Note that the operator is always EQUAL TO. You cannot define any other operator.

If you have some experience with the tab set component, you may find that it can also be used to define what components are displayed on the dashboard at what time. To achieve this, you put different UI components on different tabs, and when the user switches among tabs, different components are displayed on the single canvas. Figure 8.9 shows what's displayed on the canvas when the user switches among the tabs of the tab set component.

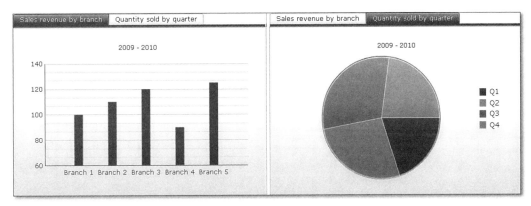

Figure 8.9 Dynamic Visibility Achieved with a Tab Set

This is a kind of dynamic visibility. In this section we'll ignore this type of usage of a tab set component and focus on how to show different UI components through the dynamic visibility property.

SAP Crystal Reports has a feature very similar to dynamic visibility. In SAP Crystal Reports, you can conditionally suppress a certain section with the Section Expert at runtime, based on the value of some data source fields or formulas.

8.2.1 When to Use Dynamic Visibility

Dynamic visibility is a very useful way to create an interactive dashboard. There are many situations where you can use it.

Give the User the Ability to Show or Hide a Single or Group of Components

This applies when you have some UI components in your dashboard as a supplement to those showing the main information, and you want the user to decide whether or not to see the additional information delivered by the supplementary components.

A typical use of this is ABOUT or HELP of the dashboard, which is a simple button at the corner of the dashboard. When it's clicked, a panel component appears showing what the dashboard is about or how to use it. Clicking the button again will hide the new component and return to the original screen.

Figure 8.10 shows an example of such a use. At first, the dashboard shows the values in a line chart, as displayed on the left. When the user clicks the ABOUT button on the top right, the line chart becomes hidden, and a panel component appears, showing some basic information such as the version of the dashboard, displayed on the right. Meanwhile, the label of the ABOUT button becomes CLOSE. Clicking on it again will revert the dashboard to its original state.

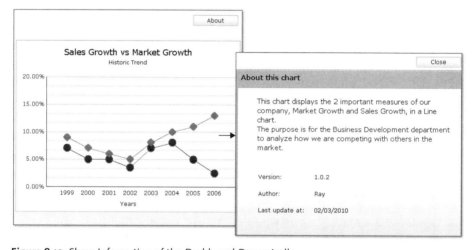

Figure 8.10 Show Information of the Dashboard Dynamically

In this example, the visibilities of both the chart and the panel are controlled by the same cell, which stores the status of the ABOUT button, which is a toggle button.

One more example in this category is when some components show the same or similar data, but in different formats, and the user doesn't need to see all of the components all of the time. The user can decide what kind of visualization he wants to see, and then the corresponding components are displayed and others become hidden. For example, let's say you added two charts, one a column chart and the other a stacked column chart, to display sales for each region and/or sales trends. Users view either of these charts instead of viewing both simultaneously by clicking a toggle button or selecting one from a combo box.

Figure 8.11 illustrates this method. The user can choose the visualization type from the combo box—a column chart or a pie chart.

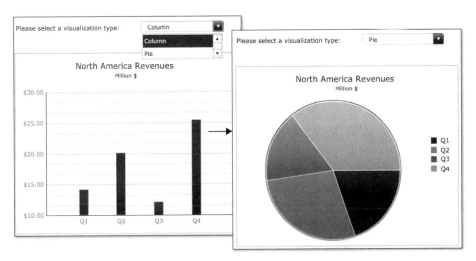

Figure 8.11 The User Can Decide to Show Different Components Based on Selection of a Combo Box

In this example, the user controls the visibilities dynamically through the combo box.

Another use of this method is for the user to choose whether or not to see supplementary information. Suppose you have some charts showing high-level aggregated data, such as the quarterly sales revenue of branches or product lines. As a supplement, you list some more detailed data, such as the daily sales revenue of each product, in a list view or a spreadsheet component. At first, the component showing the detailed data is hidden. However, a button on the dashboard functions as a hide/display switch, and the user can click it to see the details when he wants to.

Show the UI Component that Should Be Shown

The difference between this method and the situation described above is that the decision to show a UI component is controlled not by the end user, but by the logic defined at design time. This applies when your dashboard is divided into several stages or states, and in different states, different UI components need to be displayed. A typical example is when your dashboard requires the user to enter his credentials before seeing its UI components with data. When the dashboard is first loaded, the user is presented with a logon panel asking him to enter credentials such as his access key. On a successful logon, the logon panel disappears, and the charts showing the confidential data are displayed.

We'll see the effect of this and how to achieve it in the hands-on session shortly.

8.2.2   How to Use Dynamic Visibility

In Chapters 4 and 5 we described how to use dynamic visibility to control the visibility of a UI component at runtime. This property is common to most UI components. Figure 8.12 shows the typical properties related to dynamic visibility in the PROPERTIES panel.

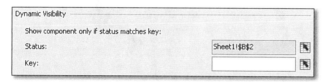

Figure 8.12 Dynamic Visibility Property in the Properties Panel

You need to specify the following two properties:

▶ STATUS
Bind STATUS to a cell that determines the visibility of the component. This cell is supposed to change at runtime.

▶ KEY
Enter a value or bind it to a cell. The component is visible when the status matches the key.

The KEY field is disabled until you have bound STATUS to a cell in the embedded spreadsheet. You can either enter a text in the field or click the BIND button to bind it to another cell.

The UI component is only displayed when the values of the two fields are equal.

Setting the dynamic visibility property of a single UI component is very straightforward. Sometimes, multiple UI components in your dashboard share the same dynamic visibility. For example, if your dashboard requires the user to enter his credentials before viewing any data, you need to provide one or more input fields for the user to enter his credentials, corresponding labels to indicate the purpose of each field, and a button to submit. All of these components share the same dynamic visibility property. Then we are faced with a question: How do you set this property for multiple components?

You can simply set dynamic visibility for each component and repeat the same steps for all of the components. This is a waste of time. Moreover, when the condition to show or hide them changes, you have to waste the time once more and try to avoid missing a component.

There are two better ways to do this, as explained in the following subsections.

Multi-Select

Some properties are available in the PROPERTIES panel when multiple components are selected. Dynamic visibility is one of these. To use this functionality, you hold down `Ctrl` on your keyboard and click to select multiple components. Then you can set the dynamic visibility property in the PROPERTIES panel once and for all.

However, when you need to update the status or key of the components' dynamic visibility property, you should try to avoid missing any component before updating them.

You can further group those UI components by clicking the GROUP COMPONENTS button on the toolbar after selecting them. This way, when in the future you need to update the condition describing when to show or hide them, you can simply click on one of the components to select them all. Thus, you'll never miss a component.

Container

Another way to include all of the components is to use a container component, described in Chapter 4, Section 4.4, and set the dynamic visibility property for the container only. The reason behind it is that when included in a container component such as a panel container, the UI components become part of the container and are shown or hidden along with it.

A typical use of this is the logon panel when your dashboard requires the user to enter his credentials and click the SUBMIT button before seeing the actual data, if he has the right to. To do this, we put all related components in a panel container and set its dynamic visibility instead of that of the related components. Figure 8.13 shows an example.

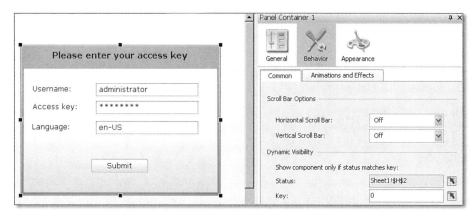

Figure 8.13 Set Dynamic Visibility Properties for Multiple Components in One Container

However, using an additional container changes the appearance of the dashboard. As you can see from Figure 8.13, the user will notice an extra header and borders around the labels, input texts, and button, which are part of the panel container. In the PROPERTIES panel of the container, you have no option to hide or remove the header or the borders. If you don't want to display these extra spaces, you can use a new component introduced in SAP BusinessObjects Dashboards 4.0, a canvas container, which is the best candidate to group multiple UI components but itself will not be visible at runtime.

8.2.3 Practice

Suppose you're going to create a dashboard showing your company's retained profit of each quarter last year, which is very sensitive information. To help protect this information, you only show the data when the user has entered the correct credentials. For simplicity, we'll assume the data is secured with an access key or shared secret. The user is granted permission to the data if he has entered correct key.

1. **Plan the data.**

   The data can be divided into four categories:

   ▶ **Metadata**: The purpose of the dashboard, the author, and the titles or labels

   ▶ **Logon data**: The access key the user has entered

▸ **Values**: The retained profit of each quarter

▸ **Indicating data**: Whether the logon is successful or not

Figure 8.14 shows what the data is like in the embedded spreadsheet in this sample dashboard. You can further customize it according to your requirements. For example, you can localize the labels and titles.

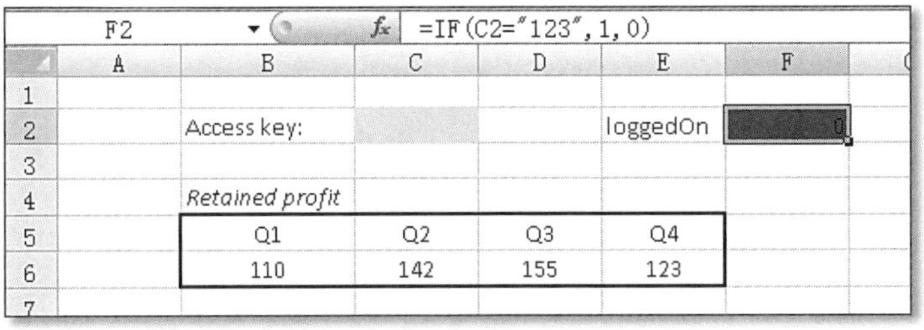

F2	▾	f_x	=IF (C2="123", 1, 0)			
	A	B	C	D	E	F
1						
2		Access key:			loggedOn	
3						
4		*Retained profit*				
5		Q1	Q2	Q3	Q4	
6		110	142	155	123	
7						

Figure 8.14 Data in the Embedded Spreadsheet

As you can see from this figure, cell Sheet1!$C$2 is used to store the access key the user has entered, and cell range Sheet1!$B5$:$E$6 stores the confidential data.

A special cell, Sheet1!$F$2, is used to check whether the user's access key is valid, as the indicating data. It's calculated with Excel formulas by checking whether the user's access key is equal to 123, which is the key the designer and the granted end user have agreed on.

2. **Set up the UI components for logon.**

We need an input text component for the user to enter his access key and a label component for the input text. We'll bind the input text's destination under DATA INSERTION to cell Sheet1!$C$2 so that the text the user enters in this field will be inserted into that cell.

When the user has entered his access key, there should be a button for him to say, "Hey, I've finished entering my access key, can you show me the retained profit now?" To do this, we add a toggle button component as the SUBMIT button. Clicking on it will trigger the calculation of cell Sheet1!$F$2.

By now, there's one label, one input text, and one toggle button on the canvas. You can move and position them as you like. Figure 8.15 shows the three components on the canvas and the PROPERTIES panel of the input text.

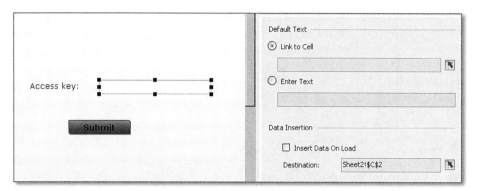

Figure 8.15 UI Components for the Logon Panel

We don't want the toggle button to look different with each click, so we'll change its on and off labels to "Submit." Similarly, make the button and the labels the same color in both the on and off status.

3. **Set up the chart for the data.**

Now let's set up the chart displaying the retained profit of each quarter. We'll drag and drop a pie chart onto the canvas, set its position, and bind its labels to range Sheet1!$B$5:$E$5 and its values to range Sheet1!$B$6:$E$6.

Figure 8.16 shows the pie chart on the canvas and its PROPERTIES panel. Note that it has masked the three components defined in the last step, because we want to show it in the same position as the three components, in the center of the canvas.

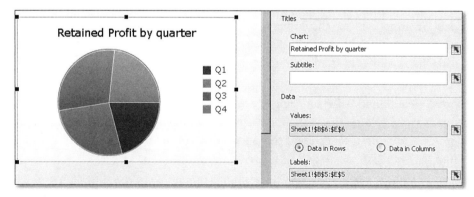

Figure 8.16 Data for the Pie Chart

4. **Set up dynamic visibility.**

Now we come to the most important step in this example—setting the dynamic visibility of each component.

As we've planned, cell Sheet1!$F$2 checks the user's access key and returns 1 if it's acceptable and 0 otherwise. You may want to bind STATUS to this cell and set KEY to 0 in BEHAVIOR • COMMON • DYNAMIC VISIBILITY for the three logon components. For the pie chart also, bind STATUS to this cell but set KEY to 1. That is, show the pie chart when the user has entered a correct access key and clicked the SUBMIT button.

The first problem you need solve is how to select each of the three logon components, because they have been masked by the pie chart. To do this, go to the Object Browser and click the SHOW/HIDE button to hide the pie chart for now, as displayed in Figure 8.17. Note that you're only hiding the pie chart at design time, not at runtime.

Figure 8.17 Hide Pie Chart through the Object Browser

To quickly find the UI component we want, we've renamed the text input and the toggle button to make them distinguishable. Refer to Chapter 2, Section 2.7 for a description of how to work with the Object Browser.

The second problem is that you're repeating the same steps to set the dynamic visibility of the three components. As mentioned in the previous section, we can use a container component to solve this problem by including all three of the components in one container and setting dynamic visibility for the container only.

To do this, drag a panel container from the COMPONENTS view and drop it onto the canvas. You might be a little puzzled about where to drop it to include the three logon components. You can initially drop it anywhere—but don't mask any of the three components—and then move each of them into the container, as displayed in Figure 8.18.

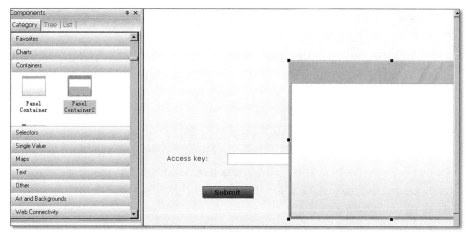

Figure 8.18 Drop the Panel Container Anywhere on the Canvas

Next, click to select one of the components, drag it into the container, and drop it there, as displayed in Figure 8.19.

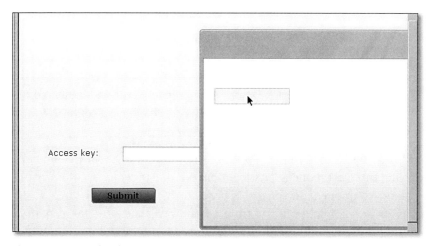

Figure 8.19 Drag the Three UI Components into the Panel Container

Repeat this step for the other two components. You may find that if you've grouped these components, you can move them all in one step and, furthermore, keep their relative positions during the move. This is a practical use of grouping components.

When you're finished, move the container to the center of the canvas and set its dynamic visibility property, as displayed in Figure 8.20.

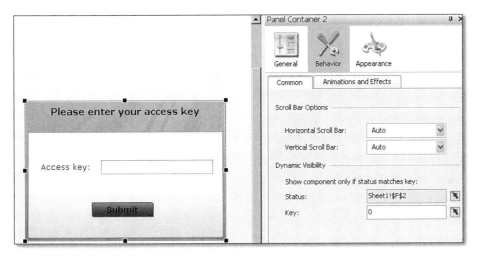

Figure 8.20 Set Dynamic Visibility for the Panel Container

Now the logon panel is done. The panel container, along with the label, the text input, and the toggle button, is only visible before the user has entered a valid access key, when the value in cell Sheet1!$F$2 is not equal to 0.

Setting dynamic visibility for the pie chart is very simple. You can select it in the Object Browser, select BEHAVIOR and then the COMMON tab, bind the STATUS field to cell Sheet1!$F$2, and set its KEY to 1, which indicates a valid access key.

At runtime, when the dashboard is loaded, the user is first presented with the logon screen. When the user clicks the SUBMIT button, SAP BusinessObjects Dashboards will calculate the value of cell Sheet1!$F$2. If it's 0—that is, if the user's access key doesn't match the agreed-on key—the dashboard remains on the logon screen, and nothing changes. However, when the user enters a valid access key and then clicks the SUBMIT button, the value in cell Sheet1!$F$2 becomes 1, causing the panel container to be hidden and the pie chart to be visible.

Figure 8.21 shows the screen before and after the user clicks the SUBMIT button with a valid access key entered in the input text.

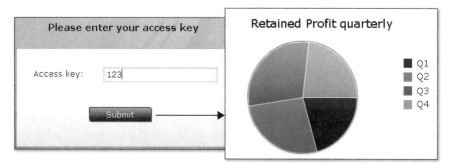

Figure 8.21 Screen Before and After the User Submits Valid Credentials

You can find the complete source file for this example at *www.sap-press.com.*

8.3 Alerts

Alerts are commonly used to call the user's attention to a specific item that has reached some predefined limit by highlighting the item in a contrasting color. The user can then focus on these items and take action accordingly. These limits are often called thresholds, targets, budgets, or benchmarks and are the standards to which an item is compared to define what category it falls in.

SAP BusinessObjects Dashboards 4.0 provides the alerts feature in a very user-friendly, easy-to-use, and flexible way, so you can show different colors for different data items in a chart, icon, grid component, and so on.

Using alerts in your dashboard is very simple and easy, as we explained in Chapter 4 in the section on column charts and as you will see in the next section. It's an important function because it allows the end user to quickly grasp the important items he should focus on with the help of your dashboard.

8.3.1 How to Use Alerts

Alerts can be enabled for UI components satisfying the following two conditions.

▶ The component is used to represent values. This includes most charts and single-value components but not selectors or containers.

▶ The component has only one series. That's why you cannot use alerts for pie charts or for charts with multiple series.

For example, you can configure alerts for a line chart with one series, but the ENABLE ALERTS checkbox will become disabled if you add one more series.

You can define alerts behavior in the ALERTS tab in the PROPERTIES panel of the UI component. Briefly, the steps to configure alerts are as follows.

1. **Activate alerts.**
   Select ENABLE ALERTS in the ALERTS tab.

2. **Select the alert method that suits your needs.**
   If you want to define the status (good or bad) by the absolute value, select BY VALUE. Otherwise, to define the status by the percentage of the absolute value against a base value, select BY PERCENTAGE and then specify the target value as a constant number or bind it to a cell in the embedded spreadsheet.

3. **Define alert thresholds.**
   Double-click on a field to update the threshold of any existing range or enter a value and click ADD to add a new threshold. If you want to dynamically define the thresholds, select USE A RANGE to bind the threshold definitions to a cell range so the user can define what values are good at runtime with the help of some other UI component, such as a slider.

4. **Define colors for each range.**
   This step is very important, because this is what the end user sees. In other words, the color you specify here for each range determines what items will get the user's attention. For example, if you highlight the values of a certain range, you can define a color that stands out for that range so the user can quickly focus on what you want him to.

   To take advantage of the software's built-in coloring mechanism, select ENABLE AUTO COLORS. In this case, you need tell SAP BusinessObjects Dashboards what values are good by selecting the corresponding option in the COLOR ORDER area.

8.3.2 Practice

As you've seen above and in Chapter 4 when we discussed column charts, it's not difficult to use alerts in your dashboard. The hands-on example here is for you to better understand alerts as a common and useful feature of SAP BusinessObjects Dashboards, not just a property of some UI components.

Suppose you're going to create a dashboard for the marketing department to find a range to define the top-sold product categories. To do this, you first create a column chart showing and comparing the quantities sold of all product categories. To highlight the top-sold categories with a very good market, you enable alerts to show them in different colors. The user can dynamically adjust the threshold at runtime. Meanwhile, for the top-sold categories, you want to know whether their total quantity sold takes up a reasonable proportion of the total quantity. As common sense, the total quantity sold is defined as reasonable if its percentage of the grand total is between 45% and 65%.

You don't know how to define a category as good or bad at design time; that is, how to define the top-sold product categories. Instead, you want the user to adjust the threshold at runtime to determine an appropriate threshold range, so that the total quantity sold of product categories above the threshold is reasonable.

You don't know how to define a category as good or bad at design time. Instead, you want the user to:

1. **Plan the data.**

   For simplicity, we won't use any data connectivity here. Instead, we'll hard-code the data in the embedded spreadsheet.

   The data in this example is very simple. We need a range to store the product categories and their corresponding quantities sold, which might be live data retrieved using data connectivity, and a cell to store the threshold value of the good categories, which the user adjusts with a slider.

   We also need to calculate some more data to determine the percentage of the quantity of the top-sold products against the grand total. To do this, we'll add a new row below the actual quantities sold by comparing the actual value with the threshold and returning the actual value for those above the threshold and 0 for others.

   Your data should be similar to what's shown in Figure 8.22.

   Note that only the data in cell range Sheet1!$B$3:$R$4 is the actual data. Other data is calculated by Excel functions. So if you want to replace the hard-coded data in this example with your live data, simply map the output values of your data connectivity to cell range Sheet1!$B$3:$R$4.

2. **Set up the UI components.**

   We need a column chart to show the quantity sold of each product category, a horizontal slider to define the threshold value of the good categories, and a gauge indicating whether the good categories are in a reasonable status.

C5		f_x	=IF(C4>Sheet1!$C$8,C4,0)				
	A	B	C	D	E	F	G	H
1								
2		data						
3	sum	category1	category2	category3	category4	category5	category6	category
4	10816	1490	263	728	409	982	231	448
5	5290	1490	0	0	0	0	0	0
6	48.91%							
7								
8		threshold	1000					
9			1000					

Figure 8.22 Data in the Embedded Spreadsheet

For this, we'll drag these components onto the canvas and position them. Binding data is very simple, and we won't go into the details here. Briefly, the data of the column chart is bound to range Sheet1!$B$3:$R$4, the horizontal slider to cell Sheet1!$C$8, and the gauge to Sheet1!$A$5. Your canvas should look something like Figure 8.23.

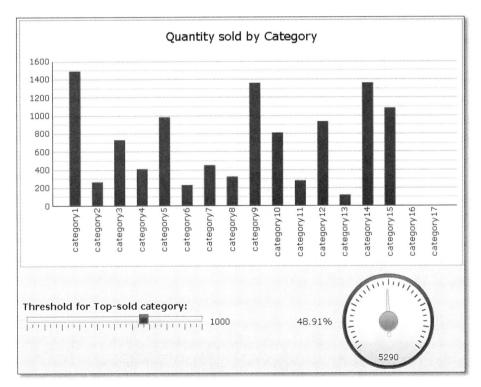

Figure 8.23 UI Components on the Canvas

467

3. **Define alerts.**

This step is the focus of this example, where we need to define appropriate alerts for each UI component.

For the column chart, after selecting the ENABLE ALERTS checkbox to activate the alerts tab, select BY VALUE because we want to distinguish the categories by their absolute quantities sold.

Only categories with a quantity sold above the user-defined value will be highlighted. To do this, select USE A RANGE, and bind the range to the cell where the user-defined threshold is stored. The software will then create two ranges at runtime based on the value of that cell: One range is from minimum to the value in the cell, and the other is from the value in the cell to the maximum. This may seem puzzling, because there are still three ranges defined in the PROPERTIES panel after you bind the range to the cell, as displayed in Figure 8.24.

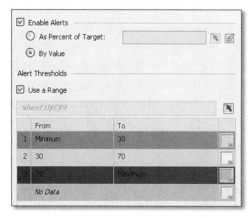

Figure 8.24 Three Ranges Displayed Only when One Threshold Is Defined

As a result, you cannot go on to set colors for each range because the cell is now empty. To solve this problem, give the cell a default value such as "1000". SAP BusinessObjects Dashboards will detect the value and update the range definition immediately.

We want to customize the colors to highlight the good categories. To do this, deselect ENABLE AUTO COLORS and set the color of the first range to a neutral one (e.g., navy) and the color of the second range to something eye-catching; green for example.

You can also customize the color to some user-defined value by clicking the color button to launch the color picker and then clicking the BIND button to bind the color to a cell in the embedded spreadsheet, as displayed in Figure 8.25.

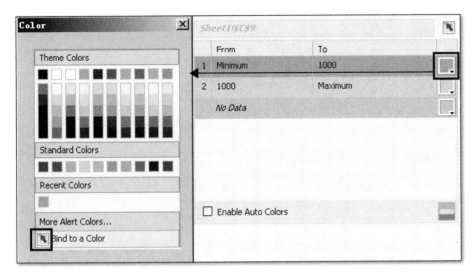

Figure 8.25 Bind a Color to a Cell in the Embedded Spreadsheet

That's all. The ALERTS tab in the PROPERTIES panel of the column chart now looks like Figure 8.26.

For the gauge component showing the status, as planned before, the alerts are defined by percentages instead of the absolute value. To do this, select AS PERCENTAGE OF TARGET and bind TARGET to cell Sheet1!$A$4, which stores the grand total of quantities sold of all categories.

In contrast to the column chart, the threshold definition is known at design time, so we needn't bind anything to the embedded spreadsheet. According to our assumption, the total quantity sold of the top-sold categories should take up 45% to 65% of the grand total. This is a kind of "middle values are good" range. To do this, uncheck ENABLE AUTO COLORS, enter 20, 45, 65, and 80 in the ENTER A VALUE field and click the ADD button one by one. These four values will generate five ranges, of which less than 20% and greater than 80% are considered bad, 20–45% and 65–80% are warnings, and 45–65% is good. Click the COLOR button to specify colors for each, as displayed in Figure 8.27. In this example, we use red to indicate bad ❶, yellow for warnings ❷, and green for good ❸.

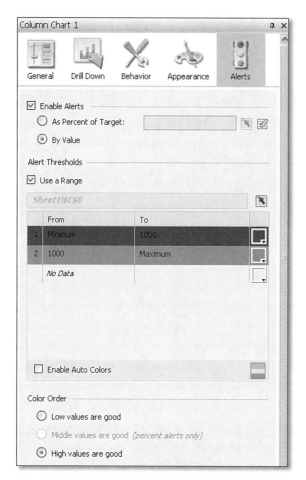

Figure 8.26 Alerts Tab for the Column Chart

Now we're done. At runtime, the user moves the horizontal slider to adjust the threshold of top-sold categories. The colors of each column in the column chart will be updated accordingly based on the corresponding quantity sold, and the needle in the gauge moves to indicate whether the user's definition is reasonable. This way the user can find an appropriate range to define the condition of a top-sold product category and make policies such as promotions and purchasing plans accordingly. In our example, we might find that it's appropriate to define the threshold between 900 and 1,100. That is, we can define any product category with a quantity sold larger than 900 and less than 1,100 as a top-sold category.

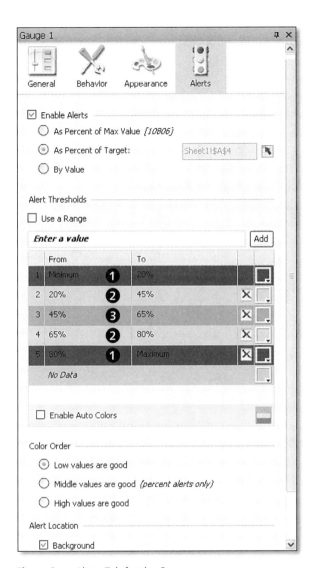

Figure 8.27 Alerts Tab for the Gauge

Figure 8.28 shows a screenshot of the dashboard at runtime.

The source file of this dashboard can be found at this book's web page at *www.sap-press.com*.

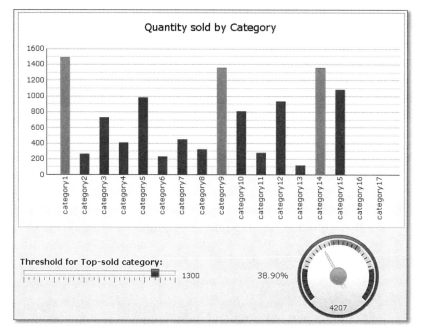

Figure 8.28 Our Dashboard at Runtime

8.4   Direct Data Binding

In Xcelsius 2008 and 4.5, the embedded spreadsheet was the only direct data source for all UI components. The data transfer between UI components and the external data source had to involve the embedded spreadsheet as an intermediate bridge.

Since the release of SAP BusinessObjects Dashboards 4.0 you can bind the data of a UI component such as values, labels, and insertion destinations directly to a Universe query without the need of the embedded spreadsheet. This feature is called *direct data binding*.

This is a useful new feature to save development time and add new possibilities. Many UI components, including all charts and some selectors, can be configured to use this functionality. But keep in mind that you can't bind their single-value properties such as title, subtitle, and series name to a Universe query. Direct data binding is not possible for single-value components, maps, texts, and some other UI components.

What's more, to use this feature, the Universe must be relational and can't be OLAP. That is, direct data binding is not possible for Universes based on an SAP BW query.

To use direct data binding, you must have defined Universe queries in your dashboard. To learn how to do this, refer to Chapter 2, Section 2.8, where we talked about how to manage Universe queries in the Query Browser.

You configure direct data binding in the PROPERTIES panel of your UI component, often in the GENERAL tab, by clicking the drop-down arrow (⧉▾) of a field and choosing QUERY DATA. In the following sections we talk about two uses of direct data binding, one for one-dimensional binding and the other for two-dimensional.

Note that you can't bind any UI component field that accepts a single value to a Universe query; for example, the title or subtitle of a chart. Their bind buttons don't have a drop-down arrow for you to choose a Universe query.

8.4.1 One-Dimensional Binding

This refers to the case when you're binding a field to a Universe query, the data of which is one-dimensional; for example, the LABELS field of a combo box, the CATEGORY LABELS field of a column chart, or the VALUES field of one series of a line chart.

To execute one-dimensional binding, click the drop-down arrow of the field's BINDING icon and select QUERY DATA. Then select one field from the RESULT OBJECTS list of a Universe query, as displayed in Figure 8.29.

Figure 8.29 Binding Labels of a Combo Box Directly to a Universe Query

As displayed in this figure, two Universe queries are available in this dashboard. Query 1 based on Universe BL_Activity has three fields returned. We bind the LABELS field of the combo box to CONTACT COUNTRY of query 1. The labels of the combo box are then dynamic.

8.4.2 Two-Dimensional Binding

This applies to the case when you are binding a field that accepts a cell range to a Universe query; for example, the DATA field for a column chart when BY RANGE is selected or the DISPLAY DATA field of a list view.

For two-dimensional binding, click on the drop-down arrow of the field's BINDING icon and select QUERY DATA. You'll see a SELECT FROM QUERY window, which lists all the Universe queries defined in your dashboard. You then select one or more fields from any Universe query and click OK. Figure 8.30 shows an example.

Figure 8.30 Binding Two-Dimensional Display Data of a List View Directly to a Universe Query

As displayed in this figure, we are binding the DISPLAY DATA field of the list view component to three fields in the RESULT OBJECTS list of query 1. The list view then displays data in three columns and several rows, depending on how many rows of data will be returned from the Universe.

8.5 Export

Export is an important feature of SAP BusinessObjects Dashboards. Basically, you create dashboards to illustrate data for information sharing and communication. Without the export functionality, you can only view the data inside SAP Business-Objects Dashboards, which makes little sense in communication with others.

You can export your dashboard as a local file, such as a PDF or Flash SWF file, or to an SAP BusinessObjects Enterprise system, thereby leveraging the power of this enterprise-level application. No matter what type you select, the exported dashboard is fully functional and interactive, instead of a plain image. The following sections will provide a detailed explanation of the various export types.

When you've come to the final stage in your dashboard design, you can export it by selecting FILE • EXPORT and choosing an appropriate type. The toolbar also provides a quick way for you to export your dashboard to PowerPoint, Word, Outlook, PDF, and SAP BusinessObjects. Let's go over your different export options.

8.5.1 Flash

Adobe Flash, formerly known as Macromedia Flash, is developed and distributed by Adobe. Flash files are generally in the SWF format, traditionally called Shock-Wave Flash movies, and usually have an *.swf* extension. It's widely used in web pages and other media types for animation. The benefits of exporting your dashboard to Adobe Flash is that it can run on almost all computers in the world and is operating system (OS) independent, so you needn't worry about whether the dashboard consumer can open your output, whether he is working on Windows, Linux, or Mac.

Select this option if you want to export your dashboard into an Adobe Flash file, with an *.swf* extension, so that the user can double-click it to run when he has stand-alone Adobe Flash Player installed or access to it via a web browser when the required plug-in is installed. You can send the Flash file as an attachment via email.

8.5.2 AIR

AIR (Adobe Integrated Runtime) is a cross-platform, versatile runtime environment that can run Flash files. Before selecting Adobe AIR from the export options list, you need to have Java 2 Runtime Environment (J2EE) and Adobe Flex 3.0 SDK installed on your system and configured so that SAP BusinessObjects Dashboards can find them.

The dashboard consumer needs to have the Adobe AIR player installed. You can get it from the Adobe website at *http://get.adobe.com/air/*.

Both Flash and AIR are Adobe file formats that can run on your desktop. You can search the Internet to learn about the differences between them. Briefly, a Flash *.swf* file cannot access a local file until it's trusted by the consumer, as discussed in Chapter 6, Section 6.3. On the other hand, AIR is browserless and can access local storage and file systems, but it needs to be packaged, digitally signed, and installed on the consumer's local file system.

8.5.3   HTML

If you select this option, SAP BusinessObjects Dashboards exports the dashboard to a Flash file and generates an HTML container. You can put the two files on a web server so others can see your dashboard from a web browser. You can also integrate the dashboard with your web portal. You can further edit the HTML file to add more content, such as an introduction to the dashboard and users' comments about it.

If you've defined a Flash Variables connection in your dashboard, the Flash variables will also be reflected in the HTML file. You can edit the HTML file to pass your customized values into the dashboard.

After clicking to select this option, you'll be prompted to enter the file name and the folder to save the HTML file in. When you click OK, the software will generate one Flash file and one HTML file with the same name.

8.5.4   SAP BusinessObjects Platform

Note that you can now only export your dashboard to an SAP BusinessObjects Business Intelligence platform through menu path FILE • SAVE TO PLATFORM or SAVE TO PLATFORM AS.

When saved, the dashboard object will contain both the definition (the dashboard model, *.xlf*) and the output (a Flash file, *.swf*). The dashboard designers can open it from the SAP BusinessObjects BI platform to view or continue your design. The consumers can view the output Flash file through BI Launchpad to get the information. For more information about the dashboard design object in the SAP BusinessObjects BI platform, refer to Chapter 1, Section 1.2.4.

The benefit of this option is that you needn't export the dashboard and then send it to each consumer via email, which may be time-consuming and inconvenient to update. Instead, you export it to a specific folder in the SAP BusinessObjects system. Then corporate users who have the required rights can access your dashboard and do further analyses.

Another benefit is that you can access other SAP BusinessObjects resources within your dashboard, without the need for the user to enter his credentials. For example, in your dashboard, if you are using Query as a Web Service (explained in Chapter 7), to access the source data, the end user needs to enter his credentials to log on to the SAP BusinessObjects Enterprise system before he can access the Query as a Web Service, which is deployed to an SAP BusinessObjects Enterprise system. However, when the dashboard has been exported to an SAP BusinessObjects platform, the platform will solve this problem when the user has logged on to the SAP BusinessObjects system.

For example, say you are in the IT department and have created one dashboard for the sales team and one for the HR team. You export them to the corresponding folder. Within SAP BusinessObjects Enterprise you grant viewing rights to the folder for each team. When a user on the sales team logs on to SAP BusinessObjects Enterprise, he can see the dashboard in the sales folder.

This command is disabled if you don't have a valid license for SAP Crystal Dashboard Design, departmental edition (formerly known as Xcelsius Enterprise).

8.5.5   PDF

You can export your dashboard to PDF (Portable Document Format), a file format created by Adobe for creating documents in a manner independent of the application software, hardware, and operating system. Your dashboard will function completely the same way everywhere, including the texts, fonts, images, and animations.

After selecting this option, you'll be prompted to enter the file name and location for the PDF file. You can send it to consumers who can then view your dashboard in the PDF file. The dashboard in the PDF file is fully functional, not just an image.

You can also choose which version of Adobe Acrobat to use, either Acrobat 6 for PDF 1.5 or Acrobat 9 for PDF 1.6. However, when exporting your dashboard to PDF through the toolbar, the exported document will always be in Acrobat 9 format.

Only one PDF file is generated in this case, with the Flash object embedded. It's different from exporting to HTML, which generates one SWF file and one HTML file.

8.5.6 PowerPoint Slide

You can export your dashboard into a Microsoft PowerPoint file, thus making your presentation more attractive and interactive.

Choose this option when you want to use the dashboard during a presentation using PowerPoint. For example, during a company conference, the sales manager can embed a dashboard showing global sales status in his presentation. This way, he can show the sales information in different quarters or branches in the intuitive dashboard, without leaving the presentation.

After selecting this option you will be prompted to enter the file name and location for the PowerPoint file. SAP BusinessObjects Dashboards will create a PowerPoint file with one slide in which your dashboard is embedded and automatically open it. Your dashboard may appear blank in PowerPoint in Edit mode, but don't worry; it will behave perfectly in Slide Show mode.

So what's behind the scenes? SAP BusinessObjects Dashboards generates a temporary Flash file in your *Users* directory (for example, *C:\Users\ray\AppData\Local\Temp*) and embeds it into a PowerPoint slide as a macro control.

Maybe you've noticed a limitation here. The generated PowerPoint file has only one slide, while usually we want to add the dashboard to an existing PowerPoint presentation. For example, say an HR manager is preparing his presentation for a year-end conference, and after the first few slides about some general information, he wants to add a dashboard to show the on-board and resignation status. To solve this problem, he can either copy the Flash object from the exported slide or manually insert the generated Flash file to PowerPoint. You can insert a Flash file into a PowerPoint slide either via the menu path INSERT • OBJECT or from the DEVELOPER tab.

SAP BusinessObjects Dashboards is not required at runtime to display the dashboard inside the PowerPoint file. Only PowerPoint and Adobe Flash Player are.

8.5.7   Outlook

You can quickly send out your dashboard via email by exporting it to Outlook. When you select this option, the software generates a temporary Flash file and launches Outlook to create a new mail message with that generated Flash file (*.swf*) as an attachment. You can then add more content to the message and send it out.

If you want to see the generated Flash file, go to the *Temporary Internet Files* folder on your computer, for example, *C:\Documents and Settings\Administrator\ Local Settings\Temporary Internet Files\Content.Outlook\A9LU74IT\swfA.swf*.

8.5.8   Word

Similar to exporting to a PowerPoint slide, after selecting the WORD option you'll be prompted to enter a file name and location for the Word document. SAP BusinessObjects Dashboards will generate a Word document embedding your dashboard, which will function the same as you see in Preview mode. You can further edit the Word document to make it more meaningful, such as adding some text around the dashboard to explain its context and purpose.

In contrast to exporting your dashboard to Microsoft Outlook or PowerPoint, when you select WORD, the dashboard is embedded into the Word document as a ShockWave Flash object; it is not linked there. You'll see that the size of the generated Word document is somewhat large—maybe over 1 megabyte.

8.6   Themes and Colors

When creating dashboards, you may wonder how the UI components are colored. For example, how is the color of each data part of a pie chart defined? This is where themes and colors come into play.

Similar to many applications such as Microsoft Windows OS, in SAP Business-Objects Dashboards 4.0, a theme defines the global styles and properties of all components, including color, font styles, and even behavior. It provides an easy way to customize the components and maintain a consistent look and feel among all components throughout your dashboard. This concept may be called a *skin* in some applications.

Color has a large impact on your dashboard. However, a misuse of color may negatively affect your dashboard and weaken the user experience. Colors define the color schema of your dashboard; that is, what color is used for each part of any UI component. The colors of the canvas background; the titles, labels, and values of a text component; and the mouse-over and selected colors are all defined in the color scheme. For example, a pie chart may have many parts, and the color of the first, second, and other parts is defined in the color scheme. A color scheme is also included in a theme, but you can further customize your components by changing the color scheme within a theme.

A theme defines what colors are used to render the UI components. However, it is not just about colors. A theme also contains information about fonts and many other visual effects. When you have many UI components on the canvas, you can see the differences when you switch to another theme. You can also change the color scheme of a theme, thereby changing the colors of the UI components while maintaining the fonts and other visual effects.

Generally, you can select from a list of available themes and colors, which have been well-defined by SAP BusinessObjects Dashboards 4.0, to quickly make your dashboard attractive and professional. You can also switch among them, thus providing a different look and feel for your dashboard without the need to modify your dashboard. You cannot create a new theme, but you can create your own customized color schemes.

8.6.1 How to Apply a Theme

SAP BusinessObjects Dashboards 4.0 provides some predefined themes such as Aqua, Aero, Nova, and Phase, as displayed in Figure 8.31. The default theme is Nova.

Each theme's name is displayed on the top left, with the color scheme on the top right, and an example on the bottom. You can get a rough idea about the styles of each theme from its colors and sample.

To apply a theme to your dashboard, simply select one from the THEMES dropdown list, as displayed in Figure 8.31. You can also achieve this by selecting FORMAT • THEMES and selecting one from the list window, as displayed in Figure 8.32.

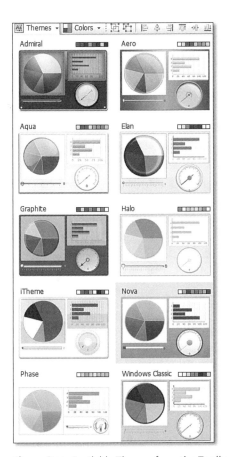

Figure 8.31 Available Themes from the Toolbar

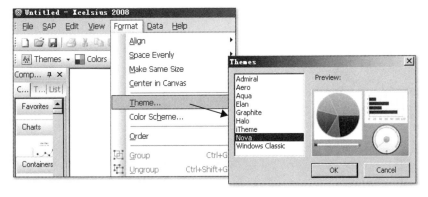

Figure 8.32 Available Themes from the Menu

When you change the theme of your dashboard, the look and feel of all of the UI components will be updated according to your selected theme, including colors, font family, font styles, and visual effects. If you have customized the colors or fonts of the UI components through the PROPERTIES sheet, they will be overwritten. You can test each theme to find out which one best fits your design.

You may underestimate the usefulness of themes when you find out that you can also customize the colors and fonts in the PROPERTIES panels. It's important to note that some other properties, such as lighting effects in some charts, are invisible in the PROPERTIES sheet.

8.6.2 How to Apply a Color Scheme

To apply a new color scheme to your dashboard, select one from the COLORS dropdown list in the toolbar area, next to THEMES, as displayed in Figure 8.33.

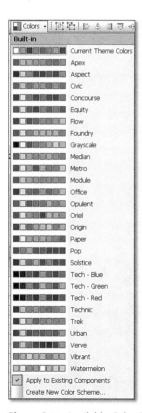

Figure 8.33 Available Color Schemes from the Toolbar

Note that the first color scheme is CURRENT THEME COLORS, which are defined in themes and are what you are currently using for the UI components in your dashboard by default, if you haven't switched to another scheme.

You can also achieve this by going to FORMAT • COLOR SCHEMES and selecting a scheme in the list window, as shown in Figure 8.34.

You can click the DELETE button on the bottom to delete a color scheme in the CUSTOM category. However, those in the BUILT-IN category cannot be deleted or edited.

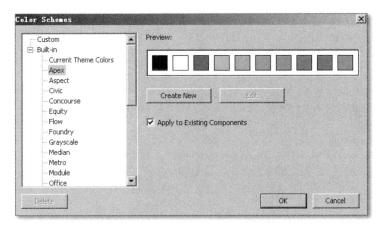

Figure 8.34 Available Color Schemes from the Menu

With both methods of selecting a color scheme you'll see the APPLY TO EXISTING COMPONENTS checkbox, which will cause the software to update the existing UI components on the canvas with the new color scheme when selected. If it's not selected, the existing UI components will keep their old colors. Whether it's selected or not, any UI component you add to your dashboard will use the new color scheme.

When you apply a new color scheme, the theme of your dashboard is not changed. That is, the UI components retain their styles and property settings but use a new color palette.

8.6.3 How to Create a Customized Color Scheme

You cannot create a custom theme for SAP BusinessObjects Dashboards 4.0, but you can create your own color schemes. The color schemes are XML files that define the color palette used to set the colors for each part of each component. You can find the XML files at *%XCELSIUS_DIR%/assets/themes*, for example, *C:\Program Files\SAP Business Objects\Xcelsius\assets\themes*. In this folder is a sub-folder called BUILT-IN, which stores all of the built-in color schemes. You can take a look at the XML files for a better understanding of color schemes.

To define a color scheme for your company so that all dashboards you and your colleagues design look similar, create a color scheme first and then send it to others. Your colleagues will apply this color scheme when designing dashboards, thus ensuring a consistent look and feel.

To do this, click CREATE NEW COLOR SCHEME... in the COLORS dropdown list in the toolbar area, or click the CREATE NEW button in the menu FORMAT • COLOR SCHEMES. A window will pop up for you to enter the name and select the colors of your color scheme, as shown in Figure 8.35.

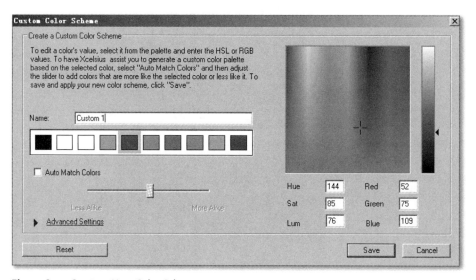

Figure 8.35 Create a New Color Scheme

To have SAP BusinessObjects Dashboards help you design your own color scheme, click on the color palette to set a base color. Then select AUTO MATCH COLORS. This will generate a custom color palette based on the selected color. You can adjust the color palette by dragging the slider bar from LESS ALIKE to MORE ALIKE. While you're dragging, the colors will be updated. If you want to change a certain color, unselect AUTO MATCH COLORS, select the color you want to change, and click the color palette on the right to set a new color.

You can also set colors in more detail by expanding ADVANCED SETTINGS and setting the color for each item, as shown in Figure 8.36.

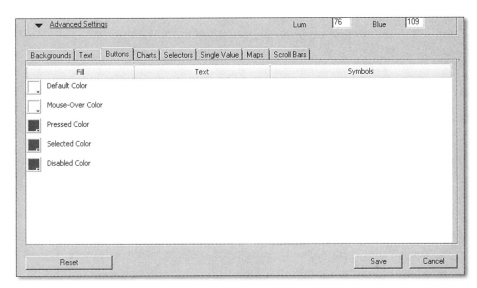

Figure 8.36 Advanced Settings for Editing a Custom Color Scheme

The color of each property is defined by the colors in the scheme. However, you can only configure 10 colors in a color scheme, although there are many more visual parts for which you may want to configure colors. So what color among the 10 is used for what visual part? You can try them out by setting an eye-catching color for each of the 10 colors listed below NAME, with AUTO MATCH COLORS unselected, and check what colors are updated in the ADVANCED SETTINGS area. For example, as displayed in Figure 8.37, we'll set the first item of a custom color scheme to a very eye-catching color—red ❶. When checking the colors of each tab in the ADVANCED SETTINGS area, we find out that this item in the color scheme controls the default colors of all items in the TEXT tab, all texts of charts, default and mouse-over colors of the label texts of selectors, the rick color of single-value components, the region border color of maps, and the button symbol color of scroll bars.

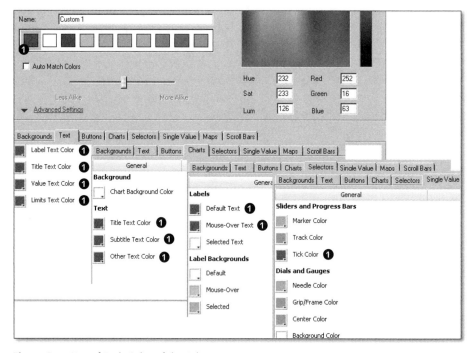

Figure 8.37 Use of Each Color of the Scheme

To change a color in the color scheme, click to select it and choose a color in the color picker to the right. Colors in the advanced settings will be updated accordingly, which may take some time, during which period input is disabled.

Table 8.1 lists what UI components are affected by each color item in a color scheme, according to our investigation.

Item	Affected UI Component Parts
1	Texts of any part of all components
2	Default and mouse-over colors of buttons, chart background, selected text color of the label and default label background of selectors, dial and gauge background, default and mouse-over colors of maps, track and button color of scroll bars
3	Canvas background

Table 8.1 UI Components Affected by a Color Scheme

Item	Affected UI Component Parts
4	Component background color, mouse-over color of selectors, selectable color of maps, thumb color of scroll bars
5	Chart series 1 (e.g., the first data part in a pie chart, the columns of the first series in a column chart, etc.), selected color of buttons, label background color of selectors when selected, marker color of sliders and progress bars, needle color of dials and gauges, region color of maps when selected
6	Chart series 2
7	Chart series 3
8	Chart series 4
9	Chart series 5
10	Disabled color of buttons, track color of sliders and progress bars, grip/frame color and center color of dials and gauges

Table 8.1 UI Components Affected by a Color Scheme (Cont.)

You can specify any color, such as the background color of each chart, in ADVANCED SETTINGS by selecting the CHARTS tab, clicking on the color next to CHART BACKGROUND COLOR, and customizing your color from the color picker. Repeat these steps for any other color you want to customize.

To save your custom color scheme, click the SAVE button. It's then saved as an XML file in a custom subfolder beneath *%XCELSIUS_DIR%/assets/themes*, for example, in *C:\Program Files\SAP BusinessObjects\Xcelsius\assets\themes\custom*. Depending on your software and operating system version, the folder may be your personal folder such as *C:\Users\Ray\AppData\Roaming\XcelsiuscustomThemes*.

To share your custom color scheme with others, send the XML file to them. They can then copy the XML file to the location on the file system where SAP BusinessObjects Dashboards is installed, for example either *custom* or *built-in* under the folder *-%XCELSIUS_DIR%/assets/themes*. The difference lies in where they will see the custom color scheme when choosing among all of the available schemes—either in the category BUILT-IN or the category CUSTOM. The color scheme cannot be edited if it's placed in the subfolder BUILT-IN.

8.7 Summary

In this chapter, we explained some common and useful properties of most UI components from the perspective of an entire dashboard, not an individual component. The features we covered here are very useful in your design, and you'll use them frequently to create professional dashboards. They include drill-down, alerts, and color schemes. We hope you've gotten a big picture of these features and will take them into consideration before choosing any UI component for your dashboard.

By now we've covered almost all aspects of SAP BusinessObjects Dash-boards 4.0. Let's move on to a comprehensive hands-on example and practice some of what we've learned.

9   A Comprehensive Hands-On Example

We've covered all that you need to create a dashboard with SAP BusinessObjects Dashboards, including all of the UI components and data connectivities. In this chapter, we'll put everything together by leading you in creating a comprehensive, though simple dashboard. This sample dashboard will contain charts, selectors, single-value components, texts, art, backgrounds, and some data connections. It will give you the chance to practice most aspects of we've presented in previous chapters.

We've already gone through some simple examples in the practice sections of some of the other chapters. The difference between this chapter and those practice sections is that the previous practices focused on a single SAP Business-Objects Dashboards feature, while the example in this chapter is more comprehensive. You'll also learn about the workflow of building a real dashboard and some general best practices of working with SAP BusinessObjects Dash-boards.

After reading this chapter, you'll be able to:

▸ Use all of the components you have learned about in this book
▸ Understand the workflow of building dashboards
▸ Apply general best practices while designing dashboards

Suppose that it's 2007 and you work for eFashion, a successful retail store selling fashion merchandise in 11 US cities. The company currently sells more than 200 products across 12 product lines. You're an analyst working at eFashion head-quarters, and your job is to produce interactive dashboards and present them to the company's management team. You're currently designing a sales dashboard covering the year 2006 to help them analyze the sales status.

The workflow of building dashboards is often in the following sequence:

▶ Plan the dashboard.

▶ Prepare the data.

▶ Organize the data in Excel.

▶ Design the dashboard in SAP BusinessObjects Dashboards.

Always start with planning. In the planning stage, you analyze user requirements and draw a draft design of what the dashboard will look like to the end user, including parameters, the canvas layout, and how the end user will access it. You might use a pencil and a piece of paper to plan your design in this phase.

Next, prepare the data your dashboard needs to present. This work can be done by you, the dashboard designer, or the IT department after negotiation. Here you need to understand the backend logic to retrieve live data with the help of some data connectivity. In addition, you need to be very clear about the data structures of both the input and output. For example, how many rows and columns of data will be returned? This is important for you to map the output data and bind it to UI components later.

Before you start to actually work in SAP BusinessObjects Dashboards, it's better to add one more step to organize your data in the embedded Excel spreadsheet. Well-organized data in Excel can greatly improve the design efficiency and make the dashboard easy to maintain. What you need to do in this step includes highlighting different kinds of data in different colors and calculating some extra data with the help of Excel functions.

Finally, you design the dashboard in SAP BusinessObjects Dashboards. You work with different kinds of UI components and data connectivities and set their properties. We'll discuss each of these steps in more detail in the following sections.

Now let's return to our example. The dashboard we're going to create will connect to live data through Live Office Connection, which in turn will fetch data via the eFashion Universe deployed in an SAP BusinessObjects Business Intelligence platform.

Maybe you cannot replicate the exact environment. For instance, you may not have an SAP BusinessObjects system, so the eFashion universe and SAP Business-Objects Live Office are not available to you, but you can easily mock-up some data and use another connection type to follow this example. You can even insert the data directly into the embedded spreadsheet. Note that we are trying to give you the idea of how a professional dashboard is created. The workflow and design practices are the focus.

9.1   Planning the Dashboard

The first step of building a comprehensive dashboard is always planning, just like what you do when you develop a piece of software, build a formatted report, or design a web page.

9.1.1   Plan the Workflow

For dashboard design, it is particularly important that you start with user requirements rather than with the data you are working with. Diving into the data at an early stage can easily cause you to get lost and miss what you actually need to focus on. You should work with business users, communicate with them, and make sure you fully understand the following items:

▸ What primary business question they want the dashboard to answer

▸ What other questions may arise

▸ What actions they would like to take

Only when the user requirements are clear can you decide which components to use and what data each of them will display.

We'll omit the planning step in our sample dashboard project because our main purpose is to lead you through the process of creating a comprehensive dashboard. We'll assume that the communication with the end user has already been conducted and the user responses are as follows:

▸ This is a sales dashboard, so the primary metric is sales revenue.

▸ The company is expanding geographically. The dashboard should show sales revenue by US states.

▸ There's a target sales revenue for each store. The dashboard should clearly illustrate the accomplishment status based on the target for each store.

▸ When a store has identified exceptions, more details on that store are needed, for example, the trend of the sales revenue and break-down of different product lines.

9.1.2 Plan the UI

Based on the planning information, we can choose the appropriate visual presentation to tackle each problem, as explained next.

▶ **Map**
A map is a very good way to display geographical data, so we'll use one to show revenue by region. From the map, we can drill down to a chart that displays the sales revenue of all of the stores in the state that is selected on the map.

▶ **Column chart**
We'll use a column chart because we'll compare sales revenue across all of the stores. Alerts should be enabled to highlight the accomplishment of the revenue target. From the column chart, we can again drill down to a line chart and a pie chart.

▶ **Line chart**
The line chart will display the monthly, quarterly, and year-to-date trends of the sales revenue. The user can choose which trend he wants to see.

▶ **Pie chart**
The pie chart will display the distribution of the sales revenue across product lines.

▶ **Gauge**
We'll add a gauge to show the sales revenue of the selected state. This is not directly derived from user requirements, but it will help correct a small flaw in the map component: The values are not visible unless the mouse is pointing to a region. In addition, adding a single-value component increases the breadth of the components we use for this dashboard, which is good for demonstration and practice purposes.

Figure 9.1 shows a mock-up of our dashboard. Please note that the mock-up is created in SAP BusinessObjects Dashboards for simplicity here, but as we explained, you should do this with a pen and paper or some dedicated mock-up tool.

Pay attention to the way we placed the components. The layout of these components follows the logical relations among them. Information is presented from left to right and top to bottom as it goes from high-level to more detailed. The map, at the upper left, carries the most high-level information, sales revenue by state. We can drill down to the store level in the column chart to the right of the map. Below the map and the column chart, we can drill down to information from single stores. This kind of layout is intuitive, so the user won't get confused by the information presented.

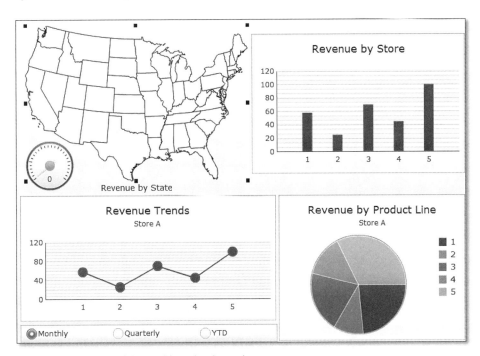

Figure 9.1 Mock-Up of the Dashboard to be Built

9.2   Preparing Data

Now that the initial design is completed, we need to consider what kind of data is needed for each component of the dashboard. The general best practice for a connected model is that you should build more connections returning fewer rows and columns instead of fewer connections returning more rows of data. The more data a connection returns, the slower your dashboard is. You'll produce a very bad user experience if you're trying to pull all of the data shown on the dashboard at once, which will probably make the user wait for tens of seconds or even minutes. Impatient users will close the dashboard before it finishes loading data.

A better way is to build more connections that return less data and trigger the connectivity only when required. Whenever more data is needed upon user interaction, the corresponding data connectivity is triggered to retrieve the extra data. The user may have to wait only a few seconds when he clicks on a chart or chooses a different item in a selector, which will be within the user's tolerance. If your databases and backend servers have enough power, this may even be unnoticeable.

We are now going to build queries that fetch only the data needed for each display component. SAP BusinessObjects Live Office is our chosen connection type in this sample dashboard project, so we're going to work in Excel and fetch data through SAP BusinessObjects Universe. If you aren't using SAP BusinessObjects Live Office, you can create web services for a web service connection or develop a web application for an XML data connection.

Now let's launch SAP BusinessObjects Dashboards 4.0 and build connections for each component and configure data mapping.

9.2.1 The US Map

The US map will display the sales revenue for each state, so we're going to build a query on the universe to get the sales revenue by state. We'll insert a Universe query into Excel. The query includes the objects STATE and SALES REVENUE, and it is filtered by year as shown in Figure 9.2.

If you aren't familiar with SAP BusinessObjects Universe, Listing 9.1 shows the generated SQL (Structured Query Language) statement for this query.

```
SELECT DISTINCT
  Agg_yr_qt_rn_st_ln_ca_sr.State,
  sum(Agg_yr_qt_rn_st_ln_ca_sr.Sales_revenue)
FROM
  Agg_yr_qt_rn_st_ln_ca_sr
WHERE
  (
  Agg_yr_qt_rn_st_ln_ca_sr.Yr  =  '2006'
  )
GROUP BY
  Agg_yr_qt_rn_st_ln_ca_sr.State
```

Listing 9.1 Generated SQL Statement for Sales Revenue by State

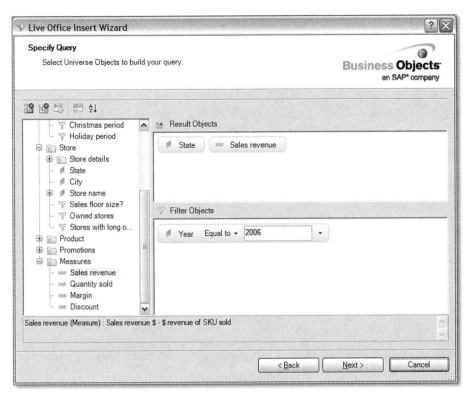

Figure 9.2 Revenue by State Query in Universe Query Panel

9.2.2   The Gauge

This single-value component shows the sales revenue for the currently selected state on the map. Because the data for it is already included in the data for the map component, we don't need to build another query for the gauge. The data for the gauge is updated when the map component inserts the data for the state selected into the destination cell range.

9.2.3   The Column Chart

The user wants to see the sales revenue by store in a column chart, and only data for the stores in the selected state should be returned, so the Universe query for the column chart includes the objects STORE NAME and SALES REVENUE, and is filtered by year and state as shown in Figure 9.3.

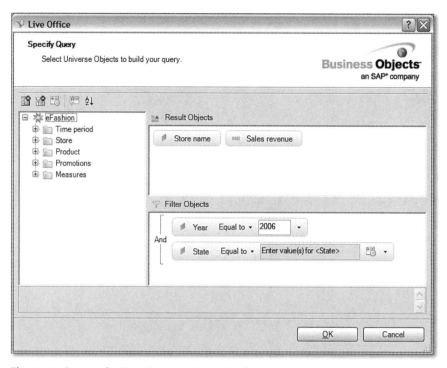

Figure 9.3 Revenue by Store Query in Query Panel

The generated SQL statement is displayed in Listing 9.2. This SQL statement is a little bit longer than that of the sales revenue by state query because some table joins are involved. You may also notice that the SALE REVENUE object and STATE object don't map to the same database fields for the two queries. The reason for this is that this query retrieves data from transactional tables, and the previous one retrieves data from a single aggregated table that is generated from transaction tables. SAP BusinessObjects Universe provides this aggregation awareness technology that can automatically determine which tables the data should be fetched from. The Universe technology is beyond the scope of this book so we won't describe it here.

The SQL statement (Listing 9.2) merely gives you an idea of what data we are pulling from the database. Another interesting aspect of this SQL statement is the @prompt function in the WHERE clause. This is a Universe function rather than an SQL function, which simply stands for a placeholder and will be replaced with a user response.

```
SELECT
  Outlet_Lookup.Shop_name,
  sum(Shop_facts.Amount_sold)
FROM
  Outlet_Lookup,
  Shop_facts,
  Calendar_year_lookup
WHERE
  ( Outlet_Lookup.Shop_id=Shop_facts.Shop_id  )
  AND  ( Shop_facts.Week_id=Calendar_year_lookup.Week_id  )
  AND
  (
  Calendar_year_lookup.Yr  =  '2006'
   AND
  Outlet_Lookup.State  =  @prompt('Enter State:','A','Store\State',
  Mono,Free,Persistent,,User:0)
   )
GROUP BY
  Outlet_Lookup.Shop_name
```

Listing 9.2 Generated SQL Statement for Sales Revenue by Store

9.2.4   The Line Chart

The line chart is to display any of the monthly trends, the quarterly, or the year-to-date (YTD) trends. We are going to utilize the dynamic visibility feature to implement this switching, so instead of using one line chart, we need three line charts. After further analyzing the data, the Universe in this case, we find that we can build a sales revenue by month query and a sales revenue by quarter query, but there is no YTD data. This problem will be solved by using Excel formulas to generate the YTD data based on the monthly data, which we'll demonstrate in the next section.

For sales revenue by month, the Universe query includes the objects MONTH and SALES REVENUE, and it is filtered by year and store name, which again is a prompt, as illustrated in Figure 9.4.

The SQL statement for this query is shown in Listing 9.3.

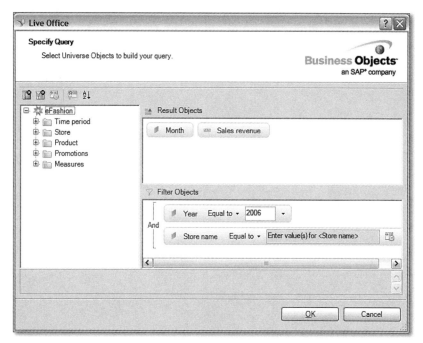

Figure 9.4 Revenue by Month Query in Query Panel

```
SELECT
  Agg_yr_qt_mt_mn_wk_rg_cy_sn_sr_qt_ma.Mth,
  sum(Agg_yr_qt_mt_mn_wk_rg_cy_sn_sr_qt_ma.Sales_revenue)
FROM
  Agg_yr_qt_mt_mn_wk_rg_cy_sn_sr_qt_ma
WHERE
  (
  Agg_yr_qt_mt_mn_wk_rg_cy_sn_sr_qt_ma.Yr  =  '2006'
   AND
  Agg_yr_qt_mt_mn_wk_rg_cy_sn_sr_qt_ma.Store_name  =
  @prompt('Enter Store name:','A','Store\Store name',Mono,Free,
  Persistent,,User:0)
  )
GROUP BY
  Agg_yr_qt_mt_mn_wk_rg_cy_sn_sr_qt_ma.Mth
```

Listing 9.3 Generated SQL Statement for Sales Revenue by Month

We can easily build the revenue by quarter query (shown in Figure 9.5) by replacing the MONTH object with the QUARTER object (Listing 9.4).

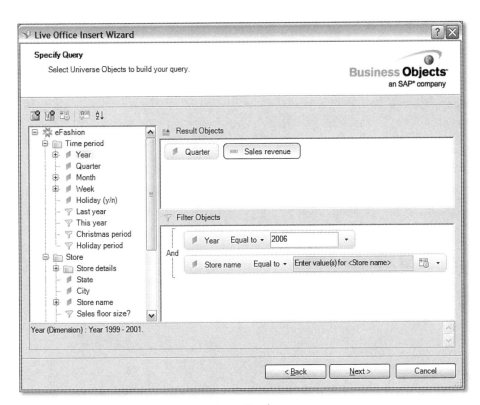

Figure 9.5 Revenue by Quarter Query in Query Panel

```
SELECT
  Agg_yr_qt_mt_mn_wk_rg_cy_sn_sr_qt_ma.Qtr,
  sum(Agg_yr_qt_mt_mn_wk_rg_cy_sn_sr_qt_ma.Sales_revenue)
FROM
  Agg_yr_qt_mt_mn_wk_rg_cy_sn_sr_qt_ma
WHERE
  (
  Agg_yr_qt_mt_mn_wk_rg_cy_sn_sr_qt_ma.Yr  =  '2006'
   AND
  Agg_yr_qt_mt_mn_wk_rg_cy_sn_sr_qt_ma.Store_name  =
  @prompt('Enter Store name:','A','Store\Store name',Mono,Free,
  Persistent,,User:0)
  )
GROUP BY
  Agg_yr_qt_mt_mn_wk_rg_cy_sn_sr_qt_ma.Qtr
```

Listing 9.4 Generated SQL Statement for Sales Revenue by Quarter

9.2.5 The Radio Button

The radio button enables the user to switch the trend displayed in the line chart. A general best practice is to retrieve everything from the database if possible, including selector labels, but in this case the labels for this radio button cannot be retrieved from the database, so we'll simply hardcode them in the Excel worksheet.

9.2.6 The Pie Chart

Similar to the line chart we're using to show the revenue trends, the pie chart is also used in our example to display more detailed information about the selected single store. It breaks the yearly revenue down to product lines. The Universe query includes the objects LINES and SALES REVENUE, and it is filtered by year and store name as illustrated in Figure 9.6. The SQL statement is shown in Listing 9.5.

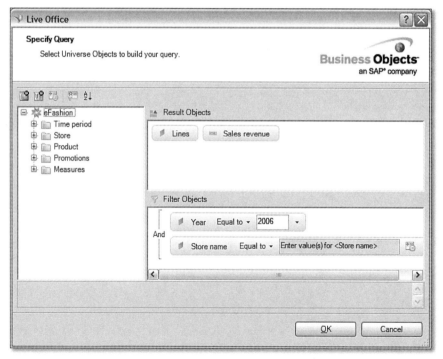

Figure 9.6 Revenue by Product Line Query in Query Panel

```
SELECT
  Article_lookup.Family_name,
  sum(Shop_facts.Amount_sold)
FROM
  Article_lookup,
  Shop_facts,
  Calendar_year_lookup,
  Outlet_Lookup
WHERE
  ( Outlet_Lookup.Shop_id=Shop_facts.Shop_id  )
  AND  ( Article_lookup.Article_id=Shop_facts.Article_id  )
  AND  ( Shop_facts.Week_id=Calendar_year_lookup.Week_id  )
  AND
  (
  Calendar_year_lookup.Yr  =  '2006'
   AND
  Outlet_Lookup.Shop_name  =  @prompt('Enter Store name:','A',
   'Store\Store name',Mono,Free,Persistent,,User:0)
  )
GROUP BY
  Article_lookup.Family_name
```

Listing 9.5 Generated SQL Statement for Sales Revenue by Product Line of a Specific Store

9.3   Organizing Data in Excel

In this phase, we're going to work with Excel to organize the data. Note that we're working in a stand-alone Excel instance with SAP BusinessObjects Live Office installed, not in the embedded Excel spreadsheet of SAP BusinessObjects Dashboards. Later we'll import this Excel file into the dashboard.

Because we're using Live Office Connection in this sample dashboard project, we already have a snapshot of data inside the embedded spreadsheet, which is helpful to the designer. However, you'll probably start with an empty spreadsheet for some other connection types. We recommend putting the data returned by each connectivity into the embedded spreadsheet and adding some dummy data so that later you can test charts and interactivity while you are designing your dashboard model inside SAP BusinessObjects Dashboards.

Figure 9.7 shows the current status of our spreadsheet. As you can see, we put the data for each component in a separate worksheet, so we have five Live Office objects in four tabs in the embedded spreadsheet. You may find that the object doesn't start at cell $A$1. We intentionally left some space above and to the left of the data so we'll have room if more logic is needed in the spreadsheet.

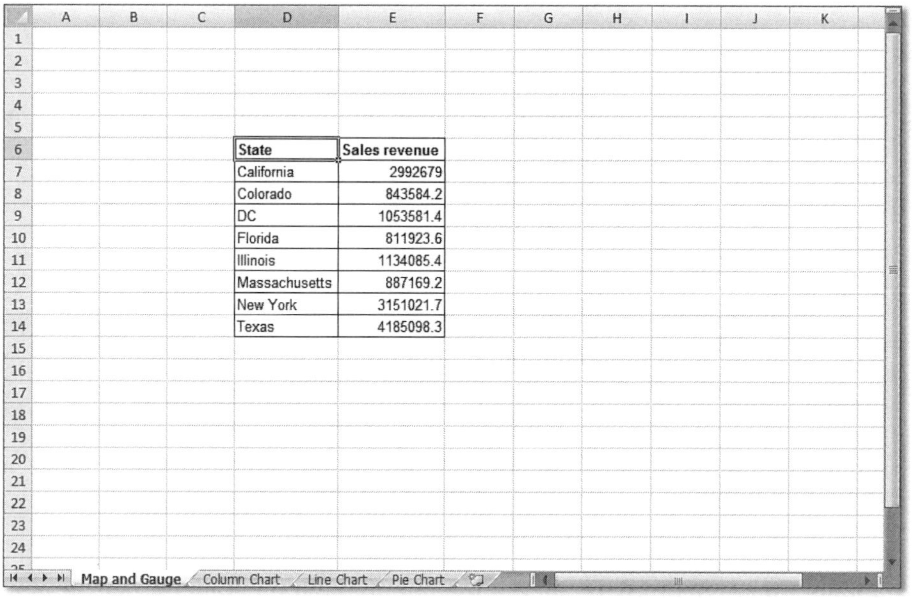

	A	B	C	D	E	F	G	H	I	J	K
1											
2											
3											
4											
5											
6				State	Sales revenue						
7				California	2992679						
8				Colorado	843584.2						
9				DC	1053581.4						
10				Florida	811923.6						
11				Illinois	1134085.4						
12				Massachusetts	887169.2						
13				New York	3151021.7						
14				Texas	4185098.3						
15											
16											
17											
18											
19											
20											
21											
22											
23											
24											

Map and Gauge / Column Chart / Line Chart / Pie Chart

Figure 9.7 Excel Spreadsheet with Live Office Objects

Another best practice is adding a *control* sheet in Excel with the UI control logic inside, such as the data insertion, calculation mechanism, and when to trigger a connection.

The following steps list how we organize data in the embedded Excel spreadsheet for our sample dashboard:

1. **Add the dashboard title.**

   We have a label component that is the dashboard title, so we'll enter the text "Sales Dashboard" in cell $E$6 and later bind it to the label component. If the title needs be updated, you can easily change it in this cell without locating the label from among many components.

2. **Reserve cells for data insertion of the map component.**

   The data for the map component is a vertical range of sales revenue by state, so we'll select Row in the INSERTION TYPE dropdown list in the PROPERTIES panel of the map component. Here, we'll highlight cell range $E$8 to $F$8 in yellow for the inserted row of data. Cell $F$8 contains the revenue of the selected state, which the gauge component will use later.

3. **Bind the prompt for the revenue by store via the Live Office connection.**

   Cell $E$8, which contains the currently selected state, will be used as the input parameter for the query retrieving the revenue by store of a state, so we need to bind the prompt for the revenue by storing Live Office object to cell $E$8.

4. **Add the column chart title.**

   Enter the text "Revenue by Store" in cell $E$10.

5. **Reserve cells for data insertion of the column chart.**

   Similar to the map component, the drill-down functionality of the column chart should also be enabled. We'll highlight cell range $E$11 to $F$11 for data insertion of the column chart.

6. **Bind prompts for the rest of the queries.**

   There are three other queries: revenue by month, revenue by quarter, and revenue by product line. The store name is used as the input parameter for all of them, so bind their prompts to cell $E$11.

7. **Add the title for the line chart.**

   Enter "Revenue Trend" in cell $E$13.

8. **Add the pie chart title.**

   Enter "Revenue by Product Line" in cell $E$15.

9. **Add labels for the radio button.**

   Enter "Monthly," "Quarterly," and "YTD" in cells $E$17, $E$18, and $E$19, respectively, which will be used for a selector component.

10. **Reserve cells for data insertion of the radio button.**

    Highlight cell $E$20, where the selected label of the radio button is inserted so we can use the label of the radio button and this cell to control the dynamic visibility of the three line chart components.

Most of our control logic is now implemented in the CONTROL tab of the Excel spreadsheet. Figure 9.8 shows the finished worksheet.

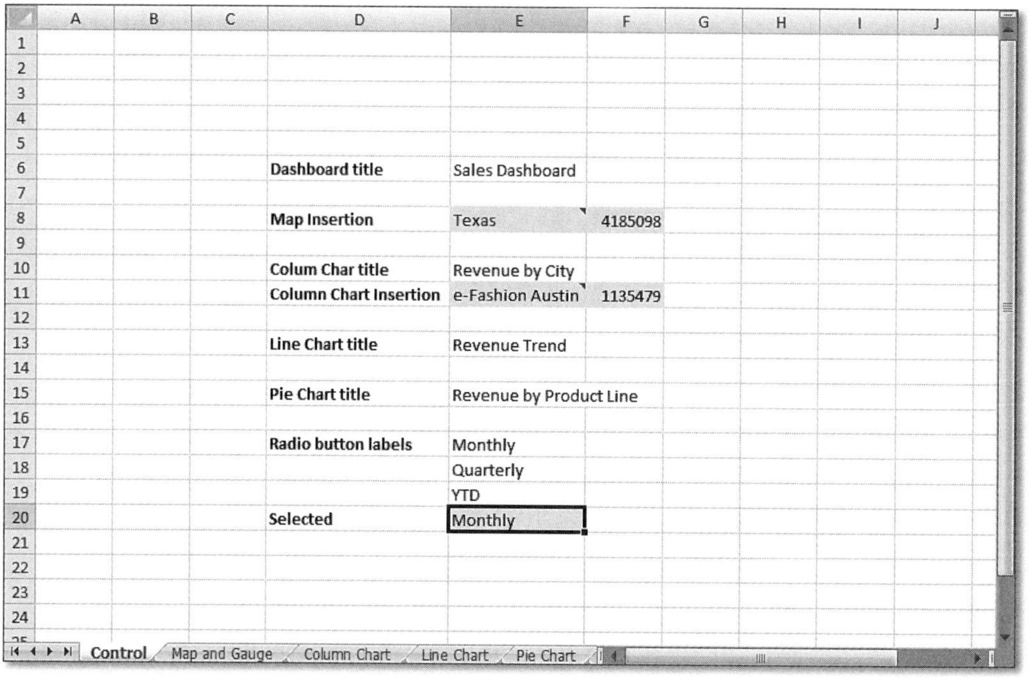

Figure 9.8 Control Tab in the Excel Spreadsheet

There is one more thing to add in the Excel spreadsheet: the YTD trend data. We'll switch to the LINE CHART tab in Excel and add an Excel formula to calculate the YTD trend based on the monthly trend data. The YTD revenue for January is just the revenue in January, so we'll make cell $F$7 equal to cell $E$7. Then, in cell $F$8, we'll add the formula SUM($E$7:E8). Notice that we've locked the first parameter of the sum function, which is the starting cell of the summation. This is necessary so we can easily copy the formula to cells below, as displayed in Figure 9.9.

Now we've finished the data organization step. You can also do this in the embedded spreadsheet of SAP BusinessObjects Dashboards while designing the dashboard, but we recommend that you first deal with data itself so you won't be distracted by the UI components. The result of this step is a well-organized Excel model that is clear and can be easily maintained.

504

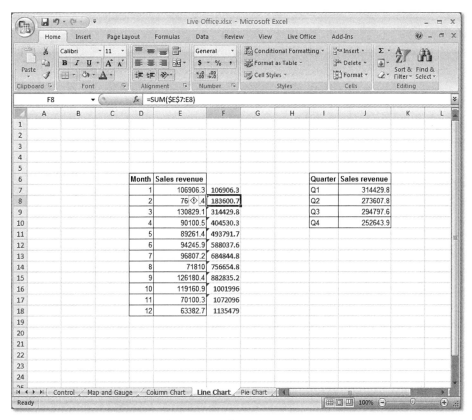

Figure 9.9 Formula to Calculate the YTD Trend

9.4 Designing the Dashboard

Now that we've finished the plan and preparations, let's start building the dashboard.

9.4.1 Position the UI Components

The first thing you're going to do is add UI components to the canvas to implement the layout you've designed.

The first problem you will meet with will probably be the canvas size. The size of the canvas is 800 by 600 by default. You can change this size in the document properties, and you can also change the default canvas size by going to FILE • PREFERENCES, as described in Chapter 2. So how big should the canvas be? The answer depends on whether you have a rigid constraint on the canvas size; for example, if you're building a dashboard that will be integrated into a web page, and the web designer reserves an area, which has an accurate width and height, on the page for your dashboard. In that case, you should set the canvas to that specific size. Otherwise, you can freely choose the size. We recommend that you start with a relatively large canvas size and lay your components on it. When you finish designing the dashboard, if there's extra space, you can easily use Fit Canvas to Components to cut out the blank space. In this example, we'll use the default 800 by 600 canvas.

Laying the components on the canvas is quite straightforward with our planned layout. Usually you should follow the up-to-down, left-to-right order.

It's worth noting that the aligning and sizing tools in SAP BusinessObjects Dashboards can save you time in placing and sizing the components. For example, you can make the map and column chart the same height and align them at their top edges. Another example is that you can add three line charts to the canvas and make them the same width and height and align them to both their top and left edges so they will exactly overlap each other. Alignment is very important for a clean appearance and for an agreeable user experience.

9.4.2 Import the Excel File

After we've added all of the required UI components, we'll import the Excel file that we edited in the previous step and continue setting the properties for each component. You can refer to the Properties panel of each component to get a clear idea what we are doing here.

The Label

Link the label's text to cell $E$6, which stores the name of this dashboard—"Sales Dashboard".

The Map

First, remove the map title because it makes little sense. Then bind the display data to the output value of the revenue by state query, which is in the cell range 'Map and Gauge'!$D$7:$E$14.

For data insertion, select Row, as it's the insertion type, and set the source data to the same range as the display data and the destination to cell range $E$8 to $F$8 in the CONTROL tab. Be aware that in our database, District of Columbia is abbreviated to DC, so you need to edit the region key as shown in Figure 9.10.

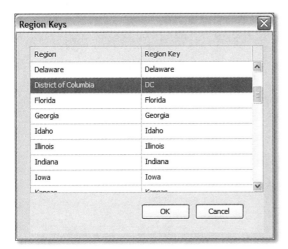

Figure 9.10 Region Keys Window

The Gauge

Bind the DATA property to cell $F$8 in the CONTROL tab and set the maximum to 5000000, which is the assumed maximum sales revenue a store can produce.

The Column Chart

Bind the column chart's title to cell $E$10 in the CONTROL tab and its subtitle to cell $E$8 so that the title of the column chart will be *Revenue by Store* and the subtitle will be the state that is currently selected on the map. Bind the display data to the result of the revenue by store query.

Because we can't determine how many stores will be in the selected state, we'll bind more rows and select IGNORE BLANK VALUES in the BEHAVIOR tab in the chart's PROPERTIES panel.

Enable drill-down and select the row insertion type. Bind the source data to the same range as the display data and the destination to cell range $E$11 to $F$11 in the CONTROL tab.

The Line Charts

The three line charts share a lot of common properties. Bind their titles to cell $E$13 in the CONTROL tab and the subtitles to cell $E$11 so that the title of the line charts will be *Revenue Trend* and the subtitle will be the name of the store that is selected in the column chart.

Then bind their display data to the monthly trend data, quarterly trend data, and YTD trend data, respectively.

We also need to set the dynamic visibility properties for these line charts. To do this, in the PROPERTIES panel of each line chart, bind their keys, which are Monthly, Quarterly, and YTD, to one cell in range $E$17 to $E$19, and bind the status to $E$20 so that when the radio button selection changes, it inserts one of the cells among $E$17 to $E$19 to cell $E$20, and the corresponding chart will be visible, with the other two hidden.

The Radio Button

Bind the label to cell range $E$17 to $E$19 in the CONTROL tab. Select LABEL in the INSERTION TYPE dropdown list and set DESTINATION to $E$20.

The Pie Chart

Bind the title to cell $E$15 in the CONTROL tab and the display data to the revenue by product line query result.

9.4.3 Connect to External Data

Now you can preview the dashboard and test the charts, the drill-down behavior, and the dynamic visibility with the sample data. If all is well, you can go on and configure the data connections.

We're using Live Office connections, so we'll simply use existing Live Office connections in the Data Manager. SAP BusinessObjects Dashboards will then automatically detect any existing Live Office connections contained in the Excel file and create one connection in the Data Manager for each.

For each connection, you can correct the session URL and set it to REFRESH ON LOAD. The only thing you need pay attention to is when to trigger each connectivity. For the Live Office connection called REVENUE BY STORE, which corresponds to the revenue by store query, we set it to refresh when cell $E$8, the selected state, changes. We'll set the other three Live Office connections, corresponding to the revenue by month query, the revenue by quarter query, and the revenue by product line query, to refresh when cell $E$11, the selected store, changes.

At this point, you can preview your work again and test the data connections to see if the correct data is fetched upon user interaction.

9.4.4   Adjust the Appearance

Now the dashboard has complete functionality. If you like, you can make it look better by adjusting the components' appearances.

As the last step of this example, we'll change some styles of the components such as font size, color, and alignment. We'll add a background below the label component to highlight the purpose of this dashboard. We'll also change the theme and the color scheme for a cooler look and feel. The final result is displayed in Figure 9.11.

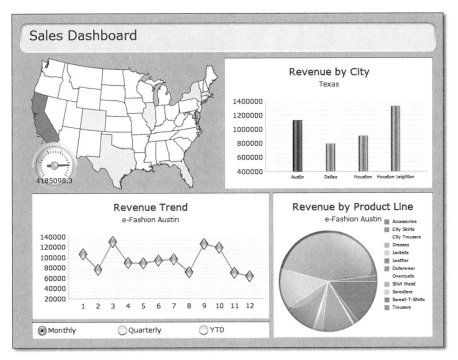

Figure 9.11 Final Version of the Dashboard

We've already explained how to change the appearance of each component, how to use the background, and how to change the theme or color scheme in previous chapters, so we'll ignore that here. According to your preferences, you can adjust the visual appearance of the dashboard, such as using different fonts or background colors.

You can get the source file of this dashboard from *www.sap-press.com*.

9.5   Summary

From this simple dashboard project, we hope that you've gained an understanding of the basic workflow of building a true dashboard and the things you need to pay particular attention to during development. You plan the dashboard, prepare the data, organize the data in a separate Excel file or the embedded spreadsheet, and design your dashboard in SAP BusinessObjects Dashboards. You can use a list view or some sample data to help debug and test your dashboard. When you're certain the dashboard is ready in both functionality and appearance after thorough testing, you can distribute it to the end users.

This chapter introduces the SAP BusinessObjects Dashboards SDK and explains some of its core functionalities, highlights common cases where the SDK can be implemented, and gives an overview of the value that it can bring to your SAP BusinessObjects Dashboards dashboard projects.

10 Introduction to the SAP BusinessObjects Dashboards SDK

SAP BusinessObjects Dashboards introduced a new level of overall dashboard power and control with the release of the SAP BusinessObjects Dashboards software development toolkit (SDK). The SAP BusinessObjects Dashboards SDK enables SAP BusinessObjects Dashboards designers and developers to extend the value of their existing SAP BusinessObjects Dashboards environments by creating custom components to address dashboard requirements that fall outside of the scope of inherent SAP BusinessObjects Dashboards functionality. This chapter will get you familiar with the concept of the SAP BusinessObjects Dashboards SDK and will help you understand the high-level value of the SDK and how to factor it in when defining dashboard project specifications.

10.1 About the SAP BusinessObjects Dashboards SDK

The SAP BusinessObjects Dashboards SDK is built on Adobe's Flex technology and consists of a foundational set of software tools, fully functional code examples, documentation files and utilities that Flex developers can leverage to create and introduce custom components into the existing SAP BusinessObjects Dashboards component library. The software technologies bundled with the SDK include a core Flex class library (*.swc* file) that facilitates communication to and from SAP BusinessObjects Dashboards as well as a set of tools and compiler utilities that make packaging and distributing custom components for use in SAP BusinessObjects Dashboards an easy process.

The SAP BusinessObjects Dashboards SDK is made available to developers as a downloadable package from the SAP website. SAP BusinessObjects Dashboards must be installed on the machine as a prerequisite to installing the SDK. For testing and debugging purposes, it's strongly advised that developers have ready access to a licensed instance of SAP BusinessObjects Dashboards that does not expire. To begin using the SAP BusinessObjects Dashboards SDK risk free, a fully functional trial version of SAP BusinessObjects Dashboards may be installed as an alternative. Instructions on where to find the SDK are included in Section 10.4.

10.2   About Flex

Flex is the technology behind the SAP BusinessObjects Dashboards SDK and is the same technology that developers use to build custom components for SAP BusinessObjects Dashboards.

Flex is an open source software framework developed by Adobe that allows developers to build rich, powerful cross-platform applications that run in the ubiquitous Adobe Flash Player. In addition to being supported by all major browsers, by leveraging the cross-operating system Adobe AIR runtime, Flex applications can also be designed to run on the desktop as well as mobile devices.

Flex provides developers with an intuitive way to create highly adaptable and functional application user interfaces as well as the logic behind them. Flex leverages a declarative markup language called MXML, which is an XML-based syntax that enables developers to design and describe user interface layouts and behaviors. To power application functionality and to define application logic, Flex also leverages the object-oriented programming language ActionScript 3. All Flex applications compile out to an SWF file, which can be deployed to a variety of environments. Developers new to Flex who are familiar with languages such as XML and JavaScript will be able to pick up the Flex concept quickly.

The Flex framework also provides developers with complete access to over 100 built-in components that can be extended and customized in an infinite number of ways. From interactive layout components and a full charting library to components that provide intuitive access to web services and databases, the Flex component library is continuously evolving. These built-in components provide developers with a measurable competitive advantage when developing applications by eliminating the need for custom development when implementing commonly used components. With a single line of code, developers can implement powerful, complex components in their applications.

To use the Flex framework, developers need access to the free SDK, which is available for download from the Adobe website. However, for a more productive and complete development experience, it's recommended that developers also download Adobe Flex Builder. Flex Builder is an integrated development environment that provides a complete framework for managing Flex projects and coding Flex applications. Features like intelligent coding, project linking, and automatic code formatting are valuable time savers when developing Flex applications. Flex Builder is available as a free trial download as well as for purchase on the Adobe website. Note that for the purpose of the SAP BusinessObjects Dashboards SDK, Flex Builder 2 or 3 should be used as opposed to the newly named Flash Builder IDE that came out with the release of Flex 4. This recommendation is due to the current release of the SAP BusinessObjects Dashboards SDK being built on an earlier version of the Flex framework.

10.3   When to Use the SDK

So often, due to rigid built-in functionality and dashboard component limitations, dashboard requirements are often scaled down, trimmed, or otherwise modified to make do with what's available in the dashboard technology package that has been bought. This has always been problematic as seemingly harmless requests, such as altering axes on a given chart slightly outside of its inherent bounds, begin to shed light on other potential stumbling blocks as dashboards begin to evolve and require finer control over the way users interact with, consume, navigate through, and visualize their data.

Meeting every dashboard use case with a default toolset is an impossible order. The inevitable fact that sooner or later unique requirements come along that drive innovation and are not found in the core toolbox is a universal problem that can only be solved by empowering developers to satisfy their custom dashboard requirements with the use of an SDK. This is exactly what the SAP BusinessObjects Dashboards SDK does: empower developers to innovate and develop new components and concepts, satisfy the most demanding business requirements, and solve new and existing dashboard challenges in a creative way.

How and when the SDK is applied to a dashboard project is completely subjective and open on a project-by-project basis. However, listed here are a few common areas where the SDK can be implemented.

Create new data connections to connect to:

▸ CSV files

▸ Encrypted data repositories

▸ Customer relationship management systems and legacy data stores

▸ Third-party tools, such as Sales Force or MailChimp

▸ Text files

▸ Website content

▸ Really Simple Syndication (RSS) feeds

Create new data visualizations:

▸ Flash or JavaScript maps

▸ Specialty charts, such as Smith charts or Gannt charts

▸ New gauges, dials, or heatmaps

Create new navigational controls:

▸ Simple buttons

▸ Coverflow navigators

▸ Hierarchical trees

▸ Complex fisheye menus

Mathematic and data processing formulas:

▸ Any math functions not supported natively by SAP BusinessObjects Dashboards

▸ Any string or text functions not supported natively by SAP BusinessObjects Dashboards

▸ Any statistical functions not supported natively by SAP BusinessObjects Dashboards

These categories are common areas where the SDK can be applied, but it's important to remember that virtually any component that can be created in Flex can easily be purposed to function as an SAP BusinessObjects Dashboards component. This new ability provides a great deal of creative latitude to the SAP BusinessObjects Dashboards dashboard designer and the Flex developer alike.

10.4 How to Use the SDK

The introduction of a new SDK is always an exciting prospect, though it can be a confusing piece of functionality as well, especially for dashboard designers or dashboard stakeholders that are not necessarily aware of what SDKs are, how they bring value, and how they're used or applied in a real-world SAP Business-Objects Dashboards dashboard project. This lack of clarity that arises is for good reason, especially in the case of SAP BusinessObjects Dashboards, because the vast majority of SAP BusinessObjects Dashboards designers and dashboard stakeholders are not and do not aspire to be software engineers. In the case of the SAP BusinessObjects Dashboards SDK, it is much more important for dashboard designers and stakeholders to know that a mechanism exists that allows software engineers who are familiar with Flex to inject custom functionality into their dashboard projects.

From a software engineer's perspective, the SAP BusinessObjects Dashboards SDK and its foundational concepts and functionality that drive core value are fairly straight forward to understand and eventually master. At this point in the evolution of the SAP BusinessObjects Dashboards SDK, functionality can be boiled down to a set of bare essentials that are highly adaptable and extremely powerful and flexible when properly applied. As the SAP BusinessObjects Dashboards product and the SDK continue to evolve, we'll certainly receive new pieces of functionality and potential down the road, but for now the SDK allows a Flex developer to create any Flex 2.0.1-compliant component and import it for use into SAP BusinessObjects Dashboards via a simple packaging process. The Flex component that you create can subsequently subscribe to data in the SAP BusinessObjects Dashboards spreadsheet model in either a read, write, or read/write manner, opening the doors to the runtime data model that your SAP BusinessObjects Dashboards dashboard relies on to consume, process, and display data.

This means that through Flex binding, you can intercept, manipulate, and re-inject data to and from the SAP BusinessObjects Dashboards model at will. With

515

this powerful concept, it starts to become clear that with foundational hooks into the SAP BusinessObjects Dashboards framework coupled with a powerful software tool (Flex), virtually anything and any component is possible.

From a nuts and bolts standpoint, getting set up to develop on the SAP BusinessObjects Dashboards SDK is a fairly lightweight and straightforward process that can see you up and running in your very own environment within a few minutes. These steps assume a general familiarity with Flex basics, including MXML, ActionScript, and project setups. If you are not familiar with basic Flex project setup or Flex concepts in general, it's best to start learning, or at least to become familiar with Flex before you begin using the SDK.

By following these steps, you'll be able to establish a Flex development environment for SAP BusinessObjects Dashboards and will be primed to begin developing custom components.

1. Download and install SAP BusinessObjects Dashboards: *http://www.sdn.sap .com/irj/boc/crystal-dashboard*

2. Download and install the SAP BusinessObjects Dashboards SDK: *http:// www.sdn.sap.com/irj/boc/xcelsius-sdk*

3. Download and install Flex Builder: *http://www.adobe.com/products/flex/*

4. Download and install the Flex 2.0.1 Hotfix 3 SDK: *http://labs.adobe.com/ technologies/Flex/sdk/Flex2sdk.html*

5. Read the tutorials and the manuals. This is a critical step that's tempting to jump past to get started, but will save significant amounts of time and energy if you take a day to familiarize yourself with the tutorials, source code, and other material that comes bundled with the SDK.

Once you've established your Flex development environment, implementing a custom component in SAP BusinessObjects Dashboards is only a few steps away. To install your component into SAP BusinessObjects Dashboards, use the Manage Add-Ons functionality as illustrated in Figure 10.1.

Here we walk through the high-level workflow (illustrated in Figure 10.2) for developing and injecting your custom component into SAP BusinessObjects Dashboards:

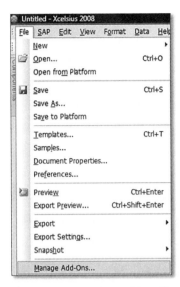

Figure 10.1 Managing and Installing Add-Ons

1. Create your component and property sheet applications in Flex, ultimately generating two SWF files, one for the component and one for the component's property sheet:

   ▹ Create a Flex project for your component.

   ▹ Set your Flex project to compile using the Flex 2.0.1 Hotfix 3 SDK.

   ▹ Add the SAP BusinessObjects Dashboards SDK SWC file to your project's build path.

   ▹ Develop and test your component.

   ▹ Compile the applications.

2. Package your component and property sheet SWF files using the SAP Business-Objects Dashboards Packager, and build the package to generate an XLX installer file.

3. Open SAP BusinessObjects Dashboards and install the XLX file generated as a result of step 2, using the SAP BusinessObjects Dashboards Add-On Manager.

4. Restart SAP BusinessObjects Dashboards and begin using and testing your new component.

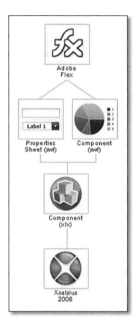

Figure 10.2 SAP BusinessObjects Dashboards Custom Component Workflow

10.5 What Can I Do with the SDK?

Flex is a creative software tool with tremendous business value that provides developers with a virtually boundless canvas for innovating and creating components. Whether they are basic charts that satisfy simple outlying requirements, cutting-edge novel navigational elements, or data visualizations that present data for interaction in a way that the SAP BusinessObjects Dashboards components cannot accommodate, by combining the SAP BusinessObjects Dashboards SDK and Flex, nearly anything is possible. A custom pie chart example with source code that illustrates the simplicity of a basic custom Flex component can be found in Figure 10.4 and Listing 10.1.

Data Visualizations

SDK developers can create powerful native components to represent any kind of data, as well as compelling mashups with third-party SDKs.

- Data visualizations with custom ItemRenderers
- Heatmaps
- Geographical mapping components as shown in Figure 10.3

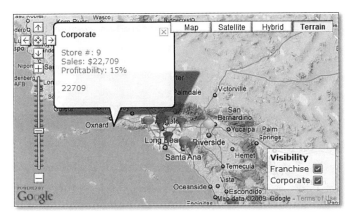

Figure 10.3 Custom Google Map

- 3D pie charts
- Hierarchical pie charts
- Multi-dial gauges
- Data meters
- Sparkline collections, bullet charts, and so on

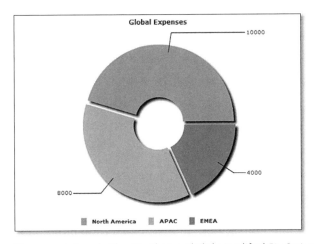

Figure 10.4 Sample Flex Pie Chart + Slightly Modified Pie Series = Fast New Custom Pie Chart

```
<?xml version="1.0"?>
<mx:Application backgroundColor="0xffffff"
  xmlns:mx="http://www.adobe.com/2006/mxml"
  backgroundGradientAlphas="[1.0, 1.0]"
  backgroundGradientColors="[#FFFFFF, #FFFFFF]">
  <mx:Script><![CDATA[
        import mx.collections.ArrayCollection;

        [Bindable]
        public var expenses:ArrayCollection = new ArrayCollection([
        {Expense:"North America", Amount:10000},
        {Expense:"APAC", Amount:8000},
        {Expense:"EMEA", Amount:4000}
    ]);
  ]]></mx:Script>
  <mx:Label text="Global Expenses" fontWeight="bold"
        color="#000000" fontSize="12"/>
    <mx:PieChart id="myChart"
        dataProvider="{expenses}"
        showDataTips="true"
        innerRadius=".3">
        <mx:series>
          <mx:PieSeries
              explodeRadius=".025"
                    field="Amount"
                nameField="Expense"
              labelPosition="callout"/>
        </mx:series>
    </mx:PieChart>
    <mx:Legend direction="horizontal"
          dataProvider="{myChart}" height="20"
                width="302" color="#000000"/>
</mx:Application>
```

Listing 10.1 Pie Chart Component Source Code

As you can see here, with a little bit of Flex code you can create an exploded doughnut pie chart in just minutes.

10.5.1 Flex Applications

SAP BusinessObjects Dashboards can host other Flex applications as children as well as communicate with any other compatible Flex SDK (and vice versa).

▶ Import entire Flex applications.

▶ Import entire supporting dashboards or dashboard modules built in Flex.

▶ Import Flex applications or modules that support data entry and write back to dashboard data marts or data warehouses.

10.5.2 Data Processors, Connections, and Functions

For advanced statistical or financial computations or other unsupported Excel functions, you can create custom functions and data processing components using SDK to:

▶ Connect to Google Adwords.

▶ Connect to homegrown data or Salesforce-type systems.

▶ Connect to data cubes and expose MDX querying capabilities.

▶ Sort and filter data using compound filters.

▶ Use the SDK to easily create mathematical, statistical, and text/string functions.

10.6 SDK Best Practices

As with any SDK, there are best practices that should be followed when scoping and developing your custom component. The best practices we'll discuss here are specifically related to the SAP BusinessObjects Dashboards SDK and workflow. Flex best practices should be followed at all times as well, though they are outside of the scope of this discussion. A working knowledge of Flex best practices is advised before moving forward with your component development.

When developing components for SAP BusinessObjects Dashboards, there are a few common themes that should be adhered to, which will save time and will provide much more rapid development, testing, and debugging cycles.

Note that SAP BusinessObjects Dashboards does not come with any kind of built-in debugging capabilities; therefore, you must leverage what is available to gain insight into component runtime behavior.

10.6.1 Use Only What You Need

In general, using only what you need cannot be overstated in software development, and developing components for SAP BusinessObjects Dashboards is no exception. The following subsections contain some guidelines to keep in mind that should expedite troubleshooting and testing cycles.

10.6.2 Bindings

The types of binding directions available to you as an SDK developer are input, output, and both. These are the binding direction options that are available when subscribing to updates for a cell or a range of cells in the SAP BusinessObjects Dashboards Excel data model. They're specified in the property sheet that accompanies your custom component and should be used with care, specifically adjusted to suit the needs of a given component property.

- **Input:** Your component writes to SAP BusinessObjects Dashboards.
- **Output:** Your component reads from SAP BusinessObjects Dashboards.
- **Both:** Your component reads from and writes to SAP BusinessObjects Dashboards.

10.6.3 Use Custom Property Sheets

The basic property sheet (*.swf*) that is included with the SAP BusinessObjects Dashboards SDK offers limited binding flexibility and virtually no customization or user experience control in the way a dashboard developer will interact with your component's properties, and should be avoided. Creating custom property sheets is an extra step but is just as important as your custom component.

10.6.4 Don't Repeat Yourself

Since it's recommended that you create your own custom property sheets, it's also recommended that you create reusable property sheet patterns to prevent code duplication in every property sheet you create. We'll explore some options around this concept in Chapter 13.

10.6.5 Develop Test Containers

Debugging at SAP BusinessObjects Dashboards runtime, aside from trace statements and alerts, is currently nonexistent. Therefore, it's crucial that you create local Flex applications that allow you to test and manipulate your component's properties before testing your custom component in SAP BusinessObjects Dashboards. This simple step will drastically cut down on your debugging revision cycles and will also allow you to leverage the built-in debugging capabilities of Flex Builder.

10.6.6 Trace and Alert

Often it isn't possible to replicate functionality in your local test container that occurs in SAP BusinessObjects Dashboards because there is no shell or harness mechanism that the SDK provides to simulate data binding through the SAP BusinessObjects Dashboards Excel model. Therefore, if you cannot troubleshoot through your test container and need to gain insight into what is happening at SAP BusinessObjects Dashboards design or runtime, you can use alerts or trace statements in your Flex component and capture the trace output via web browser tools or the Flash trace log.

10.6.7 Development Approaches (MXML versus ActionScript)

When developing a visual component for SAP BusinessObjects Dashboards that is either complex in layout or has the potential to evolve to a more complex visual layout using basic Flex components, MXML should be used wherever possible due to readability and design time editing WYSIWYG (what you see is what you get) advantages. Pure ActionScript may be favored for logic and data connectivity components or if you are developing a base class that other visual components will extend. However, if you're developing a composite component, MXML will save time in the long run and will be easier to read, maintain, and edit, should the design further evolve or need to be changed in the future.

10.6.8 Styling

The current version of the SDK presents some challenges in preserving your design time styles at runtime. Often, when imported into SAP BusinessObjects Dashboards and previewed, your component may lose some or all of its visual styles if you rely on inline MXML style directives.

A good approach to minimize the amount of style reapplication at runtime is to create your styles in a separate Cascading Style Sheet (CSS) file and to embed that CSS file for use in your component.

An alternate to the CSS file approach is manually reapplying styles through ActionScript style directives once your component has been initialized, though this approach often leads to a large amount of ActionScript style management code, which is not necessarily ideal to have in your custom component's code base.

10.7   SDK Pitfalls

There are many pitfalls common to all programming languages, though the ones we discuss in this section are specifically related to add-ons that can come back to haunt you if they are not managed up front.

10.7.1   Flash Shared Local Objects are Unreliable

With the most recent release of Flash Player 10.3, users can now delete shared local objects with ease. Individuals can always clear out SLOs, but the most recent player release made it quick and easy to accomplish. In short, custom components for SAP BusinessObjects Dashboards that rely on the use of SLOs should be reengineered, or at the very least users of the product should be notified about how SLOs are leveraged.

10.7.2   XLPs and XLXs Should Be Archived

XLPs, or SAP BusinessObjects Dashboards Add-On Packager files, generate unique XLX installer files so that end users can install custom components in their SAP BusinessObjects Dashboards environments. XLPs stamp XLXs with unique IDs that the SAP BusinessObjects Dashboards Add-On Manager uses to determine if a component that is attempting to be installed already exists in that SAP BusinessObjects Dashboards environment. If an original XLP file is lost that was used to generate and distribute the original XLX file(s) and a new XLP file has to be created to generate new XLX files for subsequent distribution to end users, installation issues will be encountered that require any preexisting component by the same fully qualified name to be uninstalled before the new one can be installed. This obviously isn't the end of the world, but it can create confusion and should be avoided if possible.

10.7.3   Common Component Classes—First in Wins

If multiple add-ons have been developed, and some or all of those components leverage a set of base classes, and those components and the base class functionality that they rely on can potentially or do evolve (get released) at different paces, be aware that the Flash Player operates using first-class-loaded-wins. This means that any components that rely on a common class will be using the first version of that class that was loaded by Flash Player. If there are any inconsistencies between the first class loaded and the class functionality that a given component is expecting, this can create some obvious and not so obvious behaviors and/or bugs at runtime. Be sure to nail down a strategy that allows all components to coexist and evolve peacefully.

10.8   Summary

In this chapter, we introduced the SAP BusinessObjects Dashboards SDK, explained some of its core functionality, highlighted common cases where the SDK can be implemented, and gave an overview of the value it can bring to your SAP BusinessObjects Dashboards dashboard projects. With the fundamental concept of the SDK in mind, the following chapters will build on this foundational knowledge to further illustrate and explain basic to advanced SDK implementation options and details.

This chapter provides a detailed walkthrough of a full property sheet and corresponding custom Flex component for SAP BusinessObjects Dashboards.

11 Get Started with Custom Component Basics

In this chapter we'll take a closer look into the core concepts of SAP Business-Objects Dashboards SDK development. We'll cover the foundational pieces that compose a custom component and work with concrete examples to get you up to speed and prepared for more advanced topics.

Let's start by gaining an understanding of the backbone of a custom component integration that facilitates all component data flow and binding communication: the custom component property sheet.

11.1 Developing Basic Add-On Property Sheets

Conceptually, property sheets will seem very similar to a developer who is familiar with SAP BusinessObjects Dashboards and interacting with the SAP Business-Objects Dashboards components offered in the default component library. A property sheet is essentially a self-contained Flex application that serves as both a user interface control and a communication proxy between the SAP Business-Objects Dashboards design environment and your custom component's publicly exposed properties that you want to give users control over.

Property sheets can serve many functions, and since they're Flex-based applications, property sheets enable the custom component developer to exercise creativity in designing the most effective user interfaces that the business users who leverage the custom component will ultimately interact with.

The basic primary property sheet features we'll cover before moving to more advanced property sheet features are:

- Property data binding
- Property value setting/getting

11.1.1 Property Sheet Data Binding

Perhaps the most powerful feature exposed by the SAP BusinessObjects Dashboards SDK is the ability to bind public properties that you specify in your custom Flex component to a variety of data ranges in the underlying SAP BusinessObjects Dashboards Excel data model. Binding types come in a handful of shapes and sizes and enable custom components to read, write, or read and write to the SAP BusinessObjects Dashboards Excel model in every way that is needed to fundamentally communicate with the two-dimensional data model (rows and columns) that's supported by the SAP BusinessObjects Dashboards implementation of the Excel model.

Bindings can be adapted to suit a variety of basic to advanced use cases. In this section we'll review the basic concepts of data binding that a custom component developer is most likely to encounter. Below are the fundamental concepts offered by the SAP BusinessObjects Dashboards SDK binding mechanism.

Here's a binding call example that specifies a read-only two-dimensional array property binding of a custom component's xcChartData property:

```
proxy.bind("xcChartData", null, bindingID, BindingDirection.OUTPUT, "",
    OutputBindings.ARRAY2D);
```

Binding Directions and Data Flow

When establishing a binding between SAP BusinessObjects Dashboards and one of your custom component's properties, you can specify whether your property should be treated as read-only, write-only, or as both a read and write property.

Reading Values from the Spreadsheet

To specify your component's property as a read-only property, meaning that your property will be a consumer of data from the SAP BusinessObjects Dashboards model, you'll need to specify a binding direction type of OUTPUT, as described below. By subscribing to the SAP BusinessObjects Dashboards model through binding as a read-only or OUTPUT consumer, your component's property value will change any time the range or cell data your custom component is bound to in the SAP BusinessObjects Dashboards data model changes, both at runtime as well as design time in the SAP BusinessObjects Dashboards environment.

To access this binding direction type, import the *xcelsius.binding.BindingDirection* namespace into your property sheet application. The fully qualified path to the OUTPUT type is:

```
xcelsius.binding.BindingDirection.OUTPUT
```

> **Note**
>
> Anything referenced in code samples needs to retain the Xcelsius name. Unfortunately this is confusing, but is the proper name until SAP renames the SDK's guts.

Writing Values to the Spreadsheet

To specify your component's property as a write-only property, meaning that your property will be a provider of data to the SAP BusinessObjects Dashboards model, you'll need to specify a binding direction type of INPUT, as described below. By subscribing to the SAP BusinessObjects Dashboards model through binding as a write-only or INPUT consumer, your component's property value will update the cell or range that it is bound to in the data model any time the data in your bound custom component property changes.

To access this binding direction type, import the *xcelsius.binding.BindingDirection* namespace. The fully qualified path to the INPUT type is:

```
xcelsius.binding.BindingDirection.INPUT
```

Writing Values to and Reading Values from the Spreadsheet

To specify your component's property as both a read and write property, meaning that your property will be a provider and consumer of data via the SAP BusinessObjects Dashboards Excel model, you'll need to specify a binding direction type of BOTH, as described below. By subscribing to the SAP BusinessObjects Dashboards model in this manner, your component's property value will update the cell or range that it is bound to in the data model any time the data in your custom component property changes, and conversely, your component's property value will change anytime the SAP BusinessObjects Dashboards Excel model is updated.

To access this binding direction type, import the *xcelsius.binding.BindingDirection* namespace. The fully qualified path to the BOTH type is:

```
xcelsius.binding.BindingDirection.BOTH
```

Binding Types

Whether your custom component's property is read, write, or both, it will need to specify what type of value it is in the `proxy.bind()` operation so the SDK can properly handle its data flow.

The options for `InputBindings` and `OutputBindings` are shown in Figures 11.1 and 11.2.

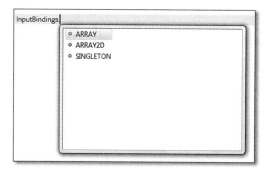

Figure 11.1 InputBinding Options

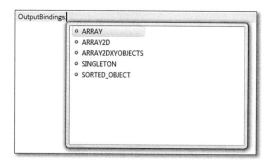

Figure 11.2 OutputBinding Options

InputBindings

▶ ARRAY

A type of ARRAY indicates that your custom component's property will be bound to and able to write to a set of cells in either a single column or row.

▶ ARRAY2D

A type of ARRAY2D indicates that your custom component's property will be bound to and able to write to a set of cells in a row and column format.

▶ SINGLETON

A type of SINGLETON indicates that your custom component's property will be bound to and able to write to a single cell.

OutputBindings

▶ ARRAY

A type of ARRAY indicates that your custom component's property will be bound to and able to read from a set of cells in either a single column or row.

▶ ARRAY2D

A type of ARRAY2D indicates that your custom component's property will be bound to and able to read from a set of cells in a row and column format.

▶ SINGLETON

A type of SINGLETON indicates that your custom component's property will be bound to and able to read from a single cell.

▶ ARRAY2DXYOBJECTS

A type of ARRAY2DXY indicates that your custom component's property will be bound to and able to read multiple columns or rows of cells output as a two-dimensional array of objects with X and Y properties.

▶ SORTED_OBJECT

A type of SORTED_OBJECT indicates that your custom component's property will be bound to and able to read a sorted object representation of a two-dimensional table.

11.1.2 Explicitly Setting Property Values

In addition to binding custom component properties to data in the SAP Business-Objects Dashboards Excel model, the ability also exists to read from and write to a custom component's property directly through the property sheet, thus bypassing the Excel model altogether.

An example of this functionality would be if you have a Flex ColorPicker control on your property sheet that is responsible for setting a color property on your component. Assuming you had a custom Flex canvas component with a public property named `xcBackgroundColor`, you could write a value to that property by using the following command specified inline in the ColorPicker's `change` event handler, where `cp` represents the ID of your MXML ColorPicker in the Flex property sheet.

```
private var proxy:PropertySheetExternalProxy =
  new PropertySheetExternalProxy();

<mx:ColorPicker left="19" top="175" id="cp"
  change="proxy.setProperty('xcChartColor',cp.selectedColor)"/>
```

11.1.3   Explicitly Getting Property Values

The ability to extract values from your custom component at property sheet design time exists as well and will be covered in Chapter 13.

11.1.4   Property Sheet Styling

While certain factors need to be considered for styling custom components, property sheet styling is direct and enables developers to leverage common styling practices in Flex such as style sheet references, inline style directives, and embedded style sheets.

11.1.5   Basic Property Sheet Overview

With some basic property sheet concepts in mind, let's walk through a functional example that highlights some of the fundamental aforementioned features. The full property sheet code is listed in breakout form of the code and accompanying code explanations in order from top to bottom.

This property sheet is designed as a basic example that is used to control a basic Flex `AreaChart` custom component with a handful of public properties. The full sample source code for the corresponding custom component is listed in Section 11.2.

Figure 11.3 highlights the overall end result of the following property sheet and component walk through by displaying the component, connected to data, and the data layout, inside the SAP BusinessObjects Dashboards designer. Figure 11.4 shows the isolated property sheet in SAP BusinessObjects Dashboards design mode.

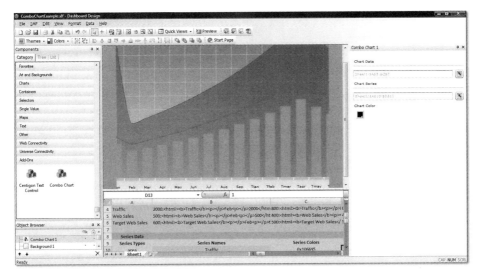

Figure 11.3 Custom Component and Property Sheet End Result

Figure 11.4 Property Sheet in Design Mode

Property Sheet Code Walkthrough

Let's take a walk through the property sheet code now, which has been broken up into the following sections.

- Main property sheet initialization event handler
- Fundamental SDK import statements
- Private SDK variables
- Supporting SDK functions
- `Proxy.Bind` dissected

Property Sheet Application Complete Event Listener

```
<?xml version="1.0" encoding="utf-8"?>
<mx:Application xmlns:mx="http://www.adobe.com/2006/mxml"
  layout="absolute" applicationComplete="init();">
```

On line 2 of the property sheet, which is a basic Flex Application MXML file, we listen for the native Flex Application event `applicationComplete`. When this event is triggered, it calls the `init()` function. In the `init()` function, we perform the routine task of initializing and executing the basic SAP BusinessObjects Dashboards SDK event listeners and callback functions needed to perform the custom component data binding and value setting tasks.

Fundamental SDK Import Statements

The import statements below provide us with a reference to the foundational classes and utilities in the SDK needed for the basic property sheet application.

```
<mx:Script>
<![CDATA[
import mx.containers.*;
import mx.controls.*;
import mx.core.Container;
import mx.events.FlexEvent;
import xcelsius.binding.BindingDirection;
import xcelsius.binding.tableMaps.input.InputBindings;
import xcelsius.binding.tableMaps.output.OutputBindings;
import xcelsius.propertySheets.impl.PropertySheetExternalProxy;
import xcelsius.propertySheets.interfaces.PropertySheetFunctionNamesSDK;
```

Here we call out and explain the import statements that are specifically related to the SDK.

```
import xcelsius.binding.BindingDirection;
```

The `BindingDirection` import statement enables you to call on binding direction constants from the SAP BusinessObjects Dashboards SDK. The binding direction options (`INPUT`, `OUTPUT`, `BOTH`) specify the direction of data flow between your SAP BusinessObjects Dashboards component properties and the SAP BusinessObjects Dashboards Excel data model when performing a bind operation through the SDK.

```
import xcelsius.binding.tableMaps.input.InputBindings;
```

The `InputBindings` import statement enables you to call on input binding constants from the SAP BusinessObjects Dashboards SDK. The input binding options (`ARRAY`, `ARRAY2D`, `SINGLETON`) specify the type of data range you want to bind to between your SAP BusinessObjects Dashboards component properties and the SAP BusinessObjects Dashboards Excel data model when performing a bind operation through the SDK. `InputBindings` should be specified when a custom component property needs to input values into the SAP BusinessObjects Dashboards Excel model.

```
import xcelsius.binding.tableMaps.output.OutputBindings;
```

The `OutputBindings` import statement enables you to call on output binding constants from the SAP BusinessObjects Dashboards SDK. The output binding options (`ARRAY`, `ARRAY2D`, `SINGLETON`) specify the type of data range you want to bind to between your SAP BusinessObjects Dashboards component properties and the SAP BusinessObjects Dashboards Excel data model when performing a bind operation through the SDK. `OutputBindings` should be specified when a custom component property needs to read values from the SAP BusinessObjects Dashboards Excel model.

```
import xcelsius.propertySheets.impl.PropertySheetExternalProxy;
```

The `PropertySheetExternalProxy` import statement provides access to the `PropertySheetExternalProxy` class, which is the backbone of the SDK integration performing all binding and value operations between the property sheet and the custom component.

```
import xcelsius.propertySheets.interfaces.PropertySheetFunctionNamesSDK;
```

The `PropertySheetFunctionNamesSDK` import statement provides access to a set of constants that tie to SAP BusinessObjects Dashboards SDK function names.

Basic Private SDK Variables
The three private variables defined in this section are key to managing custom component property data binding and property value setting through the SDK.

```
private var proxy:PropertySheetExternalProxy =
  new PropertySheetExternalProxy();
private var propertyToBind:String;
private var currentBindingID:String;
```

Let's discuss the primary private variables related to the SDK.

```
private var proxy:PropertySheetExternalProxy
```

The `proxy` variable is responsible for performing the job that its class name indicates: to serve as a proxy between the custom component's properties and the property sheet. This variable is responsible for all key communication, property data binding, and value setting in a custom component property sheet.

```
private var propertyToBind:String;
```

The `propertyToBind` variable serves as a string value that is responsible for holding the name of the custom component property that is currently being bound to during user-initiated binding operations. This value allows the developer to manage UI controls, data binding for the given property, and any other housekeeping or special functionality associated with the property. This variable is used primarily in the `initiateBind` and `continueBind` functions listed in the following section, "Supporting SDK Functions."

```
private var currentBindingID:String;
```

The `currentBindingID` variable serves as a string value that is responsible for holding the binding ID of the custom component property that is currently being bound to during binding operations. This value allows the proxy to manage data bindings for the given property. This variable is used primarily in the `initiate-Bind` and `continueBind` functions listed in the following section.

Supporting SDK Functions

A few common functions can be found across the majority of property sheet implementations. Those common functions are also included in this source code walkthrough as follows.

Initialize Values

The initValues function is responsible for retrieving the custom component's property values at property sheet initialization time and populating the property sheet's user interface controls with their property values. In this implementation, we retrieve the three values exposed by the custom component and loop through them to initialize their corresponding property sheet controls. The function code is listed here:

```
// Initializes Property Sheet on load to show the
current Xcelsius custom component property/style value.
private function initValues():void
{
    //Process the array of values for the Xcelsius custom
    //component properties.
    var propertyValues:Array = proxy.getProperties(
    ["xcChartData", "xcChartSeries", "xcChartColor"]);

    var propertyValuesLength:int = (propertyValues != null ?
                                    propertyValues.length : 0);
    for (var i:int=0; i < propertyValuesLength; i++)
    {
        // Get the property name and value.
        var propertyObject:Object = propertyValues[i];
        var propertyName:String = propertyObject.name;
        var propertyValue:* = propertyObject.value;

        // Process the property by name, either show the
        //value or show the cell address if bound to the
        //Excel spreadsheet.
        var bindingText:String = "";
        switch (propertyName)
        {
            case "xcChartData":
                bindingText=
                getPropertyBindDisplayName(propertyName);
                if (bindingText != null)
                {
                    // When bound the user cannot edit the value.
                    tiChartData.enabled = false;
                    // Show the address we are bound to.
                    tiChartData.text = bindingText;
```

```
            }
            else
            {
                tiChartData.text = "";
            }
            break;
        case "xcChartSeries":
            bindingText =
            getPropertyBindDisplayName(propertyName);
            if (bindingText != null)
            {
                tiChartSeries.enabled = false;
                tiChartSeries.text = bindingText;
            }
            else
            {
                tiChartSeries.text = "";
            }
            break;
        case "xcChartColor":
            cpChartColor.selectedColor = propertyValue;
        break;
        default:
            break;
    }
  }
}
```

Get Bound Property Display Names

The getPropertyBindDisplayName function is a utility function that's responsible for returning the Excel range address that a given custom component property is bound to once a user-initiated binding operation has been completed. This cell address value is traditionally used in all custom SAP BusinessObjects Dashboards components to visually indicate to the user through a text input control where in the Excel model the property is bound. The function code is listed here:

```
// Returns the bind display name or null if not bound.
private function
    getPropertyBindDisplayName(propertyName:String):String
{
```

```
    // Get the array of bindings for this property.
    var propertyBindings:Array = proxy.getBindings([propertyName]);
    if ((propertyBindings != null)       &&
        (propertyBindings.length  > 0) &&
        (propertyBindings[0].length > 0))
    {
        // We have at least one binding for this
        //property so pick the 1st one.
        // Note: [0][0] is 1st property in the array,
        //then 1st binding for that property.
        var bindingID:String = propertyBindings[0][0];
        return proxy.getBindingDisplayName(bindingID);
    }
    return null;
}
```

Initiating End-User Interaction Binding Operations

The initiateBind function is a utility function that is responsible for launching the SAP BusinessObjects Dashboards binding window as shown in Figure 11.5 and Excel range address that a given custom component property is bound to when the binding button for a particular property is clicked. This function allows the user to select or modify the range that a custom component's property is bound to.

Figure 11.5 Initiate Bind Window

Listed here is the function code needed to launch this utility to initiate data binding operations for a given custom component property:

```
// Allows the user to select the Excel spreadsheet cell
//to bind to an Xcelsius custom component property.
private function initiateBind(propertyName:String):void
{
    //If there is an existing binding for this property
    //show that in the Excel binding selection window.
    //Store the currentBindingID (null if there is no
    //current binding), we need this for "continueBinding".
```

```
    currentBindingID = null;
    var propertyBindings:Array = proxy.getBindings([propertyName]);
    if ((propertyBindings != null) && (propertyBindings.length > 0))
    {
        //Use the 1st binding address for the property.
        currentBindingID = propertyBindings[0];
    }

    //Store the name of the property that we are binding,
    //we need this when we "continueBinding".
    propertyToBind = propertyName;

    //Let the user choose where to bind to in the
    //Excel spreadsheet.
    proxy.requestUserSelection(currentBindingID);
}
```

Finalizing User-Initiated Binding Operations

The `continueBind` function is called as a result of the user clicking the OK button in the SAP BusinessObjects Dashboards binding control shown in Figure 11.5 once he has selected the range he wants to bind the custom component property to. This function performs the final steps via the `proxy` variable needed to establish a binding of any type between the SAP BusinessObjects Dashboards Excel model and a custom component property. Listed here is the function code needed to finalize or commit a data binding operation for a given custom component property. The remainder of the MXML code for this source code example is listed below the `continueBind` function code as well.

```
// Completes the binding when the user has finished selecting
//the cell to bind to or clear the binding.
private function continueBind(bindingID:String):void
{
    // Define common variables here.
    var propertyName:String = propertyToBind;
    var propertyValues:Array;
    var propertyObject:Object;
    var bindingAddresses:Array;

    // Clear any existing bindings - so we can re-bind.
    if (currentBindingID != null)
    {
```

```
        proxy.unbind(currentBindingID);
        currentBindingID = null;
}

// Process the property binding.
switch (propertyName)
{
    case "xcChartData":
        //User explicitly cleared binding,
        //do not create another.
        if ((bindingID == null) || (bindingID == ""))
        {

            //Fill the chart with an empty dataset
            propertyValues = proxy.getProperties([propertyName]);
            propertyObject = propertyValues[0];
            //Make sure we set the property
            //on the component as well.
            proxy.setProperty(propertyName, propertyObject.value);
            return;
        }
        //Display the range address.
        tiChartData.text = proxy.getBindingDisplayName(bindingID);

        proxy.bind("xcChartData",
            null, bindingID,
            BindingDirection.OUTPUT, "",
            OutputBindings.ARRAY2D);
        break;
    case "xcChartSeries":
        //User explicitly cleared binding,
        //do not create another.
        if ((bindingID == null) || (bindingID == ""))
        {
            propertyValues = proxy.getProperties([propertyName]);
            propertyObject = propertyValues[0];
            proxy.setProperty(propertyName, propertyObject.value);
            return;
        }

        // Display the range address.
        tiChartSeries.text = proxy.getBindingDisplayName(bindingID);
```

```
            proxy.bind("xcChartSeries",
            null, bindingID,
            BindingDirection.OUTPUT, "",
            OutputBindings.ARRAY2D);
            break;
        default:
            break;
    }
}
]]>
</mx:Script>
<mx:Canvas minWidth="268"  minHeight="350"
         width="100%" height="100%"
         backgroundColor="#FFFFFF">
    <mx:Label x="10" y="22" text="Chart Data"/>
    <mx:HRule y="39" height="10" right="10" left="10"/>
    <mx:TextInput id="tiChartData"
        y="57" right="42" left="10"/>
    <mx:Button y="56" right="10"  width="24"
        click="initiateBind('xcChartData');"
        icon="@Embed('com/assets/bind to cell.png')"/>
    <mx:Label x="10" y="87" text="Chart Series"/>
    <mx:Label x="10" y="152" text="Chart Color"/>
    <mx:HRule y="104" height="10" right="10" left="10"/>
    <mx:TextInput id="tiChartSeries" y="122"
                right="42" left="10"/>
    <mx:Button y="121" right="10"  width="24"
            click="initiateBind('xcChartSeries');"
            icon="@Embed('com/assets/bind to cell.png')"/>
    <mx:ColorPicker left="19" top="175"
                id="cpChartColor"
                change="proxy.setProperty('xcChartColor',
                cpChartColor.selectedColor)"/>
</mx:Canvas>
</mx:Application>
```

11.1.6   Proxy.Bind Explained

The SAP BusinessObjects Dashboards SDK `bind` function currently accepts ten parameters, the last five of which are optional. Let's take a look at the fundamental first six parameters, in order.

```
proxy.bind(
    "xcChartData",                <- Property
    null,                         <- Chain
    bindingID,                    <- BindingID
    BindingDirection.OUTPUT,      <- Direction
    "",                           <- InputMap
    OutputBindings.ARRAY2D        <- OutputMap
);
```

▶ **Property**
The name of the custom component property to be bound.

▶ **Chain**
An alternate array argument usually left blank for normal binding scenarios. This chain is usually reserved for subelement binding.

▶ **BindingID**
The SAP BusinessObjects Dashboards-generated `BindingID` of the custom component property to be bound.

▶ **Direction**
The `BindingDirection` constant that indicates whether the property is read, write, or read and write.

▶ **InputMap**
The `InputBindings` constant that indicates whether the property is:

SINGLETON, ARRAY, or ARRAY2D

▶ **OutputMap**
The `OutputBindings` constant that indicates whether the property is:

SINGLETON, ARRAY, ARRAY2D, ARRAY2DXYOBJECTS, or SORTED_OBJECT

11.2   Developing Basic Add-On Components

Now that we have a basic property sheet implemented and connected to the properties exposed by the custom component, we'll take a look at how the custom component's public properties are exposed, consumed, and set, and how they process their data output flow from SAP BusinessObjects Dashboards, where applicable. The full component code is listed in breakout form of the code and accompanying code explanations in order from top to bottom.

This custom component is designed as a basic example that leverages a base Flex charting component, CartesianChart, to expose a simple yet powerful and highly adaptable chart that allows for multiple series types to be combined in a single chart implementation.

Let's walk through the different custom component codes.

11.2.1 Main Component Initialization Event Handler and Import Statements

On line 2 below, we watch for the native Flex canvas event of creationComplete. When this event is triggered, in the function buildSeries() we perform the fundamental operation of the component, which is to build up the chart's data and series. The complete import code is listed below.

```
<?xml version="1.0" encoding="utf-8"?>
<mx:Canvas verticalScrollPolicy="off" creationPolicy="all"
  creationComplete="buildSeries()"
  horizontalScrollPolicy="off"
  xmlns:mx="http://www.adobe.com/2006/mxml" width="400" height="400">
<mx:Script>
<![CDATA[
    import mx.charts.series.ColumnSet;
    import mx.graphics.RadialGradient;
    import mx.graphics.LinearGradient;
    import mx.managers.ToolTipManager;
    import mx.charts.renderers.LineRenderer;
    import mx.charts.renderers.CircleItemRenderer;
    import mx.charts.series.AreaSeries;
    import mx.charts.series.LineSeries;
    import mx.graphics.Stroke;
    import mx.charts.series.ColumnSeries;
    import mx.graphics.GradientEntry;
    import mx.collections.ArrayCollection;
```

11.2.2 Private Variables

The private variable _columnSet is responsible for clustering any specified ColumnSeries for the Cartesian chart. The private variable _xcChartData is a bindable ArrayCollection that serves as the Cartesian chart's data provider. In the MXML code listed last in this section in the subsection "MXML Markup: Grid

Lines and Cartesian Chart," the Cartesian chart's `dataProvider` property is bound to the `_xcChartData` variable. Listed below are the private variables for the basic component.

```
private var _columnSet:ColumnSet = new ColumnSet();
```

```
[Bindable]private var _xcChartData:ArrayCollection = new ArrayCollection();
```

11.2.3   Public Chart Color Variable—xcChartColor

The public variable `xcChartColor` is set up as a read and write variable, and in each operation it is responsible for setting or getting the bindable internal variable `_xcChartColor`. In the MXML code listed last in this section in the subsection "MXML Markup: Grid Lines and Cartesian Chart," the Cartesian chart's color property is bound to this private variable that controls the color property of the chart. The public property function code is listed below.

```
[Bindable]private var _xcChartColor:Number = 0x000000;
public function get xcChartColor():Number
{
    return _xcChartColor;
}
public function set xcChartColor(value:Number):void
{
    _xcChartColor = value;;
}
```

11.2.4   Public Chart Series Variable

The public variable `xcChartSeries` is set up as a read and write variable, and in each operation it is responsible for setting or getting the internal variable `_xcChartSeries`. In the property sheet, this variable is defined as a two-dimensional array consumer, and each time the public variable is set, we cycle through this two-dimensional array variable to build the chart series for the Cartesian chart. Note that the function `buildSeries()` is called every time the `xcChartSeries` public set function is called, enabling the chart to completely redesign itself at SAP BusinessObjects Dashboards runtime any time the SAP BusinessObjects Dashboards dashboard designer decides it should be redesigned, making it highly adaptable. The function code is listed next:

```
private var _xcChartSeries:Array = new Array();
public function get xcChartSeries():Array
{
    return _xcChartSeries;
}

public function set xcChartSeries(value:Array):void
{
  try
  {
      _xcChartSeries = value;
      buildSeries();
   }
   catch(e:Error)
   {
      trace(e.getStackTrace());
   }
}
```

11.2.5 Public Chart Data Variable

The public variable xcChartData is set up as a read and write variable, and in each operation it is responsible for setting or getting the internal variable _xcChart-Data. In the property sheet, we have this variable defined as a two-dimensional array consumer, and each time the public variable is set, we cycle through this two-dimensional array variable to build the data for the Cartesian chart. Note that the building of the data is called every time the xcChartData public set function is called. Notice that we treat a two-dimensional array of data output from SAP BusinessObjects Dashboards exactly like any other two-dimensional array would be treated in ActionScript. We access the data in SAP BusinessObjects Dashboards by looping over the data, referencing rows and individual cells by using their ordinal position; that is, _xcChartData[rowPosition][columnPosition] = a single cell in the SAP BusinessObjects Dashboards Excel data model.

In this case, we always extract the user-specified series name for a given set of data, at position 0 on each row in the data. For brevity's sake, we then dynamically roll through each cell in any given row from position 1–N, to extract data values and associated tooltips. The data and tooltip values are specified as colon-separated in each cell in the SAP BusinessObjects Dashboards Excel model, that is, [data:tooltip] or 5,000:My Tooltip. The function code is listed next:

```
public function get xcChartData():Array
{
    return [];
}
/**
*Cycle through the 2D data Array,
*building data for each series
***/
public function set xcChartData(value:Array):void
{
    //Row[0]=SeriesName
    //Row[0-N]=Data:HTMLTooltip
    _xcChartData.removeAll();
    try
    {
        var columnStart:int = 0;
        var columnEnd:int = value[0].length;
        //Append each dataset to a
        //given month (month = key to each row)
        for (var i:int=columnStart; i<columnEnd; i++)
        {
            var data:Object = new Object();
            data.yLabel = value[0][i];
            if(data.yLabel == "" || data.yLabel == null)
                continue;
            //Build data for each month
            for (var i2:int = 1;i2<value.length;i2++)
            {
                //cell content format =
                //[dataValue : toolTip];
                var cell:String = String(value[i2][i]);
                var seriesName:String = value[i2][0];
                var dataValue:Number =
                    Number(cell.substring(
                        0,cell.indexOf(":")));
                var toolTip:String =
                    cell.substring(
                    cell.indexOf(":") + 1, cell.length);

                data[seriesName]= dataValue;
                data[seriesName + data.yLabel] = toolTip;
            }
```

```
            _xcChartData.addItem(data);
        }
    }
    catch(e:Error)
    {
        trace(e.getStackTrace());
    }
}
```

11.2.6 Chart Building Function

The `buildSeries` function is responsible for looping through the publicly set private variable, `xcChartSeries`. In the property sheet, this variable is defined as a two-dimensional array consumer, and each time the public variable is set, we cycle through this two-dimensional array variable to build the series for the Cartesian chart.

Notice that we treat a two-dimensional array of data output from SAP Business-Objects Dashboards exactly like any other two-dimensional array would be treated in ActionScript. We access the data in SAP BusinessObjects Dashboards by looping over the data, referencing rows and individual cells by using their ordinal position; that is, `_ xcChartSeries [rowPosition][columnPosition]` = a single cell in the SAP BusinessObjects Dashboards Excel data model.

For readability's sake, we have created an intermediary variable, called `series` that is an array. Essentially, the series variable represents a row of data from the SAP BusinessObjects Dashboards model, and each cell in the row provides us with a singular piece of information about the type of series the user wants to see on the chart and how he wants that series to be named and represented through the Cartesian chart. In this case, we require the user to place the series type in position 0, the series name in position 1, the series color in position 2, and the series alpha in position 3 as shown below.

```
var series:Array = _xcChartSeries[i]; RA row of data from Xcelsius
var seriesType:String = series[0];   RA cell (#1) of data from Xcelsius
var seriesName:String = series[1];   RA cell (#2) of data from Xcelsius
var seriesColor:Number = series[2];  RA cell (#3) of data from Xcelsius
var seriesAlpha:Number = series[3];  RA cell (#4) of data from Xcelsius
```

As we cycle through this data, in the switch statement below, we determine the type of series specified, style the series accordingly, and add the series to the Cartesian chart. The function code is listed here:

```
/***
*Cycle through the 2D series Array,
*styling and adding specified series types
***/
private function buildSeries():void
{
    if(chart == null)
        return;
    chart.series=new Array();
    columnSet = new ColumnSet();
    columnSet..type = "clustered";
    var st:Stroke;
    for(var i:int=0;i<_xcChartSeries.length;i++)
    {
        var series:Array = _xcChartSeries[i];
        var seriesType:String = series[0];
        var seriesName:String = series[1];
        var seriesColor:Number = series[2];
        var seriesAlpha:Number = series[3];
        //Add the correct series based on the
        //specified seriesType
        switch (seriesType.toLowerCase())
        {
            case "line":
                var ls:LineSeries = new LineSeries();
                ls.yField = seriesName;
                ls.name = seriesName;
                ls.displayName= seriesName;

                st = new Stroke();
                st.color=seriesColor;
                st.alpha=seriesAlpha;
                st.weight=2;
                st.pixelHinting=false;

                var linePointFill:RadialGradient =
                    new RadialGradient();
                linePointFill.entries =
```

```
            [new GradientEntry(seriesColor,
                              0.33, .5),
            new GradientEntry(seriesColor,
                              0.65, seriesAlpha)]

    ls.setStyle("fill",linePointFill);
    ls.setStyle("lineStroke",st);
    ls.setStyle("stroke",st);
    ls.setStyle("radius",3);
    ls.setStyle("form","curve");
    ls.setStyle("itemRenderer",
        new ClassFactory(
        mx.charts.renderers.CircleItemRenderer));
    ls.setStyle ("lineSegmentRenderer",
        new ClassFactory(
        mx.charts.renderers.LineRenderer));

    //Add the series
    chart.series.push(ls);
break;
case "column":
    var cs:ColumnSeries = new ColumnSeries();
    cs.yField = seriesName;
    cs.name = seriesName;
    cs.displayName= seriesName;

    var columnFill:LinearGradient =
        new LinearGradient();
    columnFill.entries =
        [new GradientEntry(seriesColor,
                    0.33, seriesAlpha),
    new GradientEntry(seriesColor,
                    0.65, seriesAlpha)]

    cs.setStyle("fill",columnFill);
    cs.alpha=seriesAlpha;

    //Add the series
    columnSet.series.push(cs);
break;
    case "area":
    var ar:AreaSeries = new AreaSeries();
```

```
      ar.yField = seriesName;
      ar.name = seriesName;
      ar.displayName= seriesName;

      st = new Stroke();
      st.color=seriesColor;
      st.alpha=1;
      st.weight=1;
      st.pixelHinting=false;

      var areaFill:LinearGradient =
          new LinearGradient();
      areaFill.entries =
          [new GradientEntry(seriesColor,
              0.33, .5),
          new GradientEntry(seriesColor,
              0.65, .6)]
      ar.setStyle("areaFill",areaFill);
      ar.setStyle("areaStroke",st);
      ar.setStyle("stroke",st);
      ar.setStyle("form","curve");
      //Add the series
      chart.series.push(ar);
    break;
  }
  chart.series.push(columnSet);
  }
}

private function formatDataTip(obj:Object):String
{
    return obj.item[obj.element.displayName +
        obj.item.yLabel];
}
```

11.2.7   Tooltip Function

The ability to finely control the information that end users see when they mouse over a data point in an SAP BusinessObjects Dashboards chart is an extremely important feature. By leveraging some standard Flex capabilities, you can return custom tooltips to your end users via this simple function that extracts information from the `obj:Object` parameter and returns your user-specified tooltip content, which may contain normal text as well as HTML. The function code is listed below.

```
private function formatDataTip(obj:Object):String
{
    return obj.item[obj.element.displayName + obj.item.yLabel];
}
```

11.2.8   MXML Markup: Grid Lines and Cartesian Chart

The MXML specified in this part of the component provides us with the type of grid lines we want to use for the chart as well as the basic implementation of the Cartesian chart's shell.

```
<mx:Array id="chartBg">
    <mx:GridLines alpha=".65" direction="both"/>
</mx:Array>
<mx:CartesianChart
        id="chart"
        width="100%" height="100%" showDataTips="true"
        color="{_xcChartColor}"
        dataTipFunction="formatDataTip"
        dataProvider="{_xcChartData}"
        backgroundElements="{chartBg}">
    <mx:horizontalAxis>
    <mx:CategoryAxis dataProvider="{_xcChartData}"
                    categoryField="yLabel"/>
        </mx:horizontalAxis>
    </mx:CartesianChart>
</mx:Canvas>
```

11.3   Creating Basic Component Packages

As a continuation of the custom chart component highlighted in this chapter, let's build a packager for it as the final step in preparing it for consumption by SAP BusinessObjects Dashboards.

11.3.1 Basic Component Packaging Steps

1. Open the *Packager.exe* application contained in the SAP BusinessObjects Dashboards SDK install directory *{Program Files}/SAP BusinessObjects\Xcelsius 4.0\ SDK.*

2. Enter the details related to your component as shown back in Figure 11.5, including the component name.

3. Select the VISUAL COMPONENTS tab and click ADD NEW COMPONENT.

4. Enter the component's class name, including its full package path, as well as any additional information about the component, including the path to the property sheet SWF file, component SWF file, and optional images you may define to represent the component in the SAP BusinessObjects Dashboards Object Browser and component list as shown in Figure 11.6.

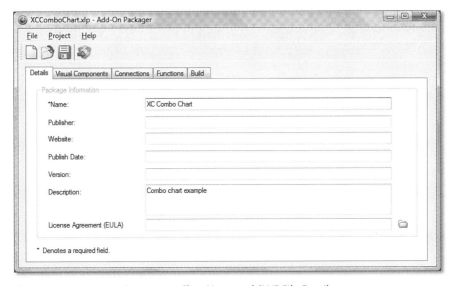

Figure 11.6 Enter your Component Class Name and SWF File Details

5. Save your packager file.

6. Build your XLX installer file and install it using the SAP BusinessObjects Dashboards Add-On Manager (in SAP BusinessObjects Dashboards, FILE • MANAGE ADD-ONS) as shown in Figure 11.7.

Figure 11.7 Build Your Component XLX Installer File

11.3.2 Packaging for Special Components

If your component isn't a visual component and is a data connection or a function component, use the CONNECTION and FUNCTION tabs accordingly to establish and build your component's installer file as shown in Figure 11.8.

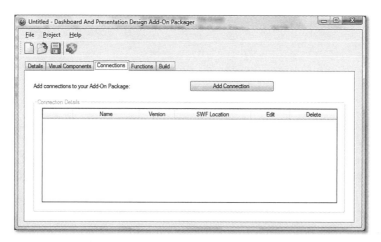

Figure 11.8 Connections Tab

11.3.3   Packaging Best Practices

While the packaging process is a simple act on the home stretch of creating your custom component, there are a handful of best practices you should adhere to during this very important process.

▶ Use relative paths when linking assets (SWF files, image files, text files) to your package.

▶ Use only one package per component to avoid installation conflicts in SAP BusinessObjects Dashboards. Each package contains a unique ID value that SAP BusinessObjects Dashboards inspects at install time and expects to be unique on a per-component basis.

▶ Don't copy components to avoid the conflict behavior described previously.

▶ Save and backup your packages, especially if you are developing products, because if a package is lost or corrupted, you'll once again run into the installation issue outlined above if you attempt to re-create the lost or corrupted package from the ground up.

11.4   Summary

In this chapter we went through a full property sheet and corresponding custom Flex component for SAP BusinessObjects Dashboards. We also dived deeper into the details of certain core pieces of SDK functionality, highlighted common functions where the SDK can be implemented, and gave an overview of how to develop a basic custom component for your SAP BusinessObjects Dashboards environment. With a functional component under our belts, we'll take a tour of some more advanced yet less advertised, very powerful concepts and utilities exposed by the SDK in Chapter 12.

A strong foundational knowledge of the advanced data binding and component communications abilities of the SDK will enable you to begin developing more advanced property sheet implementations.

12 Implement Advanced Custom Add-On Component Features

With a good grasp of the fundamentals of the SDK, we'll now take a look into the finer details of custom component development. We'll also cover some less-advertised but very powerful SDK features that when implemented can give you a more granular level of control over the user experience and component functionality, enabling you to take your custom components to the next level.

12.1 Implementing Advanced Property Sheet Features

As your components begin to get slightly more complex, it's necessary to begin to use parts of the SDK that are not fully documented and are less obvious to understand and leverage. This section will go through several common scenarios that fall under this description and will explain how to use these powerful features with short and concise functional code snippets.

▶ Subelement binding

▶ Persisting property sheet values

▶ Retrieving custom component property values

▶ Setting custom component property values

▶ Generating reusable property sheet patterns

▶ Communicating with external data services

12.1.1 Subelement Binding

Subelement binding is the act of binding one or more data ranges in the SAP BusinessObjects Dashboards Excel model to a single property in your custom component. A perfect example of this would be to define data for each series to a single component series property in an SAP BusinessObjects Dashboards column chart component. Conceptually this seems very simple, but as you get into the SDK how to actually implement this commonly requested functionality becomes less clear.

For this example, we have a property called `chartSeriesData` that needs to accomplish the goals outlined above. Using the SAP BusinessObjects Dashboards column chart's property sheet as a visual guide, let's take a look at how to set up the bindings and other functionality needed to support this feature through the SDK. Let's assume that the list containing the series names in Figure 12.1 has the ID `seriesList` in Flex.

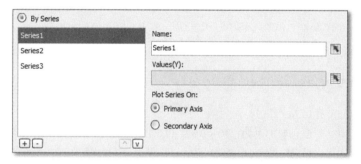

Figure 12.1 Series List Example

Subelement properties leverage the same `initiateBind` and `continueBind` functions found in the previous chapter's property sheet code walkthrough with a few exceptions.

1. We need to establish a private property sheet variable called `seriesBindingIDs` whose function is to maintain a persistent list of SAP BusinessObjects Dashboards binding IDs associated with the `chartSeriesData` property.

   ```
   private var _seriesDataBindingIDs:Array = new Array();
   ```

2. In the `initiateBind` function, we need to set the `currentBindingID` equal to the stored `bindingID` that resides at the selected index of the list control (`seriesList.selectedIndex`) in the private variable above.

```
if(propertyName == "chartSeriesData ")
{
    currentBindingID =
        _seriesDataBindingIDs [seriesList.selectedIndex];
      proxy.requestUserSelection(
        _seriesDataBindingIDs [seriesList .selectedIndex]);
}
```

3. In the `continueBind` function, we need to perform some general UI house-keeping and most importantly pass the chain `Array` variable and the `binding` `ID` to the `proxy.bind` function. This notifies the SDK that you intend to bind the specified `bindingID` at the given index specified by the chain variable.

```
case "chartSeriesData":
    //User explicitly cleared binding, do not create another.
    if ((bindingID == null) || (bindingID == ""))
    {
        txtSeriesData.enabled=false;
        txtSeriesData.text="";
        return;
    }

    txtSeriesData.enabled=false;

    //save this Binding ID in order to re-bind later
    _seriesDataBindingIDs[seriesList.selectedIndex] = bindingID;

    // create a chain to bind to
    //chartSeriesData[selectedIndex]
    var chain:Array = [seriesList.selectedIndex];

    proxy.bind("chartSeriesData", chain,
                bindingID, BindingDirection.OUTPUT,
                "", OutputBindings.ARRAY);
    break;
```

4. We also need to persist or save the private variable `seriesDataBindingIDs` stored IDs. This will enable us to save these values for the given XLF so that the next time the user interacts with the component, all of the subelement binding IDs will be saved and ready for use. This concept will be covered for this example in Sections 12.1.2 and 12.1.3.

These are the fundamental steps to establishing subelement binding. Other housekeeping operations should be performed based on the type of user interface controls used to manage these bindings; the proxy call `proxy.unbind` should also be used to clean up any legacy bindings; for example, if the user were to click the minus sign button in the list control above, to remove a given series. A fully functional subelement binding example is provided in the SDK samples directory (*{Program Files}\SAP BusinessObjects\Xcelsius 4.0\SDK\samples*) and is titled RSS-ConnectorWithTrigger.

12.1.2 Persisting Property Sheet Values

One of the less advertised but tremendously helpful features of the SDK is the ability to save variable values across sessions for a given XLF file. For example, you may want to save the selected tab index if your property sheet has multiple tabs and you want your property sheet to auto-select the tab where the user was last working. This is a basic use case, though you can store much more complex values if you want.

Let's take a look at what is needed to persist the binding IDs of the private `_seriesDataBindingIDs` variable mentioned in Section 12.1.1.

When the property sheet initializes, another event listener needs to be established alongside the standard SDK event listeners enumerated in Chapter 11.

```
proxy.addCallback(PropertySheetFunctionNamesSDK.GET_PROPERTIES_FUNCTION,
  getProperties);
```

The `GET_PROPERTIES_FUNCTION` event is triggered when the property sheet is closing or unloading and is responsible for saving or persisting any variable values you specify.

The following example illustrates how to save the set of `_seriesDataBindingIDs`. The essential duty that this function performs is to return to the SDK an array of name/value pair objects where the name is equal to the name of the property you want to persist and the value is equal to the value of the property you want to persist. It's important to note that the name property of the object can be named anything you want and does not and should not be named with the name of the corresponding custom component property it is used to assist.

```
private function getProperties():Array
{
    var persist:Array = new Array();
    var persistObject:Object = new Object();
    var seriesDataBindings:Object = new Object();
    for (var i:int=0; i< _seriesDataBindingIDs.length; i++)
    {
        seriesDataBindings[i] = _seriesDataBindingIDs [i];
    }
    persistObject.name = "seriesDataBindingIDs";
    persistObject.value = seriesDataBindings;
    persist.push(persistObject);

    return persist;
}
```

12.1.3 Retrieving Persisted Property Sheet Values

Now that we have persisted a value to the XLF file, let's take a look at how to retrieve that value when the property sheet initializes.

When the property sheet initializes, as in the `initValues()` function referenced in Chapter 11, we need to make a call to the following `loadProperties` function.

In the `loadProperties` function, we use the `proxy.getPersist` function of the SDK to retrieve the object we have persisted.

```
private function loadProperties():void
{
    //Get the property name and value of our seriesDataBindingIDs
    var propertyObject:Object =
      proxy.getPersist(["seriesDataBindingIDs"])[0];
    var propertyValue:* = persistProperties[0].value;
    for (var prop:String in propertyValue)
    {
        if (prop != null && prop != "")
        {
            _seriesDataBindingIDs[i] = propertyValue[prop];
        }
    }
}
```

The `proxy.getPersist` function of the SDK essentially accepts an array of persisted property names and returns a corresponding array of objects with the previously stored name and value properties we established in the `getProperties` function referenced above.

With these basic functions, you can store and retrieve any number of property values to either serve advanced property sheet concepts, such as Subelement binding, to store variable values for user experience management or for an unlimited variety of other purposes.

12.1.4 Setting Custom Component Property Values

Perhaps one of the most straightforward and concise concepts contained in the SDK is the ability to set a custom component's property explicitly, not through the traditional binding mechanism.

For example, if have a property on the custom component called `fontSize` that we want to set to a value of 12, the one line of code below allows us to set the value of that component property. This operation can be done for any data type supported by the SDK (arrays, strings, two-dimensional arrays, and so on).

```
proxy.setProperty('fontSize', 12);
```

12.1.5 Retrieving Custom Component Property Values

With the knowledge of how to set a custom component property, we'll undoubtedly need to extract that component's property value for use in the property sheet. Let's use the `fontSize` property example to see how we would extract the value of that property contained in the custom component.

Again, though not quite as concise, the process of extracting the currently stored value of a custom component property is fairly straightforward.

The `proxy.getProperties` function accepts an array of property names (in this case just a single element array) and returns an array of property values. Since we are only getting one property value below, we can reference position 0 in the array returned from `proxy.getProperties` and subsequently access its value property.

```
var fontSize:int = proxy.getProperties(['fontSize'])[0].value;
```

12.1.6 Generating Reusable Property Sheet Patterns

If you're creating a single component with no plans to develop future SAP BusinessObjects Dashboards Flex components, it is hardly worth the effort to abstract away repetitive property sheet functionality into a set of base classes and controls. However, if you are creating or could see creating three or more custom components in the future, we recommended creating at least some basic MXML components that abstract away the often repetitive boiler plate property sheet code necessary to facilitate binding operations and specifically subelement binding operations. If you don't take the time to create these components, you'll quickly find yourself deep in code that is repetitive in nature and difficult to debug and manage. By creating basic reusable patterns for SAP BusinessObjects Dashboards property sheets, your property sheet code base can be cut in half and in some cases, by more than 70%.

At least a 20% savings can be attributed to creating a single MXML `TextInput` component that serves as a bindable SAP BusinessObjects Dashboards text input property facilitator. With a couple of view states and a handful of properties, you'll quickly see that by leveraging the power and flexibility of the Flex framework and layout structure, you can quickly generate huge code savings with a bit of effort.

The primary three items suggested for creating MXML components or base ActionScript classes for are:

1. **The property sheet itself**
   Create a new ActionScript class that extends `mx.core.Application`, and add the common event handlers, variables, and repeated private and public functions found as a common thread through the majority of property sheets, that is:

```
package
{
    import mx.core.Application;
    import xcelsius.propertySheets.impl.
            PropertySheetExternalProxy;
    import xcelsius.propertySheets.interfaces.
            PropertySheetFunctionNames;
    import xcelsius.propertySheets.interfaces.
            PropertySheetFunctionNamesSDK;

    public class MyXCPropertySheet extends Application
    {
```

```
        public function MyXCPropertySheet()
        {
            addEventListener(FlexEvent.CREATION_COMPLETE,
                creationComplete);
            super();
        }

        protected function creationComplete(e:FlexEvent):void
        {
          proxy.addCallback(
          PropertySheetFunctionNamesSDK.RESPONSE_BINDING_ID,
          this.continueBind);

          proxy.callContainer(
          PropertySheetFunctionNames.INIT_COMPLETE_FUNCTION);

          proxy.addCallback(
          PropertySheetFunctionNamesSDK.GET_PROPERTIES_FUNCTION,
          getProperties);

          initValues();
        }

        /**
         * Fill the controls with the current values of the component.
         * **/
        protected function initValues():void
        {
        ...... . .
        }
          ...................................
          ...................................
    }
```

2. `initiateBind`

   As your property sheets grow in the number of custom component properties they are responsible for managing, the `initiateBind` function becomes a large source and primary contributor to property sheet clutter and code duplication, specifically in instances where subelement binding needs to be supported. By creating a generic `initiateBind` function with some additional embedded intelligence, you'll likely be able to account for 90% of use cases. In outlying cases where the base class' `initiateBind` function is not suitable, you still have the option to override the base class' function, implement any custom logic for your outlying use case, and then call the super class' `initiate Bind` method to support the rest of your property sheet's `initiateBind` functionality, that is, in your property sheet implementation that uses your ActionScript property sheet base class:

```
override protected function initiateBind(propertyName:String):void
{
    //Implement any custom needs here......
    super.initiateBind(propertyName);
}
```

3. `continueBind`

As your property sheets grow in the number of custom component properties they are responsible for managing, the `continueBind` function also becomes an additional large source and primary contributor to property sheet clutter and code duplication, specifically in instances where subelement binding needs to be supported. By creating a generic `continueBind` function with some additional embedded intelligence, this is another case where you'll likely be able to account for 90% of use cases. In outlying cases where the base class' `continueBind` function is not suitable, you still have the option to override the base class' function, implement any custom logic for your outlying use case, and then call the super class' `continueBind` method to support the rest of your property sheet's `continueBind` functionality, that is, in your property sheet implementation that uses your ActionScript property sheet base class:

```
override protected function continueBind(bindingID:String):void
{
    //Implement any custom needs here......
    super.continueBind (bindingID);
}
```

12.1.7 Communicating with External Data Services

Communicating with external data sources is possible in your Flex property sheets, just as it is in your Flex components. You may use the `HTTPService` class from Flex, the `WebService` class, a `URLLoader`, or any other remote data service type offered in the currently supported version of Flex for SAP BusinessObjects Dashboards. In the next section, we'll take a spin through a functional example of how to retrieve and display a simple remote XML file's contents through the SAP BusinessObjects Dashboards Excel model.

12.1.8 Implementing Advanced Component Features

With advanced property sheet functionality under our belts, let's take a look at how we can leverage the functionality where it matters most—in the custom component.

► Leveraging subelement binding from property sheets

► Advanced component overview using subelement binding plus a walkthrough of fully functional code

► Communicating with external data services

Leveraging Subelement Binding from Property Sheets

Though the process of establishing subelement binding for certain properties through the property sheet requires additional steps and binding management, using the subelement properties in your custom component is effortless and identical to the way you would interact with and process any other kind of array or two-dimensional array normal binding implementation, that is, where sub-Property is a subelement array:

```
for(var i:int = 0; i < subProperty.length; i++)
{
    //access each individual value just like usual
    var value:Object = subProperty[i];
}
```

Subelement Array Tricks

One feature that is of quite significant impact, is the ability to write multiple data ranges simultaneously back to the SAP BusinessObjects Dashboards Excel model through a single custom component property that leverages subelement binding direction of type BindingDirection.INPUT.

Let's say, for example, that we have created a subelement property binding called numericLists on the custom component. In this example, we're theoretically bound to five SAP BusinessObjects Dashboards Excel columns, each with five cells of data. Our simple yet powerful objective is, through the custom component, to set the values of these 25 combined cells to hold the numbers 1–25, respectively.

Listed below is the source code that will construct the subelement numeric list in a manner that will allow the SAP BusinessObjects Dashboards SDK to bind it to the multiple list destinations. This is a fairly simple example, though hopefully it sheds some light on more advanced, useful use cases.

This function cycles across five columns, creating a five-element array (or five cells), with each cell populated with its respective overall cell position in the entire collection, for each column array. Figure 12.2 shows the contents of the `numericListItems`.

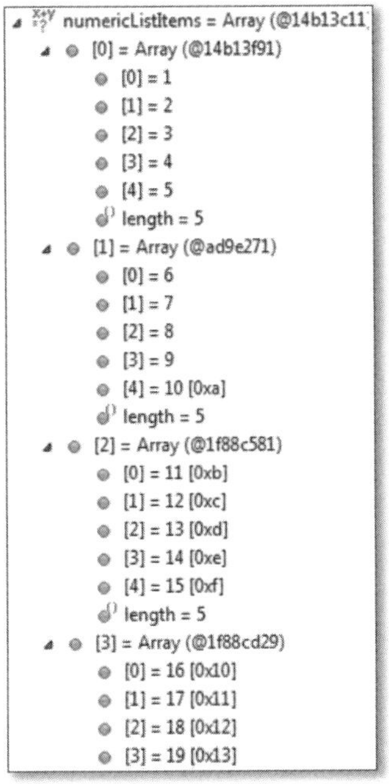

```
numericListItems = Array (@14b13c11)
   [0] = Array (@14b13f91)
      [0] = 1
      [1] = 2
      [2] = 3
      [3] = 4
      [4] = 5
      length = 5
   [1] = Array (@ad9e271)
      [0] = 6
      [1] = 7
      [2] = 8
      [3] = 9
      [4] = 10 [0xa]
      length = 5
   [2] = Array (@1f88c581)
      [0] = 11 [0xb]
      [1] = 12 [0xc]
      [2] = 13 [0xd]
      [3] = 14 [0xe]
      [4] = 15 [0xf]
      length = 5
   [3] = Array (@1f88cd29)
      [0] = 16 [0x10]
      [1] = 17 [0x11]
      [2] = 18 [0x12]
      [3] = 19 [0x13]
```

Figure 12.2 Numeric List Items Output from Flex Expressions Window

At the end of the function, we dispatch a simple event to let SAP BusinessObjects Dashboards know that the property has changed. Notifying SAP BusinessObjects Dashboards can be done a couple of ways. The most concise for our short code example is:

```
public var numericLists:Array = new Array();
private function generateSampleMultiList():void
{
    var numericListItems:Array = new Array();
    var cellValue:Number = 1;
    for(var numCols:int=0;numCols<5;numCols++)
```

```
    {
        var tmpListArry:Array = new Array();
        for(var i:int = 0; i < 5; i++)
        {
            tmpListArry[i] = cellValue;
            cellValue++;
        }
        numericListItems.push(tmpListArry);
    }
    numericLists = numericListItems;
    dispatchEvent(new Event("numericLists"));
}
```

Communicating with External Data Services

Communicating with external data sources can be achieved using a variety of different mechanisms and utilities. For this functional example, we'll connect to an XML feed on the *C:* drive and display its contents through a bindable two-dimensional input array into the SAP BusinessObjects Dashboards Excel model. The resulting property sheet properties are show in Figure 12.3.

- ▶ Property sheet code
- ▶ Component code
- ▶ End result

Figure 12.3 Property Sheet in Design Mode

Since we have already taken a verbose spin through very similar property sheet code, we've excluded a full description has been excluded and included the full source code for reference.

```
<?xml version="1.0" encoding="utf-8"?>
<mx:Application xmlns:mx="http://www.adobe.com/2006/mxml"
    layout="absolute" creationComplete="init()">
<mx:Script>
```

```
<![CDATA[
    import xcelsius.propertySheets.interfaces.
        PropertySheetFunctionNames;
    import xcelsius.propertySheets.interfaces.
        PropertySheetFunctionNamesSDK;
    import xcelsius.propertySheets.impl.
        PropertySheetExternalProxy;
    import xcelsius.binding.BindingDirection;
    import xcelsius.binding.tableMaps.input.InputBindings;
    import xcelsius.binding.tableMaps.output.OutputBindings;

    private var proxy:PropertySheetExternalProxy =
        new PropertySheetExternalProxy();
    private var propertyToBind:String;
    private var currentBindingID:String;

    private function init():void
    {
        proxy.addCallback(
        PropertySheetFunctionNamesSDK.RESPONSE_BINDING_ID,
        this.continueBind);
        proxy.callContainer(
        PropertySheetFunctionNames.INIT_COMPLETE_FUNCTION);
        initValues();
    }

    private function initValues():void
    {
        var props:Array =
            [
                "xmlUrl",
                "xmlData"
            ];

        //Process the array of values for the Xcelsius
        //custom component properties.
        var propertyValues:Array =
            proxy.getProperties(props);
        var propertyValuesLength:int =
            (propertyValues != null ?
            propertyValues.length : 0);
```

```
for (var i:int=0; i < propertyValuesLength; i++)
{
    // Get the property name and value.
    var propertyObject:Object = propertyValues[i];
    var propertyName:String = propertyObject.name;
    var propertyValue:* = propertyObject.value;

    //Process the property by name, either show the
    //value or show the cell address if
    // bound to the Excel spreadsheet.
    var bindingText:String = "";
    switch (propertyName)
    {
    case "xmlUrl":
        bindingText =
            getPropertyBindDisplayName(propertyName);
            if (bindingText != null)
            {
                txtXmlUrl.enabled = false;
                txtXmlUrl.text = bindingText;
            }
            else
            {
                txtXmlUrl.enabled = true;
                txtXmlUrl.text = propertyValue;
            }
     break;
    case "xmlData":
        bindingText = getPropertyBindDisplayName(propertyName);
        if (bindingText != null)
        {
            txtXmlData.enabled = false;
            txtXmlData.text = bindingText;
        }
        else
        {
            txtXmlData.text = "";
        }
     break;
    default:
     break;
    }
```

```
    }
}

/**
 * Allows the user to select the Excel spreadsheet
 * cell to bind to an Xcelsius custom component property.
 * **/
private function initiateBind(propertyName:String):void
{
    currentBindingID = null;
    var propertyBindings:Array = proxy.getBindings([propertyName]);
    if ((propertyBindings != null) &&
        (propertyBindings.length > 0))
    {
        // Use the 1st binding address for the property.
        currentBindingID = propertyBindings[0];
    }

    propertyToBind = propertyName;
    proxy.requestUserSelection(currentBindingID);
}

/**
 * Completes the binding when the user has finished
 * selecting the cell to bind to or cleared the binding.
 * **/
private function continueBind(bindingID:String):void
{
    var propertyName:String = propertyToBind;
    var propertyValues:Array;
    var propertyObject:Object;
    var bindingAddresses:Array;

    // Clear any existing bindings - so we can re-bind.
    if (currentBindingID != null)
    {
        proxy.unbind(currentBindingID);
        currentBindingID = null;
    }

    // Process the property binding.
    switch (propertyName)
```

```
      {
        case "xmlUrl":
            if ((bindingID == null) || (bindingID == ""))
            {
                txtXmlUrl.enabled=true;
                propertyValues = proxy.getProperties(
                             [propertyName]);
                propertyObject = propertyValues[0];
                txtXmlUrl.text = propertyObject.value;

                proxy.setProperty(propertyName,
                             propertyObject.value);
                return;
            }
            txtXmlUrl.enabled=false;
            txtXmlUrl.text = proxy.getBindingDisplayName(
                                  bindingID);
            proxy.bind("xmlUrl", null,
                bindingID, BindingDirection.OUTPUT,
                "", OutputBindings.SINGLETON);
         break;
        case "xmlData":
            if ((bindingID == null) || (bindingID == ""))
            {
                txtXmlData.enabled=false;

                propertyValues = proxy.getProperties(
                             [propertyName]);
                propertyObject = propertyValues[0];
                txtXmlData.text = "";
                return;
            }
            txtXmlData.enabled=false;
            txtXmlData.text = proxy.getBindingDisplayName(
                                     bindingID);
            proxy.bind("xmlData", null,
                bindingID, BindingDirection.BOTH,
                InputBindings.ARRAY2D,
                OutputBindings.ARRAY2D);
         break;
       default:
        break;
```

```
        }
    }
    /**
     * Returns the bind display name or null if not bound.
     * **/
    private function getPropertyBindDisplayName(propertyName:
      String):String
    {
        // Get the array of bindings for this property.
        var propertyBindings:Array = proxy.getBindings([propertyName]);
        if ((propertyBindings != null)    &&
            (propertyBindings.length > 0) &&
            (propertyBindings[0].length > 0))
        {
            // We have at least one binding for
            //this property so pick the 1st one.
            // Note: [0][0] is 1st property in the array,
            //then 1st binding for that property.
            var bindingID:String = propertyBindings[0][0];
            return proxy.getBindingDisplayName(bindingID);
        }
        return null;
    }

</mx:Script>
<mx:Canvas label="General"  width="100%" height="100%" >
<mx:RadioButtonGroup id="radiogroup1"/>
<mx:VBox height="100%" top="0" width="100%" x="0">
    <mx:Canvas width="100%" height="100%" borderStyle="solid">
        <mx:Label text="XML Data Destination"
            width="131" enabled="true" left="10" top="70"/>
        <mx:Label text="XML URL" width="106"
            enabled="true" left="10" top="16"/>
        <mx:TextInput id="txtXmlData" enabled="false"
            y="85" right="69" left="10"/>
        <mx:TextInput id="txtXmlUrl" y="40"
            visible="true" right="69" left="10"
            change="proxy.setProperty('xmlUrl', txtXmlUrl.text)"/>
        <mx:Button y="40"  icon="@Embed('bind.png')"
            click="initiateBind('xmlUrl');"
            width="24" right="35"/>
```

```
        <mx:Button y="85"  icon="@Embed('bind.png')"
             click="initiateBind('xmlData');"
             width="24" right="35"/>
    </mx:Canvas>
</mx:VBox>
</mx:Canvas>
</mx:Application>
```

Component Code

The custom XML connector component, based on the canvas object in Flex for simplicity so you can drag and drop the connector onto the SAP BusinessObjects Dashboards designer. This component could very easily be turned into a data connection by using the CONNECTION tab in the SAP BusinessObjects Dashboards Packager. The objective of the custom XML component is to process a simple XML payload in the following format.

```
<root>
    <row cell1Value="1" cell2Value="1.2"/>
    <row cell1Value="2" cell2Value="2.2"/>
    <row cell1Value="3" cell2Value="3.2"/>
    <row cell1Value="4" cell2Value="4.2"/>
    <row cell1Value="5" cell2Value="5.2"/>
    <row cell1Value="6" cell2Value="6.2"/>
</root>
```

There is no doubt that SAP BusinessObjects Dashboards has built-in utilities that are quite adept at processing XML. This demonstration, however, is to serve as a primer for connecting to a remote data source and pushing that data up through to the SAP BusinessObjects Dashboards Excel model through a custom component.

Import Statements and Public Component Variables for SAP BusinessObjects Dashboards

In the first half of this component, we import the necessary namespaces so we can leverage the Flex HTTPService class. In this section we also specify the private HTTPService variable and establish the public xmlUrl property as well as the two-dimensional array output property for SAP BusinessObjects Dashboards:

xmlData. xmlData's getter is tagged as a bindable event to force SAP Business-Objects Dashboards Excel updates.

```
import flash.events.Event;
import flash.xml.XMLNode;
import mx.containers.Canvas;
import mx.controls.Alert;
import mx.rpc.events.FaultEvent;
import mx.rpc.events.ResultEvent;
import mx.rpc.http.HTTPService;

public class XmlConnector extends Canvas
{
    private var httpsvc:HTTPService = new HTTPService();

    private var _xmlUrl:String = "";
    public function set xmlUrl(value:String):void
    {
        _xmlUrl = value;
        getXML();
    }
    public function get xmlUrl():String
    {
        return _xmlUrl;
    }

    private var _xmlData:Array = new Array();
    public function set xmlData(value:Array):void
    {
        _xmlData = value;
    }
    [Bindable(event="xmlData")]
    public function get xmlData():Array
    {
        return _xmlData;
    }
```

Listening for Our HTTPService Result

In this section we add the necessary event listeners to the HTTPService, call the super class' constructor in the constructor, and subsequently call the getXML() function so the service requests data on load. The getXML() function is a simple call to the specified XML path. At line 64, we receive the result event of the HTTPService request. The function code is listed here:

```
/**
 * Constructor
 * **/
public function XmlConnector()
{
    super();
    httpsvc.resultFormat = "xml";
    httpsvc.useProxy = false;
    httpsvc.addEventListener(ResultEvent.RESULT,httpserviceResult);
    httpsvc.addEventListener(FaultEvent.FAULT,httpFaultError);
    getXML();
}

/**
 * Call Http service
 ***/
private function getXML():void
{
    if(_xmlUrl == "" || _xmlUrl == null){return;}
    httpsvc.url = _xmlUrl;
    httpsvc.send();
}
```

HTTPService Result Processing

Once we receive the event result of the HTTPService call, we parse the XML, creating a two-dimensional array of cell data that SAP BusinessObjects Dashboards can consume through binding via its Excel model. The function code is listed here:

```
/**
 * Http service result listener
 ***/
private function httpserviceResult(e:ResultEvent):void
{
    for each(var xn:XMLNode in e.result.childNodes)
    {
        var row:Array = new Array();
        row.push(xn.attributes.cell1Value);
```

```
        row.push(xn.attributes.cell2Value);
        _xmlData.push(row);
    }
    dispatchEvent(new Event("xmlData"));
}
```

HTTPService Fault Handling

The `httpFaultError` function catches any error encountered by the `HTTPService` call. Here we have implemented a simple alert message, though something more sophisticated, like sending an error message to the SAP BusinessObjects Dashboards model so the SAP BusinessObjects Dashboards designer can define the user error experience, could easily be done as well. The function code is listed below.

```
private function httpFaultError(e:FaultEvent):void
{
Alert.show("Unable to load the following file: " + _xmlUrl + "." +
  "Please check to make sure that the specified  file " +
  "exists and is accessible.","I/O Error");
}
```

12.1.9   Communicating at the Application Level

A commonly requested feature in SAP BusinessObjects Dashboards custom components is the ability to share data between custom components, across separate SWF files. Usually, developers turn to Flash Vars or other methods of workaround, which present limitations and additional work. Fortunately, there is another more streamlined approach if you want to share data between two SAP BusinessObjects Dashboards SWFs. This method comes with a couple of caveats, the first being that the SWFs need to be loaded via the SAP BusinessObjects Dashboards SWF Loader component, and second, that the two SWFs share the same application domain (the THIS option on the SAP BusinessObjects Dashboards SWF Loader). If you can live with these two requirements, this can be a powerful approach for passing large volumes of data from component to component while completely bypassing the Excel model, if desired.

To accomplish component-to-component communication across SWFs is fairly straightforward. All that is needed is a `ModelLocator`-type singleton that both components share data through. The components don't even need to be the same; they just need to refer to the same `ModelLocator` class and corresponding `ModelLocator` variables to share data. A full code example and walkthrough can be found in Chapter 13.

12.1.10 Additional Packaging Features

Packaging visual components and connections through the SAP BusinessObjects Dashboards Packager utility are very similar processes, with a key difference being that custom components packaged using the Connections tab end up in the data menu as opposed to the component browser, for standard visual components. However, creating a function package or installer XLX is a bit different, yet even more concise. A good example of a simple SAP BusinessObjects Dashboards function component, complete with source code and packager can be found in the SAP BusinessObjects Dashboards SDK samples at:

Program Files SAP BusinessObjects\Xcelsius 4.0\SDK\samples\XcelsiusSDKfunctions

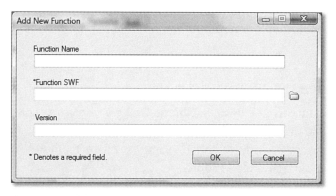

Figure 12.4 Add New Function Dialog

To use functions that have been created in your XLX installer file, add the custom component via the Add-On Manager and begin using the function in the SAP BusinessObjects Dashboards Excel model just as you would a native Excel function. To add a component in as a function as shown in Figure 12.4, click the Add Function button on the Function tab of the SAP BusinessObjects Dashboards component packager.

12.2   Where to Go from Here: Tips, Tricks, and Resources

As the SDK community continues to flourish, more resources are coming to the surface that will help developers who are new to the SAP BusinessObjects Dashboards SDK.

Below are some useful links that cover fundamental SDK subject matter and provide a forum for SAP BusinessObjects Dashboards SDK Q&A as well as helpful Flex links.

▸ SAP BusinessObjects Dashboards Blog: *EverythingXcelsius.com*

▸ Forum: *http://forums.sdn.sap.com/forum.jspa?forumID=466*

▸ Getting Started with Flex: *http://www.adobe.com/devnet/flex/*

12.3   Summary

In this chapter, we described some advanced yet commonly encountered and less-documented features of the SDK. This introduction provides a foundational knowledge of the advanced data binding and component communications abilities of the SDK, enabling you to begin developing more advanced property sheet implementations.

After reading this chapter, you'll know how to implement a Flex bubble chart with a runtime-controllable series color, tooltips (HTML or plain text), chart data, and write-back functionality to the SAP BusinessObjects Dashboards Excel model.

13 Hands-On: Develop Your Custom Add-On Component

In this chapter we'll take a hands-on, step-by-step approach to creating two commonly implemented custom component types: a custom Flex chart and an application-level data sharing component. The components that will result from this walkthrough are fairly short in the amount of source code required and are concise, with a few key properties (listed and explained below) and quick-win benefits. The overall goal of the custom chart we'll be creating is to implement a Flex bubble chart with a runtime-controllable series color, tooltips (HTML or plain text), chart data, and write-back functionality to the SAP BusinessObjects Dashboards Excel model in the form of a selected data and selected tooltip property. The overall goal of the data-sharing component is to illustrate how data can be passed between two separate SWF files while bypassing the Excel model.

13.1 Creating the Chart

Before we get started, here is a brief explanation of the custom properties.

- ▶ Bindable chart data: `xcChartData`
  - ▷ Binding type: `OutputBindings.ARRAY`
  - ▷ Binding direction: `BindingDirection.OUTPUT`
  - ▷ Purpose: To pass an array of cells to the bubble chart component, each cell with a CSV (comma separated value) format of:
  - ▷ valueX,valueY,radius,tooltip

- ▸ valueX – the X position of a given bubble
- ▸ valueY – the Y position of a given bubble
- ▸ radius - the radius of a given bubble
- ▸ tooltip – the tooltip, HTML or plain text, for a given bubble
- ▶ Bindable series color:
  - ▸ Binding type: `OutputBindings.SINGLETON`
  - ▸ Binding direction: `BindingDirection.OUTPUT`
  - ▸ Purpose: To pass a color value to control the chart's `SolidColor` color property.
- ▶ Bindable selected tooltip – Input
  - ▸ Binding type: `InputBindings.SINGLETON`
  - ▸ Binding direction: `BindingDirection.INPUT`
  - ▸ Purpose: To pass the selected tooltip value to a single cell in the SAP BusinessObjects Dashboards Excel model.
- ▶ Bindable selected data – Input
  - ▸ Binding type: `InputBindings.SINGLETON`
  - ▸ Binding direction: `BindingDirection.INPUT`
  - ▸ Purpose: To pass the selected radius/value to a single cell in the SAP BusinessObjects Dashboards Excel model.

13.2 Creating the Flex Component and Property Sheet Project

The first step in creating a custom component for Flex is to create a Flex project and file structure for your component, if one doesn't already exist.

Open Flex Builder and select FILE • NEW • FLEX PROJECT as shown in Figure 13.1.

Name your project *CustomBubbleChart* and select a logical location for the project to reside on your computer as shown in Figure 13.2. Click NEXT.

Select the LIBRARY PATH tab and click the ADD SWC... button. Browse to locate the *xcelsiusframework.swc* file *{Program Files}\SAP BusinessObjects\Xcelsius 4.0\SDK\bin* and click OPEN as shown in Figures 13.3 and 13.4.

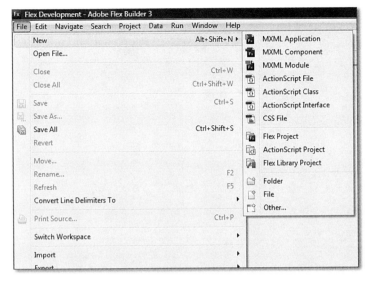

Figure 13.1 Creating a New Flex Project

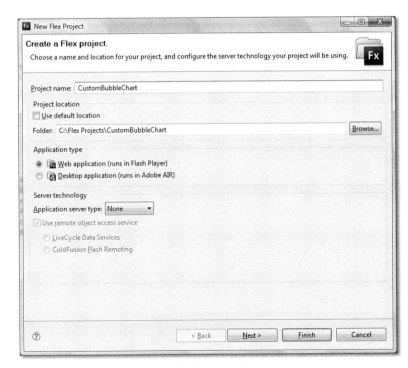

Figure 13.2 Name the Project and Select a Location

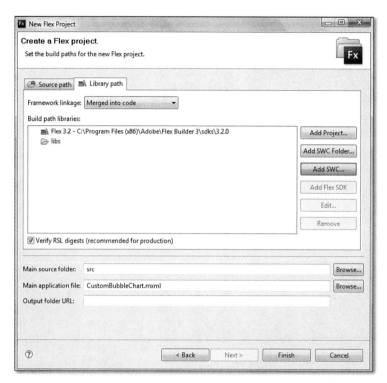

Figure 13.3 Add an SWC to the Flex Project

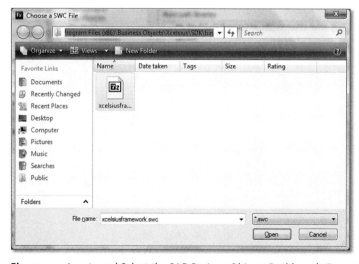

Figure 13.4 Locate and Select the SAP BusinessObjects Dashboards Framework.swc Library

Click FINISH to create your project as shown in Figure 13.5.

Figure 13.5 Click "Finish" to Create Your Flex Project

Select PROJECT • PROPERTIES as shown in Figure 13.6 to change the Flex compiler version to the 2.0.1 Hotfix 3 SDK version. Click the Flex Compiler link in the left pane, select the USE A SPECIFIC SDK option, and select the proper SDK as shown in Figure 13.7. Click OK.

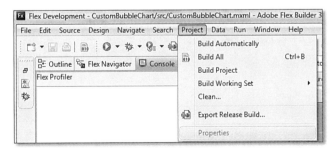

Figure 13.6 Navigating to Project Properties

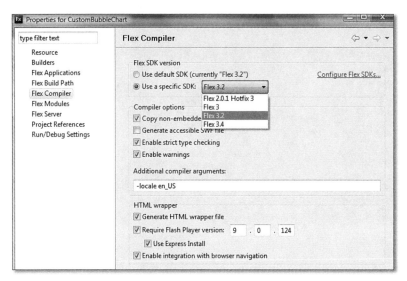

Figure 13.7 Setting the Proper SDK Version

Create three new Flex application files for your project and title them:

- ▶ CustomBubbleChartPropertySheet
- ▶ CustomBubbleChart
- ▶ CustomBubbleChartTestContainer

Create a package structure under the *src* folder to match Figure 13.8.

Figure 13.8 Project Folder Structure

Create a new MXML component under the *exc* folder by right-clicking the *exc* folder and selecting the MXML COMPONENT option as shown in Figure 13.9. As shown in Figure 13.10, choose the canvas component as the component's base, name it BubbleChartBase, and click OK.

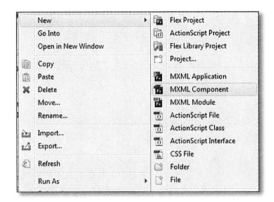

Figure 13.9 Create a New MXML Component

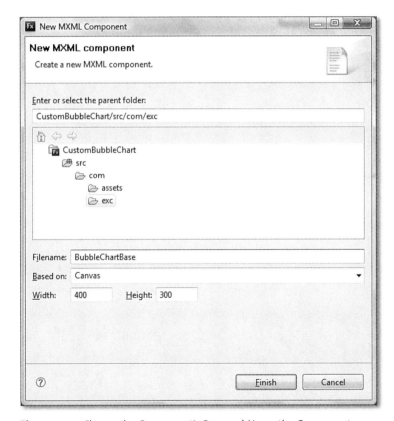

Figure 13.10 Choose the Component's Base and Name the Component

13.2.1 Creating the Flex Property Sheet

Open the *CustomBubbleChartPropertySheet.mxml* application file.

1. Add an `applicationComplete` event listener in the opening MXML application tag.

```
<?xml version="1.0" encoding="utf-8"?>
<mx:Application xmlns:mx="http://www.adobe.com/2006/mxml"
  layout="absolute" applicationComplete="init();">
```

2. Insert a script into the MXML file and import the necessary classes.

```
<mx:Script>
<![CDATA[

import mx.containers.*;
import mx.controls.*;
import mx.core.Container;
import mx.events.FlexEvent;
import xcelsius.binding.BindingDirection;
import xcelsius.binding.tableMaps.input.InputBindings;
import xcelsius.binding.tableMaps.output.OutputBindings;
import xcelsius.propertySheets.impl.PropertySheetExternalProxy;
import xcelsius.propertySheets.interfaces.PropertySheetFunctionNamesSDK;
```

3. Create the necessary private variables for the SDK.

```
private var proxy:PropertySheetExternalProxy = new PropertySheetExte
rnalProxy();
private var propertyToBind:String;
private var currentBindingID:String;
```

4. Create the `init()` function that will fire when the property sheet's `applicationComplete` event fires.

```
private function init():void
{
    proxy.addCallback(
        PropertySheetFunctionNamesSDK.RESPONSE_BINDING_ID,
        this.continueBind);
    proxy.callContainer(
        PropertySheetFunctionNamesSDK.INIT_COMPLETE_FUNCTION);
    initValues();
}
```

5. Create the `initValues()` function that will extract the custom component public variable values and populate the property sheet's controls accordingly.

```
private function initValues():void
{
    var propertyValues:Array = proxy.getProperties(
            ["xcChartColor","xcChartData",
            "selectedData","selectedTooltip",
            "xcSeriesColor"]);

    var propertyValuesLength:int = (propertyValues != null ?
                                propertyValues.length : 0);
    for (var i:int=0; i < propertyValuesLength; i++)
    {
        var propertyObject:Object = propertyValues[i];
        var propertyName:String = propertyObject.name;
        var propertyValue:* = propertyObject.value;
        var bindingText:String = "";
        switch (propertyName)
        {
            case "xcChartColor":
                cpChartColor.selectedColor = propertyValue;
            break;
            case "xcChartData":
                bindingText = getPropertyBindDisplayName(
                            propertyName);
                if (bindingText != null)
                {
                    tiChartData.text = bindingText;
                }
                else
                {
                    tiChartData.text = "";
                }
                break;
            case "selectedData":
                bindingText =
                    getPropertyBindDisplayName(propertyName);
                if (bindingText != null)
                {
                    tiSelectedData.text = bindingText;
                }
                else
```

```
                {
                    tiSelectedData.text = "";
                }
                break;
            case "selectedTooltip":
                bindingText =
                    getPropertyBindDisplayName(propertyName);
                if (bindingText != null)
                {
                    tiSelectedTooltip.text = bindingText;
                }
                else
                {
                    tiSelectedTooltip.text = "";
                }
                break;
            case "xcSeriesColor":
                bindingText =
                    getPropertyBindDisplayName(propertyName);
                if (bindingText != null)
                {
                    tiSeriesColor.text = bindingText;
                }
                else
                {
                    tiSeriesColor.text = "";
                }
                break;
            default:
                break;
        }
    }
}
```

6. Create the generic helper functions `getPropertyBindDisplayName`, and `initiateBind`.

```
private function getPropertyBindDisplayName
    (propertyName:String):String
{
    var propertyBindings:Array =
        proxy.getBindings([propertyName]);
    if ((propertyBindings != null)    &&
```

```
        (propertyBindings.length > 0) &&
        (propertyBindings[0].length > 0))
    {
        var bindingID:String = propertyBindings[0][0];
        return proxy.getBindingDisplayName(bindingID);
    }
    return null;
}

private function initiateBind(propertyName:String):void
{
    currentBindingID = null;
    var propertyBindings:Array =
        proxy.getBindings([propertyName]);
    if ((propertyBindings != null) &&
        (propertyBindings.length > 0))
    {
        currentBindingID = propertyBindings[0];
    }
    propertyToBind = propertyName;
    proxy.requestUserSelection(currentBindingID);
}
```

7. Create the binding commit function, `continueBind`.

```
private function continueBind(bindingID:String):void
{
    var propertyName:String = propertyToBind;
    var propertyValues:Array;
    var propertyObject:Object;
    var bindingAddresses:Array;

    if (currentBindingID != null)
    {
        proxy.unbind(currentBindingID);
        currentBindingID = null;
    }

    switch (propertyName)
    {
        case "xcChartData":
            if ((bindingID == null) || (bindingID == ""))
            {
                return;
```

```
        }
        tiChartData.text =
            proxy.getBindingDisplayName(bindingID);
        proxy.bind("xcChartData", null, bindingID,
            BindingDirection.OUTPUT, "",
            OutputBindings.ARRAY);
    break;
case "selectedTooltip":
    if ((bindingID == null) || (bindingID == ""))
    {
        return;
    }
    tiChartData.text =
        proxy.getBindingDisplayName(bindingID);
    proxy.bind("selectedTooltip", null, bindingID,
        BindingDirection.INPUT,
        InputBindings.SINGLETON, "");
    break;
case "selectedData":
    if ((bindingID == null) || (bindingID == ""))
    {
        return;
    }
    tiChartData.text =
        proxy.getBindingDisplayName(bindingID);
    proxy.bind("selectedData", null, bindingID,
        BindingDirection.INPUT,
        InputBindings.SINGLETON, "");
    break;
case "xcSeriesColor":
    if ((bindingID == null) || (bindingID == ""))
    {
        return;
    }
    tiSeriesColor.text =
        proxy.getBindingDisplayName(bindingID);
    proxy.bind("xcSeriesColor", null, bindingID,
        BindingDirection.OUTPUT, "",
        OutputBindings.SINGLETON);

    break;
```

```
        default:
         break;
    }
}
```

8. Implement the XML layout and controls.

```xml
<mx:Canvas minWidth="268"  minHeight="350" width="100%"
            height="100%" backgroundColor="#FFFFFF">
<mx:Label x="10" y="22" text="Chart Data"/>
<mx:Label x="10" y="277" text="Chart Color"/>
<mx:HRule y="39" height="10" right="10" left="92"/>
<mx:HRule y="295" height="10" right="10" left="92"/>
<mx:TextInput enabled="false" id="tiChartData" y="57" right="42"
            left="92"/>
<mx:Button y="56" right="10"  width="24"
            click="initiateBind('xcChartData');"
            icon="@Embed('com/assets/bind.png')"/>
<mx:Label x="10" y="87" text="Selected Data Value"/>
<mx:HRule y="104" height="10" right="10" left="92"/>
<mx:TextInput enabled="false" id="tiSelectedData" y="122" right="42"
            left="92"/>
<mx:Label x="10" y="152" text="Selected Tooltip Value"/>
<mx:HRule y="169" height="10" right="10" left="92"/>
<mx:TextInput enabled="false" id="tiSelectedTooltip" y="187"
            right="42" left="92"/>
<mx:Button y="186" right="10"  width="24"
            click="initiateBind('selectedTooltip');"
            icon="@Embed('com/assets/bind.png')"/>
<mx:Label x="10" y="217" text="Series Color"/>
<mx:HRule y="234" height="10" right="10" left="92"/>
<mx:TextInput enabled="false" id="tiSeriesColor" y="252" right="42"
            left="92"/>
<mx:Button y="251" right="10"  width="24"
            click="initiateBind('xcSeriesColor');"
            icon="@Embed('com/assets/bind.png')"/>
<mx:Button y="121" right="10"  width="24"
            click="initiateBind('selectedData');"
            icon="@Embed('com/assets/bind.png')"/>
<mx:ColorPicker id="cpChartColor"
                change="proxy.setProperty('xcChartColor',
                  cpChartColor.selectedColor)"
                x="92" y="313"/>
</mx:Canvas>
```

13.2.2 Creating the Flex Component

1. Open the *BubbleChartBase.mxml* component file.

2. Add a `creationComplete` event listener in the opening MXML tag.

```
<?xml version="1.0" encoding="utf-8"?>
<mx:Canvas creationComplete="buildChart()"
           xmlns:mx="http://www.adobe.com/2006/mxml"
           width="400" height="300">
```

3. Insert a script into the MXML file and import the necessary classes.

```
<mx:Script>
<![CDATA[
    import mx.collections.ArrayCollection;
```

4. Create the chart data provider private variable for the custom component.

```
[Bindable]private var _chartDp:ArrayCollection=new ArrayCollection();
```

5. Create the private and public custom component properties for SAP Business-
Objects Dashboards.

```
private var _xcChartData:Array=new Array();
public function set xcChartData(value:Array):void
{
    _xcChartData = value;
    buildChart();
}
public function get xcChartData():Array
{
    return _xcChartData;
}
[Bindable]private var _xcChartColor:Number = 0x000000;
public function get xcChartColor():Number
{
    return _xcChartColor;
}
public function set xcChartColor(value:Number):void
{
    _xcChartColor = value;;
}
[Bindable]private var _xcSeriesColor:Number = 0x0000ff;
public function get xcSeriesColor():Number
{
    return _xcSeriesColor;
}
```

```
public function set xcSeriesColor(value:Number):void
{
    _xcSeriesColor = value;;
}
private var _selectedTooltip:String="";
public function set selectedTooltip(value:String):void
{
    _selectedTooltip = value;
}
[Bindable(event="selectedTooltip")]
public function get selectedTooltip():String
{
    return _selectedTooltip;
}

private var _selectedData:Object;
public function set selectedData(value:Object):void
{
    _selectedData = value;
}
[Bindable(event="selectedData")]
public function get selectedData():Object
{
    return _selectedData;
}
```

6. Create the *buildChart* function to process the data from SAP BusinessObjects
Dashboards into data the bubble chart can display.

```
private function buildChart():void
{
    _chartDp.removeAll();
    for each(var s:String in _xcChartData)
    {
        var a:Array = s.split(",");
        var o:Object = new Object();
        o.valueX=a[0];
        o.valueY=a[1];
        o.radius=a[2];
        o.tooltip=a[3];
        _chartDp.addItem(o);
    }
}
```

7. Create the `formatDataTip` function to process mouse-over tooltips for the bubble series and to push the `selectedData` and `selectedTooltip` bindable properties to the SAP BusinessObjects Dashboards Excel model.

```
private function formatDataTip(obj:Object):String
{
    _selectedTooltip = obj.item.tooltip;
    _selectedData = obj.item.radius;
    dispatchEvent(new Event("selectedTooltip"));
    dispatchEvent(new Event("selectedData"));
    return "<b>" + obj.element.displayName + "</b>" + "\n" +
      obj.item.tooltip;
}
```

8. Implement the XML layout and controls.

```
<mx:SolidColor id="sc1" color="{_xcSeriesColor}" alpha=".5"/>
<mx:BubbleChart dataTipFunction="formatDataTip" showDataTips="true"
color="{_xcChartColor}" dataProvider="{_chartDp}" id="bubbleChart" w
idth="100%" height="100%">
    <mx:series>
        <mx:BubbleSeries
            fill="{sc1}"
                xField="valueX"
                yField="valueY"
                radiusField="radius"
                displayName="Bubble Series 1"

    </mx:series>
    <mx:verticalAxis >
        <mx:LinearAxis id="v1"  />
    </mx:verticalAxis>
    <mx:horizontalAxis >
        <mx:LinearAxis id="h1"  />
    </mx:horizontalAxis>
    <mx:verticalAxisRenderer>
        <mx:AxisRenderer tickLength="2" showLine="true"
                        showLabels="true"/>
    </mx:verticalAxisRenderer>
    <mx:horizontalAxisRenderer>
        <mx:AxisRenderer tickLength="2" showLine="true"
                        showLabels="true"/>
    </mx:horizontalAxisRenderer>
</mx:BubbleChart>
```

13.3   Creating the Flex Test Container

As specified in the SDK Best Practices, a local test container should always be established to test your custom component as thoroughly as possible before importing it for testing in the SAP BusinessObjects Dashboards environment. In this case, the test container will be very lean but will enable you to step through its behavior at runtime to ensure that everything is functioning as expected in Flex.

Open the *CustomBubbleChartTestContainer.mxml* component file and insert the following code, which sets the chart's data provider as expected from SAP BusinessObjects Dashboards.

```
<?xml version="1.0" encoding="utf-8"?>
<mx:Application creationComplete="init()"
               xmlns:mx="http://www.adobe.com/2006/mxml"
               layout="absolute" xmlns:exc="com.exc.*">
<mx:Script>
    <![CDATA[
    private function init():void
    {
        bubbleChart.xcChartData =
            ["1,5,20,1,<html><i><b>tooltip0</b></i>",
            "10,20,50,1,tooltip1","10,10,30,1,tooltip2"]
    }
]]>
</mx:Script>
<exc:BubbleChartBase id="bubbleChart"/>
</mx:Application>
```

13.4   Creating the Packager and SAP BusinessObjects Dashboards XLX Add-On

Now that we have the property sheet and custom component SWF files ready, the next step is to create the packager file to generate the XLX installer file.

1. Open the Packager application and create a new package called *CustomBubble-Chart.xlp*.

2. Select the Visual Components tab, click Add Component, and specify the information as shown in Figure 13.11.

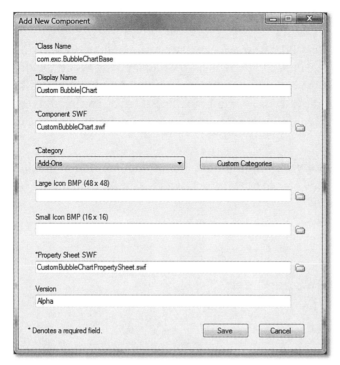

Figure 13.11 Specify the Component Details

3. Click BUILD to generate the XLX.

4. Open SAP BusinessObjects Dashboards, launch the Add-On Manager and browse to and install your newly created XLX installer file.

5. Restart SAP BusinessObjects Dashboards and drag your new add-on onto the SAP BusinessObjects Dashboards designer. You are now ready to begin testing your new component.

13.5 Creating the Data Sharing Component

In this example, we'll walk through the code needed to achieve application-level data sharing between two SWF files in an SAP BusinessObjects Dashboards application. Since we covered property sheet, project setup, and packaging concepts in detail in Section 31.1, the property sheet code has been listed in this example without comment, and the project setup has been excluded. For step-by-step instructions on general project setup, please refer to Section 13.1.

To start, let's dive straight into the component side of the equation. First, we'll take a look at the backbone of the operation, the ModelLocator singleton.

13.5.1 Model Locator

The model locator in an application is a singleton class that the application uses to store data. Since the class is a singleton, any objects that reference it refer to a single copy of the class and, therefore, a single copy of the data contained within the class.

Throughout the application, the model can be accessed in the following manner:

```
var model:ModelLocator = ModelLocator.getInstance();
```

In this simple implementation of a model locator, we simply enforce the class' singleton nature in the class constructor and include a getter and setter function for the classes' only public property, xcData. xcData will serve as the data pass-through for both of our component files, which share the same data from this variable.

```
package com.exc.model
{

    import mx.controls.dataGridClasses.DataGridColumn;
    import mx.core.Application;

    [Bindable]
    public class ModelLocator
    {

        //instance of ModelLocator
        private static var instance:ModelLocator = new ModelLocator();
        public function ModelLocator()
        {
            if (instance) { throw new Error('Cannot create a new
              instance.  Must use ModelLocator.getInstance().') }
        }

    public static function getInstance():ModelLocator
        {
            return instance;
        }
```

```
        private var _xcData:Array = [[1,2,3,4]];
        public function set xcData(value:Array):void
        {
            _xcData = value;
            dispatchEvent(new Event("xcData"));
            trace("dispatch");
            Application.application.dispatchEvent(new
                Event("xcDataOutChanged"));
        }
        public function get xcData():Array
        {
            return _xcData;
        }


    }
}
```

13.5.2 Component Files

Up next are the two input and output component files. We'll start with the input component.

Input Component

The input component is very straightforward and only contains one public property, xcData. Whenever it receives new data from the SAP BusinessObjects Dashboards spreadsheet through the xcData property, it sets the model's xcData property and dispatches an event to let any listeners know that the data has changed. The eventing shown in this example is rudimentary in its application and is specific to SAP BusinessObjects Dashboards.

```
<?xml version="1.0" encoding="utf-8"?>
<mx:Canvas xmlns:mx="http://www.adobe.com/2006/mxml"
        width="400" height="300">
    <mx:Script>
        <![CDATA[
            import mx.core.Application;
            import com.exc.model.ModelLocator;
            private var model:ModelLocator = ModelLocator.getInstance();
            private var _xcData:Array = new Array();
```

```
        public function set xcData(value:Array):void
        {
            _xcData = value;
            model.xcData = value;
            dispatchEvent(new Event("xcData"));
            Application.application.dispatchEvent(new
              Event("xcDataOutChanged"));
        }
        [Bindable(event="xcData")]
        public function get xcData():Array
        {
            return _xcData;
        }
      ]]>
    </mx:Script>
    <mx:DataGrid  dataProvider="{model.xcData}"/>
</mx:Canvas>
```

Output Component

The output component is as straightforward as the input component and only contains one public property, xcDataOut. Whenever it receives new data through the xcDataOutChanged event, it sets the SAP BusinessObjects Dashboards model's xcData property and pushes the change through to the spreadsheet, if binding to this data is desired. The eventing shown in this example is rudimentary in its application and is specific to SAP BusinessObjects Dashboards.

```
<?xml version="1.0" encoding="utf-8"?>
<mx:Canvas creationComplete="init()"
          xmlns:mx="http://www.adobe.com/2006/mxml"
          width="400" height="300">
    <mx:Script>
        <![CDATA[
            import mx.core.Application;
            import com.exc.model.ModelLocator;
            private var model:ModelLocator = ModelLocator.getInstance();
            private var _xcDataOut:Array = new Array();
            private function init():void
            {
                Application.application.addEventListener("xcDataOutChanged",
                  xcDataOutChanged);
```

```
            }
            private function xcDataOutChanged(e:Event):void
            {
                _xcDataOut = model.xcData;
                dispatchEvent(new Event("xcDataOut"));
            }
            public function set xcDataOut(value:Array):void{}
            [Bindable(event="xcDataOut")]
            public function get xcDataOut():Array
            {
                return _xcDataOut;
            }
        ]]>
    </mx:Script>
</mx:Canvas>
```

13.5.3   SAP BusinessObjects Dashboards Component Files

Up next are the two MXML application files needed to package up in an XLX file for use in SAP BusinessObjects Dashboards.

ExCDataInput.mxml

```
<?xml version="1.0" encoding="utf-8"?>
<mx:Application xmlns:mx="http://www.adobe.com/2006/mxml"
                layout="absolute" xmlns:exc="com.exc.*">
    <exc:DataShareInput width="100%" height="100%"/>
</mx:Application>
```

ExCDataOutput.mxml

```
<?xml version="1.0" encoding="utf-8"?>
<mx:Application xmlns:mx="http://www.adobe.com/2006/mxml"
                layout="absolute" xmlns:exc="com.exc.*">
    <exc:DataShareOutput width="100%" height="100%"/>
</mx:Application>
```

13.5.4 Property Sheet

Last is the glue that binds the package together: the property sheet. The vast majority of the code below is repetitive boiler plate code that is common to all property sheets, with one noteworthy piece: the `isDataShareOut` variable. Toggle this property to true or false based on the input or output component XLX file you're generating. If you're generating the input component, set the variable to false, and if you're generating the output component, set the variable to true. Both components share the same property sheet and use this simple Boolean variable to ensure that the corresponding component binds to the correct property name.

```
<?xml version="1.0" encoding="utf-8"?>
<mx:Application xmlns:mx="http://www.adobe.com/2006/mxml"
                layout="absolute" applicationComplete="init();">
    <mx:Script>
        <![CDATA[
            import mx.containers.*;
            import mx.controls.*;
            import mx.core.Container;
            import mx.events.FlexEvent;

            import xcelsius.binding.BindingDirection;
            import xcelsius.binding.tableMaps.input.InputBindings;
            import xcelsius.binding.tableMaps.output.OutputBindings;
            import xcelsius.propertySheets.impl.
              PropertySheetExternalProxy;
            import xcelsius.propertySheets.interfaces.
              PropertySheetFunctionNamesSDK;

            private var isDataShareOut:Boolean = false;
            private var propertyName:String = isDataShareOut ?
              "xcDataOut" : "xcData";
            private var proxy:PropertySheetExternalProxy =
            new PropertySheetExternalProxy();
            private var propertyToBind:String;
            private var currentBindingID:String;

            //Initializes Property Sheet on load.
            private function init():void
            {
```

```
        proxy.addCallback(
            PropertySheetFunctionNamesSDK.RESPONSE_BINDING_ID,
            this.continueBind);

        proxy.callContainer(
            PropertySheetFunctionNamesSDK.
              INIT_COMPLETE_FUNCTION);

        initValues();
    }

    private function initValues():void
    {
        var propertyValues:Array = proxy.
          getProperties([propertyName]);
        var propertyValuesLength:int = (propertyValues !=
          null ? propertyValues.length : 0);
        for (var i:int=0; i < propertyValuesLength; i++)
        {
            var propertyObject:Object = propertyValues[i];
            var propertyName:String = propertyObject.name;
            var propertyValue:* = propertyObject.value;
            var bindingText:String = "";
            switch (propertyName)
            {
                case propertyName:
                    bindingText =
                      getPropertyBindDisplayName(propertyName);
                    if (bindingText != null)
                    {
                        tiData.enabled = false;
                        // When bound the user cannot
                        // edit the value.
                        tiData.text = bindingText;
                        // Show the address we are bound to.
                    }
                    else
                    {
                        tiData.text = "";
                    }
                    break;
                default:
```

```
                    break;
        }
    }
}


protected function getPropertyBindDisplayName(
  propertyName:String):String
{
    var propertyBindings:Array =
      proxy.getBindings([propertyName]);
    if ((propertyBindings != null) &&
        (propertyBindings.length > 0) &&
        (propertyBindings[0].length > 0))
    {
        var bindingID:String = propertyBindings[0][0];
        return proxy.getBindingDisplayName(bindingID);
    }
    return null;
}


private function initiateBind(propertyName:String):void
{
    currentBindingID = null;
    var propertyBindings:Array =
      proxy.getBindings([propertyName]);
    if ((propertyBindings != null) &&
        (propertyBindings.length > 0))
    {
        currentBindingID = propertyBindings[0];
        // Use the 1st binding address for the property.
    }

    propertyToBind = propertyName;
    proxy.requestUserSelection(currentBindingID);
}

private function continueBind(bindingID:String):void
{
    var propertyName:String = propertyToBind;
    var propertyValues:Array;
    var propertyObject:Object;
```

```
var bindingAddresses:Array;

if (currentBindingID != null)
{
    proxy.unbind(currentBindingID);
    currentBindingID = null;
}

switch (propertyName)
{
    case propertyName:
        if ((bindingID == null) || (bindingID == ""))
        {
            propertyValues =
                proxy.getProperties([propertyName]);
            propertyObject = propertyValues[0];
            proxy.setProperty(propertyName,
                propertyObject.value);
            return;
        }

        tiData.text =
            proxy.getBindingDisplayName(bindingID);

        if(isDataShareOut)
        {
            proxy.bind(propertyName, null, bindingID,
            BindingDirection.INPUT,
                InputBindings.ARRAY2D, "");
        }
        else
        {
            proxy.bind(propertyName, null, bindingID,
            BindingDirection.OUTPUT, "",
                OutputBindings.ARRAY2D);
        }

        break;
    default:
        break;
    }
}
```

```
            ]]>
    </mx:Script>
    <mx:Canvas minWidth="268"  minHeight="350" width="100%"
               height="100%" backgroundColor="#FFFFFF">
        <mx:Label x="10" y="22" text="Data"/>
        <mx:HRule y="39" height="10" right="10" left="10"/>
        <mx:TextInput id="tiData" y="57" right="42" left="10"/>
        <mx:Button y="56" right="10"  width="24"
                   click="initiateBind(propertyName);"
                   icon="@Embed('com/assets/bind to cell.png')"/>
    </mx:Canvas>
</mx:Application>
```

After creating these files, your project should look similar to the structure shown in Figure 13.12.

Figure 13.12 Project Structure

Packaging It for Testing

Upon successful compilation of your project files, create an XLX for the output component with the `isDataShareOut` property in the property sheet set to true. Once this has been done, create another XLX for the input component with the `isDataShareOut` property in the property sheet set to false.

Once the two XLX files have been generated, you can implement the input and output components in separate SAP BusinessObjects Dashboards models. Once the model that implements the output component has been completed, export it as an SWF file. Next, implement the input component as desired. Once the input implementation is complete, you can import the SWF file that contains the output component by using the SWF Loader control. Be sure to set Application Domain to the This option as illustrated in Figure 13.13. From this point, run the SAP BusinessObjects Dashboards model and change the shared data to observe it pass through one component to the other.

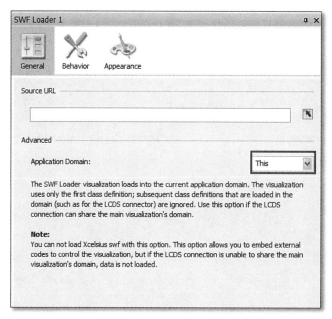

Figure 13.13 Setting the Application Domain

13.6 Summary

In this chapter we presented a hands-on step by step approach to creating a commonly implemented custom component type: a custom Flex chart. You should now know how to implement a Flex bubble chart with a runtime-controllable series color, tooltips (HTML or plain text), chart data, and write-back functionality to the SAP BusinessObjects Dashboards Excel model by way of a selected data and selected tooltip property.

Appendices

A   **Location Intelligence** 611

B   **Tips for Using SAP BusinessObjects Dashboards** 635

C   **The Authors** 669

Here you'll find an overview of location intelligence and some of its core functionalities. You'll also explore common use cases where location intelligence can be implemented in your SAP BusinessObjects Dashboards projects.

A   Location Intelligence

Location intelligence (LI) combines geographic and business data to uncover key insights, trends, and patterns, as well as to assist in more informed decision making and forward planning. The goal of viewing data within the context of a map is to provide insight into geospatial relationships not possible with standard charts and tabular data. Location intelligence can take many shapes and forms and can be implemented in a wide variety of ways. Location intelligence can be integrated in both operational and analytical dashboards to help increase productivity, drive revenue, decrease costs, and improve productivity and process efficiency.

Conservative research estimates show that on average, upwards of 70% of business data can be tied back to some sort of meaningful location-based data. With such a high percentage of data that can be viewed in a geographic context, it's often inefficient to visualize this data in a standard chart-type format because the spatial context that is so important in understanding location based data is not present. To truly understand how location impacts your business and its operations, an appropriate location intelligence solution should be included in dashboard solutions that contain location data. Location intelligence at a high level can assist in revealing trends, risks, opportunities, and actionable items of all varieties that otherwise remain unseen or difficult to detect when not presented in a geographic context.

Location intelligence comprises many individual components, techniques, and processes, though as it applies to SAP BusinessObjects Dashboards, the main focus is the resulting map that is displayed in the dashboard user interface. Fortunately, with advances in geographic and BI technology combined with the application of flexible, user-friendly consumer technologies within the enterprise, true location intelligence can now be included and delivered as a seamless component in SAP BusinessObjects Dashboards.

A.1   What Makes Up Location Intelligence?

Location intelligence is often associated with the end result that most users are familiar with—a map. However, location intelligence generally consists of not only the resulting map, but also the tools that assist in data cleansing, spatial queries, data formatting, advanced map navigation and selection tools as well as supplementary data sets, such as demographics. Listed below is a set of fundamental parts that generally compose a location intelligence solution.

A.1.1   Geocoding

Geocoding is the process of translating a physical address into its corresponding latitude and longitude coordinates, which are needed to display information on a map. Geocoders are also capable of returning coordinates for named locations such as airports, restaurants, and hotels.

A.1.2   Reverse Geocoding

Reverse geocoding is the exact opposite of the process of geocoding. Reverse geocoding is the process of translating a set of latitude and longitude coordinates into a corresponding physical address. Reverse geocoding can be useful when detailed address information needs to be known or otherwise displayed for a location.

A.1.3   Address Validation and Standardization

By transforming addresses and locations into common formats, the resulting data can be run through additional validation tools to ensure the data is in a clean and accurate form before it ends up on a map.

A.1.4   Data Mashups for Enhanced Insight

Data mashups are a key advantage of location intelligence; that is, being able to see your data plotted on a map in combination with other relevant supporting data sets to help you better understand your metrics. For example, looking at sales data on a map is informative and useful, but combining your sales data with demographic data sets provides true insight into who you are selling to and who you should be targeting in advertising campaigns.

A.1.5 Selecting Capabilities

Looking at a map is informative, but being able to interact with a map and dynamically navigate, select, and analyze any number of elements within the map brings intelligence to location intelligence. The ability to select assets within a given radius and the ability to freeform lasso multiple assets on the map shown in Figure A.1 for further comparison provide tremendous analytical advantages. As illustrated in the figure, a dashboard user can perform a distance-based selection on items in Florida to see their cumulative impact on marketing and sales.

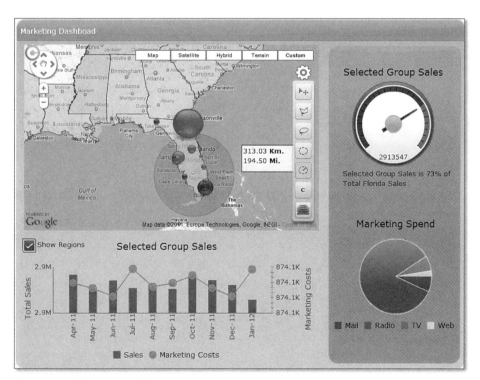

Figure A.1 Selecting Capabilities

A.2 Why Location Intelligence Is Important

Location intelligence is so important in BI because it helps users assimilate and act on metrics with a geographic dimension faster than any other method of data visualization. The quantum leap of information absorption and intuitive understanding gained through the use of location intelligence is equivalent to the power of transforming ordinary static spreadsheet data into interactive, meaningful charts.

Just as data trends and relationships are hard to understand in pure spreadsheet form, location data is equally difficult to digest and quickly understand when it is in chart form. The bottom line is that if data can be tied to a location, it should be displayed through an interactive map user interface to provide dashboard users with the best tool possible to aid in truly understanding and uncovering key relationships in data.

A.2.1 The Power of Where

Nearly every event and every transaction can be tied back to a specific location. Locations across the globe where these events and transactions occur are all unique in nature in that they contain different demographics, different infrastructure features, different buildings, roadways, natural features, and so on. Understanding exactly *where* events occur is an advantage that cannot be overstated. To get the true value out of the "where" in these events and transactions, they need to be placed into geographical context and visualized on a map. Once events and transactions are viewed in the context of a map and combined with other supporting data such as demographics, key insights are revealed, and deeper understanding of the events start to take place.

A simple yet powerful case that illustrates the power of where, is that of a major convenience store chain that monitors the sale of state lottery tickets in a localized area through a ticket sales dashboard. Upon viewing the dashboard, one of the chain's locations in Southern California had ticket sales that were literally off the charts in comparison to other stores in the nearby area. Looking at the ticket sales comparison in a traditional chart offered no insight, only the hard fact that sales were much, much higher at a single location.

Why they were higher remained an open question to the analysts who were unfamiliar with the area. However, with the addition of a basic location intelligence solution inside their ticket sales dashboard, analysts immediately had a moment of clarity when they viewed these locations in a geographical context. The location was nicely positioned straight up the road from a sports stadium, and ticket sales spiked on game day. Without location intelligence, the analysts would have to manually research outliers and assess each on an individual basis, outside of their dashboard analysis tool. The basic implementation of location intelligence immediately yielded a significant return on investment, in not only time saved and potential money to earn, but also in knowledge gained. After this discovery, targeted sales campaigns could be launched nationwide in stores near sporting events to strategically boost sales.

A.2.2   The Benefits of Where

The benefits that can be gained from location intelligence are endless and sometimes specific to the situation for which they are implemented. Many companies large and small are starting to realize and reap the benefits of location intelligence in many areas of their operations. Location intelligence is a rapidly growing area and is quickly becoming a necessity as well as a focal point in many new BI deployments and development efforts.

Since location intelligence reveals key insights, relationships, and trends, the majority of these important pieces of information have remained hidden up until the implementation of a location intelligence solution. As customers begin to get familiar with the concept of location intelligence, the realization that they've been effectively sitting on an untapped mine of extremely valuable information starts to sink in. More effective marketing, better customer service, more optimized retail store placement, better delivery routes, more targeted communications, improved disaster management, and better general awareness and understanding of business transactions are all possibilities when applying location intelligence solutions within BI dashboards.

A.3   How Does Location Intelligence Fit into SAP BusinessObjects Dashboards?

Location intelligence should fit nearly seamlessly into your SAP BusinessObjects Dashboards. A proper location intelligence solution for SAP BusinessObjects Dashboards should be portable, customizable, interactive, as well as easy to use and implement. Due to the portable nature of SAP BusinessObjects Dashboards' SWF file output, the location intelligence solution that you choose should be able to tag along seamlessly with the SAP BusinessObjects Dashboards SWF file so as to not degrade or otherwise interfere with the important factors of portability and usability that are inherent to SAP BusinessObjects Dashboards.

An optimal location intelligence solution for SAP BusinessObjects Dashboards should also be able to take part in the SAP BusinessObjects Dashboards design process as a native component. This can be achieved by the maps that come bundled with SAP BusinessObjects Dashboards or by leveraging rich third-party components that can be added on to SAP BusinessObjects Dashboards. We'll take a closer look into these options in the following subsections.

Apart from selecting an appropriate location intelligence solution, maps can be presented and designed to interact seamlessly alongside other dashboard elements such as charts, navigation, or any other dashboard elements to enable cross-filtering, drilldown, and chained interactions that SAP BusinessObjects Dashboards users have become accustomed to using.

Prepare for Location Intelligence in Dashboard Projects

As demand for location intelligence in dashboards begins to spread, anticipating where and how these solutions may be implemented is a great way to get ready for their implementation. Let's look at a few helpful tips to jumpstart your location intelligence preparation.

Identify Opportunities

Since over 70% of data can be tied back to a location, the number of places where location intelligence can be implemented are plentiful. A good point to start is by looking through existing dashboards that have already been implemented. If location-based data are present in the dashboards, is it a case where information could be more quickly assimilated with the inclusion of location intelligence? If so, think through the user experience and how the dashboard could be changed to accommodate and benefit from a mapping element.

In new dashboard projects, keep an eye out for geographic data during requirements gathering phases. This is usually a perfect time to account for and factor in location intelligence to your dashboards.

Know Your Limits

Be aware of the types of systems in place in the context of your dashboard project that are capable of providing location intelligence. Explore them at a high level so that their core capabilities are known and can be taken into account during the requirements-gathering phase.

Know Your Options

Knowing the available options is as important as knowing the limits of existing systems that are candidates for location intelligence. If your dashboard requirements exceed your current systems capabilities, it's time to readjust requirements or time to explore other options. Do you need SVG maps, web maps, or a full geographic information systems (GIS) solution? To help decide, read more in Section A.4.

Prepare the Data

In anticipation of implementing location intelligence, it's wise to get ahead of the curve and to start integrating basic geocoding and address cleansing processes into your existing data-cleansing processes. Just having their placeholders carved out in the overall process is important, because clean location data is critical to ensuring accurate analysis when implementation begins. You can read more on the topic of geocoding and cleansing in Section A.6.

A.4   Location Intelligence Options in SAP BusinessObjects Dashboards

While SAP BusinessObjects Dashboards comes packaged with a large library of maps, they fall short of addressing the wide range of business requirements for monitoring and analyzing geographic metrics. The unlimited business requirements for monitoring and tracking performance have been addressed using multiple technology approaches, all with their own set of strengths and weaknesses. The following sections contain the most common options that are presented when choosing a location intelligence solution for SAP BusinessObjects Dashboards.

Implementation details related to these options can vary widely, though links have been listed at the bottom of this section where more specific information can be obtained on how to implement each of these solutions for SAP BusinessObjects Dashboards.

A.4.1 SVG and Vector Maps

Scalable Vector Graphics (SVG) maps are a widely used solution inside SAP BusinessObjects Dashboards. This is because SAP BusinessObjects Dashboards comes with numerous predesigned scalable maps that can be colored and interacted with just like any other SAP BusinessObjects Dashboards control. The benefit of an SVG approach is that virtually no research or learning has to be done outside of SAP BusinessObjects Dashboards, and time-to-market with the dashboard will be fairly fast, given that the dashboard contains a handful or less of SVG maps. Managing many more can be cumbersome. If a dashboard requirement calls for simple color-coded noncustomizable regions, SVG maps should suit those needs. Figure A.2 shows a standard SAP BusinessObjects Dashboards map, along with some of the common properties found in all SAP BusinessObjects Dashboards maps.

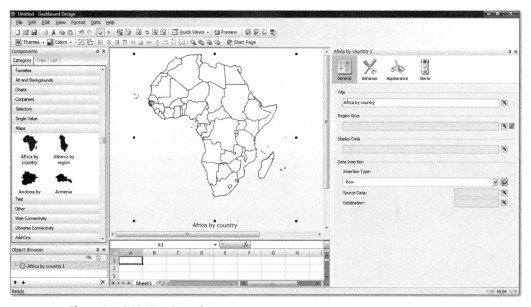

Figure A.2 SVG Map Control

A.4.2 Web 2.0 Maps

Google, Yahoo!, and Bing maps are widely adopted as the standard interface for navigating maps on the web. The flexibility to quickly navigate any geographic level provides a powerful solution to address a wide range of visualization and interactivity requirements. In recent years these consumer technologies have been repurposed and offered as enterprise "software as a service" solutions. Gartner recently reported that by 2012, one-third of analytic applications applied to business processes will be delivered through application mashups. Many organizations are now adopting these powerful APIs to provide exactly what business users require in an interactive map interface.

While Google and Bing may supply robust platforms for delivering map visualizations to business users, they are not equipped out of the box to address some of the advanced capabilities facilitated by GIS mapping solutions. Although they don't come equipped out of the box with rich functionality found in GIS, most web map APIs allow developers to build custom controls and advanced data visualization layers that rival thicker GIS solutions.

Web maps, as shown in Figure A.3, are a popular choice given their flexibility, portability, and small footprint. Not only do they fit well into the SAP BusinessObjects Dashboards paradigm, but they are controls that are used by nearly everyone outside of BI at one point or another. Nearly every human with a computer is familiar with Google, Yahoo!, or Bing maps. Because of this, most users are pre-educated on how to interact with the map, which cuts down on adoption time and increases the immersive, interactive experience provided by SAP BusinessObjects Dashboards. When dashboard users see a familiar map interface, the inclination is to dive in and start using it, which is an obvious benefit. If your needs surpass those provided by web maps, GIS may be the right solution for you.

Figure A.3 Web Map Control

A.4.3 GIS Solutions

If your mapping needs are advanced and cannot be achieved through web maps or SVG, GIS is likely the way to go, as GIS solutions can achieve just about anything having to do with location intelligence.

Geographic information systems (GIS) enable organizations to generate and edit maps, as well as to create advanced geographic planning and analysis views not possible with SVG and Web 2.0 maps. While GIS solutions provide tremendous power in the breadth and depth of analysis, most business intelligence dashboards require a small fraction of what GIS solutions are capable of delivering. Database and BI vendors have filled several capabilities traditionally managed in GIS, now allowing customers to deploy rich mapping experiences without any GIS software.

GIS solutions, as shown in Figure A.4, are used in SAP BusinessObjects Dashboards, but more sparingly, often due to cost, accessibility, maintenance implications and the need for more simplified tooling. However, if your location intelligence requirements call for the advanced capabilities found in GIS, it's possible to overlay GIS maps onto a functional SAP BusinessObjects Dashboards dashboard. This capability is provided through an SAP-certified solution and can be located in the resources box.

Figure A.4 GIS Map Control

A.5   Common Location Intelligence Use Cases

The application of location intelligence is critical in helping organizations understand how location impacts business performance and to assist in forward planning. Maps provide a powerful solution for assimilating the location of assets (people, customers, products, vehicles, etc.) and/or areas (zones, regions, etc.). Though the number of use cases for location intelligence is staggering, we'll discuss a few common cases that demonstrate the types of scenarios location intelligence can accommodate.

A.5.1   Analyze Customer Habits

By combining consumer and census data with your own business data, uncovering purchase or other behavioral habits of your customers becomes dramatically easier. When a time dimension is added to the data, a vision of how customers move and act around your stores and the general area throughout the day can be achieved.

A.5.2   Identify Underperforming Stores

By visualizing how existing store locations are performing in the context of a map, new market and customer opportunities can be revealed. If an underperforming location is surrounded by other locations with acceptable performance, the question "Why is this happening?" will probably arise immediately. Perhaps the location is not optimally serving the customers in the area based on the area's customer demographics. Does this location need to tailor the products and services it offers to more comprehensively serve its constituents? These questions are the first step in uncovering the answers needed to better understand the location's performance and to subsequently take the appropriate action.

In Figure A.5, it's evident at a glance that some impactful underperformers are present based on the red icon size and density in Southern California. By quickly lassoing this general cluster, it becomes easier to see how they're impacting Southern California's sales and how much marketing spending is currently being focused in the area. By further zooming in to the underperforming areas, additional insights may be revealed by switching to a satellite view and observing the placement of the stores relative to roadways and other influencing factors, such as competitor locations.

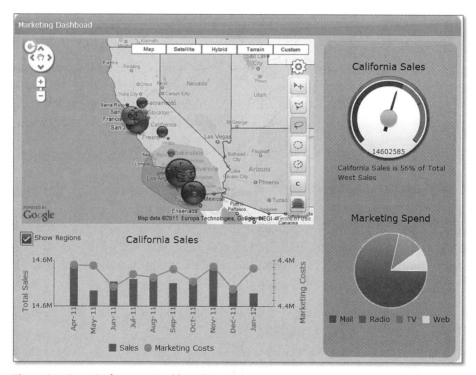

Figure A.5 Store Performance Dashboard Use Case

A.5.3   Track Sales

Tracking sales by region, illustrated in Figure A.6, is a very common use case. Location intelligence can assist in helping the viewer almost instantly ascertain where sales are good, average, or bad with a single glance.

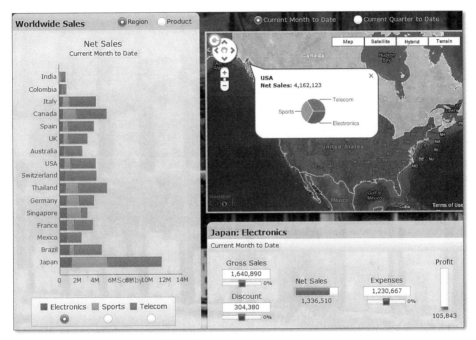

Figure A.6 Sales by Region Dashboard Use Case

A.5.4   Disaster Management

In the event of a disaster, a location intelligence solution can help you understand and plan for how the event is affecting your employees, customers, supply chain, and surrounding areas. Location intelligence solutions not only assist in effectively reacting to and assessing disasters, but they can also help forward-plan for disasters in the area based on historical disaster data. In Figure A.7, estimated and hypothetical radiation fallout from the Fukushima Nuclear Power Plant in Japan is illustrated. By visualizing the fallout zone in combination with company assets, it becomes much clearer how people, operations, and locations are affected based on their proximity to the radiation zone.

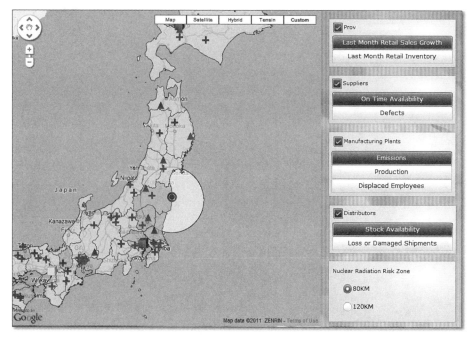

Figure A.7 Disaster Management Dashboard Use Case

A.5.5 Plan Retail Store Sites

In a retail scenario, a business can put together a comprehensive view of competitors and other influencing factors in the area, such as traffic and storefront visibility, to help identify optimal potential sites for new stores.

A.5.6 Targeted Advertising

Armed with store locations and demographic data, a marketer can create targeted advertising based on demographics. Comprehensive and thorough approaches leveraging location intelligence can turn marketing guesswork into targeted and effective campaigns and increased ROI.

A.5.7 Delivery Management

Any business that provides delivery services can instantly benefit from the application of location intelligence. Determining problematic routes, traffic patterns, and repeat late-delivery locations and planning better alternatives are all achievable goals when leveraging the right location intelligence solution. Figure A.8 illustrates how quickly one can assess where late deliveries are occurring or are about to occur. From here, proactive measures can be taken to manage customer satisfaction and service and to start understanding long-term fixes in areas with many historical late deliveries.

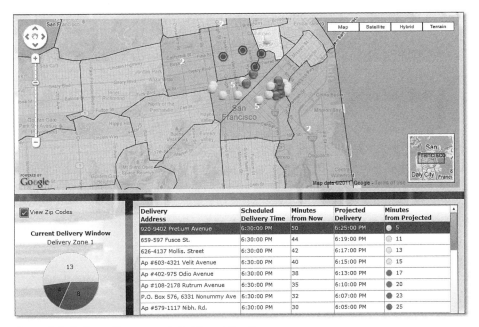

Figure A.8 Delivery Management Dashboard Use Case

A.5.8   Manage Operations

An electric company that has plants distributed across the nation can assess plant performance at a glance and take action when a plant hits associated thresholds.

A.5.9   Insurance Underwriting and Risk Management

Insurance providers can visualize historical disasters by area that they insure, providing for more comprehensive planning and understanding of rates. Further, if a disaster strikes, agents can identify affected policy holders and begin customer management procedures in a targeted and proactive manner.

A.5.10 Law Enforcement

Police officials and other law enforcement personnel can analyze crime statistics in a geographic context, resulting in better-informed decision making, such as where to increase patrols, where to install traffic cameras, where to draw back patrols, and so on. All of this information also assists in performing predictive analysis to determine when and where the next crime is likely to occur.

A.5.11 Oil/Land Management

An oil and land managers can view properties by region and immediately ascertain production rates, lease notifications, well problems, drilling status, and other pertinent information.

A.6 Location Intelligence Best Practices

Generally speaking, there are many best practices that should be followed when implementing a location intelligence solution for BI projects. Usually, SVG maps do not fall into this category of best practices in the context of SAP Business-Objects Dashboards, because their boundary data are hardcoded, though web maps and GIS solutions are relevant.

Although there are several categories of best practices, the general aim of the combined application of these practices is to ensure high performance, accurate and reliable location intelligence to your dashboard projects.

A.6.1 Geocoding

Geocoding, as shown in Figure A.9, is the process of translating a physical address into its corresponding latitude and longitude coordinates, which are needed to display information on a map. Location Intelligence solutions perform faster if geocoding is implemented correctly. In this section, we'll discuss the best practices to keep in mind when considering geocoding data for your location intelligence solution.

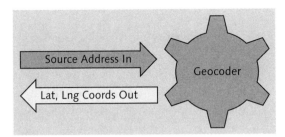

Figure A.9 Geocoding Process

A.6.2 Reverse Geocoding

Reverse geocoding, as shown in Figure A.10, is the exact opposite of the process of geocoding. Reverse geocoding is the process of translating a set of latitude and longitude coordinates into a corresponding physical address. Reverse geocoding can be useful when detailed address information needs to be known or otherwise displayed for a location.

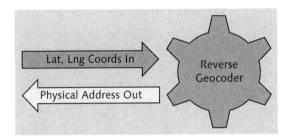

Figure A.10 Reverse-Geocoding Process

As a best practice for reverse geocoding, it's always better for performance to have the address data on-hand and ready to display as opposed to needing to run asynchronous reverse-geocoding requests on-demand at runtime. However, for certain use cases, having the address data preloaded and ready to display at runtime is not an option for one reason or another. In this case it's acceptable to send reverse-geocoding requests to your geocoder as needed. Just be sure to manage the user experience appropriately by displaying a status bar of some sort, as reverse geocoding request responses vary based on available bandwidth and other network and system factors.

Geocode Before You Map

Translations take time, and geocoding is no exception. Geocoding operations should be performed on a scheduled basis to support good performance and load times in your location intelligence–enabled dashboards. Many mapping solutions allow for runtime geocoding, but this runtime translating takes a toll on the overall user experience and slows analysis and loading time significantly. Whenever possible, these translations should happen behind the scenes so that when a location intelligence dashboard is launched, the location data is ready to be plotted without intervention or additional processing time.

Validate Source Addresses

If the geocoding process is flawed, everything downstream from the process suffers. Inaccurate addresses will produce inaccurate analysis of your location-based data. If the analysis is inaccurate, this inevitably leads to inaccurate decision making and distrust of the system. It is of great importance to ensure that the source address data and the translated latitude and longitude coordinates accurately represent the locations they are meant to represent.

Geocoding solutions at the minimum should be capable of accepting a wide variety of address types and verifying source address data accuracy before translating the source addresses into coordinates. Further, the geocoding solution should report any errant data so that it can be examined, fixed, and reprocessed.

Manual validation of this sort of process is impractical due to the potential data volume being run through the geocoding process. Thankfully, the vast majority of geocoding tools automate this sort of cross-validation and data safeguarding. Whether the data is being displayed in a GIS tool or a web map interface, be sure to confirm that the geocoding process is up to standards and provides this sort of basic functionality. If this functionality is not provided, either consider a different solution or obtain an outside tool that handles this process.

Companies like Google and Yahoo! have geocoding services, and SAP also provides SAP BusinessObjects Data Services, which offer top-quality geocoding and data accuracy and validation tools as well. To find out more about these specific service providers, please refer to their websites listed in the "Location Intelligence Resources" section.

Validate Coordinate Accuracy

There will be times when it isn't possible to deliver a set of coordinates for a given address to the center point of the object at that address. The tools you use should leverage rules to enforce accuracy to the best of their ability. For example, if the point cannot land directly on the center of an exact address point, the logic in the system should automatically select the next closest point available. Usually this concept starts with the optimal point of reference, an exact parcel point, and then moves down in levels of accuracy, such as to street, zip code, city, state, country, and so on.

Automate Geocoding Processes

When possible, geocoding and other relevant location data-cleansing processes should be integrated into existing BI processes. This will ensure that the latest and cleanest data is always available to your applications that leverage location intelligence and rely on geocoded data.

Leverage a Common Toolset

Before buying into any external geocoding tools, check into your local BI system and infrastructure first to see if anything already exists. If, for example, your business is an SAP shop and you already have Data Services running, look no further. In general, the fewer disparate moving parts you have, the more smoothly operations can be implemented and managed around location intelligence.

A.6.3 Visualizing Large Data Volumes

Visualizing hundreds or even thousands of points should not be a problem in a robust location intelligence solution. However, in cases where hundreds of thousands or potentially millions of points need to be viewed on a map at one time to get the full picture needed for analysis, remote standards such as web mapping services (WMS) should be implemented. Figure A.11 shows a map with a WMS layer comprised of tens of thousands of data points.

Standards like WMS are capable of intense data processing on the server side and simply return images that contain the requested data visualizations back to the requesting map. On receipt of the returned WMS image, the map can subsequently overlay the image on top of itself. Since SAP BusinessObjects Dashboards runs in Flash, and Flash runs locally, it's important to offload intense processing roles like this to the server side to maintain a satisfactory user experience.

WMS is an open standard, and the software needed to run it can be found in GIS solutions or it can be obtained freely from WMS software providers.

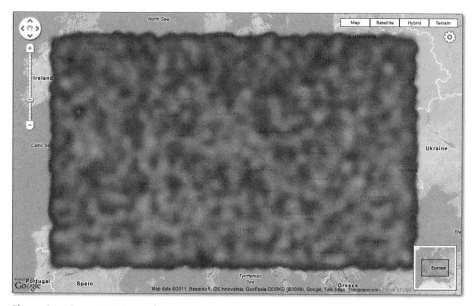

Figure A.11 Dense WMS Visualization

WMS Resources

▶ WMS Standard: *www.opengeospatial.org/standards/wms*

▶ WMS server software: *http://mapserver.org/ogc/wms_server.html*

A.6.4   Creating Reusable Data

Often when creating location intelligence–enabled dashboards, the need to reuse common assets across dashboards, like boundary data, will be an inevitable request. It's good to anticipate what kind of datasets may be reused across various projects and to package those datasets into manageable and distributable assets.

A great example of this is the use of shape files, which are a common standard in location intelligence and virtually every available GIS tool. Shape files contain boundary coordinates in a compressed and reusable standardized format. If, for example, 10 separate dashboards needed to display the United States by state, a single United States by state shapefile could be created and used to visualize those shapes across all 10 dashboards. As shown in Figure A.12, a shape file can be hosted on any file system or web server and can be accessed just like any other local or online asset. To learn more about shape files, including the shape file specification maintained by ESRI, refer to *http://www.esri.com/library/whitepapers/pdfs/shapefile.pdf/*.

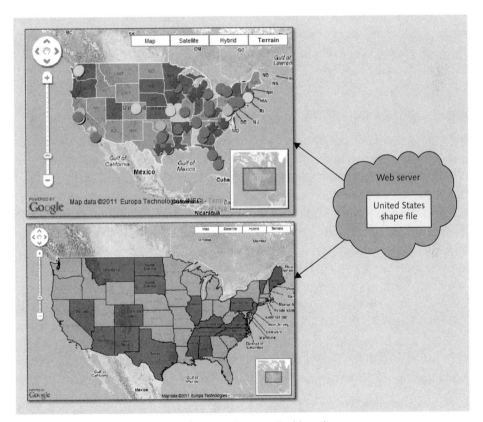

Figure A.12 Common Shape File Feeding Two Separate Dashboards

A.6.5 Filtering Data and Performance Tuning

Most location intelligence solutions inside dashboards are responsible for displaying a sizeable amount of information. However, depending on where a user is in the context of a given dashboard's navigation, there is usually only a subset of relevant data that needs to be displayed. Any location intelligence solutions should be capable of filtering the data that is on the map view based on user navigation.

For example, if a dashboard is displaying neighborhood boundaries by zip code, and the user is at a zoom level in the map that displays the entire United States, it would be both visually ineffective and non-performant to display all of this data at once. A more suitable option would be to allow users to select a state and then a city or zip code, and at this point the relevant neighborhood boundaries would be displayed. This kind of basic functionality is extremely important in managing the user experience, especially within the context of an SAP BusinessObjects Dashboards dashboard where performance is at a high premium.

A.6.6 Loosely Couple Boundary Data and Business Data

If boundary or other geographic data are being sourced from GIS to power your location intelligence solution, it's a best practice to loosely couple this data so that it is flexible and resilient to change. For example, the shape file format specification mentioned in Section A.6.4 imposes standards that are inflexible in some BI scenarios. For example, the shapefile standard at a basic level consists of an SHP shapefile that contains the boundary/coordinate data, a DBF data file that contains relevant business data, and an SHX index file that maps the business data to its corresponding shape data. For many scenarios, this is expected behavior and a potentially acceptable format. However, in cases where web maps or other non-GIS location intelligence solutions rely on shapefile data to render shapes and real-time business data together, the rigid format becomes unusable since the business data is essentially tied up on the DBF file. This means that to pull real-time data, the DBF file would need to be regenerated each time the data updates, which requires the intervention of a GIS tool.

In today's real-time data world, this is an unacceptable option, and an alternative for tying business data to shapefile shapes dynamically at runtime should be implemented if you are using a web bap option. A simple option to fix this problem is to require the data coming back from a query to be in the same order in which the shapes are defined in the shapefile. If this isn't possible, then a dynamic lookup table can be implemented in SAP BusinessObjects Dashboards to map the business data to its corresponding shape in real time.

A.7   Summary

In this chapter, we introduced the concept of location intelligence for SAP BusinessObjects Dashboards, explained some of its core functionality, highlighted common cases where location intelligence can be implemented, and gave an overview of the value it can bring to your SAP BusinessObjects Dashboards projects. With the fundamentals in mind and being armed with a variety of implementation options, it's a great time to begin exploring the capabilities of location intelligence in BI to unlock key insights, trends, and patterns that are present in your location-based data.

We want to share some additional tips for using SAP BusinessObjects Dashboards and what you need to be aware of when using it in an SAP or SAP BusinessObjects environment.

B Tips for Using SAP BusinessObjects Dashboards

In the previous chapters we discussed almost every element of SAP Business-Objects Dashboards 4.0—its design environment including menus and toolbars, all of its rich UI components, and all kinds of data connectivity. In addition, we discussed the general workflow to create a dashboard and important features such as drill-down and alerts. This is enough information for you to create enterprise-level dashboards for your company.

We also covered the SAP BusinessObjects Dashboards SDK, with which you can create custom UI components or data connectivities with the Adobe Flex programming language.

In this chapter, we'll discuss something that is very useful when building dashboards in a reporting system. After reading this chapter you'll be able to:

▶ Describe how to use SAP BusinessObjects Dashboards in an SAP Business-Objects environment

▶ Know what license to choose during purchasing

B.1 Using SAP BusinessObjects Dashboards in an SAP BusinessObjects Environment

SAP BusinessObjects Dashboards is a product of SAP belonging to its BusinessObjects BI (business intelligence) landscape and one of its query, reporting, and analysis products. Usually, SAP BusinessObjects Dashboards is used not alone, but together with other SAP BusinessObjects products including:

- ▶ SAP BW query
- ▶ SAP NetWeaver Portal
- ▶ BI portals like BI Launchpad/CMC (Central Management Console)
- ▶ Query as a Web Service
- ▶ SAP BusinessObjects Universe
- ▶ SAP BusinessObjects Live Office
- ▶ SAP Crystal Reports
- ▶ SAP BusinessObjects Web Intelligence

The following subsections will describe how SAP BusinessObjects Dashboards is used with other products of the SAP BusinessObjects family.

B.1.1   BI Launchpad/CMC

BI Launchpad and CMC are portals of SAP BusinessObjects, which can be used to host and manage the dashboards as Flash SWF objects. The portals can run on both Java and .Net web application servers, such as Apache Tomcat and Microsoft IIS (Internet Information Service). BI Launchpad is for information consumers, while CMC is for system administrators.

To use this feature, you have to save your dashboard to the SAP BusinessObjects BI platform from the FILE menu. Keep in mind that this is the only way you can export your dashboard into an SAP BusinessObjects system as a Flash InfoObject. Though you can upload the source (.xlf) or output (.swf) into SAP Business-Objects, it will be recognized not as a Flash file, but as a plain file, which cannot be viewed but can only be downloaded. In the InfoView you will find that the object type of the uploaded SWF file is format-free, instead of Flash.

The benefits of accessing your dashboard through BI Launchpad/CMC are easy and secure access.

- ▶ **Easy access**
  The end user can access the dashboard by logging on to BI Launchpad and navigating to the folder in a web browser. You don't have to save the file locally on your computer. Figure B.1 shows the InfoView where the user accesses the dashboard.

  If you are familiar with BI Launchpad, you'll notice that fewer commands are available after right-clicking a Flash object. For example, you cannot schedule it.

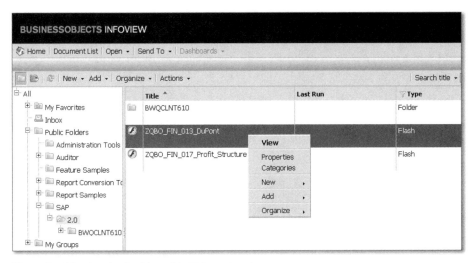

Figure B.1 Viewing the Dashboard in BI Launchpad

Whenever the dashboard is updated, the designer can update it at the backend and save it to the SAP BusinessObjects platform after testing to overwrite the original version, without interrupting the end user. The end user knows nothing about this process. He just focuses on business analysis through this dashboard, which always delivers the right information.

▶ **Secure access**
With BI Launchpad, you can configure who can access what dashboards with the enterprise-level permission control mechanism of SAP BusinessObjects. This way only users who have been granted the required permissions can access the dashboard to see the information.

You can also store the dashboard definition file (*.xlf*) of your dashboard to the SAP BusinessObjects platform, from the menu path FILE • SAVE TO PLATFORM. Later you can open it from SAP BusinessObjects again, from the menu path FILE • OPEN FROM PLATFORM. This way you use the SAP BusinessObjects platform as a central storage place, similar to a version control application such as Microsoft VSS (Visual Source-Safe) or CVS (Concurrent Version System). For example, say you work with your colleagues to design a dashboard together. When you have come to a certain stage in the dashboard design, you save it to a folder in the SAP BusinessObjects platform. Your colleagues can then continue the design by opening it from that folder.

B.1.2   SAP BusinessObjects Universe

In SAP BusinessObjects Dashboards 4.0 you can directly connect to a Universe and build a query on top of it, through the Query Browser. You can then bind data of a UI component to fields in the resulting data of a Universe query.

SAP BusinessObjects Universe is used primarily to map complex database fields into business terms that can be easily understood by non-IT business users. It can access several kinds of data sources, either relational or multidimensional.

B.1.3   Query as a Web Service

In SAP BusinessObjects Dashboards 4.0 you can use Query as a Web Service connectivities to retrieve data either from a universe or from a published block of an SAP BusinessObjects Web Intelligence document.

Query as a Web Service is used to expose partial or all data fields in a universe as a standard web service, so it can be consumed by any other application that can parse the web service. This largely expands the use of SAP BusinessObjects Universe.

If your company has SAP BusinessObjects reports, some universes may have already been created. With Query as a Web Service connectivity, you leverage the existing universes for your dashboards.

B.1.4   Live Office

SAP BusinessObjects Live Office is an integration between SAP BusinessObjects and the Microsoft Office product family. It allows you to insert SAP Crystal Reports, SAP BusinessObjects Web Intelligence documents, or Universe queries into a Microsoft Word, Excel, or PowerPoint document.

The integration between SAP BusinessObjects Dashboards and SAP BusinessObjects Live Office goes in one direction only, allowing you to consume SAP BusinessObjects Live Office data inside your dashboard. You do this by importing a Live Office-enabled Excel file and adding a Live Office connection in the dashboard. The user can see live data at runtime. If any parameter is defined in the SAP Crystal Reports or SAP BusinessObjects Web Intelligence document or the Universe query, the user will be prompted to enter values for them when accessing the dashboards.

B.1.5   SAP Crystal Reports

The integration between SAP BusinessObjects Dashboards and SAP Crystal Reports exists in both products. In your dashboard, you configure an Crystal Reports Data Consumer connectivity to define what values are to be passed in from an SAP Crystal Reports document. On the other hand, in SAP Crystal Reports, you insert the dashboard into the report as a Flash object and define how to pass values into it using Flash Vars, as explained in Chapter 7 as part of the discussion of the Crystal Reports Data Consumer connectivity.

You can also create charts within SAP Crystal Reports, but they are not as intuitive or attractive as those created in SAP BusinessObjects Dashboards. With the help of this integration, you can include interactive dashboards in your SAP Crystal Reports documents to provide a better user experience.

In SAP BusinessObjects Dashboards you can also consume data from SAP Crystal Reports by importing a Live Office-enabled Excel file with one or more SAP Crystal Reports documents embedded and creating a Live Office connection, as mentioned above and in Chapter 7 when we discussed the Live Office connectivity.

B.1.6   SAP BusinessObjects Web Intelligence

In contrast to the integration between SAP BusinessObjects Dashboards and SAP Crystal Reports, you cannot insert a dashboard into an SAP BusinessObjects Web Intelligence document. The integration goes only in one direction, for SAP BusinessObjects Dashboards to consume data in an SAP BusinessObjects Web Intelligence document.

Similar to SAP Crystal Reports, you do this by importing a Live Office-enabled Excel file with one or more SAP BusinessObjects Web Intelligence documents embedded and creating a Live Office connection in your dashboard for each SAP BusinessObjects Web Intelligence document.

Another way is to make public the data in a block of an SAP BusinessObjects Web Intelligence document as a Query as a Web Service using standard WSDL and SOAP protocols. It's much easier than the traditional way of using SAP BusinessObjects Live Office. You need pay attention to following items:

► You can only publish data from a block of the SAP BusinessObjects Web Intelligence document from Web Intelligence Rich Client, not from BI Launchpad where you edit the SAP BusinessObjects Web Intelligence document.

► To publish the data, right-click the border of a block in either structure or results mode and select PUBLISH BLOCK in the context menu.

► After publishing, you can find the WSDL URL in the properties panel after selecting the SHOW BI SERVICES checkbox. A typical WSDL URL might be *http:// bo4:8080/dswsbobje/qaawsservices/biws?WSDL=1&cuid=AVXD17CR1ixHtGzSfTT Shk8*.

Figure B.2 shows a screenshot of Web Intelligence Rich Client, where the available BI services of the given SAP BusinessObjects system are displayed, and the user has just selected a block and right-clicked.

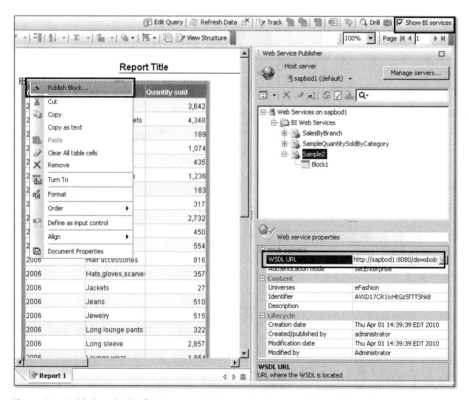

Figure B.2 Publish a Block of Data in an SAP BusinessObjects Web Intelligence Document as a Web Service in Web Intelligence Rich Client

To use the BI service in SAP BusinessObjects Dashboards, you need to add a Query as a Web Service (or web service) connection in the Data Manager, copy the WSDL URL from the PROPERTIES panel of the selected BI service in Web Intelligence Rich Client, and paste it in the WSDL URL field. You can then bind input parameters and output values of this BI service, as displayed in Figure B.3.

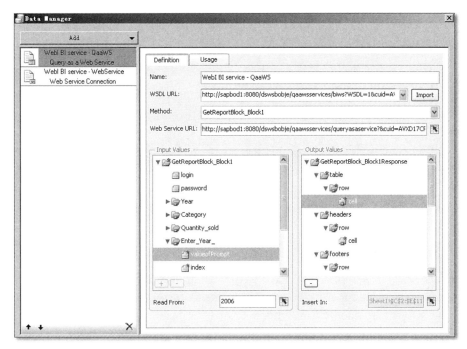

Figure B.3 Consuming Data from BI Services in SAP BusinessObjects Dashboards

Parameters are also supported in this case. As displayed in Figure B.3, ENTER_YEAR_ in the INPUT VALUES area is a parameter defined in the SAP BusinessObjects Web Intelligence document. You can use a selector component in the dashboard for the user to specify this parameter's value.

To use the returned data, bind the output values to cell ranges in the embedded spreadsheet. To do this, bind the CELL of the nodes TABLE or HEADER in the OUTPUT VALUES area. Note that data in HEADER indicates the column name of each column, such as SALES REVENUE, while that in TABLE indicates the actual value, such as $23.8. Though there's only one leaf node named CELL below TABLE or HEADER, you can bind it to a cell range with more columns, the number of which should be equal to that of the actual data. For example, in Figure B.3, the CELL of TABLE is bound to cell range Sheet1!$C$2:$E$11 with three columns, because the data from the BI service contains the three columns YEAR, CATEGORY, and QUANTITY SOLD.

The BI services are hosted in the SAP BusinessObjects system, so you need credentials to log on to it. That's why you see two input parameters, LOGIN and PASSWORD, in Figure B.3. You may or may not bind them to some input controls such as two input text components. If you are going to save the dashboard to an SAP BusinessObjects platform for end users to access through BI Launchpad or OpenDocument, you can simply ignore these two parameters because the user has already logged on to the SAP BusinessObjects system.

B.1.7 OpenDocument

OpenDocument is web application provided by SAP BusinessObjects for URL reporting, that is, to access an SAP BusinessObjects report with a URL. It can be used to view a Flash file created by SAP BusinessObjects Dashboards, an SAP Crystal Reports or SAP BusinessObjects Web Intelligence document, and so on. For example, you can view a Flash file with a URL like:

http://host:port/OpenDocument/opendoc/openDocument.jsp?iDocID=6322

where 6322 for parameter iDocID is the ID of the Flash object in the SAP BusinessObjects system. You may need to contact the administrator of your SAP BusinessObjects system to find out the ID of your dashboard.

OpenDocument can be deployed to either a Java or .Net web application server, such as a Tomcat or IIS. You need to be certain about the required parameter values such as token to append to the URL. You can refer to the link below to see how to use OpenDocument in an SAP BusinessObjects 4.0 environment:

http://help.sap.com/businessobject/product_guides/boexir4/en/xi4_opendocument_en.pdf

With this feature, you can integrate dashboards into your own portal so that users can access them within their everyday portal, by providing a link to the OpenDocument URL. A typical use is to integrate SAP BusinessObjects Dashboards with SAP NetWeaver Portal, by creating a URL iView, with its URL being an OpenDocument one, so users can access the dashboards without leaving SAP NetWeaver Portal. For more information about this topic, please refer to the next section, where we'll discuss using SAP BusinessObjects Dashboards in SAP NetWeaver Portal.

B.2 Deployment and Migration

When SAP BusinessObjects Dashboards is used in conjunction with other SAP BusinessObjects products, you need to consider how to deploy your dashboards to the SAP BusinessObjects portal or SAP NetWeaver Portal and migrate them as part of your SAP BusinessObjects system.

To deploy a dashboard to SAP BusinessObjects, go to FILE • SAVE TO PLATFORM. After logging on, specify an appropriate folder to store the dashboard. Users can access the dashboard in BI Launchpad or CMC or within another portal with OpenDocument.

Another issue is how to migrate your dashboards between SAP BusinessObjects systems, such as from a development environment to production or when upgrading to a newer version of SAP BusinessObjects. You can use the Import Wizard provided by SAP BusinessObjects for the migration, treating the dashboards as common objects such as SAP Crystal Reports documents.

If your dashboard contains one or more Query as a Web Service connectivities, the WSDL URL of that connectivity will change after migration. Migrating the dashboard objects using the Import Wizard is not enough. You need go through the following steps to make the dashboard work perfectly after migration if it contains any Query as a Web Service data connectivity.

1. **Update the Universe connection.**
   The connection of a Universe defines where to retrieve the data—from the development or the production database. After migration, the Universe and its connection are copied to the production SAP BusinessObjects system. However, it still connects to the old database. You need update the connection to connect to the new database.

2. **Update the Query as a Web Service.**
   The definition of the Query as a Web Service is copied to the production SAP BusinessObjects system after migration. However, its URL still points to the old system, such as *http://boe_dev:8080/dswsbobje/...*. To reflect the environment change, you need edit it in Query as a Web Service designer to deploy it to the new web application server of the production SAP BusinessObjects system.

3. **Update the web service URL within SAP BusinessObjects Dashboards.**

The web service URL of the Query as a Web Service has changed, so you need to update it in SAP BusinessObjects Dashboards. To do this, you need the source file (*.xlf*) of the dashboard, not the Flash object.

Note that what needs be changed is the web service URL, not the WSDL URL. If you change WSDL URL, you have to rebind the input and output values of this connectivity.

If your web service URL uses a relative instead of absolute URL, that is, no *http://host:port*, you can skip this step.

When finished, deploy the dashboard to the production SAP BusinessObjects system.

B.3   How to Use SAP BusinessObjects Dashboards with SAP NetWeaver BW and SAP NetWeaver Portal

SAP BusinessObjects Dashboards can connect to almost any kind of data source and be deployed to almost any portal on any web application server. However, as a product of SAP, it's more frequently used within an SAP environment.

Generally, SAP BusinessObjects Dashboards can be used with two SAP products.

▸ SAP NetWeaver Business Warehouse (BW)

▸ SAP NetWeaver Portal (formerly known as EP)

In the rest of this section, we'll discuss how they are used together.

B.3.1   SAP NetWeaver BW

SAP NetWeaver BW is the SAP data warehousing product that's used to store enterprise information in various types of structures including InfoCubes, InfoObjects, and Data Store Objects. It's the foundation of reporting and analysis using SAP BusinessObjects products.

In an SAP environment, SAP BusinessObjects Dashboards is often used to create dashboards on top of the aggregated data stored in SAP NetWeaver BW. The typical steps are listed below in order.

1. **Create a BW query with the necessary dimensions and measures.**
   Depending on the business requirement, you can choose what dimensions (characteristics) and measures (key figures) of an InfoCube you want to show the end user. Sometimes you may need to create restricted or calculated key figures to show the user some special data.

2. **Create a Universe based on the BW query.**
   In this step you create a Universe to connect to the BW query you just created. If multiple BW queries have to be queried to get the data for your dashboard, you need to create one Universe for each BW query.

   Any variable defined in the BW query will be detected and mapped in the Universe as filters.

   You can also create a Universe based on the InfoCube directly. However, this adds complexity for the user when creating a Query as a Web Service based on the universe in the next step, when he is faced with too many dimensions and measures. Moreover, think of the case when a restricted or calculated key figure is required. If the InfoCube is used each time in this step, many restricted or calculated key figures will be added to the InfoCube, which will confuse other users.

3. **Create a Query as a Web Service based on the Universe.**
   In this step you create a Query as a Web Service to further specify what fields are to be exposed. Pay attention to the order of the dimensions or measures in the RESULT area of Query as a Web Service. The result data will be in the same order when mapped to cell ranges in your dashboard.

4. **Create a dashboard with corresponding Query as a Web Service connectivity.**
   Now you have created a Query as a Web Service, with which you can retrieve SAP NetWeaver BW data. This step is very straightforward. Just create a Query as a Web Service connectivity and do the bindings for both input parameters and output values.

For the input parameters, you can add some UI components to the dashboard for the user to specify the parameter values. You need to consider how to set dynamic visibility properties for them so you can hide them when the result data has been returned. You can hardcode values for the parameters first, in the development or test stage, to focus on the functionality and visualization of your dashboard without a parameter prompt page. Finally, add the UI components for the user to input values, which is required for an interactive dashboard.

For the output values, pay attention to the order of the dimensions and measures defined in step 3 when doing the bindings. They will appear in the same order in the cell range of the embedded spreadsheet.

Another way to connect to data in SAP NetWeaver BW is through SAP Business-Objects Live Office. First, you create an SAP Crystal Reports document directly on top of an InfoCube or a BW query, or create an SAP BusinessObjects Web Intelligence document based on a universe on top of a BW query. Then you insert the SAP Crystal Reports or SAP BusinessObjects Web Intelligence document into a Live Office–enabled Excel spreadsheet. Finally, import it into SAP Business-Objects Dashboards and create an SAP BusinessObjects Live Office connection, as explained in Chapter 7.

B.3.2   SAP NetWeaver Portal

SAP NetWeaver Portal, formerly called Enterprise Portal (EP), is part of the SAP NetWeaver architecture. It provides a single point of access to information, enterprise applications, and services both inside and outside your company. It contains several components including knowledge management and collaboration. It's the platform for running custom Web Dynpro applications created either by SAP or by customers.

If the end users work with SAP NetWeaver Portal daily, you can use either of the two ways listed below to configure the portal so the users can access dashboards within the company's SAP NetWeaver Portal. The prerequisite is that you have deployed the dashboard onto the SAP BusinessObjects platform.

KM Integration

The first way is through the SAP BusinessObjects repository in knowledge management. After configuration, the portal user will be able to see a folder for the SAP BusinessObjects system in knowledge management. He can then navigate to the dashboard and right-click to view it, just like he does from BI Launchpad.

The SAP BusinessObjects Integration for SAP Solutions, commonly referred to as SAP IK, provides a *BusinessObjectsKM.par* file you can upload into SAP Net-Weaver Portal from the Administration Console within Portal Runtime. The SAP NetWeaver Portal administrator can follow the steps listed in the Installation and

Administration Guide of SAP IK to configure the SAP BusinessObjects repository to point to your SAP BusinessObjects system.

URL iView

Another way is through a URL iView, with the help of OpenDocument, as mentioned in the section above. The user can click an iView from within SAP NetWeaver Portal to launch a dashboard.

SAP IK brings with it some *.epa* (Enterprise Portal Archive) files. After importing it to your SAP NetWeaver Portal system, you will see three iView templates added. You can duplicate any of them, or create a new URL iView, to point to a dashboard that has been exported into an SAP BusinessObjects platform. This is a big topic and is not the focus of this book, so we won't spend too much space on it. For example, you need configure single sign-on (SSO) between SAP NetWeaver Portal and your SAP BusinessObjects system, so the user can access your dashboard from SAP NetWeaver Portal without entering credentials for the SAP BusinessObjects system again, to achieve seamless integration.

B.4   Supported Excel Functions

As you have seen in the previous chapters and from your dashboard design experience, Excel plays a very important role in SAP BusinessObjects Dashboards. External data passed in from a data connectivity is mapped to the embedded Excel spreadsheet, which can in turn be mapped to UI components in the dashboard.

Sometimes the data you want to display in the dashboard is not passed in directly from the data connectivity. For example, let's say the sales revenues of the current and the previous months are returned from a web service connectivity, but what you want to display is the growth rate. In such cases, you need to calculate the data in the embedded Excel spreadsheet, with the help of the powerful Excel functions.

Excel is popular thanks to its comprehensive and powerful functions. SAP BusinessObjects Dashboards leverages this power of Excel and supports the most frequently used functions. If you're already familiar with Excel functions, you may find this functionality very useful. In the next section, we'll list and briefly explain these functions.

B.4.1 How Excel Functions Work in SAP BusinessObjects Dashboards

At design time, you can enter Excel functions in the spreadsheet area and see the calculation results immediately. The embedded Excel spreadsheet is a separate Excel process. If you launch the Task Manager by pressing [Ctrl]+[Alt]+[Del], you'll find an Excel process in the PROCESS tab. So it's no surprise that functions at design time always return the same value as that of a stand-alone Excel program outside SAP BusinessObjects Dashboards.

However, at runtime, no Excel process is running, and functions are calculated by SAP BusinessObjects Dashboards itself. A calculation engine tries to mimic Microsoft Excel. But you'll still find that results from SAP BusinessObjects Dashboards runtime differ from those of Excel in some cases. So you should preview the dashboard to test function results before you use a new Excel function for the first time.

B.4.2 Supported Functions

The Excel functions supported by SAP BusinessObjects Dashboards 4.0 can be divided into several categories as follows. For each category, the functions' names are listed with a brief introduction for you to get a rough idea about what it does. For more information about any function, you can search the Internet or refer to any help such as *office.microsoft.com*.

Two websites, *spreadsheets.about.com* and *www.techonthenet.com*, are very helpful for understanding certain functions.

Math and Trigonometry

- ABS
  Calculates the absolute value of a number.
- ACOS/ACOSH/ASIN/ASINH/ATAN/ATAN2/ATANH/COS/COSH/SIGN/ SIGNH/TAN/TANH
  Calculates the direct/inverse trigonometric values.

▶ CEILING/FLOOR
Rounds a number up or down based on a multiple of significance, which is a parameter of this function.

▶ COMBIN
Returns the number of combinations by choosing *N* from *M* values. For example, COMBIN(10,3) = (10*9*8) / (3*2*1) = 120.

▶ DEGREES
Changes radius into degrees.

▶ EVEN
Rounds a number up to the closest even number. For example, EVEN(4.1) = 6.

▶ EXP
Returns *e* raised to the *N*th power, where *e* = 2.71828, which is the base of the natural logarithm.

▶ FACT
Returns the factorial of a given number. For example, FACT(3) = 3*2*1 = 6.

▶ INT
Returns the integer portion of a given number. For example, INT(2.8) = 2.

▶ Ln/LOG/LOG10
Returns the logarithm of a given number.

▶ MOD
Returns the remainder after a number is divided by a divisor. For example, MOD(13, 5) = 3.

▶ PI
Returns the mathematical constant called pi (the ratio of the circumference to the diameter of a circle), which is 3.14159265358979.

▶ POWER
Returns the result of a number raised to a given power. For example, POWER(2, 3) = 8.

▶ PRODUCT
Multiplies numbers and returns the product. For example, PRODUCT(2, 3, 4) = 24.

▶ QUOTIENT
Divides a number. It differs from regular division in that it only returns the integer portion of a division operation. For example, QUOTIENT(5, 2) = 2.

► RADIANS

Converts degrees into radians, in contrast to DEGREES. For example, RADIANS(120) = 2.094395102.

► RAND

Returns a random number that is greater than or equal to 0 and less than 1. A new random number is returned each time the worksheet recalculates.

► ROUND/ROUNDDOWN/ROUNDUP

Returns a number rounded to a specified number of digits. ROUNDUP rounds the number away from 0, while ROUNDDOWN rounds the number toward 0.

► SIGN

Returns the sign of a number, which is 1 when the number is positive, –1 for a negative number, and 0 for 0.

► SQRT

Returns the square root of a number. For example, SQRT(25) = 5.

► SUM

Adds all numbers in a range of cells and returns the result.

► SUMIF

Adds all numbers in a range of cells, based on a given criteria.

► SUMPRODUCT

Multiplies the corresponding items in arrays and returns the sum of the results. For example, SUMPRODUCT({1,2;3,4}, {5,6;7,8}) = (1*5) + (2*6) + (3*7) + (4*8).

► SUMSQ

Returns the sum of the squares of a series of values.

► SUMX2MY2

Returns the sum of the difference of squares between two arrays.

► SUMX2PY2

Returns the sum of the squares of corresponding items in the arrays and returns the sum of the results.

► SUMXMY2

Returns the sum of the squares of the differences between corresponding items in the arrays and returns the sum of the results.

► TRUNC

Returns a number truncated to a specified number of digits. For example, TRUNC(66.78,1) = 66.7.

Logical

▶ AND
Returns TRUE only when both operands evaluate to TRUE. Otherwise returns FALSE.

▶ OR
Returns FALSE only when both operands evaluate to FALSE. Otherwise returns TRUE.

▶ NOT
Reverses the given Boolean value.

▶ IF
Returns one value if a specified condition evaluates to TRUE or another value if it evaluates to FALSE. For example, IF(TRUE, 1, 2) = 1, and IF(FALSE, 1, 2) = 2.

Statistical

▶ AVEDEV
Returns the average of the absolute deviations of the numbers provided.

▶ AVERAGE
Returns the average (arithmetic mean) of the numbers provided.

▶ AVERAGEA
Returns the average (arithmetic mean) of the numbers provided. The AverageA function is different from the Average function in that it treats TRUE as a value of 1 and FALSE as 0.

▶ BETADIST
Returns the cumulative beta probability density function.

▶ COUNT
Counts the number of cells that contain numbers and the number of arguments that contain numbers.

▶ COUNTA
Counts the number of cells that are not empty and the number of arguments that contain values.

▶ COUNTIF
Counts the number of cells in a range that meets a given criteria.

- ▶ DEVSQ
  Returns the sum of squares of deviations of data points from their sample mean.

- ▶ EXPONDIST
  Returns the exponential distribution.

- ▶ FISHER/FISHERINV
  Returns the direct/inverse Fisher transformation at the given number.

- ▶ FORECAST
  Returns a prediction of a future value based on existing values provided.

- ▶ GEOMEAN
  Returns the geometric mean of an array or range of positive data.

- ▶ HARMEAN
  Returns the harmonic mean of a data set.

- ▶ INTERCEPT
  Returns the Y-axis intersection point of a line using X-axis values and Y-axis values.

- ▶ KURT
  Returns the kurtosis of a data set.

- ▶ LARGE
  Returns the Nth largest value from a set of values.

- ▶ MAX/MEDIAN/MIN
  Returns the largest/median/smallest value from the numbers provided.

- ▶ NORMDIST
  Returns the normal cumulative distribution for a specified mean and standard deviation.

- ▶ NORMINV
  Returns the inverse of the normal cumulative distribution for the specified mean and standard deviation.

- ▶ NORMSINV
  Returns the inverse of the standard normal cumulative distribution. The distribution has a mean of zero and a standard deviation of one.

- ▶ RANK
  Returns the rank of a number in a list of numbers.

▶ SMALL
Returns the *k*th smallest value in a data set.

▶ STANDARDIZE
Returns a normalized value from a distribution characterized by mean and standard deviation.

▶ STDEV
Estimates the standard deviation based on a sample.

▶ VAR
Estimates the variance based on a sample.

Lookup and Reference

These functions are expensive to calculate at runtime, so use them with care.

▶ CHOOSE
Returns a value from a list of values based on a given position. For example, CHOOSE(2, "x", "y", "z") returns "y".

▶ HLOOKUP/VLOOKUP
Searches for a value in the top row/left column of table_array and returns the value in the same column/row based on the index_number.

▶ INDEX
Returns either the value or the reference to a value from a table or range.

▶ LOOKUP
Returns a value from a range (one row or one column) or from an array.

▶ MATCH
Searches for a value in an array and returns the relative position of that item.

▶ OFFSET
Returns a reference to a range that is offset a number of rows and columns from another range or cell.

Database and List Management

▶ DAVERAGE
Averages the values in a field (column) of records in a list or database that match conditions you specify.

- DCOUNT
  Counts the cells that contain numbers in a field (column) of records in a list or database that match conditions you specify.

- DCOUNTA
  Counts the nonblank cells in a field (column) of records in a list or database that match conditions you specify.

- DGET
  Extracts a single value from a column of a list or database that matches conditions you specify.

- DMAX/DMIN
  Returns the largest/smallest number in a field (column) of records in a list or database that matches conditions you specify.

- DPRODUCT
  Multiplies the values in a field (column) of records in a list or database that match conditions you specify.

- DSTDEV
  Estimates the standard deviation of a population based on a sample by using the numbers in a field (column) of records in a list or database that match conditions you specify.

- DSUM
  Adds the numbers in a field (column) of records in a list or database that match conditions you specify.

- DVAR
  Estimates the variance of a population based on a sample by using the numbers in a field (column) of records in a list or database that match conditions you specify.

- DVARP
  Calculates the variance of a population based on the entire population by using the numbers in a field (column) of records in a list or database that match conditions you specify.

Financial

You need some basic knowledge of finance to use these functions.

▶ DB

Returns the depreciation of an asset for a specified period using the fixed-declining balance method.

▶ DDB

Returns the depreciation of an asset for a specified period using the double-declining balance method or some other method you specify.

▶ FV

Returns the future value of an investment based on periodic, constant payments and a constant interest rate.

▶ IPMT

Returns the interest payment for a given period for an investment based on periodic, constant payments and a constant interest rate.

▶ IRR

Returns the internal rate of return for a series of cash flows represented by the numbers in values.

▶ MIRR

Returns the modified internal rate of return for a series of periodic cash flows. MIRR considers both the cost of the investment and the interest received on reinvestment of cash.

▶ NPER

Returns the number of periods for an investment based on periodic, constant payments and a constant interest rate.

▶ NPV

Calculates the net present value of an investment by using a discount rate and a series of future payments (negative values) and income (positive values).

▶ PMT

Calculates the payment for a loan based on constant payments and a constant interest rate.

▶ PPMT

Returns the payment on the principal for a given period for an investment based on periodic, constant payments and a constant interest rate.

▶ PV

Returns the present value of an investment. The present value is the total amount that a series of future payments is worth now.

▶ RATE
Returns the interest rate per period of an annuity.

▶ SLN
Returns the straight-line depreciation of an asset for one period.

▶ SYD
Returns the sum-of-years' digits depreciation of an asset for a specified period.

▶ VDB
Returns the depreciation of an asset for any period you specify, including partial periods, using the double-declining balance method or some other method you specify.

Text and Data

▶ CONCATENATE
Allows you to join two or more strings together.

▶ DOLLAR
Converts a number to text, using a currency format.

▶ EXACT
Compares two strings and returns TRUE if both values are the same and FALSE otherwise.

▶ FIND
Returns the location of a substring in a string. The search is case-sensitive.

▶ FIXED
Returns a text representation of a number rounded to a specified number of decimal places.

▶ LEFT/RIGHT
Allows you to extract a substring from a string, starting from the leftmost/ rightmost character.

▶ LEN
Returns the length of the specified string.

▶ LOWER
Converts all letters in the specified string to lowercase. If there are characters in the string that are not letters, they are unaffected by this function.

▶ MID
Extracts a substring from a string (starting at any position).

► REPLACE
Replaces a sequence of characters in a string with another set of characters.

► REPT
Returns a repeated text value a specified number of times.

► TEXT
Returns a value converted to text with a specified format.

► VALUE
Converts a text value that represents a number to a number.

Information

► ISNA
Checks for a #N/A (value not available) error.

► ISNUMBER
Checks for a numeric value.

► N
Converts a value to a number.

Date and Time

► DATE
Returns the number that represents an Excel date-time code.

► DATEVALUE
Returns the serial number of a date.

► DAY
Returns the day of the month (a number from 1 to 31) given a date value.

► DAYS360
Returns the number of days between two dates based on a 360-day year.

► EDATE
Returns the serial number representing the date that is the indicated number of months before or after a specified date (the start_date).

► EOMONTH
Returns the serial number for the last day of the month that is the indicated number of months before or after start_date.

▶ HOUR
Returns the hour of a time value (from 0 to 23).

▶ MINUTE
Returns the minute of a time value (from 0 to 59).

▶ MONTH
Returns the month (a number from 1 to 12) given a date value.

▶ NETWORKDAYS
Returns the number of whole working days between start_date and end_date.

▶ NOW
Returns the current system date and time. This function will refresh the date/time value whenever the worksheet recalculates.

▶ SECOND
Returns the second of a time value (from 0 to 59).

▶ TIME
Converts hours, minutes, and seconds given as numbers to an Excel serial number formatted with a time format.

▶ TIMEVALUE
Converts a text time to an Excel serial number for a time.

▶ TODAY
Returns the current system date. This function will refresh the date whenever the worksheet recalculates.

▶ WEEKDAY
Returns a number representing the day of the week, given a date value.

▶ WEEKNUM
Returns a number that indicates where the week falls numerically within a year.

▶ WORKDAY
Returns a number that represents a date that is the indicated number of working days before or after a date (the starting date). For example, WORKDAY(DATE(2010,4,9),1) can be used to get the first work day after 2010/04/09. The result as a number is 40280, which is the date 2010/04/12 when viewed as Date. You may use this function to build a list of work days for the user to choose from.

▶ YEAR
Returns a four-digit year (a number from 1900 to 9999) given a date value.

▶ YEARFRAC
Calculates the fraction of the year represented by the number of whole days between two dates.

B.5   SAP BusinessObjects Dashboards Editions

SAP BusinessObjects Dashboards 4.0 is released in three editions: Departmental (or Enterprise), Personal (or Engage), and Present. You can choose what edition to use based on your requirements. Before purchasing, some knowledge of the differences will be helpful.

The basic functionalities of SAP BusinessObjects Dashboards are available in all editions, such as creating a dashboard based on Excel data and exporting it to a Flash SWF file. Some advanced features, such as some advanced UI components and data connectivity types, are not available in some editions. Sometimes you cannot export your dashboard to some format such as to an SAP BusinessObjects platform due to license constraints.

The installation files of all editions are the same. The editions, and consequently the different functionalities of each edition, are controlled by the license, or key code, you purchased.

SAP BusinessObjects Dashboards 4.0 can only be installed on a Windows operating system. After installation, the key code is written to the registry, at *HKEY_LOCAL_MACHINE\ SOFTWARE\SAP BusinessObjects\Suite XI 4.0\Xcelsius\ Keycodes*. If you have installed SAP BusinessObjects Dashboards on a 64-bit Windows system, the path may be slightly different, with an extra node, *Wow6432Node*, between *SOFTWARE* and *SAP BusinessObjects*. The date following the key code in the registry value makes little sense.

The key code is written as-is, without any encryption. You can copy it for other uses or update it with another valid key code. Changes to the registry key will take effect the next time you launch SAP BusinessObjects Dashboards.

If you have key codes for different editions, you are free to switch among them by changing the key code in the registry.

Detailed explanations of each edition are presented in the following sections. You can compare them with your requirements and make an informed choice.

B.5.1 Enterprise

This is the complete edition of SAP BusinessObjects Dashboards 4.0 with all of the functionalities mentioned in this book supported. To use all of the potential of SAP BusinessObjects Dashboards and create a powerful yet attractive dashboard, this edition is your best-fit choice.

B.5.2 Personal

This edition is quite similar to Enterprise, with most functionalities and all UI components supported. Its limitation is that it cannot use any functionality related to SAP, including:

▶ Save to BusinessObjects system

▶ Query as a Web Service connectivity

▶ Live Office connectivity

▶ SAP NetWeaver BW Connection

▶ Connect to Universes in query panel or query prowser

▶ Translation settings

▶ Lifecycle management in SAP BusinessObjects system

However, Crystal Reports Data Consumer connectivity is provided in this edition. You can integrate with SAP Crystal Reports 2008 to insert a dashboard into an SAP Crystal Reports document and pass values into it there.

You may try to hack the system by creating a web service connectivity to connect to the Query as a Web Service deployed in an SAP BusinessObjects system. Though you can see the input and output values successfully after clicking IMPORT, the connection will not be triggered, and thus no SAP BusinessObjects data will be returned.

The ability to connect to external web portals or reporting services is unavailable in this edition.

B.5.3 Present

Compared to Personal, the extra limitation of the Present edition is that it lacks the ability to connect to any external data source. This edition only allows you to create dashboards with Excel data. The dashboard can't be exported to Flash, Adobe Air, HTML, or Microsoft Outlook—only to PDF, Microsoft Excel, Word, and PowerPoint.

Present is the entry-level edition, with no ability to connect to any external data source, and some of the UI components listed in this book are not included. It's intended for users who want to create dashboards with data in the embedded spreadsheet only and to present it with some common yet powerful UI components. The Data Manager cannot be launched to create any connectivity.

Moreover, you cannot import data from an Excel file in an SAP BusinessObjects platform. In the DATA menu, this item is disabled.

This edition has a robust suite of the most commonly used UI components. However, some advanced components are not available here. These can be divided into categories as listed here:

- **Selectors**
  - Accordion menu
  - Play selector
- **Other**
  - Calendar
  - History
  - Panel set
  - Source data
  - Trend analyzer
- **Web connectivity**
  - SlideShow
  - Connection refresh button
- **Universe connectivity**
  - Query refresh button
  - Query prompt selector

This edition features the most commonly used visualization export options, such as exporting to a PDF. With Present, you can only export your dashboard to PDF, PowerPoint, or Word, but not to Flash, AIR, HTML, Outlook, or an SAP Business-Objects platform.

B.6 Tips for Creating a Good Dashboard

In this section let's go over some tips and best practices for creating a professional dashboard. Following these useful tips may save you a lot of time during your dashboard development and help you avoid some unnecessary mistakes.

B.6.1 Tips for the Embedded Spreadsheet

Plan what cells or cell ranges will be used for what purpose prior to any data mapping or binding. Be clear about how many sheets (tabs) are needed, what data will be placed in what cells, the maximum number or rows and columns of external data, any data that will be calculated using Excel functions and how, and so on.

Name the Sheets

By default there are one to three sheets in the embedded spreadsheet, called Sheet1 and so on. These don't tell you much about what they're about. It's a best practice to give each sheet a descriptive name so you or others can better understand your design thoughts, for example, Info, Labels, and Input Data.

Generally, you can use some of the following sheets in your dashboard.

Info

You can put some general metadata such as purpose, author, creation date, and some other assumptions like your coloring mechanism in a sheet called Info. If you are going to include HELP or ABOUT in your dashboard, their content can also be stored here. You may prefer to write them in a separate sheet, and that's up to you.

If there are some known limitations of your current dashboard or something that you want to update in future, you can document that here as well. This is a required sheet.

Data

You need this sheet to store the raw data from any data connectivity or the static data you entered at design time. The values passed in from the container at runtime can also be placed here, such as the data from FS Commands or Flash Variables. This is a required sheet.

Display

Many kinds of data for UI components can be stored in this sheet, including the titles, labels, candidate items of selectors, and destinations of data insertion of selectors or drill-down. For most UI components, either for user input or for displaying data, you should set the title properties or add a label component in front of each to tell the user about what they are. For example, you can add a label that says "Please enter your password (6-10 chars):" in front of an input text, telling the user that he needs to enter his password here, which is 6 to 10 characters long. You can use a dedicated sheet called something like Label to store such data, or include it in this sheet. The user can then bind the title or text of UI components to a cell or cell range in this sheet instead of entering the text directly in the PROPERTIES panel.

You can place the candidate items of selectors such as combo boxes in this tab if they are static.

Sometimes you need to display part of the raw data in a list view. For example, data of 10 rows and 4 columns is returned, but you want to display only the data in the first and the third columns in a list view. For the binding to work, you need to map data in the two columns into a cell range of 10 rows and 2 columns. You can put such data in this sheet, because it will be displayed in a list view or in the CalculatedData sheet, as mentioned below, because it's calculated from the raw data.

CalculatedData

Sometimes you need to create new data fields by making calculations based on the raw data. You can put them in the same Data sheet as the raw data if there are only a few fields or in a new sheet called something like CalculatedData when there are many calculated fields. For example, the sales revenues of each branch in two consecutive years are returned from a web service connectivity, and you are going to use a trend icon to show whether the total sales revenue is going up or down on a yearly basis. You can calculate the difference using Excel functions and store the data in the CalculatedData sheet, so you can easily make changes when the calculation method of some fields has changed.

We recommend that you include the calculation logic in this sheet as well, to explain how a new field is calculated.

Use Different Colors for Different Kinds of Data

There are many kinds of data in the embedded spreadsheet: general information, input parameters, external data, calculated data, and so on. You can use different colors to highlight different kinds of data to keep things clear.

What color you use for what kind of data depends on your preferences. The only requirement is that you keep it consistent and define the colors in the Info sheet. Later, when another designer is not sure whether some data is from user input or from an external data source, he can refer to the color definition in the Info sheet.

In addition, you can use a thick box border to outline the area for certain data, such as the data returned from a web service connection. This way you or another designer can easily know the boundary of the data and avoid cell overlap.

Make Extensible Cell Ranges for Data Binding

When mapping the output of a data connectivity to a cell range in the embedded spreadsheet, usually you cannot know the accurate numbers of rows or columns. For example, you cannot be quite sure about how many branches there will be two years from now.

To make your dashboard usable several years later, you need make the cell range large enough to hold possible future entries.

When binding a UI component to this cell range, which may currently contain some blank rows or columns, remember to select IGNORE BLANK CELLS in both values and series.

Explain the Cell Ranges

It's a good idea to write some explanatory words about a cell above or to the left of a cell or cell range to show what it's about. Otherwise, you will have difficulty identifying the origin and target of that cell range.

Avoid Using Complex or Expensive Excel Functions

Flash is more complex than plain HTML and costs more time in loading. Using too many complex or expensive Excel functions will weaken performance, resulting in a worse user experience.

We recommend that you avoid using expensive Excel functions including SUMIF, COUNTIF, MATCH, and INDEX. If you really need this data, try to calculate it on the server side and pass it to your dashboard with some type of data connectivity instead of calculating it at runtime. Remember that SAP BusinessObjects Dashboards is best at visualization, not calculation.

B.6.2 Tips for the UI Components

UI components can be different for each business. Keep the following in mind when planning your UI components.

Use the Right UI Component

To choose the right UI component for your business scenario, you need a good understanding of the advantages and disadvantages of all the components covered in Chapters 4 and 5. For example, you can choose a panel to include a group of related components, but don't use a big gauge to indicate the status when there's insufficient space in the dashboard.

Keep a Consistent Look and Feel among Components

It looks ugly if the styles of the UI components on the canvas are inconsistent, for example, if the font size of one component is much bigger than that of some others.

The topic of look and feel includes font, colors, entry effects, alignments, and backgrounds. You can select a group of related components and align them to any direction (top, left, bottom, or right).

Use Custom Colors Carefully

To make a customized dashboard, you can use your preferred colors for UI components instead of the default ones. For example, you may want to customize the color of each slice of your pie chart. Furthermore, you can create your own color scheme.

An agreeable coloring mechanism will result in an outstanding and extremely attractive dashboard. A bad one will cause the user to hesitate to give your dashboard a second look, making it completely useless despite its powerful functionality.

Figure B.4 displays some recommended colors that you can use in your dashboard. Generally, use light and neutral colors for the banners, the navigation tabs in a component like a tab set, and the borders. You can use brighter colors to display key messages. Light blue, light gray, and beige are always good choices. And, of course, you need to ensure that the entire dashboard is consistent in color.

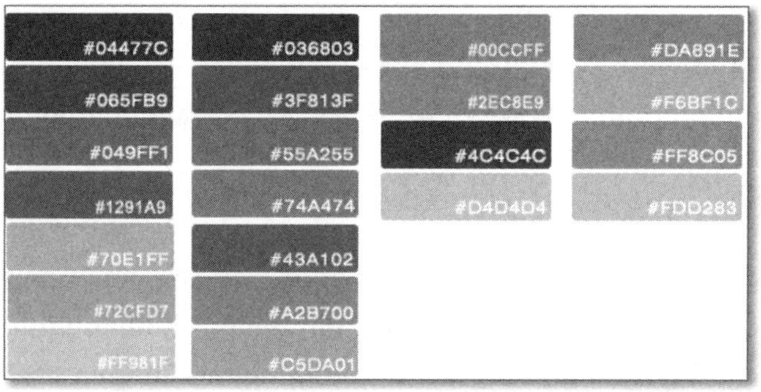

#04477C	#036803	#00CCFF	#DA891E
#065FB9	#3F813F	#2EC8E9	#F6BF1C
#049FF1	#55A255	#4C4C4C	#FF8C05
#1291A9	#74A474	#D4D4D4	#FDD283
#70E1FF	#43A102		
#72CFD7	#A2B700		
#FF981F	#C5DA01		

Figure B.4 Some Agreeable Colors for a Dashboard

If you are not confident about your sense of colors or aesthetic standard, you can fall back on the predefined color schemes.

Use "Fit Canvas to Components" with an Extra Component to Define the Size

There are two ways to adjust the canvas size of your dashboard.

▸ Use the INCREASE CANVAS, DECREASE CANVAS, FIT CANVAS TO COMPONENTS, or FIT CANVAS TO WINDOW button in the toolbar.

▸ Set the width and height in pixels from the menu FILE • DOCUMENT PROPERTIES • CANVAS SIZE.

The best way to adjust the canvas size is to use FIT CANVAS TO COMPONENTS with the help of an extra component to define the border. The steps are as follows:

1. Drop a rectangle component onto the canvas.

2. Resize it to the size you want, with all existing UI components included in it.

3. Click the FIT CANVAS TO COMPONENTS button in the toolbar.

4. Delete the rectangle.

The rectangle component here is used to define the border. An ellipse, a background, or even a chart can be used as well, but a container may not be a good choice, because it might include some existing UI components, adding difficulty to step 4 when you delete this extra component.

Add Help and/or About to Your Dashboard

From the end user's standpoint, it's good if the dashboard provides a HELP or ABOUT for him to easily understand the dashboard, such as how to use it, what kind of input values are accepted, where the data is retrieved, how some data is calculated, and the meaning of each chart.

The HELP or ABOUT can be displayed in a big label inside a container component. The user can click a button to show it and click it again or a click a CLOSE button in the container to hide it. You can achieve this with a toggle button and dynamic visibility.

Prompt the User for each Input

Give the user a hint about what he is supposed to input or select and the format of a valid input. For selectors such as a checkbox or combo box, you display the hint in its title. For a text input component, you can add an extra label.

B.6.3   Design Tips

These may seem like simple steps, but will save you from making time-consuming mistakes.

Begin with a Pencil

Before working with your dashboard inside SAP BusinessObjects Dashboards, we strongly recommend getting away from the computer and designing with paper and pencil. Think well before you act, and a pencil can help you think.

You should think thoroughly about your dashboard, from end to end. On the paper, you can illustrate the data flow and the mapping among UI components, the embedded spreadsheet, and external data. Also, you need to work out a draft of the layout and the interaction with the end user using the pencil, including which components are initially displayed, which become hidden or visible on what user interaction, and when to trigger what connection.

If Detail Is Required, Use a Link

SAP BusinessObjects Dashboards is used to visualize high-level aggregated data, not details. However, sometimes the user may want to see the more detailed information to find out the root cause of something. For example, say the user has drilled down to a store that contributes a lot to the company's total sales revenue, and then he want to see the sales information of each product every day for that store.

Instead of displaying these details in a list view or spreadsheet inside the dashboard, you can create an SAP Crystal Reports or SAP BusinessObjects Web Intelligence document for this purpose, with a parameter for the user to specify a store. After being deployed to SAP BusinessObjects, the detailed report can be accessed with an Open Document URL, as explained in Chapter 8. In your dashboard, a URL button is used to link to the report, with the ID of the currently selected store appended to the OpenDocument URL.

Use a Spreadsheet or List View for Debugging

Usually, the external data is not visualized directly in some UI components. Instead, it's reorganized or calculated before being bound to.

When previewing the dashboard to check the workflow, you may suspect something is wrong with the data but not be sure whether it's a problem with the original data from the external source or with your manual calculation or reorganization. In such circumstances, you can use a spreadsheet or list view component to help with debugging.

The original data, retrieved from a data connectivity, is mapped to a cell range in the embedded spreadsheet. You can use a spreadsheet, list view, or even a grid component to display this data in the canvas by binding its data to the range you are interested in. You can then compare what's displayed in the component in your dashboard with your original data to determine whether the problem lies here.

C   The Authors

Ray Li is a passionate business intelligence professional currently working for Lodestone Management Consultants, providing BI consulting services in the retail, pharmaceutical, manufacturing, and insurance industries. He previously worked for SAP BusinessObjects as a software engineer where he developed the integration kit for SAP Solutions and designed and delivered dashboards in several projects. In his spare time he enjoys music and badminton.

Evan DeLodder is a software engineer focused on applying cutting-edge technologies in the business intelligence and data visualization space. Evan has led the development and implementation of numerous business intelligence software products and applications and continues to innovate and apply new ideas that compliment the SAP Business Intelligence platform. Evan is an SAP BusinessObjects Dashboards SDK guru on the popular website *EverythingXcelsius.com*, an SAP author, and a frequent contributor to the growing SAP BusinessObjects Dashboards development community.

Index

A

About Dashboard Design, 75
Accordion menu, 255
   example, 258
ActionScript 3, 512
ActionScript class, 563
ActionScript language, 417
Actual value, 263
Add-On Manager, 578, 598
Add-On Packager files, 524
Address validation, 612
Adjust appearance, 509
Adobe Acrobat, 477
Adobe Flash, 417, 475
Adobe Flash Player, 342, 411, 512
Adobe Flex technology, 511
Adobe Integrated Runtime (AIR), 475, 512
Adobe LifeCycle Data Service, 440
Advanced charts, 221
Advanced component features, 566
Advanced custom add-on component features,
   557
Advanced data connectivity, 375
Advanced selectors, 255
Advanced single-value components, 273
Aggregation awareness technology, 496
Alert, 151, 158, 199, 464, 523
   method, 465
   thresholds, 153, 465
Alignment, 68, 506
AnyMap component, 300
Appearance, 122, 157
Application level, 577
Area chart, 171
Art, 292
Assist dashboard layout, 210
Auto drill-down, 451
Auto play, 265
Axes tab, 149

B

Background component, 318, 321
Backgrounds, 211
Bar chart, 111, 163
Basic add-on components, 532
Behavior, 119, 138, 157, 166
Benchmarks, 464
Best fit, 320
Best practices, 521
BI, 614
BI Launchpad, 53, 129, 476
   CMC, 636
   InfoView, 60
Bind, 383
   color, 132
   data, 98, 113
   data by range, 252
   display data, 281
Bindable chart data, 581
Bindable selected data, 582
Bindable selected tooltip, 582
Bindable series color, 582
Binding directions, 522
Binding directions and data flow, 528
Binding types, 530
BindingID, 543
Border, 123, 126
Bound property display names, 538
Bubble chart, 168
BubbleChartBase.mxml, 594
Budgets, 464
Build background, 210
Build number, 76
Build query, 90
Bullet chart, 251
   horizontal, 252
BW query, 645
By range, 134
By series, 135

C

Calendar, 270
  limits, 272
Candlestick chart, 239
Canvas, 84, 467, 518
  container, 210, 458
  size, 505
  size in pixels, 44
  sizing, 66
Canvas and spreadsheet, 66
Cascading combo boxes, 271
Cascading Style Sheet (CSS), 523
Cell, 99
Census data, 621
Chain, 543
  variable, 559
Chart area, 122
Chart background, 250
Charts, 361
Checkbox, 185
Child dashboard, 315
Child panels, 329
Color, 131
  dynamic, 132
  order, 155
  picker, 126
Column chart, 111, 133, 258, 492, 495
Columns, 383
Combination chart, 227, 362
Combo boxes, 184
Comparative marker color, 254
Comparative value, 252
Comparison, 25
Complex formatting, 401
Component code, 574
Components browser, 36, 82
Connect to external data, 508
Connection refresh button, 305
Connections, 73
Consumer, 438
Container, 206, 457
Control sheet, 502
Credentials, 456
Cross-tab, 404
Cross-Tab Expert, 406

Crystal Reports Data Consumer connectivity, 400
CSV files, 514
Currency, 129
Custom add-on component, 581
Custom component, 516, 527
  development, 557
  property values, 562
  public variable values, 589
Custom policy file, 380
Customized color scheme, 480, 483

D

Dashboard
  data marts, 521
  embed, 401
Dashboard Design Departmental edition, 477
Data, 133
  binding, 65, 361
  cleansing, 612
  formatting, 612
  insertion, 507
  labels, 127, 226
  mashups, 612
  menu, 37, 71
  meters, 519
  part, 111
  point, 126
  processing, 401
  sharing component, 598
  source, 156
  visualization capabilities, 23
  visualizations, 518
Data connectivity, 344
  basics, 335
  capabilities, 27
Data Consumer connection, 401
Data Manager, 341, 347, 360, 377, 387, 402, 412
Data source write-back, 364
Data-change-tracking function, 322
Date/time, 131
Debugging, 522, 668
Default selection, 119
Delivery management, 624

Demographics, 612, 614
Description, 44
Device fonts, 45
Dial, 252
Dial and gauge, 200
Dialog box, 207
Direct data binding, 21, 135, 137, 472
Disable mouse input on load, 356
Disaster management, 623
Discrete, 164
Display several dashboards, 328
Distribute the output, 106
Distribution, 28, 29, 111
Divisions, 146
Document, 46
Document properties, 43
Drill, 384
Drill-down, 100, 102, 115, 441
Drill-down behavior, 137, 361
Dual slider, 273
Dummy data, 501
DuPont Financial analysis system, 317
Dynamic, 178
    data, 98
    visibility, 121, 293, 452, 456, 497

E

Edit menu, 62
Embedded Excel spreadsheet, 85, 336
Embedded files, 293
Embedded JPEG or SWF, 329
Embedded spreadsheet, 98, 346, 350, 383,
    449
Enable data animation, 122
Enable data insertion, 115, 443
Enable load cursor, 356
Enable range slider, 140
Enable run-time tools, 139
Enable sorting, 120
Encrypted data repositories, 514
End-user interaction binding operations, 539
Enterprise data warehouse (EDW), 386
Entry effect, 122
Excel, 21, 501
    database and list management, 653

Excel, 21, 501 (Cont.)
    date and time, 657
    financial, 654
    formulas, 65
    functions, 183, 647
    information, 657
    Live Office, 391
    logical functions, 651
    lookup and reference, 653
    math and trigonometry, 648
    options, 49
    statistical functions, 651
    text and data, 656
Excel file, 98
    import, 506
Excel XML Map, 369
Explicitly getting property values, 532
Explicitly setting property values, 531
Exploded doughnut pie chart, 520
Exponential, 319
Export, 53, 72, 474
    preview, 53
    settings, 54
Extensible cell ranges, 664
External data, 103
External data services, 565, 568
External Interface connection, 424, 428

F

File, 36
Fill, 123, 126
Fill types, 296
Filter, 181
    data, 632
    rows, 177
Fisheye menu, 191
Fixed label size, 144
Flash, 56
Flash Data Expert, 406
Flash file, 342
    temporary, 479
Flash movies, 411
Flash Player, 367, 417
Flash trace log, 523
Flash Var, 272, 291, 639

Flash Variables, 407, 411
Flex, 512
  applications, 521
  binding, 515
  class library, 511
  framework, 512
  property sheet, 588
  test container, 597
Flex 2.0.1 Hotfix 3 SDK, 516
Flex Builder, 513, 582
Flex component, 582
  create, 594
Flex project
  create new, 583
Font, 44, 46
Format, 68, 79
  texts, 127
FS Command, 417
Function
  buildChart, 595
  continueBind, 565, 591
  formatDataTip, 596
  getPropertyBindDisplayName, 590
  HLookup(), 326
  init(), 588
  initiateBind, 564, 590
  initValues(), 589
  Rand(), 326
Fundamental SDK import statements, 534

G

Gannt charts, 514
Gauge, 252, 261, 492, 495
  component, 469
General tab, 113
Generic helper functions, 590
Geocoding, 612, 626
Geographical representation, 299
Geography, 614
GIS solutions, 620
Google maps, 618
Graphical background, 293
Greenwich Mean Time (GMT), 385
Grid, 47, 63, 289

H

Hierarchical pie charts, 519
History, 321
Hotfix 3 SDK, 585
HTML, 56
  container, 476
  file, 411
HTTPService, 576
  result, 575

I

Icon, 261
Ignore blank cells, 119, 138, 258
Image component, 292
Images through URLs, 189
Import, 71
  data from an Excel file, 340
  from platform, 72
Import Wizard, 643
Index, 115
Input component, 291, 600
Input parameters, 384
Input variables, 367
InputBindings, 531
InputMap, 543
Insertion, 114, 137, 157
Installation, 20
Insurance underwriting and risk management, 625
Integrated data warehouse (IDW), 386
Integrated development environment (IDE), 35
Interaction options, 118
Interactive analysis, 316
Interactive dashboard, 453
Interactivity, 26

J

Java, 346
Java Servlet, 358, 450
JavaScript code, 417, 428
JavaScript maps, 514

L

Label, 176, 261
Languages, 48
Launch, 59
Law enforcement, 626
Layout, 122
LCDS (Adobe LifeCycle Data Services)
    connections, 313, 431
Legacy bindings, 560
Legend, 125
License manager, 75
Line chart, 155, 362, 492, 497
Linear function, 319
Lines, 127, 298
List, 84
List builder, 192, 193
Live Office
    compatibility, 51, 392
    connection, 388, 490, 501
Load, 349
    status, 356
Local file, 107
Local scenario button, 315
Location intelligence (LI), 611
Logarithmic, 143, 319
Logo, 293
Logon panel, 456
Loosely couple data, 632
LOV, 381

M

Manage add-ons, 56
Manage operations, 625
Manual (Y) axis, 143
Map, 299, 492
Marker overlap, 225
MDX querying capabilities, 521
Measures, 164
Menu, 36
Metadata, 383, 458
Method
    GetReportBlock, 383
    runQueryAsAService, 383
Microsoft Office Excel, 336

Model locator, 599
Mouse click, 101, 118
Mouse events, 213
Mouse sensitivity, 280, 291
Mouse tracking, 203
Multi-dial gauges, 519
Multiple add-ons, 525
Multiple value axes, 240
Multi-select, 457
MXML, 512, 523
    application files, 602
    components, 563
    file, 588
    markup, grid lines and Cartesian chart, 552
My workspace, 66

N

New command, 36

O

Object Browser, 64, 88, 97, 207
OHLC chart, 229, 248
OHLC series, 233
Oil/land management, 626
One-dimensional binding, 473
One-dimensional cell range, 99
OpenDocument, 642, 643
Organizing data in Excel, 501
Outlook, 56, 479
Output component, 601
Output values, 383
OutputBindings, 531

P

Packager and SAP Dashboards XLX add-on,
    597
Packaging best practices, 555
Panel container, 208, 462
Panel set, 328
PDF, 477
Percent, 130
Percentage, 24
Performance color, 254

Performance metric, 242
Persisting property sheet values, 560
   retrieve, 561
Picture menus, 188
Pie chart, 96, 99, 110, 492, 500
Plan UI, 492
Plan workflow, 491
Planning the dashboard, 491
Play control, 276
Play selector, 263
Plot area, 123, 250
Polynomial, 319
Portal data, 435
Position, 115
Power, 319
PowerPoint, 56, 478
PowerPoint/Word document, 342
Preferences, 46
Preferred viewing locale (PVL), 129
Preparing data, 493
Preview, 52, 53
Primary measure values, 252
Print button, 324
Private SDK variables, 533
Private variable, 559
Progress bar, 200, 252
Properties, 64
   panel, 112, 371
Property data binding, 528
Property sheet, 36, 85, 517, 527, 563, 603
   code base, 563
   controls, 589
   custom, 522
   data binding, 528
   initializes, 561
   styling, 532
Property value setting/setting, 528
Provider, 440
Proxy.Bind, 542
proxy.getPersist, 562
proxy.unbind, 560
Public component variables, 574
Publish, 58

Q

Query as a Web Service, 376, 403, 477, 638
   methods, 380
   workflow, 377
Query as a Web Service Designer, 383
Query Browser, 64, 89, 638
Query prompt selector, 216
Query refresh button, 215
Quick views, 64

R

Radar chart, 240
   filled, 243
Radio button, 500
Range list, 350
Range slider, 157
Ratio, 110
Region, 299
Region keys, 301
   default, 303
Relative size, 111
Reset button, 324
Resize, 339
Reusable data, 630
Reusable property sheet patterns, 563
Reverse geocoding, 612, 627
Rich Internet application, 431
Row/column, 117
Rows, 383
   maximum number of, 383
RSS feeds, 514
Run locally, 342
Run on a web server, 343
Runtime performance, 293
Runtime tools, 157

S

Samples, 40
SAP BEx query default values, 388
SAP Business Intelligence platform, 38, 107
SAP BusinessObjects, 19
SAP BusinessObjects BI launchpad, 343

SAP BusinessObjects BI platform, 636
  export to, 476
SAP BusinessObjects Dashboards
  best practices, 662
  Departmental Edition, 38
  deploy, 643
  editions, 659
  Enterprise, 660
  Personal, 660
  Present, 661
  workspace, 35
SAP BusinessObjects Dashboards Excel model,
  558
SAP BusinessObjects Dashboards Packager,
  517
SAP BusinessObjects Dashboards software
  development toolkit (SDK), 511
SAP BusinessObjects Dashboards SWF Loader
  component, 577
SAP BusinessObjects Enterprise, 371, 477
SAP BusinessObjects Live Office, 33, 501, 638,
  646
  connections, 403
SAP BusinessObjects portfolio, 33
SAP BusinessObjects Universe, 638
SAP BusinessObjects Universe Designer, 33
SAP BusinessObjects Web Intelligence, 33,
  442, 639
SAP BW query, 473
SAP Crystal Reports, 33, 388, 399, 639
  insert SWF object, 404
  native cross-tab, 406
SAP GUI, 386
SAP HANA, 386
SAP IK, 647
SAP menu, 58
SAP NetWeaver BW, 58, 107, 384, 644
  connection, 385, 386
SAP NetWeaver Portal, 646
Scale, 142, 290
  algorithm, 253
  options, 140
  values, 252
Scenario, 316
Scroll, 187
  bars, 209

SDK, 585
Secondary axis, 133
Security, 367
  issues related to accessing external data, 341
  restriction, 389
Select a single item, 175
Select assets, 613
Selected item, 258
Selectors, 174
Series, 156, 157
Set appearance, 162
Set default currency format, 130
Shape files, 630
Shapes, 294
Shared local objects, 524
Single cell, 99
Single numeric value, 194
Singleton, 599
Skin, 479
Slide show, 312
Slide speed, 257
Slider, 195
Sliding picture menu, 191
Snapshot, 55
SOAP protocols, 639
Sound, 180
Source data, 325, 444
Space evenly, 68
Sparkline chart, 247
Spatial queries, 612
Spinner, 275
Spreadsheet, 99
  table, 285
SQL (Structured Query Language), 494
Stacked area chart, 227
Stacked bar, 227
Stacked column chart, 222
  visualized, 225
Standard, 78
Start page, 74
Status list, 116
Subelement
  array tricks, 566
  binding, 558, 566
  properties, 558
SVG and vector maps, 618

SWC, 584
SWF document, 401
SWF file, 380, 577, 598, 616
SWF loader, 314
SWF movies, 312

T

Tab set, 209
Table, 280
  grid, 289
  list view, 280
  spreadsheet, 285
Targeted advertising, 624
Targets, 464
Templates, 39
Test container, 522, 597
Text formats, 150
Themes, 79
Themes and colors, 479
Third-party tools, 514
Three-dimensional analysis, 168
Thresholds, 464
Ticker, 186
Ticks, 266, 278
Title area, 124, 250
Titles, 133
Toolbar, 68, 77
  buttons, 80
Tooltip function, 551
Trace statements, 523
Track sales, 623
Transaction
  MDXTEST, 387
Translation Manager, 52
Translation settings, 52, 60
Transparency, 126, 263
  slider, 148
Tree map, 245
Trend analysis algorithm, 318
Trend analyzer, 318
Trend icon, 317
Trends, 497
Trigger connections, 305
Two-dimensional binding, 474
Two-dimensional cell range, 100

U

UI component, 68, 96, 258, 441, 455
  add, 505
  art, 292
  best practices, 665
  web connectivity, 304
UI control logic, 502
UI controls, charts and gauges, 22
UI elements, 22, 39
Undo/redo, 62
Universe connectivity, 214
Universe query, 89, 98, 116, 135, 157, 214,
  281, 337, 472
  prompt, 264
  prompts, 117
URL, 344
  button, 307
  reporting, 642
Use current excel data, 55

V

Value, 116, 176
  change trend, 317
  component, 278
Variable values
  save across sessions, 560
Vertical axes, 240
View menu, 63

W

Web 2.0 maps, 618
Web connectivity, 304
Web Intelligence documents, 388
Web Intelligence Rich Client, 34, 90, 214, 376,
  383, 640
Web Mapping Services (WMS), 629
Web service connection, 22, 364, 365
Web service URL, 379
What-if analysis, 325
Word, 479
Working with charts, 110
Wrap components, 207
Wrap several components, 206

X

X-axis, 133
X-axis scale by series, 254
.xlf, 38
XLF file, 560
.xls, 36
.xlsx, 36
XML data, 343, 344
XML data connectivity, 360, 450
XML feed, 568

XML file, 346
XML layout, 596
XML layout and controls, 593
XML schemas, 369
XY chart, 164

Y

Y-axis, 133, 142
Y-axis scale, 143
YTD trend, 504

Interested in reading more?

Please visit our website for all
new book releases from SAP PRESS.

www.sap-press.com